In a nonmodal Windows application more than one application window can be opened on the desktop at once, and the operator can switch back and forth among them using the mouse or the Window pulldown.

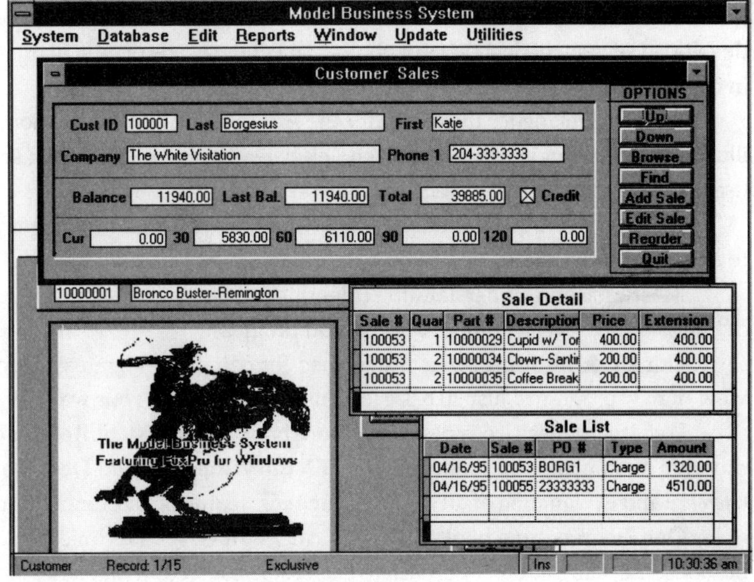

During sale invoice entry a BROWSE window comes in handy for displaying sale items. You can also select items for edit by highlighting them in the BROWSE window and then clicking a push button. Other application windows can be minimized to keep them out of the way until they are needed again.

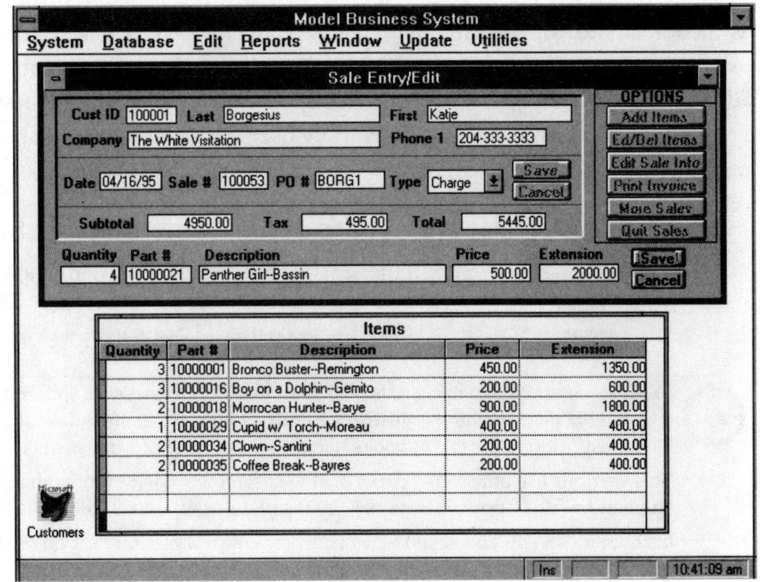

PROGRAMMER'S GUIDE TO FOXPRO® 2.6

Second Edition

Howard Dickler, Ph.D.

SYBEX®

SAN FRANCISCO • PARIS • DÜSSELDORF • SOEST

Acquisitions Editors: David Clark, Joanne Cuthbertson
Developmental Editor: David Peal
Editor: Dusty Bernard
Technical Editor: Maurice Frank
Contributing Editor: Sheldon M. Dunn
Project Editors: Michelle Nance, Michelle Khazai
Book Designer: Suzanne Albertson
Production/Layout Artists: Claudia Smelser, Suzanne Albertson
Screen Graphics: Cuong Le, Suzanne Albertson
Typesetter: Ann Dunn
Production Assistant/Proofreader: Lisa Haden
Indexer: Matthew Spence
Cover Designer: Archer Design
Cover Photographer: David Bishop
Photograph Art Director: Ingalls + Associates
Screen reproductions produced with Collage Plus.
Collage Plus is a trademark of Inner Media Inc.
SYBEX is a registered trademark of SYBEX Inc.

Library of Congress Card Number: 94-66851
ISBN: 0-7821-1609-4

Manufactured in the United States of America
10 9 8 7 6 5 4 3 2 1

Warranty

SYBEX warrants the enclosed disk to be free of physical defects for a period of ninety (90) days after purchase. If you discover a defect in the disk during this warranty period, you can obtain a replacement disk at no charge by sending the defective disk, postage prepaid, with proof of purchase to:

SYBEX Inc.

Customer Service Department

2021 Challenger Drive

Alameda, CA 94501

(800) 227-2346

Fax: (510) 523-2373

After the 90-day period, you can obtain a replacement disk by sending us the defective disk, proof of purchase, and a check or money order for $10, payable to SYBEX.

Disclaimer

SYBEX makes no warranty or representation, either express or implied, with respect to this software, its quality performance, merchantability, or fitness for a particular purpose. In no event will SYBEX, its distributors, or dealers be liable for direct, indirect, special, incidental, or consequential damages arising out of the use of or inability to use the software even if advised of the possibility of such damage.

The exclusion of implied warranties is not permitted by some states. Therefore, the above exclusion may not apply to you. This warranty provides you with specific legal rights; there may be other rights that you may have that vary from state to state.

Copy Protection

None of the programs on the disk is copy-protected. However, in all cases, reselling these programs without authorization is expressly forbidden.

For Molly and Morris,

my real and imaginary children

ACKNOWLEDGMENTS

Writing this book was no mean task. It took every ounce of strength I could muster over a nine-month period, beginning when I first received a beta test copy of FoxPro for Windows and found myself obliged to bury myself in books on FoxPro 2.0 in order to catch up on FoxPro's vast extension of the Xbase programming language. As my developmental editor at Sybex, David Peal, commented, FoxPro programmers would need a lot of help. As a dBASE specialist migrating to FoxPro to take advantage of its implementation of Windows programming, I could easily attest to the fact. This was not Kansas anymore. The encouragement to continue working on the book came from several sources, including David Peal, David Clark, and Sheldon M. Dunn, author of the indomitable *Xbase Cross-Reference Handbook* (Sybex, 1993), all of whom saw the need for a book that would help readers bridge the gap that had opened between standard Xbase programming and the wily Fox with its power tools, new program file types, and hundred and one new commands and functions. Their belief that I could deliver such a book helped to make it so.

I am grateful to Sheldon Dunn as well for providing technical advice and for his instructions on the use of the FoxPro Distribution Kit, which I had little time to explore. I also owe no end of thanks to Maurice Frank, my technical reviewer. In several instances he answered questions that found no answer in the FoxBeta forum or from Microsoft's Tech Support. He is also directly responsible for steering me away from many errors and for providing a great number of user tips that I have done my best to incorporate in the text. His comments and criticisms were invaluable; I thank him for every post-it he attached to the manuscript.

I also came to depend upon Dusty Bernard, my editor, who smoothly handled the many stages each chapter went through as it passed rapidly from hand to hand. (And they said computers would lead to a more leisurely existence!) Her expertise allowed me to concentrate on writing the next chapter, assured there was someone on board to save me from embarrassing grammatical errors and remind me of promises made in previous chapters.

Special thanks are also owed to Michelle Nance and Michelle Khazai, my project editors at Sybex, for their calm rescheduling of due dates and excellent oversight of the project; to Jim and Marilyn Solk of the Solk Foundry of Los Angeles, for allowing me to make use of images taken from their catalog of bronze replicas in this book; and to the many participants in the FoxBeta Forum who responded to my questions while I struggled to learn FoxPro for Windows.

Finally, I would like to thank my wife, Annette Leddy, my daughter, Molly-Max, and our dog, Jack, for their patience and support over the long period it took to complete the *Programmer's Guide to FoxPro 2.6*. At last, we can go to the beach.

CONTENTS AT A GLANCE

TABLE OF CONTENTS

INTRODUCTION

The *Programmer's Guide to FoxPro 2.6* provides programmers familiar with any version of the Xbase programming language with a crash course in developing business and accounting systems using Microsoft's new FoxPro 2.6 for Windows. The book leads you through the development of a full-featured accounts receivable system capable of maintaining customer accounts, printing sale invoices, and producing customer statements—to mention only its major features. The Model Business System, or *MBS,* included on disk at the back of this book also provides facilities for generating customer, sales, and payments reports, for maintaining an inventory and price list, and for producing mass personalized form letters and labels. Most important, it provides the quickest means of introducing readers to the exciting new world of Windows programming with FoxPro 2.6.

FoxPro 2.6 is a *maintenance upgrade* of FoxPro 2.5. Important enhancements include greater international and cross-platform compatibility, making it easier than ever to write applications that will function smoothly in different environments. With respect to the FoxPro programming language and interface, however, what's really new to FoxPro 2.6 are the enhancements that make it downwardly compatible with dBASE IV. With a few simple revisions and a bit of testing, you can now make your existing dBASE IV applications run smoothly under FoxPro 2.6. (See Appendix C for instructions.)

How This Book Is Organized

Part I, "Learning the Ropes," begins with an overview of the MBS customer database. In Chapters 1 and 2 we examine the Customer, Sales, and Payments tables and how they are linked together for input of customer account and transaction data and for output of customer invoices and statements. Then, in Chapters 3 through 6—the most important ones for Xbase programmers learning how to create Windows applications—we review the MBS screen programs used for entry and update of Customer, Payments, and Sales and Sales Transaction table records. We also take time out in Chapter 4 to examine the use of index tags and Rushmore optimization in establishing record order, performing record lookup, and controlling record output.

In Part I you will examine the core MBS screen programs, starting with the simplest—overseeing data entry to the Customer table—and ending with the most complex—the two screen programs used for entry of sales and production of invoices. You will learn about screen objects like popups, pick lists, push buttons, radio buttons, and check boxes. You will become familiar with intra-window and extra-window events and with modal and nonmodal application windows. By the end of Part I you should be sufficiently at home in the world of Windows programming to take a top-down approach to the process of application development.

In Part II, "Creating a Windows-Style Interface," we begin re-creating the process by which the Model Business System was put together. Chapter 7 starts out from the FoxPro Project Manager, which provides a Windows interface for creating and managing all the files belonging to each of your projects and a Build facility for producing an application (.app) file—or, if you have the FoxPro Distribution Kit, an executable (.exe) file—based on all the files included in a project. In Chapter 8 we begin piecing together the MBS, starting with the main (startup) program. A typical Xbase program, Bigbiz.prg, establishes the environment required by our application programs and then activates the system menu so the operator can begin using them. In Chapter 9 we examine the FoxPro Menu Builder in depth. In addition to using the Menu Builder to reproduce the MBS system menu, we supply a full account of FoxPro menu programs, the commands they contain, and how the system menus they execute work.

The first nine chapters of this book are intended to prepare you fully for the material covered in Chapter 10, "Event Handling in a Windows Application," where we show how all the major components of the MBS are made to work together at once. We study the procedures and functions we use in the MBS to make it function like any other well-wrought Windows application, focusing our attention on the use of Foundation READ and its special VALID clause to control what happens in the system when the operator switches from one application window to another.

If you are new to FoxPro, you will want a helping hand in learning how to use the Screen Builder and Report and Label Writers to their full potential. Part III, "Using the Screen Builder," provides a full account of screen program architecture and shows how to use the Generate Sceen and Edit Screen Set dialogs to produce screen programs with multiple READ windows. We also take time to review the MBS screen programs that serve as an operator interface. In Part IV, "Executing Reports," we examine how to use the Report and Label Writers to create the forms required by the MBS. By the end of Part IV, you will be ready to plan and execute your own applications, taking full advantage of the FoxPro power tools. In the MBS you will also have a model for emulation and a library of screen, menu, report, and program files that you can adapt for your own use.

Appendix A provides instructions for installing the MBS on your hard disk and for building and running the MBS application. It also includes a list of all files present on the companion disk and a brief description of their functions in the MBS system. If you have purchased the FoxPro Distribution Kit in order to build and distribute your applications as executable programs, you will find further assistance in Appendix B, which is devoted to the use of the Distribution Kit. Appendix C provides useful information for those migrating from dBASE IV to FoxPro.

Installing and Using the Model Business System

The companion disk at the back of the book contains a complete copy of the MBS with the exception of MBS.app, the executable MBS application file, and screen and menu source code files; these files can be regenerated automatically using the FoxPro Project Manager. In Appendix A you will find complete instructions for installing the MBS on your hard disk and for opening the MBS project file, MBS.pjx, in the FoxPro Project Manager so you can rebuild MBS.app and optionally regenerate all screen and menu source code files. This can be done at any time, but if you are familiar with earlier versions of FoxPro, you are likely to benefit most from the MBS if it is available on disk from the outset. Though the *Programmer's Guide* does not require you to execute MBS.app or to open and explore any of the tables, programs, or other files included in the system, you will learn everything more quickly if you take the time to run the application as you make your way through Part I. If you are new to FoxPro, you will probably want to wait until Chapter 7, where we discuss the use of the FoxPro Project Manager, to reopen the MBS project file. From that point on, you will gain valuable hands-on experience in the use of the FoxPro power tools and in the organization and functioning of event-driven applications like the MBS if you open and explore the MBS menu, screen, program, and report and label files as they are discussed in the text.

Conventions Used in This Book

In the code listings in this book, long commands are often entered on more than one line using the line-continuation character (;). This makes the program code easier to read, but it is not necessary. When entering the program code yourself, you may enter longer commands using a single line. Just omit the line-continuation character (;).

Program code listings often include comment lines. In FoxPro, as in most versions of Xbase, the word *NOTE* or an asterisk (*) is placed at the beginning of a command line to instruct FoxPro to ignore the entire line. That way the line can be devoted to explaining program action to other programmers and to yourself. Also, && may be placed after a FoxPro command to use the rest of the command line for comments. We use * and && throughout the text and in the MBS programs to display helpful comments along with the FoxPro commands or program code segments under discussion.

TIP

When entering FoxPro commands and functions, it is not necessary to enter entire command words and function names. Like other versions of Xbase, FoxPro recognizes most commands, functions, and command keywords by their first four letters. MODIFY COMMAND bigbiz, for example, can be entered as MODI COMM bigbiz.

FoxPro commands are typically entered using uppercase characters for all FoxPro command verbs, functions, and keywords and using lowercase characters for everything else—file, field, array, and memory variable names and the names of all user-defined objects, including windows and menus. These conventions are rigorously followed in the MBS program code. However, for the sake of clarity, such names begin with an uppercase letter in the text. The only exception is memory variables. In a FoxPro program, memory variables are typically entered with the memvar prefix m. to distinguish them from table fields with the same name. (The alternative memvar prefix, m->, is also available.) The m. prefix distinguishes the names of memory variables when they are cited in the text, where the memory variable names themselves are presented in lowercase letters.

Limitations of the MBS

While the MBS may be depended on to work as described in this book, remember that it was developed as a learning aid. While I have attempted to be as consistent as possible in writing the core screen programs, illustrations of different ways to achieve similar ends using different FoxPro commands result in a certain inconsistency in programming style that you would not want in an application produced for your clients. (Variations also require more testing.)

The more advanced you become in your use of FoxPro, the more you will rely on program routines that can be used with any data set because they receive their instructions through passed parameters or access them from memory arrays or tables specially designed to serve as data dictionaries. While we introduce these techniques in this book, for the most part the MBS is designed to fence-sit between intermediate and advanced programming techniques, the better to help you get over the fence without falling on your face. For this reason, pay special attention to tips and notes inserted in the text where we discuss alternative ways of writing routines that will make them useful in other applications without modification.

Finally, be aware that the MBS Help file, Mbshelp.dbf, has not been filled in. By reading through the *Programmer's Guide to FoxPro 2.6,* though, you will end up knowing far more about the MBS than could possibly be spelled out in a Help file. You will know it as a developer. Also be sure to take a look at Readme.txt, included on the companion disk. It informs you of any significant last-minute changes to the MBS that couldn't be incorporated in the text. Additional tips and notes on the MBS are also provided on the disk in a file named Readme.txt.

NOTE

The text of this book provides substantial coverage of all programs included in the MBS with the exception of the Backup MBS Tables, Update MBS Index Tags, and Pack MBS Tables programs listed on the MBS system menu's Utilities pulldown. However, these programs are quite simple and can be easily understood with the aid of the program comments placed in them. The Backup MBS Tables program is executed by Backup.spr, a screen program, while the Update MBS Index Tags and Pack MBS Tables programs are combined in Tablefix.prg. You can look them over once you feel at home in the Project Manager.

PART I

Learning the Ropes

CHAPTER

ONE

Designing the Customer Database

- Planning the Customer database
- Arranging customer accounts
- Using tables in a multi-table view
- Handling sales invoice entry and statement production
- Linking tables in a multi-table view

The Model Business System featured in the *Programmer's Guide to FoxPro 2.6* is designed to give you a model to emulate. It therefore sticks as closely as possible to the specifications for the most basic of business applications: an accounts receivable system operating on a stand-alone basis. To make the Model Business System (or MBS) as useful as possible, we will presume to be writing it for a small firm with an international clientele. Its basic functions will be

- Maintaining customer accounts
- Orchestrating invoice data entry for all sales, including cash sales and charges
- Producing customer statements on a monthly basis

Other MBS features include maintenance of an Inventory table and price list, maintenance of a letter library, and the ability to generate a variety of reports in addition to mass personalized form letters and mailing labels.

Maintaining Customer Accounts

The first thing we need to know is whether the system must handle multiple customer accounts. This is not typical of most accounts receivable systems but will be required by firms that do the majority of their business with contractors. From the standpoint of database design, it is also an important consideration since it determines the very definition of customers and accounts. Where there is a one-to-one relation between customers and accounts, we may not only speak of them interchangeably but may also store customer account data directly in the Customer table. Where multiple customer accounts are required, two tables are needed—one to hold customer information and another to hold account information.

In the one-customer/one-account system, we assign each customer listed in the Customer table a unique customer number, or *Custno*. The customer number is then used to identify the customer's record in the Customer table with the records of his or her sales and payments, which are typically stored in separate transaction tables, according to the schema illustrated in Figure 1.1. Using this strategy, our system may readily accommodate as many sales and payments as a customer cares to make. We just add additional records to the Sales and Payments table, being sure to assign each record the correct customer number. This is how multiple transactions are best handled in any DBMS.

FIGURE 1.1:

A unique customer number is used to identify customers with their multiple transactions.

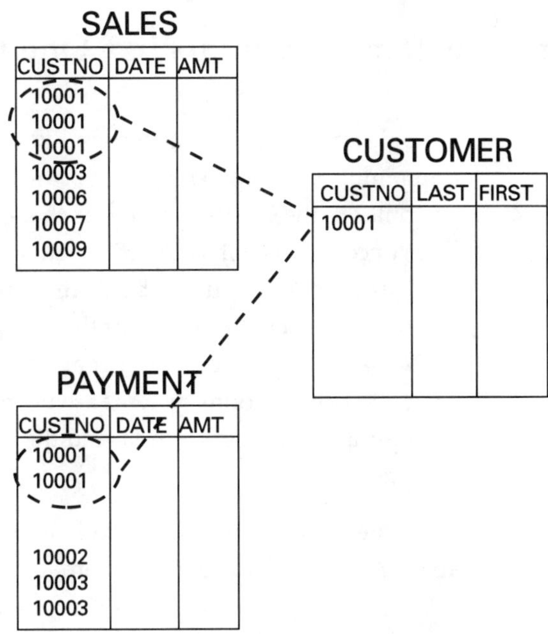

With multiple accounts per customer, things are a bit more complex since, from the standpoint of database design, we must handle each customer's account separately and associate sales or payments with the correct account. For this we require a customer number to identify each customer listed in our Customer table with the records of the customer's accounts in an account table and a unique account number to identify sales and payments with the correct account. This, of course, alters the definition of a customer. From the standpoint of the system, a *customer* is the combination of a customer number identifying a record in the Customer table and an account number identifying a record in the Accounts table.

The strategy used to devise multiple customer account systems roughly simulates the strategy that must be employed in any case to manage the relation between the Sales table, typically designed to hold only summary information about each sale, and a Sales Detail (or Transaction) table, used to hold records of the multiple items that may be included in any sale. Thus we may avoid unduly weighing ourselves down in an endless discussion of transaction-table processing by sticking to a one-customer/one account system.

Multiple Customer Accounts in a One-Customer/One-Account System

A single customer account system like the MBS is, nonetheless, capable of handling multiple customer accounts. You can simply place as many records for each customer in the Customer table as that customer has accounts in the system. This, of course, is not standard practice and should be regarded as a system level work-around. But you will be more than justified in using it in systems in which multiple customer accounts are the exception and not the rule. There is only one aspect of MBS's behavior that you must modify to use it in this way; one-customer/one-account systems are normally designed to inhibit operator entry of duplicate customer records, and the MBS is no exception to this rule. (See Chapter 3.)

To further legitimize using a single-customer account system in this way, you can add an account field to the Customer table and supply each record representing a different account (but the same customer) a distinct account number, using 01, for example, for the customer's first record (and account) in the table, 02 for the second, and so on. This will help make things more orderly.

Orchestrating Sales Invoice Entry

NOTE Here and elsewhere in the text, the word *orchestration* is used in discussions of the programmer's conception and execution of a DBMS. This is because managing the various relations among the multiple tables participating in a DBMS is similar to arranging the themes in a musical score. Both activities require the careful consideration of how the different themes—in our case, tables—contribute to the whole, and how they must appear, disappear, and reappear in the course of composition.

Turning now to the second item on our specifications list, we need to know what the process of sales invoice entry entails with respect to data input and storage. As mentioned above, in a typical acounts receivable system, two tables are used to store information about customer sales: the Sales table, holding summary information about each sale, and the Sales Detail table, designed to hold records of the specific items included in each sale listed in the Sales table. You handle the relation between the two tables by assigning each sale a unique sale number, or *Saleno*. Thus we form a chain of relations among several tables since we identify sales with customers through their assigned Custnos and sales detail records with records in the Sales table by their assigned Salenos.

Using an Inventory/Price List

Experienced programmers are familiar with these issues. What attracts their attention is fleshing out the relation (assuming there is to be one) between the Sales Detail table and the Inventory table. This is because an Inventory table, listing the names and prices of all items available for sale, is typically used during the process of sale invoice entry as a lookup table, making it unnecessary for the operator to do more than enter the quantity and part number (*Partno*) of each item required in a sale. The part descriptions and prices of the items can be supplied automatically by the Inventory table.

Where a stable inventory/price list is used, it is, moreover, unnecessary to store such information in the Sales Detail table. We need include only a sale number to identify its records with a corresponding record in the Summary Sales table, a part number to identify its records with a record in the Inventory table, and a quantity. We can calculate the total cost of each item in a sale—the *extension*—on the fly by multiplying the quantity of an item, stored in the Sales Detail table, by the price of the item, stored in the Inventory table.

Variations in the Use of an Inventory/Price List

Things get a bit more complex when we deal with firms that change item prices so often or use so many different prices for different customers that it becomes necessary for the operator to enter item prices manually—or at least to be able to overwrite prices supplied by the Inventory table. Where this is the case, our Sales Detail table must accommodate item prices. All we may reliably fetch from the Inventory table is the part description—that is, assuming the list of items sold by the firm is stable enough to warrant using an Inventory table at all. Where this is not the case, the Sales Detail table will have to accommodate part descriptions as well so the operator can key them in.

Once again, sticking to the most typical arrangement, the MBS is designed to make use of an Inventory table for automatic lookup of part descriptions and prices, though we can change this by simply altering the structure of the MBS Sales Detail table and changing the screen program employed for entering and editing sales. (These procedures are discussed in Chapter 6.)

Storing Multiple Item Records in the Inventory/Price List

Systems that depend on an inventory/price list for automatic input of item descriptions and prices during sales invoice entry and printing are not inflexible. For example, if you (or your client) have a stable inventory list but use two or more standard prices for each item, multiple records can be placed in the Inventory table for each item. When entering an item in a sale, the operator need enter only the part number corresponding to the record with the desired price. The point is to find out how the business really operates before wasting time creating a sale entry routine that forces the operator to input data that, in the majority of cases, can be supplied directly from an Inventory or other lookup table.

Handling Cash and Charge Sales

The ability to handle customer cash sales is essential in a DBMS designed to hold customer accounts. There are two aspects to this problem: how the system stores and uses cash sales data and distinguishes between cash and charge sales (only charge sales must be used to update the customer account), and how much information should be stored in the Customer table about any given customer. Indeed, must a customer be listed at all in order to print out an invoice?

We can handle the first issue easily by placing a data field in the Summary Sales table that can subsequently be used to identify each record as a cash sale or charge. The value stored in that field—say 1 for cash sale and 2 for charge, the simple schema used by the MBS Sales table—can then be used to determine how each sale entered in the system should be processed. (This is discussed in Chapter 6.)

Entering Cash Sales without Entering a Customer

The second issue is a bit more complex since you may wish to prepare for a variety of different situations. You may, for example, want to store name and address information for every customer, even those without an active (charge) account, for the sake of advertising. This in itself poses no problem, as long as the system is designed to distinguish between cash and charge sales. But a problem can arise when one or more customers (or even the majority of customers) making cash purchases do not want to be listed in the Customer table or when it is simply inconvenient and a waste of time to list them.

We can handle this problem easily, however, by using another system work-around. With the MBS, for example, it is necessary to enter or locate a customer in the Customer table before a sale can be entered. To enter sales not attached to any specific customer, we simply create a record in the Customer table using a last-name entry of Cash Sale and leave the rest of the record blank. (Of course, MBS assigns a customer number to the record.) Then, whenever a customer who is not already listed in the Customer table comes in to make a quick purchase, the operator simply accesses the Customer table record for Cash Sale and continues with data entry. Since the MBS is designed to keep track of a customer's total charge and cash sales in a special History field, the total cash sales made to customers not specifically listed in the Customer table will appear in the History field of our Cash Sale record. All we'll have to do to make use of this particular system work-around is to make sure our invoice-printing program will not require additional name-and-address information from the Cash Sale record but will simply print *Cash Sale* and leave it at that.

Producing Customer Statements

The third item on our requirement list, the production of customer statements, is usually routine. Generally speaking, you need only ask how often customer statements must be generated—usually, once a month—if interest rates are to be levied against customers with delinquent accounts, and if so, what defines a delinquent account.

Of course, from the standpoint of database design, things are not so simple. The new FoxPro programmer will want to know where all the data included in customer statements comes from. The master programmer might shrug and say,

"From the Customer database, where else?"—all the better to help novices to understand the multiple tables that must be employed to produce statements as a single data source, or *database,* that can be viewed in a variety of ways. It is only when producing customer statements that we need to view all the data stored in the Customer database at once.

MBS Handling of Interest Charges

In most instances, *delinquent accounts* are those with debts outstanding for more than three months; interest charges are levied at a set rate against such debts. This is how the MBS is designed to handle them—though, as you will see in Chapter 2, the interest rate employed by the system for calculating interest charges can be altered at whim by the operator. It is not hard coded.

Looking at the sample statement produced by the MBS in Figure 1.2, we see the combined output from three tables. The Customer table supplies name-and-address information, the summary customer account data (representing customer debits over a several-month period), and the customer's balance forward. (Of course, when a separate Accounts table is required for handling multiple customer accounts, the account data and balance forward will be taken from the Accounts table.) The Sales table pumps in sales for the *current* statement period—the only sales that need be detailed on the statement. (There is no need here to include sales detail information). The Payments table supplies all other customer transactions made during the current period, including payments, refunds, interest charges, bookkeeping adjustments, and the like. The statement-printing program performs all the calculations.

Organizing the Customer Database for Fast Output of Data

Arranging our tables for instantaneous output of the data required by our statement-printing program—or by our customer sales or payment reports program—is a rather simple matter. This is because FoxPro can read data from several tables at once, provided they can be linked together through the use of a common field like

FIGURE 1.2:

Statement production draws data from all the tables in the Customer database.

```
04/01/95        Customer Statement                                      1

                Howard Dickler
                PO Box 34293
                Los Angeles, CA 90034
                310-204-2780

  Statement for: 100010
                Dr. Katje Borgesius
                The White Visitation
                Entertainment & Therapy
                34012 Pennsylvania Ave.
                Washington DC 02043-2222
                USA
                204-333-3333
```

Date	Invoice	Charge	Credit	Type	Balance
				Balance Forward:	0.00
03/04/95	100004	3,410.00		Sale	3,410.00
03/04/95	100006	1,870.00		Sale	5,280.00
03/04/95	100007	5,940.00		Sale	11,220.00
03/04/95	100012	15,290.00		Sale	26,510.00
03/04/95	100004		3,410.00	Payment	23,100.00
03/04/95	100006		200.00	Return	22,900.00
03/04/95	100006	100.00		Bk Adj (db)	23,000.00
03/04/95	100012		10,000.00	Payment	13,000.00
03/04/95	100012		450.00	Return	12,550.00
03/04/95	100007		5,940.00	Payment	6,610.00
03/08/95	100012		500.00	Payment	6,110.00
	Totals:	26,610.00	20,500.00		

Current	30 Days	60 Days	90 Days	120 Days+
6,110.00				
		Please Remit Present Balance of:		$6,110.00

Variable Uses of the Payments Table

Since payments, unlike sales, generally have no detail, the table used to enter and store payments offers an ideal way to hold all customer transactions other than sales. All that is required is a Transaction Code field to indicate the function of each record so the system will be able to recognize it as a debit or credit and use it as such. A Payments table designed to hold different types of transactions can even accommodate sales charged to a customer's account and can be so used when no sale invoice is required. (We see how to do all of this in Chapter 5.)

Custno. In fact, FoxPro can handle the job in a variety of ways. Sticking for the moment to commands familiar to the Xbase programmers, we can create the database view required for printing our statements with the following FoxPro commands:

```
USE customer ORDER names
USE sales ORDER sales IN 0
USE payments ORDER payments IN 0
SET RELATION TO custno INTO sales
SET RELATION TO custno INTO payments ADDITIVE
SET SKIP TO sales, payments
```

Quick Notes on Work Areas and Tables

In FoxPro as in other versions of Xbase, one table can be opened in each available work area. With FoxPro, however, there are 255 available work areas, each of which can be identified by work area number—1 through 255—or, after a table has been opened, by the name of the table open in it. When FoxPro initiates action, work area 1 is selected as the current work area, and a table opened with USE <file> will be opened in it. (If you execute USE <file> to open a table in a work area already employed by another table, FoxPro will close the open table before opening the new table.) To open a table in another work area, use SELECT <work area> before issuing USE <file> or employ the USE command's IN <work area> option to specify the work area in which the file should be opened. (Note that unlike SELECT, USE IN <work area> does not change the current work area to open the indicated table.)

Since work areas can be identified by the tables open in them—a topic upon which we expand as we move along—it will be unnecessary to trifle with work area numbers, provided that we can instruct FoxPro to select or open a table in an unused work area. FoxPro allows us to do this by using 0 with SELECT and USE IN <work area> to designate the lowest unused work area—a feature we use in the commands shown above. (Again, we will have much more to say about work areas and the conventions used with them in the following chapters.)

Returning now to the commands shown above, we begin by issuing USE <file> three times, twice with IN 0, to open the tables required to form our multifile database view. Moreover, we employ the USE command's ORDER option to activate an index with each of our tables. An index, however, is not required to include the table in the multifile view in the case of Customer.dbf; but index tag Names will help to arrange the records included in the view in alphabetical order by customer last and first names. (Customer table index tags are discussed in Chapter 4.)

The case is different with index tags Sales and Payments, activated with Sales.dbf and Payments.dbf, respectively, to arrange the records in each table by Custno. With the aid of these two index tags, FoxPro can instantaneously look up all sales and payments listed in the two tables by Custno. It is therefore ready to link the records in the Payments and Sales tables with whatever record may be current in the Customer table. The two SET RELATION commands that follow instruct FoxPro to enable the links. Figure 1.3 indicates the resulting database view as it would appear in FoxPro's View dialog box. We discuss the effects of SET RELATION with greater precision in just a moment.

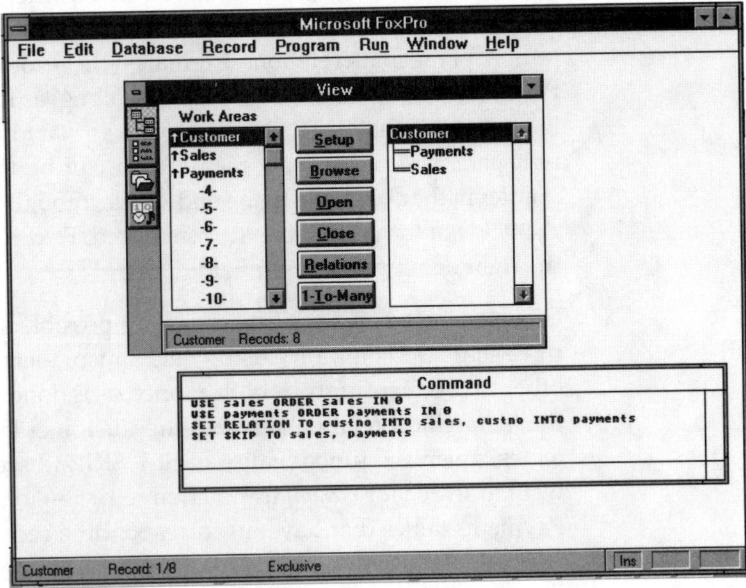

FIGURE 1.3:
The FoxPro View dialog with the MBS Customer database open

With FoxPro, two or more relations can be specified at once with SET RELATION. We can, for example, link the Customer file into Sales and Payments with

```
SET RELATION TO custno INTO sales; custno INTO payments
```

To do the same thing using two commands, we must be certain to use the keyword ADDITIVE in the second SET RELATION command; otherwise it will undo the link set with the first.

TIP

When you build a multi-table database view with the View dialog, FoxPro echoes the commands used to execute the view in the Command window. You can therefore transfer the commands executing the view to any program file by copying them into the Clipboard and then pasting them into the program.

Parent-Child Table Relations

The particular relation formed by SET RELATION among the three tables is that of a parent table to two child tables. In effect, wherever we move the record pointer in Customer.dbf—which we refer to as the *parent table* because it is from Customer.dbf that both relations originate—the record pointers used with the Sales and Payments tables—the *child tables*—tag along, as it were, moving to the first record in either table that has the same Custno as that found in the Custno field of the current parent record. (If no such record can be found, FoxPro moves the record pointer in the *child* table to the end-of-file, though this causes no error.) If and when the fields of the child table are referenced, FoxPro simply returns empty values of the right data type for each field.

Of course, other types of relations are possible among the three tables. Since all three share the common Custno field, any of them might be made the parent of the other two, either singly or both at once, as is done here. Still, it is unusual to reverse the hierarchical relation between the Customer table and the Sales and Payments tables, given the functionality of SET SKIP (discussed in a moment), unless you want to search for *orphan* transaction records—in this case, records in the Sales and Payments tables that have no corresponding record in the Customer table, owing to accidental deletion of Customer table records.

Locating Orphan Transaction Records

To find orphan records in a transaction table, just reverse its relation to the table to which it normally stands as a child to a parent with SET RELATION. Then issue the command SET FILTER TO NOT FOUND( ):

```
USE customer ORDER custno

USE sales IN 0

SELECT sales

SET RELATION TO custno INTO customer

SET FILTER TO NOT FOUND("customer")

LIST
```

When we issue the LIST command, only those records in Sales.dbf that have no corresponding record in Customer.dbf will be included in the view. The childless parent records, in the present view, are the parentless children in our normal database view and, owing to the action of SET RELATION, will always remain out of sight and out of mind unless a deliberate effort is made to find them. To only look at Sales.dbf records that are not orphan records in our normal view—or, stated with respect to the present view, to look only at *parent* records that have no records in a *child* table—just change SET FILTER TO FOUND().

Now that we have properly linked the Sales and Payments tables to our Customer table, we can scroll through the records of our Customer table and view their contents along with that of the first child record in either table. Such is the action of SET RELATION. To print our statements, however, we must gain access to all their child records—or at the very least to all sales and payments falling in the current billing period. In the FoxPro View dialog this is referred to as a *one-to-many relation*, and it is achieved with the SET SKIP command. SET SKIP directs FoxPro to stop at every parent record it comes to while executing any of the FoxPro sequential commands, such as LIST, DISPLAY, SUM, and REPORT FORM, and skip through all the child records it can find for the current parent record before moving on to read the next record in the parent table.

Though you are as yet unfamiliar with all the data field names used by the MBS Customer, Sales, and Payments tables, Figure 1.4, showing sample output from a LIST command referencing fields from all three tables, should help you understand the action of SET SKIP. (As previously mentioned, whenever FoxPro finds no child record to include in the view in either child table, it just outputs empty values.)

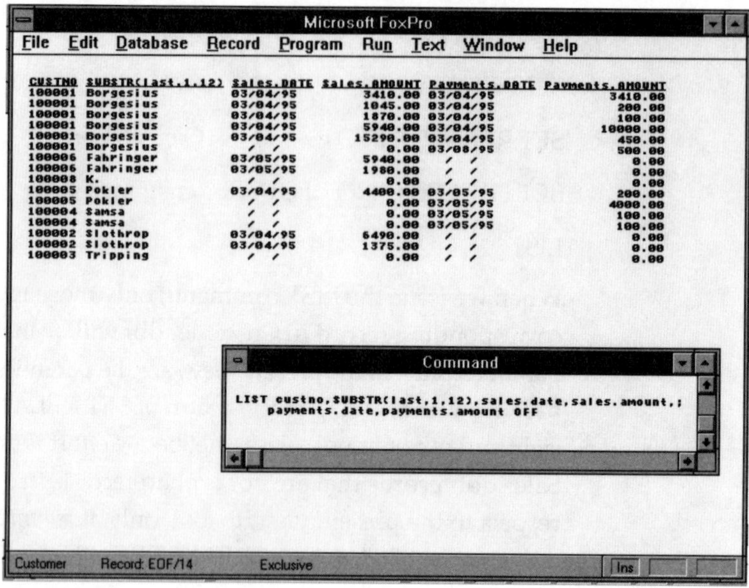

FIGURE 1.4:
Sample output from a parent-multiple child view

TIP

If you are new to the one-to-many views formed with SET RELATION and SET SKIP, you will find them easier to understand by playing around with a single parent-child view. Consider the effects of reversing the relation, as well as the possible effects of conditional filters, including SET FILTER TO FOUND() and NOT FOUND(), on the resulting view. This will prepare you to deal with parent-multiple child table relations when they turn up—and grandchild tables as well.

More provocative yet, for those who are new to FoxPro, will be the display produced by the FoxPro BROWSE command, which does not repeat the data in a parent record when reporting multiple child records. (See Figure 1.5.) If you look closely at the BROWSE table you will find six records listed for Last = "Borgesius", though only the first cites data from the parent (Customer) table. Since Borgesius has six records in the Payments table, FoxPro must include six records in the view to display them all. As she has only five records on file in the Sales table, the fields of her sixth record, which would otherwise display her sixth sale, remain blank. The display format used by BROWSE with multi-table views makes them easier to read.

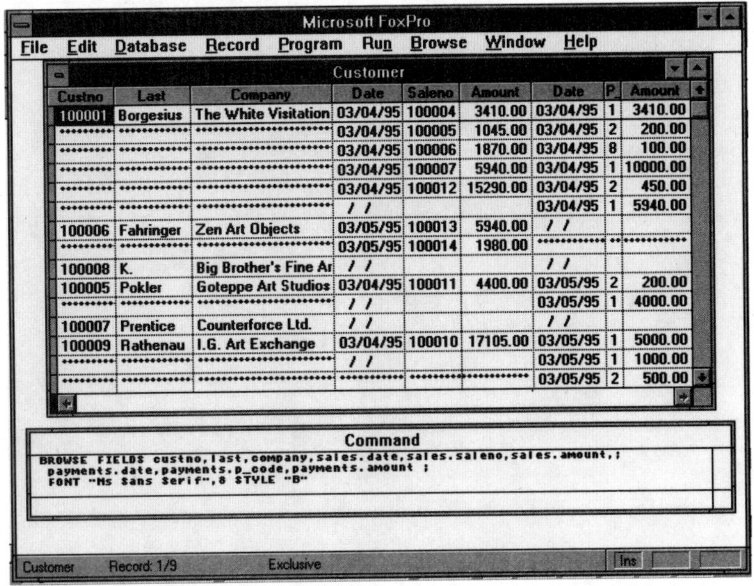

FIGURE 1.5:
FoxPro's BROWSE command makes it easy to view records in a multi-table view.

Still, with regard to outputting data from our Customer database, this is just the tip of the iceberg, since FoxPro has another and faster way to execute most multi-table views: SQL-SELECT. There are also the potential uses of Rushmore optimization to consider. But these tools are dedicated to data output. While we introduce them in Chapter 4, our primary concern throughout Part I is data input in a multi-table environment. When linking tables for purposes of data entry and display, SET RELATION and SEEK and SEEK( ), also discussed in Chapter 4, are the tools of choice.

TWO

2

Designing the Customer Table

- Defining an international Customer table
- Managing customer accounts
- Program assignment of customer numbers
- Using system value tables

As we saw in Chapter 1, the MBS Customer database is made up of three tables that can be linked instantly through the use of a common customer number, or Custno, field. These include our Customer table, Customer.dbf, which stores summary customer account data, our Payments table, Payments.dbf, which holds records of all customer transactions other than sales (though it can be used to hold them too), and the Sales table, Sales.dbf, which holds summary information about customer sales. In the following chapters we deal with each of these tables, focusing on the function and use of each within the system, the index tags and auxiliary files with which they are used, and the data entry or *screen* programs we must devise for putting them to work in a business environment.

The MBS Customer Table

According to the specifications laid out in Chapter 1, the Customer table must hold name-and-address information for an international clientele and customer account data suitable for the production of monthly statements. We achieve these two goals and throw in a few frills by employing the table structure shown in Figure 2.1. Note

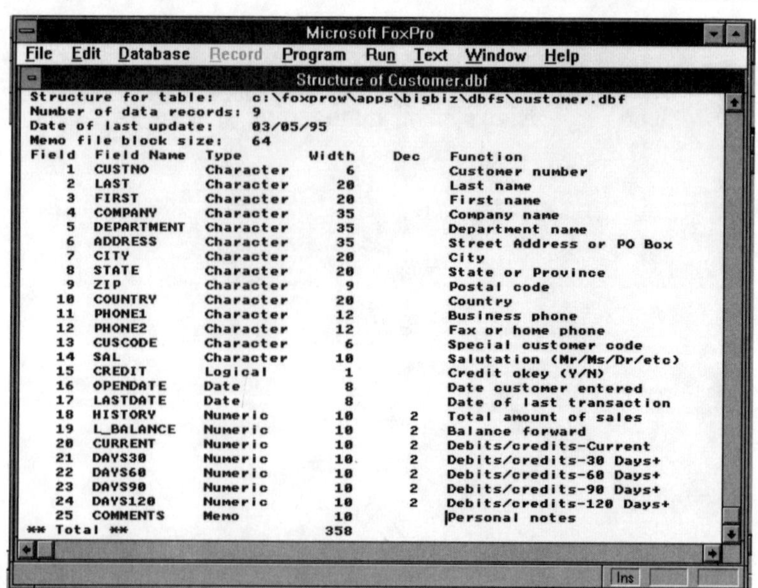

Microsoft FoxPro

File Edit Database Record Program Run Text Window Help

Structure of Customer.dbf

Structure for table: c:\foxprow\apps\bigbiz\dbfs\customer.dbf
Number of data records: 9
Date of last update: 03/05/95
Memo file block size: 64

Field	Field Name	Type	Width	Dec	Function
1	CUSTNO	Character	6		Customer number
2	LAST	Character	20		Last name
3	FIRST	Character	20		First name
4	COMPANY	Character	35		Company name
5	DEPARTMENT	Character	35		Department name
6	ADDRESS	Character	35		Street Address or PO Box
7	CITY	Character	20		City
8	STATE	Character	20		State or Province
9	ZIP	Character	9		Postal code
10	COUNTRY	Character	20		Country
11	PHONE1	Character	12		Business phone
12	PHONE2	Character	12		Fax or home phone
13	CUSCODE	Character	6		Special customer code
14	SAL	Character	10		Salutation (Mr/Ms/Dr/etc)
15	CREDIT	Logical	1		Credit okey (Y/N)
16	OPENDATE	Date	8		Date customer entered
17	LASTDATE	Date	8		Date of last transaction
18	HISTORY	Numeric	10	2	Total amount of sales
19	L_BALANCE	Numeric	10	2	Balance forward
20	CURRENT	Numeric	10	2	Debits/credits-Current
21	DAYS30	Numeric	10	2	Debits/credits-30 Days+
22	DAYS60	Numeric	10	2	Debits/credits-60 Days+
23	DAYS90	Numeric	10	2	Debits/credits-90 Days+
24	DAYS120	Numeric	10	2	Debits/credits-120 Days+
25	COMMENTS	Memo	10		Personal notes
** Total **			358		

Ins

FIGURE 2.1:

Field structure of the MBS Customer table, Customer.dbf

that the output of LIST STRUCTURE has been altered to include a description of each field's function in the table. (The Index column of the display has also been omitted, to save space.)

Making Your Customer Table International

We can easily revise a Customer table dedicated to storing names and addresses of customers living in the United States for use with an international clientele by adding a Country field and increasing the width of the State field so it will be large enough to accommodate province and state names. The width of Phone fields should also be increased to accommodate country codes. Since Zip Code fields, like all code fields, should be type C (Character) and not type N (Numeric), they should require no revision to hold postal codes employing alphabetical characters.

While the data fields used to store name-and-address information for each customer should be clear from Figure 2.1, this is not the case with the customer account and supplementary Customer table fields.

The Customer Account Fields

The Current, Days30, Days60, Days90, and Days120 fields are used by the MBS as *debt-aging fields*. They are used to break down customer debt by billing period. Since all debts older than 120 days are allowed to accrue in the Days120 field, the total of all debt-aging fields will always provide us with the customer's present balance:

```
pres_bal = current + days30 + days60 + days90 + days120
```

When a customer's account shows a balance in the customer's favor, the Current field is employed to indicate the credit. For reasons discussed below, none of the other debt-aging fields are designed to hold or represent customer credits.

Although the finished system will allow the operator to enter data in these fields through the use of the Customers window shown in Figure 2.2, this should be necessary only when installing the MBS system, if old customer accounts must be manually carried over to the new system.

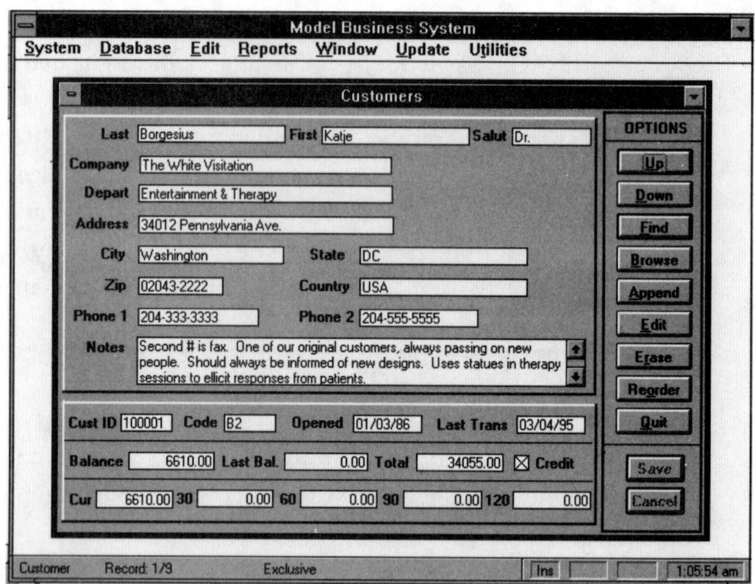

FIGURE 2.2:
MBS Customers window

System Update of the Customer Account Fields

Customer account data, as our simplified MBS flow chart indicates (see Figure 2.3), is updated whenever a customer sale or payment is entered. The sale or payment is recorded in the Sales or Payments table, respectively, under the customer's assigned Custno. The sum of the payment or sale, assuming it is a charge, is then used to update the customer account's debt-aging fields. (We do not update the debt-aging fields with cash sales since they create no debt, nor do they require mention on statements.)

FIGURE 2.3: The flow chart indicates the movement of customer account data in the system.

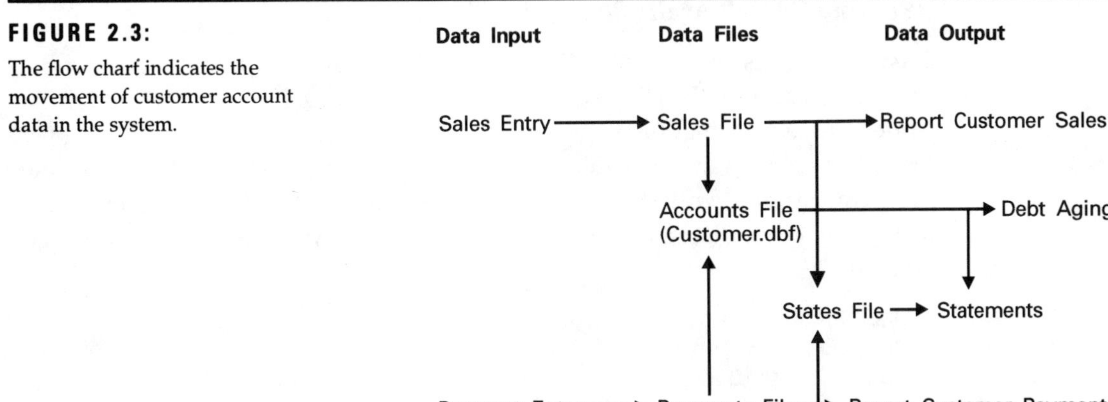

Handling Customer Debits

In the case of customer sales (and the set of other customer debits that may be recorded in the Payments table), the sum is added to the Current field, which indicates current customer debits or credits, with the following command, where m.amount is a memory variable used to temporarily hold the sale amount:

```
REPLACE current WITH current + m.amount
```

As this should imply, debits will be represented in the customer account fields and treated internally by the MBS system as positive numbers, while customer credits will be represented as negative numbers.

At the end of the month, after statements are written, the system is prepared for the entry of sales belonging to the billing period just beginning. Whatever debit appears in the Current field must be passed on to the Days30 field since the debit will be more than 30 days old, supposing it is not paid off, by the time of the next billing. The same thing is done with debits held in the other debt-aging fields. Whatever debit is found in Days30 is passed on to Days60, and so on. Again, debts of 120 days or older are allowed to accrue in the Days120 field since three months is the usual amount of time allowed before interest charges can be levied. With respect to the generation of interest charges, there is therefore no need to track debt over a longer period.

Handling Customer Credits

Customer credits entered in the Payments table are used to update the customer account fields differently. They are automatically subtracted from customer debts recorded in the customer debt-aging fields in reverse order—that is, beginning with the oldest debts found. The following procedure accomplishes this. It is executed programmatically with the command DO subtract WITH m.amount, where m.amount (and therefore memvar m.amount2 as well) represents the credit amount.

```
PROCEDURE Subtract
PARAMETER m.amount2
IF days120 <> 0.00
    IF days120 - m.amount2 >= 0.00
        REPLACE customer.days120 ;
            WITH customer.days120 - m.amount2
        RETURN
    ENDIF
    m.amount2 = m.amount2 - days120
    REPLACE days120 WITH 0.00
ENDIF
IF days90 <> 0.00
    IF days90 - m.amount2 >= 0.00
        REPLACE days90 WITH days90 - m.amount2
        RETURN
    ENDIF
    m.amount2 = m.amount2 - days90
    REPLACE days90 WITH 0.00
ENDIF
* Repeat same commands for days60 and days30 and then place any
* remaining amount in the current field
REPLACE current WITH current - m.amount2
RETURN
```

If a customer credit remains after all debits are wiped out, it remains in the Current field, where the system will automatically apply it against new customer debits (though it can also be wiped out by entering a record representing a *refund* in the Payments table). This means that when we update the customer account debt-aging fields immediately after printing out monthly statements and, preferably, a copy of the Customer Account (debt-aging) report, described below, we must refrain from passing a customer credit, appearing in the Current field, over to Days30. Only debits are passed.

Using a Balance Forward Field

When printing statements, we must also have access to the Customer's *balance forward*—that is, the account balance at the time of the last monthly billing. This is the function of the L_balance, or Last Balance, field. It too must be updated immediately after monthly statements are produced.

Batch Update of Customer Account Fields

In accordance with their use, the customer account fields of all records in Customer.dbf must be updated in batch at the outset of each new billing period. We achieve this by executing the Update Customer Accounts program, available on the MBS main menu's Update pulldown. (See Figure 2.4.) However, since it will be impossible to reverse the results of the batch update without restoring the Customer table from a backup copy, the program requires action validation from the operator (See Figure 2.5) before executing the following REPLACE command:

```
SELECT customer
m.orig_ord = ORDER()
m.eof = EOF()
m.cus_rec = RECNO()
SET RELATION TO
SET ORDER TO
REPLACE ALL l_balance ;
    WITH current+days30+days60+days90+days120, ;
    days120 WITH days120+days90, ;
    days90 WITH days60,days60 WITH days30, ;
    days30 WITH IIF(current > 0.00,current,0.00), ;
    current WITH IIF(current < 0.00,current,0.00) ;
    FOR l_balance <> 0.00 AND current <> 0.00
SET RELATION TO custno INTO payments, custno INTO sales
SET ORDER TO (m.orig_ord)
IF NOT m.eof
    GO m.cust_rec
ENDIF
```

Since the Customer table will already be open and linked into the Sales and Payments tables, as indicated at the end of Chapter 1, we prepare for the REPLACE command by deactivating Customer.dbf's master index (since no record order is required) and by breaking off Customer.dbf's relation with the Sales and Payments table (since REPLACE addresses only data fields in Customer.dbf). Both actions speed up REPLACE, as does the use of the conditional filter, which prevents FoxPro from wasting time shuffling zeros about in inactive accounts.

FIGURE 2.4:

MBS main menu with the Update pulldown open

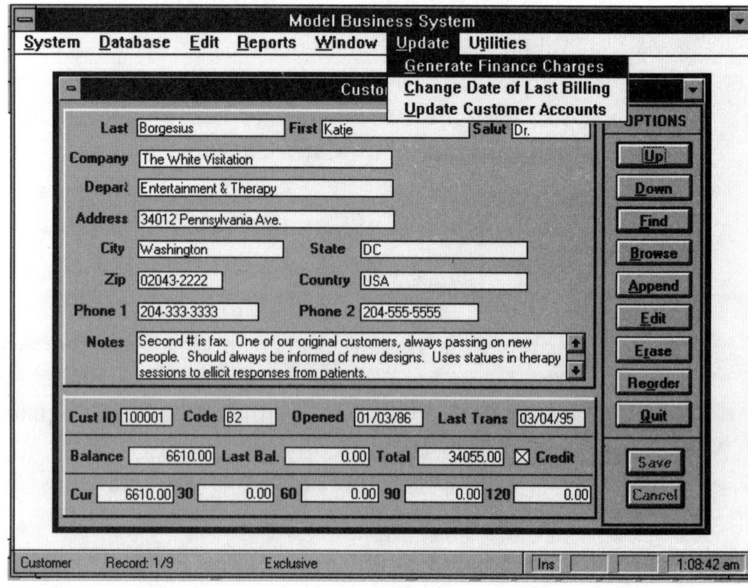

FIGURE 2.5:

Whenever an action is irreversible, MBS requires action validation from the operator.

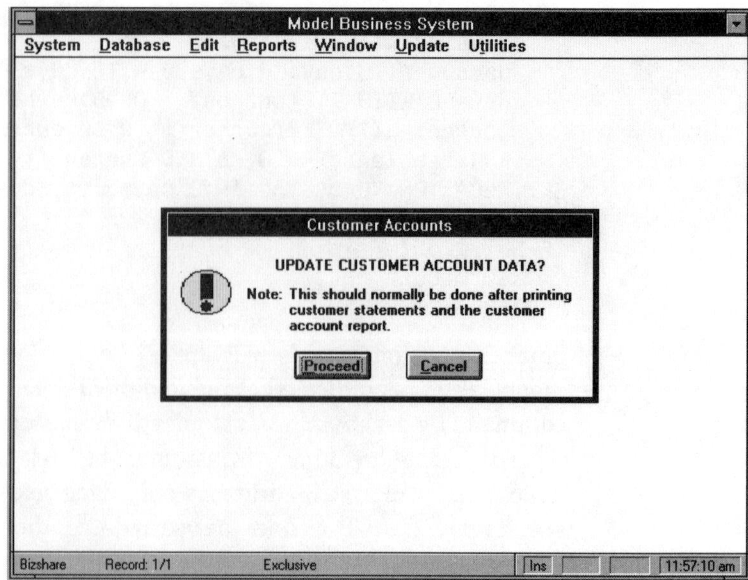

NOTE

We need not test all debt-aging fields to identify active accounts since L_balance will always be greater than 0 if there is anything in Days30-Days120. We must, however, test Current since the figure it holds will not be reflected by L_balance. Note that we do not use the condition L_balance + Current <> 0.00 because the value in the two fields could cancel each other out, supposing one were a credit and the other a debit. ABS(L_balance) + ABS(Current) <> 0.00, however, will do since the absolute values of the two fields, added together, cannot cancel each other out.

TIP

If you must select a table to perform an operation and then reselect whatever table was current before the action, just store the value of ALIAS(), indicating the name of the current table, to a memvar. After the action is completed, issue the command SELECT (memvar). (We discuss the use of alias names later in this chapter.)

Having saved the name of the master index and current record number to memvars, we can reengage the master index after REPLACE is done and even return FoxPro to its original position in the Customer table. Note, however, that we also save the value of EOF(), indicating whether the end of the table has been surpassed, to a memvar and subsequently use the memvar with IF to control execution of GO m.cus_rec. This is a necessary precaution since GO m.cus_rec may result in an error if EOF() was .T. when m.cus_rec was initialized.

WARNING

RECNO() returns a value of 1 when EOF() is .T.—or when FoxPro is positioned to the first record of an unindexed table. If you store RECNO() to a memvar when EOF() is .T. and subsequently issue GO memvar, FoxPro therefore goes to the first record in the table. However, if the table is empty or record 1 is deleted and SET DELETED is ON, GO memvar results in an error.

Focusing on the action of the REPLACE command, first we sum the debt-aging fields and store the total in the L_balance field, representing the customer's balance forward. Then we update the debt-aging fields in reverse order, which is necessary to obtain the correct results. When we come to the Days30 and Current fields, we must arrange things so that a credit appearing in Current does *not* get passed on to Days30. Again, we must leave the credit in Current so it can be applied against sales and other debits entered during the billing period just beginning. This is handled in the REPLACE command using the IIF(), or *immediate IF,* function, which allows us to conditionally control which of two values is used to update Days30. If the value of *Current* is greater than 0, indicating a customer debit, the value is placed in Days30; otherwise, the Days30 field is zeroed out. We also use IIF() to control the update of Current. If the field holds a debit (already passed on to Days30), it is zeroed out. If it holds a customer credit, its current value is left untouched. In effect, this approach allows the field to update itself.

Once the REPLACE command has completed its action, the customer account fields are set for the period just beginning since the Current field is set to 0 (or holds a balance in the customer's favor) to begin receiving debits accrued over the next month. The rest of the debt-aging fields are set to hold the history of customer debits as they will stand at the end of the month, supposing they are left unpaid.

WARNING Beware of using a master index tag with REPLACE if any of the fields slated for replacement are included in the index tag's <key expression> and the command's scope includes more than one record. If a record's position in the indexed table is altered by the replacement, FoxPro moves the record pointer to that record's new position. This prevents it from processing the rest of the table records in sequential order.

The Customer Account or Debt-Aging Report

As you may surmise, the debt-aging fields provide an immediate profile of our customer accounts, and though the business for which you are developing a system may have no need of it, the MBS is designed to make use of this data in producing a Customer Account (or Debt-Aging) report. This report, a sample page of which is shown in the screen display in Figure 2.6, is generally produced immediately *after* printing statements and *before* updating the account fields. This way, if it is employed, for example, as a tickle-file report for contacting customers with problem accounts, its data will be completely up to date. Still, like other customer reports including statements, you can print out the Customer Account report at any time and even limit the output in a variety of ways. (We return to this in a moment.)

FIGURE 2.6:

Sample output from the MBS Customer Account report

Model Business System

File Edit Database Record Program Window Help

03/31/95 Customer Accounts 1

Cust ID--Name/Company	Phone	Pres Bal.	Last Bal.	Current	Days30	Days60	Days90	Days120
100001--Borgesius, Katje The White Visitation	204-333-3333	6110.00	0.00	6110.00	0.00	0.00	0.00	0.00
100002--Slothrop, Hogan Aloha Noveltiesn	800-333-3445	9365.00	1500.00	7865.00	600.00	900.00	0.00	0.00
100003--Tripping, Geli Just Say NO!	209-333-3333	0.00	0.00	0.00	0.00	0.00	0.00	0.00
100004--Samsa, Gregor, Samsa Culture Clinic	212-222-2222	400.00	600.00	0.00	300.00	100.00	0.00	0.00
100005--Pokler, Franz Goteppe Art Studios	011-233-3223	-700.00	3500.00	-700.00	0.00	0.00	0.00	0.00
100006--Fahringer, Max Zen Art Objects	314-567-5677	7920.00	0.00	7920.00	0.00	0.00	0.00	0.00
100007--Prentice, Pirate Counterforce Ltd.	01222333-456	200.00	200.00	0.00	200.00	0.00	0.00	0.00
100008--K., Joseph Big Brother's Fine Art	617-322-4532	900.00	900.00	0.00	0.00	0.00	300.00	600.00
100009--Rathenau, Walter I.G. Art Exchange	213-757-4566	10605.00	0.00	10605.00	0.00	0.00	0.00	0.00
100010--Bloom, Leopold Eccles St. Galleries	012-326-7775	1200.00	1200.00	400.00	200.00	600.00	0.00	0.00
100011--Boylan, Blazes Boilin' Art Enterprises	208-345-2245	500.00	500.00	0.00	300.00	200.00	0.00	0.00
100012--McDowell, Gerty McDowell Studioy	212-345-6788	400.00	400.00	400.00	0.00	0.00	0.00	0.00
100013--Dingham, Pat Charon's Place Gallery	402-556-7655	1000.00	1000.00	200.00	100.00	0.00	400.00	300.00
100014--Cunningham, Martir Cunningham Art Objects	310-345-6789	12000.00	12000.00	2000.00	2000.00	3000.00	4000.00	1000.00

Alternative Strategies for Updating Customer Account Fields

Bear in mind that the techniques used by the MBS for updating the customer account fields, though relatively straightforward, do not provide safeguards against errors. If the figures appearing in the debt-aging fields are thrown off for one reason or another, the routines employed to update the fields during data entry of sales and payments or in preparation for the new billing period will not correct them. The alternative is to refer exclusively to the Sales and Payments tables whenever updating the account fields. Since all records in the Sales and Payments tables bear a date, you can, for example, use SUM or CALCULATE to recalculate the proper entries for each of the debt-aging fields.

Though it will require yet more programming, a routine that recalculates debt-aging fields by referring to the transaction data can also be further refined to link payments to specific invoices. By working in this way, you can ensure that the values displayed in the debt-aging fields are precise with regard to the actual dates of the invoices that have yet to be paid. In the MBS, we lump all debits together with respect to any payment or other customer credit; but doing so will be far too simplistic in many systems.

Be aware that using transaction data to recalculate debt-aging fields will not require you to keep all customer transactions permanently on file or to make FoxPro read them all when making its calculations. For example, recalculating a customer's debt-aging fields may show that the customer has no debts of 120 days or older. If this is the case and all transactions in the Sales and payments tables include invoice numbers, allowing payments to be related to invoices, you can mark all sales of 120 days or older for deletion and then do the same to all payments bearing upon the deleted invoice. (Instead of deleting them, you can also add a field to the Sales and Payments tables to indicate when a sale or payment should not be considered when recalculating the debt-aging fields.) A simpler strategy that does not depend upon matching payments with sales by invoice numbers is to mark all customer sales and payments for deletion when recalculation shows that the customer's balance is 0 or, again, to use a field to indicate that the sales and payments should no longer be included in the calculations. However you do it, the point is to supply your program (and FoxPro) with a means of limiting the transactions that must be considered when recalculating the debt-aging fields to those that matter.

Supplementary Customer Table Fields

The MBS Customer table also includes several supplementary fields that will be of use in most businesses. If you (or your client) maintain personal contacts with customers, you will want a place to record personal information or notes about them. This is the function of the Comments field. The Comments field is created as a field of type M (Memo) so it will hold as much or as little information about each customer as is needed. As you will note, the contents of the Comments field are displayed in a scrollable box on the Customers window, where it is labeled as Notes. (Again, see Figure 2.2.) If you are familiar with FoxPro 2.0 or later, you know that this is achieved with the @ EDIT command, not with @ GET, which is used to display all other Customer table fields.

As for the Cuscode, Opendate, Lastdate, and History fields, these too are used in MBS for informational purposes only. Their function in the system, however, is most easily illustrated by the dialog that appears when the operator selects Customer Database from the MBS main menu's Reports pulldown. (See Figure 2.7.) Suppose, for example, that a business wishes to write letters advertising the sale of certain items. The operator may elect to print letters to all customers on file or fill in the data entry fields in the lower portion of the Customer Database Reports window to target customers by country, by zip-code range, by the total amount of a

FIGURE 2.7:

All MBS Customer table reports are executed with a single dialog.

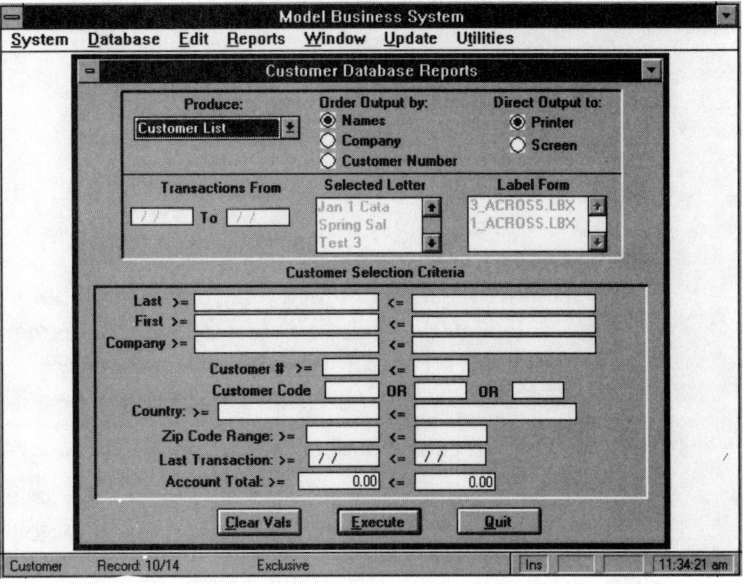

customer's purchases (History), by any of up to three customized customer codes of the user's own devising (Cuscode), or by the date upon which the customer made its last purchase (Lastdate). Only Opendate—the date the customer was added to the Customer table—is excluded from use, though it is displayed during data entry of sales and payments.

> **NOTE**
>
> Although we must update the History field each time a customer makes a purchase it cannot, strictly speaking, be regarded as a customer account field. This is because it is updated to reflect the total purchases made by a customer, whether they are made by cash or charge. The field is specifically used to help target customers for special mailings and the like.

The Customer Number Field

As previously mentioned, each customer entered in Customer.dbf is assigned a unique customer number, or custno, which is subsequently used to identify the customer with its transactions in the Sales and Payments tables. Since the accidental assignment of the same Custno to more than one customer will obviously wreak havoc with our system—the customers will receive bills listing the debits and credits of all other customers with the same Custno—customer number assignments are best handled programmatically.

In the MBS, the operator entering a new customer is allowed to make entries to all Customer table fields with the exception of Custno. (During the process the Custno field will display a value of n/a, for *not available*.) As soon as the operator signals that he or she is finished and wishes to save the new record, the system creates a unique Custno for the new customer. Since our Custno field is defined as a character field with a width of 6, this is done by incrementing the last-used customer number in the series of numbers 100000 through 999999. Once the system has the last-used customer number in hand, producing the next is easy:

```
new customer number = STR(VAL(last custno)+1,6)
```

The algorithm simply converts the character string containing the last used Custno to a numeric value (as must be done before employing it in an arithmetic computation) with the VAL() function, adds 1, and then converts the resulting numeric value back to a character value for storage in our Custno field with the STR() function.

But where are we to get the last used customer number? We can handle this in a variety of ways—even by placing the Customer table's records in order by Custno using an index tag and going to the bottom of the table to fetch it—but there is, in fact, only one approved way of proceeding, owing to the level of security it permits, its ease of use, and its suitability in network (multiuser) applications. This involves the use of a system value table.

Using a System Value Table

A *system value table* is a table specifically designed to hold values required by your application. The system value table used by the MBS is Bizshare.dbf. Its structure is shown in Figure 2.8.

FIGURE 2.8:

Bizshare.dbf, the MBS system value table

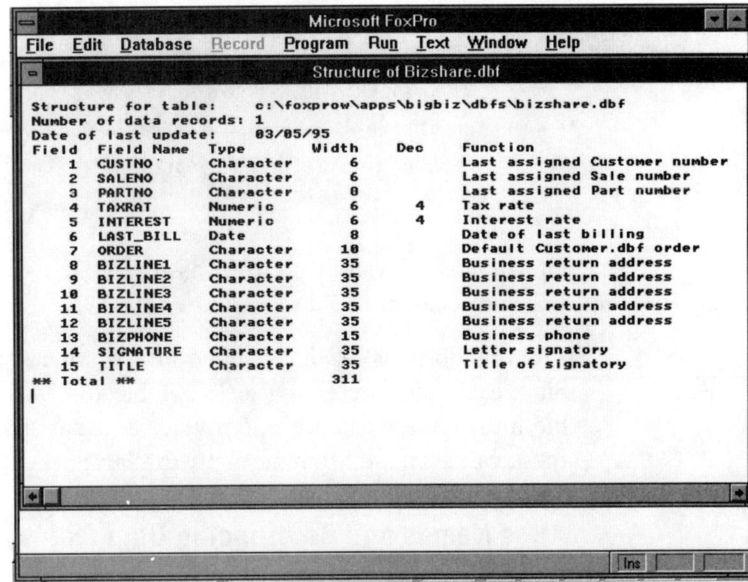

Microsoft FoxPro

File Edit Database Record Program Run Text Window Help

Structure of Bizshare.dbf

Structure for table: c:\foxprow\apps\bigbiz\dbfs\bizshare.dbf
Number of data records: 1
Date of last update: 03/05/95

Field	Field Name	Type	Width	Dec	Function
1	CUSTNO	Character	6		Last assigned Customer number
2	SALENO	Character	6		Last assigned Sale number
3	PARTNO	Character	8		Last assigned Part number
4	TAXRAT	Numeric	6	4	Tax rate
5	INTEREST	Numeric	6	4	Interest rate
6	LAST_BILL	Date	8		Date of last billing
7	ORDER	Character	10		Default Customer.dbf order
8	BIZLINE1	Character	35		Business return address
9	BIZLINE2	Character	35		Business return address
10	BIZLINE3	Character	35		Business return address
11	BIZLINE4	Character	35		Business return address
12	BIZLINE5	Character	35		Business return address
13	BIZPHONE	Character	15		Business phone
14	SIGNATURE	Character	35		Letter signatory
15	TITLE	Character	35		Title of signatory
** Total **			311		

Ins

Program Assignment of Customer, Sales, and Part Numbers

Bizshare.dbf holds only one record. But that's all it needs. Since Bizshare's Custno is used to store the last customer number assigned by the system, as long as Bizshare is open we may proceed to increment its value for Custno while simultaneously using that value to place a unique customer number in each new Customer table record. This is done with the following REPLACE command:

```
REPLACE bizshare.custno WITH STR(VAL(bizshare.custno)+1,6)), ;
    customer.custno WITH bizshare.custno
```

If you write multiuser applications, you will appreciate this arrangement since the REPLACE command establishes an automatic record lock on Bizshare's single record and does not relinquish it until the newly generated customer number is safely placed in Customer.custno. This prevents other operators, who may also be entering new records into Customer.dbf, from gaining access to the same new Custno. Their requests must wait until the automatic record lock is relinquished.

NOTE With respect to network applications, there is a downside to using REPLACE in this way. Since it performs replacement on fields in two tables at once, it must establish record locks in two tables instead of one. In a busy network this will be undesirable since the same thing can be achieved with two separate commands, requiring the use of only one record lock at a time.

Of course, at system startup, assuming the Customer table is empty, we set Bizshare's Custno field to a value of 100000.

The functions of Bizshare.saleno and Bizshare.partno require little explanation. Since each sale entered in the Sales table and each part entered in the Inventory table must have a unique sale invoice and part number, respectively, we generate these values in the MBS in exactly the same way that we generate unique Custnos.

Alias Names and Referencing Data Fields in a Multi-Table Environment

In a multi-table environment, you must reference all data fields using their alias prefixes, unless they are found in the the currently selected table. This is what allows us to use the same field name in several different tables without confusion; the alias prefix points FoxPro to the field of a specific table. When no such prefix is supplied, FoxPro looks only in the currently selected table—and if no such field can be found, FoxPro reports an error.

Each table is assigned an alias name when it is opened with the USE command. Here are three examples:

```
USE customer ALIAS c1
USE customer
USE customer AGAIN ALIAS cus2 IN 0
```

In the first command, the ALIAS option is deliberately used to assign an alias name: c1. We must subsequently reference Customer.dbf's fields as C1.custno, C1.last, and so on, when Customer.dbf is not the currently selected table. In fact, we must also identify Customer.dbf, when using the SELECT command, for example, as C1 and not as Customer. Once it is opened with an alias name, that's how FoxPro *knows* the table—by its *alias*.

In the second command, the ALIAS option is not used. FoxPro therefore uses the table's name (without the file extension) as the alias name by default. When Customer.dbf is not the active table, we must reference its fields as Customer.custno, Customer.last, and so on, because Customer is the table's assigned alias.

The third command explains the reliance on alias names rather than actual file names for referencing tables as well as the fields of tables in unselected work areas. With it, we open the Customer table in yet another of FoxPro's 225 work areas by using the USE command's AGAIN option. With the Customer table open in two work areas, we must obviously have a means of distinguishing between their fields and distinguishing between the tables. This, and the difficulty of using work area letters and numbers to identify tables and fields in different work areas—the only alternative—is the reason for using alias names. With Customer.dbf open in one work area as Customer and in another as Cus2, we can switch between the two tables (or rather the work areas in which they are open) with SELECT Customer and SELECT Cus2. We can, of course, reference their fields from any work area by using alias prefixes.

Bear in mind that alias prefixes can be formed in one of two ways in FoxPro: In the first, the alias name is separated from the field name by a single period; in the other, it is separated by a hyphen and a right angle (->).

WARNING

While we use periods as separators throughout the MBS because they are shorter, there is one place where they cannot be used in this way. During macro substitution with &<variable>, FoxPro interprets a period as separating the variable name from literal characters we intend it to add on to the end of the expanded value. For example, if we create a table Files.dbf that holds the names of all tables included in the MBS in a field named Filename, we can open our files with USE &filename—that is, when Files.dbf is the active table. However, if we use &Files.filename, FoxPro regards Files as the name of the variable to be expanded and Filename as a literal string it must tag on to the end of the expanded value. We prevent this from happening by using &Files->filename instead.

System Storage of Tax and Interest Rates

As for Bizshare.dbf's other fields, they are included as a means of making the MBS as flexible as possible. Try to avoid hard-coding such things as tax or interest rates, since they are likely to change during the life of the application. If we place these values in our system value table, they can be altered at any time without our having to alter the program code. Bizshare.taxrat holds the current tax rate for use with all sales, while Bizshare.interest holds the interest rate to be employed if and when the operator chooses to generate finance charges for delinquent accounts prior to statement production.

NOTE

Mail order firms have special needs when it comes to sales tax since tax must be applied according to the customer's state or locality. This can be effectively handled only by creating a special table, also known as a *data dictionary,* listing the tax rates used in each of the states or localities in which the firm does business. The table can then be used during invoice entry and elsewhere to look up and use the appropriate tax rate. (While the MBS does not include a tax table, it does include several data dictionary tables, and you can adopt the techniques used with them to implement use of a tax rate table as well.)

System Tracking of the Billing Period

Bizshare.last_bill, a Date field, is vital to statement production and several other aspects of MBS's operation. It holds the date on which the last set of monthly statements was printed. This is important to MBS protocol, which stipulates that monthly statements must be produced and the customer account data updated first thing in the morning on the day the new billing period is supposed to begin. Assuming the operator sticks to this practice and, moreover, updates Bizshare.last_bill to hold the current system date immediately after updating customer accounts (done automatically through use of the dialog shown in Figure 2.9), Bizshare.last_bill will not only indicate the date on which statements were last printed, it will also indicate the date on which the present billing period begins. The next time we print monthly statements, we can therefore use Last_bill to determine which sales and payments stored in the Sales and Payments tables (all of which include their dates of entry) should be included in the current run of statements.

Note that we also reference the data held in Bizshare.last_bill at MBS program startup to see if a month has passed since the last printing of statements. If so, MBS warns the operator that it is time to print statements even as the MBS main menu appears on the screen. Bizshare.last_bill is also used during data entry of sales and

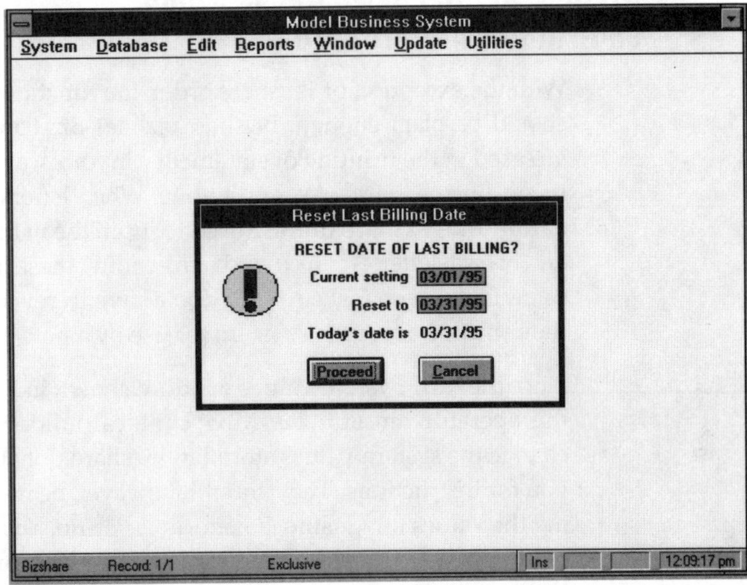

FIGURE 2.9:

At the end of monthly billing, a dialog is used to update the system value indicating the date of last billing.

payments to prevent the operator from entering a transaction date belonging to a previous period and, during the editing of sales, to prevent the operator from editing any sale not falling in the current period. We will see how this is done in Chapter 5 and Chapter 6.

WARNING

From the standpoint of the professional programmer, the MBS's dependence upon a specific date to determine when the current billing period begins will seem a bit risky since it assumes that the operator is bright enough not to enter sales and payments on the same day prior to printing statements and updating the customer accounts—unless the operator knows how to do it safely. If the operator or operators cannot be relied on, the program should be altered so that billing activities are automatically initiated upon system startup if MONTH(DATE()) <> MONTH(Bizshare.Last_bill)—that is, if the month has changed. We will have more to say about this important matter in the chapters that follow.

System Storage of Business Name-and-Address Information

With the exception of Bizshare.order, the function of our remaining system values should be plain enough. Bizshare.bizline1-Bizshare.bizline5 and Bizshare.bizphone are used in the printing of statements, invoices, and letters to input the MBS user's name, business address, and phone. When letters are being printed, Bizshare.signature and Bizshare.title are used to input the name and title of the signatory at the end of each letter. Again, avoid hard-coding these items in the Report forms you use to perform these tasks so you don't have to revise your Report forms every time they employ or revise a system for use by a new client.

Since the MBS System Values window, shown in Figure 2.10, is directly available to the operator through the MBS Utilities pulldown, your clients can, moreover, change the system values stored in Bizshare.dbf at any time without having to call you for instructions. They should, however, be instructed in the dangers of changing the values for Custno, Saleno, and Partno. You might even render these values read-only since they can warrant changing only once the system is under way if a serious error has occurred and they are thrown out of whack. In network applications, all access to system values should be restricted to authorized users, using the techniques discussed in Chapter 9.

As should be clear from the sample data displayed in the MBS System Values window, business return address and phone number information should be input exactly as you or your customer wants it to appear at the top of statements and sales invoices. Each of the fields Bizshare.bizline1-Bizshare.bizline5 represents one possible line in the return address. Enter each line of the return address in order, just as you would type them in a letterhead or mailing label. Here alone, such things as a comma separating city and state and (in Bizphone) the hyphens separating area codes and prefixes should be entered directly in the data. (This is never done elsewhere in the system since FoxPro is perfectly capable of inserting hyphens, for example, in a customer's phone number when displaying it on the screen.)

FIGURE 2.10:
Data entry/display window used with the MBS system value table, Bizshare.dbf

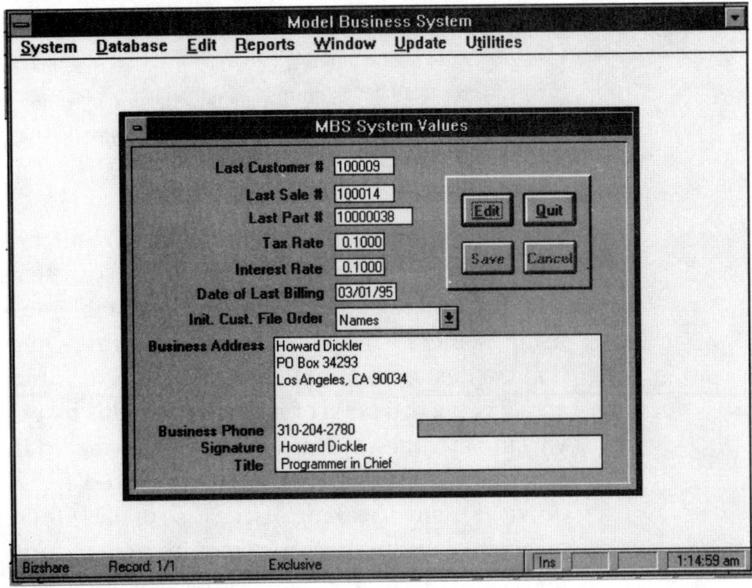

System Storage of Operator Preference for Database Order

Finally, Bizshare.order is used to specify the default order of the records in our Customer table. Since we will use several index tags with Customer.dbf so we can instantly access or display its records in order by Name (Last + First), Company, or Custno, it will be altogether easier to permit the MBS operator to determine which index tag will always be engaged when the table is first opened. We can do this in the MBS with the following commands:

```
USE bizshare ALIAS bizshare IN 0
m.order = TRIM(bizshare.order)
USE customer ALIAS customer ORDER (m.order) IN 0
```

Here again, we employ the USE command's IN <work area> option with 0 to tell FoxPro to open each of the tables in the lowest unused work area. Thus, the first command opens Bizshare.dbf in one work area, the second command stores the value of Bizshare.order in a memory variable (while also trimming off any trailing blanks), and the third command opens Customer.dbf in another work area and activates the index tag specified by the value held in the memvar m.order.

TIP

In FoxPro, you can prefix memory variables with either m. or m->. This tells FoxPro to look for a memory variable wherever a table field with the same name may be available. (m. is normally used except when employing memvars in macro substitution, where, you may recall, the period has special meaning.)

The last command also illustrates how memory variables (or array elements—or even the values contained in data fields) can be used to supply FoxPro commands with the name of a desired object, be it a table, an alias name, or an index tag. When using memory variables in this way, however, in most cases you must signal FoxPro that the memory variable included in the command line is exactly that and not the actual name of a table or index tag. Do this by placing the memory variable (memvar) in parentheses. This tells FoxPro to regard the memvar as a name expression. Macro substitution can also be employed for this purpose, but it slows FoxPro down. (Strictly speaking, in the case of SET ORDER and USE ORDER, parentheses or macro substitution is not required when supplying the index tag name with a memvar. SET ORDER TO m.order will also work without error.)

The default order of the Customer table is not the only preference we may allow an operator to select. Two index tags, for example, are used with the Inventory table, though we hard-code MBS to select one that arranges inventory records by Partnos at system startup. Still, this is only intended as an example, though it is a useful one since some firms will mostly deal with companies and others with individuals who must be located by name. Why force operators to change (or select) the index tag used with the Customer table every time they start work?

CHAPTER

THREE

3

Designing the Customer Data Entry Program

- **Understanding how screen programs work**
- **Controlling screen programs with READ**
- **Using push buttons and @ GET VALID**
- **Using READ CYCLE and READ SHOW**
- **Creating modal dialogs**

Activated by operator selection of the Customer option on the MBS main menu's Database pulldown, the Customer table entry window, shown in Figure 3.1, is designed to oversee manual update and display of Customer table records in a controlled fashion suited to a business environment.

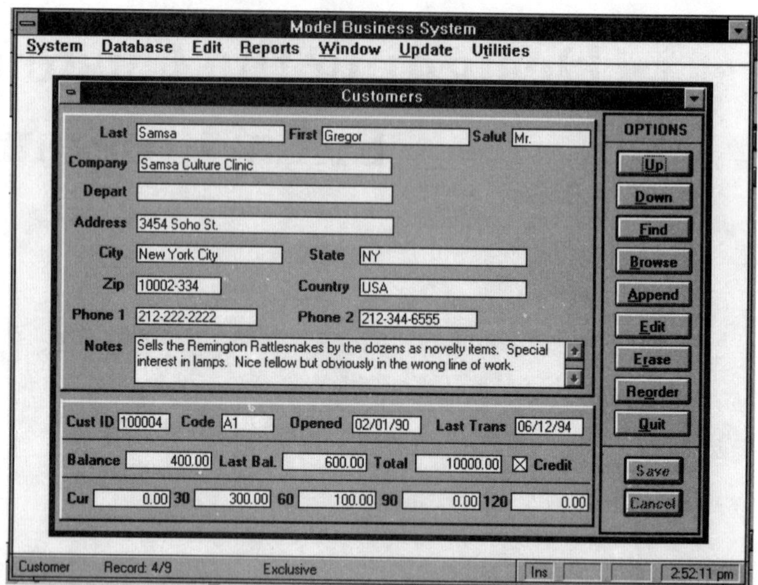

FIGURE 3.1:

MBS Customer table entry window

The *control panel* on the right side of the Customers window is made up of two sets of vertically arranged *push buttons*, divided for esthetic reasons by a horizontal line. Taken together, the set of push buttons at the top provides the operator with an easily understandable menu of options. Not so clear is the way they work—or the way FoxPro manages their repeated use. For here we are not dealing with a typical Xbase .prg (program) file, though FoxPro still uses them, but with an .spr, or *screen program,* that relies on the READ command and its various options—and not DO WHILE .T.—to control program action and repetition.

Since the READ command and all other commands and functions discussed in this chapter can also be employed in a .prg file, if you are as yet unfamiliar with FoxPro screen programs, feel free to read along as though we were discussing a typical .prg file. This way we can introduce the commands, functions, and routines that are most often found in screen programs but that are still functional in traditional Xbase .prg files without having to deal head on with the complexities of screen program architecture and directives. We will, however, take note of various aspects of screen programs as we move along and also show how the FoxPro Screen Builder is employed to semi-automatically create some of the more challenging pieces of program code found in screen programs.

Also, following the strategy outlined in the Introduction, we begin our discussion of the customer data entry program by focusing on *intra-window events*—that is, the events taking place inside the Customers window. By the end of the chapter, however, we will begin to take inter-window or window-level events into account. For now, we stick to READ and the set of related FoxPro commands you must master to create a Windows-style data entry program suitable for operation in a business or accounting environment.

NOTE

For those who are coming to FoxPro from another Xbase language, additional assistance in comprehending the Customer table data entry program is provided in the section "A Bird's-Eye View of the Customer Entry Program," where we compare its organization with that of a standard Xbase program working under the control of a DO WHILE loop. This section of Chapter 3 has been placed near the end of the chapter since it is primarily intended as a means of reviewing the components of the Customer table entry program after you are familiar with them, but you can turn to it at any time if you find yourself confused by FoxPro's way of handling repetition within a program with READ.

Controlling Program Repetition with READ

The FoxPro READ command is able to take over the function of DO WHILE .T. as a means of controlling program action whenever a user-interface screen is required, owing to a variety of features and commands that were introduced with FoxPro 2.0. Push buttons, for example, are produced with a variant form of @ GET <variable>, as are check boxes, radio buttons, popups, and pick lists. And like all other @ GET commands, they are activated by READ. In fact, all the push buttons in the control panel with the exception of the *disabled* Save and Cancel push buttons at the bottom are created with a single command, though it is generated semi-automatically by FoxPro, based upon our use of the Screen Builder. (The name of the user-defined function called with VALID <expL> is created by FoxPro.)

```
@ 2.538,95.600 GET m.but1 ;
    PICTURE"@*VN\<Up;\<Down;\!\<Find;\<Browse;\<Append;"+ ;
    "\<Edit;E\<rase;Re\<order;\?\<Quit" ;
    SIZE 1.692,11.000,0.385 ;
    DEFAULT 1 ;
    FONT "MS Sans Serif", 8 ;
    STYLE "B" ;
    VALID _qco0yp0h5()
```

NOTE

In FoxPro, push buttons, check boxes, radio buttons, popups, and the like are created with a variant form of @ GET <variable>, using special @ GET FUNCTION and PICTURE symbols. The fact that you create these items semi-automatically through the use of the FoxPro Screen Builder, however, makes it unnecessary to learn the symbols and syntax used to define them, though it doesn't hurt to learn how to read the commands.

All we need do when designing the Customers window is fill in the Screen Builder's Push button dialog, as shown in Figure 3.2; designate the name of a memory variable—in this case, m.but1 (short for *button set 1*)—to hold the value returned by operator selection of one of the push buttons; and enter any MESSAGE, WHEN, or VALID clause—all standard features of @ GET <variable>—using the available entry area for each item. (Position, Sizing, Font, Style, and the like are handled when the dialog is ended and the push buttons are placed in the Screen Builder's layout editor, which contains a mockup of the data entry window being created.) Owing to the facilities of the Screen Builder, it is scarcely necessary to know how to write such commands—or any other @ SAY or @ GET commands placing data fields, check boxes, popups, push buttons, and the like—in our data entry window. But how do they work?

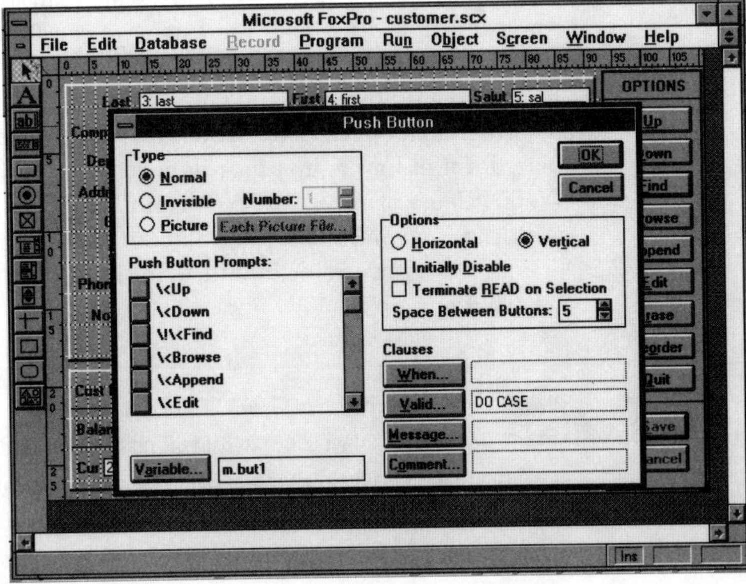

FIGURE 3.2:

Screen Builder Push Button dialog

NOTE

The Push Button dialog can be used to create a single button or a set of buttons, as is done here. When several buttons are to be used together, it is easier to create them all at once so they are executed with a single @ GET push button command. However, many programmers prefer to define each button as a separate @ GET push button since this makes it easier to alter the attributes of individual buttons.

READ CYCLE and CLEAR READ

When the Customers window is first activated by selecting the Customer option on the MBS main menu's Database pulldown, we place all data for the current customer record on the screen with @ GET <variable> and @ EDIT <variable>. The READ command is subsequently issued using the READ CYCLE option. This tells FoxPro not to terminate the READ, as would happen without CYCLE, when the operator passes the last @ GET on the screen, but to *cycle* back to the first @ GET and vice versa. This way, READ begins to function like DO WHILE .T.

In addition to using Esc and Ctrl+W, which can still be used to terminate the READ command unless we alter their use, we can terminate READ CYCLE (or READ alone) with the CLEAR READ command. This, in a sense, substitutes for the EXIT command, traditionally used with DO WHILE .T. in most Xbase programs to break the program loop. CLEAR READ can be executed any time READ is active if it is placed, for example, in a user-defined function (UDF) called with the VALID or WHEN clause of any @ GET command. This means that the Customers window, inasmuch as it represents a program, can be programmatically terminated upon operator entry to any field, though, in the MBS, we use it only with our *control* (menu) push buttons.

NOTE As an alternative to CLEAR READ, a push button can be defined to terminate READ when it is selected by checking Terminate READ on Selection in the Push Button Options dialog. (Again, see Figure 3.3.) However, with the Customers window, this would be useful only if the Quit button were defined as a separate push button since the Terminate READ option will apply to all buttons defined with a single push button.

Use of @ GET WHEN to Control Cursor Access to Fields

At the outset of the Customer table entry program, Customer.spr, we arrange for the @ GET representing our control push buttons to be the only *active* GET on the screen by using a simple trick. All other @ GET commands, with the exception of the @ GET overseeing the operation of our manually disabled Save and Cancel push buttons, are rendered off limits to the cursor through the use of @ GET WHEN <expL>, as suggested by the program fragment shown below. (Row and column coordinates are omitted since they are immaterial to the discussion. Ellipses are used to indicate other omitted portions of commands.)

```
m.doit = .F.
@ GET customer.last WHEN m.doit
@ GET customer.first WHEN m.doit
@ GET m.but1 PICTURE...VALID <expL>
READ CYCLE
```

TIP

Using @ GET WHEN with a memvar that can change in value from .T. to .F. is the simplest means of conditionally controlling operator access to input fields.

As long as the value of memvar m.doit remains .F., the operator cannot address the GET input fields using WHEN m.doit. The cursor will remain active in @ GET m.but1, designating our control push buttons, allowing the operator to cycle through them and make a selection.

Using @ GET VALID to Execute Program Routines

To control program action when the operator presses a push button, we use @ GET VALID with the UDF shown in Figure 3.3. Again, if we do not name the UDF by beginning it with the FUNCTION <function name>, it is because Genscrn.prg, the FoxPro program designed to write our screen programs based upon our work with the Screen Builder, takes care of those matters we would naturally have to attend to ourselves were we actually placing the UDF in a .prg file.

FIGURE 3.3:

UDF used with @ GET (push button) VALID to control program action

Microsoft FoxPro - customer - m.but1 Valid

File Edit Database Record Program Run Text Window Help

```
DO CASE
CASE m.but1 = "Up"
   IF NOT BOF()
      SKIP -1
   ENDIF
   IF BOF()
      WAIT WINDOW "At first record in file." NOWAIT
   ENDIF
CASE m.but1 = "Down"
   IF NOT EOF()
      SKIP 1
   ENDIF
   IF EOF()
      WAIT WINDOW "At last record in file." NOWAIT
      IF NOT BOF()
         SKIP -1
      ENDIF
   ENDIF
CASE m.but1 = "Find"
   DO Cus_Find.spr WITH "Locate Record"
CASE m.but1 = "Browse"
   * Procedures Browcust, Hide, and Unhide are in procedure file bizlib.prg.
   * Procedures Hide and Unhide are explained in Chapter 10.
   DO hide WITH "CUSTOMERS",""
   DO Browcust
   DO unhide
CASE m.but1 = "Append"
   STORE .T. TO m.doit,m.doappend
   DO Cus_Find.spr WITH "Append Record"
CASE m.but1 = "Edit" AND NOT EMPTY(m.custno)
   STORE .T. TO m.doit,m.doedit
CASE m.but1 = "Erase"
   IF l_balance = 0.00 AND current = 0.00
      DO Erase.spr
   ELSE
      WAIT WINDOW "Cannot delete a customer with an active account!" NOWAIT
   ENDIF
CASE m.but1 = "Reorder"
   DO Cus_Find.spr WITH "Reorder File"
CASE m.but1 = "Quit"
   CLEAR READ
ENDCASE
SHOW GETS
RETURN .F.
```

Customer Record: 1/14 Exclusive Ins

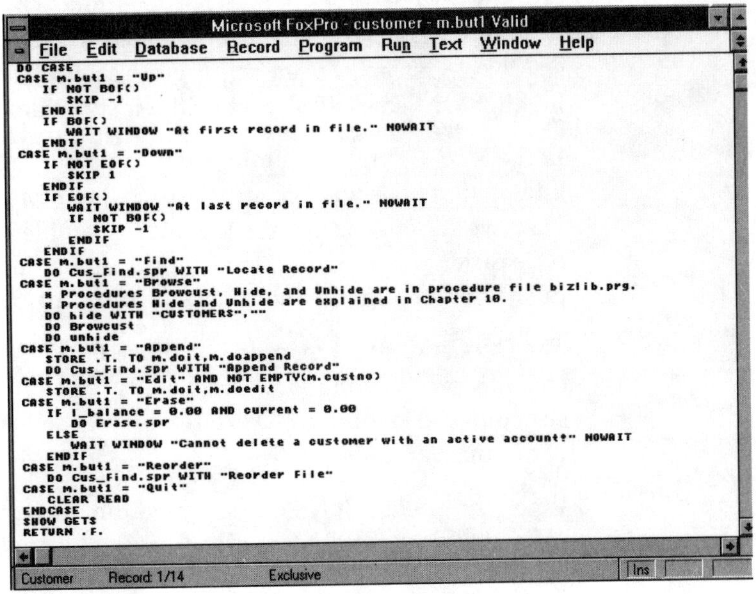

@ GET Push Button Return Values and @ GET DEFAULT <value>

When generating program code, Genscrn.prg is in the habit of assigning a DEFAULT <value> to every @ GET we place in the Screen Builder's Design window. This is intended to help prevent program crashes. If a variable referenced by @ GET doesn't exist, FoxPro creates it on the fly using the DEFAULT value. With respect to @ GET push buttons in particular, FoxPro uses DEFAULT 1 and assigns a numeric value 1 through *n* to each of the buttons controlled by a single @ GET. When the operator selects a button, FoxPro returns an integer value to the <variable> corresponding to the order of the selected button in the Push Button Prompts box. (See Figure 3.2).

We can make FoxPro return the character string used to label each button instead by manually changing the DEFAULT <value>—or better yet, since it is more suitable to working with the Screen Builder, by initializing the variable referenced by @ GET push buttons as a character string in advance of its use with @ GET.

```
m.but1 = "Up"
@ GET m.but1 PICTURE...
READ CYCLE
```

Note that while this determines the type and default value of the memvar used with @ GET PUSH BUTTON, it does not determine which of several buttons, defined by a single @ GET, will be initially highlighted when the @ GET becomes the current cursor object. (A small dotted box appears around the button label when the button is highlighted.) This will always be the first button in the set.

In the MBS we employ numeric return values only when using pictures stored in bitmap files (instead of character strings) to represent push button options. Otherwise, we stick to character values for the simple reason that it makes our program code easier to read. Using character values also allows us to change the order of the push button options without revising our program code.

The DO CASE structure called by our @ GET VALID clause (again, see Figure 3.3) contains precisely the same commands we would expect to see in the DO CASE structure used within a DO WHILE loop to achieve the actions suggested by each of our push buttons.

When the operator presses the Up button, thereby placing the string value "Up", corresponding to the button's label, in memvar m.but1, FoxPro executes the VALID clause. If FoxPro is not already at the top of the file (which we test for with the beginning-of-file function, BOF()), it executes SKIP –1, moving to the previous record in the Customer table. As an additional frill, the routine then checks again for BOF() and, if the beginning of the file has been passed, executes WAIT WINDOW <expC> NOWAIT to display an appropriate message on the screen using the FoxPro System Message window.

FoxPro's WAIT Command

FoxPro's WAIT command includes several options that make it especially useful in a Windows program. WINDOW is used to display the message in the FoxPro System Message window at the top right of the screen. It is sized as needed to accommodate the message. Thus you do not need to worry about creating a window to display run-of-the-mill messages. As in standard Xbase, the message remains on the screen until the operator presses a key, unless the NOWAIT option is employed. Then the message is displayed until the operator presses a key or moves the mouse. TIMEOUT <expN> can also be used to clear the message after <expN> seconds, supposing the operator takes no action. As with all other Xbase languages, FoxPro's WAIT also stores the keystroke used to clear the message to a memory variable if the more traditional WAIT TO <memvar> option is employed.

As soon as the Up action is performed, FoxPro moves past ENDCASE and comes to SHOW GETS. Having SKIPped a record in the file, the @ GET input fields displayed in the Customers window are no longer current. They must be rewritten, or *refreshed.* In a single command SHOW GETS does this, so the new (current) customer record is displayed. The UDF then terminates with a value of .F., leaving the cursor still active in the push button—though given our use of memvar m.doit, there is no place for it to go in any case. (Since push buttons are designed to be used in this way—that is, with VALID clauses that return a value of .F.—no error message is generated.) The operator is therefore free to select the same or another push button. The operator may also start any of the other programs on the MBS main menu while leaving the Customer window open on the screen— a matter we return to in Chapter 5.

To terminate the customer entry and close the Customers window, we provide a Quit push button. It is designed to execute the CLEAR READ command, terminating READ CYCLE.

Using BROWSE to Display and Locate Records in Sequential Order

Other push button options are rigged to execute nested procedures and screen programs. The Browse push button, for example, executes procedure Browcust, which is actually stored in the MBS procedure file Bizlib.prg, owing to its use by several different screen programs, including Customer.spr.

```
PROCEDURE Browcust
m.fields = "Department,Address,City,State,"+ ;
    "Zip,Country,Phone1,Phone2,Cuscode:H='Code',Credit,"+ ;
    "Opendate,Lastdate,Comments,History,"+ ;
    "Balance=Current+Days30+Days60+Days90+Days120,"+ ;
    "Last_Bal = L_Balance,Current,Days30,Days60,Days90,Days120"
DO CASE
CASE ORDER() = 'NAMES'
    BROWSE PREFERENCE "Cust1" NOEDIT NOAPPEND NOMENU ;
        NODELETE NORMAL ;
        LOCK 1 WIDTH 15 IN SCREEN TITLE "Table of Customers" ;
        FIELDS Last,First,Company,Custno:H="Cust_ID", &fields
CASE ORDER() = 'COMPANY'
    BROWSE PREFERENCE "Cust2" NOEDIT NOAPPEND NOMENU ;
        NODELETE NORMAL ;
        LOCK 1 WIDTH 15 IN SCREEN TITLE "Table of Customers" ;
        FIELDS Company,Last,First,Custno:H="Cust_ID", &fields
CASE ORDER() = 'CUSTNO'
    BROWSE PREFERENCE "Cust3" NOEDIT NOAPPEND NOMENU ;
        NODELETE NORMAL ;
        LOCK 1 WIDTH 15 IN SCREEN TITLE "Table of Customers" ;
        FIELDS ,Custno:H="Cust_ID",Last,First,Company, &fields
ENDCASE
RELEASE WINDOW "Table of Customers"
RETURN
```

Use of a DO CASE structure permits us to BROWSE the Customer table using slightly different field lists, based upon which of the three main Customer table index tags is currently selected as the *controlling*, or active, index. (The ORDER() function returns the name of the controlling index in uppercase characters.) We review the index tags Names, Company, and Custno in the next chapter. For now, suffice it to say that they arrange Customer.dbf's records in order by last and first name, company, and Custno, respectively. We thus devise our three BROWSE commands so they will display the fields used by the current controlling index in the left-hand column(s) of the BROWSE table. We also use LOCK <expN> to isolate those fields in the BROWSE table's left partition so that, regardless of where the operator may move in the right partition, the locked fields will still be visible. Figure 3.4 shows the BROWSE table produced by CASE ORDER = "NAMES".

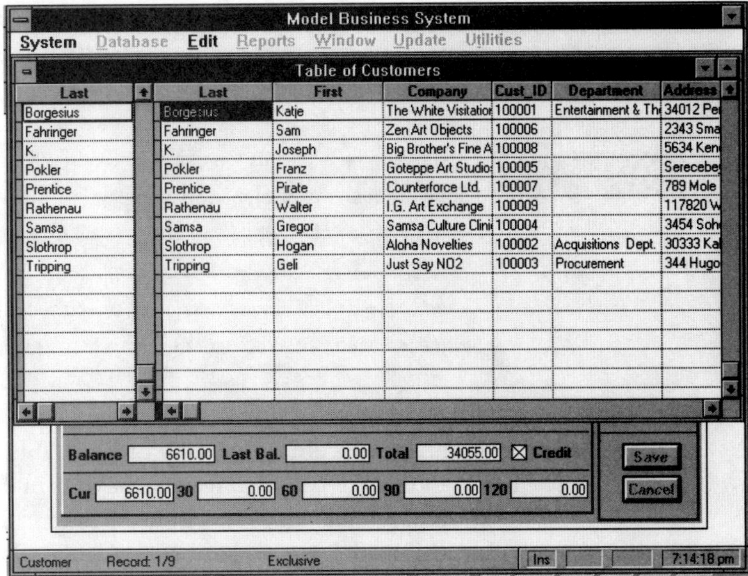

FIGURE 3.4:
The BROWSE command provides an easy way of reviewing records quickly.

WARNING

When using macro substitution with &, avoid entering a memvar with the memvar prefix m. since the period has a special use in macro substitution. It indicates that the following characters should be appended to the macro. In this instance, if we use &m.fields, FoxPro will mistake *m* for a memvar. If you must distinguish between a memvar and a data field value with the same name, use the alternative memvar prefix, m->.

To avoid having to write out a lengthy field list three times over, we store the portion of the BROWSE FIELDS list that will be the same for all three commands to a memvar, m.fields, and enter it where needed, using macro substitution with &fields. When the column heading supplied by a field name can be improved upon, we use the BROWSE field heading option, :H=<expC>, to supply a better one. This is done with Cuscode, L_balance, and Custno. We also employ a calculated field for displaying the present balance, using the calculated field formula: <heading>=<exp>.

Since we do not want BROWSE to open within the active window, we use the IN SCREEN option to tell FoxPro to open a special BROWSE window on top of the Customers window. The first record in the table will be the current customer record. We also use the TITLE option to give the BROWSE window a special title. Otherwise, FoxPro uses the current table's alias name.

NOTE

In Chapter 5 we discuss the use of BROWSE PREFERENCE <expC> since its use depends upon the availability of an open FoxPro resource file—a topic that would take us too far afield at this point. Suffice it to say at this point that our use of PREFERENCE will allow FoxPro to recollect the size, position, field list, and title of each of our BROWSE windows when we close them and to reuse this information when we open BROWSE with the same preference once again.

More important, we employ a slew of BROWSE options, including NOAPPEND, NOEDIT, and NODELETE, to render the data in the BROWSE table read-only. Bear in mind that NOEDIT does not in itself render the BROWSE table read-only. Records can still be deleted and appended unless NOAPPEND and NODELETE are used as well. NOMENU prevents FoxPro from adding the Browse pulldown menu (always available when working with BROWSE in the interactive mode) to the MBS main menu, where it would only indicate actions we have disallowed.

Noting that the small entry area provided by the Customers window makes viewing large Memo field entries difficult, we are bound to include Comments in our BROWSE field list. An operator who wants more space to view comments can pan right to the Comments field and press Ctrl+PgDn or click twice on the Memo marker to open the customer's memo in a sizable system window, as shown in Figure 3.5. Still, entries cannot be made using the window since the NOEDIT keyword

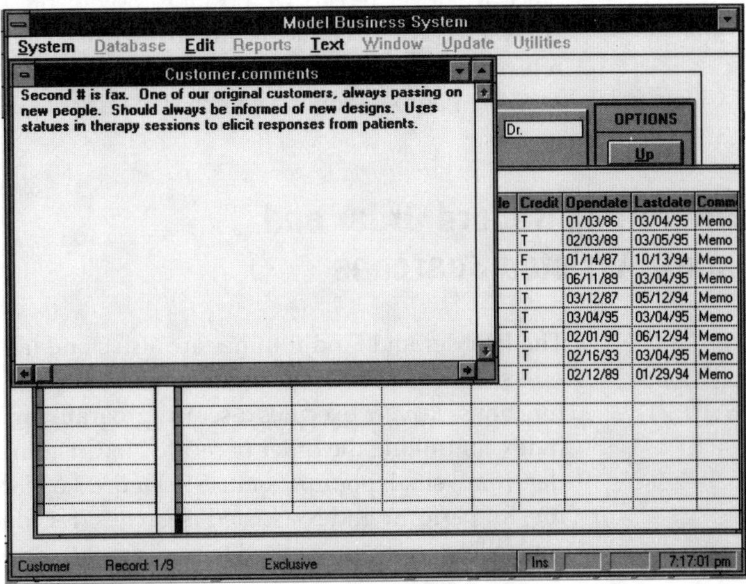

FIGURE 3.5:

BROWSE provides a special system window for viewing Memo and General fields.

renders all fields in the BROWSE table, including Comments, as read-only. The same thing can be done with General fields used, for example, to hold pictures.

As you can see in Figure 3.5, when the Comments field is opened with BROWSE, the Text menu pad automatically appears in the MBS main menu. This allows you to alter the font and spacing used in the window. (This book does not discuss the Text pulldown at length because it is the same menu used by FoxPro in the interactive mode.) The Edit pulldown, also available in FoxPro's interactive mode, can be used to select and copy text to the Windows Clipboard and to perform searches, but unlike the Text pulldown, it is always available on the MBS main menu and can be activated and used, for example, when addressing the Customers window.

Still, with respect to the operation of our Customers window, BROWSE offers us more than a means of simply viewing records in a tabular fashion. It can also help us locate records quickly in the vicinity of the record current in the Customers window, using the scroll bar and/or the ↑, ↓, PgUp, and PgDn keys. When the operator closes the BROWSE window (by clicking outside its border, pressing Esc or Ctrl+W, or clicking Close in the window control box), the BROWSE window is released, procedure Browcust is terminated, and program control is returned to our push button VALID clause, where FoxPro will subsequently come upon the SHOW GETS command.

Since whatever record we position to with BROWSE automatically becomes the current record, that's the record FoxPro displays in the Customers window on our return. Such *point-and-click* (or *shoot*) use of BROWSE to target a record for subsequent manipulation is a standard feature of all MBS data entry programs.

Controlling Record Order and Index-Assisted Searches

The Reorder and Find routines are also standard features of MBS data entry windows. These routines are discussed in Chapter 4, but for now we can review their functions. *Reorder* executes a screen program enabling the operator to change the index controlling the order of records in Customer.dbf by selecting the desired order from a small popup menu. (See Figure 3.6.) Find, for its part, enables the operator to perform index-assisted searches for data records and to change the controlling index as required to perform the correct search.

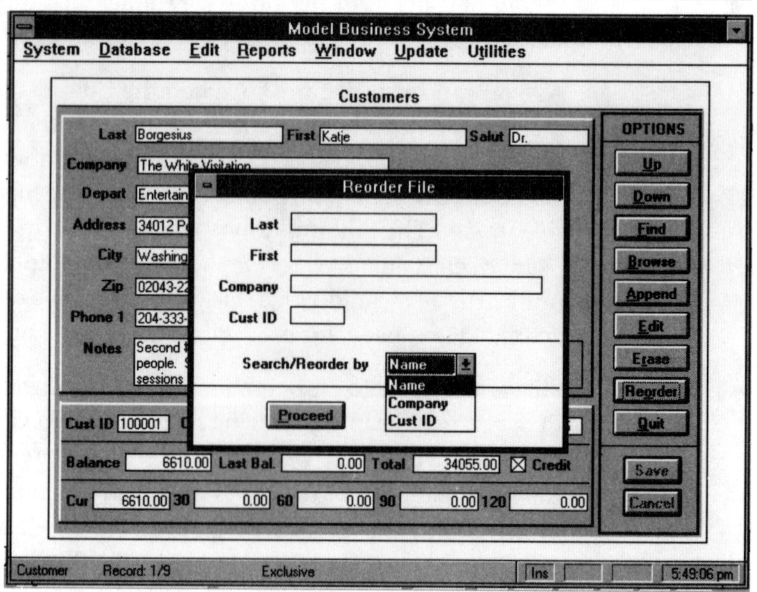

FIGURE 3.6:
A dialog box is used to reorder or find customer records using index tags.

Since both operations provide a means of changing the controlling index, we consolidate the two routines in the same screen program, Cus_find.spr. When executing Cus_find.spr with DO <program> in our push button VALID clause, we pass it a single parameter (Reorder Datafile or Locate Customers), supplying Cus_find.spr with a suitable title for the dialog box as well as a means of conditionally determining which specific activities are to be performed. (Note that Cus_find.spr is also executed when m.but1 = "Append". We discuss this use of Cus_find.spr below.)

Writing the Record Append and Edit Routines

In introducing the function of READ in controlling program action in FoxPro, I attempted to simplify matters by pretending to place Customer.dbf's fields directly in the Customers window with @ GET. This is not really what happens. When writing programs for use in a business environment, it is always wise to limit the operator's contact with actual data fields by using memory variables instead. What appears in the Customers window with @ GET <variable> is a set of memory variables initialized to hold the values stored in the current record. This process, which has long been standard to Xbase programming, is made easier than ever with FoxPro, owing to the SCATTER and GATHER commands. The following program fragment is intended to suggest their function:

```
SCATTER MEMVAR MEMO
@ GET m.last
@ GET m.first
@ GET m.company
* Additional @ GET commands displaying other Customer table
* fields.
@ EDIT comment
READ    && Without CYCLE terminates when user surpasses last GET.
GATHER MEMVAR MEMO
```

Use of Memory Variables during Data Display and Update

SCATTER MEMVAR creates a memory variable for each of the fields in the current table. Each memvar has the same field type and width as the corresponding data field and, moreover, shares the field's name. (We must therefore reference the memvar, when we want it, instead of the data field of the same name by using the memvar prefix m. or m->, at least as long as the table is open in the current work area.) Note that SCATTER MEMVAR will not place Memo field data into memvars with corresponding field names unless the MEMO option is used. BLANK is another important SCATTER option; it initializes memory variables suitable to represent all table fields but leaves them blank. This will be helpful when we want to add new records to a table.

NOTE

SCATTER and GATHER include additional options. FIELD <field list> controls which values are scattered to and gathered from memvars. If you prefer working with arrays instead of individually named memory variables, use TO <array> instead of MEMVAR to transfer data values to and from the named array. (With SCATTER, if the array doesn't exist, FoxPro creates it on the fly. If an existing array has an insufficient number of elements, FoxPro adjusts its size.)

GATHER MEMVAR is SCATTER's companion command. It looks for memory variables with names corresponding to current table fields and uses the values they contain to update those fields after the fashion of REPLACE but without having to specify field names and values. The MEMO keyword must be used if Memo fields should be updated as well.

The program fragment shown above may thus be used to edit the fields of the current customer record indirectly, through the use of memory variables, without our having to do much work to make it happen. We can also alter the program fragment into a record Append routine by making just a few adjustments:

```
SCATTER MEMVAR MEMO BLANK
@ GET m.last
@ GET m.first
@ GET m.company
* Additional @ GET commands displaying other Customer table
* fields.
@ EDIT comment
READ
APPEND BLANK
GATHER MEMVAR MEMO
```

As previously mentioned, SCATTER's BLANK option directs FoxPro to create a set of *empty* memory variables corresponding to the current table fields. And once we use APPEND BLANK to add a new empty record to the table, GATHER MEMVAR will suffice to place the data entered into the memory variable with @ GET/EDIT and READ into the new record.

Using READ SHOW for Conditional Control of READ Action with IF

Referring back to Figure 3.3, showing the text of the UDF executed by the VALID clause of our @ GET push buttons, SCATTER, GATHER, and APPEND BLANK are nowhere to be seen. Looking at the CASE executed when the operator selects the Edit push button, we see this instead:

```
CASE m.but1 = "Append"
    STORE .T. TO m.doit,m.doappend
    DO Cus_Find.spr WITH "Append Record"
CASE m.but1 = "Edit" AND NOT EMPTY(m.custno)
    STORE .T. TO m.doit,m.doedit
* Other cases.
ENDCASE
SHOW GETS
RETURN .F.
```

So where does all the action take place? The answer to this question is found in yet another optional READ clause—the aptly named SHOW clause, which can be optionally used to execute a UDF when READ is first issued and *every time the SHOW GETS command is executed.*

Still, with regard to explaining the functionality of the READ SHOW clause, a picture is worth a thousand words. Displayed below is the program code used in the UDF executed by Customer.spr's READ SHOW clause:

```
IF m.doit
    IF m.doappend
        SCATTER MEMVAR MEMO BLANK
        m.custno = "N/A    "
            * Values of m.lastfnd, m.firstfnd, and m.companyfnd
```

```
            * are supplied by Cus_find.spr, used at outset of
            * append action to prevent entry of duplicate
            * customer records.
        m.last = m.lastfnd
        m.first = m.firstfnd
        m.company = m.companyfnd
        m.opendate = DATE()
        m.country = "USA"
        m.credit = .T.
        m.pres_bal = 0.00
    ENDIF
    SHOW GET m.verify ENABLE
    SHOW GET m.but1 DISABLE
    _CUROBJ = OBJNUM(m.last)
ELSE
    SCATTER MEMVAR MEMO
    m.pres_bal = current+days30+days60+days90+days120
ENDIF
```

NOTE

When SHOW GETS is executed and a READ SHOW clause is in effect, FoxPro reads through and executes the commands in the SHOW clause (or UDF) before refreshing the GETs.

The easiest way to comprehend the SHOW is to step through the different ways it can be executed when our push button VALID clause issues SHOW GETS. First, all VALID clause actions used to locate or otherwise reposition FoxPro in the Customer table will leave the value of m.doit set to .F. (This is the value initially assigned m.doit at the beginning of Customer.spr.) As a result, the SHOW clause will initialize memvars for the new current record with SCATTER, calculating the customer's present balance (Pres_bal) as indicated by the sum of the current record's debt-aging fields. Upon termination, program control is passed back to the SHOW GETS command in the VALID clause and the @ GETs on the screen are refreshed. The cursor remains active in our push buttons (the last selected button will still be selected) since m.doit = .F. gives it nowhere to go.

NOTE With FoxPro it is unnecessary to include the RETURN command at the end of a UDF unless the RETURN command is needed to return a value other than .T. with RETURN <exp>. RETURN is also generally omitted at the end of procedures since FoxPro has no need of it to determine where one procedure or function appearing in a program file begins and ends.

On the other hand, suppose the Append or Edit push button is selected. In both instances m.doit, which is used globally in the MBS to indicate that data entry is under way, will be set to .T. But here we're also dealing with two other memvars, m.doappend and m.doedit, which, like m.doit, are used in Customer.spr as flags. Like m.doit, at the outset of the program they are initialized with a value of .F. In our VALID clause, CASE m.but1 = "Edit" changes m.doedit to .T. but leaves m.doappend alone. Thus, if the Edit push button is selected, when FoxPro comes to the SHOW, it bypasses the commands embedded in IF m.doappend. It therefore executes the two SHOW GET (without the *S* in GETS) commands and resets the value of the FoxPro current object system memory variable _CUROBJ before returning to our VALID clause SHOW GETS and refreshing all the @ GETs in the Customers window.

Using SHOW GET to Enable/Disable GETs

With SHOW GET, we come to the last really vital command used in controlling action within a screen program. Since memvar m.doit is set to .T., the moment the screen is refreshed by SHOW GETS (after the SHOW clause terminates), all the @ GETs using WHEN m.doit become accessible for data input. (Note that the field values of the record current at the time the operator selected Edit will already be on the screen before SHOW is executed. There is no need for SCATTER.) But as an added touch, we execute SHOW GET m.but1 DISABLE to manually dim and disable our push buttons so they cannot be accessed while the operator edits the @ GET <variables> representing our data fields. We also take advantage of the FoxPro current object system memory value, _CUROBJ, and OBJNUM(), the object number function, to send the cursor to a specific @ GET input field (namely, m.last), where data entry (or edit) will begin.

At the same time that the Edit (and Append) SHOW routine disables our control push buttons with SHOW GET m.but1 DISABLE, it also uses SHOW GET m.verify

ENABLE to activate the second set of push buttons appearing in the Customers window. (Since the Save and Cancel push buttons are drawn using @ GET <variable> DISABLE, they initially appear dimmed on the screen and cannot be selected regardless of the value of m.doit, which obviously has nothing to do with them.)

```
m.verify = "Save"
* As with m.but1, we initialize the value of m.verify in advance
* so the @ GET m.verify push buttons will return the string value
* of the push button labels.
@ 22.154,97.400 GET m.verify ;
    PICTURE "@*VN \!\<Save;\?\<Cancel" ;
    SIZE 1.769,8.500,0.308 ;
    DEFAULT 1 ;
    FONT "MS Sans Serif", 8 ;
    STYLE "B" ;
    VALID _qcq11vlbk() ;
    DISABLE
```

@ GET m.verify, representing our Save and Cancel push buttons, is actually executed *before* m.last and the rest of the @ GET input fields (which are otherwise initialized in order, row by row), starting out with the cursor in @ GET m.last with READ CYCLE in effect. Thus m.verify will be the last @ GET the operator comes to when Tab is used to move through the other @ GETs—though the mouse can obviously be used to move directly to them.

Using _CUROBJ and OBJNUM() to Position the Cursor

FoxPro is designed to recognize every @ GET and @ EDIT <variable> by a number indicating the order in which it was executed prior to READ:

```
@ GET m.last WHEN m.doit VALID <expL>
@ GET m.first WHEN m.doit
@ GET m.but1 VALID <expL>
READ CYCLE SHOW <expL>
```

With regard to these three commands, GET m.last is 1, GET m.first is 2, and GET m.but1 is 3.

During READ, we may discover where the cursor is at any time by simply referencing the value of _CUROBJ. It returns the number (type N) of the current cursor object or GET. However, we may also use _CUROBJ at any time to immediately move the cursor to another object. This is often done, for example, in the VALID or WHEN clause of one @ GET to send the cursor backward or forward to a related @

GET. To do this, we need only manually alter the value of _CUROBJ just as we alter the value of any other memory variable, though we must enter an integer corresponding to an existing @ GET. Thus we might use _CUROBJ = 3 in @ GET m.last VALID to send the cursor immediately to @ GET m.but1, though the operator can manually move back to m.last or m.first using the mouse or Tab key.

Of course, knowing the number—or rather, the *order* of @ GETS in a window with dozens of @ GETs—will be easier for FoxPro than it will be for most programmers. We depend upon the mnemonic names of our variables. To make things easier, FoxPro supplies the OBJNUM() function, which simply returns the order number of the referenced variable. Thus, with regard to our three @ GETs, we can send the cursor to GET m.but1 at any time by executing the command _CUROBJ = OBJNUM(m.but1).

Bear in mind, however, that from the standpoint of FoxPro, @ GET push buttons and radio buttons may represent more than one object. In fact, they will represent as many objects as they have buttons. Here, however, we must make do with numbers:

```
_CUROBJ = OBJNUM(m.but1)
_CUROBJ = OBJNUM(m.but1) + 3
```

The first command places the cursor on Up, the first button created with @ GET m.but1. The second command places the cursor on the fourth button, Browse.

Of course, the fact that @ GET push buttons can represent multiple objects throws a monkey wrench into most efforts to address specific @ GETs without OBJNUM(), but that's why OBJNUM() was created. With OBJNUM(), we need not worry about the order in which we execute our push buttons relative to the other @ GETs since we will not use @ GET order numbers to move the cursor where we want.

```
@ GET m.but1 VALID <function>
@ GET m.last WHEN m.doit
@ GET m.first WHEN m.doit
READ CYCLE SHOW <function>
```

For this reason, we are free to initialize our @ GET push buttons first, as is generally done in the MBS screen programs. This cuts down on the amount of flashing that will occur, if and when the window holding our @ GETs—also known as the *Read window*—must be redrawn (the controls being the most prominent objects on the screen). It also makes the selection of the push buttons automatic upon execution of READ without recourse to _CUROBJ—or the optional OBJECT <object number> clause of READ, which can also be used for this purpose.

SHOW GET's Intricate Options

To begin with, unlike SHOW GETS, SHOW GET affects only the referenced variable, not all active GETs. Nor, because of its more limited action, does it execute the READ SHOW clause.

Used without the ENABLE/DISABLE keyword, SHOW GET simply refreshes the designated <variable>. This is quite useful since it allows us to alter the value of one or more @ GETs programmatically and redisplay the new values without having to redisplay all @ GETs in the READ window. However, with regard to push buttons, SHOW GET is capable of not only disabling or enabling specific buttons but also of altering push button labels:

```
SHOW GET m.but1 ENABLE
SHOW GET m.but1, 3 PROMPT "Locate"
SHOW GET m.but1, 9 DISABLE
```

NOTE

Like SHOW GET, SHOW GETS uses the ENABLE/DISABLE keywords. But with SHOW GETS, ENABLE/DISABLE affects all active @ GETs at once. You can, however, use SHOW GETS ENABLE/DISABLE to affect all active GETs and then use SHOW GET ENABLE/DISABLE to selectively enable/disable specific @ GETs.

The first command enables our control push buttons—@ GET m.but1. The second command changes the prompt (label) used with the third push button in the set from Find to Locate. The third command selectively disables the ninth push button, Quit. This should suffice to show the level of discrimination of which FoxPro is capable when executing @ GET/READ.

If and when you know the order number of an @ GET object, you can address it using SHOW OBJECT instead of SHOW GET. SHOW OBJECT has the same action as SHOW GET and includes the same options. The only difference is that it allows you to reference @ GET objects by order numbers instead of variable names.

Specifying Default Values during Append

If the operator selects the Append instead of the Edit button, setting the value of m.doappend to .T. (and leaving m.doedit=.F.), all the commands listed in the READ SHOW clause under IF m.doit are executed.

```
IF m.doit
    IF m.doappend
        SCATTER MEMVAR MEMO BLANK
        m.custno = "N/A    "
        * Values of m.lastfnd, m.firstfnd, and m.companyfnd
        * are supplied by Cus_find.spr, used at outset of
        * append action to prevent entry of duplicate
        * customer records.
        m.last = m.lastfnd
        m.first = m.firstfnd
        m.company = m.companyfnd
        m.opendate = DATE()
        m.country = "USA"+SPACE(17)
        m.credit = .T.
        m.pres_bal = 0.00
  ENDIF
  SHOW GET m.verify ENABLE
  SHOW GET m.but1 DISABLE
  _CUROBJ = OBJNUM(m.last)
ELSE
```

The effect of selecting the Append button should be clear. Before enabling and disabling our two sets of push buttons with SHOW GET and sending the cursor to @ GET m.last, where it will appear when SHOW GETS refreshes the screen, SCATTER ... BLANK is used to create empty memvars suitable for holding all data for a new record. The memvar initialization commands that follow reset selected memvars so they will hold suitable default values, which of course can be changed by the operator during data entry. We do not, however, create a new record with APPEND BLANK at this point since we want to make it as easy as possible to cancel the new record.

Screening Out Duplicate Customer Records

Here we must pause to take special note of memvars m.lastfnd, m.firstfnd, and m.companyfnd, used immediately above to supply default values for the Last, First, and Company fields of new customer records. Going back to our @ GET m.but1 VALID clause, we find these commands listed under m.but1 = "Append":

```
CASE m.but1 = "Append"
    STORE .T. TO m.doit,m.doappend
    DO Cus_Find.spr WITH "Append Record"
```

The STORE command alters the values of m.doit and m.doappend so they will trigger the right action during execution of READ SHOW. The next command, however, calls the same nested screen program used by the Reorder and Find buttons for reordering or finding records. (Again, see Figure 3.6.) In this case, though, owing to the passed parameter, the window will use the title Append Record instead of Reorder File or Locate Records.

The function of the Reorder/Locate/Append dialog box when executed as part of the Append routine is simple. We ask the operator to begin the Append routine by entering the new customer's name (last and first) or company. We capture the entries in the memvars m.lastfnd, m.firstfnd, and m.companyfnd and then use them to search the Customers table for a preexisting record for that customer. If such a record is found, Cus_find.spr is written so as to change the values of m.doit and m.doappend back to .F. before terminating. The append action will therefore be countermanded before execution of READ SHOW, and the record located by Cus_find.spr will be sent to the screen just as though it had been deliberately accessed through use of the Find routine.

On the other hand, if Cus_find.spr turns up no record corresponding to the operator's entry, the values of m.doit and m.doappend are left set to .T., and the SHOW clause prepares memvars for the new record. It even places the values entered by the operator when using Cus_find.spr into m.last, m.first, and m.company so they need not be reentered when SHOW GETS activates the Customers window for data entry to the new record.

The use of the customer search routines in Cus_find.spr thus serves to prevent the entry of duplicate customer records to Customer.dbf, though, in order to be most effective, the operator must specifically be instructed to use it to this end. For example, when entering a record for *Doubtful Enterprises Ltd.*, it is best to enter the *Doubtful* and perhaps the *Enterprises* in the dialog box's Company entry area. That way, if a record has been entered for *Doubtful Enterprises Inc.*, FoxPro won't miss it owing to the change of *Inc.* to *Ltd.* On the other hand, if two people or companies have the same name, we can easily prevent Cus_find.spr from countermanding the append action and displaying the existing record by slightly altering the new customer's name. If a record for *Gregor Samsa* is already on file, the Append button can be reselected and Cus_find.spr instructed to search for *Gene Samsa.* When the Customers window reappears, the operator can then change *Gene* back to *Gregor* before entering data in the other fields. (We will take a closer look at Cus_find.spr in Chapter 4.)

WARNING

There is one main weakness in the way we screen for duplicate customer records in the MBS. Once the operator accesses the Customers window to enter the new record, he or she can freely alter the entries for m.last, m.first, and m.company. Moreover, during the Edit action, no effort is made to prevent the operator from changing these key fields to values used in another record. If you are concerned about preventing operators from taking such actions, you can check for duplicate values once again when the operator presses the Save button to save the new record or to save the edited record values.

Using @ GET <variable> (Input Fields) to Best Advantage

We can now move on to the final actions performed by our Append and Edit routines. With the execution of SHOW GETS (after READ SHOW has terminated), the Customers window displays all memvars representing the current customer record (called for edit) or the set of empty memvars (some filled in with default values), now ready for data entry by the operator owing to the present value of m.doit (.T.). As a result of the two SHOW GET commands, the Save and Cancel push buttons are also active, while our control push buttons remain disabled and dimmed on the screen. Figure 3.7 shows the Customers window awaiting data entry for a new customer.

Additional Uses of @ GET WHEN

Since we intend to control data entry of Custno programmatically, there is no sense in allowing the operator to address @ GET m.custno. In fact, we must strictly forbid it during the edit action. Another field useless for the operator to address is the Balance field, the value of which is actually held by memvar m.pres_bal, since the customer's balance is not stored in Customer.dbf but is always calculated on the fly by summing the debt-aging fields. We therefore inhibit access to these two @ GETs, which are used for display purposes only, by using @ GET WHEN with a literal value of .F.

FIGURE 3.7:

Customers window during data entry of a new record

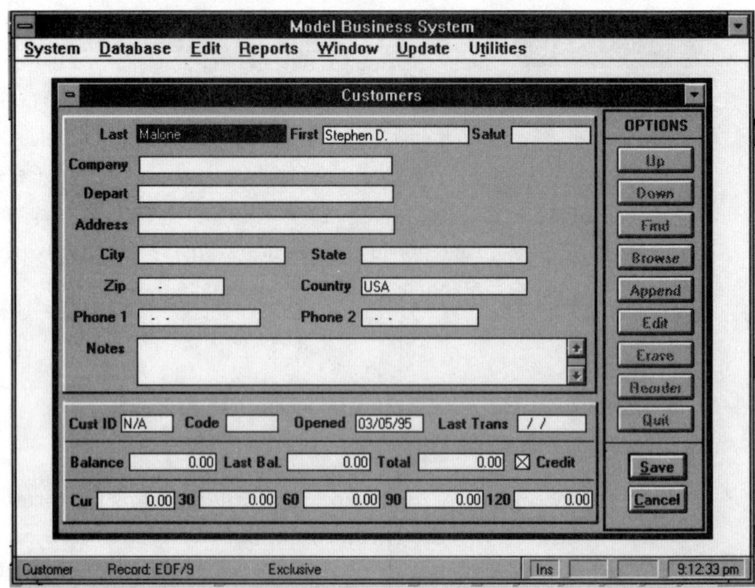

NOTE

An alternative way of displaying read-only data is with @ SAY output fields. @ SAY, for example, is used to display all the labels that appear in the Customers window in front of our @ GET input fields. If we use @ GET instead of @ SAY to display our read-only data, it is because we want the data to be displayed in a bordered box like all other data values. This cannot be done with values displayed with @ SAY.

Of course, this is the simplest possible use of @ GET WHEN. Our use of WHEN m.doit was already more complex. But as previously noted, we can do much more with WHEN <expL>. For example, we can use it with a UDF designed to test data entries to other GETs before permitting operator entry. If operator entry is to be inhibited based upon some condition, _CUROBJ can be used to send the cursor somewhere else. But then, we can do literally anything we want in WHEN <expL>, just as we more or less did in our @ GET m.but1 VALID using a function. CLEAR READ, SHOW GET, and SHOW GETS, not to mention other screen programs, can be launched from WHEN. All that is wanting is a reason for taking such action.

TIP

@ GET WHEN can be used to activate a popup containing possible entries to a field when it is more convenient to do this with DEFINE POPUP PROMPT and ACTIVATE POPUP than @ GET popup or list. We will see how to do this in Chapter 6.

Use of @ GET PICTURE Template and FUNCTION Symbols

If you are already familiar with the basic uses of @ GET PICTURE and FUNCTION in controlling data input and formatting, there should be no secret about how we display phone numbers and zip codes with delimiting hyphens without actually including them in the raw data. Here, for example, are the @ GETs used with m.phone1, m.phone2, and m.zip, pared down to the essentials:

```
@ GET m.zip PICTURE "@KR XXXXX-XXXX" WHEN m.doit
@ GET m.country PICTURE "@K!" WHEN m.doit
@ GET m.phone1 PICTURE "@KR XXX-XXX-XXXXXX" WHEN m.doit
@ GET m.phone2 PICTURE "@KR XXX-XXX-XXXXXX" WHEN m.doit
```

Using the PICTURE template symbol X, we allow the operator to enter any keyboard characters in the memvars. The hyphens, however, do not belong to the set of available PICTURE template symbols, which used to control which keyboard entries will be accepted. (As you may recall, 9s can be used to accept only numbers, while *A*s can be used to accept only alphabetic characters.) FoxPro therefore regards the hyphens entered in the PICTURE template as literal values. It would even treat them as actual data if it were not for the @R function placed in front of the template. The @R function symbol tells FoxPro to regard all *literals* appearing in the PICTURE template as being supplied for reasons of data display only. (The hyphens are regarded not as data but only as part of the data display.)

The reason we use Xs in the PICTURE template to allow any keyboard characters instead of 9s to allow only numbers is simple: We must be prepared for international and not just national phone numbers and postal codes, which may contain alphabetic characters.

Also shown above is the PICTURE clause used with m.country. The PICTURE function @! is used to force all data entries to uppercase. As for the PICTURE function @K, it is used to select the entire @ GET <variable> for editing, though you need not concern yourself about it when designing screens with the Screen Builder since FoxPro automatically inserts it. But you can appreciate its importance if you consider what will happen when the display size of a field is made smaller than the largest possible entry to the field. This is often the case when proportional fonts are used with @ GETs. Without @K, the operator will be limited to the number of characters that will fit in the variable as determined by its display size in the window, not by the variable's actual width. With it, FoxPro will scroll in the display as needed to accommodate entry to the entire field.

Of course, when you design a data entry screen with FoxPro's Screen Builder, dialog boxes help you along in specifying your @ GET input field PICTURE clauses. Figure 3.8, for example, shows the Field dialog box used to define @ GET m.zip. Also open on the screen is the Format dialog box, activated by clicking the Field dialog box's Format push button. It is intended to aid you in entering an appropriate PICTURE clause for your output fields. We will return to these Screen Builder dialog boxes in Chapter 11, though we will not discuss available PICTURE templates or function symbols at length. (For a listing of all available PICTURE template and function symbols, refer to your FoxPro documentation or Help file. The Help file is always immediately available when you use the Screen Builder.)

FIGURE 3.8:
Screen Builder's Field dialog box with the Format dialog box also displayed

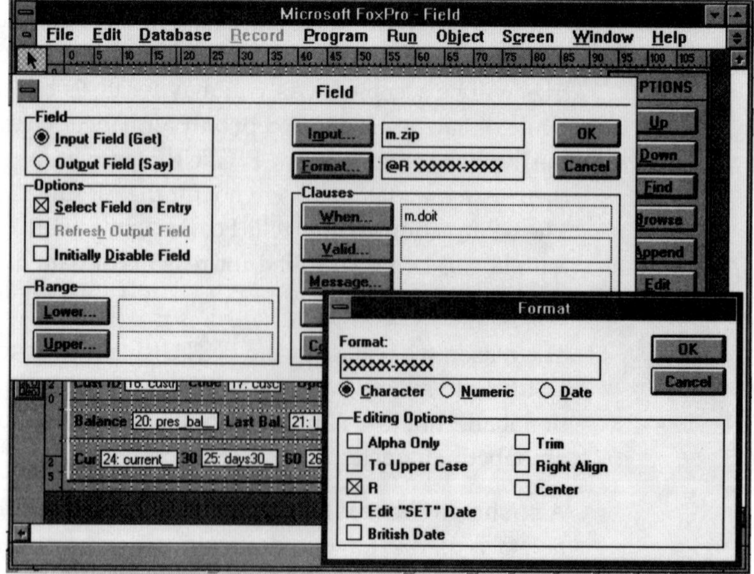

NOTE

The Field dialog can be used to define *input fields* with @ GET <variable> or *output fields* with @ SAY <exp>. Output fields are for data display only and, in the case of the Customers window, might be used to display the customer's present balance—or any other data field or value that will not be altered during data entry. In the MBS, however, we generally work with input fields only, though in the case of the customer's present balance, we need to calculate the balance and stick it in a memvar before displaying it on the screen with @ GET <variable> WHEN .F. You will find it advantageous to work in this way only if you use borders around all your @ GET input fields, as we do in the MBS. Since @ SAY <exp> will not use a border, using it in conjunction with @ GETs employing a border will generally result in an unappealing screen display.

Idiosyncrasies of Proportional Fonts in the Data Entry Screen

If you take another look at Figure 3.7, you will note that the hyphens located in the display of the Phone and Zip fields—and the date delimiters in the blank Last Trans field, representing Customer.lastdate—are shifted toward the left. This is one of the idiosyncrasies of using proportional fonts in data entry fields with FoxPro. Since it does not yet know where the delimiters will actually be positioned once data has been entered, owing to the variable width of each character in the font, FoxPro shifts them to the left in anticipation of the smaller characters and then shifts them back to the right as needed when entries are made. If you do not like this effect, you can simply avoid using proportional fonts in your Read windows. You can, for example, use a monospaced font like FoxFont.

To keep things simple, MBS sticks to the Windows default fonts: MS Sans Serif, 8, regular for data and bold for labels, though we change to TrueType font when producing reports.

Using @ GET RANGE, VALID, and ERROR in Data Validation

Our Customers window offers no useful examples of how to use @ GET input field VALID or RANGE to exert greater control over which entries may be made to a field. But taken together, the two @ GET options make it possible to do almost anything in this regard. RANGE is used with variables of types N and D (Numeric and Date) to establish lower and upper bounds for the operator's entry. You just plug in the numbers or dates you want to use, employing literal values or expressions. With VALID, a logical expression or UDF can be employed. With @ GET VALID, ERROR <expC> can also be used to display an error message in the status bar when the operator makes an invalid entry to the @ GET. With @ GET RANGE, FoxPro uses the entries for Lower and Upper to display the correct range in the System Message window. ERROR <expC> is not used. We see several examples of these @ GET options in Chapter 5 and Chapter 6.

Record-Level Data Validation with Push Buttons

We have arranged our data Edit and Append routines so that both will terminate when the operator presses either the Save or Cancel button. As with our (menu) control push buttons, we use @ GET VALID once again to control program action. The UDF used by @ GET m.verify is shown in Figure 3.9. It should be easy enough to follow at this point. However, before discussing the various actions controlled by IF, we will do well to reflect on the commands at the end of the UDF, all of which are executed regardless of which button the operator selects.

FIGURE 3.9:

UDF executed by the VALID clause of the Save and Cancel push buttons

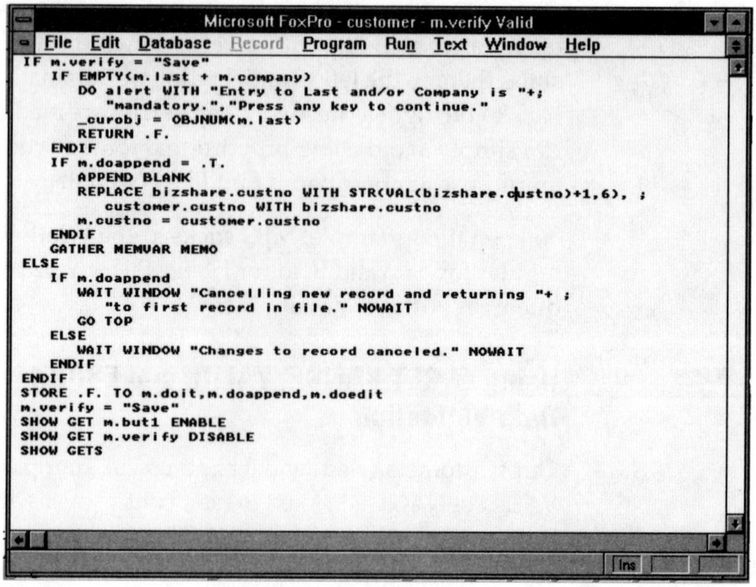

Microsoft FoxPro - customer - m.verify Valid

File Edit Database Record Program Run Text Window Help

```
IF m.verify = "Save"
   IF EMPTY(m.last + m.company)
      DO alert WITH "Entry to Last and/or Company is "+;
         "mandatory.","Press any key to continue."
      _curobj = OBJNUM(m.last)
      RETURN .F.
   ENDIF
   IF m.doappend = .T.
      APPEND BLANK
      REPLACE bizshare.custno WITH STR(VAL(bizshare.custno)+1,6), ;
         customer.custno WITH bizshare.custno
      m.custno = customer.custno
   ENDIF
   GATHER MEMVAR MEMO
ELSE
   IF m.doappend
      WAIT WINDOW "Cancelling new record and returning "+ ;
         "to first record in file." NOWAIT
      GO TOP
   ELSE
      WAIT WINDOW "Changes to record canceled." NOWAIT
   ENDIF
ENDIF
STORE .F. TO m.doit,m.doappend,m.doedit
m.verify = "Save"
SHOW GET m.but1 ENABLE
SHOW GET m.verify DISABLE
SHOW GETS
```

Ins

To begin with, the STORE command resets the memvars controlling the action of our READ SHOW clause so that when the latter is reexecuted, as it will be by the SHOW GETS command at the end of the UDF, FoxPro will prepare to display the current customer record. Here are the pertinent commands:

```
ELSE
    SCATTER MEMVAR MEMO
    m.pres_bal = current+days30+days60+days90+days120
ENDIF
```

Not incidentally, we also reset the initial value of m.verify to Save so that when the Edit and Append routines are executed once more, Save will again be the default button. (If this were not done and Cancel had been selected, "Cancel" would remain in memory as m.verify's value and would be used as the default.)

More important, we use SHOW GET ENABLE/DISABLE to reenable our control push buttons, @GET m.but1, and to disable our Save and Cancel push buttons until they are needed again.

Finally, SHOW GETS reexecutes the READ SHOW clause and, upon termination, passes control of the Customers window back to our control push buttons. Since m.doit is once again set to .F., no other @GET input fields or objects can be selected.

Moving back to our IF statements, we can now readily review our conditionally controlled actions. If the operator selects Cancel, we can simply throw out the memvars currently displayed on the screen. In the case of Edit, no further action need be taken since READ SHOW will execute SCATTER, thus restoring the @GET input fields to their original values prior to refreshing the screen. With Append, however, we must consider which record should next be displayed. (My own preference is to simply GO TOP.) In any case, as a courtesy to the operator we indicate the action taken by using WAIT WINDOW to send a suitable message to the screen.

More interesting are the actions taken when the operator selects Save. We must, after all, prevent the operator from accidentally saving records that may be empty or have no entry in the most important (*key*) data fields. We do this at once with the following commands:

```
IF EMPTY(m.last + m.company)
    DO alert WITH "Entry to Last and/or Company is "+;
        "mandatory.","Press any key to continue."
    _CUROBJ = OBJNUM(m.last)
    RETURN .F.
ENDIF
```

First, notice the use of the FoxPro EMPTY() function. It can be used with data of type C to determine if an expression is filled with blanks or contains a null string, though it can be used to test for empty expressions of all data types. (With data of type N, it returns .T. if the value is 0; with data of type D, it returns .T. if no date has been entered.)

Using a Global Alert Procedure

The next command, DO Alert, calls a nested procedure and passes it two strings. This is the MBS system Alert procedure, which was first designed as a screen program using the Screen Builder and then removed to the MBS procedure file, Bizlib.prg, where it was altered for greater speed of execution. Executed at this point in our program, it provides the operator with due warning of what is required. (See Figure 3.10.)

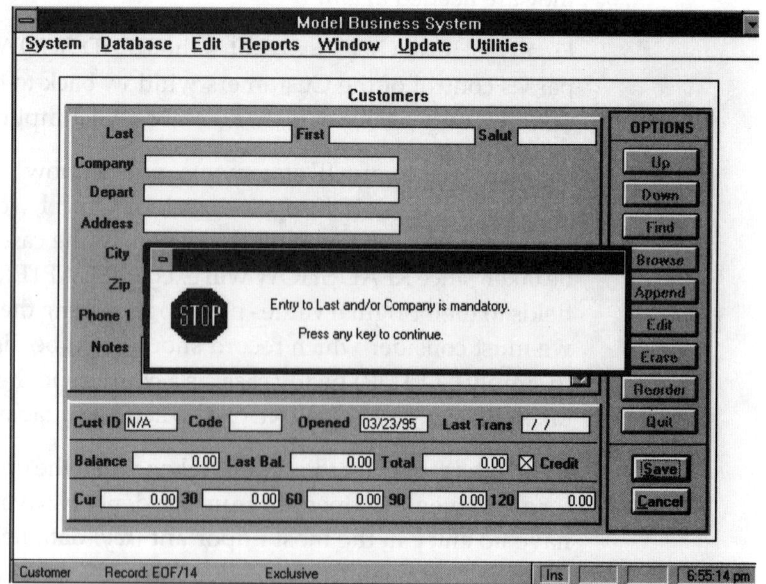

FIGURE 3.10: The MBS Alert window provides the operator with needed instructions or warnings.

TIP

User-defined windows created with DEFINE WINDOW will have *half-height* title bars like the window Alert unless the SYSTEM attribute keyword is used or a font is specified with the FONT clause, though any window can be made to use a half-height title bar if you use the HALFHEIGHT keyword.

TIP

When displaying a character string, use the PADC() function—PADC(<expC>,<expN>[,<expC2>])—to supply the string <expC> with a specific length, <expN>, and if <expC> is shorter than <expN>, to center the string within the display area by padding it with an equal number of blanks on both ends. (Use the optional <expC2> to specify a different character to use as padding.) The PADL() and PADR() functions are also available for padding strings only on the left or right, respectively, to right or left justify them in the display area. We use PADC() in procedure Alert to center the two-line Alert message in the Alert window.

Figure 3.11 shows that all procedure Alert does is draw a window and display the two line messages passed to it with DO WITH <parameters> under a small picture of a stop sign, sent to the screen with @ SAY <.bmp file> BITMAP. The procedure then comes to a halt owing to the use of WAIT. (SET CURSOR OFF is used to prevent the cursor from appearing in the window.) When the operator presses any key to continue program execution, program control returns to our @ GET m.verify VALID clause, which reestablishes m.last as the current GET object with _CUROBJ and issues RETURN .F. to reactivate the cursor. Back in the Customers window, the operator can make entries to the key fields or choose Cancel to break off the action.

Though we cannot discuss the use of .bmp files to display pictures on the screen with @ SAY at this point, you will see in Chapter 11 that the Screen Builder makes it quite easy—provided you have on hand the bitmap files holding the drawings or pictures you want to use. (This is why I designed the Alert window with the Screen Builder rather than writing it by hand.)

FIGURE 3.11:

Procedure Alert is used as a system-wide alert and message window.

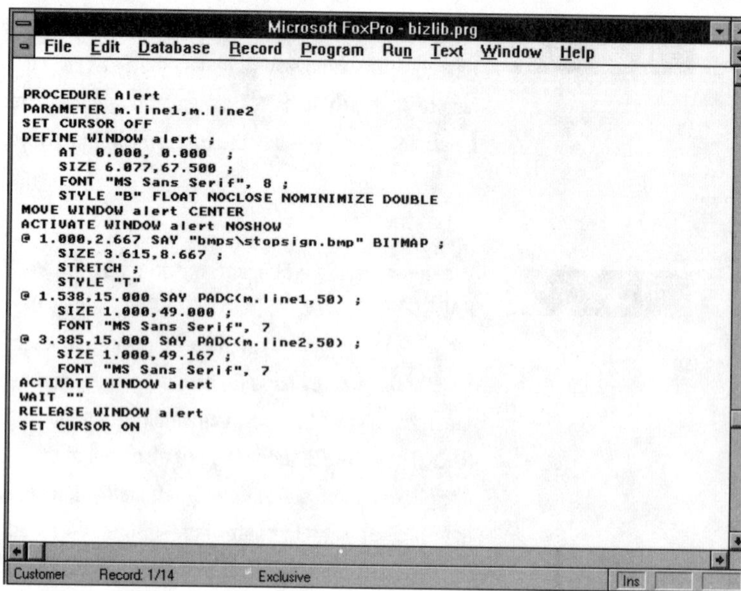


```
PROCEDURE Alert
PARAMETER m.line1,m.line2
SET CURSOR OFF
DEFINE WINDOW alert ;
    AT  0.000, 0.000  ;
    SIZE 6.077,67.500 ;
    FONT "MS Sans Serif", 8 ;
    STYLE "B" FLOAT NOCLOSE NOMINIMIZE DOUBLE
MOVE WINDOW alert CENTER
ACTIVATE WINDOW alert NOSHOW
@ 1.000,2.667 SAY "bmps\stopsign.bmp" BITMAP ;
    SIZE 3.615,8.667 ;
    STRETCH ;
    STYLE "T"
@ 1.538,15.000 SAY PADC(m.line1,50) ;
    SIZE 1.000,49.000 ;
    FONT "MS Sans Serif", 7
@ 3.385,15.000 SAY PADC(m.line2,50) ;
    SIZE 1.000,49.167 ;
    FONT "MS Sans Serif", 7
ACTIVATE WINDOW alert
WAIT ""
RELEASE WINDOW alert
SET CURSOR ON
```

TIP

Happily, the FoxPro sample applications come complete with plenty of bitmap files that you can put to use in your own applications. The stop sign used by procedure Alert and the exclamation point used in the dialogs presented in Chapter 2 were both taken from the store of bitmaps found in \FoxProw\Goodies\Bitmaps. Of course, these bitmaps and a few others are supplied with the MBS and will be found in \Foxprow\Apps\Bigbiz\Bmps when you install the MBS on your hard disk.

Updating Customer Records during Append or Edit

Finally, we come to the real Save action, where we must distinguish between Append and Edit.

```
IF m.doappend = .T.
    APPEND BLANK
    REPLACE bizshare.custno WITH STR(VAL(bizshare.custno)+1,6), ;
    customer.custno WITH bizshare.custno
    m.custno = customer.custno
```

```
ENDIF
GATHER MEMVAR MEMO
```

In the case of Append, we now add a new record to the Customer table and use REPLACE, as described in Chapter 2, to update Bizshare.custno, representing the last-used customer number assigned by the system. This creates the unique Custno required by our new record. Next, anticipating that it will be easiest to complete the Append and Edit actions together with GATHER MEMVAR, we must remember that m.custno, which remains unaltered by REPLACE, still holds the value n/a assigned it at the outset of the Append routine. We must therefore reinitialize it to hold the new Custno before executing GATHER MEMVAR or else overwrite Customer.current. (Given the number of fields in Customer.dbf, this is a lot easier than using GATHER MEMVAR FIELDS <field list>.) Once GATHER MEMVAR MEMO is executed, we can go on with the SHOW by executing the commands at the end of the VALID clause as described above.

Network Append and Edit Routines

If you write network applications, you'll be especially appreciative of the way the MBS Append and Edit routines are written. Indeed, they are already network ready. Automatic record and file locking will be kept to an absolute minimum, owing to the use of memvars with SCATTER, APPEND BLANK, REPLACE, and GATHER. Customer number assignments are also handled in a way that will automatically prohibit the assignment of duplicate Custnos, even when many operators are simultaneously adding records to the Customer table. Again, this is done by using a system value table and the REPLACE command to control Custno assignments.

In fact, with regard to network operation, the customer data entry program has only one defect: It is possible for two or more operators to update the same customer record simultaneously. Simply put, the memvars displaying a record in the Customers window can become out of date, even as an operator begins editing them, owing to another operator's use of the same record. This problem is compounded by the way the Payments and Sales programs are designed to update customer account fields. Those updates, if made while another operator is working on a customer record, will be overwritten, for example, by the GATHER command used by the Edit routine. Clearly, this must be prevented.

In a small network involving only a few operators working in close quarters, the problem can be minimized through cooperation and planning. The Customer table can be divided up alphabetically among the users so that one operator handles customers with names beginning with letters A–F, another handles G–M, and so on. This eliminates conflicts and ensures the integrity of data in the Customer database. (Of course, the practice must extend to the entry of sales and payments as well as to entry and edit of customer records with the Customers window.)

Controlling Operator Access to Records

In medium and large network applications, we cannot expect to get by with such measures. All programs that update the Customer database must be written so as to prevent two or more operators from updating the same customer account. This is best handled by using the record-locking function, RLOCK() or LOCK(), to place a lock on the record before allowing data edit. (RLOCK() and LOCK() are just two names for the same function.) We can, for example, put LOCK() to work to make the Edit action conditional on FoxPro's success in locking the record for the operator by inserting the following commands in our @ GET push button VALID clause:

```
CASE m.but1 = "Edit" AND NOT EMPTY(m.custno)
    IF LOCK()
        STORE .T. TO m.doit, m.doedit
     ELSE
        WAIT WINDOW "Sorry, customer record locked by other "+ ;
            "operator." NOWAIT
    ENDIF
```

If the record is available, the LOCK() function locks it and returns a value of .T., thereby resetting the values of m.doit and m.doedit so that READ SHOW, when executed, will enable data editing of the current record. On the other hand, if the record is locked by another operator, we use WAIT to indicate that the record is not available and leave the values of m.doit and m.doedit unchanged.

Of course, at the end of the edit action—that is, in the VALID clause of our Save and Cancel push buttons—we must execute the UNLOCK command to relinquish the record lock. Otherwise FoxPro will maintain the lock even as the operator goes on to perform other work.

Controlling Record and File Locking with SET REPROCESS

The FoxPro command SET REPROCESS TO <expN> [SECONDS] / TO AUTOMATIC can be used to control the action of commands establishing automatic record or file locks as well as the functions used to establish manual record and file locks when the locking action is unsuccessful. Use TO <expN> to make FoxPro retry the command or function <expN> times before an error is generated by commands using automatic record or file locking or when a function establishing a manual record or file lock returns .F. Use TO <expN> SECONDS to retry the lock for <expN> seconds.

When SET REPROCESS TO 0 (the default value) is in effect, FoxPro attempts to lock the record or file indefinitely and displays the message "Attempting to lock... Press Escape or Cancel" in the System Message window. If the record or file cannot be locked, the operator must press Esc to cancel the command or return a value of .F. with the manual record- and file-locking functions. However, FoxPro responds in this way only if ON ERROR <command> is not used to establish a system error-handling routine. If an ON ERROR routine is in effect, SET REPROCESS TO 0 automatically triggers it when the record or file lock is unsuccessful. If you want to allow SET REPROCESS to ignore the ON ERROR routine until the operator presses Esc, use SET REPROCESS TO AUTOMATIC (or –2). You can also force FoxPro to retry a lock indefinitely without executing a standing ON ERROR routine and without providing the operator with an opportunity to break off the action by using SET REPROCESS TO –1. (See Chapter 8 for a brief discussion of ON ERROR <command>.)

A Bird's-Eye View of the Customer Entry Program

TIP

To make a complex program easier to understand or create, outline it in *pseudocode*—that is, in a combination of English and FoxPro. You can then execute the program by filling in the outline with the required FoxPro commands.

Though the customer entry program reviewed in this chapter is elementary by FoxPro standards, it is bound to give pause to those who are coming to FoxPro from other Xbase languages that do not depend upon READ and its many clauses to control program action. Still, if all this is new to you, take heart by considering how effects similar to those achieved with the @ GET push buttons VALID, SHOW GET/S ENABLE/DISABLE, _CUROBJ, READ CYCLE, and READ SHOW might be obtained using traditional DO WHILE loops. Simply put, one would be faced with a programmer's nightmare. To refresh all @ GETs in a window, you would be required to place READ within a DO WHILE loop, terminate the READ, for example, by placing KEYBOARD '{Ctrl+W}' in the VALID clause of an @ GET, and repaint the screen from scratch:

```
DO WHILE .T.
    @ GET variable
    @ GET variable VALID <including KEYBOARD command>
    READ
    IF <expL>
        LOOP
    ENDIF
    EXIT
ENDDO
```

Controlling which @ GET the cursor is sent to would require the use of additional memvars to conditionally disable all other @ GETs with WHEN <expL>. And this would be only the beginning. We would still be a long way from attaining the look and feel of a Windows-style data entry program.

On the other hand, with the commands and functions provided by FoxPro beginning with version 2.0, our programmer's nightmare is reduced to a few compact routines and a single strategy with near-global application.

1. Initialize all memvars required as flags: m.doit, m.doappend, m.doedit.
2. Initialize default values for our two @ GET push buttons.
3. SELECT customer and prepare memvars for @ GET variables.
4. Define and activate a window and issue all @ GETs.
5. Execute READ CYCLE SHOW.
6. Write a UDF used by the VALID clause of our control push buttons, relying on DO CASE.
7. Write a UDF used by READ SHOW, relying on IF, SHOW GET, and SCATTER.
8. Write a UDF used by the VALID clause of our Save and Cancel push buttons, relying on IF, APPEND BLANK, GATHER, and SHOW GET/S.

This will be more or less standard practice with all our data entry programs.

Of course, we must also write the various nested screen programs called out by control push buttons, including Cus_find.spr and the far simpler Erase.spr, which is used by all the MBS data entry programs for the same purpose—to DELETE the record currently displayed in the READ window. We close out this chapter by taking a look at this relatively simple program—or at least so it will appear once it is stripped down to the bare essentials and presented in pseudo-code fashion.

Additional Comments on SHOW GETS and READ SHOW

The SHOW GETS command includes two important options for controlling its effect when a READ SHOW clause is employed. If you must refresh the screen but do not want to execute READ SHOW, use SHOW GETS ONLY. If you want to execute READ SHOW but do not want to refresh the @ GETs on the screen, use SHOW GETS OFF. These two SHOW GETS options were omitted above so we could concentrate on the use of SHOW GETS in Customer.spr.

With respect to READ SHOW in particular, as noted above, it is executed once when READ is activated. It is subsequently reissued whenever SHOW GETS is executed, unless ONLY is employed. The Screen Builder's penchant for generating @ GETs using a DEFAULT <value> makes it unnecessary to initialize the memvars used by our @ GET input fields (in step 3 of our pseudo-code version of Customer.spr) prior to executing READ and READ SHOW. As long as m.doit is .F., SCATTER MEMVAR and the command initializing the memvar representing the customer's present balance (both located in READ SHOW) will see to it that the memvars displaying the fields of the current customer record are properly loaded when the screen program is first executed. The only difference is that the @ GET input fields will briefly display the *empty* DEFAULT values on the screen until FoxPro finishes with READ SHOW. (Since I prefer to have the @ GETs appear with the proper values already loaded, I always use SCATTER MEMVAR in my screen program setup code, prior to executing @ GET and READ.)

Designing a Global Delete Program

When the operator selects the Erase button in the Customers window, we execute the following commands in our push button VALID clause:

```
CASE m.but1 = "Erase"
    IF l_balance = 0.00 AND current = 0.00
       DO Erase.spr
    ELSE
        WAIT WINDOW "Cannot delete a customer with an "+ ;
            "active account!" NOWAIT
    ENDIF
```

Since it is not good policy to allow an operator to erase a customer record representing an active account, we first use IF to see whether or not the account is active. If it is, L_balance and/or Current will not equal 0, and FoxPro will display the WAIT WINDOW message and take no further action. On the other hand, if the account is inactive, FoxPro executes Erase.spr, which sends the dialog box shown in Figure 3.12 to the screen. The dialog does no more than ask the operator to confirm the erase action by selecting one of two buttons: Proceed or Cancel.

FIGURE 3.12:

MBS Erase Record dialog box

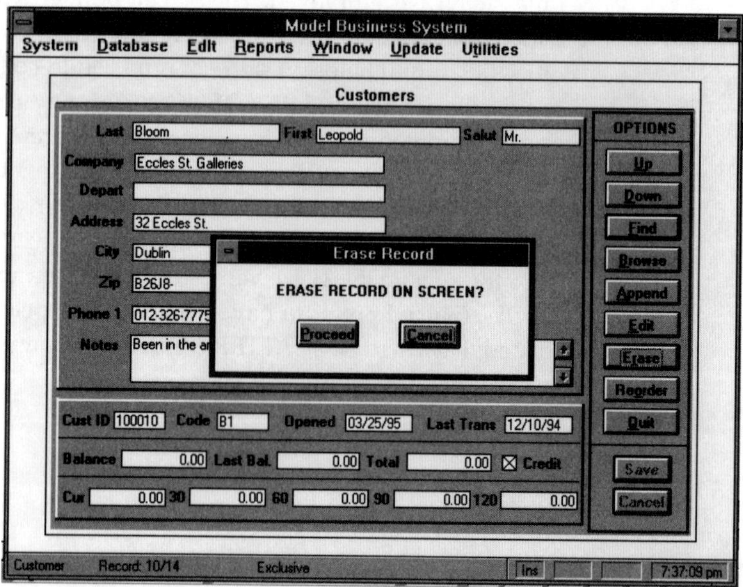

Erase.spr is quite simple. All that is involved is the definition and opening of a window; the display of a message along with one set of push buttons; execution of the READ CYCLE command; and execution of one UDF, written for execution with @ GET VALID following the same format as was used with the Customers window's Save and Cancel push buttons.

```
* Pseudo-code version of Erase.spr.

* We may reuse memvar m.verify without affecting the value of
* m.verify used in Customer.spr if we declare it Private to
* Erase.spr.
PRIVATE m.verify
m.verify = "Cancel"

* Define and activate a suitable window.
DEFINE WINDOW erase...
ACTIVATE WINDOW erase

* Send message and push buttons to active window.
@ GET m.verify PICTURE "@*HT \!\<Proceed;\?\<Cancel" VALID <udf>
@ SAY "ERASE RECORD ON SCREEN?"

* Execute READ with CYCLE and MODAL keywords.
READ CYCLE MODAL

* Release window after @ GET push button VALID <udf>
* is executed and READ is terminated.
RELEASE WINDOW erase
```

So much for the central portion of the program. There are only two things that are new here. First, unlike our other sets of push buttons, we define @ GET m.verify with the Screen Builder's Push Button dialog to Terminate READ on Selection by checking the appropriate Options check box. (See Figure 3.13.) Since we also select the radio button designating *horizontal* push buttons, this results in the @ GET push button PICTURE clause using functions "@*HT" for push buttons (*), horizontal (H), and terminate READ on selection (T). As a result, we do not need to execute CLEAR READ in our VALID clause. A return value of .T. will clear the READ for us. (The function symbol V is used instead when the *vertical* radio button is selected. Function symbol N, short for *No terminate,* is used when the terminate READ on selection check box is unused. This prevents push button selection from terminating the READ.)

The other significant thing about Erase.spr is its use of the READ MODAL keyword.

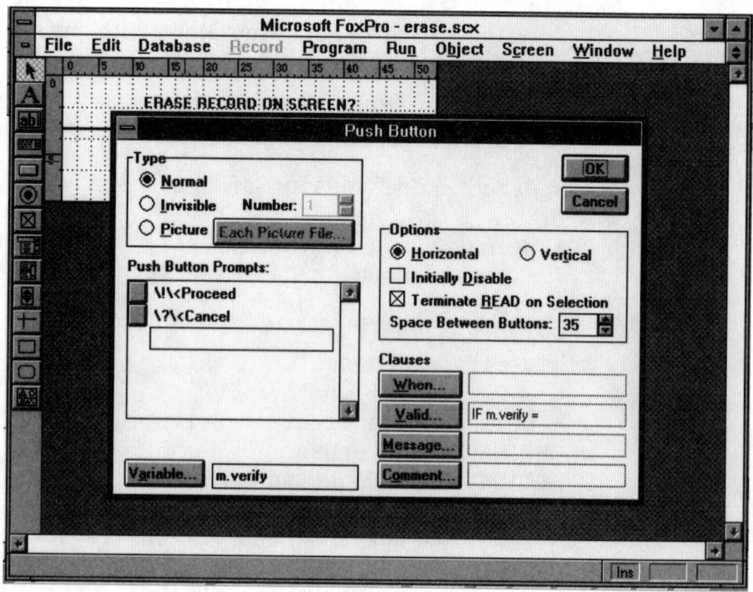

FIGURE 3.13: Use the Screen Builder's Push Button dialog Options box to control push button attributes.

Using READ MODAL in Dialog Boxes

Simply put, MODAL is used to prevent the operator from selecting any other window not employed in the current READ—and we do have another window on the screen: Customers. In other contexts we might have several.

Still, what is essential about a dialog box is that the operator is supposed to enter additional information about an action already launched. That is what the *dialog* is about. And following traditional Windows practice, we want the operator to finish with the dialog before going on to something else. This is achieved in this instance (as it was with Cus_find.spr, described above) by using READ MODAL.

The Delete Records Routine

The @ GET VALID clause used by Erase.spr's push buttons is quite simple. If the operator presses Cancel, no action is taken. The UDF automatically returns .T., Erase.spr terminates, and no record is deleted.

```
IF m.verify = "Proceed"
   DELETE
```

```
    IF .NOT. EOF()
        SKIP
        IF NOT EOF()
            WAIT WINDOW "Record Deleted. Moving to "+ ;
                "next record in file" NOWAIT
            RETURN .T.
        ENDIF
    ENDIF
    WAIT WINDOW "Record Deleted. Moving to "+ ;
        "first record in file" NOWAIT
    GO TOP
ENDIF
```

On the other hand, if Proceed is selected, we execute the DELETE command. So far so good. But now for the conundrum.

In the MBS we generally work with SET DELETED ON, which prevents FoxPro from displaying records marked for deletion with DELETE. However, a current record marked for deletion will not be ignored with SET DELETED ON until the record pointer is moved in the table. We must therefore move the record pointer so that when the operator returns to the Customers window, the deleted record will not appear on the screen. We do this with SKIP.

Though it is a minor point, you may note that we test for EOF() before executing SKIP even though EOF() will never be .T. if a record is actually deleted. But recollecting that when the application is first installed, Customer.dbf is likely to be empty, we are forced to consider what will happen if an operator selects Erase instead of Append. Is this even worth worrying about? While there are various opinions on this matter, one thing is clear. If Erase.spr is inadvertently used to delete records from an empty table, the only command in it that will generate an error is SKIP. The test for EOF() prevents this from happening. (Again, GO TOP will not generate an error even in an empty table.)

The alternatives are simple. You may prevent Erase.spr from being run when the current table is empty, using SHOW GET DISABLE in Customer.spr's READ SHOW clause to disable the Erase button or using m.but1 = "Erase" AND NOT EMPTY(m.custno) to prevent it from being executed if the Erase button is selected. (The second strategy is actually used to impede execution of Edit when Customer.dbf is empty.) You can also attempt to write an error-handling routine dexterous enough to recognize and suppress such innocuous errors without bringing the system to a crashing halt. However, this is not advised for the simple reason that the error generated by SKIP when a table is empty may also occur when an index tag or a table has become damaged. It is therefore best to deal up front in the program code with the kind of errors that can be generated when the system files are empty —and to do it, as we attempt to in the MBS, with a minimum of fanfare.

Finally, looking over the text of Erase.spr, one thing should be clear. There is not a single command in it that addresses a particular table. No fields are referenced. The only thing assumed by Erase.spr is that a table is open in the current work area. What this means is simple. We can use Erase.spr to delete records from any table whatsoever, and we can therefore use it over and over without modification with all our applications.

CHAPTER

FOUR

Using Index Tags with FoxPro

4

- Using index tags to perform data retrieval
- Creating and using structural compound index files
- Designing record locate and reorder dialogs
- Controlling window events during modal dialogs
- Using Rushmore optimization to assist in searches

Anyone familiar with the fundamentals of Xbase knows the importance of indexes. They provide the means of instantaneously placing table (or database) records in a logical order on the basis of the content of one or more table fields. Moreover, with the aid of SEEK, SEEK(), FIND, and LOOKUP(), they can be used to deliver us to any one of millions of records in the bat of an eyelash. If our intention is to process a group of records in order by their position in the indexed table, we can even use an index to control our command's scope. Once we find the first record we want, for example, with SEEK, we can then use WHILE <condition> to tell FoxPro where to stop processing records when executing any of the *sequential commands.* These include COUNT, CALCULATE, LIST, DISPLAY, COPY, REPLACE, INDEX, SCAN, REPORT, and LABEL, all of which direct FoxPro to process database records, one by one, in sequence. As previously mentioned, index tags are also the *sine qua non* of SET RELATION; without them FoxPro (and other versions of Xbase supporting SET RELATION) would have no means of instantly cross-referencing the records in a multi-table view.

Beginning with FoxPro 2.0 and the introduction of Rushmore technology with SET OPTIMIZE ON and SQL-SELECT, index tags have taken on yet greater significance. This is because they can now be used as a means of filtering records from the view when you use such old Xbase workhorses as SET FILTER TO <condition> and the FOR <condition> clauses of the various sequential commands, including all those mentioned above, though several caveats apply. Rushmore, for example, cannot be used by FoxPro when executing a sequential command that processes a multi-table database formed with SET RELATION TO. This must be done using SQL-SELECT, which works quite differently than the sequential commands.

But what is *Rushmore optimization*? To be brief, when SET OPTIMIZE is ON—its default setting—and SET RELATION is not in effect, entry of a sequential command using a conditional filter that is formed with any of the standard Xbase comparison operators (=, >, >=, <, <=, #, <>) prompts FoxPro to check the key expressions of all open index tags and tables to see if one or more of them can be used to figure out which records actually meet the specified condition without having to actually read through and evaluate the condition for each record. The effect is similar to that obtained, for example, in dBASE IV 1.5 and 2.0 with SET KEY and in FoxPro itself with the BROWSE command's KEY clause, but it is far more wide ranging in effect. This is because SET KEY (not available in FoxPro because of the availability and effect of SET OPTIMIZE) and BROWSE KEY are wholly dependent on the master (actively engaged) index tag. Not so the wily Fox, which can refer to all available index tags and use whichever ones can help. If the filter condition—or part of a compound filter condition formed with the logical operator AND and OR—can be referred to an existing index, FoxPro will automatically use it, making the filtering of records as instantaneous as looking up records with SEEK. We will have more to say about this after we have introduced the primary index tags used with Customer.dbf.

The Primary Customer Table Index Tags

To aid the operator in locating records in our Customer table *and* database, we provide three main index tags for use with Customer.dbf. They are listed here along with their key expressions:

Index Tag Name	**Key Expression**
Name	UPPER(last + first)
Company	UPPER(company)
Custno	Custno

These and other Customer.dbf indexes are placed in the *structural compound index file*—a special compound (or multiple) index tag file. Like other compound index tag files (extension .cdx), a structural compound index file can hold any number of index tags. What is special about a structural compound index file like Customer.cdx is that it is given the same name as the table with which its index tags are used. Whenever we open Customer.dbf, FoxPro automatically looks for and opens Customer.cdx if it can be found. This makes using the index tags stored in a structural compound index easy; all we need do is open the table to which it is associated in order to have use of its indexes.

Creating a Structural Compound Index

A structural compound index file is created automatically when you issue the command INDEX ON <key expression> TAG <tag name>, provided that you do not use the INDEX command's OF <.cdx file> clause to place the new index tag in a compound index file with another name. Indeed, you can omit entering the OF <.cdx file> clause altogether.

A structural compound index file will also be automatically created (if it doesn't already exist) when a tag is specified for any data field while creating or modifying a table with CREATE or MODIFY STRUCTURE. Both commands activate the FoxPro Table Structure dialog shown in Figure 4.1, though the dialog can also be accessed automatically through FoxPro's system menu in too many ways to warrant mention.

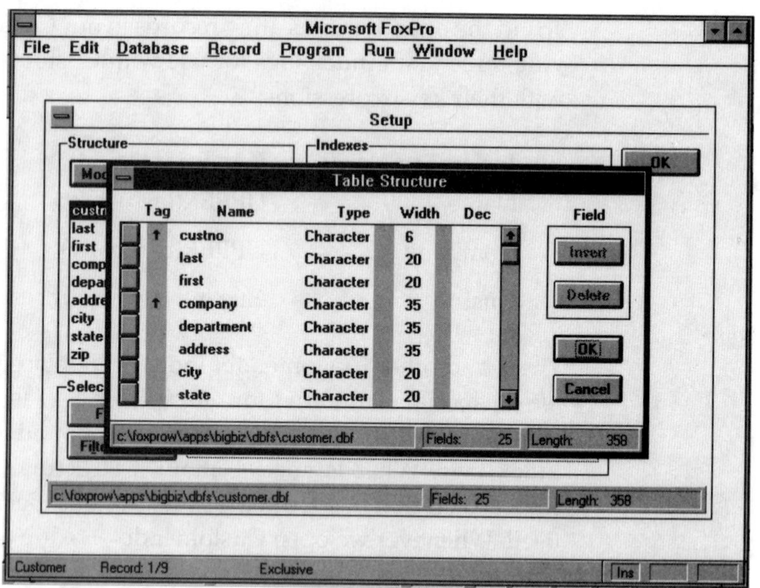

FIGURE 4.1: Single-field index tags can be created using the FoxPro Table Structure dialog.

Use of the Table Structure dialog, however, will only suffice to create index tags based upon the contents of a single data field *as is*. If you want to use functions in the index key expression or create a compound index key, referring to the contents of two or more data fields or parts thereof, the index tags must be created with the INDEX command. We might, for example, create all three of the index tags listed above, placing them in Customer.dbf's structural compound index file with the following commands:

```
USE customer
INDEX ON custno TAG custno
INDEX ON UPPER(company) TAG company
INDEX ON UPPER(last + first) TAG names
```

When we select one of these index tags as the active or controlling index with SET ORDER TO <tag> or the ORDER <tag> clause of the USE command, FoxPro arranges the records of Customer.dbf in order according to the ASCII value of each record's key in the index. When engaged as the controlling index, the index tag Names obviously arranges the Customer table's records in ASCII order (of which alphabetical order is a subset) on the basis of a customer's last and first name. The UPPER() function is used so that differences in upper- and lowercase characters will be ignored when FoxPro creates the index. All index keys are forced to uppercase.

The Company and Custno index tags can be engaged to arrange the Customer table records in order by the ASCII values of the Company field (again, forced to uppercase) or Custno field, respectively. Again, we place all the index tags used with Customer.dbf in the structural compound index file, Customer.cdx, as a matter of convenience. This way we never need open the the .cdx file manually, and all index tags will automatically be updated when the table is edited—whether or not an index tag is engaged.

ASCII Order and Index Tags

FoxPro employs ASCII order when creating index tags (or index files) based upon key expressions of type C (Character). With regard to alphabetical characters and numbers (of type C), this means that the numbers 0–9 come first in the resulting index order, followed by uppercase alphabetical characters. The lowercase alphabetical characters come next. (Blank spaces have a lower ASCII value than numbers, which is why records containing blanks in the key field or fields of a controlling index always appear first in the indexed table.)

Given the different ASCII values of the set of upper- and lowercase characters, true dictionary order can only be obtained using an index tag if the UPPER(), LOWER(), or PROPER() function is employed when creating the index. UPPER() forces all index keys to uppercase, while LOWER() forces all index keys to lowercase. PROPER() forces the first character of every word in the index key to uppercase and all other characters to lowercase. Of course, index tags and index files can be created using ascending or descending ASCII order—ascending being the default order—by using the INDEX command's ASCENDING or DESCENDING option.

FoxPro's SET ORDER TO command includes an ASCENDING/DESCENDING option that allows you to automatically reverse the order of records in an indexed table. There is no need to create two different index tags in order to obtain either order. With the availability of SET ORDER TO <tag> ASCENDING/DESCENDING on hand, one will do.

Operator Selection and Use of Index Tags in the MBS

In the MBS, we make it possible for an operator to take full advantage of our Names, Company, and Custno index tags by providing the dialog shown in Figure 4.2. As we saw in Chapter 3, the dialog is activated through operator selection of the Reorder and Find push buttons, which are standard features not just of the Customers window but of all windows dedicated to update and display of the Customer database. As also mentioned, the Reorder/Locate dialog, executed by Cus_find.spr, is also used at the outset of the customer Append routine to help prohibit the entry of duplicate customer records. Still, to spare the reader the difficulty of distinguishing among the variant uses of Cus_find.spr as controlled through the use of so many IF/ENDIFs, we focus exclusively on the program's use in performing table lookup and omit code segments not strictly dedicated to this function.

Requirements of the Customer Table Locate Dialog

The requirements of the lookup dialog should be readily apparent from what it offers. The presence of the Proceed and Cancel push buttons implies the ability to return to whatever index order and record were current before the execution of the program. The Search/Reorder by option, represented by a popup menu listing available index orders (shown closed in Figure 4.2) also implies the ability to change indexes and so too the means by which lookup is performed without leaving the dialog. Since we can make use of SHOW GET to selectively enable/disable the @ GET input fields used for operator entry of search strings, we will naturally want to use it to activate only those @ GETs corresponding to the selected controlling

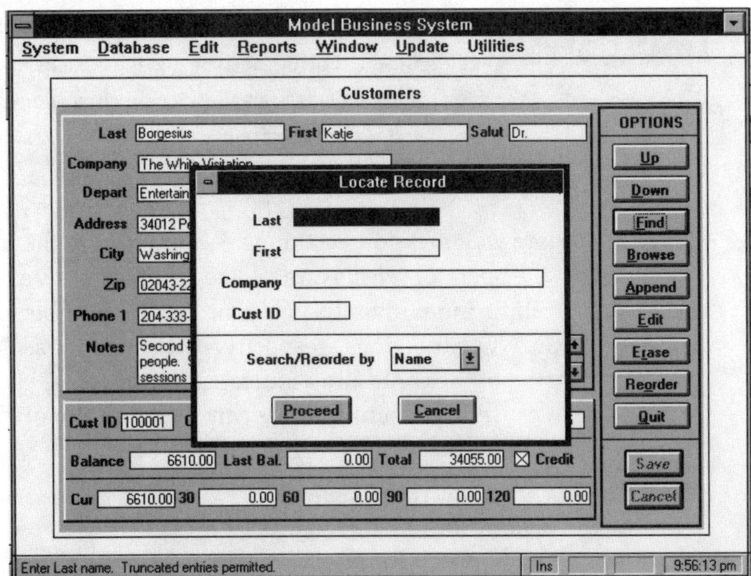

FIGURE 4.2: MBS Customer table Reorder/Locate dialog

index, though this index can be changed. All this is readily handled by READ SHOW. But first, a few preliminaries.

The following program code is taken from Cus_find.spr's setup, which establishes the environment for proper execution of the central portion of the program under the control of READ.

```
m.ord_choi = IIF(ORDER() = "NAMES","Name",;
    IIF(ORDER() = "COMPANY","Company","Cust ID"))
m.orig_ord = ORDER()
m.orig_rec = RECNO()
m.new_ord = " "
PRIVATE m.verify
m.verify = "Proceed"
STORE SPACE(20) TO m.firstfnd,m.lastfnd
m.companyfnd = SPACE(30)
m.custnofnd = SPACE(6)
```

NOTE FoxPro functions used to return information about the current status of a table, like ORDER() and RECNO(), assume that the table being queried is the currently selected table, unless an alias or work area number is supplied to direct FoxPro to another table or work area.

Here we must do two things. We must store the information that will be required if the operator selects Cancel. We achieve this by saving the name of the current controlling index and the current record number, returned by the ORDER() and RECNO() functions, respectively, to memvars. (Note that ORDER() returns the name of the controlling index tag in uppercase characters.) If the operator chooses to cancel the operation, we can return to the original settings with the following commands:

```
SET ORDER TO m.orig_ord
IF NOT BOF() AND NOT EOF()
    GO m.orig_rec
ENDIF
```

(Since the GO command will result in an error if Cus_find.spr is executed when Customer.dbf is empty, we embed it in an IF that will test for this condition. Remember, RECNO() returns 1 and not 0 when a table is empty!)

Defining @ GET Popups

There is also the issue of what *order* will initially appear in the Search/Reorder by popup as the default when the window is first drawn. Figure 4.3 shows the Screen Builder Popup dialog used to create our Search/Reorder by popup.

As the Popup dialog indicates, we use memvar m.ord_choi, short for *order-choice,* to hold the value returned by the popup. As two radio buttons in the Options box of the Popup dialog indicate, we can specify two different types of popups. With *list popups,* like our @ GET ord_choi, we simply list the options we want displayed in the Popup Prompts scroll box. (The small button to the left of each option can be used to drag and reposition the option name in the list with the mouse.) *Array popups,* on the other hand, take their options automatically from a memory array that has been predefined to hold the desired prompts. (We will see an example of an array popup in Chapter 5.)

FIGURE 4.3:

With the Screen Builder, @ GET popups are easily defined with the Popup dialog.

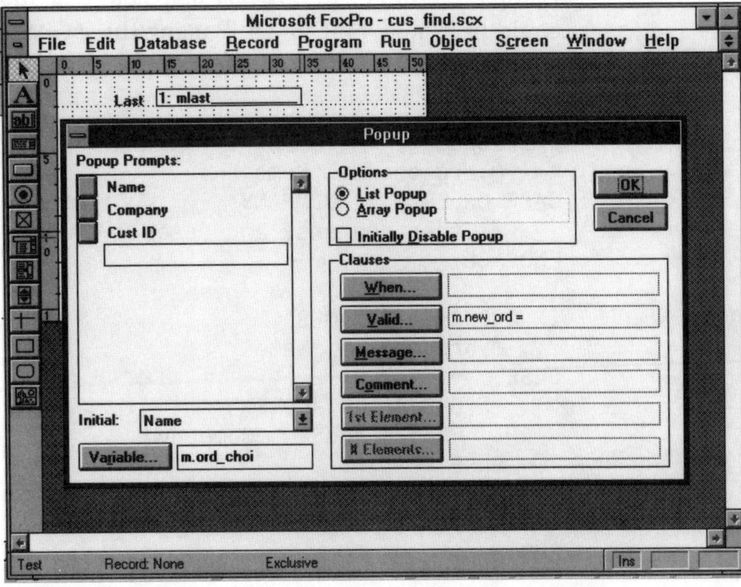

If the three entries in our prompt list don't exactly match the names of our index tags, it is simply because it seemed preferable to use a more explicit name for Custno—Cust Id—and, given that change, to use Name as the label for index tag names. As a result, whenever the operator selects an option from the popup, we must perform a translation, using the prompt label to arrive at the index tag name. In addition to m.ord_choi, holding the value returned when the popup is used, we therefore need another memvar to store the name of a newly selected index. We use m.new_ord for this purpose.

Though we supply m.ord_choi with a default value of Name in the Popup dialog, this is not the prompt we will actually want to use as the popup's default. We can determine which prompt is displayed in the (closed) popup as the default by assigning memvar m.ord_choi the desired value (that is, the name of the desired option) in advance. Note that the command used to do this employs IIF() with the ORDER() function to assign m.ord_choi the prompt corresponding to the index tag serving as the controlling index when Cus_find.spr begins.

```
m.ord_choi = IIF(ORDER() = "NAMES","Name",
    IIF(ORDER() = "COMPANY","Company","Cust ID"))
```

Using nested IIF()s in this way helps us write more compact code. The same thing could be done with DO CASE using three CASEs or two or three IF/ENDIFs, depending upon how you put them together.

```
DO CASE
CASE ORDER() = "NAMES"
    m.ord_choi = "Name"
CASE ORDER() = "COMPANY"
    * Other commands and cases.
ENDCASE

IF ORDER() = "NAMES"
    m.ord_choi = "Name"
ELSE
    IF ORDER() = "COMPANY"
        m.ord_choi = "Company
    ELSE
        m.orch_choi = "Cust ID"
    ENDIF
ENDIF
```

The single command using nested IIF()s performs the same action as the nested IF/ENDIFs using nine commands.

The other memvars in our screen program setup code—m.custnofnd, m.lastfnd, m.firstfnd, and m.companyfnd—will be used with @ GET for operator input of search strings and are initialized to have the same data type and width as the data fields used by our index tags. Memvar m.verify will once again be used to hold the value returned by our push buttons. To prevent whatever value m.verify is given in Cus_find.spr from affecting the value of m.verify used by the Save and Cancel push buttons in Customer.spr (or any other program calling Cus_find.spr), we declare it PRIVATE before setting its default value.

Memvars Public and Private

To facilitate memvar management, all memory variables created during program execution are defined as private to the program (procedure or function) in which they are initialized or declared. By convention, this means that the memory variables are accessible to the program and to all programs (procedures or functions) executed by it. (The latter are referred to as nested programs.) When the program terminates, the private memory variables are automatically flushed from memory.

Note that changes made to a memory variable by a nested program are retained upon return to the calling program. This is standard practice.

FoxPro's handling of memvars, however, can be modified in several ways. A nested program can use the same memory variable name as a calling program without altering the value of the memvar in the calling program. This is done, as shown above, by using PRIVATE <memvar list> to declare the memory variable private—though this should be regarded as a special form of privacy. When the PRIVATE command is issued in a nested program, FoxPro *hides* the preexisting memory variable of the same name (if it exists) and restores its value to memory only when the nested program terminates. Again, if this is not done, changes to the value of the existing memvar will be retained when the nested program terminates.

Parameter passing with DO <program> WITH <parameters> and the PARAMETER <parameter list> is designed to work in a similar way. Memvars created with the PARAMETER command are automatically declared private. If a memory variable of similar name already exists, it is hidden.

On the other hand, a memory variable created in a nested program can be made available to all calling programs by declaring it public with PUBLIC <memvar list>. Memory variables declared public will also be retained in memory after a program terminates and control returns to the FoxPro Command window unless they are manually released from memory with RELEASE <memvar list>/ALL or CLEAR ALL, though the CLEAR ALL command also closes all open tables and releases other memory objects.

A list of all defined memory variables, their types, and the names of the programs in which they are initialized is available through use of DISPLAY or LIST MEMORY. Note that memory array elements are handled exactly like memvars since that is how FoxPro handles them internally.

Controlling Dialog Action with @ GET VALID and READ SHOW

Stepping through Cus_find.spr, we next define and activate our window and execute our @ GETs and READ command. I have stripped down and otherwise altered the code used to perform these actions, even omitting mandatory portions of certain commands, in order to stick to the essentials.

```
DEFINE WINDOW cus_find...FLOAT, CLOSE, NOMINIMIZE
ACTIVATE WINDOW cus_find
@...SAY "Last"
@...SAY "First"
@... SAY "Company"
@...SAY "Cust ID"
@...SAY "Search/Reorder by"
@...GET m.lastfnd PICTURE "@K" ;
    MESSAGE "Enter Last name.  Truncated entries permitted."
@...GET m.firstfnd PICTURE "@K" ;
    MESSAGE "First name is optional, but can only be used "+ ;
    "when full last name is entered."
@...GET m.companyfnd PICTURE "@K" ;
    MESSAGE "Enter Company to search for."
@...GET m.custnofnd PICTURE "@K 999999"
@...GET m.ord_choi PICTURE "@^ Name;Company;Cust ID" ;
    VALID _qcb0xlqns()
@...GET m.verify PICTURE "@*HN \!\<Proceed;\?\<Cancel" ;
    VALID _qcb0xlqz6()
READ CYCLE MODAL DEACTIVATE _qcb0xlrja() SHOW _qcb0xlrjk()
```

UDFs are once again employed to control program action.

Referring first to @ GET m.ord_choi, executing our Search/Reorder by popup, note that popups, like push buttons, are no more than a special case of @ GET. They are created through the use of PICTURE function @^, which is then immediately followed by the items in our list popup. Still, you need not remember the function symbols used to create popups, push buttons, and the like since FoxPro generates the program code for us, based upon the entries we make using the various Screen Builder dialogs. (It also supplies the names of the UDFs we enter for use with @ GET VALID.)

Assigning Push Button Default, Escape, and Hot Keys

What is notable about the @ GET m.verify push button command are the \<, \!, and \? appearing before the push button labels. These are actually entered into the Push Button dialog (see Figure 4.4), from which FoxPro copies them precisely as entered. The symbols \< are used to define a *hot key* for each push button. Specifically, FoxPro uses the first label character following the \< as the button hot key and underlines that character on the screen, as shown earlier in Figure 4.2. When @ GET m.verify is the current cursor object, we can choose either button by pressing the underlined hot key for that item. This is slower than using the mouse but faster than using the arrow keys and Enter.

Of course, the more push buttons you use, the more significant hot keys become. All the control push buttons in Customer.spr, for example, have assigned hot keys. When two options begin with the same letter—as with the Customers window Edit and Erase buttons—you can simply move the \< symbols as needed to select another character in a label as the hot key. For example, we make *R* the hot key for Erase with E\<rase.

FIGURE 4.4: When defining push buttons, use \< to define hot keys and \! and \? to define Default and Escape keys.

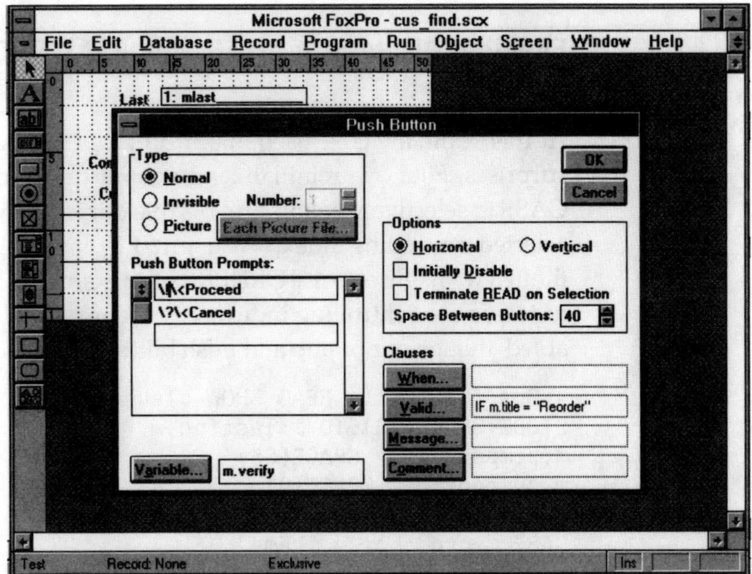

Hot keys work only when @ GET (push button) is the current cursor object. In addition, you can link the action of Ctrl+W and the Esc key—normally used, respectively, to save and terminate READ and to terminate READ without saving changes to the current READ object—to specific buttons. For example, by placing the symbols \! in front of Proceed, we make it possible for the operator to execute Proceed from any cursor position in the READ window—except when @ GET (push button) is the current cursor object—by pressing Ctrl+W. This gives us a READ-level default save and terminate key. Placing \? in front of Cancel, on the other hand, gives us a default Escape key. In both cases, however, it is our push button VALID clause that determines what action actually takes place.

Note that the default key, Ctrl+W, behaves slightly differently than a defined Escape key. This is because Ctrl+W will execute any push button if it is the current cursor object, while Escape always executes the defined Escape push button. In other words, Ctrl+W can execute Cancel, when Cancel is the current cursor object, but Escape cannot execute Proceed. (In Customer.spr, we use Quit as the Escape push button, and though we define Find as the default push button, it has no real function. In the Customers window all other @ GETs are disabled with @ GET WHEN m.doit when the control push buttons are active.)

Enabling/Disabling @ GETS with READ SHOW and SHOW GET

At this point, the UDF used in our program's READ SHOW clause should hold no surprises. First, we reinitialize our input fields to hold blanks. Then we use DO CASE to selectively enable and disable our input fields on the basis of the currently selected controlling index. (We use m.ord_choi, the selected popup value, to do this, though we might also use ORDER().) For example, when the Company index tag is selected as the controlling index, only the input field for m.companyfnd will be enabled, though our popup and push buttons, unmentioned here, will still be enabled.

```
* Cus_find.spr's READ SHOW clause.
STORE SPACE(20) TO m.lastfnd,m.firstfnd
m.companyfnd = SPACE(35)
m.custnofnd = SPACE(6)
DO CASE
CASE m.ord_choi = "Name"
    SHOW GET m.lastfnd ENABLE
    SHOW GET m.firstfnd ENABLE
    SHOW GET m.companyfnd DISABLE
    SHOW GET m.custnofnd DISABLE
    _CUROBJ = 1
CASE m.ord_choi = "Company"
    SHOW GET m.lastfnd DISABLE
    SHOW GET m.firstfnd DISABLE
    SHOW GET m.companyfnd ENABLE
    SHOW GET m.custnofnd DISABLE
    _CUROBJ = 3
CASE m.ord_choi = "Cust ID"
    SHOW GET m.lastfnd DISABLE
```

```
    SHOW GET m.firstfnd DISABLE
    SHOW GET m.companyfnd DISABLE
    SHOW GET m.custnofnd ENABLE
    _CUROBJ = 4
ENDCASE
```

Again, we use _CUROBJ to send the cursor to a particular @ GET, though here we identify the desired object by its order number. (m.lastfnd is 1, m.firstfnd is 2, m.companyfnd is 3, and m.custnofnd is 4.)

Depending as we do on READ SHOW to enable/disable our input fields as indicated by the currently selected controlling index, we must see to it that the SHOW clause is reexecuted each time the operator changes the controlling index using our popup. Indeed, both actions are accounted for by the UDF employed in the popup's VALID clause, shown here:

```
* VALID clause of @ GET m.ord_choi (popup).
m.new_ord = IIF(m.ord_choi="Name","NAMES", ;
    IIF(ord_choi="Company","COMPANY","CUSTNO"))
SET ORDER TO m.new_ord
SHOW GETS
RETURN
```

The action is quite simple. Using the value returned by the operator's selection from the popup, we again use nested IIF()s to come up with the actual name of the desired index tag. After establishing the new index as the controlling index with SET ORDER TO, we execute SHOW GETS to reexecute READ SHOW before refreshing the screen. Upon execution of RETURN (which, again, uses a default return value of .T. when no return value is supplied), the cursor will consequently appear in the input field designated by the value of _CUROBJ set in READ SHOW.

Index-Assisted Searches with SEEK and SEEK()

Finally, we come to the VALID clause used by our Proceed and Cancel push buttons. It is used to execute the index search and terminate the program, whether or not a search is performed. As you will note, the portion of the function dedicated to handling operator selection of Cancel is placed first but does not include the commands necessary to return the Customer table to its original state prior to execution of Cus_find.spr. That portion of the code is placed in our (screen) program after the READ command, in what is referred to as the *cleanup code*, for reasons explained below.

```
* @ GET m.verify VALID clause
IF m.verify = "Cancel"
    CLEAR READ
    RETURN .T.
ENDIF
DO CASE
CASE m.ord_choi = "Name"
    m.search = UPPER(TRIM(m.lastfns + m.firstfnd))
CASE m.ord_choi = "Company"
    m.search = UPPER(TRIM(m.companydnd))
CASE m.ord_choi = "Cust ID"
    m.search = TRIM(m.custnofnd)
ENDCASE
IF EMPTY(m.search)
    WAIT WINDOW "Make an entry!" NOWAIT
        _CUROBJ = IIF(m.ord_choi="Name",1, ;
    IIF(m.ord_choi="Company",3,4))
    RETURN .T.
ENDIF
IF SEEK(m.search)
     CLEAR READ
ELSE
    WAIT WINDOW "No Such Customer on File." NOWAIT
        _CUROBJ = IIF(m.ord_choi="Name",1, ;
    IIF(m.ord_choi="Company",3,4))
ENDIF
RETURN .T.
```

The logic of the UDF is fairly straightforward. Cancel simply terminates READ by issuing the CLEAR READ command. All subsequent program code refers to Proceed.

To keep the code as compact as possible, we perform the search with a single command, IF SEEK(m.search). The utility of using the SEEK() function rather than the SEEK command is that SEEK() not only performs the index tag search but also returns a value of .T. or .F. indicating the success or failure of the search. By employing it with IF, we can perform the search and determine program *branching*—that is, which of two or more actions will be subsequently taken—at once. SEEK is less efficient since we must follow it with a separate IF, using FOUND() or EOF() to test the result of the search, as shown here:

```
SEEK m.search
IF FOUND()
    * Commands to perform when search is successful.
ELSE
    * Commands to perform when search is unsuccessful.
ENDIF
```

To prepare for SEEK(m.search) we must transfer the entered search string—whether it is stored in mlast and (optionally) mfirst, mcompany or in mcustno—to m.search, while also making an effort to ensure that the format of the search string corresponds to the index key. For example, since we created index tag Company using the expression UPPER(Company), we must perform all our searches using search strings in which all characters are uppercase—or fail in the effort to find anything at all.

If we want the operator to be able to search for records using partial entries, we must also be sure to eliminate all trailing blanks from our search strings with TRIM(). This is because SEEK and SEEK() are designed to look for an exact match between the search string and an index key—that is, for as many characters as are entered for the search string. If blanks are included at the end of the search string, FoxPro will not ignore them.

Use of Truncated Search Strings

Truncated search strings—that is, search strings shorter than actual index keys—must be truncated from the right and can be used when searching index keys based on fields (or converted data) of type C, unless SET EXACT is ON. (SET EXACT ON forces FoxPro to search for exact matches between a search string and an entire index key.) This is not true, however, when searching index keys based on noncharacter fields. With index tags based upon expressions of type N (Numeric) or D (Date), FoxPro can search only for exact matches, though SET NEAR ON (also functional when using index tags based on fields of type C), can be used to position FoxPro to the first record with an ASCII, numeric, or date value greater than the entered search string.

When preparing for searches using compound index keys, care must also be taken to ensure that the spacing between the various components of the search string matches that used in the index. For example, in the case of index tag Names—key expression UPPER(TRIM(last + first))—the index keys will be 40 bytes in width with the last name beginning at byte 1 and the first name beginning at byte 21. Thus we will waste time searching for "BorgesiusKatje" or "Borgesius Katje" when her key in the index will have 11 blank spaces following her last name, owing to the width of Customer.last, which is 20. In Cus_find.spr this poses no problem since the memvars we use to get the operator's entry for last and first names are given widths conforming to the widths of Customer.last and Customer.first. Thus UPPER(TRIM(m.lastfnd+m.firstfnd)) produces a search string conforming to our needs. If the operator enters part or all of a first name, it will be concatenated properly with the entry for last name.

TIP

The MESSAGE clause of all @ GET commands can be used to supply the operator with additional information. When the cursor enters an @ GET, the MESSAGE <expC> is displayed in the status bar.

There is one other problem: The operator must be warned not to use a truncated entry for m.lastfnd if he or she wants to enter part or all of a first name. Entering anything for the first name without entering the full last name will be futile unless, of course, Customer.dbf holds records with first names but no last names. To take care of this issue, we need do no more than use the MESSAGE clause of @ GET m.firstfnd to warn the operator against misuse of first names:

```
@ <coords> GET m.firstfnd PICTURE "@K" ;
    MESSAGE "First name is optional, but can only be" + ;
    "used when full last name is entered."
```

Returning now to our @ GET m.verify VALID clause, before executing the search we perform a cursory test of m.search to make sure the operator has in fact entered a search string. If not, we request the operator to make an entry and send the cursor back to the appropriate input field as determined by the current controlling index.

```
IF EMPTY(m.search)
    WAIT WINDOW "Make an entry!" NOWAIT
```

```
    _CUROBJ = IIF(m.ord_choi="Name",1, ;
        IIF(m.ord_choi="Company",3,4))
    RETURN .T.
ENDIF
```

Next we perform the search. If it is successful, FoxPro is positioned to the correct record and we can terminate Cus_find.spr to return (for example) to Customer.spr—just in time for SHOW GETS. The located record will therefore be displayed in the Customers window.

```
IF SEEK(m.search)
     CLEAR READ
ELSE
    WAIT WINDOW "No Such Customer on File." NOWAIT
    _CUROBJ = IIF(m.ord_choi="Name",1, ;
        IIF(m.ord_choi="Company",3,4))
ENDIF
RETURN .T.
```

On the other hand, if no record has been found, we inform the operator of the outcome and send the cursor back to the appropriate input field so the operator can try another entry.

Closing Windows with the Control Box

One of the thornier issues in writing Windows programs is that there is usually more than one way of executing or terminating a screen program. Cus_find.spr is a case in point. Since a dialog box is used to perform a subsidiary action based upon the operator's instructions, it should be required to conform to the general style of dialog boxes used by all Windows programs, including FoxPro. The Screen Builder, of course, assists us in this matter. Since each screen program is designed for operation in a particular READ window, the Screen Builder provides a Windows-style dialog for specifying the type of window we want. And though we may cook up windows to order, owing to Windows conventions, we generally stick to the basic offerings and the window attributes and border that go with them. When defining window Cus_find, we therefore employ the FoxPro defaults for a dialog box. As indicated by the check boxes that are automatically filled in with our selection from the Type popup, the window attributes used with dialog boxes are Close and Move, and the border is Double. (See Figure 4.5.)

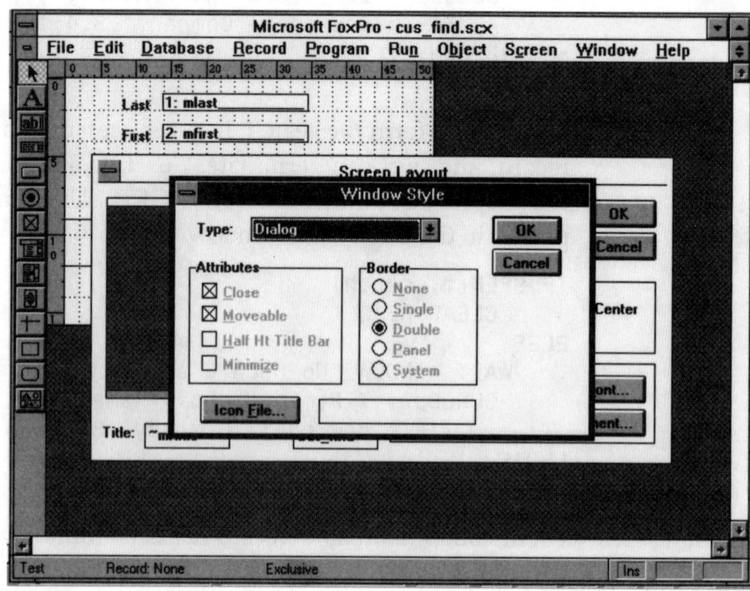

FIGURE 4.5:
Screen Builder Window Style dialog as used with Cus_find.spr

Taking another look at our READ command, we can quickly make sense of the consequences.

```
READ CYCLE MODAL DEACTIVATE _qcb0xlrja() SHOW _qcb0xlrjk()
```

As in earlier examples, we use CYCLE so that the READ will not terminate automatically if and when the operator moves past the last GET. SHOW should require no further explanation. Note, however, that like Erase.spr (discussed at the end of Chapter 3), we use READ MODAL. Again, this has the effect of making it impossible for the operator to click another window or use Ctrl+F6 to activate the next window. Just as important, READ MODAL has the effect of disabling the MBS main menu. The consequence is that the operator must finish with the dialog before going ahead with other work. (Though this is the typical way of programming and using dialogs, with regard to READ MODAL, there are many ways to alter FoxPro's behavior. We can, for example, reactivate the main menu or gain access to other windows during MODAL READ, as described in Chapter 9.) So far, so good.

A problem arises, however, when we make it possible for the operator to *close* the window—as we must do if we want our window to conform to the typical attributes of dialog boxes. Owing to the selection of Dialog in the Screen Builder's Window Style dialog, window Cus_find is defined as follows:

```
DEFINE WINDOW cus_find... <coordinates, size, title, etc.> ...;
    FLOAT CLOSE NOMINIMIZE DOUBLE
```

The FLOAT keyword enables us to move the window about the screen by dragging its title bar. NOMINIMIZE prevents the window from being reduced to an icon. (What would be the point, since no further action can be taken until the dialog is terminated?) DOUBLE gives the window a double-line border. CLOSE places the Close option in the window control box along with Move (Float) and Next Window, as shown in Figure 4.6. Next Window is actually nonfunctional here owing to the use of MODAL with a single READ window. The Close option will allow the operator to close the window and terminate the program without selecting one of the push buttons since it has nearly the same effect as CLEAR READ.

We can see how this can cause a problem with Cus_find.spr by referring back to the action of Erase.spr, the MBS Global Erase dialog. If Erase.spr were closed through use of the window control box, nothing would happen—that is, other than program control being returned to the calling program. This is because the action immediately

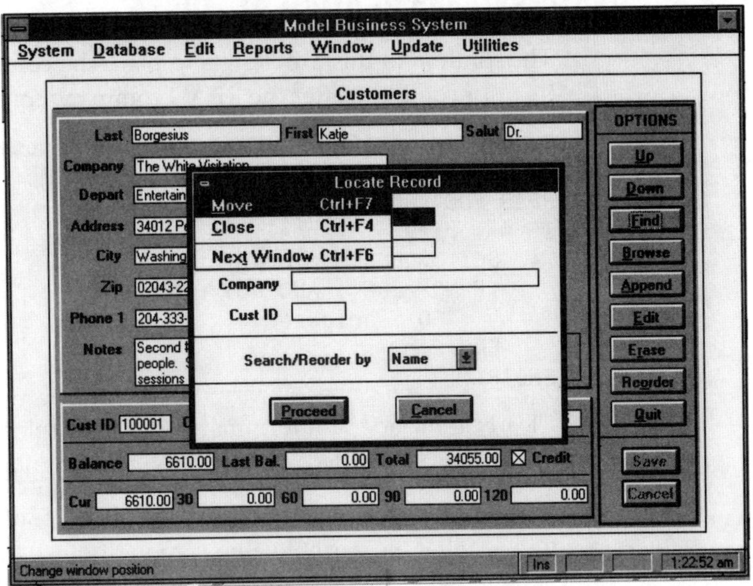

FIGURE 4.6:

The normal attributes of dialog boxes are Close and Move.

terminates the READ, thereby bypassing @ GET VALID as well as any and all commands in Erase.spr affecting our tables or the program environment. Using Close in this instance has the same effect as selecting the Cancel button; neither of them does anything except terminate the READ.

In the case of Cus_find.spr, however, our Cancel action must *do* something—that is, supposing the operator has already changed the index or repositioned FoxPro in the table while attempting to find a record. It thus falls to Cancel (if selected by the operator) to execute the commands that restore the Customer table to its original state as indicated by memvars m.orig_ord and m.orig_rec. (As you will recall, they are initialized at the outset of Cus_find.spr to hold the name of the controlling index and the current record number.) What, then, if we Close the window, thereby automatically terminating the READ, without executing the commands associated with Cancel? If FoxPro is at EOF() owing to an unsuccessful search—the primary reason for canceling the search—the Customers window will reappear on the screen displaying the blank dummy record at the end of the Customer table, and any command depending on the presence of a real current record will cause an error. This will foil our attempt to return the Customer table to its original state.

Controlling Cleanup Code Execution with READKEY() and READ DEACTIVATE

The solution to this problem is to place the commands restoring Customer.dbf to its prior condition after the READ command, in a screen program's cleanup code:

```
@...GET m.verify PICTURE "@*HN \!\<Proceed;\?\<Cancel " ;
    VALID _qcb0xlqz6()
READ MODAL CYCLE...SHOW...
IF m.verify = "Cancel"
    SET ORDER TO m.orig_ord
    IF NOT EOF() AND NOT BOF()
        GO m.orig_rec
    ENDIF
ENDIF
```

Clearly, if the operator terminates READ by selecting the Proceed push button, the commands embedded in the IF/ENDIF are ignored.

Still, one further action must be taken, since use of the control box to close the dialog will not alter the current value of m.verify. One might consider changing the memvar's initial value to "Cancel" instead of "Proceed," but that will not help since the operator might try several searches with Proceed before giving up and closing the dialog with the control box, thus leaving the value of m.verify set to Proceed. FoxPro offers two rather straightforward tools for handling this problem. The first is by far the simplest. We simply rewrite our IF to include another condition:

```
IF m.verify = "Cancel" OR READKEY(1) = 4
```

Traditionally, the READKEY() function is designed to return a value indicating how READ is terminated. Its use here is no different, though we now pass it a numeric expression so it will tell us exactly how our READ window was deactivated. These are the values it can return and what they mean:

Value	Terminating Action
1	None of the following...
2	CLEAR READ issued
3	Terminating control selected
4	READ window closed
5	READ DEACTIVATE clause returns .T.
6	READ timed out

By placing OR READKEY(1) = 4 in our IF <condition>, we ensure that closing the dialog using the control box will have the same effect as Cancel. The commands that must be issued when the operator selects Cancel will also be automatically executed if the operator terminates the READ by selecting Close in the window control box.

As for the other window-related READKEY(<expN>) values, 1 and 2 should already make sense; 3, terminating control selected, pertains to the use of @ GET push buttons when they are defined to terminate READ on selection, while 6, READ timed out, pertains to the use of READ TIMEOUT <expN>, where <expN> indicates the number of seconds that may elapse without the operator taking any action before the READ is automatically terminated. We do not employ either of these options in the MBS.

This brings us to the second tool we can use to control the way our screen program terminates when the operator selects Close from the window control box: READ DEACTIVATE <expL>. Far more wide ranging in effect than READKEY(<expN>), the optional READ DEACTIVATE clause, about which we will have much more to say in the following chapters, is executed when a window (or dialog) is closed by any other means than CLEAR READ (or QUIT). In FoxPro terms, READ DEACTIVATE is triggered by any window-level event that alters the value of WONTOP(), the FoxPro function that returns the name of the *window on top* (the active window). WONTOP() will therefore be changed when window Cus_find is closed using the control box, just as, under other circumstances, it will be changed whenever the operator is permitted to use the mouse, the Windows pulldown, or Ctrl+F1 to select and activate another window. (In Cus_find.spr the latter actions are prohibited through the use of READ MODAL.) Thus we can make FoxPro execute the commands listed under IF m.verify = "Cancel" in Cus_find.spr's cleanup code by placing the following command in the UDF executed by READ DEACTIVATE, noting that it will be issued only when the operator selects Close from the window control box.

```
m.verify = "Cancel"
```

Since the UDF will return a default value of .T., the READ command is terminated; and since m.verify will now hold "Cancel", the commands in our IF statement following READ will be properly executed.

As you will soon see, this is a quite simplistic use of READ DEACTIVATE, which is more generally used to conditionally determine whether or not READ should be terminated using IF/ENDIF.

NOTE When READ DEACTIVATE is triggered by operator selection of Close from the window control box and the DEACTIVATE clause allows the READ to terminate, READKEY(<expN>) will return 5, attributing the event to the DEACTIVATE clause and not to the use of Close (4).

Variations in MBS Execution of the Find/Reorder Dialog

We call upon a nested screen program (Cus_find.spr) to execute the Find and Reorder actions for Customer.spr for several reasons. First, the same actions will be required by the other data entry programs involving the Customer database—Payments.spr and Sales.spr. If we place the routines in a separate screen program, they will be available to all programs accessing the Customer table. Moreover, with respect to our Customers window, given the number of fields in Customer.dbf, there is little space available on the screen for the data input fields required for the Find and Reorder actions. With other tables employed in the MBS, including the Inventory and Letters tables, space is not such a pressing issue. Nor, for that matter, do any of the primary index tags used with these tables employ compound index keys, requiring us to provide the operator with two or more input fields for entering an appropriate search string.

For these reasons, when creating the data entry windows employed with the MBS Inventory and Letters (library) tables, we include the input field(s) and popup required to execute the Reorder and Find dialogs directly in the data entry window, as shown in Figure 4.7.

Leaving until later the use of a General field to store pictures in Inventry.dbf, simply note how Find and Reorder are made to operate as distinct dialogs within the Inventory READ window. This is achieved through the use of READ SHOW, which has the function of selectively enabling the GET objects in the Find and/or Reorder box at the bottom of the window using SHOW GET when the operator selects the Find or Reorder push button. The strategy employed is exactly the same as that used to launch the Append and Edit routines in Customer.spr. In the READ window control push button VALID clause, we set memvars m.dofind and m.doord,

FIGURE 4.7:

Data entry window used with Inventry.dbf, the MBS Inventory table

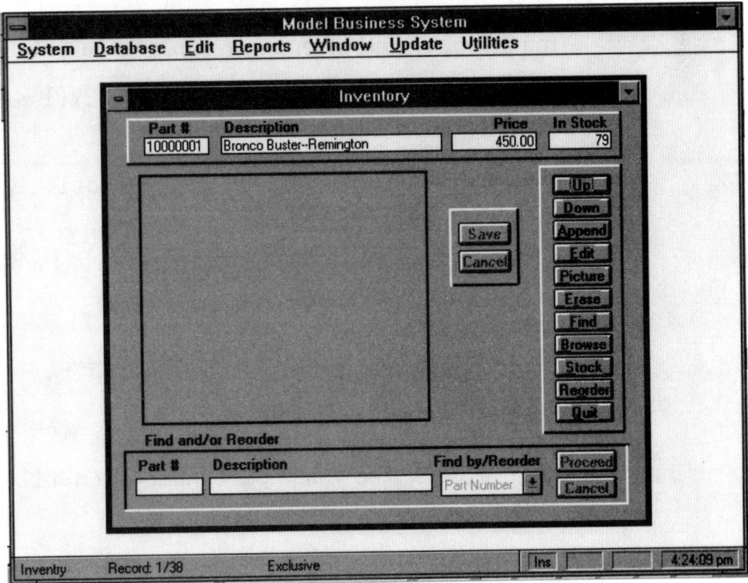

controlling execution of the Find and Reorder actions, respectively, to .T. Then in READ SHOW we enable the @ GETs used by the called dialog while disabling the main control push buttons, @ GET m.but1.

```
DO CASE
CASE m.doit
    * Commands preparing Append or Edit action.
CASE m.dofind
    SHOW GET m.partno2 ENABLE
    SHOW GET m.p_descrip2 ENABLE
    SHOW GET m.ord_name ENABLE
    SHOW GET m.locate ENABLE
    SHOW GET m.but1 DISABLE
    _CUROBJ = IIF(m.order = "PARTNO", ;
        OBJNUM(m.partno2), OBJNUM(m.p_descript))
CASE m.doord
    SHOW GET m.ord_name ENABLE
    SHOW GET m.locate ENABLE
    SHOW GET m.but1 DISABLE
* Other CASES...
ENDCASE
```

When executing the Find action, however, we do not wait for the operator to select Proceed to execute the search, as we do in Cus_find.spr. Instead, we perform the search directly in the VALID clause of the @ GET input field used for operator input of the search string. Here, for example, is the VALID clause used with @ GET m.partno2 to find inventory records by part number:

```
IF NOT EMPTY(m.partno2) AND LASTKEY() <> 27 AND ;
    SEEK(TRIM(m.partno2))
    m.partno2 = inventry.partno
    m.p_descrip2 = inventry.p_descript
    SHOW GET m.partno2
    SHOW GET m.p_descrip2
    _CUROBJ = OBJNUM(m.locate)
    RETURN .T.
ENDIF
IF EMPTY(m.partno2) OR LASTKEY() = 27
    _CUROBJ = OBJNUM(m.locate)+1
    RETURN .T.
ENDIF
WAIT WINDOW "No such part number on file." NOWAIT
RETURN .F.
```

Upon operator entry of the part number to look for, the function immediately performs the search with IF SEEK(), provided that the operator did not leave m.partno2 blank or press the Escape key, setting the value of LASTKEY() to 27, the ASCII value of Escape. If a search string was entered and SEEK() is successful, we display the full part number and description of the newly located record in the Find and/or Reorder dialog box and send the cursor along to the Proceed and Cancel push buttons, represented in this case by @ GET m.locate, so the operator can choose to display the record in the (main portion of the) READ window or cancel the action.

In fact, we have two reasons for testing EMPTY(m.partno2) and LASTKEY() before executing SEEK(). If we use only IF SEEK(), as shown here, we will box ourselves in:

```
IF SEEK(TRIM(m.partno2))
    * Other commands cited above.
    RETURN .T.
ENDIF
WAIT WINDOW "No such part number on file." NOWAIT
RETURN .F.
```

If SEEK() fails and the function returns .F., the operator will find it impossible to leave @ GET m.partno2 without making a valid entry. We avoid this by using @ GET MESSAGE to instruct the operator from the outset to "Enter part number of desired record or press Escape to break out" and by using LASTKEY() = 27, first to bypass SEEK() and then to send the cursor to the Cancel push button (_CUROBJ = OBJNUM (m.locate)+1) and RETURN .T., thus enabling FoxPro to leave @ GET m.partno2.

Our use of IF EMPTY(m.partno2) is no less important, given our use of the expression TRIM(m.partno2) with SEEK(). The fact is, SEEK() will always return .T. when used with a null string. And TRIM(m.partno2) will produce a null string if m.partno2 is left blank. We must therefore prevent SEEK() from being executed when m.partno2 is blank or FoxPro will behave as though it has successfully found a record, even though it has done no more than position to the first record in the indexed table.

We subsequently use EMPTY(m.partno2) and LASTKEY() = 27 again to indicate when the operator wants to break off the search. The only other alternative is that the operator made an entry but SEEK() failed, in which case we send an appropriate message to the screen and leave @ GET m.partno2 active with RETURN .F. so the operator can try another entry.

Of course, a much simpler @ GET VALID clause can be used to oversee the Find routine:

```
@...GET m.partno2 VALID SEEK(TRIM(m.partno2)) ;
    ERROR "Sorry, no record with your entry can be found."
```

Here everything is done using a simple expression. If we want to provide the operator with a means of leaving the @ GET without having to enter a valid part number, we just add the necessary conditions: VALID EMPTY(m.custno) OR LASTKEY()=27 OR SEEK(TRIM(m.partno2)). Owing to the order of the three conditions and the use of OR, when m.partno2 is left empty, FoxPro won't even bother to test SEEK().

Creating a Table-Independent Find/Reorder Dialog

Though we do not do this in MBS, it is possible to develop a Find/Reorder dialog that is not table dependent. Assuming that index tags listed in the Reorder popup always come from the structural compound index, we can use the TAG(), SYS(14), and TYPE() functions to do this.

The first issue is to create the Reorder popup, listing the available index tags. As previously mentioned, an @ GET popup may take its options from an array. Using TAG() we can create an array that holds the names of all index tags in the structural compound index of the current table as follows:

```
mno = 1
DO WHILE .T.
    IF EMPTY(TAG(mno))
        EXIT
    ENDIF
    mno = mno + 1
ENDDO
mno = mno -1
DECLARE indexer[mno]
```

To keep things simple, we begin by using DO WHILE .T. to count the number of tags in the structural compound index. For FoxPro, index tag order in the structural compound index corresponds to the order of index tag creation. The TAG(<expN>) function returns the name of the index tag created in the order indicated by the supplied number. If no index tag exists for the indicated number, TAG() returns a null string. We can then find out how many index tags are in the structural compound index by supplying TAG() with numbers in the series 1, 2, 3, and so on, until it returns a null string. That number –1 is the number of available index tags, and we can use it with the DECLARE array command to create a memory array with a suitable number of elements to store their names.

Next we must fill the array's elements with the names of our index tags. This is just as easily done.

```
mno2 = 1
DO WHILE mno2 <= mno
    indexer[mno2] = TAG(mno2)
    mno2 = mno2 + 1
ENDDO
```

We can even shorten the last commands by using FoxPro's FOR/ENDFOR command, which is specifically designed to replace DO WHILE .T. when looping is dependent upon number comparison.

```
FOR count = 1 TO mno
    indexer[count] = TAG(count)
ENDFOR
```

FOR/ENDFOR is designed to use and automatically increment the memvar we create with FOR <memvar> = <expN>. Recursion continues until the memvar's value exceeds that of TO <expN>—in this case supplied by memvar mno, which indicates the number of index tags in our structural compound index file.

Of course, the fact that FoxPro permits us to increase the size of memory arrays without losing the data stored in their existing elements will allow us to create the array without knowing its final size in advance.

```
mno = 1
DO WHILE NOT TAG(mno) == ""
    DECLARE indexer[mno]
    indexes[mno] = TAG(mno)
    mno = mno + 1
ENDDO
```

Here we embed the DECLARE command within the loop so FoxPro will adjust its size as needed.

NOTE

The TAG() function and the FOR/ENDFOR commands include various options that render them quite flexible. We use them here in a bare-bones fashion. Refer to your FoxPro documentation or Help file to review their full syntax and potential.

Since the routines laid out above are generic and can be used with any current table, as long as it has a structural compound index file, the array they produce can be used to supply @ GET popup automatically with a list of available index tags. (With regard to the Screen Builder's Popup dialog, all we need do is specify Array popup and supply the name of the memory array that is to be used.)

We must also supply the operator with a generic search string input field. There is a variety of ways to do this. You can, for example, aid the operator by using @ SAY to display the <key expression> used by the currently selected controlling index. This is returned by SYS(14,<expN>), where <expN> is the order of the index tag in the structural index. If you need to discover the data type of the index <key expression>, you can use the TYPE() function with SYS(14,<expN>). Your generic Find dialog may include one input field for every possible index tag type or just one input field of type C for all data types. You can again use SYS(14) and TYPE() to determine which of several input fields to activate. If you use only one input field, they will also serve to indicate how the string must be converted for use with SEEK().

Still, having laid out the means by which a generic Find/Reorder dialog can be created, it is left to you to determine how best to proceed, if at all. Bear in mind that when you use the FoxPro Application Generator—activated through selection of the Application option on the Run pulldown—to create a quick application, FoxPro generates generic reorder and index tag search dialogs, like those discussed here, for use with the current table. (FoxPro names the Reorder dialog Getorder.spr and the Search dialog Appsrch.spr.) You may therefore find additional assistance in writing your own generic routines by executing a quick application and examining the program code FoxPro places in Getorder.spr and Appsrch.spr.

NOTE

Another alternative preferred by many programmers is to create a data dictionary—that is, a table listing the names, key expressions, and types of the index tags used with each of your tables. Such a table can then be used with DEFINE POPUP <name> PROMPT FIELD or with @ GET list to provide the operator with a pick list of available indexes. One of the notable advantages of this method is that a field can be used to hold a label for each index tag. When the popup or list is executed, the index tag labels can then be displayed instead of the index tag names, which are sometimes unavoidably cryptic. (We will see how to use DEFINE POPUP and @ GET LIST to create pick lists based upon the data in a table in Chapter 6 and Chapter 11.)

Selection of Index Tag Order When Producing Customer Database Reports

The three index tags, Name, Company, and Custno, are also used when creating Customer table or database reports to control the order of record output and, optionally, to control the scope or conditional filtering of records in the defined view. This is done through the aid of the Customer Database Reports window, shown in Figure 4.8 with its report selection popup open. Two sets of radio buttons are used to select the record order and output device, while operator entry of optional filter criteria is handled directly with @ GET.

Still, we may not venture to discuss the screen program executing the Customer Database Report window until Chapter 12. I show it now only to alert you to the options available when producing Customer database reports. Some of them will figure in our discussion of Rushmore optimization below.

Additional Aspects of FoxPro Indexes

While you should check the FoxPro documentation or Help file for complete coverage of the commands overseeing the creation and use of index tags and index files, the discussion now touches on a few additional aspects of FoxPro indexes before delving into their use in executing record filters.

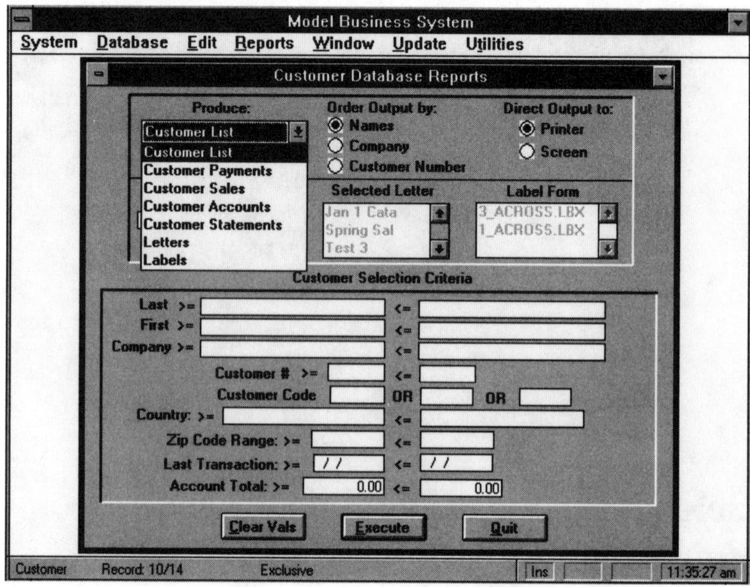

FIGURE 4.8:

Customer Database Reports window with the report selection popup activated

TIP

When converting dates to character values for use in a compound index key expression, true date order will be lost unless you use DTOS() instead of DTOC() to perform the conversion. The DTOS(), or date to string, function returns the date (as a character string) in the format YYYYMMDD—for example, 19950305.

Compound index tags, like index tag names, are based upon the content of two or more data fields (or portions thereof) of type C, concatenated with + or –. (The – tells FoxPro to place all blank spaces appearing between the two strings after the second string.) We can include data fields of other types in a compound index tag by first converting the values they hold to type C. They can then be concatenated with the other values used in the index key expression. Use DTOC() or DTOS() to convert data of type D for this purpose, STR() to convert data of type N, and IIF() to convert data of type L, as shown by the following expression:

```
Last + DTOS(opendate)+STR(history)+IIF(credit,'Y','N')
```

Forming Compound/Complex Index Tags

Complex index tags are simply index tags that use one or more functions in their <key expression>. In addition to the functions used for data conversion, you can, for example, use SUBSTR(), LEFT(), or RIGHT() to select only a portion of a character field for inclusion in an index, or SOUNDEX to create a *sound-alike index,* listing records in order phonetically instead of by ASCII value. We have already seen the use of TRIM() and UPPER(). Expressions used in index tags of type C can also be forced to lowercase characters with LOWER(). You can also use PROPER() to force the first letter of all words in the expression to uppercase and all other letters to lowercase. Leading blanks can also be trimmed from an <expC> with LTRIM(), and ALLTRIM() can be used to trim leading and trailing blanks with a single function.

Unique and Filtered Index Tags

Though we do not make use of them in the MBS, FoxPro also supports unique and filtered index tags, which can be created using the UNIQUE or FOR <expL> clause of the INDEX command. A *unique index* is one that excludes duplicate keys from the index. When activated as the controlling index, it therefore excludes duplicate records (as judged by the data field values included in the index key) from the database view. (Where two or more records with duplicate keys appear in the table, only the first record is included in the unique index.) A *filtered index* excludes keys for all records not satisfying the filter condition. When such an index is engaged as the controlling index, records without keys in the index are automatically excluded from view.

TIP

Use DISPLAY or LIST STATUS to list the names of all open tables, along with their available index tags, set relations, and filters. Tables are listed in order by work area number. The currently selected table is also indicated.

Use of Index Files and Compound Index Files

Old-style index files (file extension .idx) capable of holding only one index are still supported by FoxPro 2.6. Also created with the INDEX command's TO <.idx file> option, they are most useful when you need to use one or more temporary indexes. When they are no longer needed, just eliminate them from disk with ERASE. You may also find it convenient to use (nonstructural) compound index files to hold temporary index tags or sets of related index tags. Of course, unlike the structural compound index files, other compound index files must be explicitly opened with the OF <.cdx> option of the USE or SET ORDER command. Index tags stored in any compound index file, including the structural compound index, can be erased one by one or all at once using DELETE TAG <tag name> / ALL. (See your FoxPro documentation or Help file for more on the creation and use of old-style and compound index files.)

TIP When creating temporary index (.idx) files, use the INDEX command's COMPACT option to create a more efficient index file. (Index files created without using the COMPACT keyword are written to conform with index files used by prior versions of FoxPro, and they will be less efficient than COMPACT index files.)

Index Tags and Rushmore Optimization of Record Filters

When we write the various Customer database reports listed in the Customer Database Reports window (see Figure 4.8 above), we will want to supply the operator with a means of controlling which records are included in the report using filters. Given the availability of Rushmore optimization with SET OPTIMIZE ON and SQL-SELECT, this means supplying FoxPro with whatever additional index tags will prove most useful in executing our filters. If you are unfamilar with Rushmore and SQL-SELECT, however, you will first want to know how FoxPro relates a filter condition to an index tag.

Optimizable Filters with FoxPro's Rushmore

When executing a record filter with SET FILTER, the FOR <condition> clause of the various sequential commands, or with SQL-SELECT, FoxPro first stops to determine if the filter <condition> is optimizable. *Optimizable conditions* include any condition formed using a relational operator to compare the values held in one or more data fields with another value of the same data type. If the condition is optimizable, FoxPro next looks for an index tag that can be used to optimize the execution of the filter.

With SET FILTER and FOR <condition>, FoxPro is limited to using whatever index tags or index files are available in *open* compound or old-style index files. With SQL-SELECT, on the other hand, if a suitable index tag is not available—and with SQL-SELECT it need not be open to be available—FoxPro creates a temporary index tag to assist in record filtering if it determines that doing so will speed up its performance. Under these circumstances, we can go a long way in expediting FoxPro's execution of the record filters we plan to use in the MBS or any other system by creating the necessary index tags in advance.

With regard to the index tags we already have on hand in our structural compound index file, Customer.cdx, we can optimize any filter involving the use of customer number, company, and/or customer last and first name, provided that we specify filters that conform with the key expression used in creating our Custno, Company, and Name index tags. We must also avoid using the substring ($) operator since no simple condition using it is optimizable.

This means that the following filters are fully optimizable, since the condition or conditions used can be evaluated with the use of the index tags already present in Customer.cdx.

```
USE customer
LIST FOR custno = "100225"
LIST FOR custno >= "1005" AND custno <= "120"
LIST FOR custno <= "1005" OR custno >= "120"
LIST FOR UPPER(company) = "M"
LIST FOR UPPER(company) >= "M" OR  UPPER(company)<= "X"
LIST FOR UPPER(last + first) = "Milton"
LIST FOR (UPPER(last + first) > "Milton" ;
    AND NOT custno < "8") OR UPPER(company) >="X"
```

TIP

With FoxPro, the logical Xbase operators .AND., .OR., and .NOT. can be entered without using the periods as delimiters. AND, OR, and NOT will do. The logical operator NOT can also be entered using an exclamation point (!) instead.

As our list of optimizable filters suggests, you can create optimizable compound conditions just as you like and even use the logical operator NOT to reverse FoxPro's evaluation of any condition, provided that each condition can be related to an existing index tag. The following commands will fail the test since the conditions they use do not match our index key expressions:

```
LIST FOR UPPER(custno) = "1"
LIST FOR company = "The Firm"
LIST FOR last = "Borgesius"
```

FoxPro will still be able to execute these commands, but it must do so without the use of an index tag. It must read through the records in the Customer table sequentially and test the condition for each record.

Using SET NEAR to Locate Groups of Records

When using SEEK to locate a group of records in index order, issue the command SET NEAR ON. This tells FoxPro to stop at the first record with an index key greater than the value of the entered search string rather than moving to the end of the table when no exact match is found. If an exact match is found with SET NEAR ON, FOUND() returns a value of .T. and EOF() a value of .F. If no exact match is found but FoxPro finds and stops at a *near* record, both FOUND() and EOF() return .F.

Still, let's consider how Rushmore works by seeing how we might LIST all customers with a Company > "B" AND Company < "D" in the fastest possible way, using the standard Xbase tools, also available with FoxPro. Here again, we assume the existence of index tag Company.

```
USE customer ORDER company
SET NEAR ON
SEEK "B"
LIST WHILE UPPER(company) < "D"
```

This, however, will not work as fast as LIST FOR <condition> using Rushmore since WHILE <condition> still requires FoxPro to continue evaluating the condition for every record until it comes to the first record for which the condition evaluates .F. (This is where FoxPro stops when WHILE is employed.) But not only will FoxPro execute LIST FOR Company > "B" AND Company < "D" faster using Rushmore, since it needs to scan the index tag only once to find the first and last records belonging in the LIST; with Rushmore, FoxPro can also execute filters indicating more than one range of records (with respect to the same index tag), as suggested by the following command:

```
LIST FOR Company < "B" AND Company > "W"
```

This would require two separate LIST WHILE <condition> commands, one to LIST all the records with Company < "B" and another to LIST those with Company > "W". The compound filter doesn't represent a single range of records, but two. The other advantage of Rushmore is that it is not limited to the use of the controlling index, as is WHILE <condition>, but can refer to all open index tags and tables in evaluating the various parts of compound conditions.

Partially Optimizable Conditions

In FoxPro, conditions fall into three categories: opimizable, nonoptimizable, and partially optimizable. *Partially optimizable conditions* are those compound conditions formed with AND and OR that include both optimizable and nonoptimizable conditions. For example, FoxPro will view the following condition as partially optimizable. This is because any condition formed with a comparison operator is potentially optimizable and conditions using the substring operator are not.

```
LIST FOR custno >= "1" AND custno <= "5" AND "Inc." $ company
```

FoxPro will proceed by using index tag Custno to filter records on the basis of the first two conditions and then perform sequential filtering of those records that have passed muster using the nonoptimizable condition formed with the substring operator.

However, as logic would dictate, change the AND preceding the last condition to OR in the above command and you end up with a nonoptimizable rather than partially optimizable compound condition.

```
LIST FOR custno >= "1" AND custno <= "5" OR "Inc." $ company
```

With OR <condition>, FoxPro must check through all records in the table to determine if their Company field includes "Inc." as a substring. With AND <condition>, FoxPro can just look through the subset of records that have already satisfied the optimizable filters.

Availability of Rushmore

As previously mentioned, Rushmore optimization of conditional filters entered with SET FILTER or the FOR <condition> clause of the various sequential commands is available only when SET OPTIMIZE is ON. Rushmore optimization is also disabled when you use the WHILE <condition> clause of any sequential command. Again, Rushmore optimization can only assist in the filtering of records in a multi-table database view when SQL-SELECT is used to create the view, as discussed in Chapter 12. If you need to filter records in a multi-table view created with SET RELATION, you must stick to the traditional Xbase tools: SEEK, SET NEAR, WHILE <condition>, and (nonoptimized) SET FILTER TO and FOR <condition>.

Implications of Rushmore Optimization on System Design

Because Rushmore brings the lightning-fast action of index searches to bear on the execution of record filters, we must alter the way in which we proceed in planning a DBMS. To begin with, if the system under development must handle extremely large tables, you will suddenly find it possible to perform a wide variety of operations involving conditional filters that you would otherwise avoid like the plague. With the aid of Rushmore, however, you can COUNT FOR, CALCULATE, LIST, or REPORT records by a wide variety of criteria with the utmost speed, provided that you stick to optimizable conditions and, moreover, provide FoxPro with the index tags it will require to execute them. This will usually mean maintaining many index tags for important tables in addition to those specifically used with SET RELATION, SET ORDER, and SEEK for establishing multi-table views, controlling record order, and performing index key searches. We must now include index tags designed specifically to optimize our filters.

When it is necessary to provide operators with the capacity to filter records—for example, when producing reports, letters, or labels—we must not only determine which filters should be available, but how best to make what's available conform with what's optimizable. This may involve doing without conditions using the substring operator unless they are absolutely crucial or can be used in compound conditions in such a way as to make an overall filter partially optimizable.

There is another issue to consider. Since every index tag we care to add to our structural compound index file for the sake of using Rushmore must be updated as changes are made to the table—that is, when key fields used by an index tag are altered—the more index tags we have, the more drag we put on the overall performance of the system. The additional index tags will also require disk space. We are therefore compelled to find a middle way, balancing our decision about which additional index tags to include to speed up record filtering by considering the adverse consequences that must follow if we get carried away.

Turning our attention to Customer.dbf, we can now ask which searches we want to optimize or, stated differently, which filter criteria our operators will most want to use when writing reports or letters using the Customer table. As Figure 4.9, showing output from DISPLAY STATUS, suggests, my own decision was to include index tags to optimize filtering with the Country, Zip, History, Cuscode, and Last_date fields. Along with our Names, Company, and Custno index tags, these additional index tags will help to optimize record filtering with every report produced using the Customer Database Reports window. Again, this is not necessary, but it will help make report output nearly instantaneous, regardless of how many filters are applied.

FIGURE 4.9:

Use DISPLAY STATUS to list open tables and index tags.

```
Microsoft FoxPro - temp.txt
File  Edit  Database  Record  Program  Run  Text  Window  Help

Processor is 80386
Currently Selected Table:
Select area:  1, Table in Use: C:\FOXPROW\APPS\BIGBIZ\DBFS\CUSTOMER.DBF
  Structural CDX file:    C:\FOXPROW\APPS\BIGBIZ\DBFS\CUSTOMER.CDX
             Index tag:   COMPANY              Key: UPPER(COMPANY)
             Index tag:   CUSTNO               Key: CUSTNO
             Index tag:   NAMES                Key: UPPER(LAST+FIRST)
             Index tag:   DELETED              Key: DELETED()
             Index tag:   COUNTRY              Key: UPPER(COUNTRY)
             Index tag:   ZIP                  Key: ZIP
             Index tag:   HISTORY              Key: HISTORY
             Index tag:   LASTDATE             Key: LASTDATE
             Memo file:   C:\FOXPROW\APPS\BIGBIZ\DBFS\CUSTOMER.FPT
        Lock(s): Exclusive USE

Alternate File: c:\foxprow\apps\bigbiz\temp.txt
File search path:
Default directory: C:\FOXPROW\APPS\BIGBIZ
Print file/device:   PRN
Work area   =    1
Margin      =    0
Decimals    =    2
Memowidth   =   50
Typeahead   =   20
Blocksize   =   64
Reprocess   =      0
Refresh     = 0,5 SECONDS
DDE Timeout =    2000
DDE Safety  = on

Date format: American
Macro Hot Key = SHIFT+F10

Ins
```

Using the Expression Builder or RQBE

If you want to go to the trouble of training operators in the use of FoxPro expressions, you can, of course, write a report dialog that calls the FoxPro Expression Builder with GETEXP TO <memvar> and allows the operator to enter a filter condition manually. This will provide much greater freedom for applying filters than hard-coding the optional use of specific filters. As long as you do not compile your program as an executable (.exe) program with the FoxPro Distribution Kit but allow FoxPro to execute it, you can also call and allow the operator to make use of the RQBE window in your application by issuing the command CREATE or MODIFY QUERY. This, however, will require even more training on the part of the operator.

Helping Rushmore Do Its Work

Referring again to Figure 4.9, there is one remaining index tag that requires explanation. This is index tag Deleted, which uses the DELETED() function as its key expression. Throughout the majority of the MBS system, we use the command SET DELETED ON to exclude from view records marked for deletion in all our tables. This is traditional Xbase usage and allows us to perform the time-consuming job of actually erasing records marked for deletion from our tables with PACK when there's time to spare. (How often PACK is used, if at all, depends on the number of deleted records in the system tables.) In the meantime, SET DELETED ON keeps out of sight those records marked for deletion with the DELETE command.

SET DELETED ON, however, slows record filtering with Rushmore—unless we provide FoxPro with an index tag it can use to optimize its execution of SET DELETED ON. This is the function of our Deleted index tag.

```
USE customer
INDEX ON DELETED() TAG deleted
```

Once index tag Deleted—or any other index tag with a key expression of DELETED()—is placed in the structural compound index, we can use it in one of two ways to filter out deleted records.

```
SET DELETED ON
LIST FOR zip >= "4" AND zip <= "49999"
```

Once we set DELETED ON, when we execute a sequential command, FoxPro refers automatically to index tag Deleted to filter out records marked for deletion. We can, however, achieve the same thing manually with SET DELETED() OFF by including the expression NOT DELETED() in the record filter.

```
SET DELETED OFF
LIST FOR NOT DELETED() AND zip >= "4" AND zip <= "49999"
```

Given the existence of index tags Deleted and Zip, FoxPro will begin pouring out records meeting the indicated conditions the moment you press Enter. Since it is easier, in the MBS we work with SET DELETED ON and let FoxPro refer to index tag Deleted on its own.

Bear in mind that Rushmore optimization is also slightly slowed when a controlling index is engaged. If a controlling index is not required to obtain the desired result, as, for example, it will never be with COUNT FOR <condition>, be sure to disengage it before executing an optimizable command. (Use the controlling index only when the order of record output is important, as it will be in most reports, unless the data is prepared with SQL-SELECT.) If you need to reengage the controlling index after executing the optimized commands, just use memvars and SET ORDER to do it.

```
m.orig_ord = ORDER()
m.orig_rec = RECNO()
SET ORDER TO 0
COUNT FOR zip >= "4" AND zip <= "49999" ;
    AND history >=  1000.00
SET ORDER TO (orig_ord)
IF NOT EOF() AND NOT BOF()
    GO orig_rec
ENDIF
```

In the above commands, we again use IF to test for an empty table before issuing GO since GO <record number> will produce an error if the table (or defined view) has no records.

Deactivating Rushmore

Rushmore can be disabled in two different ways. Use SET OPTIMIZE OFF to disable it globally. To disable it when executing specific sequential commands, however, you can employ the NOOPTIMIZE option available with most sequential commands.

Note that it may not always be desirable to disable Rushmore when executing REPLACE FOR <condition>, even when one or more of the data fields updated by the replacements are included in the index tag(s) Rushmore must use. This is because Rushmore determines its action at the outset of the command, using the index tag as it stands before any replacements occur. Thus the REPLACE command presented in Chapter 2 for updating customer accounts in preparation for a new billing period can be regarded as optimizable.

```
REPLACE ALL;
    l_balance WITH current+days30+days60+days90+days120, ;
    days120 WITH days120+days90,days90 WITH days60, ;
    days60 WITH days30, ;
    days30 WITH IIF(current > 0.00,current,0.00), ;
    current WITH IIF(current < 0.00,current,0.00) ;
    FOR l_balance <> 0.00 AND current <> 0.00
```

To arrange for this command to be optimized, however, we would have to maintain two additional index tags, one for L_balance and another for Current—or only one, if we used the condition ABS(l_balance) + ABS(current) <> 0 and an index tag with a key expression of ABS(l_balance) + ABS(current) instead. To be blunt, we do not do this in MBS since the command will only be executed once a month and we have no other reason at present to maintain any of these indexes.

We turn our attention in Chapter 5 to the MBS Payments entry program, Payments.spr. Discussion of SQL-SELECT is delayed until Chapter 12, where we show how to use it as a query tool with single tables and multi-table database views.

CHAPTER

FIVE

Creating a Multi-Window Data Entry Program

5

- Designing the Payments table
- Using lookup files as aids in data entry
- Designing the Payments entry program
- Using BROWSE in a screen program
- Handling interest charges

While data entry of new customers requires the use of only one table, things become a bit more complex when dealing with customer transactions. This is because transaction records, stored in the Payments or Sales table, must be identified through use of the Customer table. Moreover, when entering transactions for any given customer, the operator will generally want to have direct visual accesss to the transactions already on file for that customer. As you will see in this chapter, which examines the MBS Payments entry program, these requirements are easily met by including BROWSE windows in a screen program.

In the Payments entry program we also begin making use of additional tables as lookup tables to aid the operator in data entry. This is the first topic with which we deal as soon as we lay out the design of the MBS Payments table.

Designing the Payments Table

In itself, the MBS Payments table, *Payments.dbf*, is a rather simple affair. Its structure is shown in Figure 5.1, though I have altered the output of the LIST STRUCTURE command once again to include a description of each field's function.

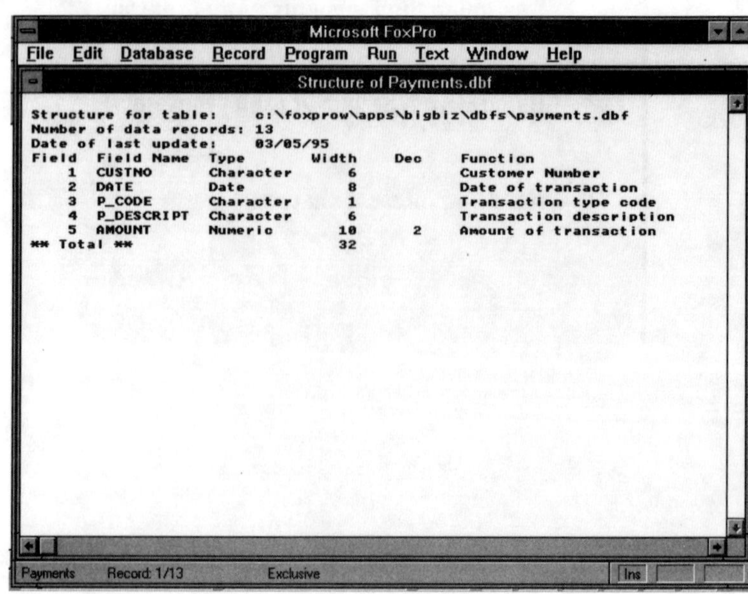

FIGURE 5.1:
Structure of the MBS Payments table, Payments.dbf

The word *payments*, when applied to this table, is something of a misnomer. This is because the MBS Payments table is designed to accommodate a variety of customer transactions in addition to payments on account. The system must, after all, have a means of storing interest charges, returns, refunds, and the like if it is to be able to report all customer transactions and not just sales and payments when it produces statements. The sum of every transaction, whether it be a debit or a credit, must also be used to update the customer account fields in Customer.dbf. Customer credits are deducted from the debt-aging fields, Current through Days120, in reverse order, while customer debits are added to the Current field, using the program routines discussed in Chapter 2.

Handling Multiple Transactions in a Single Table

As previously mentioned, the MBS processes customer debits as positive numbers and customer credits as negative numbers. This affects the Payments table since we use only one Amount field to store all transaction amounts, whether they are debits or credits. To make data entry easier on the operator, however, we store *all* amounts as positive numbers while identifying the function of each through use of a payment code, or *P_code.* Since the number of possible transactions is less than ten, we can devise our code using the ASCII characters (or numbers) 0 through 9 and simply use the values 0–4 to represent customer credits and 5–9 to represent customer debits. Other than that, the assignment of numbers 0–4 and 5–9 to specific types of credits and debits is arbitrary. In the MBS, we use them as follows:

P_code	Transaction
1	Payments
2	Return
3	Refund
4	Book Adj (cr)
5	Sale
6	Interest
7	Book Adj (db)

As you will note, not every possible P_code is used. But that is intended, since the system must have some built-in flexibility for change. Other customer transactions can be added.

More important, by referring to the P_code field, we can readily determine whether the customer transaction is a debit or credit with a simple algorithm: p_code < "5". If and when we want to represent or employ the amount as it must actually be used by the system, we use the following expression to perform the translation:

```
IIF(p_code < "5", -amount,amount)
```

This is used, for example, with the BROWSE command employed to display customer payments on the screen during the payment entry program, and it is responsible for the negative figures appearing in the payment Amount column when the transaction is a credit.

Using a Transaction Code Lookup Table

Whenever displaying payments, we can also substitute the full transaction name for every P_code through use of a *lookup table*. This is the function of table P_codes.dbf. We show its structure in Figure 5.2, along with LIST output of all its present records.

FIGURE 5.2:

A lookup table can be used to translate transaction codes into full descriptions.

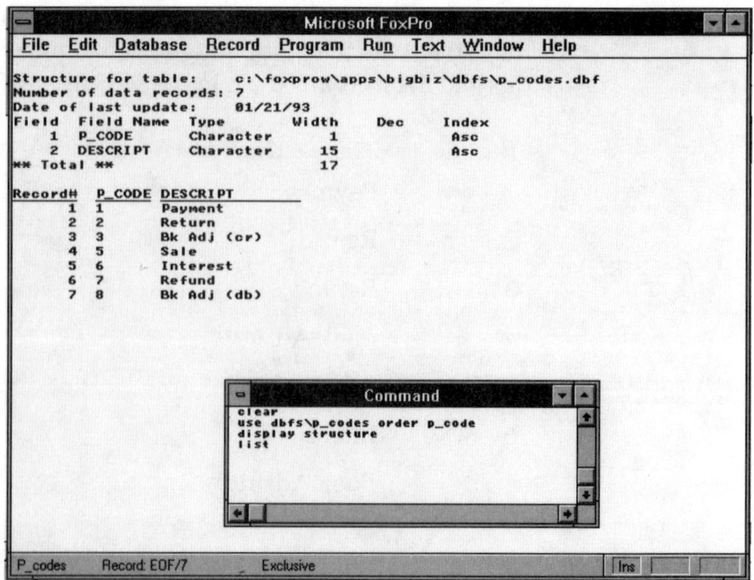

Linked into Payments.dbf with the following commands, P_codes.dbf will enable us to display full transaction code descriptions in place of our code element names:

```
SELECT payments
USE p_codes ORDER p_code IN 0
SET RELATION TO p_code INTO p_codes
LIST date, p_codes.descript, p_descript, amount
```

P_codes.dbf must use a controlling index based on a key expression of P_code in order to support the relation. Since it is not a compound index, we simply name the index tag P_code.

Operator Selection of Payment Type

A secondary function of the payments code lookup table, P_codes.dbf, is to assist the operator during data entry to the Payments table by supplying a list of possible transaction types, as shown in Figure 5.3. This way, the operator won't have to remember our less-mnemonic payment codes. This is readily accomplished through the use of @ GET popup, which takes the popup's list of values from a memory array that was previously created to hold P_codes' record information. We create the array with these commands:

```
SELECT p_codes
COUNT TO arrayno
PUBLIC ARRAY p_cs[arrayno,2]
COPY FIELDS descript, p_code TO array p_cs
```

By creating the array P_cs prior to execution of the Payments entry program, we free P_codes.dbf to perform its other duties unhindered in the Payments entry program.

In defining the array, we first select P_codes.dbf as the active table and count its records. The PUBLIC ARRAY command is subsequently used to define a two-dimensional array with a suitable number of rows to accommodate P_codes' records. We then use COPY FIELDS TO <array> to copy the data into the array. Our reason for using PUBLIC rather than DECLARE or DIMENSION to create the array is simple. We will be creating the array in a nested procedure of the MBS main program file, Bigbiz.prg, at system startup. We must therefore make the elements of the array *public* so they will not be released when the nested procedure is terminated. Otherwise they will not be available to the Payments entry program. (We look at the single procedure used to open all MBS tables and establish all system default relations in Chapter 6 and Chapter 8.) The order in which we specify the fields in

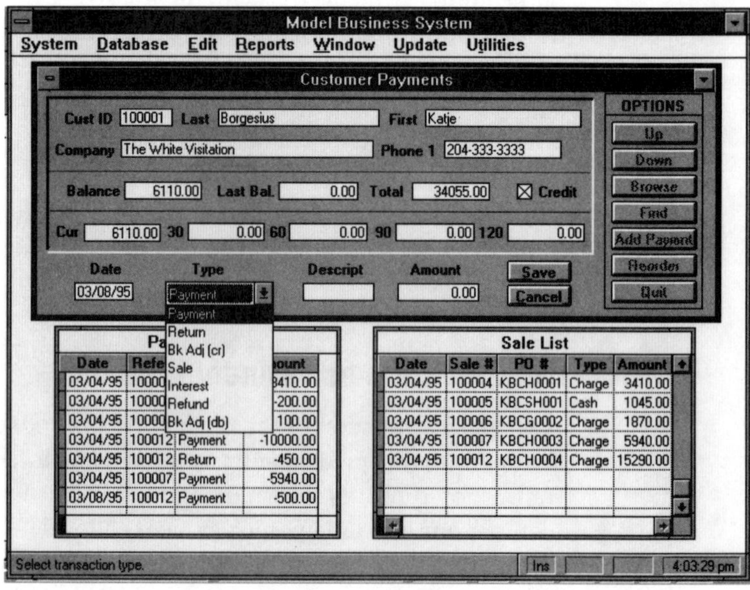

FIGURE 5.3:

Customer Payments window with the Type selection popup open

the COPY command is also significant. When we define the array popup, using the Screen Builder's Popup dialog (see Figure 5.4), the array popup will use only the elements found in the first column of the array. Given the native structure of P_codes.dbf, we must therefore take action to place our P_code descriptions in the array's first column.

TIP

SQL-SELECT provides an alternative and faster way of creating arrays based on the contents of a table. In this particular case, we can use the command SELECTdescript, P_code FROM P_codes ORDER BY P_code INTO ARRAY P_cs to achieve the same result. (See Chapter 12 for a discussion of SQL-SELECT.)

We will look at the MBS Payments entry program in a moment, but it is perhaps best to review how the popup will be used in advance. As with push buttons, @ GET popups will return a numeric value corresponding to the position of the selected option in the popup unless FoxPro is instructed to return the option names

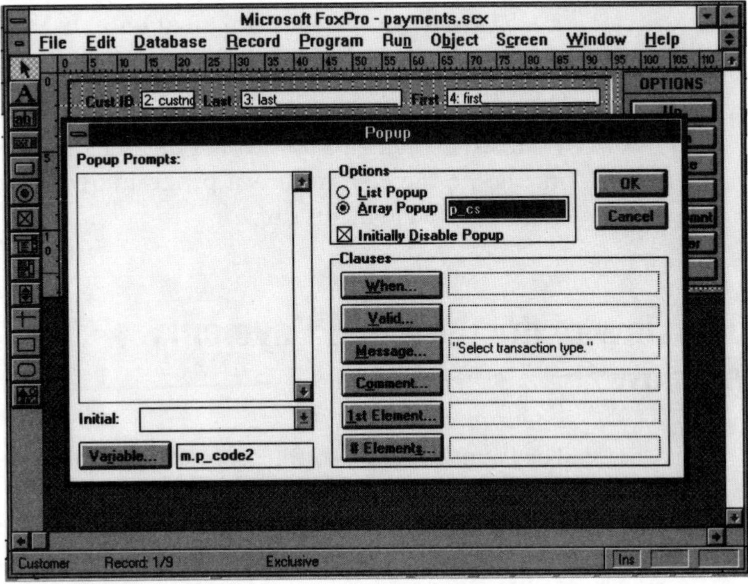

FIGURE 5.4:

Use the Screen Builder's Popup dialog to create a popup using data from a memory array.

instead. Using the option names, however, will make it far easier to access the corresponding P_code for storage in Payment.dbf since we can perform the lookup using memory array P_cs.

```
m.p_code =  p_cs[ASCAN(p_cs,TRIM(m.p_code2))+1]
```

The operator's selection is stored to @ GET m.p_code2. We can therefore TRIM() any trailing blanks from the return value and use the ASCAN(), or *array scan*, function to return the element number of array P_cs in which that value appears. Since the array is two dimensional, holding the payment type description in the first column and the corresponding P_code in the second, we can consequently add +1 to the value returned by ASCAN() to indicate the array element number holding the correct P_code. Using a single command, we thus manage to look up the correct P_code and place it in m.p_code, for later storage in a Payments.dbf record, without having to access the value from P_codes.dbf. (This is just quicker.)

Of course, in order to make our @ GET popup return the character value of the selected option instead of a numeric value corresponding to the option's position in the popup, we must initialize m.p_code2 prior to execution of the @ GET to hold the character value we want to use as the popup's default. This can also be done by filling in the Popup dialog's Initial value setting, but I find it easier to set all @ GET default values manually in a screen program's setup code before execution of the @ GETS so I can review them all at once. In the case of our Type popup, we use the command m.p_code2 = "Payment" in the Payments entry program's setup code to establish "Payment" as the default.

We discuss Payments.dbf's other data fields after reviewing the attributes of Payments.spr, the FoxPro screen program overseeing the entry of customer transactions with Payments.dbf.

Overview of the Customer Payments Window

The Payments entry screen program, activated by selecting the Payments option on the MBS main menu's Database pulldown, uses not one but three windows. (See Figure 5.5.) We refer to the main window at the top of the screen as our READ window because it contains all the @ GET commands that are actuated by the READ command. Referring to it by title, we use the Customer Payments window to look up and display customer records using a set of control push buttons with much the

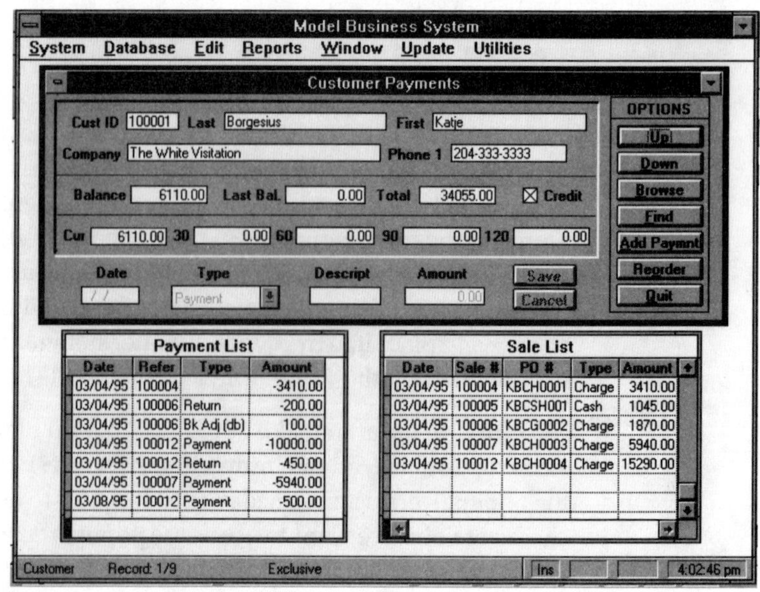

FIGURE 5.5:

The Customer Payments data entry screen employs a READ window and two BROWSE windows.

same options as we used in Customer.spr. What is missing are the push buttons used for appending, erasing, and editing Customer table records.

NOTE The @ GET input field commands used to display Customer table data in the Customer Payments window all use WHEN .F. to prohibit operator access to the fields without dimming and disabling them.

To save space on the screen, only data immediately pertinent to the operator is displayed from Customer.dbf: customer name, company, and phone number and, of course, all the customer account fields that may require updating whenever a customer transaction is entered into the system. (Displaying the customer account fields on the screen allows the operator to check the effects of each transaction on the customer account balance and, moreover, keep an eye on the overall integrity of the data in the customer account.) If the operator wants to see the complete Customer table record, however, the Customers window, under the control of Customer.spr, is only one click of the mouse away—though this is the sort of thing we will not begin to address in earnest until the next chapter. In the normal run of things, entering transactions to Payments.dbf will not, in any case, involve manual update of records in Customer.dbf using the Customers window unless there has been a change of address or phone number or additional comments must be entered.

To enter a customer transaction, the operator first looks up the correct customer account in Customer.dbf, using the available push button controls. When the correct customer appears in the window, pressing the Add Paymnt push button enables the initially dimmed and disabled @ GETs in the bottom row of the READ window so a new transaction can be entered. Because the record of the customer making the transaction remains current in Customer.dbf, the value of Customer.custno, displayed in @ GET m.custno at the top of the window, is immediately available. If the transaction is saved, we simply transfer it to Payments.custno. Other than that, the process of data entry more or less follows the same pattern employed in Customer.spr. Besides enabling the @ GET input fields used for data entry, Add Paymnt activates the Save and Cancel push buttons, used to save or cancel the new transaction record, while deactivating the control push buttons used for Customer table searches. Here again, we use SHOW GETS, READ SHOW, SHOW GET, ENABL/DISABLE, and _CUROBJ to perform the work.

Writing Reusable Screen Program Code

One look at the VALID clause employed by the Customer Payments window control push buttons reveals the degree of standardization of program code in the MBS. Not only do we use the same program structures and routines whenever possible—a practice encouraged by the Screen Builder, which allows us to copy, paste, and otherwise hack all portions of existing screen programs, including the screen layouts, when designing new screen programs—we also take pains to reuse the same memory variables over and over.

```
DO CASE
CASE m.but1 = "Up"
    IF NOT BOF()
        SKIP -1
    ENDIF
    IF BOF()
    WAIT WINDOW "At first record in file." NOWAIT
ENDIF
CASE m.but1 = "Down"
    * Commands omitted for sake of brevity.
IF NOT EOF()
CASE m.but1 = "Find"
    DO Cus_Find.spr WITH "Locate Record"
CASE m.but1 = "Browse"
    DO Browcust
CASE m.but1 = "Add Paymnt"
    STORE .T. TO m.doit, m.doappend
CASE m.but1 = "Reorder"
    DO Cus_find.spr WITH "Reorder File"
CASE m.but1 = "Quit"
    CLEAR READ
ENDCASE
SHOW GETS
RETURN .F.
```

Here, for example, we use m.but1 once more to hold the value of our @ GET push buttons. Memvars m.doit and m.doappend are also used to control access to the @ GETs representing transaction data. We even use m.verify once more for our Save and Cancel push buttons.

Working in this way will make it far easier to read through and revise any screen program in the system since the functions of each of these memvars will be readily apparent regardless of which program we are revising. That we have no reason to declare these reused memvars private to Payments.spr, as we do, for example, with m.verify, used by the nested Cus_find.spr, will be explained in Chapter 6. For now, suffice it to say that even though the Customers window can appear on the screen at the same time as the Customer Payments window, only the memvars belonging to the active READ window will reside in memory. Neither program is nested within the other, though Cus_find.spr is nested in and available to both.

Using BROWSE in a Screen Program

Below our READ window are two BROWSE windows, so called because they are each produced with a BROWSE command. While not necessary for the entry of customer transactions, a list of each customer's transactions (stored in Payments.dbf) and sales (stored in Sales.dbf) will often be helpful to the operator while working on a customer's account. In fact, there are many companies that like to link customer payments to specific sales on the customer's statement. This requirement is anticipated in the MBS by the Payments.descript field, the width of which is suitable for storing MBS sales numbers, though the field can be otherwise employed to hold any data further descriptive of the transaction. (In the Payment List window this field is labeled Refer#, short for *reference number,* to denote its typical usage.) The requirement is also anticipated by the very presence on the screen of the Sale List window, which, along with the Payment List window, is immediately updated as the operator moves through Customer.dbf with the Up, Down, Find, Reorder, or Browse (Customer.dbf) push button.

The simultaneous display of data from the three tables forming our customer database is achieved, as described in Chapter 1, through the use of SET RELATION and BROWSE—though, for the sake of adding full transaction type descriptions to our BROWSE display of payments, we also throw in the link between Payments.dbf and P_codes.dbf.

```
USE customer
USE payments ORDER payments IN 0
* Index tag Payments uses Custno as its key expression.
SELECT payments
USE p_codes ORDER p_codes IN 0
SET RELATION TO p_code INTO p_codes
USE sales ORDER sales IN 0
* Index tag Sales uses Custno + Saleno as its key expression.
SELECT customer
SET RELATION TO custno INTO payments, custno INTO sales
```

Once this view is established, we can select the Payments and Sales tables, each in turn, and issue BROWSE to view all payments and sales belonging to the parent record in Customer.dbf. Moreover, if we leave the BROWSE tables open on the screen, as long as the SET RELATION commands are in effect, wherever we move in Customer.dbf, FoxPro will immediately update the BROWSE tables to display only those transactions belonging to the current customer. (There is no need to enter SET SKIP to view the multiple transactions or to reselect the Sales or Payments tables to update the BROWSE windows.) As for displaying the full payment descriptions in the Payment List window, that's simply a matter of including P_codes.descript in the BROWSE command issued while Payments.dbf is the active table.

Executing BROWSE with READ ACTIVATE or READ WHEN

Though the BROWSE commands can be issued in our program setup code before the @ GETs and READ activating our READ window, the sequence in which the three windows appears will be most pleasing to the operator if we execute the READ window first, followed by the two BROWSE windows, beginning with the one on the left. After executing the Payments entry window set, we will then want to leave the cursor active in the READ window control push buttons, since that is where the operator must begin the process of entering customer transactions. To get this effect, however, two things are wanted: first, a means of executing BROWSE at the very outset of the READ and, second, a means of preventing BROWSE from bringing program execution to a halt, as it does when used in the FoxPro interactive (Command window) mode. (The operator must either close the BROWSE window or manually click another window to end or temporarily halt the BROWSE session. This is more or less how BROWSE is employed to view customer records in Customer.spr and Payments.spr when the Browse push button is selected.)

The first problem is readily handled through use of yet another READ clause—READ ACTIVATE <expL>—though READ WHEN <expL> can also be used. The following commands illustrate this:

```
* Screen setup code
* Screen window code, including DEFINE/ACTIVATE WINDOW and all @
* GETs used in the READ window.
READ ACTIVATE doact() SHOW showfunc()
* Screen cleanup code.
RETURN && Ending screen program.
```

```
FUNCTION doact
IF NOT WVISIBLE("Payment List")
    SELECT payments
    BROWSE PREFERENCE pbrow1 ;
        NODELETE NOAPPEND NOEDIT NOMENU NOWAIT ;
        IN SCREEN TITLE "Payment List" ;
        FIELDS date,p_codes.descript:H="Type", ;
        p_descript:H="Refer", ;
        Amount = IIF(p_code < "5",-amount,amount) ;
        KEY customer.custno
ENDIF
IF NOT WVISIBLE("Sale List")
    SELECT sales
    BROWSE PREFERENCE pbrow2 ;
        NODELETE NOAPPEND NOEDIT NOMENU NOWAIT ;
        IN SCREEN TITLE "Sale List" ;
        FIELDS date,saleno:H="Sale #",pono:H="PO #", ;
        Type=IIF(s_code="1","Cash","Charge"),amount ;
        KEY customer.custno
ENDIF
SELECT customer
RETURN
```

The READ window is displayed before execution of READ. However, before activating the first @ GET for data entry, FoxPro checks for the existence of READ WHEN, ACTIVATE, and SHOW and, if they exist, executes them in the stated order before activating the cursor in the READ window. Since we have already discussed READ SHOW, we focus here on WHEN and ACTIVATE.

Though both clauses can be used to prevent the actual activation of the READ—you can simply design the UDFs or conditions they employ to RETURN .F.—they can also be used, as ACTIVATE is employed here, to control extra-READ window events before initiation of data entry. (SHOW is used for controlling intra-READ window events, primarily with SHOW GET.) This gives us ample opportunity to place our BROWSE windows on the screen.

With regard to our BROWSE tables, once again we make them read-only by using the NODELETE, NOAPPEND, NOEDIT, and NOMENU options. We also prevent FoxPro from suspending program execution when BROWSE is issued by using the special NOWAIT option. This option, available only during program execution, tells FoxPro to execute the BROWSE table and then go on with our program. (An operator who wants to BROWSE either table after the READ window is activated can do so at that point just by clicking the desired window.)

Again, we use the IN SCREEN option to tell FoxPro to orient the BROWSE windows in relation to the full screen and not to open them in the active READ window. We also go to pains to supply each of our BROWSE tables with suitable column titles when the actual field names will be unattractive, using the field heading option: <field>:H=<column title>. To display customer credits using negative numbers—since this will make them easier for the operator to scan—we also place a calculated field in the Payment List table using the formula <column title>=<exp>. And though we use the BROWSE KEY <index key> option to explicitly limit the display to those transactions belonging to the current customer (parent table) record, identified by Customer.Custno, strictly speaking it is not required. However, as my own tests have shown, if you remove the KEY <index key> clause when using BROWSE in this way, FoxPro is sometimes slow to update the tables properly. It is therefore best to give FoxPro explicit instructions with BROWSE KEY.

TIP

Like BROWSE, MODIFY COMMAND and MODIFY FILE <file> can be used in conjunction with a READ window to display and/or enable editing of text files in separate windows. The conventions overseeing the names and titles of the windows they use is similar to that employed with BROWSE, though they do not include a TITLE option. Unless opened in a predefined window, their window name and title are the same as the name of the file they open.

When we begin placing several windows on the screen at once, we must ensure that each window is assigned a unique name. With the DEFINE WINDOW command, used to draw our READ windows, this is no problem; the DEFINE WINDOW command allows us to specify a window name, using up to ten alphanumeric characters (and embedded underscores), in addition to a more explicit window TITLE that can include spaces and be as long as you want to make it, though the actual size of the window will determine how much of a longer title is displayed. With respect to the various FoxPro functions used to test the status or existence of windows, the window *name* is the means by which we will normally reference the windows we create with DEFINE WINDOW. The DEFINE WINDOW <name> is also the name FoxPro automatically displays for the window when it is open in the MBS Window pulldown. (See Figure 5.6.)

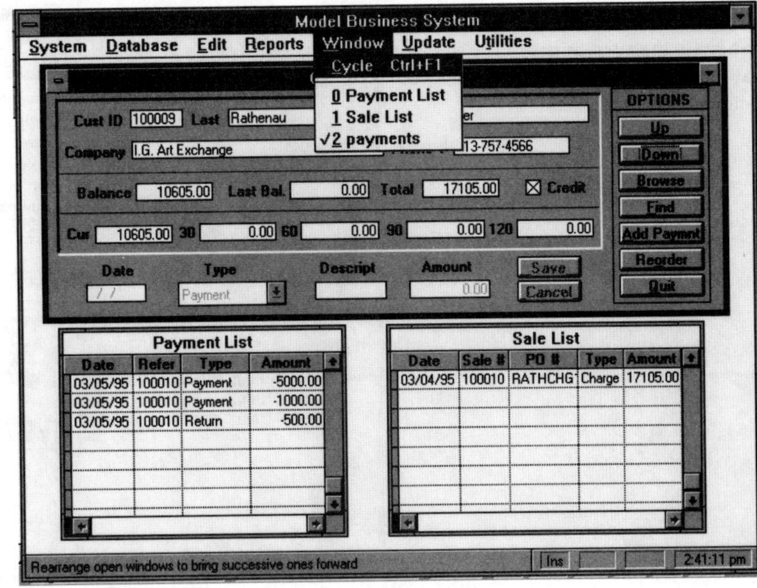

FIGURE 5.6:
To activate an open window, click it with the mouse or select its name from the Window pulldown.

DEFINE WINDOW Name and BROWSE Window Title Conventions

Given the conventions we must observe in naming windows with DEFINE WINDOW and the desirability of making the Window pulldown available to the operator, it is best to assign the major READ windows employed in a system with the most obvious names. Thus we can give our READ window the title Customer Payments, but we will want to name the window Payments. (Note that window names always appear in the Window pulldown in lowercase letters regardless of how you enter them with DEFINE WINDOW, though this may be changed in future versions of FoxPro.) In the MBS, we name the customer entry READ window Customers, the payments entry READ window Payments, the sales entry READ window Sales, and so on. This way, if and when all these windows are open on the screen at once, as shown in Figure 5.7, the operator will have no difficulty in selecting the correct window (and corresponding screen entry program) from the Window pulldown.

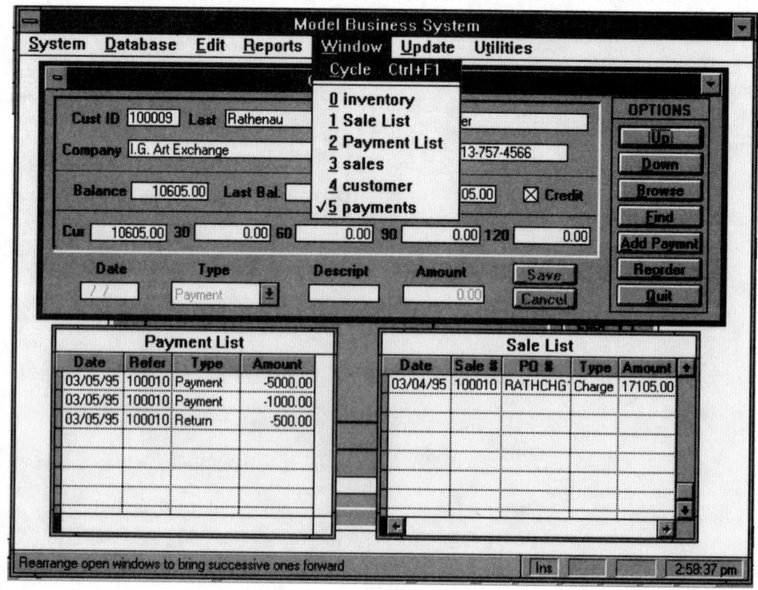

FIGURE 5.7:
Enhance the value and attractiveness of the Window pulldown by following consistent window-naming conventions.

Of course, following conventions that will make things easier on the operator will also make things easier on us as programmers. This is because we must control our window-level events using a variety of FoxPro functions and commands designed to identify windows by name. WONTOP(), for example, returns the name of the currently active (or foremost) window, while WEXIST(<window name>) returns a .T. or .F. indicating whether the referenced window is currently defined. To use these functions effectively, we will want to have a good handle, so to speak, on our window names, and this means sticking to clearly defined naming conventions.

When we turn to the names of windows used by BROWSE, however, FoxPro follows different conventions, a fact that is certain to annoy many programmers. Though we can define a window in advance in which to subsequently open our BROWSE tables—the strategy we ultimately follow in Payments.spr (see below)—when not employed in this way, the BROWSE window name defaults to the supplied BROWSE TITLE. Thus our BROWSE windows are listed in the Window pulldown as Payment List and Sale List.

Bear in mind, however, that if no BROWSE TITLE is supplied, FoxPro uses the name of the table active when BROWSE is issued as the default window title *and* name. The confusion this can lead to will be readily apparent if you consider what will happen if we do not supply the BROWSE command issued with Payments.dbf a specific title. Since our READ window is created with DEFINE WINDOW payments, FoxPro will mistake it for the window in which BROWSE (payments) must be opened—even though we explicitly instruct it to BROWSE IN SCREEN! Clearly, if we want to stick as closely as possible to the practice of giving the same names to our READ windows as those employed by the tables they update and the programs that execute them, we must take care to avoid running into conflicts with our BROWSE window names by always supplying them through use of a specific BROWSE TITLE.

Matching Screen Program and READ Window Names

If you are an experienced programmer you will immediately understand the desirability of using the same name for a screen program and its main READ window. Not only does it offer a superior mnemonic, or memory-schema, but there are situations in which we will find it desirable to execute a screen program when its main READ window becomes WONTOP(), owing, for example, to its selection from the Window pulldown. These matters are discussed in Part II of this book. The drawback of working in this way—which otherwise provides the most desirable window-naming conventions—follows from the different conventions overseeing the naming of programs, which are limited by DOS to no more than eight characters, and windows, which can use up to ten characters like all other FoxPro memory objects. For example, the best we can do when naming our inventory screen program is Inventry.spr. But do we want *inventry* or *inventory* to appear in the Window pulldown? *Inventory* will obviously be preferable, at least from the standpoint of the operator. For reasons discussed in Part II, you may determine otherwise. At this point, however, simply notice how the limitations imposed by DOS file-naming conventions may force us to occasionally forego following the best conventions for us as programmers for the sake of giving the operator the most explicit window names.

Note that we do not, for example, name our BROWSE payments window Payments by Customer to avoid assigning a window name that is not discrete by virtue of the first (and often only) word included in the title. This may make no difference to the operator but will make a world of difference to FoxPro when you use the window test functions to check on the status of your windows. WONTOP(), WEXIST(), WVISIBLE(), and the like, when used to check on a BROWSE window with a name (supplied by TITLE) of more than one word, will be content to consider only the *first word* of the name (title). This can lead to chaos. Since Payments is the name we use for Payments.spr's READ window, WEXIST("payments") will return .T. if the Payments READ window doesn't exist but the Payments BROWSE TITLE "Payments by Customer" does!

WARNING Be certain to supply your BROWSE windows with specific titles since FoxPro will employ them as the windows' names. And since FoxPro functions like WEXIST() and WVISIBLE() will test positive if supplied only the first word of a multiword BROWSE window name supplied by BROWSE TITLE, be sure to supply BROWSE titles that are unique at least with regard to the first word in the title.

This may be a lot to swallow at one time. It is only necessary to be aware of the difficulties around which we must steer with FoxPro 2.6 when naming our windows with DEFINE WINDOW and BROWSE. If we want to give operators access to the FoxPro Window pulldown (which is incorporated and modified in the MBS main menu) and simultaneously use a mess of BROWSE windows, we must be sure that DEFINE WINDOW names are explicit and that BROWSE TITLEs do not repeat the first word of any other window that may appear on the screen at the same time. We achieve this goal with respect to our current BROWSE windows by using the titles Payment List, which differs from our READ window's name Payments by the solitary but still significant final *s*, and Sale List. (Not incidentally, our Sales entry READ window is named Sales.)

Window Names, Window Functions, and the Window Pulldown

The names of all windows created with DEFINE WINDOW will appear in the Window pulldown in lowercase characters, regardless of whether you enter the names that way with DEFINE WINDOW. This is not true, however, of BROWSE window names, which appear exactly as entered with TITLE. Moreover, if no title is entered and FoxPro uses the active BROWSE table name instead, the name will appear with the first character capitalized and the rest of the characters in lowercase. This in itself poses no problems and will even help an experienced programmer identify the function of each window by looking at the format FoxPro uses to display the window name in the pulldown.

TIP

You can ignore differences in upper- and lowercase characters when using functions like WONTOP() and WOUTPUT(), which returns the name of a window, by using the UPPER() function to force the returned window name to uppercase. For example, UPPER(WONTOP()) = "SALE LIST".

Looks, however, can be deceptive, since the window test functions, when they take upper- and lowercase characters seriously, do not test window names in the same way as they are displayed in the Window pulldown. To be succinct, all window test functions that take a window name as an argument and return a logical value do not give a hoot about upper- and lowercase. WEXIST() and WVISIBLE, for example, will return .T. whether you enter WEXIST("payments"), WEXIST("PAYMENTS"), or WEXIST("PaYmEnTs"). On the other hand, window functions designed to return the name of a window are quite exacting in their use of upper- and lowercase characters. WONTOP(), for example, returns a window name in uppercase characters if the window was created with DEFINE WINDOW. (This is exactly the opposite of how the window name would be displayed in the Window pulldown.) If the window is a BROWSE window with a name supplied by BROWSE TITLE, WONTOP() returns the entire name (title) exactly as it was entered with BROWSE TITLE <expC>. But where a BROWSE window name defaults to the name of the active table, WONTOP() returns the name in uppercase characters, just as though the window had been created with DEFINE WINDOW.

In the future, I expect to see changes in the conventions used by FoxPro for identifying windows by name since the present conventions are confusing and require more explanation than is warranted by what should be a straightforward topic. In any case, you will not have to overly concern yourself about these matters if you are careful to give your windows discrete names.

Using READ DEACTIVATE to Control Window-Level Events

An additional problem arises when including BROWSE windows in a screen program controlled with READ. To be responsive to operator selection of another window on the screen using the mouse, the Window pulldown, or Ctrl+F6, READ is designed to terminate when any of these *window-level* events take place. In effect, this means that once our READ window is fully activated, operator selection of either BROWSE window will automatically terminate our READ and our program.

To prevent this from happening, we can once again rely upon READ's DEACTIVATE clause, which is triggered when an attempt is made to terminate READ by means other than CLEAR READ. If the DEACTIVATE clause RETURNs .T., READ is allowed to terminate and the next window is selected—that is, supposing it is not released by the terminated screen program. On the other hand, if DEACTIVATE RETURNs .F., READ is not terminated. We can thus prevent the termination of READ overseeing our Payments entry program when the operator switches from the READ window to one of the BROWSE windows by simply entering a DEACTIVATE clause with a literal value of .F. This, however, will not do entirely. DEACTIVATE .F. will negatively affect another window-level event we want to allow with our Customer Payments window—namely, closing the window (and terminating the program) by selecting the Close option in the window control box. We must therefore write a small UDF to distinguish between the different events:

```
IF UPPER(WONTOP()) $ "PAYMENT LIST SALE LIST"
    RETURN .F.
ENDIF
RETURN .T. && command not required.
```

Here we use the WONTOP() function, which returns the name of the window on top—that is, the window just selected by the operator—to check to see if DEACTIVATE was triggered as the result of operator selection of one of our BROWSE windows. If it was, the function returns .F. and prevents READ from terminating. Mind, this does not prevent the selected window from being brought forward and made the active window, or window on top. The event, in fact, has already happened. It is what triggers READ DEACTIVATE. If we want to disallow it, we must do so manually by using the ACTIVATE WINDOW command to forcibly reactivate our READ window, as shown here:

```
IF UPPER(WONTOP()) $ "PAYMENT LIST SALE LIST"
    ACTIVATE WINDOW payments
```

```
   RETURN .F.
ENDIF
RETURN .T. && command not required.
```

This would prevent either BROWSE window from staying on top since ACTIVATE WINDOW immediately reactivates window Payments. The READ itself is never terminated.

In the case of both routines, only the first of which is really useful to us, any other event triggering DEACTIVATE—for example, selecting Close from the control box or selection of a window other than the READ window or the two named BROWSE windows—terminates the READ.

TIP

Use RETURN <exp> in a UDF to evaluate and return the <exp> with one command. We can, for example, shorten the first UDF cited above by reducing it to a single command: RETURN UPPER(WONTOP()) $ "PAYMENT LIST SALE LIST". This will suffice as long as we do not need to perform any other action in the READ DEACTIVATE clause.

With regard to WONTOP() itself, note that we used the UPPER() function to force its return value to uppercase. This is generally wise since both WONTOP() and WVISIBLE(), the latter of which tests to see if a window is active but not hidden (an issue which we take up in Part II), return window names exactly as they were entered with DEFINE WINDOW or BROWSE TITLE. We can therefore avoid problems arising from inconsistent use of upper- and lowercase characters in our window names by using UPPER() along with WONTOP() and WVISIBLE(), and test everything in uppercase.

Going back to our DEACTIVATE clause, if we want to give the operator access to other windows without terminating the READ, we need only add them to the list of window names tested with UPPER(WONTOP()) $ <window name list>. Likely candidates are the windows employed by the FoxPro desk accessories—the Calculator, Calendar/Diary, and Puzzle—all of which are incorporated in the MBS and are accessible through the System pulldown, shown open in Figure 5.8.

However, we have more pressing issues to deal with before showing how to incorporate the desk accessories into your applications, though this is easily done when creating our system menu.

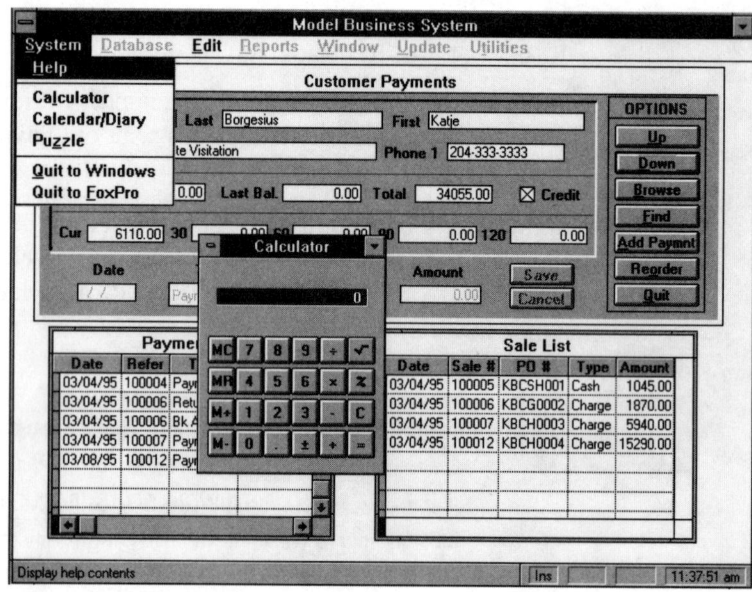

FIGURE 5.8:
The MBS System pulldown accesses the FoxPro Calculator, Calendar/Diary, and Puzzle.

Using READ ACTIVATE to Reopen a Manually Closed BROWSE Window

Unlike DEFINE WINDOW, BROWSE includes no options for controlling window attributes—that is, the list of options that appear in the BROWSE window control box. Instead, BROWSE automatically derives its window attributes from the last window opened with ACTIVATE WINDOW (in this case, our READ window) unless the BROWSE NORMAL keyword is employed. NORMAL tells FoxPro to open the BROWSE window in the *normal* way—that is, with the same window attributes assigned it when opened in the FoxPro interactive mode (when no other window is active).

Because we do not use NORMAL when opening our two BROWSE windows, they take on the attributes of our READ window. (See Figure 5.7.) Since the READ window is defined with the CLOSE MINIMIZE and FLOAT keywords, the BROWSE windows naturally include these options. But even were this not so, we should still face the problem with which we are concerned here. Take away the BROWSE control box, and an operator can still close either of our BROWSE windows by pressing the Esc key or Ctrl+W when either window is active. The BROWSE window closes, automatically activating the next window in the stack, where window order is determined, inversely, by the order in which each window was activated. And that's that; the BROWSE window disappears from the screen.

NOTE BROWSE windows do not include activate and deactivate clauses. For this reason, we must control their opening and closing in a screen program through use of READ ACTIVATE and READ DEACTIVATE.

To prevent this from happening we must make use, once again, of the READ ACTIVATE clause, which is triggered not just when the READ window is first activated, but every time it is reactivated. In other words, every time the operator moves back to our READ window after activating one of the BROWSE windows (or one of the desk accessories), FoxPro will reexecute the DEACTIVATE clause if it is defined. As this suggests, however, it will not be sufficient just to reexecute our BROWSE commands in the ACTIVATE clause; we will also want to avoid reexecuting BROWSE when it is not necessary to do so. (In most cases, the operator will only close a BROWSE window accidentally.) This explains our use of the IF/ENDIFs in which we embedded our BROWSE commands. We repeat one of them here:

```
IF NOT WVISIBLE("Payment List")
    SELECT payments
    BROWSE...
ENDIF
```

This way, if the BROWSE window is not visible on the screen, as is certain to be the case when READ ACTIVATE is triggered at the outset of the program, the BROWSE window will be activated. If it is already present on the screen, FoxPro won't waste time redrawing it.

Using a Resource File to Control Size and Placement of BROWSE Windows

It is likely that those new to FoxPro have read through the previous pages all the while wondering how we control the placement of our BROWSE windows on the screen as well as the sizing of each BROWSE window's fields. If we have ignored addressing these issues until now, it is because they are so easily managed through the use of a FoxPro *resource file*.

Limitations of Control over Two or More BROWSE Windows

The strategy employed above to ensure that BROWSE windows are not manually closed and released during READ works imperfectly with two or more BROWSE windows. This because only activation of a READ window—that is, a window actually containing @ GET commands activated with READ—will trigger READ ACTIVATE. If only one BROWSE window is used, closing that window will automatically activate the remaining READ window. But if two or more BROWSEs are employed, closing one of them may activate another BROWSE rather than the READ window. (In the case of the Payments entry program, for example, because of the order in which the windows are initially activated, closing the Sale List BROWSE window will activate the Payment List.) The manually closed BROWSE window will not reappear on the screen until the READ window is reactivated.

FoxPro resource files—and a slew of other FoxPro features, including FoxPro Help files—came into existence when somebody had the bright idea of using tables to store system-level information. With regard to BROWSE windows and, indeed, all other FoxPro system windows and desk accessories, why not store the operator's choice of field sizing, window position, and the like in a special table. This way, whenever a specific BROWSE window is opened, for example, FoxPro can refer to that window's listing in the table to find out how the window was arranged when the operator last used it. With such information available, it would then be possible to reopen the window just as the operator left it, making it unnecessary to continually resize fields or bother to use the BROWSE command's <field>:<expN> column-width option to do this. Thus were FoxPro resource files born, and FoxPro uses one at system startup by default: Foxuser.dbf. You will find it listed in your FoxPro home directory.

TIP

To automatically control the appearance of BROWSE windows on the screen, include a resource file in each of your applications and issue BROWSE LAST or PREFERENCE <expC>.

Although you can open a FoxPro resource file with the USE command, this is not how a resource file is pressed into service. A resource file is opened as the current resource file with the command SET RESOURCE TO <file>. To change back to the default FoxPro resource file, you can issue the command SET RESOURCE TO foxuser or enter SET RESOURCE TO without specifying any file. FoxPro automatically reengages the default resource file, provided it has not been erased from the disk.

Creating an Application Resource File

The best practice is to create a specific resource file for use with every application. To do so, open Foxuser.dbf with USE and employ COPY STRUCTURE TO <file> to create an empty table with the correct structure. However, as you will discover, you cannot USE Foxuser without first closing it as the resource file. This is done by issuing the command SET RESOURCE OFF. Thus we can re-create the resource file used with the MBS by issuing the following commands:

```
SET RESOURCE OFF
USE \foxprow\foxuser
COPY STRUCTURE TO bigbiz
USE
SET RESOURCE TO
```

Note that the last command reengages Foxuser.dbf as the current resource file. (The command SET RESOURCE ON, turning the resource file on, is automatically issued when SET RESOURCE TO is issued.) Still, there is a simpler alternative. FoxPro's use of a resource file does not prevent you from opening it a second time with USE <file> AGAIN.

TIP

The name, including the drive and full path, of the current resource file is returned by the SYS(2005). The name and on/off status of the current resource file can also be referenced with the SET(<parameter>) function. To return the name, enter ? SET("RESOURCE",1). On/off status is returned if you enter ? SET("RESOURCE").

When we want to engage our new resource file, all we need do is issue the command SET RESOURCE TO Bigbiz. FoxPro will then begin using Bigbiz.dbf as the active resource file instead of Foxuser.dbf. If and when we want to change back to Foxuser.dbf, we reissue the command SET RESOURCE TO.

NOTE

Be aware that the FoxPro default resource file holds the definitions of label layouts. To preserve them in the new resource file, instead of COPY STRUCTURE, create the new resource file with COPY TO <file> FOR Id = "LABELLYT". This way the label layout definitions will be available when creating Label forms when the new resource file is in use as the current resource file.

Using BROWSE LAST and BROWSE PREFERENCE

Every BROWSE window's position and field sizes are saved in the active resource file. Suppose, for example, we issue the following commands when Bigbiz.dbf is the current resource file:

```
USE customer
BROWSE FIELDS custno,last,first
```

Once the BROWSE window appears on the screen, we can move it where we choose by dragging it with the mouse. We can also resize its fields, not to mention the dimensions of the window itself. Once the window is closed with Ctrl+W or by choosing Close from the window control box, FoxPro stores the field list and field sizes, as well as the dimensions and position of the BROWSE window, in the resource file under the name of the active table. The next time we open Customer.dbf, we can choose to open the BROWSE window using the configuration stored in the resource file by issuing BROWSE LAST. We can also open the BROWSE window again without taking advantage of the resource file configuration by simply issuing BROWSE without LAST. However, this will also remove the BROWSE LAST configuration for the table from the resource file.

Regardless of how we reinitiate BROWSE, if we move or resize the fields or window before closing the table, FoxPro will update the record in the resource file for the window. Since this may not always be desirable, FoxPro follows one simple rule: If you close the window by pressing Ctrl+Q, it will not update the record in the resource file, making it possible to return to the previous BROWSE configuration. (Note that you can use BROWSE LAST without error even when opening the table for the first time.)

Still, BROWSE LAST has one major shortcoming. When you use BROWSE or BROWSE LAST, FoxPro saves the BROWSE field list and window configuration information in the resource file under the name of the active table—in this case, Customer. FoxPro is not sensitive to window names entered with BROWSE using the TITLE option, nor does it store a title in the resource file. (It does, however, store any FIELD list, regardless of how complicated, along with the size and position of the window and the display size of the fields.) This means we can replicate only one BROWSE view for each table with the aid of BROWSE LAST unless we resort to using alias names for the table.

To get around the limitation, FoxPro allows us to use BROWSE PREFERENCE <expC> instead of LAST:

```
USE customer
BROWSE PREFERENCE "Cust1"
BROWSE PREFERENCE "Cust2"
```

Each of the BROWSE PREFERENCE window configurations will subsequently be stored in the resource file under the name of the PREFERENCE: Cust1 and Cust2. Indeed, we can create as many preferred views of the Customer table as we want by working in this way. And this is obviously what we do in executing the two BROWSE windows belonging to the Payments entry program, using BROWSE PREFERENCE "pbrow1" and "pbrow2".

Setting Up BROWSE Resource Settings during System Development

When creating a data entry program using BROWSE windows, it is customary to execute the program (with the system resource file open), position and size the windows and fields to your own satsifaction, and then close them manually with Ctrl+W or the Close option in the control box. Since Payments.spr's BROWSE windows will be immediately reopened by READ ACTIVATE as soon as we reselect the READ window, we can see the results at once. Once we have done this, our work with respect to shape, size, and position of our BROWSE windows is over.

TIP

You can speed up the reexecution of BROWSE by READ ACTIVATE by executing the BROWSE windows first in the screen setup code, writing out the full field lists. Then, in READ ACTIVATE, you need only BROWSE LAST or BROWSE PREFERENCE, though you must also include such BROWSE options as are not stored in the resource file—for example, TITLE, KEY, NORMAL, and NOWAIT.

However, having set up your BROWSE windows to your own satisfaction, you may want to fix things so that even though an operator can feel free to resize and reposition any BROWSE window, it will always appear on the screen when the program begins exactly the way you configured it. This is easily done by making some manual changes to your application's resource file:

```
SET RESOURCE TO bigbiz
USE customer
BROWSE LAST
BROWSE PREFERENCE "Cust1"
BROWSE PREFERENCE "Cust2"
SET RESOURCE OFF  && Close Bigbiz.dbf as resource file.
* Or use SET RESOURCE TO to close Bigbiz.dbf as the resource
* file while re-engaging Foxuser.dbf.
USE bigbiz
BROWSE
```

In the above commands, we establish the new resource file, Bigbiz.dbf, created above, as the current resource file; open Customer.dbf; and issue BROWSE three times, once using LAST (though the LAST keyword is optional except when renewing the BROWSE table) and twice with PREFERENCE, using two different preference names. This is intended to mimic what would happen during system development, where we can BROWSE the customer database in a variety of ways from program to program, using LAST or PREFERENCE to restore a prior BROWSE window configuration. Once our BROWSE windows are arranged as we want them, we return to the FoxPro Command window, close our system resource file (if it is not automatically closed by our program), open it like any other table, and execute BROWSE, EDIT, or CHANGE to display and edit its records. Figure 5.9 shows what we'd see.

FIGURE 5.9:

FoxPro resource file opened with USE and BROWSE

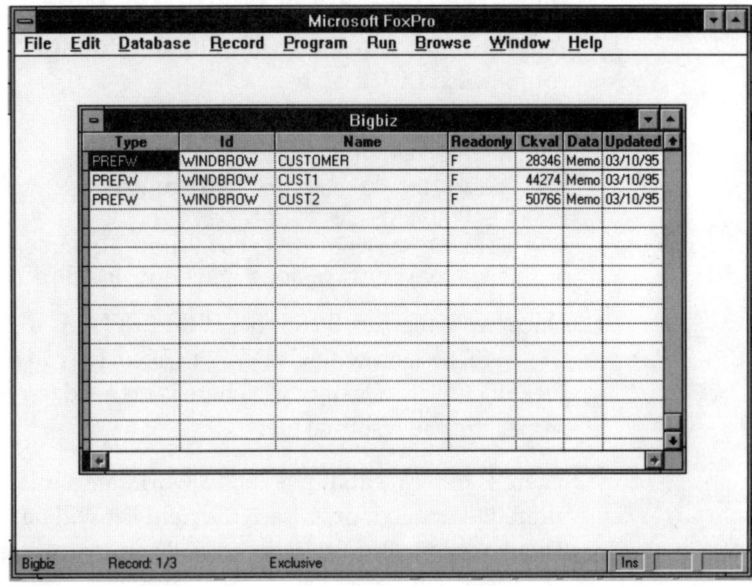

Obviously, all resource files have the same structure and, as the second-to-last column of the BROWSE window indicates, include a Memo field to hold configuration instructions. The only field you will want to play with, however, is the Readonly field, the value of which determines whether or not FoxPro continues to update the resource file record for the BROWSE window identified by name. (Of course, Customer is the name assigned the window produced with BROWSE LAST, and Cust1 and Cust2 represent the BROWSE windows produced with BROWSE PREFERENCE "Cust1" and "Cust2", respectively.) To make the current configuration instructions for any of the three windows permanent (at least when Bigbiz.dbf is the current resource file), we need only alter the value of the window's Readonly field in the resource file to .T. before terminating the BROWSE session. Note that no MBS resource file records have Readonly values set to .T. If the operator alters the position and sizes of BROWSE windows, the BROWSE windows will later reappear just as they were left, except where BROWSE tables are opened in windows predefined with DEFINE WINDOW.

Resource File Storage of BROWSE Field List

As noted above, resource files hold onto BROWSE field lists, regardless of how complicated they may be:

```
USE customer
USE payments ORDER payments IN 0
SET RELATION TO custno INTO payments
BROWSE PREFERENCE "Cust_pay" ;
    FIELDS Name=last+first,Cust_ID=custno, ;
    Type=payment.p_code,payment.amount
```

Once we save the BROWSE PREFERENCE to the resource file by ending the BROWSE session with Ctrl+W or Close, we can simply reinitiate it with BROWSE PREFERENCE "Cust_pay". There is no need to reenter the FIELD list since FoxPro stores it in the resource file.

There is one caveat, however, to working in this way: If the resource file becomes altered, damaged, or erased, the field list will be lost along with the configuration. This is why the BROWSE commands we use to open our Payment List and Sale List BROWSE windows include the desired field list. (Were there other occasions in the Payment entry program, following execution of the ACTIVATE clause, where we might be required to reexecute the BROWSE windows, however, we might safely omit citing the field lists.)

Using a resource file with each of your systems will also enable the operator to position the Calculator, Calendar/Diary, and Puzzle on the screen just where desired. For more information about the variety of uses of FoxPro resource files, refer to your FoxPro documentation. In the MBS, we employ a resource file for the sake of controlling BROWSE and for providing the operator control over the FoxPro desk accessories used by the system. Other uses are incidental to our purpose.

Gaining Additional Control over BROWSE Window Attributes

As we have already noted, BROWSE does not include options for controlling BROWSE window attributes. Unless the NORMAL keyword is employed, the BROWSE window takes on the attributes of the window in which it is opened. This is either the main FoxPro window, if BROWSE is opened IN SCREEN (the default orientation), or in the specified user-defined window, if BROWSE is opened using BROWSE WINDOW <name>. This, however, provides a means of exerting control over which options may or may not appear in the BROWSE window control box. You can, for example, create a window with DEFINE WINDOW, provide the window with the attributes you want BROWSE to adopt, and then open BROWSE using WINDOW <name>.

NOTE

Use BROWSE IN WINDOW <name> instead of BROWSE WINDOW <name> if you do not want the BROWSE window to take on the attributes of the window in which it is opened.

In fact, this is what we do with the two BROWSE windows employed in Payments.spr in order to prevent the BROWSE window control box from displaying the Close option. Here we limit ourselves to the commands used in the READ ACTIVATE clause to place the Payment List BROWSE window on the screen.

```
IF NOT WVISIBLE("Payment List")
    DEFINE WINDOW pbrow1 FROM 14,6 TO 25,55 ;
        SYSTEM GROW FLOAT NOZOOM NOCLOSE ;
        FONT "MS Sans Serif", 8
    SELECT payments
    BROWSE PREFERENCE pbrow1 ;
        NODELETE NOAPPEND NOEDIT NOMENU NOWAIT ;
        WINDOW pbrow1 TITLE "Payment List" ;
        FIELDS date,p_codes.descript:H="Type", ;
        p_descript:H="Refer", ;
        Amount = IIF(p_code < "5",-amount,amount) ;
        KEY customer.custno
    RELEASE WINDOW pbrow1
ENDIF
```

Using DEFINE WINDOW, we create a window that can be sized (GROW) and positioned (FLOAT) and that has the look of a system window (SYSTEM) but cannot be enlarged to fill the entire screen (NOZOOM) or closed (NOCLOSE). As a consequence, we restrict the options appearing in the control box to Resize, Float, and Next Window. Moreover, we take this occasion to define the font that will be adopted by BROWSE once it is opened in the window, though this could be done using BROWSE's font option instead.

Next we issue our BROWSE PREFERENCE command using the WINDOW option to open BROWSE in our predefined window. It is not necessary to activate the window first. (We give the PREFERENCE the same name as the window, pbrow1, only as a matter of convenience.)

Note that the following command, RELEASE WINDOW, will not close the BROWSE window; but it does remove the window definition from memory. For us, this is an important step. If we fail to release window Pbrow1, it will be listed in the Window pulldown along with Payment List and the rest of the windows used by the Payments entry program. As this is unattractive and will, moreover, distract the operator, we release the window the moment its job is done.

Creating DEFINE WINDOW Coordinates for Use with the BROWSE Window

Still, this leaves us with a small headache. When BROWSE PREFERENCE "pbrow1" opens, its position and size will be predetermined by the window coordinates provided by DEFINE WINDOW pbrow1. The BROWSE PREFERENCE can give us control only of field list sizes and definitions; it no longer controls window position, size, or attributes. And unfortunately for us, we cannot create a user-defined window with DEFINE WINDOW using a preference. The coordinates must be hard coded.

To take care of this matter, we simply resort to cunning. We begin by preparing Payments.spr to work with BROWSE PREFERENCE IN SCREEN. We omit all mention of the window. In this way, we can depend upon BROWSE PREFERENCE to hold the desired window position and size. Next we issue the following command before executing Payments.spr:

```
ON KEY LABEL Alt+F7 DO dimens
```

When running the application, we target each of our BROWSE windows in turn and press Alt+F7 to execute Dimens.prg, the small program file shown below, though we strip it of a few inessential commands.

```
SET ALTERNATE TO dwindows.txt ADDITIVE
wcom = "DEFINE WINDOW FROM " + ;
    LTRIM(STR(WLROW(WONTOP()))) + "," + ;
    LTRIM(STR(WLCOL(WONTOP()))) + " TO " + ;
    LTRIM(STR(WLROW(WONTOP())+WROWS(WONTOP()))) + "," + ;
    LTRIM(STR(WLCOL(WONTOP())+WCOLS(WONTOP()))) + ;
    " SYSTEM GROW FLOAT NOZOOM NOCLOSE"
    FONT "MS Sans Serif", 8
```

```
SET CONSOLE OFF
SET ALTERNATE ON
? wcom
SET ALTERNATE OFF
SET ALTERNATE TO
SET CONSOLE ON
RETURN
```

Dimens.prg's action is simple. It opens a text file with SET ALTERNATE TO. (We use the ADDITIVE option so FoxPro will open the text file without erasing its content if the file already exists.) In the next command, we build the DEFINE WINDOW command required to create a window with the current position and size of the active BROWSE window, the name of which is referenced with WONTOP(). All of this is stored to the memory variable wcom. The coordinates are supplied by way of four special window functions. WLROW() and WLCOL() return numeric values indicating the row and column coordinates, respectively, of the BROWSE window's upper-left corner. Since WROWS() and WCOLS() return the number of rows and columns in the window, adding their return values to WLROW() and WLCOL() supplies us with the coordinates of the lower right-hand corner of the window. (LTRIM() and STR() are obviously used to convert the numbers to character strings and trim off leading blanks.)

In the rest of the program, we turn the console off momentarily, turn on output to the text file, and send the window definition to the text file before closing the test file and turning the console back on. Program control is then returned to Payments.spr, though we can reexecute Dimens.prg again by pressing Alt+F8 at any time.

After executing Dimens.prg once for each of our BROWSE windows, we need only call Payments.spr for edit, open the text file with MODIFY FILE, and use the Clipboard to paste each of the DEFINE WINDOW commands into place in Payments.spr. We need only give the windows names, edit the BROWSE commands to use the new windows, and enter the RELEASE commands. Thus is a knotty problem cut down to size. (You will find Dimens.prg on disk with the MBS in the prgs directory used for all program files.)

Be aware that other methods and tools are available for getting hold of the coordinates required by the windows we use with BROWSE. We will see some of them in Chapter 6, when we deal with the related problem of defining windows for use with pick lists executed with DEFINE POPUP PROMPT <fields> and ACTIVATE POPUP rather than @ GET popup or @ GET list.

TIP

You can use SET TEXTMERGE as a more sophisticated alternative to using SET ALTERNATE to create and send output to text files. Unlike SET ALTERNATE, SET TEXTMERGE is specially designed to handle output of fields, functions, and expressions without having to evaluate them first. (See your FoxPro documentation or Help file for a discussion of SET TEXTMERGE.)

The Payments Entry Program Up Close

Now that we have covered the major elements that distinguish Payments.spr from Customer.spr, we can examine it up close. Bear in mind, however, that while we have covered a variety of issues pertaining to the use of BROWSE windows in our program, we have yet to deal with window-level events involving windows not created and used by Payments.spr itself. We therefore confine our treatment of the screen program to the work it is specifically intended to perform and omit mention of how the program is designed to respond to other extra-window events. We will nonetheless continue moving, as we already have, toward filling in the gaps as we review Payments.spr's action.

The appropriate table view, linking Customer.dbf into Payments.dbf and Sales.dbf and linking Payments.dbf into P_codes.dbf, is already established by the MBS before the program begins. Bizshare.dbf, the MBS system value table, is also open and the memory array P_cs, used for display and entry of payment codes, is already on hand. (With the exception of Bizshare.dbf, the role and interrelations of all these files are discussed earlier in this chapter, as is memory array P_cs. For a discussion of Bizshare.dbf, see Chapter 2.)

The Payments Program Setup Code

Like Customer.spr, Payments.spr begins by establishing the environment required for subsequent execution of the @ GETs included in our READ window:

```
SET SKIP OF BAR 2 OF Database .T.
SET TOPIC TO topic = "Payments File"
SELECT customer
SCATTER MEMVAR
m.pres_bal = current+days30+days60+days90+days120
```

```
m.but1 = "Up"
m.verify = "Save"
m.last_bill = bizshare.last_bill
STORE .F. TO m.doit,m.doappend,m.hide
SELECT payments
SCATTER FIELDS date,p_descript,amount MEMVAR BLANK
m.p_code = p_cs[1,2]
m.p_code2 = p_cs[1,1]
SELECT customer
```

The first two commands, which are also used in Customer.spr with slightly different settings, are incidental to our needs. The first deactivates the Payments option on the MBS Database pulldown. This inhibits recursive execution of Payments.spr. (Since Payments.spr does not use READ MODAL, it does not automatically deactivate the MBS main menu.) The second command establishes a specific entry in the MBS Help file as the default topic. If the operator presses F1 or selects Help from the MBS System pulldown, the entry listed in the Help table under Payments File will appear on the screen. We will return to these matters later and mention them now only to familiarize you with the commands used to achieve these relatively simple ends.

The rest of the commands require little explanation. Since the READ window includes fields from both Customer.dbf and Payments.dbf, we initialize the required memory variables in advance. (The second SCATTER command is used with a FIELD list to prevent FoxPro from blanking out m.custno, which now holds the value of Customer.custno. We use BLANK to create empty memvars for a new payment record.) Other memory variables are initialized to serve as default values for our two sets of push buttons and as flags for controlling the action of READ SHOW. (We do not discuss the function of m.hide at this point; it is used to help us control window-level events.)

The two commands used to initialize m.p_code and m.p_code2, representing Payments.p_code and the @ GET popup used for operator selection of payment type, respectively, take their values from the elements in the first row of our two-dimensional array P_cs. (Remember, payment type descriptions are in column 1 of the array, while the corresponding P_codes are in row 2.)

The Payments Program READ Window

Here we touch briefly on a few aspects of our READ window. Like all other MBS data entry windows, the Payments window (title: Customer Payments) is created by the Screen Builder with the following attributes: CLOSE, MINIMIZE, and FLOAT. The @ GET input fields in the top portion of the window display memvars holding values taken from the current Customer table record. Once again, all of these @ GETs use WHEN .F. to prevent the operator from addressing them. (Remember, *disabling* an @ GET also dims it. This is why we use WHEN .F.)

The @ GETs, offset in a 3-D rectangular box at the bottom of the window, display the empty memvars prepared for entry of a new payment, though instead of displaying P_code, we display the @ GET m.p_code2 popup, which takes its values from memory array P_cs. (Payment will appear as the default value as long as it has the lowest P_code value in P_codes.dbf, the table used to load the array with values, as discussed earlier in this chapter.) Since these @ GETs along with @ GET m.verify, overseeing the use of the Save and Cancel push buttons, are initially disabled through the use of @ GET DISABLE, only the window control push buttons, represented by @ GET m.but1, are active when READ is issued.

Since we already looked at the VALID clause used by @ GET m.but1 above and have, moreover, covered our READ ACTIVATE clause, setting up our BROWSE windows in some depths, we move directly to READ SHOW, noting only that operator selection of the Add Paymnt push button sets the value of m.doit to .T.

The Payments Program READ SHOW Clause

Payments.spr's READ SHOW clause holds no surprises. It's almost exactly like the one used with Customer.spr. (The ELSE clause of IF/ENDIF is exactly the same since all control push button operations except for Add Paymnt and Quit are designed to reposition FoxPro in the Customer table.)

```
IF m.doit
    m.date = DATE()
    SHOW GET m.date ENABLE
    SHOW GET m.p_code2 ENABLE
    SHOW GET m.p_descript ENABLE
    SHOW GET m.amount ENABLE
    SHOW GET m.verify ENABLE
    SHOW GET m.but1 DISABLE
    _curobj = OBJNUM(m.date)
ELSE
    SCATTER MEMVAR
    m.pres_bal = current+days30+days60+days90+days120
ENDIF
```

If the operator presses Add Payment, the commands listed under IF m.doit are executed. The only memvar we need to initialize is m.date, which is *empty* at this point in the program owing to the use of SCATTER in the setup code. We supply m.date with a default value of DATE(). The SHOW GET commands that follow enable all @ GETs employed in transaction entry while disabling the main control push buttons, @ GET m.but1. The cursor is then sent to the first @ GET requiring input during transaction entry, and SHOW GETS—located at the end of @ GET m.but1 VALID, triggering READ SHOW—refreshes the READ window display. The operator can begin entering the transaction.

Using SHOW GETS ONLY and OFF

In the case of Append Paymnt, it is not really necessary to refresh all @ GETs with SHOW GETS (at the end of @ GET m.but1 VALID). It is only necessary to trigger READ SHOW. Thus we might speed action slightly by altering the last commands in @ GET m.but1 VALID to read as follows:

```
DO CASE
* CASEs testing m.but1.
ENDCASE
IF m.doit
    SHOW GETS ONLY
ELSE
    SHOW GETS
ENDIF
RETURN .F.
```

As mentioned in Chapter 3, SHOW GETS ONLY will trigger READ SHOW without refreshing all @ GETs. Since READ SHOW itself redisplays the one variable that changes value in READ SHOW with SHOW GET m.date, there is no need to refresh the entire READ window. Again, SHOW GETS OFF, not used here, will refresh all @ GETs without triggering READ SHOW.

Using READ SHOW with Output Fields

If you look over the READ SHOW clause carefully, you will note that there is no reason not to issue RETURN .T. immediately after _curobj = OBJNUM(m.date). Indeed, we might revise the READ SHOW clause as follows:

```
IF m.doit
    * Commands preparing Append action.
    _curobj = OBJNUM(m.date)
    RETURN .T.
ENDIF
SCATTER MEMVAR
m.pres_bal = current+days30+days60+days90+days120
```

The reason we do not write our READ SHOW clause this way is simple. Though we use @ GET input field to place our customer's present balance on the screen, using a memvar to recalculate it as needed, the job of representing data on the screen that is not subject to editing can just as easily be arranged by using an *output* field instead. (Ouput fields are also defined with the Screen Builder Field dialog.) All we do is supply FoxPro with the expression to use. If we do not do this to display our customer's present balance, it is because @ GET enables us to display the balance with the same screen colors and border as our other @ GETs without going to additional trouble—though we must write out the calculation for m.pres_bal ourselves and stick it in READ SHOW.

Still, suppose we were to use an output field instead of an input field for our customer's present balance. FoxPro uses @ SAY to calculate and display the balance and, when generating the screen program, based upon our work with the Screen Builder, places the @ SAY command at the very end of READ SHOW!

Though it would not make much difference in the case of Payments.spr, FoxPro's behavior in this regard will make it bad policy to use RETURN in the midst of READ SHOW unless you specifically do not want FoxPro to refresh any defined output fields. If you bear this in mind, you will avoid being puzzled one day by FoxPro's failure to update your output fields properly. This usually happens when RETURN terminates READ SHOW before FoxPro gets to @ SAY.

Controlling Operator Entry and MBS Processing of Transaction Records

Having reviewed the use of @ GET popup to trap the operator's selection of payment type (P_code), the rest of the process of payment entry would require no comment were it not for *system-level* considerations.

Owing to the use of Payment table records in producing customer statements, the date the operator enters is not immaterial to the system. As you may recall, statements will detail all customer account transactions with dates falling within the current billing period as defined by the setting of Bizshare.last_bill. Every transaction with Date >= Bizshare.last_bill will be processed. (Again, unless otherwise changed, Bizshare.last_bill holds the date on which statements were last produced *and* the customer account fields updated. Following MBS protocol, according to which these activities are conducted first thing in the morning, Bizshare.last_bill also represents the date on which the new period begins.)

In the face of such system-level requirements, we court disaster if we give the operator complete freedom to overwrite the default transaction date offered by @ GET m.date. We must either prevent the operator from making any change to the default date or place some constraints on the operator's action. Anticipating the possibility that the operator may wish to enter payments left over the night before statements must be produced and will therefore want to change the default date to an earlier date in order to include them in statements (without having to subsequently worry about the setting of Bizshare.last_bill), we choose to allow changes to m.date but use @ GET RANGE to hold the operator to dates falling in the current period. As the Screen Builder Field dialog box used to define @ GET m.date indicates (see Figure 5.10), we easily achieve our end by plugging m.last_bill (initialized in the setup code to hold Bizshare.last_bill) into the Lower and DATE() into the Upper Range box, respectively. This way, entries outside the defined range will be automatically rejected and the operator forced to make a valid entry.

To assist the operator in knowing what's required, we also plug a character string into the @ GET MESSAGE box, though the complete expression is not visible in the Field dialog box. When the cursor is activated in @ GET m.date, FoxPro evaluates and displays the MESSAGE, shown below in its entirety, in the status bar at the bottom of the screen.

```
"Enter transaction date between "+ DTOC(m.last_bill)+ ;
    " and "+DTOC(DATE())+"."
```

Using DTOC() to convert the two dates to type C, we manage to include the date range in the message. Of course, if the operator makes an improper entry, falling outside the indicated RANGE, FoxPro automatically uses the values entered with RANGE to display an appropriate error message in the FoxPro System Message window also used by WAIT window, as shown in Figure 5.11.

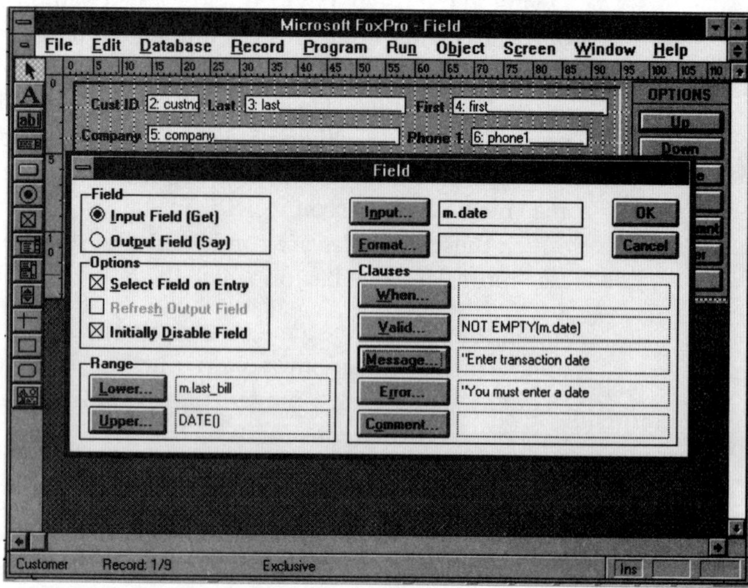

FIGURE 5.10:

Data entry of transaction date is controlled through use of @ GET RANGE.

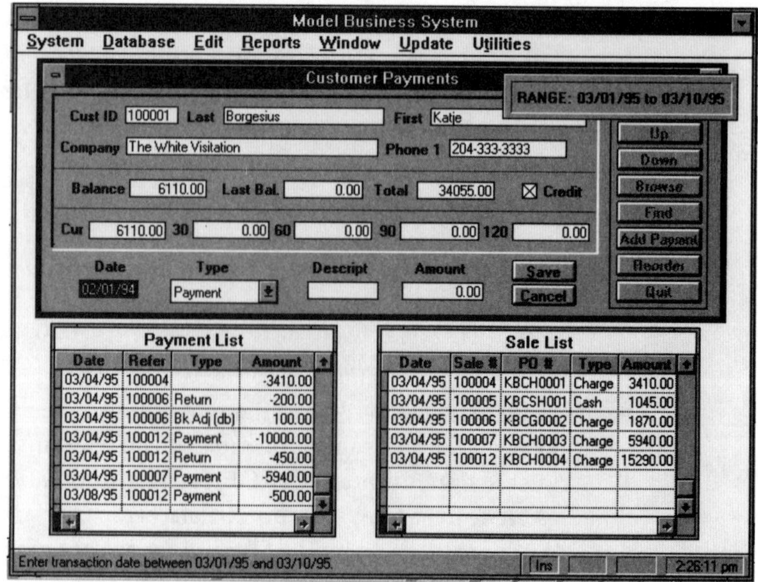

FIGURE 5.11:

FoxPro uses its own error message when an operator's entry falls outside @ GET RANGE.

We also use an @ GET VALID condition of NOT EMPTY(m.date) to make sure the operator doesn't erase the default date and then leave the field blank.

Another thing we must take into consideration is operator entry of amounts. Since we display negative amounts in the Payment List BROWSE window for customer credits but actually expect the operator to enter positive values for both debits and credits, we must be certain to inhibit the accidental entry of negative values. This we do, once again, using @ GET RANGE with m.amount to establish a lower bound of 0.00 and MESSAGE to supply the operator with appropriate instructions. In Figure 5.12, we show the Field dialog for @ GET m.amount with its nested Message dialog, used to enter a lengthy expression or a procedure (actually a UDF) returning an <expC>, open on the screen. If the operator makes an inappropriate entry to @ GET m.amount, FoxPro will automatically use the entry for Lower Range as an error message.

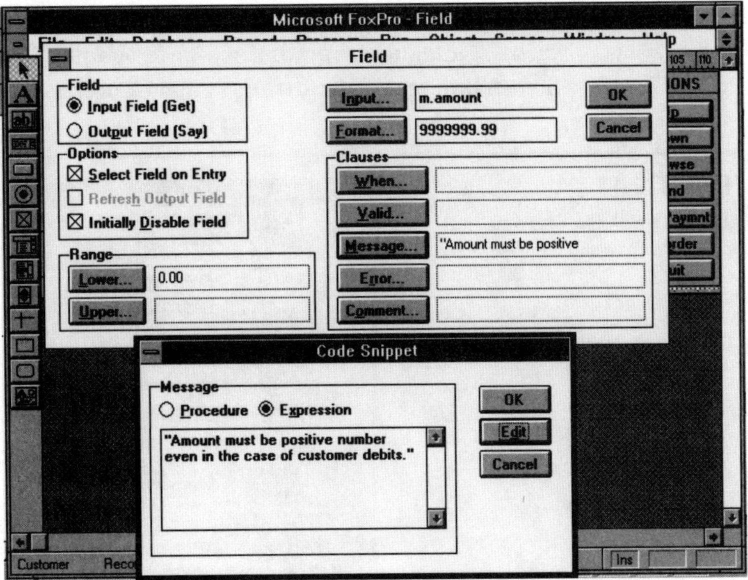

FIGURE 5.12: Use @ GET MESSAGE to aid the operator in making data entry.

TIP

The VALID clause of @ GET can be used to return error messages without the use of the ERROR clause. Just use WAIT WINDOW <expC> in the VALID clause to display the message. This gives greater flexibility since you can specify different error messages and determine which one is displayed through use of IF. Some programmers avoid using RANGE, choosing instead to use VALID to test the range and issue error messages as needed. This cuts down the number of clauses that need to be entered with a single @ GET.

Once again, operator entry of transaction P_descript is optional. We label it Refer, short for *Reference,* in the Customer Payments window to suggest its typical use for linking payments to sales in the customer statement through operator entry of an MBS sale number.

Turning now to the @ GET push button VALID clause overseeing program action when the operator selects Save or Cancel (see Figure 5.13), there should be no surprises. Note, however, that we once again define our push button options in the Screen Builder Popup dialog so that Cancel is automatically selected if the operator

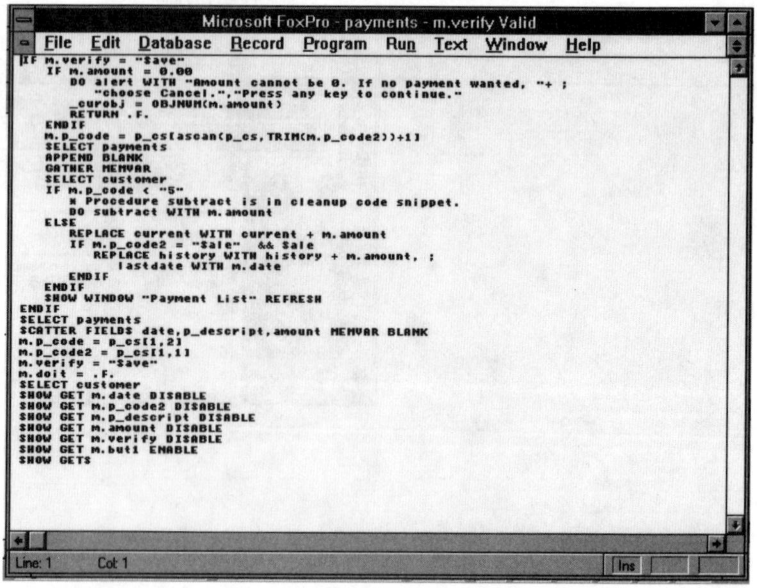

FIGURE 5.13:

UDF used with the Payment program's Save and Cancel push buttons

```
Microsoft FoxPro - payments - m.verify Valid
File  Edit  Database  Record  Program  Run  Text  Window  Help
IF m.verify = "Save"
   IF m.amount = 0.00
      DO alert WITH "Amount cannot be 0. If no payment wanted, "+ ;
         "choose Cancel.","Press any key to continue."
      _curobj = OBJNUM(m.amount)
      RETURN .F.
   ENDIF
   m.p_code = p_cs[ascan(p_cs,TRIM(m.p_code2))+1]
   SELECT payments
   APPEND BLANK
   GATHER MEMVAR
   SELECT customer
   IF m.p_code < "5"
      * Procedure subtract is in cleanup code snippet.
      DO subtract WITH m.amount
   ELSE
      REPLACE current WITH current + m.amount
      IF m.p_code2 = "Sale"  && Sale
         REPLACE history WITH history + m.amount, ;
            lastdate WITH m.date
      ENDIF
   ENDIF
   SHOW WINDOW "Payment List" REFRESH
ENDIF
SELECT payments
SCATTER FIELDS date,p_descript,amount MEMVAR BLANK
m.p_code = p_cs[1,2]
m.p_code2 = p_cs[1,1]
m.verify = "Save"
m.doit = .F.
SELECT customer
SHOW GET m.date DISABLE
SHOW GET m.p_code2 DISABLE
SHOW GET m.p_descript DISABLE
SHOW GET m.amount DISABLE
SHOW GET m.verify DISABLE
SHOW GET m.but1 ENABLE
SHOW GETS
Line: 1     Col: 1                                   Ins
```

presses the Esc key. (This is done by placing the symbol \? in front of the Cancel prompt in the Push Button dialog, as described in Chapter 4.)

With respect to our UDF, if Save is selected, we first check to make sure an actual amount has been entered. If not, we execute procedure Alert, discussed in Chapter 3, to warn the operator of the problem and send the cursor back to the Amount field. However, assuming the amount passes muster, we use ASCAN() as previously described to look up the P_code corresponding to the operator's popup selection of payment Type in memory array P_cs. Since we leave Customer.dbf current while executing Payments.spr, we must SELECT Payments before using APPEND BLANK and GATHER MEMVAR to create and update the new transaction record. There is no need to worry about payment.custno receiving the right value since m.custno, the value used by GATHER to update the field, takes its value from Customer.custno (in READ SHOW) and not from Payments.custno. This obviously makes no difference to FoxPro when we issue GATHER MEMVAR.

Once the record is created, we turn our attention to updating the account fields of the current customer record. Here we use the payment code, held in m.p_code, as described earlier in this chapter, to determine whether the transaction is a debit or credit. If it is a credit—P_code < "5"—we execute procedure Subtract, as described in Chapter 2, to subtract the credit from the debt-aging fields, working our way from Days120 to Current. If it is a debit we simply add the amount to the Current field. As an additional consideration, supposing the transaction is intended to represent a customer sale—P_code = "5"—we also use the amount to update Customer.history, indicating the customer's total purchases (whether cash or charge) and use m.date to update Customer.lastdate, indicating the date of the customer's last purchase. (Bear in mind, if you change the function of P_code = "5" in P_codes.dbf, holding the payment type codes, you may want to prevent Customer.history and Customer.lastdate from being updated. Simply strip out the REPLACE command and the IF/ENDIF overseeing its execution.)

Refreshing BROWSE Windows during READ

The last command specifically issued with Save is SHOW WINDOW "Payment List" REFRESH. This must be issued in order to immediately update the Payment List BROWSE window to include the payment just entered. The SHOW WINDOW command is normally used to redisplay windows and, optionally, to control their ordering (front-to-back placement) on the screen. We will use it for this purpose in Chapter 10. Here, however, we use it with REFRESH, which is specifically designed to update a BROWSE window without having to reselect it.

Having come to the end of the update activity, we finish the routine by preparing to execute SHOW GETS. Here we join hands with the Cancel action, which must perform the same tasks. Since SHOW GETS will execute our READ SHOW routine, all we need do is reset our memvars to their values prior to execution of Append Payment (repeating much the same commands used in our setup code) and use SHOW GET to disable the @ GETs used for transaction entry and to reenable our Up/Down...Quit push buttons. Then we are ready to go on with the SHOW.

Editing Payment Table Transactions

Unlike its handling of sales, the MBS includes no facility for editing transactions entered with Payments.spr. This is usual practice in accounting systems since it is easy to key in a book adjustment correcting an erroneous entry and difficult, if not impossible, to program the adjustments that must be made to the customer account fields owing to the editing of a customer credit. We would require a means of recalling the settings of the customer's debt-aging fields at the time the transaction was entered in order to restore the account fields to their correct settings. Rather than venture into a programming nightmare entirely fruitless in a system designed for generic uses, we therefore stick to the traditional approach. Instead of editing or erasing transactions in Payments.dbf, the operator must enter Book Adj transactions.

The Payments Program READ DEACTIVATE and Cleanup Code

When the operator selects the Quit push button, terminating READ with the CLEAR READ command, the Payments entry program ends by issuing the following commands:

```
IF but1 = "Quit"
    RELEASE WINDOW "Payments"
```

```
ENDIF
RELEASE WINDOW "Payment List"
RELEASE WINDOW "Sale List"
SET SKIP OF BAR 2 OF Database .F.
SET TOPIC TO
```

As should be clear, we use our cleanup code—the name used to refer to the commands following READ in a screen program—to manually release our windows. We also use SET SKIP OF BAR to reactivate the Payments option on the Database pulldown and SET TOPIC TO without any parameter so that F1 or Help will access our Help file's table of contents instead of a specific entry.

The only surprise in the cleanup code is that the release of our READ window is made conditional on the operator's selection of the Quit push button. Why should we do this? The answer is simple. Here we prepare for a window-level event. In the MBS we will allow the operator to have several READ windows associated with different screen programs on the screen at once. Figure 5.14, for example, shows Payments.spr being run with the READ window belonging to Customer.spr still on the screen in the background. (I have moved the windows to show the Window pulldown open without covering the READ window titles.) Suppose the operator were to use the mouse to click the Customers window or select it from the Window pulldown? Such an event, were we to allow it, would change the value of WONTOP(). It would therefore trigger the DEACTIVATE clause of our current READ. And as you will recall, the DEACTIVATE clause for Payments.spr is designed only to RETURN .F. and prevent the READ from terminating when the operator selects either of our BROWSE windows. The UDF otherwise RETURNs .T., terminating the READ without use of the Quit push button.

When this happens, assuming again that we allow such an event to take place, READ terminates as expected and our BROWSE windows are released, but our READ window, no longer the foremost (or active) window, is not released. It remains visible on the screen. The Customers window will be WONTOP(). How this triggers reexecution of Customer.spr is discussed in Chapter 10. For now, simply take note of how we prepare our Payments program for such an event.

Additional Uses of READ DEACTIVATE

Still, having broached the subject of this additional function of READ DEACTIVATE, it is well to take note of two additional functions of READ DEACTIVATE. Assuming we want to allow the operator to switch to another open READ window and rely on READ DEACTIVATE to terminate READ without closing the Customer

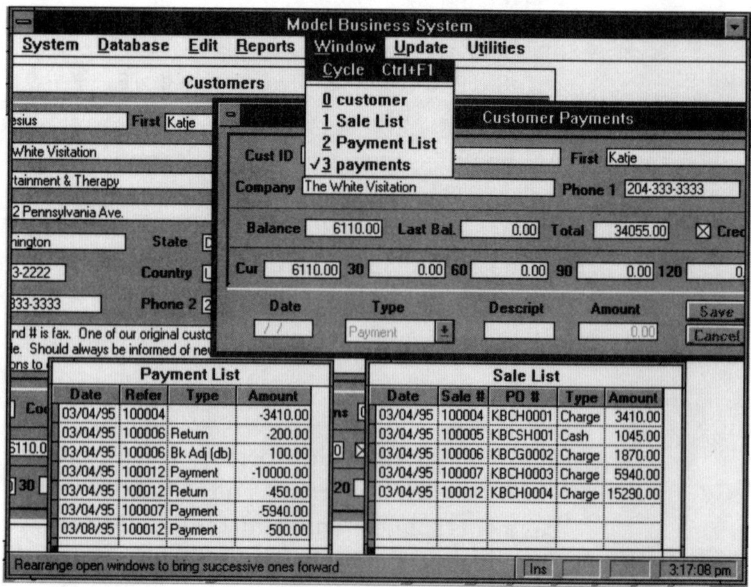

FIGURE 5.14:

In the MBS, the operator can select among programs by clicking the appropriate READ window.

Payments window (again, we bypass the command owing to the value of m.but1 when Quit is not selected), won't this negatively affect operator use of the Close option in the control box? Close also triggers READ DEACTIVATE, but it should also release the Payments window. As it stands, it will not do so unless we rework the DEACTIVATE clause to reinitialize m.but1 = "Quit" if Close has been selected. Since Close does in fact close the window before DEACTIVATE is consulted, we can test for this state of affairs by testing WVISIBLE("payments").

Before showing how we can rewrite our DEACTIVATE clause to take care of this matter, there is one further consideration. Suppose the operator is in the midst of entering a payment—or, more generally, entering or editing data with any other MBS data entry program. Do we want to enable the operator to terminate the READ by using Close or by selecting another (inactive) READ window?

Though this will rarely cause problems in the MBS, owing to the use of memvars during data entry and edit, it is not wise to enable such events while data is being entered since whatever data has been entered but not saved with the READ window will not reappear on the screen if and when the window is reactivated. (We explain why this is so in Chapter 6.) Where programs work directly with data fields or in situations in which the Append and Edit routines are not programmed as discrete actions that can be abandoned without adversely affecting the integrity of other data values, this should be strictly forbidden.

Given the way MBS data entry programs are written to set memvar m.doit to .T. whenever an Append or Edit routine is launched, we can disallow closing of the window during data entry (when the Quit push button is inaccessible) by simply testing the value of m.doit.

Here, then, is a revised DEACTIVATE clause that will take charge of these several matters:

```
IF UPPER(WONTOP()) $ "PAYMENT LIST SALE LIST"
    RETURN .F.
ENDIF
IF m.doit
    DO alert WITH ;
        "Cannot change windows until editing is over.", ;
        "Press any key to continue."
    ACTIVATE WINDOW payments
    RETURN .F.
ENDIF
IF NOT WVISIBLE("payments")
    m.but1 = "Quit"
ENDIF
RETURN .T.
```

The first IF/ENDIF prevents the termination of READ owing to operator selection of either BROWSE window, as discussed earlier in this chapter. The second uses m.doit to make sure that use of the Close push button or operator selection of another (inactive) READ window fails. Procedure Alert is called to advise the operator that the action will not be allowed before ACTIVATE WINDOW is used to reinstate the window Payments as WONTOP(). (Note that our READ window is not released by Close, nor does clicking another READ window or selecting a READ window from the Window pulldown release the current window. These events simply *deactivate* the window. For this reason, we are not obliged to redraw window Payments. Everything is still there.) RETURN .F. then renews the append or edit action just where it was broken off.

Having dispensed with the conditions that lead us to prevent READ from terminating, we need only distinguish between the effects of operator selection of Close and operator selection of another READ window. Only in the case of Close do we want to release the Payments window. The effect must be the same as selecting Quit; and to make it so, we simply initialize m.but1 = "Quit" if the Payments window is no longer visible (indicating use of Close). In all other cases, however, RETURN .T. is executed, the READ is terminated, and the cleanup code is executed as the program comes to an end, thus conditionally managing the releasing of the Payments window.

A Word of Caution in Learning Window-Level Event Handling

Now that you have been introduced to most of the window-level events we must plan for in designing our screen programs, I must nonetheless caution you to go slowly. The most important thing at this point is to gain a competent knowledge of the various possible events and the commands and functions than must be used to allow or disallow them.

In the disk version of the MBS, for example, the Payments DEACTIVATE CLAUSE is yet more complicated, though not by much. We have yet to address the issue of accessing the FoxPro desk accessories during READ. How should that be managed? Whenever BROWSE windows are included in the READ, this also leads to further complications if we determine to allow switching to other (inactive) READ windows. As you may recall—and this is an important detail to hold on to—BROWSE does not count as a READ window. When one of our BROWSE windows is WONTOP(), Payments is still the active READ window. (This would be indicated by the WREAD() function, which is specifically designed to return the name of the active READ window.) Consequently, were we to switch to BROWSE and then click an inactive READ window, that window would become WONTOP(), but Payments.spr's READ DEACTIVATE clause would not be triggered. The new WONTOP() will appear dead on the screen since FoxPro, never having executed READ DEACTIVATE, is still waiting to continue working with WREAD(). Only leaving the READ window triggers DEACTIVATE.

Bear in mind also that it is quite unnecessary to allow all the window-level events we are describing. If we go to pains to make the MBS a fairly compex nonmodal application, this is because it is designed to show you how to write a well-wrought windows program. But it is hardly necessary to go so far. Recall the use of READ MODAL with Erase.spr and Cus_find.spr to prevent the operator from selecting any other window or using the MBS main menu while the dialog box is active. Both screen programs must be terminated with Close or through selection of a push button executing CLEAR READ. We might just as easily make Payments.spr and Customer.spr (which also employs a READ DEACTIVATE clause similar to Payments') into simpler MODAL READ programs. In the case of Payments, we can still allow the operator access to the BROWSE windows and even to the FoxPro desk accessories during a modal READ, provided that we use the optional READ WITH clause to supply FoxPro with a list of the windows we want to make accessible. Any window not included in the associated window list with WITH <windows> remains inaccessible. Were we to work in this way, the present READ DEACTIVATE clause would be perfectly satisfactory to our needs, though we might need to expand the list of windows tested in the first line with IF WONTOP() $ to include the names of all the windows listed in the READ WITH <associated window> clause.

We will have more to say about these matters, including modal reads, in Chapter 6 and Chapter 10. So go slowly and just take in the possibilities.

NOTE

Assuming you create your screen programs as you should using the FoxPro Screen Builder, you will not specify READ MODAL or an associated window list until you generate the screen program. This is simply done with the Generate Screen or Edit Screen dialog, discussed in Chapter 11.

MBS Generation and Handling of Interest Charges

Though we provide the MBS operator with the ability to enter interest charges against customer accounts using Payments.spr, this is not the way they will be typically entered into the system—supposing they are used at all. As mentioned in Chapter 2, the debt-aging fields are arranged to give us immediate access to customer debts, which, according to most state laws, are legally subject to interest charges. That amount will be found in Customer.days120. If interest charges are to be levied on a monthly basis, this is best done programmatically and always, as a matter of MBS protocol, immediately before the generation of statements, to avoid the danger of generating interest charges twice over in one month.

WARNING If you don't need to generate finance charges in your system, it's best to remove the Generate Finance Charges option from the MBS main menu. Accidents will happen, and it will be difficult to reverse the effects of this program without some effort.

To generate finance charges, the operator selects the Generate Finance Charges option from the Update pulldown. This executes Finance.spr, a simple modal screen program that uses the dialog shown in Figure 5.15. Like Erase.spr, which served as a template for creating it, Finance.spr does no more than request action validation before executing finance charges.

The Cancel and Close options in the control box can both be used to break off further execution of the program. Proceed, on the other hand, triggers execution of procedure Generate, which, for the sake of convenience, is placed directly in Erase.spr after the RETURN following the cleanup code that terminates the actual program. (We discuss FoxPro program and screen program architecture in Chapters 8 and 11.)

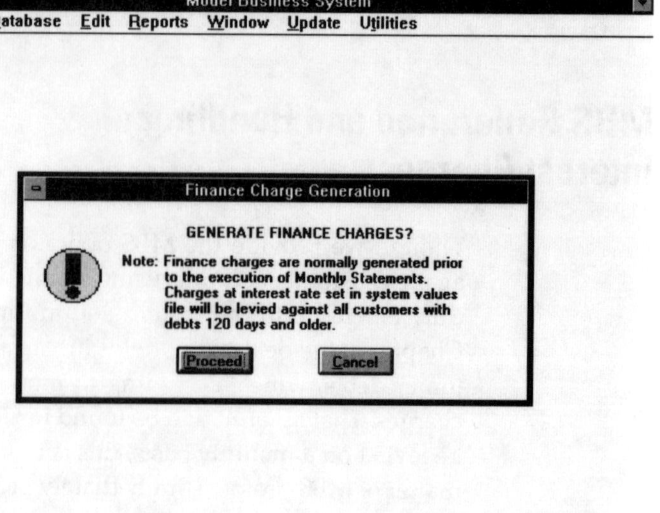

FIGURE 5.15: Action dialog used during finance charge generation

WARNING

Finance charges are automatically given a P_code of "6", corresponding to the P_code values currently stored in P_codes.dbf and used by the MBS system. If you change the payment code schema, altering the P_code used to represent interest charges, you must change the value used in Finance.spr as well.

As stated in Chapter 2, MBS regards interest charges levied against customers as *current* debits. They are consequently used to update Customer.current and not Customer.days120. So that finance charges will be detailed in the customer statements about to be written, not only must we store them in Payments.dbf, we must also give them a Payment.date of DATE()–1. Otherwise, if Bizshare.last_bill is updated to hold DATE() after statements are printed, the finance charges will be dated as falling in the next billing period. (Since we use only a lower bound to define the current period during statement production, they will, moreover, be included in the current run of statements as well.) In any case, be aware of the significance of the assigned date if you alter MBS statement-printing protocol. We naturally assign the records added to the Payments table a P_code of "6", corresponding to the P_code currently assigned to represent interest charges in P_codes.dbf. The simplest version of procedure Generate will include the following commands:

```
m.interest = Bizshare.interest
SELECT customer
SET RELATION OFF
SET ORDER TO
SCAN FOR customer.days120 > 0.00
    m.charge = ROUND(customer.days120 * m.interest,2)
    INSERT INTO payments (custno,date,P_code,amount) ;
        VALUES (customer.custno,DATE()-1,"6",m.charge)
    REPLACE customer.current WITH customer.current + m.charge
ENDSCAN
```

TIP

With FoxPro you can use SQL-INSERT to append a blank record to the end of any table, whether it is open or not, while also placing values in the fields of the new record. This is faster than using APPEND BLANK and REPLACE.

Here we simply scan Customer.dbf for customers with outstanding debts of 120 days or more. Whenever such a record is found, we calculate the interest charge on the basis of Bizshare.interest, the MBS system value for interest rate. (Again, this can be changed at any time using the MBS System Values option on the Utilities pulldown.) We then use the SQL-INSERT command to append a record to the end of Payments.dbf while filling its referenced fields with the indicated VALUES, execute REPLACE to update Customer.current accordingly, and move on to the next record.

To work most quickly, the relation between the two tables should be set off and any master index disengaged. Since no index tag is maintained for Customer.days120, SET OPTIMIZE cannot help. If you choose, however, you can add an index tag for Days120 to make the routine execute more quickly with the aid of Rushmore.

Using SQL-INSERT

Unlike the Xbase INSERT command, which is still supported by FoxPro, SQL-INSERT is designed to add a record to the end of the table designated with INTO <file>. Since it works more quickly than APPEND BLANK and REPLACE, it is the preferred tool when adding records to a table. (If the table referenced with INTO <file> is not open, FoxPro automatically opens it to insert the new record.) In our example command, repeated below, we use the field and VALUE list options to direct specific values to fields designated by name:

```
INSERT INTO payments (custno,date,P_code,amount) ;
   VALUES (customer.custno,DATE()-1,"6",m.charge)
```

Note that unlike traditional Xbase syntax, we are expected to place our field and value lists in parentheses. Each data value in the VALUES list is transferred to the corresponding field in the field list. Still, the field list is optional. When omitted, the values are transferred to fields according to the fields' order in the table structure.

Giving SQL-INSERT even greater functionality are the FROM MEMVAR and FROM ARRAY <array> options, which allow you to use INSERT FROM MEMVAR and INSERT FROM ARRAY in place of APPEND BLANK and GATHER MEMVAR or GATHER FROM ARRAY <array>. In the case of INSERT FROM MEMVAR, FoxPro will fill the new record with data taken from memvars having the same name as table fields. With FROM ARRAY, the fields are filled with array elements according to field order in the table structure. Where memvars or array elements are unavailable to update fields, the fields are left empty.

Making an Intelligent Batch Update Routine

The obvious shortcoming of procedure Generate, as presented above, is that it is wholly unprotected against power failures, computer lockups, crashes, and the like. Still, if disaster occurs in the midst of running procedure Generate, we can make it unnecessary to immediately restore yesterday's backup copies of the MBS tables before running the procedure again—that is, supposing our tables otherwise survive the crash intact. We do so by making the program intelligent enough to avoid generating duplicate interest charge records to any customer even if the program is run than once on the same (billing) day. This will, naturally, run a good deal more slowly than the simpler version, but in the long run it is probably the safer way to go. Here then are the crucial commands in procedure Generate as it appears in Generate.spr:

```
m.interest = bizshare.interest
SELECT customer
SET RELATION OFF INTO sales
* Relation to Payments.dbf is still active.
orig_rec = RECNO()
orig_ord = ORDER()
SET ORDER TO
SCAN ALL FOR customer.days120 > 0.00
    IF NOT EOF("payments")
        SELECT payments
        LOCATE WHILE custno = customer.Custno ;
            FOR p_code = "6" AND date = DATE() - 1
        IF FOUND()
            SELECT customer
            LOOP
        ENDIF
    ENDIF
    m.charge = ROUND(customer.days120 * m.interest,2)
    INSERT INTO payments (custno,date,P_code,amount) ;
        VALUES (customer.custno,DATE()-1,"6",m.charge)
    REPLACE customer.current WITH customer.current + m.charge
    SELECT customer
ENDSCAN
SET RELATION TO custno INTO sales ADDITIVE
SET ORDER TO orig_ord
IF NOT BOF AND NOT EOF()
    GO orig_rec
ENDIF
```

As we start with our default customer database view, we deactivate Customer.dbf's relation to Sales.dbf, since it is not involved in the batch update, and deactivate the master index while saving its name and the current record number to memvars. We then begin our SCAN of Customer.dbf. When a customer account with a debit of 120 days or older turns up, we test the value of EOF("payments") to see if SET RELATION has located a record. If payment records are on file for that customer—EOF() = .F.—we SELECT Payments and use LOCATE WHILE to search only the payments on file for that customer. We obviously do so to see if an interest charge has been entered bearing the date assigned by procedure Generate. If such a record is already on file, we move back to the Customer table and execute LOOP to go on with the SCAN. On the other hand, if no payment records are found—or no payment that meets the criteria by which we check for an interest charge entered by a previous run of the program—we go ahead and create the payment record and update the customer account fields accordingly. When the SCAN ends, we finish by restoring Customer.dbf's relation to Sales.dbf, reset the master index, and return FoxPro to the record that was current before the procedure was executed. (Here again, the GO command will produce an error when Customer.dbf is empty. We therefore arrange to bypass it if that is the case.)

You can decide for yourself to leave the more complex procedure Generate in Finance.spr or change to the simpler one.

NOTE

Though we have only mentioned the index tag Payments key expression, Custno, in this chapter, be aware that Payments.dbf includes two additional indexes in its structural compound index file. Index tag Deleted (key expression: DELETED()) and index tag Date (key expression: Date) are both maintained for use with SQL-SELECT when preparing customer payment reports. (See Chapter 12.)

Converting the MBS into a Donation-Tracking System

Bear in mind that most donation-tracking systems involve only two main tables: a donors table, listing name and address information about each donor, and a donations table, listing all contributions. The functions of these two tables are, of course, easily handled by Customer.dbf and Payments.dbf, even as they are presently used by MBS. You can therefore readily convert the MBS for use as a donation-tracking system by first stripping out all portions of the program related to sales, inventory, and the production of customer statements. Then turn your attention to modifying the Payments entry program with the Screen Builder to exclude the Sale List BROWSE window, change the available P_codes to functions as needed, and change the labeling of the @ GETs in the READ window. Of course, other cosmetic changes will be necessary. Whenever the word *Customer* appears, you will want to change it to *Donor,* and wherever *Payment* appears, you will want to change it to *Donation*. Note, however, that tables and fields need not be renamed since the operator need never see them. If you're concerned about *Customer* appearing in the status bar when the Customer table is current, just SET MESSAGE TO "". This will keep the status bar message area blank except when it is used by @ GET MESSAGE/ERROR and the like. You can also use SET MESSAGE TO <expC> to display any other message in the status bar when it is not being otherwise employed. Where inappropriate field names are used as BROWSE column headings, simply use the <field>:H=<expC> or heading option to change them. The rest should be easy.

CHAPTER

SIX

Designing the Sales Entry Program

- Working with a default multi-table view
- Using nested screen programs
- Creating and using nonmodal screen programs
- Linking nonmodal screen programs
- Creating a Sales Transaction entry program
- Automatic input of data with pick lists

Designing a Sales entry program is a different kettle of fish. This is because, unlike payments, sales include line items. Moreover, if any errors are made in entering sale items, reasonable facilities must be offered for fixing them, whether by adding, deleting, or editing items. Too much work goes into entering a sale to toss it aside when a close look at the invoice turns up an error. Indeed, out of sympathy for the operator, we may even go so far as to enable editing of invoices after they have been saved to disk. Imagine, for example, the chagrin of the poor sod who punches in a long sale, prints it out, and saves it to disk and then discovers that it was really a charge and not a cash sale. But giving the operator the capacity to change a sale after the fact is no mean task since it requires us to make adjustments to the customer's account as well.

With regard to the user interface supplied by our Sales program, we must also be aware of the operator's need for an orderly procedure with built-in safeguards. While we want to supply the operator with every convenience afforded by the FoxPro programming language, we don't want to get carried away, leaving the operator awash in a sea of windows, wildly clicking one after the other in order to finish with an invoice—though this problem is, admittedly, diminished if we allow the operator to recall and edit a sale that was accidentally closed and saved to disk.

Designing the Sales Table

As mentioned in Chapter 1, the MBS employs three tables in addition to Customer.dbf during sales invoice entry, as shown in Figure 6.1. The Summary Sales table, Sales.dbf, is designed to hold information about each sale that will be required during statement production. The Custno field serves to link the table as a child to Customer.dbf with SET RELATION. Saleno, our sales number field, is used to store a unique sales number in the series 100000–999999. A sales number is assigned to each sale by incrementing the value of Bizshare.saleno, which is designed to store the last Saleno assigned by the system. (See Chapter 2 for more on the use of the MBS system value table, Bizshare.dbf.)

As for our S_code, or sales code, field, we use it to distinguish between cash and charge sales, assigning a 1 to cash sales and a 2 to charges. If at any time we need

FIGURE 6.1:
Structure of the MBS Sales, Sales Detail, and Inventory tables

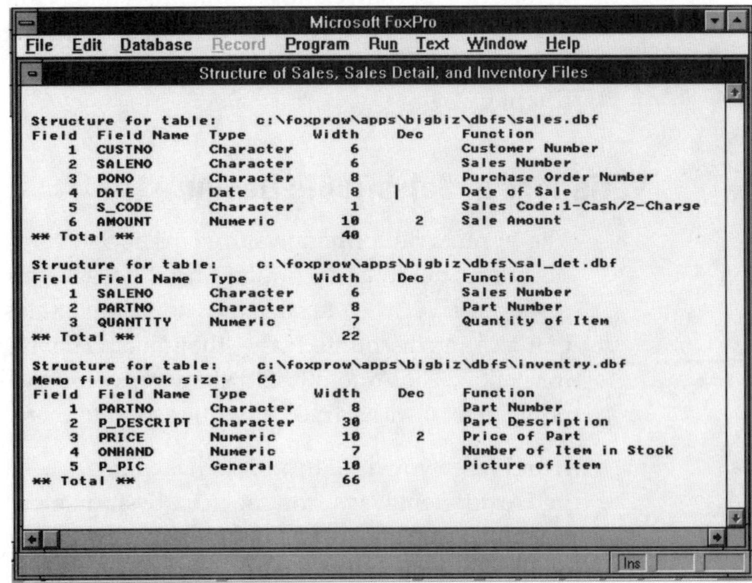

to distinguish between the two—for example, when displaying records on the screen—we simply use the following algorithm:

```
IIF(s_code = "1","Cash","Charge")
```

The function of the other fields should be readily apparent, though once again, we must give thought to the Date field. As with Payments.date, we must be certain that no date is entered that falls outside the current period. Moreover, if we are to permit the editing of sales, we must also be sure that only *current* sales can be so manipulated. (Fixing the books to handle changes to sales outside the current period is not only unconventional, it would also be impossible to program, at least with regard to properly updating the customer account fields.) In any case, changes to the customer account resulting, for example, from return of goods, can be adequately handled through Payments.spr. Indeed, though we programmatically restrict editing of sales invoices to those falling in the current period, operators should be advised to use the edit sale facility yet more conservatively. It is intended to make day-to-day work easier; it should not be used as a means of playing around with week-old sales.

In order to support its relation to Customer.dbf, Sales.dbf is indexed on Custno. However, we makes Sales.dbf's master index, Sales, a compound index tag, using the expression Custno + Saleno. This way, customer sales will always be arranged in their order of entry into the system. (The Sales table's structural compound index also includes index tags based on Date and DELETED() since these are required for optimization of Sales reports through the use of SQL-SELECT, as discussed in Chapter 12.)

Variations in Sales Table Design

The summary information stored in the Sales table should be suitable for most applications, but it has its limitations. It does not, for example, include a Tax field to distinguish between taxable and nontaxable sales; nor does it provide any means of indicating discounted sales, though our client may wish to keep track of such information. The Amount field shows only the total of the sale; it does not indicate how the total was arrived at with respect to these things.

If and when you need to add such facilities to a Sales Entry program, you can work in two different ways. You can actually add fields to Sales.dbf, for example, to indicate the actual tax or discount rate applied with a sale. Or you can choose instead to alter the sales code schema used with S_code to include more options. There is no need to limit it to cash and charge. You can add cash-taxed, charge-tax, and the like, as long as you revise the Sales program and related reports to handle the additional codes. The more elaborate payment codes used with Payments.spr will provide you with an example of how to go about doing this.

Entering Nontaxable Sales with the MBS

Though the MBS is not designed to distinguish between taxable and nontaxable sales, the Sales program can be made to enter and print invoices for nontaxable sales, owing to the storage of the present tax rate in the system value table, Bizshare.dbf. If you need to enter nontaxable sales, the value of Bizshare.taxrat can be set to 0.00. Of course, you must be certain to set the system tax rate back to its usual value when you are through or go on entering nontaxable sales. Still, this is a work-around, not a design feature. Bizshare.taxrat is used to make the system flexible in the face of changing tax rates. That it also enables the system to support nontaxable sales will prove to be a blessing if used with care. (The same stricture applies to entering sales with different tax rates.)

Designing the Sales Detail and Inventory Tables

As you already know, the Sales Detail table, Sal_det.dbf, and the Inventory table, Inventry.dbf, go together in the MBS, the latter primarily serving as an inventory/price list for use during sales invoice entry. On the other hand, the Inventory table is sophisticated enough to include an Onhand field. This is used to keep track of the quantity of each inventory item still in stock, though its use is optional. Still, from the standpoint of inventory management, a solitary Onhand field is mere child's play. It may, for example, be necessary to keep a detailed account of the quantity of each item sold in a week, a month, over several months, or over a year. This will require an array of additional fields, as well as programming code and reports to take advatange of them. They can be added to Inventry.dbf or stored in a transaction table that can be linked into Inventry.dbf through the use of Partno. It may also be necessary to include item cost so, along with sales figures, the system can produce reports indicating the relative profitability of items or even serve as an aid in projecting profits as based upon different price schemas. Inventry.dbf does not include a Cost field, and the MBS is not prepared to report on the profitability of sales items.

Our present Inventory table does include an additional General field that is used by the MBS to store pictures or drawings of each inventory item. The Inventory window, shown in Figure 6.2, however, is the only place in the MBS where we use or display the pictures stored in Inventry.p_pic, though the window is accessible during sales invoice entry in case the operator or customer wants to refer to it. Here we need only note that pictures stored in a General field are displayed as output

Tracking the Number of Items Sold

Because of the way Inventry.onhand is updated by the Sales transaction program, it can be used in a roundabout way to keep track of the quantity of each item sold rather than the quantity of each item still in stock. Just leave the Onhand field of each record set to 0 when entering items in the Inventory table. When the item is sold, the figure in Onhand will be decreased by the number of items presumably taken from stock. Thus the number of each item sold will appear in Onhand, though it will be represented by a negative number. Needless to say, if you use Onhand in this way, you cannot use it to track stock levels. If you need to do both, you must add a field to Inventry.dbf.

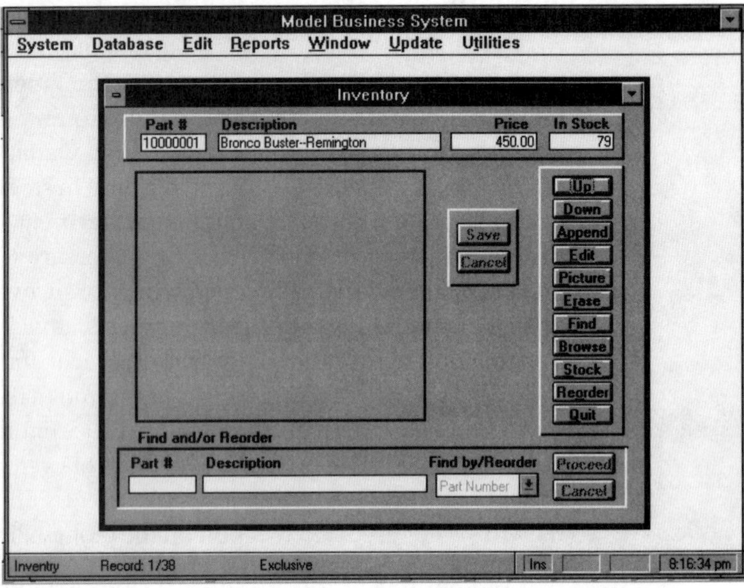

FIGURE 6.2:

The MBS Inventory table, Inventry.dbf, uses a General field to store pictures of inventory items.

fields using @ SAY, though they are defined in the Screen Builder with the Screen Picture dialog shown in Figure 6.3, not with the Field dialog. (The Screen Picture dialog is discussed in Chapter 11.)

Owing to its function as a lookup table, Inventry.dbf uses two index tags, Partno (key expression: Partno) and P_descript (key expression: UPPER(P_descript)). Index tag Partno allows us to link Inventry.dbf as a child table into Sal_det.dbf with SET RELATION so it will supply any display of sales items with the necessary part descriptions and prices. Sal_det.dbf, the table used to store records of each item included in a sale, need only hold the part number, or Partno. The two index tags, taken together, also supply us with a means of looking up items in the Inventory table by part number or by description, and we use both index tags for this purpose whenever the Inventory table must be consulted.

As already pointed out, the structure of our Sales Detail table, Sal_det.dbf, is determined by the role Inventry.dbf is designed to play during invoice entry. Since the Inventory table is used to supply part descriptions and prices automatically, Sal_det.dbf need hold no more than the Partno and Quantity of each item—and a Saleno linking it to a record in Sales.dbf. The total cost of each item (the extension) can be calculated on the fly. There is no need to store it in the table.

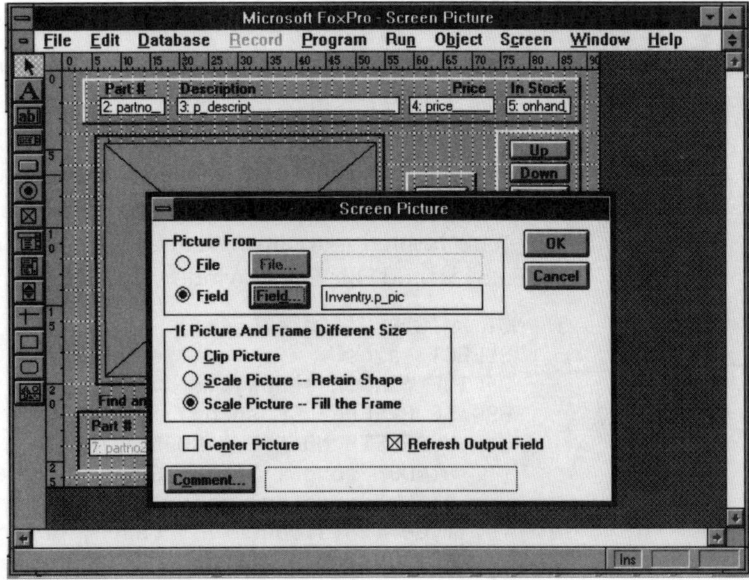

FIGURE 6.3:

Use the Screen Builder's Screen Picture dialog to place and size pictures in a window.

Still, as mentioned in Chapter 1, if you are dealing with an unstable inventory/price list, you will have to revise Sal_det.dbf and the MBS Sales entry program accordingly. If prices or part descriptions must be entered by the operator or if the operator is to be allowed to change the default price for items supplied by the Inventory table, Sal_det.dbf must be altered to include fields to hold item prices and/or descriptions, though here again, the system has some built-in flexibility. For example, if an item is to be sold at one or another price, two or more records can be entered in Inventry.dbf using the same part description but with different prices. During invoice entry, it will only be necessary for the operator to look up the part with the correct price.

Note that the only index tag employed with Sal_det.dbf uses a compound index key: Saleno + Partno. Since the table is always used with index tag Sal_det, the items displayed with any sale will always be arranged in order by Partno. This is intended to make it easier for the operator to find items entered into a sale and to check the printed invoice for errors.

We now turn our attention to the process of entering sales into our system.

Overview of the Sales Entry Program

The MBS Sales entry program begins innocuously enough with Sales.spr, which oversees the operation of the screen set shown in Figure 6.4. Once again, we have one READ window and two BROWSE windows. The function of the READ window is to locate the customer making the purchase or requiring a modified invoice. The function of the BROWSE windows is to display the customer's sales as well as the line items belonging to any given sale. The BROWSE commands used to supply the Sale List and Sale Detail windows are shown here:

```
IF NOT WVISIBLE("Sale List")
    SELECT sales
    DEFINE WINDOW sbrow1...
    BROWSE PREFERENCE sbrow1 ;
        NODELETE NOAPPEND NOEDIT NOMENU NORMAL NOWAIT ;
        WINDOW sbrow1 TITLE "Sale List" ;
        FIELDS date,saleno:H="Sale #",pono:H="PO #", ;
        Type=IIF(s_code="1","Cash","Charge"),amount ;
        KEY customer.custno FOR date > = m.last_bill
    RELEASE WINDOW sbrow1
ENDIF
IF NOT WVISIBLE("Sale Detail")
    SELECT sal_det
    DEFINE WINDOW sbrows2...
    BROWSE PREFERENCE sbrow2 ;
        NODELETE NOAPPEND NOEDIT NOMENU NORMAL NOWAIT ;
        WINDOW sbrow2 TITLE "Sale Detail" ;
        FIELDS sal_det.saleno:H="Sale #", ;
        Quantity:4,partno:H="Part #", ;
        invsales.p_descript:H="Description":12, ;
        invsales.Price:8, ;
        Extension = quantity * invsales.price:10 ;
        KEY sales.saleno
    RELEASE WINDOW sbrow2
ENDIF
```

At this point, however, there should be nothing particularly remarkable about these windows. Both are opened in the Sales program's READ ACTIVATE clause using predefined windows, which are immediately released (without erasing the BROWSE windows) in order to prevent them from being listed in the Window pulldown. Sale List and Sale Detail will be listed in the Window pulldown; Sbrow1 and Sbrow2 will not. (See Chapter 5 for the rules for the naming of windows used by BROWSE.)

FIGURE 6.4:

MBS Customer Sales window

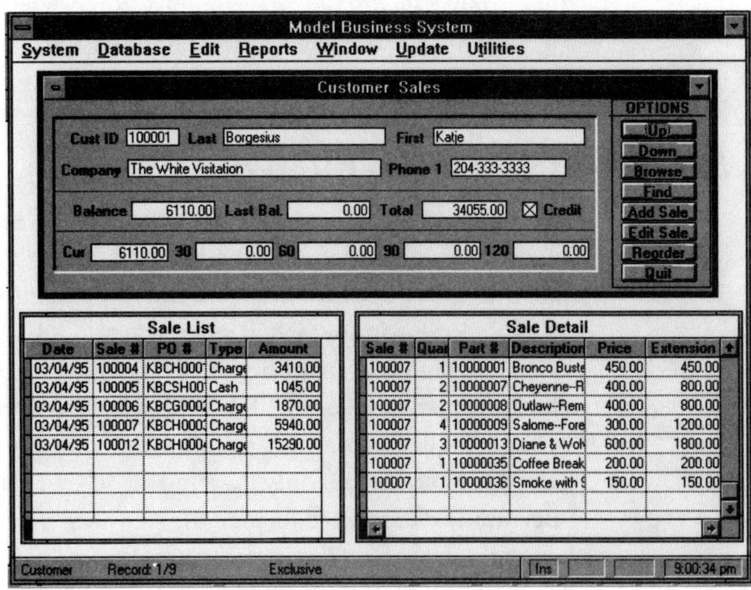

As with the BROWSE commands used by Payments.spr, wherever field names are unsuitable for use as column headings, we substitute special headings with the field heading option, :H = <expC>. We also include calculated fields, defined with <Calc. field name> = <exp>, as needed.

Because the tables referenced by the two BROWSE commands are linked in a chain with Customer.dbf, as discussed in the next section, wherever we go into Customer.dbf, the Sale List window is updated to show the current customer's sales, while the Sale Detail window is updated to show the line items included in the first sale appearing in the Sale List. To doubly enforce FoxPro's filtering of records appearing in the BROWSE windows (which to my mind is done somewhat clumsily using SET RELATION alone), we once again use KEY <index key> to make our needs explicit. (Again, with KEY, filtering is performed instantaneously using the master index.)

With respect to the first BROWSE command, we also use FOR date >= m.last_bill, where m.last_bill is initialized at the outset of the program to hold Bizshare.last_bill, representing the date on which the current billing period begins. This prevents the BROWSE window from including records of sales not belonging to the current period. And since all existing sales called for edit must first be made the current Sale.dbf record using the BROWSE window, this effectively prevents an operator from editing sales falling outside the current period.

Waiting for the Inactive BROWSE Highlight

Bear in mind that the current record in a BROWSE window is highlighted only when the cursor is active in the window. (Actually, only the current field is highlighted.) This makes it difficult, if not impossible, to tell which record is current in a BROWSE window when it is not active. We can hope to see an inactive BROWSE highlight in future versions of FoxPro, but under the present circumstances, having to work without it can lead to difficulties. For example, referring again to Figure 6.4, can you possibly determine which sale is current in the Sale List? Yes, you can, but only by referring to the Sale Detail window, which was specifically designed to display the sale number, Saleno. An inactive BROWSE highlight in the Sale List would make the use of Saleno in Sale Detail redundant. However, without it we would have no way of knowing which sale the items in the Sale Detail window belong to—quite aside from knowing which sale is current in the Sale List window. When using separate BROWSE windows to display data from two or more tables linked with SET RELATION, you must be prepared to display the key expression used in the child table(s) as a means of identifying its records with a parent record in an inactive BROWSE window or find some means of temporarily marking the current parent record.

Since the only significant action performed by Sales.spr, besides locating the right customer, is the actual launching of another screen program, its READ SHOW clause is quite simple:

```
IF EOF("sal_det")
    SHOW GET m.but1,6 DISABLE
 ELSE
    SHOW GET m.but1,6 ENABLE
ENDIF
SCATTER MEMVAR
m.pres_bal = current+days30+days60+days90+days120
```

In addition to preparing memvars for display of the current customer record, READ SHOW does no more than enable or disable the Edit Sale push button, depending upon whether or not the current sale actually has items on file in Sal_det.dbf.

With regard to the VALID clause of our @ GET push buttons, it is basically the same as what we have already seen with Customer and Payments.spr, except for the fact that Append and Edit Sale execute another screen program to perform the action. As we shall see, however, the called program is executed in an unusual way. It is not executed as a nested program (or dialog) of Sales.spr, like Cus_find.spr, our Customer table Find/Reorder dialog, but rather as a semiautonomous screen program with the same status as Customer, Payments, and Sales.spr, except for this one difference: It cannot be executed directly from the Database pulldown. It is always launched from within Sales.spr. (We will return to this shortly.)

Entering New Customers during Execution of the Sales Program

Looking at the push buttons available in the Customer Sales window, a non-Windows programmer would be likely to notice the absence of some option for entering new customers. Such an option might be superfluous in a Payments entry program since payments generally presuppose the existence of an active customer account. But with respect to sales, we must be prepared for purchases by customers not already listed in Customer.dbf.

In a Windows application, however, an Add Customer option would be redundant since the operator can simply go back to the Database pulldown and execute Customer.spr on top of Sales. There are, however, two different ways to go about doing this, depending upon whether or not READ MODAL is used in Customer and Payments.spr. If READ MODAL is used—in which case, we are bound to add, special reservations must be made to keep our system menu active—the operator can launch Customer.spr on top of Sales.spr but must finish and close the Customers window (and terminate Customer.spr) before program control can be returned to Sales.spr and the Customer Sales window. (Owing to our default table view, discussed in the next section, a newly added customer will immediately appear in the Customer Sales window, provided that the window is refreshed with SCATTER MEMVAR and SHOW GETS.) In other words, though Customer.spr is launched from the Database pulldown and not from within the VALID clause of Sales.spr's control push buttons, Customer.spr is still treated by FoxPro as a nested program. (Of course, the arrangements that must be made to handle the process with READ MODAL generally make it easier to be redundant and add another push button to the Customer Sales window so Customer.spr can be called by the push button VALID clause. This would have the virtue of making the display of a new customer record, entered with Customer.spr, automatic since the call to the nested screen program would be followed in the VALID clause by SHOW GETS.)

The alternative strategy followed by the MBS is to avoid using READ MODAL with our data entry programs, though we employ it with their subsidiary dialogs—for example, Cus_find.spr and Erase.spr—and with screen programs designed to oversee batch update or maintenance of the system tables. By avoiding using READ MODAL, we can make the jump from Sales.spr to Customer.spr using the Database pulldown, but we need not release the Customers window when we return to Customer Sales. Indeed, we can continually switch between the screen sets belonging to the two programs and even place others on the screen as well. (See Figure 6.5.) We can work in this way because the programming strategy we use without READ MODAL does not actually involve running one program on top of the other; in fact, as you will see, it only involves running one screen program at a time. The added

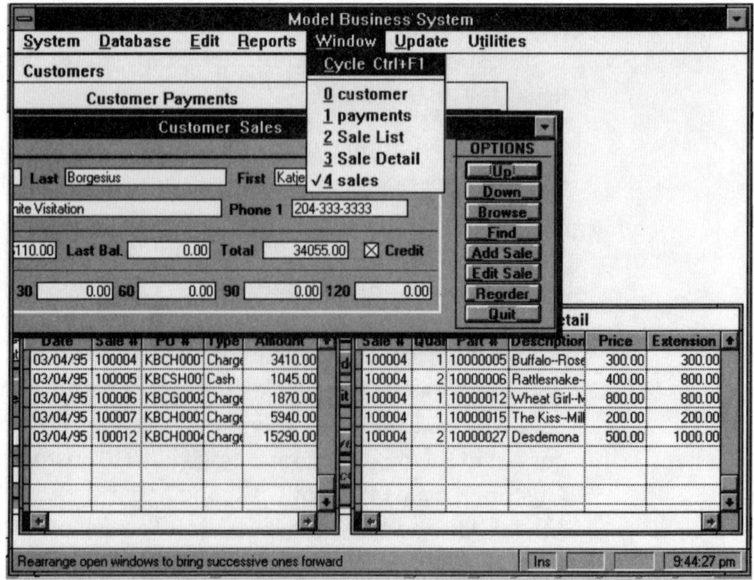

FIGURE 6.5:

After entering a new customer, the operator can switch back to the Sales program.

advantage of working without READ MODAL, except when dealing with true dialogs, is that we do not need to take any special steps to keep our system menu active. It is always available—that is, until one of our application programs calls a dialog or we execute one of the screen programs listed on the Update or Utilities pulldown, all of which employ READ MODAL for the sake of keeping the operator out of trouble.

We will return to this topic as soon as we have examined the MBS default database view.

Working with a System-Wide Default View

The database view supporting the Customer Sales window with its two BROWSE windows should be clear, except for a few small details.

```
USE bizshare
m.def_order = TRIM(bizshare.order)
USE customer ORDER m.def_order IN 0
USE payments ORDER payments IN 0
USE p_codes ORDER p_code IN 0 NOUPDATE
USE sales ORDER sales IN 0
USE sal_det ORDER sal_det IN 0
USE inventry ALIAS invsales ORDER partno IN 0
SELECT customer
SET RELATION TO custno INTO payments,custno INTO sales
SELECT payments
SET RELATION TO p_code INTO p_codes
SELECT sales
SET RELATION TO saleno INTO sal_det
SELECT sal_det
SET RELATION TO sal_det.partno INTO invsales
SELECT customer
```

Though Payments.dbf doesn't figure in the Sales entry program, we nonetheless include it as well as its child table, P_codes.dbf, in the view in case the operator should suddenly wish to switch to the Customer Payments window (Payments.spr) to survey the customer's account before continuing with sales. In fact, if we work with this database view *always* in effect as a system default view, much time will be saved in moving from one program to another. Not only will we avoid wasting FoxPro's time opening and closing tables since we need only SELECT the required table, we also save the operator's time since switching among the Customers, Sales, and Payments windows will always turn up the same (current) record in Customer.dbf.

Using Tables Multiple Times with USE ALIAS, AGAIN, and NOUPDATE

Use of a system-wide default table view that can be established at system startup is further encouraged by FoxPro, owing to its ability to hold multiple copies of the same table open in different work areas, as long as each copy of the table employs a different alias. (See Chapter 2 for a discussion of alias names.) If our default view is to be truly functional, we must take advantage of USE <file> AGAIN ALIAS <alias> to steer clear of situations in which we would otherwise have to disengage one or more of our tables from a set of relations for temporary, independent use. Otherwise, we will go batty constantly resetting our default view.

For example, during the process of sales entry, we must use Inventry.dbf as a lookup table, linked into our Sales Detail table, Sal_det.dbf. The Sale Detail BROWSE window in Figure 6.4 already uses it this way. But looking forward to the process of sales item entry, we will also want to use it to supply the operator with an inventory pick list. Instead of keying in the part numbers of items included in a sale, the operator can select the items by part number or even by part description from a popup pick list created with DEFINE POPUP PROMPT FIELD <field>. Then too, taking full advantage of our Windows environment, why not allow the operator to wander over to the Inventory entry program to place items not found in the Inventry.dbf, but required by the current sale, directly into the Inventory table before returning to the Sales entry program to add the new items to the sale? If we used only one copy of the Inventory table, we would constantly be changing Inventry.dbf with GO, SET ORDER, and SET RELATION in order to fulfill its many roles in the system. But we simply avoid these pitfalls by opening Inventry.dbf in *four* different work areas at system startup so a copy of the table can be dedicated to each of Inventry.dbf's functions in the overall system.

```
USE inventry ALIAS invsales ORDER partno IN 0

USE inventry AGAIN ALIAS inpick1 ORDER partno IN 0 NOUPDATE
DEFINE POPUP parts FROM 0,0 ;
    PROMPT FIELD inpick1.partno+" "+inpick1.p_descript+ ;
    STR(inpick1.price,10,2) SCROLL
ON SELECTION POPUP parts DEACTIVATE POPUP parts

USE inventry AGAIN ALIAS inpick2 ORDER p_descript IN 0 NOUPDATE
DEFINE POPUP descript FROM 0,0 ;
    PROMPT FIELD inpick2.p_descript+" "+inpick2.partno+ ;
    STR(inpick2.price,10,2) SCROLL
ON SELECTION POPUP descript DEACTIVATE POPUP descript

USE inventry.dbf AGAIN ALIAS inventry ORDER partno IN 0
```

We have already seen the first command; it opens Inventry.dbf for its use as a lookup table for Sal_det.dbf. Since it is the first command to open Inventry.dbf, we need not issue it with AGAIN. However, we do use ALIAS to assign it an alias name that will identify it according to its role. (Invsales is my own abbreviation of *Inventory-in-Sales*. This should be easy enough to remember.)

The next two USE commands open additional copies of Inventry.dbf for use in the two inventory popup pick lists that we will make available to the operator during sales item entry. In Inpick1, we order the inventory records by part number; in Inpick2, we order them alphabetically by part description. The DEFINE POPUP commands that follow the opening of Inpick1 and Inpick2, respectively, use the special PROMPT FIELD <exp> option to define popup menus listing the field values of Inventry.dbf's records. To make the pick lists as meaningful as possible, however, we use string concatenation to include part numbers, part descriptions, and part prices in both popups, the ordering of Partno and P_descript in the two popups being incumbent upon the master index engaged with the referenced table. When activated during sales item entry (see Figure 6.6, which displays popup Inpick1), the popups will make operator input of part numbers a breeze, provided the Inventory table is not endless.

NOTE

Pick lists created with DEFINE POPUP PROMPT FIELD <fields> will not work efficiently with large tables. When tables with more than a thousand records must be used, it is best to create the pick list using BROWSE instead.

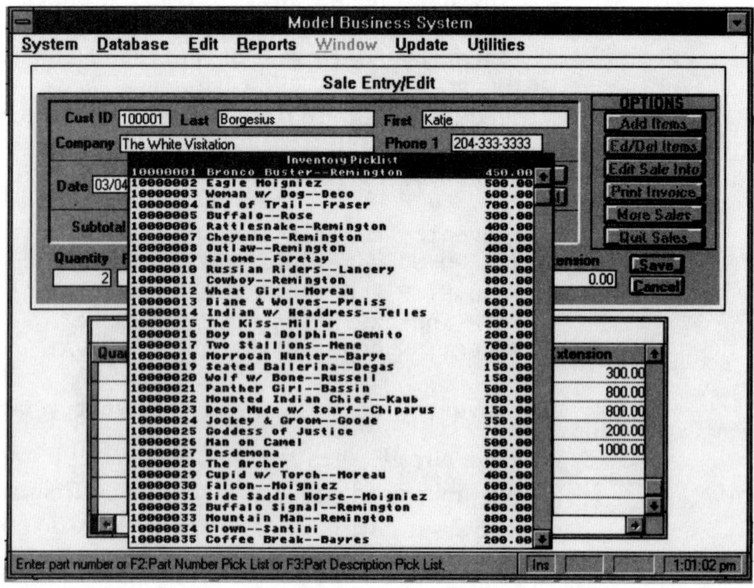

FIGURE 6.6:
The MBS uses the Inventory table as a popup pick list during sales item entry.

The fourth copy of the Inventry.dbf we open for use with the Inventory entry program. This is why we allow FoxPro to assign it the default alias name of Inventry. As with all tables that are opened multiple times, we reserve the default alias for the copy of the table that will be used during data update. Note, however, that this does not prevent us from altering Inventry.dbf by making changes to the other copies of the table. All copies of the table are updatable unless USE NOUPDATE is employed, as shown above, to render a copy read-only—though this does not prevent the copy from being immediately updated when another copy of the table is altered. If we change an inventory record by switching to the Inventry.spr in the midst of a sale, when we return to the sale, the new or changed items will appear in the pick lists.

Clearly, by using tables multiple times we create a rational table environment in which to work. By opening all our tables at once at the outset of the program, not only do we prepare FoxPro to run as quickly as it can, freeing it to dedicate its time to executing our window events, but we also make it easier on ourselves as programmers. If there's any question as to which alias we want to employ at any given time, or if we happen to forget our alias names, there's only one place we need go to in our program to find out what's available and what the current assignments are. Working in this way also makes experimenting with slightly different views affecting multiple programs in the system easy since we can see at a glance what's going on. (Procedure Opendata, which opens the MBS tables, is located in Bigbiz.prg, the MBS startup module.) As the commands used to open Inventry.dbf multiple times indicate, all open copies of the table can use the same set of index tags.

Using Modal and Nonmodal Screen Sets

The window or windows that participate in a single READ are commonly referred to as a *screen set*. Up to now, our screen sets have included only one READ window, though this need not be the case. The MBS Letter Library entry program, for example, includes two READ windows, one for performing data entry and lookup of letters and another to display the control push buttons. (See Figure 6.7.)

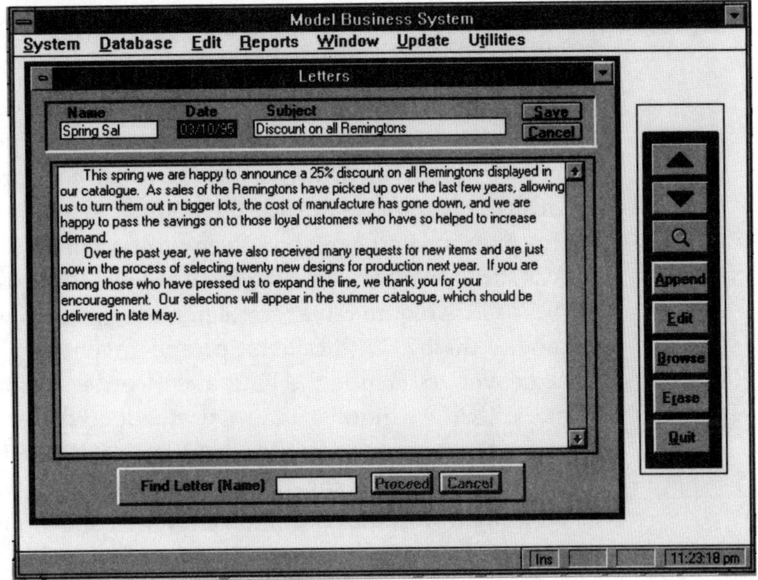

FIGURE 6.7:

The MBS Letters window uses two READ windows.

Use of a separate READ window to display control push buttons is much the fashion in FoxPro programming since the same window can be used over and over with different data entry windows, but the practice does have its limitations. It is most useful when the same set of push buttons is required by all, or at least the majority, of data entry programs and when sufficient space is available on the screen—though the window can be placed or moved on top of other windows belonging to the screen set.

I have avoided using a standard control push button window in the MBS, in part because of the space requirements of the screen programs updating the customer database and in part because they assume a greater degree of standardization of push button controls than is found in most applications. Where they are used consistently in an application, one usually finds a second set of control push buttons placed in the main READ window to take care of actions specific to each screen set. This strikes me as too much work. Moreover, with respect to the MBS as a learning tool, use of a separate push button control window would have needlessly complicated your introduction to Windows programming by forcing us to discuss the window-level events and programming required for using two READ windows from the start. We include two READ windows in Letters.spr, however, to provide the reader with a straightforward example of how to work with a separate control push button window. (See Chapter 11.)

With respect to the process of sales invoice entry and edit, we are especially hard pressed for space on the screen. Though FoxPro permits us to define our windows as we please, even using negative row and column coordinates, we cannot direct @ GETs to coordinates outside the bounds of our screen. In the case of Payments.spr this presented no hardship. Even with a READ and two BROWSE windows, there was sufficient space left over on the screen to expand the READ window to include the @ GETs required for transaction entry, which we handle as an embedded (non-modal) dialog. With Letters.spr and Inventry.spr sufficient space was available, moreover, to include the Find and Reorder dialogs directly in the READ (or primary READ) windows, again as embedded dialogs. The case of the Sales entry program, however, is more like Customer.spr, Payments.spr, and Sales.spr itself with respect to Cus_find.spr. The actual entry and editing of line items in a sale must be performed with the additional screen set shown in Figure 6.8.

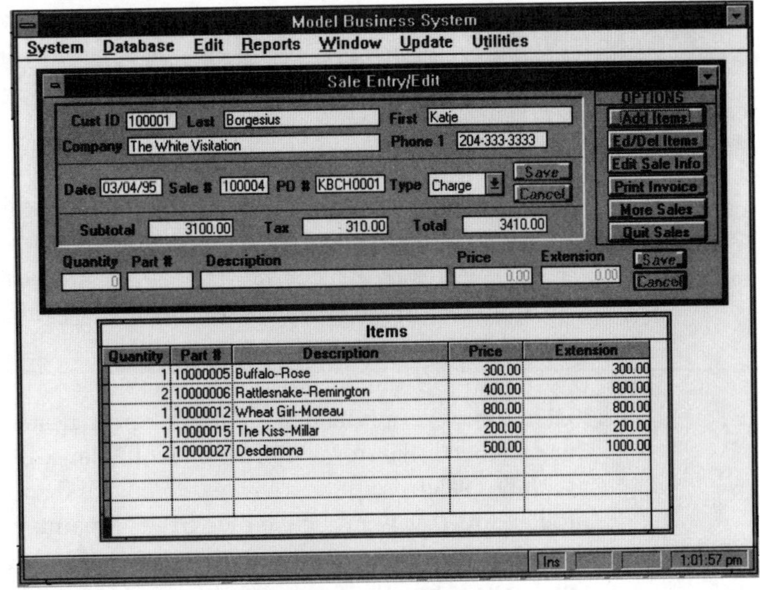

FIGURE 6.8:

Sales entry requires two screen sets: one to locate the customer and another (shown here) to enter and edit sale items.

Referring back to the Customer Sales (Sales.spr) screen set shown in Figure 6.4, if a new sale is to be entered, the operator locates the right customer and selects the Add Sale push button. If the intention is to edit an already existing sale, the operator first highlights the sale requiring update in the Sale List (BROWSE) window and then selects or clicks the Edit Sale push button. Both actions take the operator to the Sale Entry/Edit screen set.

Multiple (Nested) READs with Windows

Taken together, the Customer Sales and Sale Entry/Edit screen sets, executed by Sales.spr and Saletrns.spr (short for *sales transactions*) provide us with an example of how two or more screen programs based upon READ can be used to affect a multi-tiered screen program.

NOTE

As we will see in Chapter 11, FoxPro does include facilities for creating multi-page screen programs. For example, if the Customer table included more fields than could appear in one window, we might use the Screen Builder to create two overlapping READ windows and then combine them in a single screen program using multiple READs. During execution of the resulting screen program, the operator can use PgUp and PgDn to move back and forth between the two READ windows. However, this method works best when the input fields in the multiple READ windows come from the same table and there is no need to open and close associated BROWSE windows depending upon which page is on top.

Of course, we might make Saletrns.spr a nested MODAL READ program. We would then call it from within the VALID clause of Sales.spr's control push buttons with DO saletrns.spr, just as we call Cus_find.spr to perform data lookup in Customer.dbf. This would have the virtue of maintaining a rigorous hierarchical relation between the two screen sets, essentially turning Saletrns.spr into a modal dialog used by Sales.spr. Not until the operator finishes with data entry to a sale and returns to Sales.spr and the Customer Sales READ window can that operator venture elsewhere. We might even do this and still get away with allowing the operator to execute Inventry.spr, the Inventory entry program, whether from the Database pulldown or by inserting another push button in Saletrans.spr's READ window. This would enable the operator to make changes to the inventory/price list without leaving the sale. As with Saletrns.spr in relation to Sales.spr, we would execute Inventry.spr as a nested MODAL READ program or dialog belonging to Saletrns.spr—though in executing Inventry.spr in this way we would be pressing FoxPro to its limits with respect to the number of active READs it can handle at one time.

Limits on READ Levels

NOTE

With FoxPro you can have up to five nested READs. Each READ, in the order executed, represents a distinct READ LEVEL. Use the read-level function, RDLEVEL(), to return the current read level—0 through 5.

Though READ is used to control the action of each of our screen programs, FoxPro is at present limited to five active (nested) READs. For those who want to use READ MODAL to place strict controls over operator access to windows not directly associated with the current screen set, however, this is not such a great burden. With regard to the MBS, for example, we must use a special form of READ, called a *Foundation READ,* to place FoxPro under program control throughout the execution of our application, and we must do this whether or not we use READ MODAL with all our screen programs. (We discuss the use of the Foundation, or getless, READ Chapter 10. That accounts for one READ. Our Customer Sales screen program, Sales.spr, represents RDLEVEL() = 2. Executing the Sale Entry/Edit screen program, Saletrns.spr, gives us three nested READs; and if the operator executes Inventry.spr again as a nested screen program, we have four READ levels. Finally, since Inventry.spr uses Erase.spr to delete records, supposing it is employed, we reach the FoxPro limit. But then there would be little reason for going further, supposing we preferred to control the operator's actions by employing READ MODAL in all our screen programs.

The Cunning of the Modeless (or Nonmodal) System

We can avoid having to think about read levels with regard to the execution of our application programs (as opposed to their nested dialogs) by working without READ MODAL. This does not involve much additional programming, but it requires good planning and not a little bit of cunning. In fact, you have already seen how this works through our discussion of the Customer and Payments screen programs. Each is designed to be wholly self sufficient. Whatever actions they take, upon termination they return the system to a known condition that does not conflict with the execution of other screen programs. Using READ DEACTIVATE, they are, moreover, perfectly capable of monitoring window-level events initiated by the operator and, on the basis of the instructions we supply, determining whether or not to give way to another screen program. This is where the cunning comes in.

As you are aware, we designed the Payments.spr so it would terminate in one of two ways. If Quit or Close is selected, the READ window is released at program termination. However, under other circumstances (for example, when the operator selects another screen program from the Database pulldown or clicks an inactive READ window belonging to a previously terminated screen program), Payments.spr terminates but leaves its READ window behind. (Again, with READ

MODAL, we would not work in this way. Since each screen window operates like a dialog, it is useless to leave an inactive READ window on the screen. With READ MODAL we can run one program on top of the other as a nested program, but doing so presupposes that we do not terminate the first program.)

For example, if the operator launches Customer.spr from the Database pulldown without quitting or closing the Payments window, the Payments READ is terminated but the Payments window remains in an inactive state on the screen. Consequently, when the Customers window opens, it appears as though two READ programs are being run simultaneously, especially since we can click back and forth between the two READ windows to reactivate either program. But only one program is being run at a time: the one controlling the foremost READ window. Not forgetting our Foundation READ, working in this way we can execute all the data entry (or application) programs listed on the Database and/or Reports pulldown and have all the READ windows on the screen at once, besides being able to switch between them as we choose, without exceeding RDLEVEL() = 2. This gives us leeway for up to three levels of nested dialogs, supposing we had any need of them. But how is this done?

For now the discussion touches only briefly on how to execute screen programs from the Database pulldown one after the other without manually closing each screen set in turn and without increasing the READ level. (Full explanation is provided in Chapter 10.) Instead of executing each of our programs with DO Customer.spr, DO Payments.spr, and so on, we execute them indirectly from the main menu through the use of procedure Dospr, a simplified version of which is shown here:

```
PROCEDURE dospr
PARAMETER m.sprtodo
IF RDLEVEL() >  1
    CLEAR READ
ENDIF
DO (m.sprtodo)
RETURN
```

Instead of executing Customer.spr, for example, with DO Customer.spr, we execute it with DO dospr WITH "customer.spr". Working in this way, if another screen program using READ is still active on the screen when we make our menu selection, CLEAR READ will be triggered, automatically terminating the active program, before Customer.spr is executed through indirect reference with DO (m.sprtodo). Here again, our Foundation READ represents READ level 1. We can thus test for an active screen program with RDLEVEL() > 1.

In the case of our Sales entry program, the same basic strategy is employed to execute Saletrns.spr, controlling the Sale Entry/Edit window. Within the @ GET push button VALID used in Sales.spr, we include the command DO Dospr WITH "Saletrns.spr" instead of DO Saletrns.spr. In this way, Sales.spr—itself initiated by procedure Dospr—is terminated by CLEAR READ in procedure Dospr before that procedure launches Saletrns.spr. (That this does not involve recursive use of procedure Dospr is due to the action of our Foundation READ, discussed in Part II. As you may suspect, it is our Foundation READ that also enables us to switch back and forth between screen programs by clicking the inactive READ windows left on the screen.)

Overview of the Sales Transaction Entry Program

Turning our attention to the MBS Sales Transaction entry program, Saletrns.spr, we are bound to admit that it poses several problems if we do not execute it as a modal dialog of Sales.spr. Regardless of how we execute it—here, with a mind to giving the operator free access to the other programs on the Database pulldown without worrying about READ level—logically speaking it is not an independent program. Not only is it executed by Sales.spr, but it must be executed in that way since it makes no sense to begin appending a sale without first selecting the right customer and even less to begin editing a sale without first selecting the customer and finding the sale we want to edit. This is why Saletrns.spr is not listed on the MBS Database pulldown but is executed as an option of Sales.spr.

Moreover, suppose we want to temporarily leave the Sale Entry/Edit window in order to add new inventory items. If we really terminate Saletrns.spr while leaving its READ window on the screen so it can be immediately reselected when the operator finishes with Inventry.spr (by clicking its inactive READ window or selecting it from the Window pulldown), we must design Saletrns.spr so that when it is re-executed it automatically returns us to the sale we were working on without forcing us to start again in Sales.spr.

Using the Setup and Cleanup Code to Restart a Temporarily Interrupted Program

Quite simply, we prepare Saletrns.spr to operate independently of Sales.spr—in effect, as a nonmodal dialog of the latter program—by making one compromise in our programming practice. Normally, in Xbase, we do not create a summary sales record in Sales.dbf or assign a new Saleno until the operator has finished entering the items belonging to a new sale. This protects us from having to create and then DELETE a Sales.dbf record if the operator chooses to abandon the sale. (In a network application, it also protects us from having to throw out sales numbers if and when new sales are abandoned.)

However, if we create a Sales.dbf record and assign it a new Saleno the moment the operator selects the Add Sale push button in Sales.spr, when the Sale Entry/Edit window appears, the operator will always be editing an existing sale.

```
* Fragment from VALID clause of Sales.spr @ GET push buttons
* executing Saletrns.spr.
CASE m.but1 $ "Add Sale Edit Sale"
    SELECT sales
    IF m.but1 = "Add Sale"
        APPEND BLANK
        REPLACE sales.custno WITH customer.custno, ;
            bizshare.saleno WITH STR(VAL(bizshare.saleno)+1,6), ;
            sales.saleno WITH Bizshare.saleno,date WITH DATE(), ;
            sales.s_code WITH "1"
    ENDIF
    DO dospr WITH [saletrns.spr]
* Other cases...
```

Following the same strategy we used to assign new Custnos, we use the value of Bizshare.saleno to create our new Saleno. (We do not use SQL-INSERT to create the new Sales.dbf record since, in a network, we will want to use REPLACE in any event to handle the simultaneous update of Bizshare and Sales.dbf. Since REPLACE will place an automatic record lock on the current record in both tables at once, using REPLACE ensures that no other operator can get at Bizshare.saleno until we are done with it.)

Because we always begin Saletrns.spr with a specific Sales.dbf record, we can permit the operator to temporarily terminate the program, leaving the inactive window on the screen, and then reselect it to go back to work on the current sale, provided we include the necessary code for restarting Saletrns.spr in this way. And given our use of a default system table view, this is quite easy. Assuming the default view is unchanged, we can come back to a sale by repositioning FoxPro in Customer.dbf and Sales.dbf to the appropriate Custno and Saleno, respectively. (Sal_det and Inventry.dbf—alias invsales—as linked tables, will take care of themselves.) This naturally means storing this information away after the READ is terminated—in Sales.spr's cleanup code.

```
READ...
DO salclose
IF but1 $ "Quit Sales More Sales"
    SET SKIP OF BAR 3 OF Database .F.
    RELEASE WINDOW Sale_trans
ELSE
    stc_recno = RECNO("customer")
    stc_custno = customer.custno
    sts_saleno = sales.saleno
    SAVE ALL LIKE st* TO stmem
ENDIF
RELEASE WINDOW "Items"
SET TOPIC TO
```

For the moment the only commands we are interested in are those embedded within the ELSE clause of the IF/ENDIF. They are executed only when the READ window is left inactive on the screen—that is, when the operator has not selected the Quit Sales or More Sales push button. (Of course, we also make reservations in our READ DEACTIVATE clause so operator selection of Close will change m.but1 to Quit Sales and so release the READ window.) The first three commands save the information we need to restart Saletrns.spr with the present sale to a group of memvars using unique prefixes; the fourth command SAVEs the three memory variables to a memory file. Clearly, using unique prefixes with the memvars makes it possible to address them as a group with SAVE's ALL LIKE <skeleton> option.

Since such information will always be on hand when restarting Saletrns.spr, we only need to check for the prior existence of its READ window (named Sale_Trans) in Saletrns.spr's startup code to determine whether or not the program (or window) is being reselected. We use the window existence function, WEXIST(), to make this determination.

```
IF WEXIST("SALE_TRANS")
    IF NOT FILE("stmem.mem")
        DO alert WITH ;
            "Something went wrong. Cannot return to sale "+ ;
```

```
                "you were editing","Press any key to continue."
            RELEASE WINDOW Sale_trans
            RETURN
        ENDIF
        RESTORE FROM stmem ADDITIVE
        ERASE stmem.mem
        SELECT customer
        m.orig_ord = ORDER()
        SET ORDER TO custno
        IF NOT SEEK(stc_custno)
            DO alert WITH...
            * Reset original order and release window Sale_trans.
            RETURN
        ENDIF
        SELECT sales
        IF NOT SEEK(stc_custno+sts_saleno)
            DO alert WITH...
            * Reset original order and release window Sale_trans.
            RETURN
        ENDIF
    ENDIF
```

Though we have left out several commands, the action of the routine should be clear enough. If the window is present, the program was temporarily terminated and is, in any case, not being started by Sales.spr. We therefore restore the memvars from memory file Stmem and get on with the task of editing the sale—though not without doing some checking to make sure everything's all right. We use the FILE() function to make sure the memory file is actually on disk and SEEK() to make sure the Custno and Saleno to which we must return are still present in the Customer and Sales tables. If any of these tests fail, we alert the operator to the problem and promptly terminate Saletrns.spr before its READ can be reactivated with RETURN.

Of course, if Saletrans.spr is being executed by Sales.spr, the commands are bypassed. No actions are required since Sales.spr has already positioned FoxPro to the correct customer and sales records. We can get on with the business of adding or editing records belonging to the sale—that is, after initializing the other memvars required by the program.

Controlling Available Options during Execution of a Nonmodal Screen Set

Since we have elected to go the nonmodal route in executing Saletrns.spr, the operator is free to interrupt work on a specific sale and execute any program on the MBS System pulldown. But is this wise? Focusing specifically on the options available on the Database pulldown, there is one action we may not want the operator to take: reexecuting Sales.spr while Saletrns.spr's READ window is still on the screen. This is simply a matter of protocol. Given the relation between the two programs, we will confuse the operator if we don't make Saletrns.spr behave in a uniform way when started from Sales.spr. To maintain the hierarchical relation between our otherwise independent programs, we therefore establish and enforce our own protocols. Indeed, we have already set out in this direction by not listing Saletrns.spr on the Database pulldown. It must be initially started through Sales.spr.

As is customary with all nonmodal MBS application programs, each program on the Database pulldown begins by using the command SET SKIP OF BAR <number> OF _msysmenu .T. to disable the launched program's option in the pulldown. (Actually, it will make no difference if the option is reselected since the reexecution of any program through the auspices of procedure Dospr automatically terminates the called program before it is reexecuted. Thus, if we prohibit the action with SET SKIP OF BAR, we do so to prevent FoxPro from wasting its time.) When the program is terminated in any fashion whatsoever, we normally reactivate the option on the menu bar with SET SKIP OF BAR <number> OF _msysmenu .F.

In the case of Sales.spr, however, we do not reactivate the Sales option on the Database pulldown when it terminated by starting Saletrns.spr. We arrange to reactivate the option only when Saletrns.spr is terminated with Quit Sales or Close, thereby establishing either of these actions—or selection of the More Sales push button—as the means of properly terminating work with a specific sale. (Though it is a minor point, we can also reenable the menu option with More Sales since Sales.spr will immediately disable it once again. This just saves us from having to include an embedded IF to distinguish among the actions.)

Along these same lines, if we are to leave the Window pulldown active during execution of Saletrns.spr so the operator can use it to switch among the available windows, we will be defeating our own purpose if we do not release Sales.spr's READ window before executing Saletrns.spr. Otherwise, having prevented the operator from reexecuting Sales.spr with the Database pulldown, we provide two other ways of reexecuting it in our nonmodal environment by clicking its READ window or by selecting the READ window from the Window pulldown. This, however, is taken care of in Sales.spr's cleanup code. (Remember, procedure Dospr's CLEAR READ command will terminate Sales.spr's READ and thus trigger execution of Sales.spr's cleanup code when Sales.spr launches Saletrns.spr with DO Dospr WITH "Saletrns.spr".)

```
* Sales.spr cleanup code.
IF m.but1 $ "Quit Add Sale Edit Sale"
    RELEASE WINDOW Sales
ENDIF
IF NOT m.but1 $ "Add Sale Edit Sale"
    SET SKIP OF BAR 3 OF Database .F.
ENDIF
RELEASE WINDOW "Sale List"
RELEASE WINDOW "Sale Detail"
SET TOPIC TO
```

As should be clear, Sales.spr's READ window will remain on the screen only if Sales.spr is not terminated with Quit or Close or with one of the options executing Saletrns.spr.

The Sales Transaction Entry Screen Set

Returning now to the screen set employed by Saletrns.spr (again, see Figure 6.8), we can now begin to descibe its use. The READ window consists of three sets of push buttons. @ GET m.but1 oversees the control push buttons, while @ GET m.versum and @ GET m.veritem control the two sets of Save and Cancel push buttons used for updating @ GETs representing the fields of Sales.dbf and Sal_det.dbf, respectively. The Items BROWSE window, executed in the usual way by READ ACTIVATE, provides a list of all records in Sal_det.dbf belonging to the current record in Sales.dbf, which is selected as the active table while Saletrns.spr is running.

```
IF NOT WVISIBLE("Items")
    SELECT sal_det
    DEFINE WINDOW stbrow FROM 13.5,13 TO 25,112 ;
        SYSTEM GROW FLOAT NOZOOM NOCLOSE ;
        FONT "MS Sans Serif", 8
    BROWSE PREFERENCE "d_items" NODELETE NOAPPEND ;
        NOEDIT NOMENU NOWAIT ;
        WINDOW stbrow TITLE "Items" ;
        FIELDS quantity,partno:H="Part #", ;
```

```
        invsales.p_descript:H="Description", ;
        invsales.price,Extension = Quantity * invsales.price ;
        KEY sales.saleno
    RELEASE WINDOW stbrow
ENDIF
SELECT sales
```

Releasing BROWSE Windows

By now you have noticed that we always release our BROWSE windows regardless of how our nonmodal screen programs are terminated. The only window we leave on the screen when the operator switches to another program without terminating the active screen program is the latter's READ window. While this is admittedly not in keeping with the spirit of Windows programming, it is nonetheless necessary because FoxPro has no means of detecting when an operator moves from one BROWSE window to another. True, the action will activate the newly selected BROWSE window and change the value of WONTOP(); but it cannot trigger READ DEACTIVATE or any other event-sensitive program routine. Only moving from the active READ window to another window, be it a BROWSE window or another inactive READ window, will trigger an event detectable by a program. As a result, leaving a mess of BROWSE windows on the screen along with inactive READ windows can only lead to confusion since one can move from one BROWSE window to another without causing FoxPro to consider terminating the current screen program. This will be inappropriate when the selected BROWSE window is not associated with the active program and can, moreover, lead to program errors if the view required by the selected window is no longer current.

Here again, we place BROWSE in a window defined with DEFINE WINDOW NOCLOSE in order to remove the Close option from the BROWSE window control box. (Given the BROWSE window's subordinate relation to the READ window, closing it manually can only retrigger READ ACTIVATE, thus opening the BROWSE window once again.)

Altering the Action of FoxPro Default Control Keys

When a BROWSE window included in a screen set is selected as WONTOP(), the Esc key, Ctrl+Q, and Ctrl+W will still close it unless ON KEY LABEL is used to change FoxPro's response to operator use of these standard FoxPro keystrokes. Though we do not do this in the MBS, it can be accomplished by placing the commands in the READ DEACTIVATE clause so they will not be executed until the operator moves off the READ window to BROWSE.

```
ON KEY LABEL Esc memvar = ""
ON KEY LABEL: Ctrl+Q memvar = ""
ON KEY LABEL Ctrl-W memvar = ""
```

Here we use ON KEY LABEL to assign the three keys the superfluous duty of executing a command initializing a memvar that has no function in the program. This effectively disables the keys' default actions.

Since we may again have use of these keys, when the operator returns to the READ window (recall that a push button can be assigned the function of responding to Esc or Ctrl+W), we can reset the keys back to their normal FoxPro functions in READ ACTIVATE by simply issuing ON KEY LABEL <keystroke> without any command. You can add this feature to the MBS programs employing BROWSE if you so choose.

As with the two BROWSE windows used with Sales.spr, the function of the Items BROWSE window is not limited to display. When a sales item must be edited or deleted from the invoice, it must first be *targeted* (made the current record) in the Items window. Then, selecting the Ed/Del Items push button in the READ WINDOW will automatically load the targeted item into the input fields displayed in the last row of the READ window, where further action can be taken.

The Add Items push button, on the other hand, activates the same input fields for entry of a new sales item, while the Edit Sale Info push button activates the @ GETs representing the fields of the Sales summary table, Sales.dbf. By selecting Edit Sale Info, the operator can enter or change the sale's invoice date, purchase order number, or cash/charge status. Like the Sale # field, the @ GETs displaying Subtotal, Tax, and Total are read-only. They are updated on the fly as the operator enters or edits line items.

The functions of the remaining control push buttons should be clear. Print Invoice prints out an invoice for the current sale; More Sales reexecutes Sales.spr while terminating Saletrns.spr; and Quit Sales terminates Saletrns.spr without reexecuting Sales.spr. All this is managed by a UDF placed in the @ GET push button VALID clause.

```
DO CASE
CASE m.but1 $ "Add Items Ed/Del Items"
    STORE .T. TO m.doitem,m.doit
CASE m.but1 = "Edit"
    STORE .T. TO m.doit,m.dosum
CASE m.but1 = "Print"
    DO Invoice
CASE m.but1 $ "Quit Sales More Sales"
    IF m.amount <> 0.00 OR
        question("SALE AMOUNT IS ZERO. CANCEL?","")
        IF m.but1 = "More Sales"
            DO dospr WITH [sales.spr]
        ENDIF
        CLEAR READ
    ENDIF
ENDCASE
SHOW GETS
RETURN .F.
```

TIP

You can make your programs easier to read and revise by placing comments directly in your program files. FoxPro ignores a command line if it begins with an asterisk (*) or with NOTE. You can also place comments at the end of a command line by following the executable command with &&s.

While we once more use the global memvar m.doit to indicate when data entry has been initiated, the fact that we have two different data sets to deal with forces us to employ additional memvars as flags. Here we use m.dosum to indicate when the Edit Sale Info push button has been selected for alteration of our sale summary record in Sales.dbf, and we use m.doitem to indicate when Add Items or Ed/Del Items has been selected to initiate work on records in Sal_det.dbf. The setting of these memvar values is intended to control the action of Saletrns.spr's READ SHOW clause. Before viewing it, however, we will do well to pick up the action with Saletrns.spr's setup code—that is, following the routine employed to restart

Saletrns.spr when its READ window is already present on the screen. This will permit us to preview all actions taken during the show.

```
* Initialize memvars used with push buttons to their default
* values.

m.but1 = "Add Items"
m.versum = "Save"
m.veritem = "Save"

* Initialize memvars used as flags.

STORE .F.TO m.doit,m.dosum,m.doitem,m.hide

* Initialize values required by @ GET input fields. Tax rate is
* taken from system value table bizshare.dbf.

m.taxrat = bizshare.taxrat
SELECT customer
SCATTER MEMVAR
SELECT sales
SCATTER MEMVAR

* Initialize value of popup--@ GET m.s_code2--used to select
* "Cash" or "Charge" sale, corresponding to s_code values of "1"
* or "2", respectively. Note that if a new sale has been
* initialized by Sales.spr, Sales.s_code = "1"

m.s_code2 = IIF(m.s_code="1","Cash","Charge")

* Now use sales detail records to calculate figure for sale
* subtotal and to recalculate sales tax and sales total. Note
* that these figures must be updated as items are added, edited
* or deleted from the sale. Of course, if the sale has just been
* initialized by Sales.spr, EOF("sal_det") will be .T. We can
* therefore set m.subtot to 0. (If we allow FoxPro to calculate
* m.tax and m.amount in any event, it's just to avoid adding
* two more commands to the code.

GO RECNO()
IF EOF("sal_det")
    m.subtot = 0.00
ELSE
    SELECT Sal_det
    SUM sal_det.quantity * invsales.price ;
```

```
        WHILE saleno = m.saleno TO m.subtot
    SELECT sales
    GO RECNO()
ENDIF
m.tax = ROUND(m.subtot * m.taxrat,2)
m.amount = m.subtot + m.tax

* Initialize empty display values for @ GET input fields used for
* item entry or edit.

STORE 0.00 TO m.quantity,m.price,m.exten
m.partno = SPACE(8)
m.p_descript = SPACE(30)

* Initialize memvar for temporary storage of current record
* number in Sales Detail table.
* This will be used in the event that the operator chooses to
* move the record pointer in the BROWSE window while editing a
* line item. Before the edited record is saved it is necessary to
* move FoxPro back in Sal_det.dbf to the item selected for edit.

m.sd_rec = 0
```

Looking at the Sale Entry/Edit window as it will appear when Saletrns.spr is executed by Sales.spr with Add Sale (see Figure 6.9), we can now distinguish among its parts. The @ GET input fields at the top of the window naturally take their values from the current Customer table record. @ GET WHEN .F. is used to prevent the cursor from entering any of these fields during sale invoice entry. They are read-only.

Next we have the @ GET input fields that take their values from the current record in Sales.dbf, an @ GET popup representing our sale code field, indicating a cash or charge sale, and a set of Save and Cancel push buttons. With the exception of the push buttons, which are initially disabled, data entry to these @ GETs is controlled with WHEN m.dosum. (As you have seen, m.dosum is set to .T., along with m.doit, when the operator selects the Edit Sale Info control push button.) m.dosum is initially set to .F. to prevent the cursor from entering these fields when READ is first executed. To make things easy on ourselves, we give the name m.versum, short for *verify-summary,* to the @ GET push buttons used to terminate edit of the summary Sales table data with Save and Cancel.

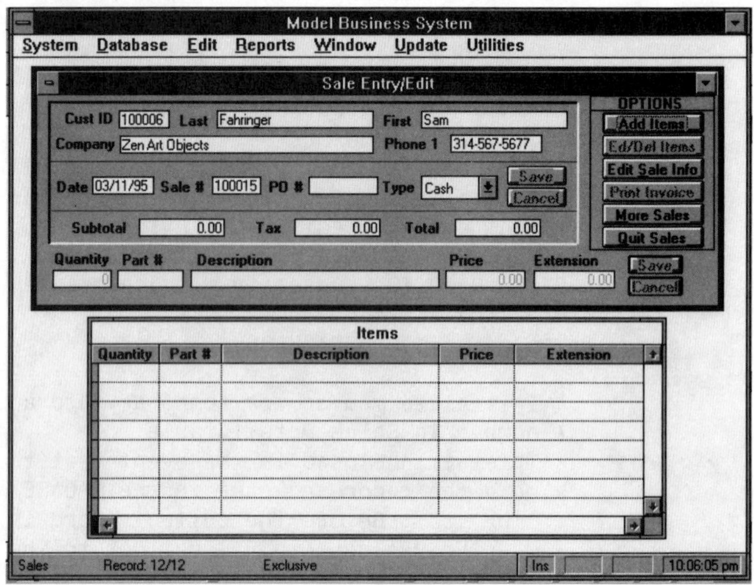

FIGURE 6.9:
MBS Sale Transaction screen set at outset of Append Sale action

Just below our summary sales data are the @ GET input fields used to display our running figures for sales subtotal (m.subtotal), tax (m.tax), and sale total (m.amount). Only the last memvar holds a value corresponding to a table field, Sales.amount, though we take the initial figure for m.amount not from the table field but from the SUM of Sal_det.quantity * Invsales.price for all items currently listed in the sale plus tax. Though this is the long way to go about getting m.amount, it is a good deal safer than using Sales.amount, owing to the freedom we intend to provide the operator. Either changing the price of items in the Inventory table or changing the value of Bizshare.taxrat will render Sales.amount unreliable when the Sale Entry/Edit window is used to edit a sale. We must, therefore, always recalculate Sales.amount at the outset of Saletrns.spr to ensure that we have the right total. Since the operator has no need to address these input fields, we send them to the screen with @ GET WHEN .F.

The last row of items in our READ window is used for entry or edit of sales items. Since they do not display any useful information until data entry or edit of a sale item is enabled, they are initially dimmed and disabled with @ GET DISABLE. This is simply achieved using the Initially Disable check box in the Screen Builder's Field dialog, as shown in Figure 6.10. While these @ GETs must be enabled with

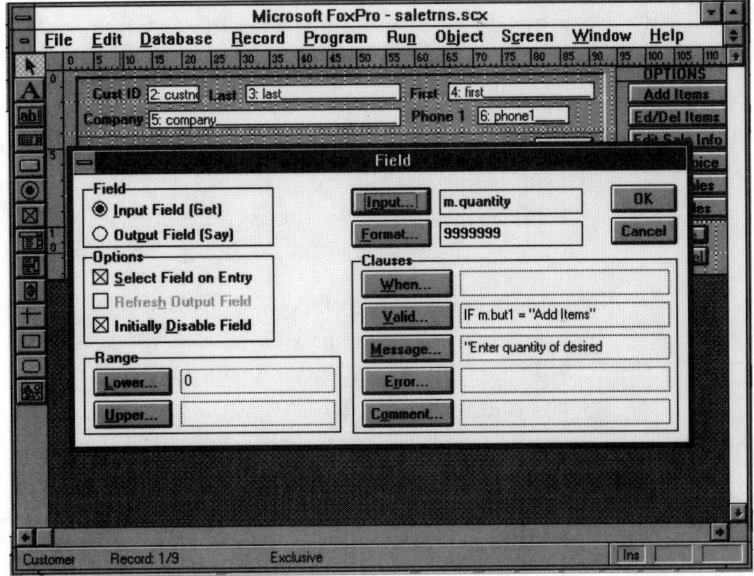

FIGURE 6.10:

The Screen Builder's Field dialog can be used to initially disable an input field.

SHOW GET before data entry or edit of a sale item, several of the input fields are used for data display only.

If Add Items is the selected action, the operator must make entries to @ GET m.quantity and @ GET m.partno. These are the only values that need be entered since, using m.partno, FoxPro can look up the item in Inventry.dbf and supply the description (m.p_descript), price (m.price), and extension (m.exten = m.quantity * m.price) automatically.

On the other hand, if Ed/Del Items is the selected action, the @ GETs are loaded with values taken from the current record in Sal_det.dbf, as determined by the position of the record pointer in the Items BROWSE window. However, data entry is enabled only to @ GET m.quantity. In other words, the edit action allows only a change in quantity. If the operator's intention is to erase the item from the sale, this is accomplished by setting m.quantity to 0.

Since the other input fields are made read-only with WHEN .F., the only input field that must be made conditionally accessible to the operator is @ GET m.partno. To prevent the cursor from entering unless the Add Items routine has been selected we use a WHEN clause, the first line of which includes the compound condition m.but1 = "Add Items" AND m.quantity > 0. The second part of the condition ensures that the operator makes an entry to m.quantity before entering a part number. (@ GET m.quantity also employs a lower RANGE of 0 to ensure that all quantities are entered using positive integers.)

The Save and Cancel push buttons store their value to m.veritem, short for *verify-item.* When Add Items is the action, saving an item immediately places it in the BROWSE window, where it can be reselected for edit. Following the use of Save, running figures for subtotal, tax, and total are all updated.

Finally, when the Quit Sales or More Sales push button is selected or any other action terminating the READ is taken, the program cleanup code executes procedure Salclose, which is designed to make final updates to Sales.dbf and to update the customer account fields (Customer.current, Customer.history, and Customer last-date) as required by the entry or edit of the sale.

Controlling Multiple Actions with READ SHOW

Despite its use to control data entry to two different data sets, Saletrns.spr's READ SHOW clause is actually quite commonplace.

```
IF m.doit
    SHOW GET m.but1 DISABLE
    IF m.dosum
        SHOW GET m.versum ENABLE
        SHOW GET m.but1 DISABLE
        _CUROBJ = OBJNUM(m.date)
    ELSE
        IF m.but1 = "Ed/Del"
            SELECT sal_det
            sd_rec = RECNO()
            SCATTER MEMVAR
            m.p_descript = invsales.p_descript
            m.price = invsales.price
            m.exten = quantity * m.price
            SELECT sales
        ENDIF
        SHOW GET m.quantity ENABLE
        SHOW GET m.partno ENABLE
        SHOW GET m.p_descript ENABLE
        SHOW GET m.price ENABLE
        SHOW GET m.exten ENABLE
```

```
        SHOW GET m.veritem ENABLE
        _CUROBJ = OBJNUM(m.quantity)
    ENDIF
ELSE
    IF EOF("sal_det")
        SHOW GET m.but1,2 DISABLE  && Ed/Del
        SHOW GET m.but1,4 DISABLE  && Invoice
    ELSE
        SHOW GET m.but1,2 ENABLE  && Ed/Del
        SHOW GET m.but1,4 ENABLE  && Invoice
    ENDIF
ENDIF
```

If and when Add Items, Ed/Del Items, or Edit Sale Info is selected, our @ GET push button VALID clause (see above) alters the values of m.doit, m.dosum, and m.doitem as required to signal the correct action in READ SHOW. When none of these actions is indicated, the SHOW clause does no more than check on the existence of items in the sale. If no items are currently listed in the sale, SHOW GET DISABLE is used to disable the Ed/Del Items and Print Invoice push buttons. When items are present in the sale, these same push buttons are enabled.

Since the rest of our READ SHOW does little we haven't seen before, we mention only one small but important detail related to launching the Ed/Del Items action. While loading our memvars with values taken from Sal_det.dbf, we also store the current record number to memvar sd_rec. This is necessary since we do not prevent the operator from moving back to the BROWSE window while editing a sale item and moving the record pointer. Since the Save edit routine is designed to update the current record in Sal_det.dbf, we may thus end up updating the wrong record unless we make certain FoxPro is positioned to the Sal_det.dbf record that was current at the time Ed/Del Items was launched. Sd_rec gives us a means of doing this.

The Add and Ed/Del Items Routines

The Add and Ed/Del Items routines are closely monitored using @ GET WHEN, RANGE, and VALID. When data entry is enabled, the cursor is sent to @ GET m.quantity, which prohibits entry of negative numbers with a lower RANGE of 0. (Again, see Figure 6.10.) Operator entry to @ GET m.quantity also triggers the following VALID clause:

```
IF m.but1 = "Add Items"
    IF m.quantity = 0
        _CUROBJ = OBJNUM(m.veritem)+1
    ELSE
        _CUROBJ = OBJNUM(m.partno)
    ENDIF
ELSE
    IF m.quantity = sal_det.quantity
        _CUROBJ = OBJNUM(m.veritem)+1
    ELSE
        m.exten = m.quantity * m.price
        SHOW GET m.exten
        _CUROBJ = OBJNUM(m.veritem)
    ENDIF
ENDIF
```

If the action is Ed/Del Items, @ GET m.quantity is the only field that is addressed. We can therefore check to see if the operator has actually changed the item Quantity by comparing m.quantity with Sale_det.quantity. If they are the same, no real edit has been made and we can send the cursor to Cancel. On the other hand, if Quantity was changed, we recalculate and display the new extension and send the cursor to Save. (Since m.partno remains unchanged, there is no need to update m.p_descipt or m.price; the values displayed are taken from the current Invsales record.)

In the case of Add Items, the UDF first checks to see if 0 was entered as the quantity. If so, we assume the operator has had a change of heart about entering the item and send the cursor to the Cancel push button. If a quantity greater than 0 is entered (negative numbers being prohibited by RANGE), we send the cursor along to @ GET m.partno so the operator can enter a part number.

Using Pick Lists for Menu-Assisted Item Entry

Moving the cursor to @ GET m.partno results in the execution of the following WHEN clause:

```
IF m.but1 = "Add Items" AND m.quantity > 0
    ON KEY LABEL F2 DO picks WITH "F2"
    ON KEY LABEL F3 DO picks WITH "F3"
    RETURN .T.
ENDIF
RETURN .F.
```

The IF/ENDIF followed by RETURN .F. ensures that the cursor cannot enter the input field unless Add Items is the selected routine and a quantity has already been entered. On the other hand, if these criteria are met, we use ON KEY LABEL to activate function keys F2 and F3 before enabling the cursor in the field. So that the operator will be informed of the availability of function keys F2 and F3, we display the message "Enter part number or F2:Part Number Pick List or F3:Part Description Pick List." in the status bar with @ GET MESSAGE <expC>. Figure 6.11 shows the Screen Builder Field dialog used to define @ GET m.partno with the embedded MESSAGE clause Code Snippet dialog open on the screen.

Once the cursor is enabled, the operator can enter a part number or use F2 or F3 to select an item by part number or description from one of our two pick lists. Still, regardless of how the part number is entered, @ GET VALID is used to check the entry by looking up the item in Inpick1 (the copy of Inventry.dbf used by the popup that lists inventory records in order by Partno) and, if it is found, to arrange the display of the part description, price, and extension with SHOW GET. We use Inpick1 rather than Invsales, the copy of Inventry.dbf linked to Sal_det.dbf, to avoid adversely affecting the BROWSE display, which is dependent on Invsales.

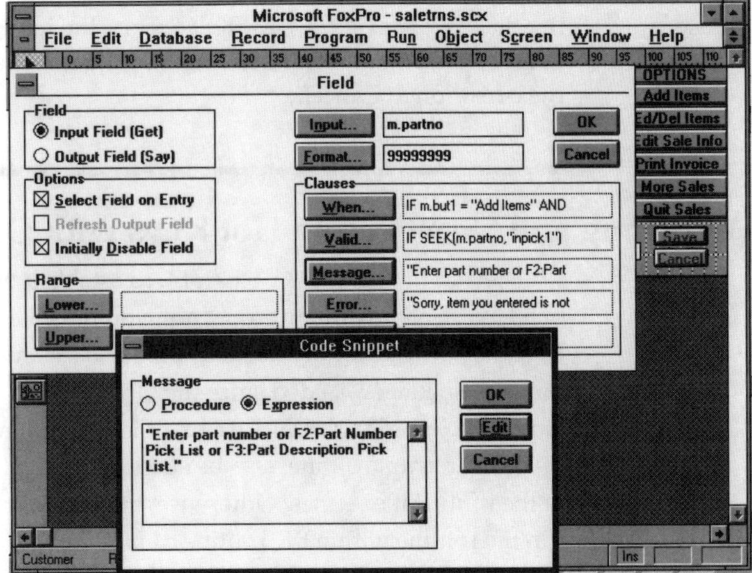

FIGURE 6.11:

The Screen Builder's Field dialog uses embedded dialogs for entering optional @ GET clauses.

```
ON KEY LABEL F2
ON KEY LABEL F3
IF SEEK(m.partno,"inpick1")
    m.p_descript = inpick1.p_descript
    m.price = inpick1.price
    m.exten = m.quantity * m.price
    SHOW GET m.p_descript
    SHOW GET m.price
    SHOW GET m.exten
    _CUROBJ = OBJNUM(m.veritem)
    RETURN .T.
ELSE
    IF EMPTY(m.partno)
        _CUROBJ = OBJNUM(m.veritem)+1
        RETURN .T.
    ENDIF
ENDIF
ON KEY LABEL F2 DO picks WITH "F2"
ON KEY LABEL F3 DO picks WITH "F3"
RETURN .F.
```

The cursor is then sent on to the Save push button.

If the part number is not listed in Inpick1, the VALID clause RETURNs .F., triggering the display of @ GET ERROR "Sorry, the item you entered is not present in Inventory table"—that is, unless the input field is left blank, in which case we send the cursor on to Cancel.

Activating and Deactivating Hot Keys with ON KEY LABEL

Whenever you use ON KEY LABEL to establish hot keys for operator execution of a FoxPro command or procedure, you must be extra careful to activate the hot keys only when they are needed. This also means deactivating them the moment they are no longer needed since the ON KEY LABEL <command> will stay in effect until cleared with ON KEY LABEL. To prevent recursive use of an ON KEY LABEL interrupt routine, also be sure to deactivate the hot key at the outset of the routine it executes. Otherwise, the operator can press the key again and run the routine within the routine *ad infinitum.*

Of course, of much greater moment is procedure Picks, which is used to handle the optional entry of part numbers to @ GET m.partno using two different pick lists—one arranging the inventory/price list by Partno, the other arranging it alphabetically by P_descript. Here we recall the definitions of the two popups used for this purpose:

```
USE inventry AGAIN ALIAS inpick1 ORDER partno IN 0 NOUPDATE
DEFINE POPUP parts FROM 0,0 ;
    PROMPT FIELD inpick1.partno+" "+inpick1.p_descript+ ;
    STR(inpick1.price,10,2) SCROLL
ON SELECTION POPUP parts DEACTIVATE POPUP parts

USE inventry AGAIN ALIAS inpick2 ORDER p_descript IN 0 NOUPDATE
DEFINE POPUP descript FROM 0,0 ;
    PROMPT FIELD inpick2.p_descript+" "+inpick2.partno+ ;
    STR(inpick2.price,10,2) SCROLL
ON SELECTION POPUP descript DEACTIVATE POPUP descript
```

To speed up execution of Saletrns.spr, we define these two popups in procedure Opendata, at the outset of Bigbiz.prg (the MBS startup program), when we open the copies of Inventry.dbf from which they take their data. However, beware! When executing a popup with ACTIVATE POPUP instead of @ GET list, the popup will automatically assume the font used by the current output window. Since we plan to invoke our popups when Saletrns.spr's READ window, Sale_Trans, is active, this means the popup will assume @ GET m.partno's font: MS Sans Serif, 8. In the normal run of things this will be no problem. But here we use string concatenation to place data from three different fields—P_descript, Partno, and Price—in our popups. If the popup is to look at all pleasing, the data from the three fields must be arranged in even columns in the popup bars, as shown in Figure 6.12. This will not happen if the popup assumes a proportional font.

Controlling Popup Attributes and Font with User-Defined Windows

As with BROWSE, we can gain greater control over a popup menu executed with ACTIVATE POPUP by activating it in a window defined with the attributes and font we want the popup to assume. However, defining the window is not as easy as defining a window for use with BROWSE. (See Chapter 5.) This is because popups are not windows. This means you cannot display a popup on the screen and trap its row and column coordinates with WLROW(), WLCOL(), and the like. The process of defining the window will be more trouble, and for this reason alone,

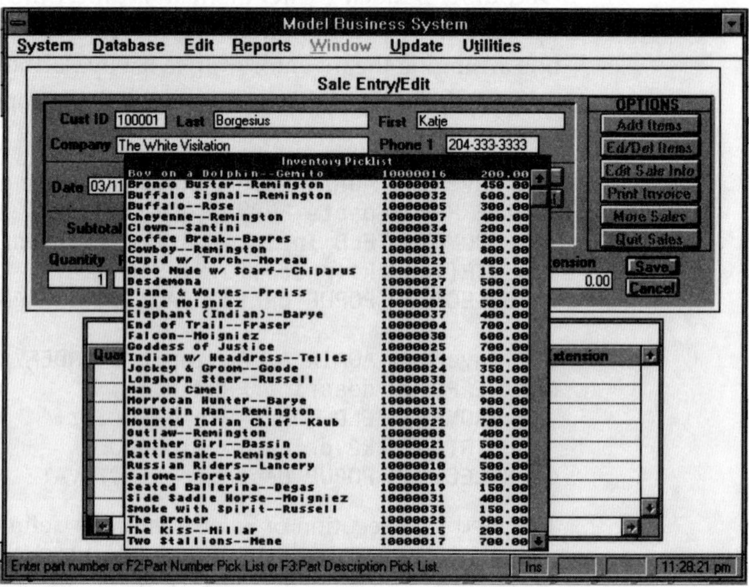

FIGURE 6.12:
Using string concatenation, popups can be defined using data from more than one field.

it will always be easier to display popups on the screen using @ GET lists, provided that there's room enough in the READ windows for the list. This is clearly not the case with the popups we use with Saletrns.spr.

The best way to go about the task of defining a window for controlling popup position and attributes is to begin by using DEFINE POPUP and ACTIVATE, SHOW, MOVE, and SIZE POPUP to locate the popup in the correct position on the screen. If no windows are active or DEFINE POPUP IN SCREEN is used, the popup will derive its font from the main FoxPro window. You can, however, change the font and attributes of the main FoxPro window with MODIFY WINDOW SCREEN. Use it to establish an appropriate monospace font for the popup when it is defined. (Note that DEFINE POPUP requires only FROM coordinates. If you omit TO coordinates, FoxPro will set them automatically to accommodate the data displayed in each row of the popup.)

Once you have the popup properly displayed, define a window with the desired font and attributes. You will want to use DEFINE WINDOW <name> with FLOAT and GROW so the window can be properly sized and positioned around the popup using the mouse. (You can also use MOVE and MODIFY WINDOW to move the window into position.) You can then trap the window's coordinates with WLROW(),

WROWS(), WLCOL(), and WCOLS() or use the utility program Dimens.prg, supplied with the MBS (discussed in Chapter 5) to record the coordinates and write a suitable DEFINE WINDOW command for use with the popup.

If the window is to extend to the bottom of the screen, you can also use SROWS(), the screen rows function, to supply the window's TO <row> coordinate since SROWS() returns an <expN> indicating the last available row on the screen. The value it returns will naturally depend upon the font being used, but that is all the more reason to use it, though we may prefer to use SROWS() –2 so the bottom of the popup will be positioned just above the status bar. (Though we have no use for it here, SCOLS(), the screen column function, is also available for returning the number of columns on the screen.)

Finally, if the popup is intended to fill the window, use DEFINE POPUP FROM 0,0 to execute it in the first row and column of the active window. Again, if no lower right-hand (TO) coordinates are specified for the popup, column width will be determined by the width of the popup's bars, and they will extend beyond the active window if it is too small to accommodate them.

Trapping Pick List Entries

Windows defined for special use with popups will be listed in the Window pulldown. For this reason, though we define our popups at the outset of the MBS while establishing our default table view, we do not define the window we use with them until the very last moment. This is done in procedure Pick, which, as you may recall, is executed by ON KEY LABEL with DO Picks WITH "F2" or DO Picks WITH "F3", depending upon which function key is used. To prevent the operator from accessing the Window pulldown while the popup is active, we use SET SKIP OF PAD <pad> OF <menu> .T. to disable the Window pulldown. We can then reenable the Window pulldown by reissuing the command with a value of .F. the moment the popup is deactivated and the window released.

```
PROCEDURE Picks
PARAMETER m.key
ON KEY LABEL F2
ON KEY LABEL F3
DEFINE WINDOW stpick FROM 5,20 TO SROWS()-2,92.5 ;
    NOGROW NOFLOAT NOZOOM NOCLOSE HALFHEIGHT ;
    TITLE "Inventory Picklist" FONT "Foxfont", 8
SET SKIP OF PAD _msm_windo OF _msysmenu .T.
ACTIVATE WINDOW stpick
```

```
SET CONFIRM ON
IF m.key = "F2"
    ACTIVATE POPUP parts
ELSE
    ACTIVATE POPUP descript
ENDIF
SET CONFIRM OFF
RELEASE WINDOW stpick
SET SKIP OF PAD _msm_windo OF _msysmenu .F.
 IF LASTKEY() <> 27
    KEYBOARD IIF(m.key="F2",inpick1.partno,inpick2.partno)
ELSE
    ON KEY LABEL F2 DO picks WITH "F2"
    ON KEY LABEL F3 DO picks WITH "F3"
ENDIF
RETURN .T.
```

After storing the passed parameter indicating which function key was pressed to execute it to memvar m.key, procedure Picks deactivates the ON KEY LABEL hot keys. It then defines and activates window stpick before activating the popup corresponding to the operator's choice. Popup Parts is defined so as to list our inventory items in order by Partno, each part number being followed by the part description and price, while popup Descript lists the parts alphabetically by part description, each part description being followed by the part number and price.

Because of the use of ON SELECTION POPUP <name> DEACTIVATE POPUP, whichever popup is used is immediately deactivated when the operator makes a selection or presses the Esc key to leave the popup without making one.

TIP

When using a popup created with DEFINE POPUP PROMPT FIELD, operator entry of a keyboard character will position FoxPro to the first popup option beginning with that character, if one can be found. However, this feature will not be very useful if entry of a character not only moves to the first option beginning with that character but also selects it automatically. We inhibit this with SET CONFIRM OFF. With SET CONFIRM OFF, the operator must explicitly press the Enter key to select the highlighted popup option.

The last step is remarkably simple. If the last key pressed by the operator was not Esc (LASTKEY() <> 27), we use the KEYBOARD command to input the Partno of the present record in the table used by the popup. Upon return to @ GET m.partno, the effect is the same as if the operator had keyed in the Partno using the keyboard. Since the input value will fill @ GET m.partno, it will automatically trigger its VALID clause, cited in full above. We repeat the crucial lines here:

```
IF SEEK(m.partno,"inpick1")
    m.p_descript = inpick1.p_descript
    m.price = inpick1.price
    m.exten = m.quantity * m.price
    SHOW GET m.p_descript
    SHOW GET m.price
    SHOW GET m.exten
    _CUROBJ = OBJNUM(m.veritem)
    RETURN .T.
ELSE...
```

If we allow FoxPro to repeat the lookup using the Partno supplied by KEYBOARD, it is just to save us from having to write additional code to distinguish between operator entry of Partnos using procedure Picks, which must always supply us with a valid Partno, and manual entry of Partnos that will have to be tested. Little time is wasted. (Again, we refer to Inpick1, the copy of Inventry.dbf used by our Parts pick list, as opposed to Invsales, linked into Sal_det.dbf, to avoid adversely affecting our BROWSE display of sales items. Moving the record pointer in Invsales with SEEK() will result in the disappearance of data in the current record in the BROWSE window.) Once we load m.p_descript, m.price, and m.exten with the proper values, we place this information on the screen with SHOW GET and move the cursor on to the Save push button.

Alternative Ways of Handling Part Number Entries

Needless to say, there are a variety of other ways to handle operator entry of Partnos. To begin with, it is not at all necessary to employ an @ GET input field for entry of part numbers if the operator will always select the part from a pick list. Where this is the case, @ GET popup, @ GET list, or DEFINE POPUP will be sufficient to trap the operator's selection. An input field is required only in situations where the operator is likely to become familiar with the part number of many inventory items or where items are ordered by part number. In these instances it will be faster to type them in instead of searching around in a pick list for the right item, even if the pick list is automatically activated—that is, without requiring the operator to press a function key.

Of course, in programs in which an input field serves no useful purpose, @ GET popup and @ GET list can be used to display the pick list directly in the READ window. With @ GET list, the items included in the list can be taken from an array or directly from a table or predefined popup. (The options are the same as those offered with DEFINE POPUP PROMPT.) With @ GET popup, the items must be taken from an array.

Still, whether or not you use an input field, the way you go about producing your pick list depends upon the number of options it must display. If the inventory list includes more than a thousand items, using a pick list created with DEFINE POPUP, @ GET popup, or @ GET list may become quite slow. FoxPro just can't manage them with the speed and efficiency with which it handles tables. Where this will be a problem, the best solution is to use a BROWSE window to display the pick list instead. For example, in place of DEFINE and ACTIVATE POPUP, we can easily rewrite procedure Picks so that operator entry of function key F2 or F3 opens a BROWSE window listing inventory records in the desired order. We might even include a nested dialog, activated, for example, by another function key, to allow the operator to search for items in the BROWSE window. In any case, when the operator leaves the BROWSE window, we simply use the current record as the operator's selection—that is, unless the operator closes the window using the Esc key, Close, or some other keystroke assigned the function of indicating that no selection has been made.

Termination of Add Items and Ed/Del Items Action

Like all append and edit operations in MBS, the Add and Ed/Del Items actions terminate with a Save/Cancel, @ GET push button VALID routine. Noting the use of SHOW GETS in the last line, we can use the Add Items routine over and over without returning to our control push buttons by simply leaving the values of m.doit and m.doitem unchanged. We take advantage of this, however, only when Save is used with Add Items since we must regard selection of Cancel as a signal to end sales item entry. In the case of Ed/Del Items, such repetition is not desirable because each item called for edit must first be targeted in our BROWSE window. To prepare for termination of Add and Ed/Del Items or repetition of Add Items, we also see to it that the @ GET input fields related to item entry are blanked out prior to execution of SHOW GETS. We also use SHOW WINDOW REFRESH to update our BROWSE window as needed, without having to reactivate it.

```
* VALID clause used with Save/Cancel push buttons
* terminating Add and Ed/Del Items.
IF m.but1 = "Add Items"
    IF m.veritem = "Save"
        * If the item was saved, check to make sure that entries
        * were actually made for quanity and part number. If so,
        * save the item and update running totals for sale. If
        * not, warn operator and do not add the item to sale.
        IF m.quantity <> 0 AND m.partno <> " "
            INSERT INTO sal_det (saleno,quantity,partno) ;
                VALUES (sales.saleno,m.quantity,m.partno)
            REPLACE invsales.onhand ;
                WITH invsales.onhand - m.quantity
            m.subtot = m.subtot + m.exten
            m.tax = ROUND(m.subtot * m.taxrat,2)
            m.amount = m.subtot + m.tax
            SHOW WINDOW "Items" REFRESH SAME
        ELSE
             WAIT WINDOW "Inappropriate entry for quantity "+ ;
                 "or part number...discarding." NOWAIT
        ENDIF
        * As operator may need to enter additional items to
        * the sale, leave values of m.doitem and m.doit
        * launching Add routine in READ SHOW unchanged.
        * However, if item was canceled, use this as signal
        * to terminate Add routine by altering these memvars.
    ELSE
        STORE .F. TO m.doitem,m.doit
    ENDIF
ELSE
    * During edit item routine, operator may have switched to
    * BROWSE window to look at other items already in sale.
    * If so, we must reposition FoxPro back to the item selected
    * for Ed/Del action or we will update the wrong item.
    SELECT sal_det
    IF sd_rec <> RECNO()
        GO sd_rec
    ENDIF
    * If Ed/Del action was terminated with Save, no action need
    * be taken if operator decided not to change the quantity.
    * However, if quantity was changed, running totals for sale
    * must be recalculated by first deducting original figures
    * for item from sale and then adding new figures to it. This
    * must be done before the sale item record is actually
    * changed. (Inventry.onhand must also be adjusted.)
```

```
    IF m.veritem = "Save" AND m.quantity <> sal_det.quantity
        m.subtot = m.subtot - (sal_det.quantity * invsales.price)
        REPLACE invsales.onhand ;
            WITH invsales.onhand + sal_det.quantity
        * A quantity of 0 indicates that item is to be deleted.
        * Test quantity and respond accordingly.
        IF m.quantity <> 0
            m.subtot = m.subtot + m.exten
            REPLACE sal_det.quantity WITH m.quantity, ;
                invsales.onhand WITH invsales.onhand - m.quantity
        ELSE
            DELETE
        ENDIF
        * After reselecting Sales we use GO RECNO() to make
        * FoxPro reposition in child table Sal_det to the first
        * record in the current sale. This will be required to
        * move FoxPro off a deleted record.
        SELECT sales
        GO RECNO()
        m.tax = ROUND(m.subtot * m.taxrat,2)
        m.amount = m.subtot + m.tax
    ENDIF
    SHOW WINDOW "Items" REFRESH SAME
    STORE .F. TO m.doitem,m.doit
ENDIF
* Renew input field values so that they will be blank when
* SHOW GETS is executed.
m.quantity = 0
m.partno = SPACE(8)
m.p_descript = SPACE(30)
m.price = 0.00
m.exten = 0.00
* If Add items routine is not to be reexecuted reset
* GETs for reactivation of main control push buttons
* in READ SHOW.
IF NOT m.doit
    SHOW GET m.quantity DISABLE
    SHOW GET m.partno DISABLE
    SHOW GET m.p_descript DISABLE
    SHOW GET m.price DISABLE
    SHOW GET m.exten DISABLE
    SHOW GET m.veritem DISABLE
    SHOW GET m.but1 ENABLE
ENDIF
SHOW GETS
```

On the whole, the portions of the VALID clause devoted to updating data updates with Add and Ed/Del Items should be straightforward enough—provided you have a cursory grasp of the different sets of values that are affected by entering and editing sales items.

With regard to Add Items, we first check to make sure entries have been made to m.quantity and m.partno. If they have, we use SQL-INSERT to place the new record in Sal_det.dbf. We then use m.quantity with REPLACE to update Invsales.onhand to reflect the number of items taken from stock and update our running totals for the sale. (We can refer to Invsales instead of Inpick1 here when updating Inventry.dbf's Onhand field since INSERT IN Sal_det will automatically move Invsales, as Sal_det.dbf's child, to the correct record.)

On the other hand, if appropriate entries are not made with Add Items, we warn the operator of the problem with WAIT WINDOW. Since the values of m.doit and m.doitem remain unchanged in either case, the memvars used with the @ GET input fields will be blanked out at the bottom of the VALID clause and SHOW GETS will renew data entry with @ GET m.quantity. Again, Add Items must be terminated with Cancel. (Because SHOW GETS will also trigger the READ SHOW clause, these last commands will be redundant if data entry goes on since READ SHOW also issues them. With Add Items/Save we might use SHOW GETS ONLY instead to avoid triggering READ SHOW.)

In the case of Save with Ed/Del Items, we must go to more effort to make sure our running totals and the figure held in Inventry.onhand for the sale item are properly updated. If a change in quantity has actually been made, we must begin by subtracting the total cost of the unedited item from our figure for subtotal and subtract the quantity of the unedited item from Invsales.onhand. We rely upon the values of the current record in Sal_det to do this. This allows us to begin with a clean slate since the running totals and Onhand field value will be returned to the values they would have if the item was never entered. We can then readjust these values as indicated by the new item quantity and use REPLACE to update Sal_det.quantity and Invsales.onhand. If m.quantity is set to 0, however, no further adjustments need be made. We can simply DELETE the item in Sal_det.dbf. Using the subtotal, we can then recalculate our figures for tax (m.tax) and total (m.amount).

NOTE

Another way to manage the running totals for a sale is to simply recalculate them from scratch after each sale item is added or changed using SUM, as we did at the outset of Saletrns.spr. Many programmers find this easier. If you choose to work in this way, place the commands calculating the running figures for the sale in a UDF and place it in the screen program's cleanup code.

As previously noted, before taking any action with Ed/Del Items, we take care to ensure that FoxPro is positioned in Sal_det.dbf to the record that was current when the routine was launched. This is done using sd_rec, which holds RECNO() in Sal_det as it stood when READ SHOW was executed. (Again, the Ed/Del Items routine does not prevent the operator from returning to BROWSE and moving the record pointer. We must therefore see to it that the correct record gets updated.)

The Edit Sale Info Routine

With regard to the editing of the summary sales record in Sales.dbf, there is no need to dwell further on the input fields used in the process. However, when saving changes to the sales summary record following operator selection of the Save push button, we must be prepared to alter Customer.current if the sale is changed from "Cash" (s_code = "1") to "Charge" (s_code = "2"). Note that we are not interested at this point in updating Customer.current with the current, running sale total stored in m.amount. This will be done when the operator is finished with the sale during execution of Saletrns.spr's cleanup code. We are only interested in making sure that Customer.current will be correct with respect to the total (Sales.amount) of the sale as it stood before a sale was called for edit.

```
IF m.versum = "Save"
    IF m.s_code <> sales.s_code
        IF m.s_code = "1"
            REPLACE customer.current ;
                WITH customer.current -sales.amount
        ELSE
            REPLACE customer.current ;
                WITH customer.current +sales.amount
        ENDIF
        m.current = customer.current
```

```
    ENDIF
    IF sales.date <> m.date OR sales.pono <> m.pono ;
        OR sales.s_code <> m.s_code
        REPLACE date WITH m.date,pono WITH m.pono, ;
            s_code WITH m.s_code
    ENDIF
ELSE
    m.temp = m.amount
    SCATTER MEMVAR
    m.amount = m.temp
    m.s_code2 = IIF(sales.s_code="1","Cash","Charge")
ENDIF
m.pres_bal = customer.current+customer.days30+ ;
    customer.days60+customer.days90+customer.days120
STORE .F. TO m.dosum,m.doit
SHOW GET m.versum DISABLE
SHOW GET m.but1 ENABLE
SHOW GETS
```

The only other aspect of the VALID clause used with @ GET m.versum push buttons worth mentioning is our use of a temporary memvar to hold on to m.amount, the running total for our sale, before using SCATTER MEMVAR to renew our memvars if the operator selects Cancel. Since SCATTER MEMVAR overwrites m.amount with the total of the sale prior to its manipulation by Saletrns.spr, we will lose the running total for the sale unless we use SCATTER MEMVAR FIELD to exclude it from SCATTER's action or prepare to restore it from another memvar after SCATTER overwrites m.amount.

Printing the Sale Invoice

Selecting the Print Invoice push button executes procedure Invoice, designed to oversee the execution of a FoxPro Report form. Here is its code:

```
PROCEDURE Invoice
IF NOT PRINTSTATUS()
    DO alert WITH "Printer not ready! Please fix and "+ ;
        "try again.", "Press any key to continue."
    RETURN
ENDIF
SELECT Sales
sal_rec = RECNO()
```

```
SELECT customer
cus_rec = RECNO()
SET SKIP TO sales,sal_det
GO cus_rec
REPORT FORM invoice TO PRINT NOCONSOLE NOEJECT ;
    WHILE customer.custno = m.custno ;
    FOR sales.saleno = m.saleno
SET SKIP TO
GO cus_rec
SELECT sales
GO sal_rec
RETURN
```

As a precaution, we design the procedure to begin by using the PRINTSTATUS() function to make sure the printer or print device is ready to receive output. If it is not, we inform the operator of the problem and break off further execution. (The operator can take whatever action is necessary to get the printer on line and then reselect Print Invoice.)

Given the multi-table view used during sales invoice entry, we have little to do to prepare for execution of Report form Invoice. However, since execution of REPORT FORM, like any other sequential command, will alter FoxPro's position in our tables, we store the record numbers of the current Customer.dbf and Sales.dbf records to memvars so we can later return to our @ GET push buttons with our tables in proper order. Then it is only a matter of making Customer.dbf the current table and issuing SET SKIP to prepare FoxPro to skip through multiple child records, specifically in Sal_det.dbf, when outputting data with REPORT FORM.

The fact that we are using SET RELATION makes our REPORT FORM command nonoptimizable, but this hardly matters since we are already positioned in our multi-table database to the sales belonging to the correct customer. We can thus use WHILE <condition> to limit FoxPro's sequential read of the database to only those records belonging to Customer.custno = m.custno—and use FOR <condition> to pinpoint only those records belonging to the current sale as indicated by the value of m.saleno. When the invoice has been printed, the procedure restores the prior view and then returns program control to the VALID clause of our control push buttons.

While we do not discuss the use of the Report Writer until Chapter 13, there is really nothing very remarkable about Report form Invoice. Data for the business return address is drawn, as in customer statements, from Bizshare.dbf. Customer name and address information is drawn from Customer.dbf; sales invoice, date, and purchase order number are taken from Sales.dbf; and line item information is drawn from Sal_det.dbf and Inventry.dbf. The Report form performs all calculations on the fly. Figure 6.13 shows a screen shot of a sample MBS invoice.

FIGURE 6.13:

MBS sale invoices are produced using a FoxPro Report form.

Model Business System

File Edit Database Record Program Window Help

03/31/95 Invoice #100012 Cust #100001 PO #KBCH0004 1

FROM:Howard Dickler
PO Box 34293
Los Angeles, CA 90034
310-204-2780

TO: Dr. Katje Borgesius
The White Visitation
Entertainment & Therapy
34012 Pennsylvania Ave.
Washington DC 02043-222
USA
204-333-3333

Item	Quantity	Part #	Description	Price	Extension
1	6	10000001	Bronco Buster--Remington	450.00	2700.00
2	3	10000004	End of Trail--Fraser	700.00	2100.00
3	3	10000006	Rattlesnake--Remington	400.00	1200.00
4	5	10000009	Salome--Foretay	300.00	1500.00
5	3	10000013	Diane & Wolves--Preiss	600.00	1800.00
6	4	10000021	Panther Girl--Bassin	500.00	2000.00
7	2	10000027	Desdemona	500.00	1000.00
8	2	10000030	Falcon--Moigniez	600.00	1200.00
9	2	10000034	Clown--Santini	200.00	400.00

Subtotal 13,900.00

CHARGED to Customer Account Tax 1,390.00

Total $15,290.00

Note that Report form Invoice is the only printed report in the MBS system that is not executed from the Reports pulldown. This is owing to typical practice in most small businesses, where invoices are printed the moment they are entered and before another sale is entered. In some systems, however, sales invoices are executed in a batch at the end of the day. Since Report form Invoice is defined as a Group report, it can be easily adapted to printing sales invoices in batch. The Print Invoices (in batch) option would naturally find its way onto the Reports pulldown since it would be unsuitable in Saletrns.spr.

We discuss the creation of Report form Invoice in Chapter 13.

Terminating the Sales Entry/Edit Program

Finally, we come to the last important routine in Saletrns.spr, the one used to make final updates to the current sale's record in Sales.dbf and to the customer account fields in Customer.dbf. However, the fact that we always use Saletrns.spr in an edit sale mode (new records being added to Sales.dbf in Sales.spr before Saletrns.spr is called) greatly simplifies what we must do. The only real issue with which we must deal when READ is terminated is whether or not the sale has been zeroed out. This will happen if all items are deleted from a sale called for edit or if no items are entered in a new sale. In any case, if the sale is empty—m.amount = 0.00—we must DELETE the sale's record in Sales.dbf, whether or not the sale is new. However, if the sale is not new, as will be indicated by Sales.amount <> 0.00, its Sales.amount will already be reflected by the values of Customer.current (if the sale is a charge) and Customer.history. We must therefore take action to see to it that these customer fields are properly adjusted to reflect the deletion of the sale. We take care of these matters with the first portion of procedure Salclose, shown below. Again, a *new* sale can be identified by Sales.amount = 0.00 since the Sales.amount field is *not* updated until procedure Salclose is executed.

```
* Procedure updating customer account fields before termination
* of Saletrns.spr.
PROCEDURE Salclose
SELECT sales
IF m.amount = 0.00
    IF sales.amount <> 0.00
        m.current = m.current - ;
            IIF(m.s_code = "2",sales.amount,0.00)
        m.history = m.history - sales.amount
        REPLACE customer.current WITH m.current, ;
        customer.history WITH m.history
    ENDIF
    DELETE
ELSE
    IF sales.amount <> 0.00
        m.current = m.current - ;
            IIF(m.s_code = "2",sales.amount,0.00)
        m.history = m.history - sales.amount
    ENDIF
    m.current = m.current + IIF(m.s_code = "2",m.amount,0.00)
    m.history = m.history + m.amount
```

```
    REPLACE customer.current WITH m.current, ;
        customer.history WITH m.history, ;
        customer.lastdate WITH sales.date
    REPLACE sales.amount WITH m.amount
ENDIF
```

If the sale has not been zeroed out, we must take steps to update Customer.current, Customer.history, and Customer.lastdate to reflect the new or edited sale and, finally, update Sales.amount to hold the total amount of the sale. Here again, we must take special care when dealing with a sale previously used to update Customer.current and Customer.history. We will get the correct results only if we set the figures held by m.current and m.history (which are not otherwise affected by Saletrns.spr) back to what they would have been had the original sale not been entered. Once we have done so, we can get the right results by updating the fields just as though we were dealing with a new sale. End of program—that is, except for the other lines of our cleanup code.

Controlling Termination of a Nonmodal Data Entry Program

As you are aware, Saletrns.spr is not written as a modal dialog. The operator is free to call and execute other MBS screen programs while leaving the inactive READ window, representing the current sale, on the screen, ready to be reactivated as soon as the operator reselects it. Again, this can be done by selecting window Sale_trans from the Window pulldown, by clicking the window, or by using Ctrl+F6 or Cycle (also Ctrl+F1) on the Window pulldown to switch to it.

From the standpoint of the operator, unfamiliar with how FoxPro manages to reactivate a window—namely, by relaunching the program executing the window from scratch—it seems as though the Sales entry program is merely suspended. We know differently; it is terminated. But we also know that it is terminated and started in such a way—that is, when the READ window is left on the screen—as to promote the illusion that the program is only temporarily suspended. When READ is terminated without use of Quit Sales, More Sales, or the Close option in the window control box, the READ window is not released and the parameters required to restart Saletrns.spr with the current sale are saved to a memory file, as discussed above. Saletrns.spr's startup code is designed to check for the prior existence of window Sale_trans and, if it exists, to use the parameters stored in the memory file to reinitiate editing of the sale displayed in the inactive window. Moreover, all data update actions performed by Saletrns.spr are so written as to permit the sudden temporary or permanent termination of the program. For example, procedure Salclose, described above, finishes with the sale in such a fashion that it really makes no difference whether or not the operator returns to the deactivated READ window. The operator can even use the Exit to Windows or Exit to FoxPro option on the System pulldown to break off MBS operations while the deactivated READ window is still on the screen. Because procedure Salclose has already taken care to record the sale as if it were final, it makes no difference.

Still, every strategy has its weak spots, and Saletrns.spr is no exception. Having gone to the effort of supporting the illusion that Saletrns.spr can be temporarily suspended at any time, we should not be surprised to find the operator attempting to suspend the program before entering any items to a new sale. One look at procedure Salclose will reveal that this is counterindicated by the program. In procedure Salclose we use m.amount = 0.00 to determine when a sale is empty and should be deleted. On the other hand, if we do not take this precaution—given the fact that we add records for new sales to Sales.dbf in Sales.spr before Saletrns.spr is called—we are likely to end up with a lot of abandoned sales records with Sales.amount = 0.00 in Sales.dbf.

Using a Global Action-Confirmation Dialog

The way around this problem is simple, though it involves making a small compromise and writing some additional code to enact it. We must warn the operator against the consequences of terminating Saletrns.spr when no items are present in a sale or, more precisely, when m.amount = 0, and provide a means of countermanding the terminate action if the operator so chooses. This is easily done by creating a small dialog, designed to inform the operator of the potential problem and to register the operator's response: Proceed or Cancel. We can then insert the dialog wherever we need it.

TIP Create a global dialog for use within your system whenever the operator must be required to confirm an action.

Since we are likely to find other places in the MBS where we will require such a dialog, we have every reason to make it generic, like procedure Alert, so it will display any message we care to send it. This will make it useful in different contexts. Moreover, to streamline its usage, instead of calling it as a FoxPro procedure, we write it as a UDF. The text of our generic UDF, function Question, is shown below. Like procedure Alert, function Question was first created with the Screen Builder. After the screen program was generated, the code was revised and the function moved to the MBS procedure file Bizlib.prg.

```
FUNCTION Question
PARAMETER m.line1,m.line2
PRIVATE m.verify
m.verify = "Cancel"
DEFINE WINDOW question...FLOAT CLOSE NOGROW NOZOOM ;
    NOMINIMIZE DOUBLE
MOVE WINDOW question CENTER
ACTIVATE WINDOW question NOSHOW
@...SAY "qmark.bmp" BITMAP...
@...SAY PADC(m.line1,50)...
@...SAY PADC(m.line2,50)...
@ 5.385,20.167 GET m.verify ;
    PICTURE "@*HT \!\<Proceed;\?\<Cancel"...
ACTIVATE WINDOW question
READ CYCLE MODAL DEACTIVATE .T.
RELEASE WINDOW question
IF m.verify = "Proceed" AND READKEY(1) <> 5
    RETURN .T.
ENDIF
RETURN .F.
```

Since function Question() makes use of READ MODAL, it functions as a dialog, deactivating the system menu and inhibiting any effort by the operator to select another open window until the action is complete and the READ is terminated. Like procedure Alert, it uses a bitmap file to display, in this case, the picture of a question mark at the left of the dialog box, followed on the right by two @ SAYs displaying the two-line message it receives as parameters when called. (Again, as in procedure Alert, we center the message passed to m.line1 and m.line2 by using PADC(). If either string is shorter than 50 characters, the maximum width allowed, it will be padded with an equal number of blank spaces at both ends before it is displayed in the window.) But unlike procedure Alert, which uses WAIT simply to bring program execution to a halt (and therefore doesn't affect the READ level), function Question uses @ GET push buttons and READ CYCLE to return an answer. Note that closing the window with the Close option in the window control box will force

Question to RETURN .F. owing to the use of the compound condition in the IF statement following termination of READ. The IF statement will be true only when m.verify = "Proceed" and the window was not closed by using the control box to trigger READ DEACTIVATE. Now all we need do is put Question in place.

Controlling READ Terminate Events with a User Dialog

TIP

Window Question is first activated with the command ACTIVATE WINDOW NOSHOW. The NOSHOW keyword tells FoxPro to activate the window without making it visible on the screen. This makes it possible to send all output to the window before making it visible on the screen. When we are ready to show it, we reissue ACTIVATE WINDOW without the NOSHOW keyword.

To make proper use of function Question as a means of warning off operators if they unintentionally attempt to leave an *empty* sale, we must insert our dialog in three different places. First, as a courtesy, and as a check against accidental use of the Quit Sales and More Sales options, we must place it in the VALID clause of our main control push buttons. Though we have already seen the code, the pertinent lines are repeated here:

```
CASE m.but1 $ "Quit Sales More Sales"
    IF m.amount <> 0.00 OR ;
        question("SALE AMOUNT IS ZERO. CANCEL SALE?","")
        IF m.but1 = "More Sales"
            DO dospr WITH [sales.spr]
        ENDIF
        CLEAR READ
    ENDIF
ENDCASE
```

Since function Question will not be called unless m.amount <> 0.00 is False, the dialog will only appear, as shown in Figure 6.14, when a sale is empty. (This is because of the way FoxPro evaluates compound conditions formed with OR. If the first condition is True, FoxPro goes no further. Change the OR to AND, and Question will only be asked if the first condition is True. We see examples of this below.)

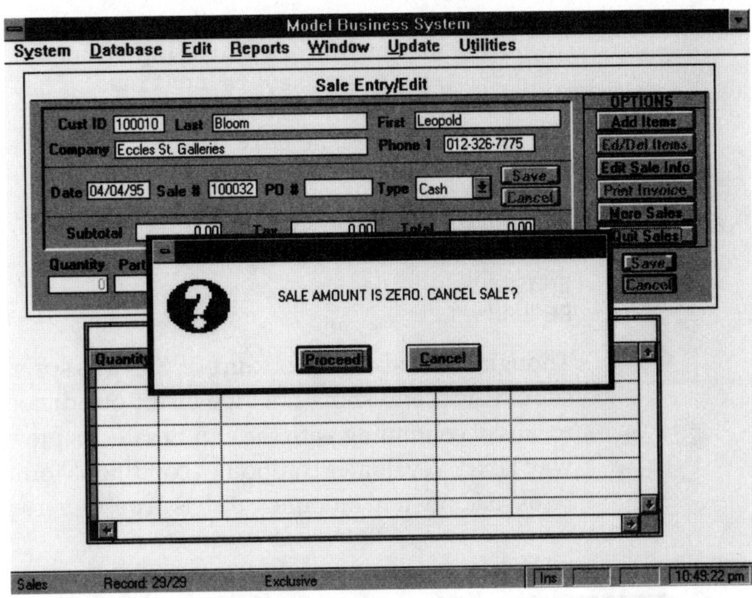

FIGURE 6.14:

The MBS action-confirmation dialog is executed by a user-defined function.

If the operator selects Cancel or closes the window using the control box, the CLEAR READ command is bypassed; the operator can go on working on the sale. However, if m.amount <> 0.00 OR the operator selects Proceed when the dialog is called, CLEAR READ is executed unless More Sales was the selected option. If it was, we restart Sales.spr, just as we started Saletrns.spr, by placing a call to procedure Dospr and allow procedure Dospr, presented earlier in this chapter, to execute CLEAR READ before executing Sales.spr. Either way, CLEAR READ terminates the READ and executes Saletrns.spr's cleanup code.

Still, the operator can terminate the program in other ways: by switching to another deactivated READ window still open on the screen, by selecting Close from the window control box, or by executing another nonmodal screen program from the Database pulldown. Since the first two events will trigger READ DEACTIVATE, we can simply insert the Question there.

```
IF m.amount = 0.00 AND
    NOT question("SALE AMOUNT IS ZERO. CANCEL SALE?","")
    ACTIVATE WINDOW items
    ACTIVATE WINDOW sale_trans
    RETURN .F.
ENDIF
```

```
IF m.doit
    DO alert WITH "Sorry, you must complete append/edit "+ ;
        "action before changing windows.", ;
        "Press any key to continue."
    ACTIVATE WINDOW items
    ACTIVATE WINDOW sale_trans
    RETURN .F.
ENDIF
IF UPPER(WONTOP()) = "ITEMS"
    RETURN .F.
ENDIF
RETURN .T.
```

Though this is but a mock-up of Saletrns.spr's READ DEACTIVATE clause, it should suffice to show how we insert our dialog to provide the operator with a means of continuing with the empty sale. As previously mentioned, because of the way FoxPro evaluates compound conditions formed with AND, our Question will be asked only if m.amount = 0.00 is True. Otherwise, FoxPro goes no further.

NOTE

If the operator selected Close from the window control box, window Sale_trans will already be deactivated by the time READ DEACTIVATE is triggered. Though RETURN .F. prevents the READ from being terminated, it will not of itself reactivate window Sale_trans or the BROWSE window. This is why we issue ACTIVATE WINDOW prior to RETURN .F.

The other IF/ENDIFs cited in the DEACTIVATE clause are used to prohibit termination of the READ (owing to the events we are currently discussing) while data editing is still going on (m.doit = .T.) or when the operator switches from the READ to the BROWSE window. Since we have already touched upon such uses of DEACTIVATE in connection with Payments.spr, however, we will say no more about them until Chapter 10.

This brings us to the third place in which we must insert our dialog: directly in procedure Dospr itself. Bear in mind that the procedure shown below is intended only to suggest how procedure Dospr functions; its actual text is significantly different, as we will see in Chapter 10.

```
PROCEDURE dospr
PARAMETER m.sprtodo
IF RDLEVEL() >  1
    IF m.doit
        DO alert WITH "Sorry, cannot execute program until "+ ;
            "append/edit operation is completed.", ;
            "Press any key to continue."
        RETURN
    ENDIF
    IF WONTOP() = "SALE_TRANS"
        IF m.amount = 0.00 AND NOT ;
            question("SALE AMOUNT IS ZERO. CANCEL SALE?","")
            RETURN
        ENDIF
    ENDIF
    CLEAR READ
ENDIF
DO (m.sprtodo)
RETURN
```

If Saletrns.spr or any other screen program is being used, the READ level will be greater than 1. Thus, if the operator selects another program from the Database pulldown while in the midst of adding or editing a record with any of the data entry programs, the action will be automatically countermanded by IF m.doit. (As should be clear by now, m.doit is always set to .T. in MBS during data entry or edit.)

We must be more cautious, however, when checking to see if the operator's action must terminate Saletrns.spr with an empty sale since, unlike m.doit, m.amount is a private (or local) memvar and will only exist when Saletrns.spr is being executed. (If we simply ask IF m.amount = 0.00 and Saletrns.spr or another program using m.amount is not being executed, our procedure Dospr will crash with the error "Variable cannot be found.") To avoid this error, we test the water first by using WONTOP() to see if Saletrns.spr is being run. If it is, we can then safely test m.amount and, if m.amount = 0.00, ask our Question(). In both cases, RETURN functions suitably to countermand the menu selection. If RETURN is executed before CLEAR READ is reached, the screen program active at the time the menu selection was made will continue uninterrupted.

With our Question dialog in place, the weak spot in our nonmodal screen program will cause us no trouble.

PART II

Creating a Windows-Style Interface

CHAPTER

SEVEN

Setting Out from the Project Manager

- Working with the Project Manager
- Loading an existing application into a project
- Using project files as tools
- Distributing your applications
- Alternative ways of starting applications

While there are a hundred and one ways to proceed in writing an application, the best way is to work through FoxPro's built-in *Project Manager.* This will be as clear as day to those who have already taken advantage of the Project Manager—and a bit difficult to swallow for those who are moving over to FoxPro from another Xbase language. The Project Manager will, after all, induce anxiety in anyone used to entering CREATE/MODIFY COMMAND <file> and setting out from scratch in the wide-open space of a text editor. There is, moreover, little you can do in the Project Manager that you can't do, although with greater difficulty, from the Command window. But that's as it should be since the Project Manager is designed to automate the use and update of files belonging to specific projects as well as the building of application (.app) or executable (.exe) program files based upon the files included in a project.

The Project Manager's simplest use is as an organizational tool, holding a list of all files, classified by type, belonging to any particular application. Figure 7.1, for example, shows the MBS project file open in the Project Manager. In the scrollable list are the names of all the files included in the MBS, listed in alphabetical order along with their file type. Though the files included in the list span several directories, they are all here, gathered in one place. We can open any table or open, modify, and/or execute any program or report by simply highlighting it in the list and selecting the Edit push button. In the case of a table, Edit opens it for use in BROWSE. You can then manipulate it in any fashion whatsoever, just as though you had opened it from the Command window. In the case of Report and Label forms, Edit executes MODIFY REPORT or MODIFY LABEL, respectively, and activates the Report/Label Writer for modification and/or execution of the indicated form.

Still, this is only the beginning. With the Project Manager you are still working in the interactive mode. Not only is the Command window immediately available, but the FoxPro system menu is still in place, though added to it you will find the Project pulldown, which is present only when the Project Manager is in use. In this case, use of the Project Manager reconfigures the FoxPro interactive mode, adding to it a variety of tools that will make it easier for you to open and modify all the files belonging to specific projects and to build your applications.

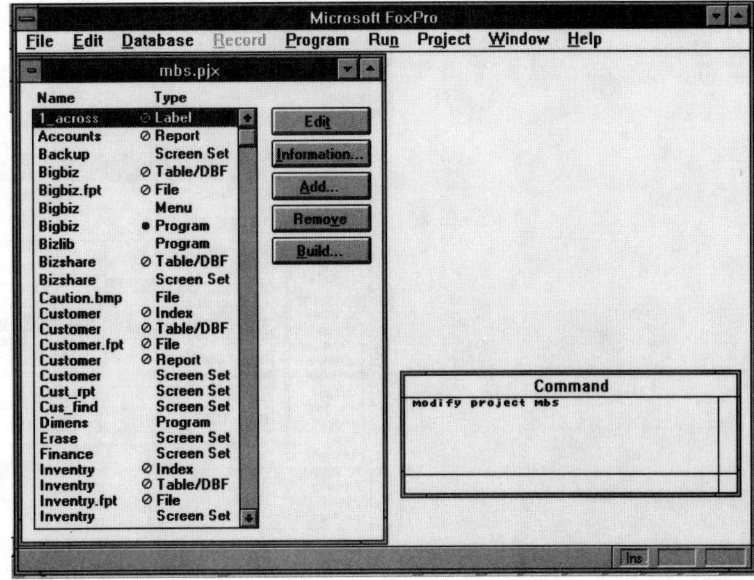

FIGURE 7.1:

The Project Manager provides a list of all files included in a project.

Starting a Project

While I recommend using the Project Manager from the outset, this does not mean that the Project Manager cannot be brought into play at any point in an application's development. Most beginners, for example, will create tables and index files, a few screen sets, and the like, working from the Command window before starting the Project Manager. Once they have the basic building blocks for their project, they use CREATE/MODIFY PROJECT <file> or the New file dialog, accessed from the FoxPro File pulldown, to start a new project. Then it's just a matter of using the Project Manager's Add File dialog, shown open in Figure 7.2, to add files to the project files list.

Loading an Existing Application

If you have already written a complete application made up of a number of program, screen, menu, and report files, you can immediately begin working with it through use of the Project Manager by creating a new project with CREATE/MODIFY PROJECT <file>. When the Project Manager appears on the screen, you simply

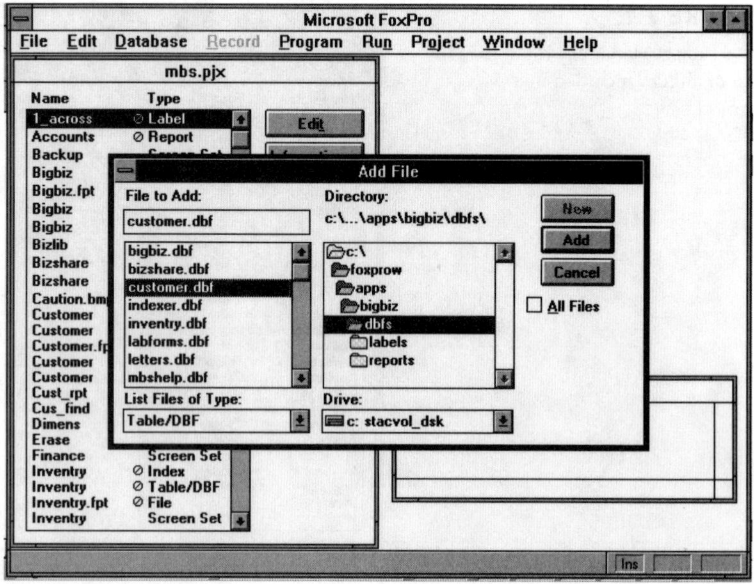

FIGURE 7.2:

Add files to a project with the Add File dialog.

add the application's startup (or main) program to the project with the Add File dialog, select the Build button to open the Build Option dialog, shown in Figure 7.3, select the Rebuild Project radio button, and press the OK button to rebuild the project. You can then continue working on the application just as though you had started it from the first using the Project Manager.

What happens is that the Program Manager reads through the program that it automatically selects as the startup, or *main*, program (a point we will return to in a moment) and looks for any and all files it references—that is, with the exception of tables and indexes. If those files are in the same directory as the main program or are located in the FoxPro file path set with SET PATH TO <path>, FoxPro adds them to the project while also taking note of their type, their directory location, and the file creation date and time. In the case of screen and menu programs generated through the use of the Screen and Menu Builder, respectively, FoxPro looks for the screen and menu (design) files on which each program is based. It then uses the screen or menu (design) file to regenerate the corresponding .spr (screen) or .mpr (menu) program and adds both versions of the file to the project, taking note, once again, of their file creation date and time. In this way, FoxPro is able to determine when a screen or menu program is out of date, following modification of the design

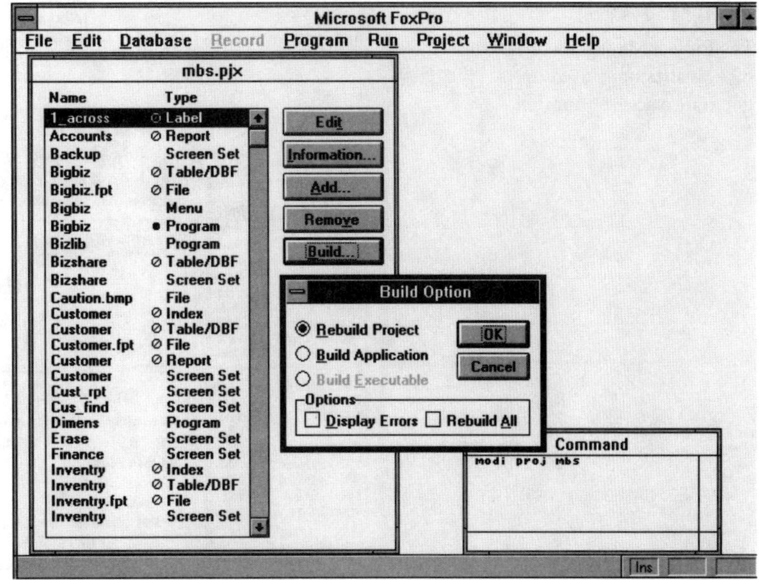

FIGURE 7.3:

Choose the Rebuild Project radio button in the Project Manager's Build Option dialog to build a project based upon an existing application.

file, and will take steps to regenerate it automatically whenever we rebuild the project or build the application. Without the Project Manager, each of these programs must be generated and compiled manually, using the Generate and Compile options on the FoxPro Program pulldown, and this will certainly be slower going.

With respect to screen programs, moreover, the Project Manager is capable of hanging on to the instructions with which FoxPro must be supplied every time you generate a screen program, while working in the Screen Builder, with the Generate Screen dialog. This same information need be entered only once with the Edit Screen Set dialog, shown in Figure 7.4. This dialog is the same as the Generate dialog except in title and in the availability of the Edit push button for activating the Screen Builder. (Chapter 11 discusses the actual use of the Screen Builder to design screen sets and generate screen programs.)

When you are working with the Project Manager, FoxPro will also automatically compile all program files, making it unnecessary to use the Program pulldown's Compile option or the COMPILE <file> command to regenerate object code files after modifying a program. The compiled code is, moreover, stored directly in the Project file. Date and time stamps are also noted so the object code version of any program can be automatically recompiled from the source when the latter is changed.

FIGURE 7.4:

The Project Manager keeps track of all instructions used to generate a screen program.

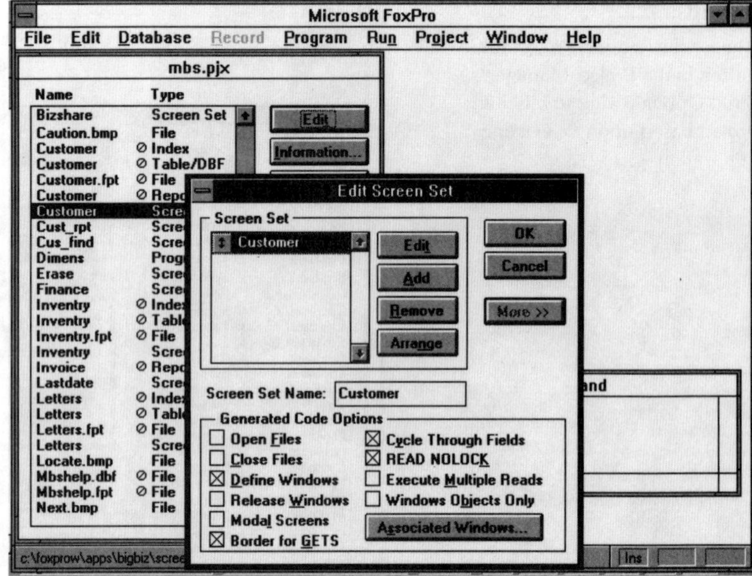

Using the Locate Dialog

When rebuilding a project based upon an existing application, FoxPro will be unable to find files referenced by the main program or any of its subordinate, nested programs if they are not located in the current directory or another directory listed in the SET PATH. When this is the case, FoxPro pauses and asks you to locate the missing file using the Locate File dialog, shown in Figure 7.5. Once FoxPro has been directed to a specific directory for one file it will not ask you before trying to locate another file in the same directory. It will check that directory again before asking for your assistance.

WARNING

If you have two or more files using the same file name in different directories in the current path (or in directories to which you have pointed the Project Manager using the Locate dialog) and the file is included in the application, the Project Manager will use the first file it comes to. It cannot be expected to know which version of the file you expect it to use.

FIGURE 7.5:

When rebuilding a project, FoxPro asks you to locate a file it is unable to find on its own.

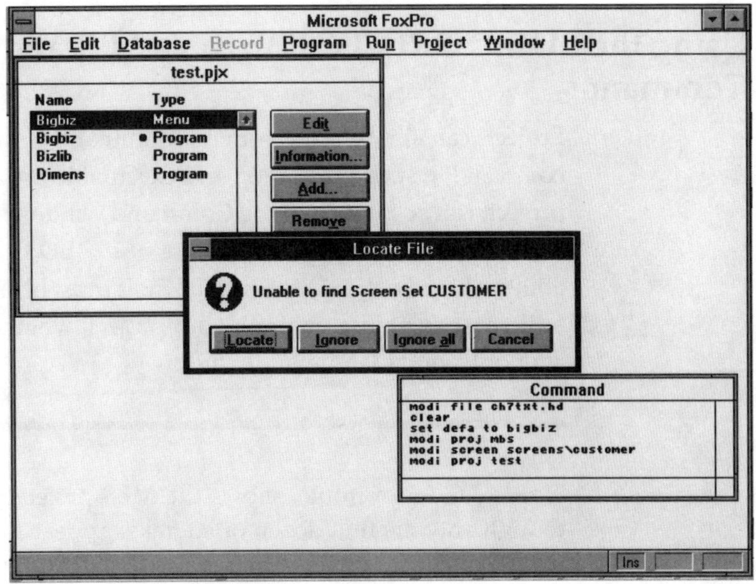

Adding Tables, Indexes, and Memo Files

Once again, when the Project Manager is used to build a project based upon an existing program, as described above, it will not automatically add tables, indexes, and memo files to the project. Though FoxPro has good reason to ignore them, you may nonetheless wish to add their names to the project files list so you can open and BROWSE your tables with the Edit push button and, perhaps more important, employ the files list as a tool in file management.

Using Project Files

All information entered into a project is stored in a FoxPro *project file*. Like resource files, project files are FoxPro tables with a special structure. (Project files use a .pjx extension, while their associated memo files use a .pjt extension.) As such, project files can be opened, browsed, and manipulated like any other table, though it is rare to use them in this way except for purposes of file management, as described later in this chapter, and as a means of better understanding how the Project Manager works.

Using the BUILD PROJECT, BUILD APP, and BUILD EXE Commands

Projects can also be built from the Command window using the BUILD PROJECT command, just as application and executable programs, based upon an existing project, can be built from the Command window with the BUILD APP and BUILD EXE commands, respectively. (Use of BUILD EXE will depend upon the availability of the FoxPro Distribution Kit. It must be installed on your computer to build an .exe file, based upon your project, whether working from the Project Manager or from the Command window.)

Figure 7.6, for example, shows the MBS project file, MBS.pjx, open in BROWSE, though only the first dozen or so fields appear in the window. Each record represents a file in the project, though the first record in a project file, denoted by *H* (for *Header*) in the Type field, is used to hold general information about the project.

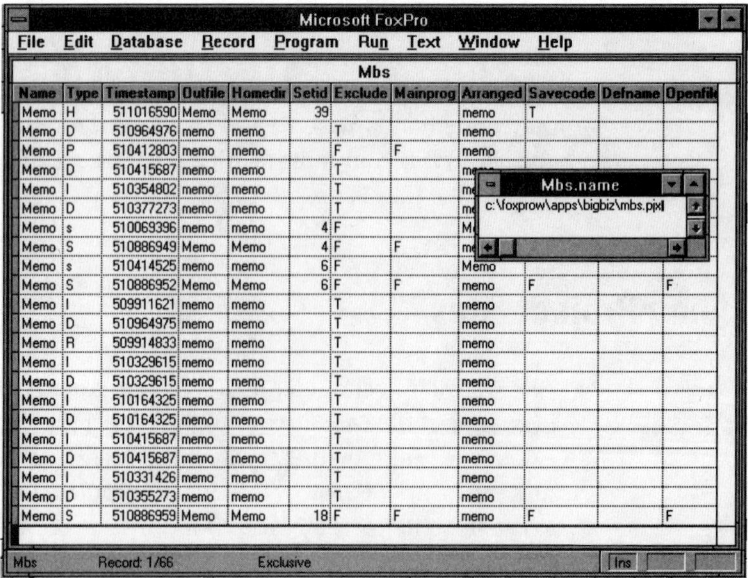

FIGURE 7.6:
MBS project file, MBS.pjx, as viewed in BROWSE

The Project Home Directory and Project File Names

The Homedir field of the project header record is quite significant since it is used to store the full path of the directory in which the project file is located and the application is to be built. Because FoxPro automatically selects the current directory as the project's home directory and stores its path to Homedir when you create a project, you will never need to address this field—or any of the other fields in the project file, for that matter, though understanding its function will be helpful.

The importance of the project's home directory is readily explained by the way FoxPro stores the names of the files listed in the project. (Again, see Figure 7.6, where the Memo field entry for Customer.dbf's Name in the project is displayed in the open window.) The Name field entry for each file in the project includes the path FoxPro must take from the project's home directory to find the file. Since files are located by their relative path from the home directory, any project including files stored in subdirectories can be easily moved to other (home) directories, provided the project subdirectories and the files they hold are moved with it. This is obviously intended to encourage the use of project subdirectories, as discussed later in this chapter. When you reopen the project, FoxPro immediately notes if the home directory has changed. If the home directory has changed, FoxPro asks if you want it to rebuild the project in the new location. If you have moved the project's subdirectories and all its files to the new home directory as well, the rebuild action will proceed smoothly, without need of the Locate File dialog, since the relative paths of the files listed in the project file will still be valid.

The Project File Type Field

While the type of each file included in a project is sensibly labeled in the Program Manager's file list, in the project file itself Type is more economically denoted by a one-letter code: *P* for program, *S* for screen set, *R* for report, *D* for data file, *I* for index, *B* for label, and *X* for other. Note that the project file will include two records for menu and screen programs, one for the design file and another for the generated source code file. The design file is indicated with an uppercase character, while the source code file is indicated with a lowercase character.

Selecting the Main (Startup) Program

Mainprog, a logical field, is used to indicate the .prg, screen, or menu program selected as the application's startup or main program module. When the application is built, combining all files included in the project (and not specifically excluded from the application) in a single application (.app) or executable (.exe) file, this is the program that is assigned the function of starting the application. By default, FoxPro selects the first program added to a project as the main program and places a bullet in the scrollable file list to the left of its entry in the file Type column. This is shown in Figure 7.7, where Bigbiz.prg is selected as the main program. You can select or change the main program, however, using the Set Main option on the Project pulldown, which is also shown open in Figure 7.7. The record in the project file representing the main program is the only one that will have a value of .T. in the Mainprog field.

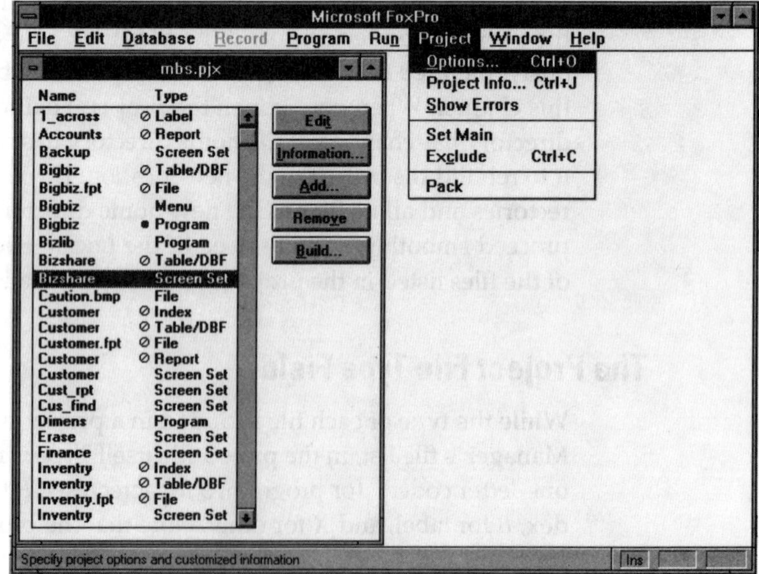

FIGURE 7.7: Use the Project pulldown to set the main program and to exclude/include files in the project.

Available Information about a Project

In the normal run of things, you will want to include all files used by an application in the project. This way, the Project Manager will be able to provide complete information about the project as a whole and about each file included in it. Figure 7.8, for example, shows the Project Information box, accessed through the Project pull-down, for MBS.pjx while it was still under development. Among other things, the Project Information box will immediately tell you if any executable files are out of date.

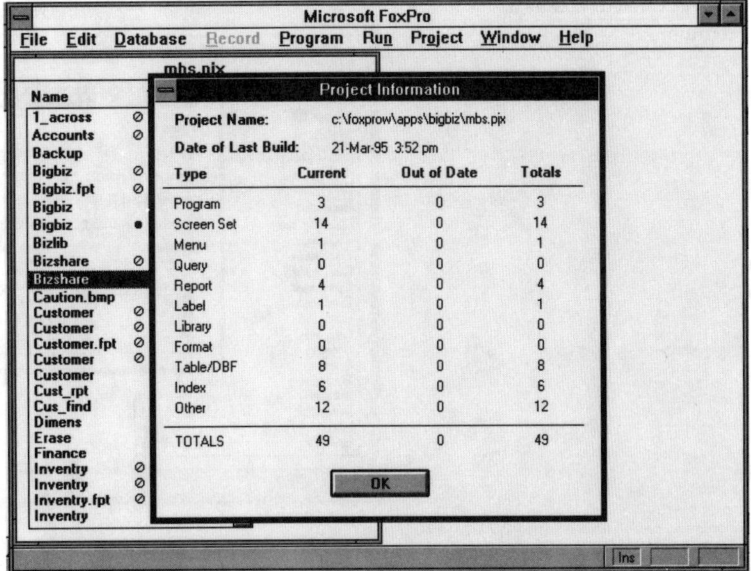

FIGURE 7.8:

The Project Information box provides summary information about all files in the project.

NOTE

There is one disadvantage to listing all files in an application in the project. If the application is very large, files listed in the Project Manager but not actually included in the compiled .app file may clutter up the file list and make it harder to use. The only files that must be included in the file list are those that will be included in the .app (or .exe) file.

You can also access information about any specific file in the project by highlighting it in the Project Manager's file list and selecting the Information push button. The File Information box shows the name, type, and creation dates for the highlighted file. In the case of programs, as shown in Figure 7.9, it also displays the symbol (name), type, and form of usage of all non-table objects referenced by the program, including executable programs, procedures, functions, reports, labels, and arrays.

FIGURE 7.9:

The File Information box lists all the objects referenced by a program.

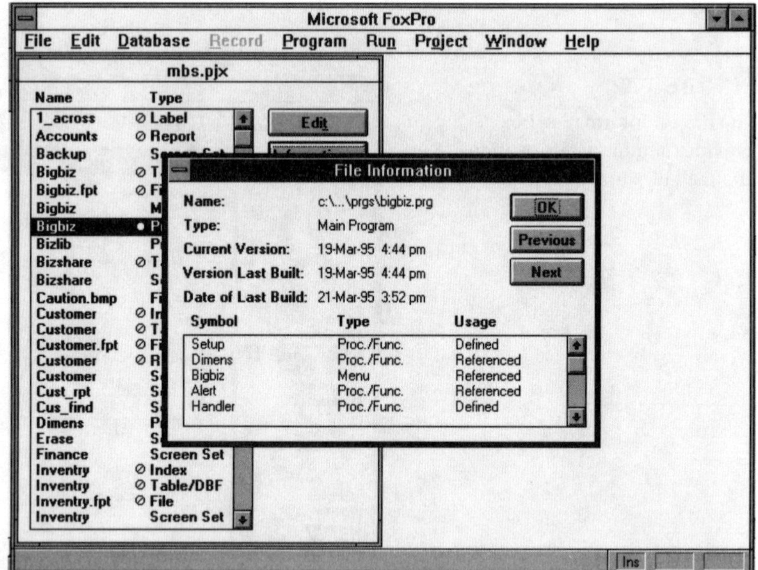

With respect to usage, symbols can be referenced, defined, or unknown. Defined symbols represent objects created by the program, while referenced symbols represent objects only referenced by it. Unknown symbols are objects referenced by the program that cannot be located by the Project Manager for one reason or another. The fact that a symbol is listed as unknown, however, does not always point to a real problem, assuming the object in question actually exists. Unknown references most often appear when name expressions or macro substitution is used to reference objects indirectly through the use of memvars, array elements, or data field values. (As you will recall, for example, procedure Dospr, discussed in Chapter 6, is used to launch screen programs using name expressions.) Unknown references may also appear when a referenced procedure or function is located in a calling (rather than nested) program or in the application's procedure file or when an array is referenced by a nested program. However, when the application file is built and executed, in the majority of instances FoxPro has no difficulty finding the unknown objects because they have been incorporated into the application itself.

Responding to Unknown References

If an error occurs when testing an application because FoxPro is unable to locate an object, check first to make sure you haven't misspelled it in the calling program. If it is not misspelled and the problem persists, in all likelihood it is owing to unresolved indirect object reference or to reference of a file that was not added to the project (or was added to the project but *excluded from the application*, for reasons discussed below) and cannot be found by means of the application's SET PATH.

If the error is owing to indirect reference, you can alert the Project Manager to the name or names of the referenced objects by adding them (or the files defining them) to the project or by using the EXTERNAL command to list them directly in the source code:

```
* m.dreport can have a value of "invoice", "statements", or
* "customer".
EXTERNAL REPORT invoice, statements, customers
REPORT FORM (dreport) TO PRINT
```

Here, for example, we use EXTERNAL to make the Project Manager aware of the three Report forms that can be referenced by the REPORT command. The Project Manager will add them to the project when we rebuild it. Note that EXTERNAL is also used to clear up problems related to the use of arrays, which may not be recognized by a nested procedure or function. (See the FoxPro documentation or Help file for more information about EXTERNAL when you have a problem that won't go away.)

With respect to files that must be excluded from the application (but may be included in the project), you must clear up an unknown reference causing an error by supplying the file's path or by pointing the application to the file's directory with SET PATH.

Putting the Project File to Work

By using a project file as a table, you can readily produce reports indicating the names, types, and status of all files included in the project. An abridged version of the project file, using only the Name and Type fields, can also be created with the COPY command and included in the project itself as a lookup file. The project file can be used, for example, to supply the operator with a list of files that can be selected or to supply the application with the names and locations of files to be PACKed or REINDEXed. Project files also have a potential role to play in file management, as we will see below.

Including Files or Excluding Files in the Application

While you will generally want to include all files used by the application in the project, if only for the sake of keeping tabs on them, not all files included in the project should be included in the application or executable file. (Remember that an .app or .exe file can include everything from program object code to tables and bitmaps.) The reason for this is simple. Since an .app or .exe file cannot be altered once it is built, files incorporated in it can be used only on a read-only basis. In other words, if you include your system tables in the application file, no records can be added to them and no records already present in them can be edited or erased. For this reason, the Project Manager allows you to mark files included in a project for exclusion from the application or executable program file.

You can mark and unmark files for exclusion from the application by highlighting them in the scrollable list and pressing Ctrl+C or by using the Exclude/Include option on the Project pulldown. (The Exclude/Include option is a toggle. If the current file in the list is included, the Exclude option is displayed in the menu. If the current file is excluded, the Include option is displayed.) When a file is excluded, the Greek character theta (θ) appears to the left of its Type field in the file list. With respect to the project file, the include/exclude status of a file is indicated by the value of the project file's Exclude field, which is .T. if the file is marked for exclusion and .F. if it is not.

In determining which files should be excluded from the application, only one question is pertinent: Should the operator be free to modify the file? For the most part, this is easily determined. Tables and their memo files and indexes must be excluded from the application, except when a table is used as a lookup file, the records of which are expected to undergo no changes during the lifetime of the application. .fll library (API) files, if used, must be excluded. Generally speaking, all other files are included in the application, though reports and labels are often excluded, as they are from MBS.app, so they can be easily modified with FoxPro without having to rebuild the entire project.

TIP

To produce a list of all files included in the project but excluded from the application, open the project file with USE <file.pjx> and then LIST FIELDS name,type FOR exclude. By using the project file in this way, you can also write a program that will copy all excluded files belonging to the project to a distribution disk. We show how to do this below. Of course, to use the project file in this way, you must be certain to list all files excluded from the application in the project file.

Typical Initiation of a Project

Once again, if you are relatively new to FoxPro, you will probably want to turn to the Project Manager after making some headway with a new project. You may, for example, create your tables and indexes, a menu program, and several screen programs to get a feel for the application and for the tools FoxPro offers for creating these objects. Still, you are unlikely to go very far, for example, in creating and testing your screen programs before you tire of the necessity of using the Program pulldown, while working in the Screen Builder, to manually generate and compile screen program source and object code. It is far easier to open a project, make changes to several files at once, and, when you're ready to retest the lot, access the Build dialog and let FoxPro do all the work.

Of course, if you do not have a main program that calls and executes the other programs in the project, you must proceed by opening a new project and using the Add File dialog to add files to the project one by one. It is, nonetheless, easily done, and you will soon have a project file with which you can deal in further developing your application. (As an alternative you can use BUILD PROJECT <file> since it allows you to supply FoxPro with a list of files that should be included in the new project.)

Developing Applications from the Top Down

By the time you become more advanced in your usage, you will have an additional pretext for moving to the Project Manager right away. This is because you will gradually build a library of procedures and programs that will prove useful in the majority of your applications. Since this will typically include a main (startup) program, a menu program, and a procedure file holding your errorhandler, alert, and question procedures (standard features of most applications, including the MBS), there is every reason to add such files to a project from the very start and develop the rest of the application in a top-down fashion, working directly from the Project Manager. Using what is called *program stubbing,* you can create a fully functional menu program that lists all the programs you intend to add to the application but takes no action or simply delivers a WAIT MESSAGE "Sorry Charlie, you have yet to write this!" when you select a program option that still awaits your attention. Working in this way, you can proceed to develop the application by using the menu as an outline to be filled in as you add new files to the project. Moreover, since the portion of the application that is completed is fully functional, you can finish each round of revisions by opening the Build Option dialog (again, see Figure 7.3) and selecting the Build Application radio button to create the .app file. You can then test the application as it will actually be used when it is finished with DO <file.app>.

TIP

Another way to begin a new project is by copying an existing project file. You can then remove all files specific to the old project, leaving only those files that will be used in the new application, and then begin adding and modifying files as needed.

Using the Build Option Dialog

When building the application, FoxPro begins by executing the routines also performed by the Rebuild Project option. It automatically scans and updates the project file as needed and regenerates and compiles any menu or screen programs that have undergone modification since the project was last rebuilt. Only then does FoxPro build the application file.

Program errors discovered while the project is being rebuilt are duly noted by the Project Manager, which will either signal the number of errors it has found in the status bar or display them on the screen in a text-editing window if the Build Options Display Errors check box is checked. You can also display the errors by selecting the

Project Errors option from the Project pulldown. (Program errors are stored in a text file with the same name as the project file, but with an .err extension. The .err file is automatically overwritten each time the project is rebuilt. It is erased if no error is encountered.) FoxPro identifies the source code file in which the error occurs, the nature of the problem, and, if it is a compilation error, the specific line number and command producing the error.

TIP

Use the Build Option dialog's Rebuild All check box only if you want the Project Manager to regenerate and recompile all programs in the project, even if they have not been modified. This option should be used when changes have been made to one or more programs in a project that affect commands issued in others.

Building an Executable (.exe) Program

The Build Executable option is disabled unless you have the FoxPro Distribution Kit installed on your computer in the FoxPro program directory. However, even when the final goal is to build a program that will run unaided by FoxPro, it is typical to run and test the application as an .app file during development, though one must be aware of the FoxPro commands that cannot be used in an .exe file. For instructions on how to create .exe files with FoxPro, see Appendix B, which is devoted to the use of the Distribution Kit.

Note that there are no advantages to testing an application by running the compiled source code files instead of the application file, though this can certainly be done. For example, the MBS can be launched by executing the main program with DO bigbiz.prg instead of DO MBS.app. However, you won't get far unless you alter Bigbiz.prg, which is not stored in the project home directory, to include the paths of all files included in the application file in addition to the paths of the excluded files belonging to the project. The .app file, after all, has no need to know how to find included files. (You will not have greater difficulty in debugging the application file since FoxPro is able to trace program errors to their place of origin in the offending source code file, as long as you check the Debugging Information check box in the Project Options dialog, which we discuss after examining several issues bearing on your use of it.)

NOTE

When executing a program with DO <file> without supplying an extension, FoxPro will first look for an .app file with the indicated file name and, if it cannot be found, will then look for a .prg file with the file name. .spr (screen) and .mpr (menu) programs must be invoked using their file extensions. Still, FoxPro does not execute the source code files but first uses them to generate object code files with slightly different extensions if they do not already exist on disk or if they are out of date. (If an object code file already exists, you can invoke it with DO <file> instead of the source code file, provided you supply the correct file extension—for example, .spx for screen and .mnx for menu code object file.) However, if you work, as I recommend, with an .app file, the object code files will never appear on disk, since object code is compiled and stored directly in the project file and then placed in the .app file when it is built.

Distributing the Application

Which files you deliver to your clients depends upon what you expect them to do with the finished application. If you intend them to run it under FoxPro as is, you need only supply them with the application (.app) file and a copy of the excluded files belonging to the overall application. On the other hand, if you wish to give them access to the application's source code and even to the application's project file so they can alter and use any portion of the application as they choose, you must supply them with copies of all files included in the project along with the project file. This is how the MBS is distributed.

NOTE

When supplying the source code for the application, it is unnecessary to include the generated menu and screen programs since these can be automatically regenerated by the Project Manager, provided the menu and screen design files are included along with the project file.

Of course, unlike an .app file, which must be executed by a full copy of interactive FoxPro, an .exe file has no use of FoxPro. When distributing an .exe file you must, however, include all excluded files belonging to the application. (Again, see Appendix B for instructions on how to use the FoxPro Distribution Kit to build an .exe file.)

Use of Directories in Your Application

While projects can be built using a single directory for all files, this is not the most orderly or efficient way to work, given the large number of files likely to be included in any application. While you are working, moreover, you will probably have occasion to experiment with different versions of files or to test out routines in isolation using small .prg files before employing the Clipboard to place the tested code in an included program file. Because the Project Manager is designed only to add or remove files from the project (though it will also create new files when the Add option is selected), you will therefore find it convenient to use the Filer or Windows File Manager in the background for copying, renaming, and/or deleting files. These tools will be more easily employed if you place files of different types in subdirectories of the application's home directory and supply each subdirectory with a name denoting the type of file to be found in it. This way, regardless of the number of directories you employ, any file can be easily located.

WARNING

The more files you store in a directory, the more time it will take the operating system to locate any one of them. Placing all files belonging to an application in the same directory therefore tends to slow execution. This is another reason for making use of subdirectories as described in these pages.

The directory structure used in developing the MBS, shown in Figure 7.10, is similar to that recommended in the *FoxPro Developer's Guide* as that most suited for creating portable applications. (If you followed the instructions supplied in Appendix A for installing the MBS on your hard disk, you will have the same directories on your hard disk.)

FIGURE 7.10:

Managing the files included in an application is easier if you use subdirectories.

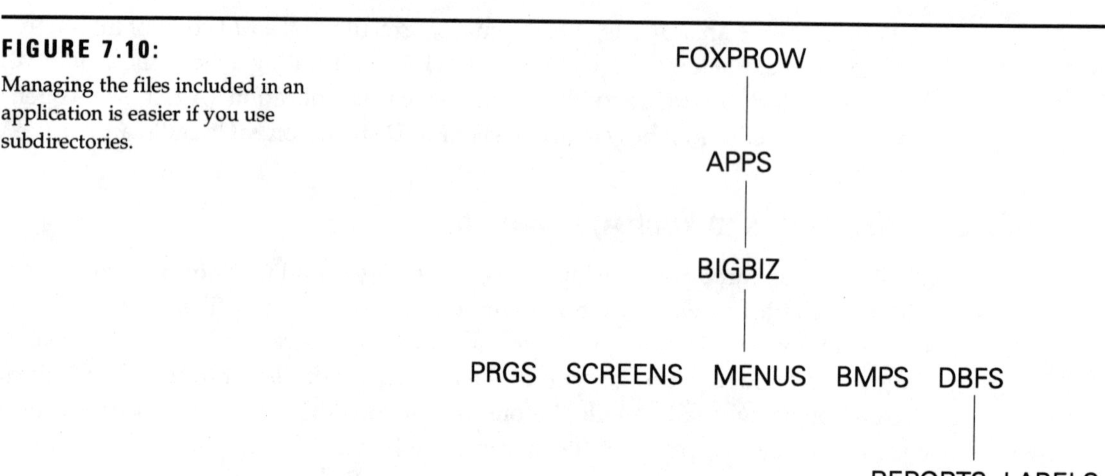

The APPS directory, listed in the FoxPro home directory for the sake of convenience, is used for organizational purposes only. Here it lists only one subdirectory, BIGBIZ, the MBS home directory. But as you begin developing your own projects, you can use APPS to hold their home directories as well. With regard to file management, this will create an orderly environment since APPS will list all your projects as directories. It will also serve as a hub through which you can move from project to project in search of files that can be incorporated directly into a new application or copied into one of the subdirectories of a new project, where it can be modified and used as needed.

> **TIP**
>
> If you don't intend to include source code with your distributed application, you need not move or copy files belonging to one project in order to include them, unchanged, in another. Just add them to the new project, though they are referenced in subdirectories not listed under the current project's home directory; this makes no difference. When you build the application, the Project Manager will incorporate them in the .app file as instructed. If you find you have many programs that can be used unchanged or as templates for others, place them in a LIBRARY directory just off APPS or in subdirectories of LIBRARY. That will make referencing them easier.

Listed under the MBS home directory, BIGBIZ, are separate directories for each type of file included in the MBS. However, REPORTS and LABELS are created as subdirectories of DBFS since, like the tables, memo files, and indexes stored in DBFS, they are to be excluded from the .app file. (Again, Report and Label forms are often excluded from the build so they can be modified without rebuilding the application.) This serves to place all excluded files to one side.

Still, the felicity of this arrangement is best appreciated when it is necessary to prepare the system for distribution—whether or not the source code is to be included. Since the .app file can be executed from any directory with DO <file>, provided the home directory is first selected as the default, the application can be installed in any directory on the host computer's hard disk as long as the subdirectories holding the excluded files are moved to that directory as well. Only the application's home directory changes. Everything else remains the same.

Where source code is not employed, the MBS is therefore easily installed on a hard disk using the directories shown in Figure 7.11.

FIGURE 7.11: When installing an application, just re-create the application's directory structure on the host computer, beginning with the application's home directory.

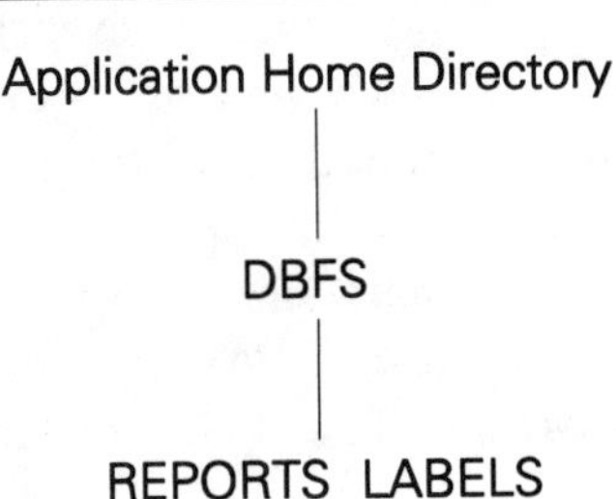

Since the files listed in PRGS, SCREENS, MENUS, and BMPS are all included directly in the .app file, these directories and the files they hold are no longer needed. The name of the application's new home directory is also unimportant, though it must be made the default before starting the application. This way, the command SET PATH TO dbfs; dbfs\reports; dbfs\labels, issued at the outset of MBS.app, will suffice to give the application access to all excluded files without our having to go to greater effort.

Making an Application Directory Independent

Though it is possible to design your application so it can be executed from any directory—that is, without selecting its home directory as the default—this is usually more trouble than it is worth, owing to the added necessity of controlling the directories into which temporary files created and used by most applications are placed. However, if the application's new home directory is stored in a system value table, just as it is stored in the Homedir field of a project file during development, it can be inserted into the paths cited with SET PATH TO at application startup by using a memvar in a name expression:

```
m.dpath = bizshare.homedir + "dbfs; " ;
    + bizshare.homedir + "dbfs\reports" ;
    + bizshare.homedir + "dbfs\labels"
SET PATH TO (dpath)
```

In this way FoxPro can be directed to the excluded files using absolute rather than relative path names, which means that it can find them regardless of the default directory. (Note that FoxPro itself uses system variables citing the full path and names of its excluded files in order to find them from any directory.)

If management of temporary files is an issue, the system's stored value for the home directory can also be used to provide commands creating temporary files with the full path names, so there will be no problem in finding or erasing them.

If the application must be executable by FoxPro from any directory but it makes no difference which directory is the default (while the application is being run), you can use the stored value (full path) for the home directory with SET DEFAULT TO at the outset of the application to make the home directory the default. This is far easier to manage since temporary files can then be created by default in the home directory and SET PATH can be used to find the excluded files using relative addresses only. (This is not done in the MBS, which assumes that its home directory is made the default before it is executed, though you can certainly revise it—or, rather, Bizshare.dbf—to store the name of the MBS home directory and use it as I have described.)

Distributing Your Application

When preparing copies of your application for installation on other computers, you will want to make use of the FoxPro Distribution Kit's SetupWizard, if you have it. While it is specially designed for creating distribution disks and a suitable Windows setup program for installing a Windows executable program, complete with icon, on a computer, using Windows' Run command, the Distribution Kit can also be used to install an .app program. The difference, again, is that the .app file must be run by interactive FoxPro; an .exe runs on its own. The SetupWizard, which is discussed in Appendix B, is capable of producing the necessary distribution disks for all files in an application semi-automatically, splitting (and during installation rejoining) files that are too large for a floppy, and, moreover, using file compression and decompression techniques to keep to a minimum the number of floppies that must be used to install an application.

However, for those who do not have the Distribution Kit and who are preparing applications for operation under FoxPro as .app files, there is no need for the SetupWizard except insofar as it offers exemplary facilities for handling larger applications than will fit on one disk without using file compression. This is because applications run under FoxPro can be installed simply by copying all files to a computer's hard disk and using DOS. Since even sizable .app files, unlike .exe files, will usually fit on a single high-density floppy (.exe files must include the FoxPro Runtime library and can therefore run up to 2 to 3 megabytes), this can be done using XCOPY. While the method is useless when working with .exe programs, it does have its merits when delivering applications complete with source code for use by other programmers since XCOPY leaves intact all files placed on distribution disks. This means that while you can include a DOS batch file to oversee the installation of the application, the person receiving the application can also pick and choose which files to copy from the distribution disks.

The remainder of this section is devoted to showing how to prepare floppy disk copies of an application that must run under FoxPro using DOS commands and how to go about using a DOS batch file to oversee the installation of the application on another computer. If you already know how to do this or have the Distribution Kit and plan to make use of the SetupWizard, feel free to skip the following pages and move on to the section "Setting Project Options," which discusses the various ways you can control FoxPro's behavior when rebuilding a project or building an application.

Preparing Copies of Your Application with DOS

Distributing an application developed using the directory structure described above is a relatively simple matter, whether or not you need to supply your clients with source code. With respect to the MBS, if the project file and all source code are required, we simply make BIGBIZ the default directory while working in DOS or the Windows MS-DOS window and issue the following DOS commands:

```
ATTRIB +A *.* /s
XCOPY *.* A: /m /s
```

The first command sets the archive bit of all files in BIGBIZ and its subdirectories. XCOPY is then used to copy all files in BIGBIZ, including its subdirectories and their files, to a disk in drive A. Files in the project home directory are copied to the root directory, while the files in the project's subdirectories are copied to subdirectories of A:\ bearing the same names as the project's subdirectories. (The /s parameter of both commands instructs DOS to include all subdirectories in the action.) Since XCOPY is used with the /m parameter, DOS will unset the archive bit of each file as it is successfully copied. For this reason, if and when XCOPY runs out of space for files on drive A, it will cease action with the message, "insufficient disk space." But you can simply place another disk in drive A and reissue the XCOPY command. Ignoring the files already copied (with an unset archive bit), XCOPY will continue copying the rest of the files in the application until it again runs out of space. By repeating the XCOPY command as many times as is required to copy all the files in the application, you end up with a set of distribution disks that can be used to install the system (along with its required subdirectories) on any computer, using XCOPY. (COPY can also be used, but it won't handle subdirectories automatically.)

```
MD <application directory>
CD <application directory>
XCOPY A:*.* /s /v
```

Here we use the DOS MD (or MKDIR) command to create a directory for the application; we then make the new directory the default with CD (or CHDIR). Then it is only a matter of copying the files from the distribution disks to the application's new home directory using XCOPY /s so DOS will be sure to create the required subdirectories and place the files belonging to them in their proper place. (The verify parameter /v tells DOS to verify that the new files can be read.) The XCOPY command must be repeated with every distribution disk. Still, this is the easiest way to go about distributing your application.

When source code files are not required, the distribution disks must be made by issuing XCOPY to target only the application's home directory and those directories holding excluded files. This is most easily handled by using ATTRIB to unset the archive bit of all files belonging to the project and then to selectively set the archive bit of the .app file and of all files in the small directory tree holding the excluded files prior to executing XCOPY:

```
ATTRIB -A *.* /s
ATTRIB +A *.app
ATTRIB +A DBFS\*.* /s
XCOPY *.* A: /m /s /v
```

NOTE

ATTRIB –A will also be useful when supplying full source code and the project file to exclude menu and screen source code files from XCOPY's action. Again, .spr and .mpr programs can be automatically regenerated if you supply the menu and screen design files. Without the menu and screen design files, however, the menu and screen programs cannot be modified using the Screen or Menu Builder. (Chapter 9 discusses the Menu Builder and Chapter 11 the Screen Builder.)

When the application file or any other file that must be distributed with it becomes too large to fit on a single disk, you must use BACKUP and RESTORE instead of XCOPY since XCOPY is unable to copy a file onto more than one disk. However, BACKUP and RESTORE are generally avoided by most programmers owing to the availability of data compression programs like PKZIP that can be used to reduce the size of large files so that XCOPY can handle them. (The main shortcoming of BACKUP and RESTORE is that files placed on disks with BACKUP must be RESTOREd to the same directories from which they were originally copied. Add to this the fact that files created by BACKUP with one version of DOS may not be restored with the RESTORE command belonging to another and you have two good reasons to avoid using them.)

As mentioned above, if you have the FoxPro Distribution Kit, you can use the Setup-Wizard to produce your distribution disks. Not only does it use file compression to reduce the number of disks that will be required to install your application on another computer, it also automatically handles files that are too large to fit on a single disk. We illustrate how to create distribution disks for your application with XCOPY only because it is already available to you. Bear in mind, however, that even if you use XCOPY as described above, you will want to include a small DOS batch file to oversee installation of your application on the host computer.

Using a DOS Batch File to Oversee System Installation

In the case of the MBS, we use a DOS batch file, Install.bat, to copy the MBS to the host computer's hard disk. For the batch file to work properly, the operator is required to make the disk drive holding the MBS distribution disk the default disk drive and then enter INSTALL <drive:directory>, where <drive:directory> is used to point XCOPY to the application's new home directory.

Since parameters entered with a batch file can be referenced by any batch file command with *%n*, where *n* is an integer representing the order of the desired parameter in the parameter list, we can use %1 to pick up the operator's entry for the MBS home drive and directory. We therefore use the following batch file commands to oversee the installation:

```
ATTRIB +A *.* /s
ATTRIB -A install.bat
XCOPY *.* %1 /s /v /m
```

The first two commands set the archive bit of all files on the distribution disk with the exception of Install.bat. Then we use %1 to direct XCOPY to copy all files and directories on the distribution disk that have a set archive bit to the drive and directory the operator has selected to use as the MBS home directory.

Several questions arise. What will happen, for example, if the operator forgets to enter the target directory or enters it incorrectly? To take care of this, we start the batch file with the following commands:

```
IF "%1" == "" GOTO instruct
IF exist %1 GOTO nodir1
IF not exist %1\nul GOTO nodir2
```

The first IF command tests to see if any parameter was entered. If not, "%1" will be a null string and the command GOTO instruct will send DOS to the section of the batch program listed under label :instruct.

```
:instruct
ECHO To install the MBS you must enter:
ECHO.
ECHO INSTALL drive:directory
ECHO.
ECHO where drive:directory indicates the hard disk drive
ECHO and directory where MBS should be installed.
ECHO.
PAUSE
GOTO end
```

Here the operator is informed of the proper way to execute INSTALL before GOTO end sends DOS to section :end, where the batch file terminates. (See Figure 7.12.)

FIGURE 7.12:

The MBS installation program is a simple DOS batch file.

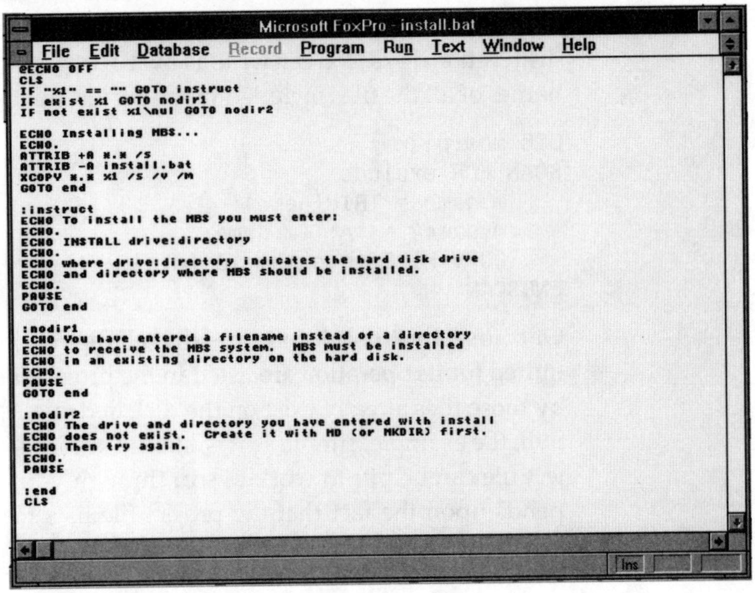

However, even if the operator has entered a parameter, how do we ensure that it is a proper one? This is achieved with the second and third IF commands. The second one tests to make sure the operator hasn't accidentally entered the name of a file instead of a directory using IF exist <file>. If %1 exists—that is, as a file—GOTO sends the batch program to another section where the operator is warned of the error. The third IF command then tests to see if the directory indicated by %1 actually exists. (Note that IF exist cannot be used to test directly for a directory. But it can test for the null device that is present in every directory with 1%\nul.) If the directory exists, only then are the ATTRIB and XCOPY commands executed. If it does not exist, GOTO is once again used to move DOS to a section of the batch program warning the operator of the problem before terminating the batch program. We thus exert fair control over operator use of the installation program.

Additional batch file commands must obviously be used if the application uses more than one disk. Still, Install.bat is intended only to serve as a simple example of what can be done. (Refer to your MS-DOS documentation for more information about the use of DOS batch files.)

Using FoxPro to Prepare the Distribution Disks

As previously mentioned, the project file can also serve as an aid in creating your distribution disks. You can write a FoxPro program that refers to it, for example, for the names of all the files included in the project but excluded from the application file:

```
USE mbs.pjx
SCAN FOR exclude
    m.name = TRIM(name)
    m.name2 = "A:"+m.name
    COPY FILE (m.name) TO (m.name2)
ENDSCAN
```

Of course, this routine assumes that all files excluded from the application but required for its operation are listed in the project file and that all subdirectories used by those files already exist on the disk in drive A. COPY FILE cannot create them. Still, the example, simple as it is, should suffice to make you aware of how the project file can be put to work to sort through your files. (The routine obviously depends upon the fact that the project file lists the names of files along with their relative paths from the home directory.)

Setting Project Options

Having surveyed the various issues that come into play when developing an application for distribution to others, we can now turn our attention to the Program Manager's Options dialog, which is accessed through the Project pulldown. (See Figure 7.13.) The information we enter here is stored in the first record of the project file.

FIGURE 7.13:

Use the Options dialog to control the Project Manager's behavior.

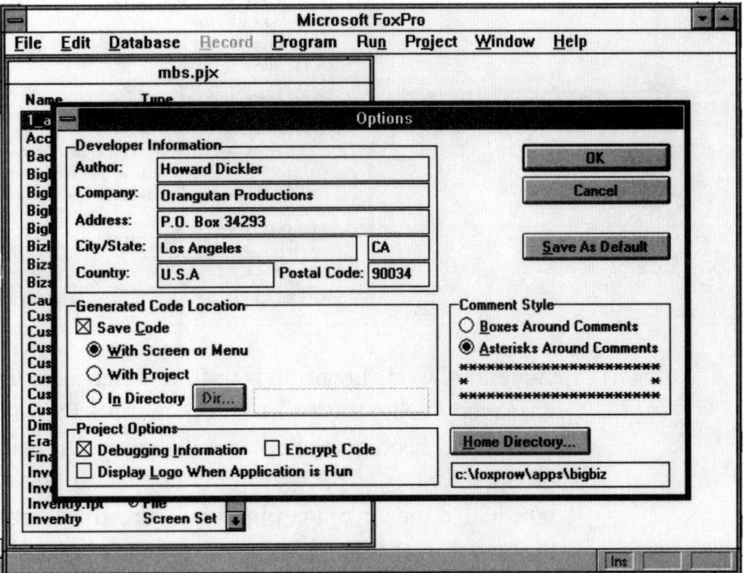

If you have already generated screen or menu programs (without the aid of the Project Manager), you may recognize the Options dialog since it is also invoked through the Generate Screen and Generate Menu dialogs, though several of the options are only available when working with the Project Manager.

Developer Information, if you care to enter it, is used in the header of source code files generated by the Project Manager. Comment Style determines whether FoxPro uses asterisks or boxes to denote automatically generated program notes, including the header. Figure 7.14, for example, shows the opening lines of Customer.spr, which was generated using the options indicated in the previous figure.

FIGURE 7.14:
Screen and menu source code files include generated code as well as extensive program comments.

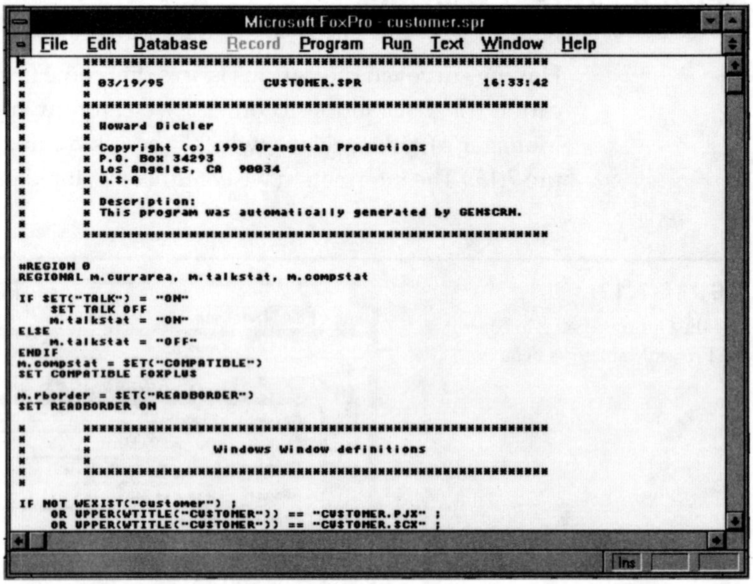

```
Microsoft FoxPro - customer.spr
File  Edit  Database  Record  Program  Run  Text  Window  Help
*       *********************************************************
*       *
*       * 03/19/95              CUSTOMER.SPR              16:33:42
*       *
*       *********************************************************
*       *
*       * Howard Dickler
*       *
*       * Copyright (c) 1995 Orangutan Productions
*       * P.O. Box 34293
*       * Los Angeles, CA  90034
*       * U.S.A
*       *
*       * Description:
*       * This program was automatically generated by GENSCRN.
*       *
*       *********************************************************

#REGION 0
REGIONAL m.currarea, m.talkstat, m.compstat

IF SET("TALK") = "ON"
    SET TALK OFF
    m.talkstat = "ON"
ELSE
    m.talkstat = "OFF"
ENDIF
m.compstat = SET("COMPATIBLE")
SET COMPATIBLE FOXPLUS

m.rborder = SET("READBORDER")
SET READBORDER ON

*       *********************************************************
*       *
*       *                 Windows Window definitions
*       *
*       *********************************************************
*

IF NOT WEXIST("customer") ;
    OR UPPER(WTITLE("CUSTOMER")) == "CUSTOMER.PJX" ;
    OR UPPER(WTITLE("CUSTOMER")) == "CUSTOMER.SCX" ;
```

Generated Code Location is used to determine whether generated source code files are saved during the build. If you uncheck the Save Code box, source code is erased after it has been compiled and the compiled code stored in the project file. If you do not intend to supply source code files along with your application, this provides you with a means of keeping your directories free of them. Bear in mind, however, that source code files are necessary to testing and debugging your application. If an error occurs and the Debugging Information box is checked, FoxPro will be able to open the source code file in an edit window and point you to the command that resulted in the error. If the source code doesn't exist, FoxPro cannot do this.

Moreover, when the source code is available, you can execute the application file through the Trace window and review the program source code as it is executed—again, assuming Debugging Information is selected. When Save Code is checked, the radio buttons can be used to specify where the source code files should be placed on disk. Select With Screen or Menu to save the screen and menu source code files in the same directories as the screen and menu (design) files.

As for the Project Option dialog, we have already explained the function of the Debugging Information check box. Bear in mind that including the debugging information in the .app file will make it larger by 2 bytes for each program line. This is the information required to reference the source code file. When you finish debugging your application, you can therefore choose to uncheck Debugging Information and rebuild the application file to make it as compact as possible.

Display Logo When Application is Run has bearing only on .exe files built through the Project Manager. Check the box before building the .exe file if you want it to display the FoxPro logo when it is started. Leave the box unchecked if you do not want the FoxPro logo to appear.

While .app files are extremely difficult to read, since the compiled code is tokenized, literal string values will remain legible, providing the curious hacker with keys for identifying segments of code. If you want to render your .app files unintelligible to even the most adept hackers, select Encrypt Code to instruct FoxPro to encrypt them.

Selecting the Save As Default push button instructs FoxPro to store the information entered in the Options dialog in the current resource file and to use it by default with other projects. It will also be used by default when the Generate option on the Program pulldown is used to generate screen or menu programs separately.

Using the MBS

If you have installed the MBS on your hard disk following the instructions provided in Appendix A, the MBS project file, MBS.pjx, and the MBS application file, MBS.app, now reside in \FOXPROW\APPS\BIGBIZ. To execute the MBS or open the project file, start FoxPro and execute the following commands. (We assume \FOXPROW is the default directory at the outset.)

```
* To execute MBS.app.
SET DEFAULT TO apps\bigbiz
DO mbs

* To open the project file.
SET DEFAULT TO apps\bigbiz
MODIFY PROJECT mbs
```

Needless to say, if you installed MBS in a different directory, you must use SET DEFAULT to make that directory current before attempting to start it.

NOTE The MBS distribution disk includes menu and screen design files but not the menu and screen programs, though they are not needed to run the application or open and work with the MBS project file. To regenerate them automatically, simply open the MBS project file and use the Build Option dialog to rebuild the project. (Make sure the Rebuild All check box is selected.) You will not need to use the Project Option dialog since I have left the Save Code check box selected. Menu and screen program source code files will be placed in the same directories used by the menu and screen design files, respectively.

Alternative Ways of Starting an Application

Of course, when you install an .app program like the MBS on a client's computer, you will scarcely want the client or operator to start the program through FoxPro. In fact, on the whole, you will want to keep them as far away as possible from FoxPro unless you know them to be competent users and there is good reason for giving them *carte blanche* to any and all tables and a menu of options for destroying them. With respect to business programming in a secure environment, this is totally out of the question. What we want instead is for FoxPro to execute our application automatically the moment it is started and to terminate when the application is quit. This can be accomplished in a variety of different ways.

First, we can place the following lines in Config.fpw, the FoxPro configuration file:

```
DEFAULT = APPS\BIGBIZ
COMMAND = DO mbs.app
```

Since FoxPro will execute these commands the moment it is started instead of initiating the interactive mode, it will execute our application. To make FoxPro terminate when the operator exits MBS, all we need do is issue the QUIT command when the operator selects the Exit option from our system menu.

TIP

As you have probably noticed, the MBS actually uses two options for quitting the program: Quit to FoxPro and Quit to Windows. Both are listed in the System pulldown. During testing the Quit to FoxPro option is essential; without it you must restart FoxPro to continue work on the project. Moreover, if the environment in which the finished application is run is reasonably secure, you can choose to leave the Quit to FoxPro option intact during the first few months of the application's use. With the aid of an adept operator or through the use of a communications program enabling you to take over the host computer by modem, this may make it easier for you to diagnose and fix errors. To be on the safe side, include a small routine in your program that will make it impossible for an operator to quit to FoxPro without entering an appropriate password.

A second way to start MBS automatically is by altering the instructions contained in the Windows Program Item Properties dialog for FoxPro. (See Figure 7.15.) Since Windows will select the working directory as the default before executing the command line starting FoxPro, we change it from its usual setting (in my own system) of C:\FOXPROW to the MBS home directory, C:\FOXPROW\APPS\BIGBIZ. Then it is only a matter of entering the name of the program we want FoxPro to launch when it starts in the command line, immediately after FOXPROW.EXE. Still, this is only one of the parameters FoxPro will accept in its command line. We can, for example enter FOXPROW.EXE –t to suppress the FoxPro logo.

TIP

A special DOS environment variable, SET FOXPROSWX=<parameters>, can also be used to make FoxPro execute a program and/or to inhibit display of the FoxPro logo with the –t switch. Set the environment variable as needed from the DOS prompt or in Autoexec.bat prior to executing FoxPro. However, a file or switch placed in the command line will take precedence over instructions supplied with SET FOXPROSWX.

To further deemphasize FoxPro's underlying use, the item's description and icon can also be changed with the Properties dialog, though you must provide Windows with the icon you want it to use. (The description can be changed without additional effort.) You can also choose to create and use a new Windows program item

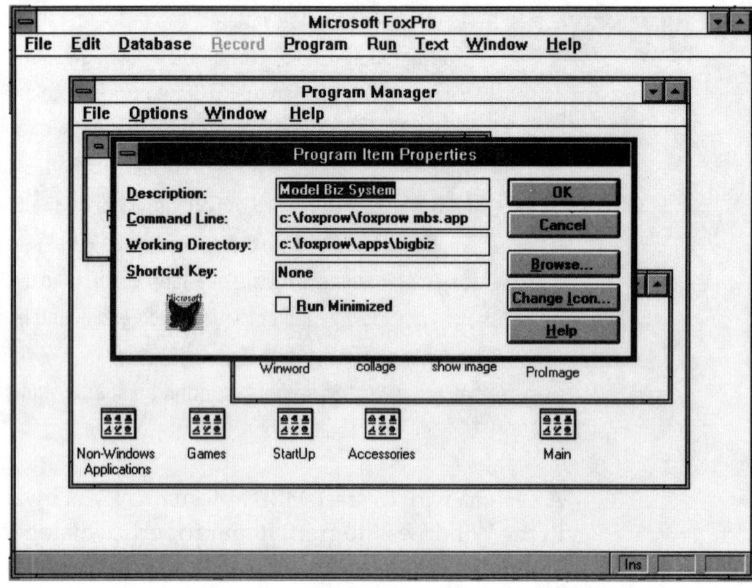

FIGURE 7.15:
Use the Windows Properties dialog to make FoxPro execute a program automatically.

instead of altering the one used by FoxPro. This is readily done by selecting New from the Program Manager's File pulldown and filling in the Properties dialog as needed.

Finally, when starting FoxPro, we can also direct it to draw its startup instructions from a configuration file other than Config.fpw. We can therefore achieve our end by placing the commands cited above (for placement in Config.fpw) in another file—say, Config.biz, located in the MBS home directory—and execute FoxPro with the following command line:

```
C:\FOXPROW\FOXPROW.EXE -cc:\foxprow\apps\bigbiz\config.biz
```

The symbol –c must be placed just in front of the configuration file name, with no spaces. One of the added advantages of controlling application startup through a configuration file is that the configuration file can be used to control certain aspects of FoxPro's behavior that cannot be altered once FoxPro is fully initialized. These include its use of available memory (memlimit), the values of system variables referencing FoxPro's excluded files, and the directories it uses to store temporary files. (See your FoxPro documentation for more information about the various uses of FoxPro configuration files.)

Tip

Which configuration file FoxPro uses at startup can also be determined through the use of another special DOS environment variable, SET FOXPROWCFG=<file>, which can be initialized in Autoexec.bat or from the DOS prompt. (If –c<file> is issued in the command line, the configuration file it specifies takes precedence over that set with SET FOXPROWCFG.)

Making Yourself at Home in the Project Manager

As mentioned at the outset of this chapter, those who are new to FoxPro may be hesitant to dive right in with the Project Manager. It does, after all, have the foreboding aspect of a black box upon which one must depend, all the while hoping that nothing goes wrong. Still, the basic explanation of how the Program Manager functions as supplied in this chapter should suffice to dissolve much of the mystery. The rest will dissolve from using it.

In the following chapters we begin reviewing the major components of the MBS in the order in which they were pieced together using the Project Manager. If you are new to the Project Manager's use, you can gain some experience with it, as well as greater familiarity with the portions of the MBS you may want to alter and use in your own applications, by opening MBS.pjx and selecting each file for edit as it is discussed in the text.

CHAPTER

EIGHT

Writing the Main (Startup) Program

- Writing the setup procedure
- Saving current memory objects and the view
- Taking over the FoxPro main window
- Replacing the FoxPro system menu
- Writing the cleanup procedure
- Creating an application help facility

In an application like the MBS, the main (or startup) program is used to execute the application. This function entails several responsibilities, some of which may be delegated to a FoxPro configuration file, supposing the application is to be started automatically from Windows, as described in Chapter 7. However, so that our application can be started without revision from within FoxPro or directly from Windows, we perform all required actions directly in our main program, Bigbiz.prg. These include

- Setting the file search path required to locate all files included in the project but *excluded* from the application file. (As you will recall, we select the application's home directory as the default directory prior to executing it. We can thus set the file search path using a relative address.)
- Issuing all SET <environment parameter> commands required to configure FoxPro for operation with our application.
- Opening application procedure, resource, and Help files, assuming these FoxPro resources are used.
- Modifying the FoxPro main window for use by the application and activating the application's main menu within it.
- Placing the application in a *wait state,* which means that the operator can begin using the programs and facilities available through the application's main menu one after the other without terminating the application.

Of course, these are the main program's responsibilities only with respect to the application, and this is all you need to care about if the application is to be launched directly from Windows. But suppose it is to be used with other FoxPro applications or launched at will by an operator working in the interactive mode? In both cases, the application must restore the FoxPro environment to its prior condition, which must be ascertained and stored away in memory before we change it. By giving our application the capacity to restore the FoxPro environment, we also render it fit for integration into a larger system; and here it is well to recall that accounts receivable is only one end of the bargain. A complete business system will require other applications, including accounts payable, general ledger, inventory tracking, and job costing, to mention only the main candidates. It is therefore best, at least with respect to the MBS, to fashion the main program so that the application will fit in well with others. This means that it must clean up after itself like a good camper.

The MBS Main Program As an Example

Turning our attention to the writing of our main program, we take advantage of FoxPro program architecture to make the executable program as short and legible to other programmers as possible. Because we can include procedures and functions at the end of any program file after the executable program, we need not dump all the detail work into the program itself. Instead we put it aside (or rather, below) in several procedures to which we assign names connoting their function. This gives the program the aspect of an outline that can be readily revised, which is precisely our object since we intend to use our startup program module as a template in creating other applications. Here, then, is the text of Bigbiz.prg. Though we omit their code, we include mention of the procedures listed in Bigbiz.prg so our program file structure will be explicit.

```
* Text of MBS main program, Bigbiz.prg.
* Procedure Setup executes procedure Opendata, establishing
* default database view, and establishes system error-
* handling routine.
DO setup
ON KEY LABEL F1 HELP
* ON KEY LABEL Alt+F7 DO prgs\dimens
* ON KEY LABEL Alt+F8 DO cleanup IN prgs\bigbiz
* ON KEY LABEL Alt+F9 SUSPEND
* ON KEY LABEL Alt+F6 SET SYSMENU TO DEFAULT
STORE .F. TO m.breakout,m.doit,m.hide
STORE "" TO m.donext,m.dhidden
MODIFY WINDOW SCREEN TITLE "Model Business System" ;
    NOCLOSE FLOAT MINIMIZE ;
    FONT "FoxFont,7"
DO bigbiz.mpr
IF Month(bizshare.last_bill) <> MONTH(DATE())
    DO alert WITH ;
    "WARNING: A month has passed since last billing!", ;
    "Press any key to continue."
ENDIF
READ VALID handler()
DO cleanup
RETURN

PROCEDURE setup
* Text of Procedure omitted.
RETURN
```

```
PROCEDURE opendata
* Text of Procedure omitted.
RETURN

PROCEDURE cleanup
* Text of Procedure omitted.
RETURN
```

Not counting the ON KEY commands turned into comment lines with the use of an asterisk, the executable program consists of only 11 commands, allowing it to read like a program script. The three procedures listed below the executable program and the menu program, executed by the command DO Bigbiz.mpr, do the real work.

The first command, DO Setup, executes procedure Setup, which takes care of establishing the application's environment and resources. The next command of significance (since the others could just as easily be moved to procedure Setup) is MODIFY WINDOW SCREEN, which alters the title and attributes of the FoxPro main window in keeping with the needs of our application. Then, DO Bigbiz.mpr replaces the FoxPro system menu with one that lists our application programs, in addition to whatever default FoxPro system menu options we care to include in it.

Following this, since the program is still in motion, we use IF to check the date to see if a month has passed since the last billing by comparing MONTH(DATE()) with MONTH(bizshare.last_bill), the latter value being available owing to procedure Setup's call to procedure Opendata, which establishes the default MBS database view, described in Chapter 6. If the month has changed, we warn the operator by using procedure Alert to display an appropriate message on the screen. (Procedure Alert, you may recall, is situated in the MBS procedure file. It too is opened by procedure Setup.) This, of course, stops the program only until the operator presses any key to clear the message.

Next we issue our Foundation, or Getless, READ, so called because it activates no @ GET objects but is used instead to place FoxPro in a wait state so the operator can execute one program after another from our system menu without terminating the application. Moreover, we use READ VALID <expL> to prevent our application from terminating when a screen program is terminated with CLEAR READ and to otherwise gain control over when and how the operator can quit the application. As long as the READ VALID <condition> is .F., FoxPro returns to a wait state until the operator launches another program or makes a menu selection that alters the VALID <condition> to .T., thereby terminating the Foundation READ and, in effect, breaking our program loop. We discuss the use of Foundation READ in depth in Chapter 10.

> **TIP**
>
> Those who are new to the use of a Foundation READ may find it helpful to conceive of it as having a role in the application analogous to that of READ CYCLE in the screen programs discussed in Part I. The analogy can, moreover, be extended as follows: The main menu plays the role of @ GET push buttons in the screen program, while READ VALID plays the role of the @ GET push button VALID clause and the READ SHOW clause.

When the Foundation READ is terminated, procedure Cleanup is launched, restoring the FoxPro environment to what it was before the execution of our application; then, with the unnecessary terminating RETURN, our application ends. So much for the script; now for the parts.

Adding Programs to the FoxPro Interactive Mode

Though most applications will make use of a Foundation READ to keep FoxPro in a wait state under program control, there is one major alternative to the practice. Take away the Foundation READ and the DO Cleanup and Bigbiz.prg terminates, returning FoxPro to the interactive mode but leaving our system menu still active. It is now the FoxPro interactive system menu and all options available on it will still work to the extent that they do not depend upon FoxPro being in a wait state under program control. Following this methodology, programmers add their own utilities or otherwise reorder FoxPro's facilities to meet their own needs.

Writing the Setup Procedure

Procedure Setup bears the responsibility of establishing the MBS environment and of saving the preexisting environment to memory for subsequent restoration by procedure Cleanup. If you have the MBS loaded on your computer, you may want to open MBS.pjx at this time with MODIFY PROJECT mbs, access Bigbiz.prg for edit—or, as an alternative, open it with MODIFY COMMAND bigbiz—and scan through the commands listed in procedure Setup as we review the most important of them below. We show the first screenful of them in Figure 8.1.

FIGURE 8.1:

Use a setup procedure to reconfigure FoxPro at the beginning of an application.

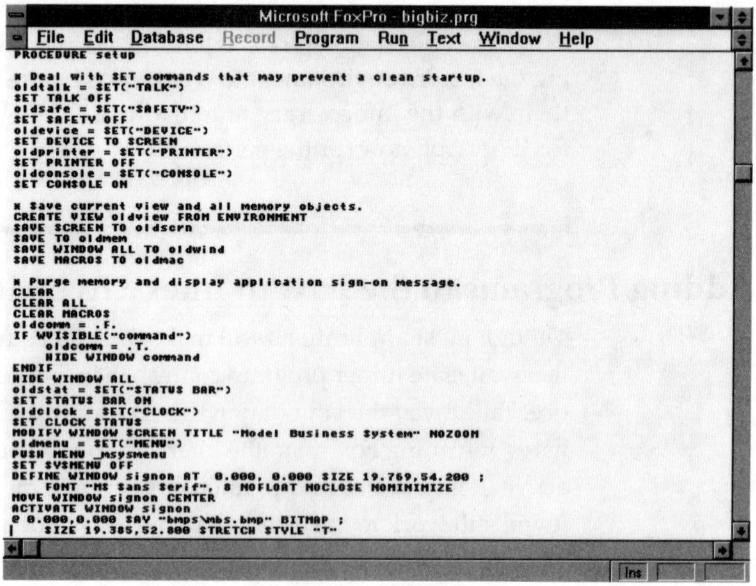

Microsoft FoxPro - bigbiz.prg

File Edit Database Record Program Run Text Window Help

```
PROCEDURE setup

* Deal with SET commands that may prevent a clean startup.
oldtalk = SET("TALK")
SET TALK OFF
oldsafe = SET("SAFETY")
SET SAFETY OFF
oldevice = SET("DEVICE")
SET DEVICE TO SCREEN
oldprinter = SET("PRINTER")
SET PRINTER OFF
oldconsole = SET("CONSOLE")
SET CONSOLE ON

* Save current view and all memory objects.
CREATE VIEW oldview FROM ENVIRONMENT
SAVE SCREEN TO oldscrn
SAVE TO oldmem
SAVE WINDOW ALL TO oldwind
SAVE MACROS TO oldmac

* Purge memory and display application sign-on message.
CLEAR
CLEAR ALL
CLEAR MACROS
oldcomm = .F.
IF WVISIBLE("command")
    oldcomm = .T.
    HIDE WINDOW command
ENDIF
HIDE WINDOW ALL
oldstat = SET("STATUS BAR")
SET STATUS BAR ON
oldclock = SET("CLOCK")
SET CLOCK STATUS
MODIFY WINDOW SCREEN TITLE "Model Business System" NOZOOM
oldmenu = SET("MENU")
PUSH MENU _msysmenu
SET SYSMENU OFF
DEFINE WINDOW signon AT  0.000, 0.000 SIZE 19.769,54.200 ;
    FONT "MS Sans Serif", 8 NOFLOAT NOCLOSE NOMINIMIZE
MOVE WINDOW signon CENTER
ACTIVATE WINDOW signon
@ 0.000,0.000 SAY "bmps\mbs.bmp" BITMAP ;
    SIZE 19.385,52.800 STRETCH STYLE "T"
```

Ins

TIP

If you are curious as to the function of any of the SET commands we do not mention, just click the Command window or select it from the Window pulldown. You can then use HELP <command name> to access and read the command's entry in the FoxPro Help file.

Ensuring a Clean Startup

Our first concern in procedure Startup is to take care of any environment settings that will get in the way of a clean startup. Though it is unlikely that the printer will be set on with SET PRINTER ON or SET DEVICE TO PRINTER or that the console will be set off, you can never be certain of these things unless the application is executed directly from Windows. We therefore take steps from the outset to ensure that SET CONSOLE is ON and that the screen will be used as the output device until our application deems otherwise. And though it is difficult to conceive of a situation in which the operator would want the printer turned back on or the console turned off when our application terminates, following what will be our normal practice, we save the prior setting of these commands to memvars. This is done, as shown in Figure 8.1, by referencing the current value of each set command with the SET() function.

On the other hand, we issue SET SAFETY OFF out of necessity, while again storing its prior setting to a memvar. SET SAFETY OFF will allow our application to issue commands overwriting or erasing files without FoxPro getting nervous about it and asking the operator to confirm the action, as it is wont to do in a program or in the interactive mode when SET SAFETY is ON (the default setting).

As for SET TALK OFF, we include this primordial Xbase command at the beginning of procedure Setup primarily for the sake of nostalgia. While it is required in the MBS to prevent FoxPro from displaying the results of commands like REPLACE, DELETE, INDEX, and COUNT on the screen, it is not needed since it is, for example, in dBASE or FoxPro for DOS, to prevent FoxPro for Windows from reporting values stored to memvars. For this reason, it need not be executed first.

Of course, if we use a common prefix—in this case *old*—for all memvars (and files) used to store the prior setting of these commands, we do so for the sake of making it possible to manipulate them as a group with SAVE TO <file> or RELEASE ALL LIKE <skeleton>. Later on, in procedure Cleanup, we will have no trouble resetting these and other SET commands to their prior settings by using RESTORE FROM <file> to restore the memvars to memory. We can then use the memvars to supply the same SET commands with the appropriate values or keywords required to restore the prior environment.

Saving Memory Objects and the Current Database View

Our next bit of business is to save the current database view and all existing memory objects to memory before purging them. The first command we issue is CREATE VIEW <file>. This creates a view file in which FoxPro will store all the information it requires to restore the current database environment with SET VIEW TO <file>. Those who are new to FoxPro should bear in mind that in addition to storing information about open tables, indexes, and relations, CREATE VIEW saves the current settings of many SET commands, including ALTERNATE, FORMAT, PATH, FIELDS, FILTER, PROCEDURE, HELP, RESOURCE, SKIP, and BRSTATUS (browse status). This means that when we next use SET PATH, SET PROCEDURE, SET RESOURCE, and SET HELP to establish the MBS file search path and to open the MBS procedure, resource, and Help files, we will not have to save their prior settings in memvars. The view file will take care of restoring these things for us.

The SAVE commands that follow next are used to save existing memory objects to files—with the exception of SAVE SCREEN, which saves a snapshot of the screen to a memvar. (SAVE WINDOWS saves the definitions of all current user-defined windows, while SAVE MACROS stores the contents of all keyboard macros, including those set with SET FUNCTION.) All these objects can be restored to memory by procedure Cleanup using RESTORE SCREEN, RESTORE WINDOWS, and RESTORE MACROS FROM <file>.

Note that we place the less explicit SAVE TO <file> command, which saves all existing memory variables to a memory file, after SAVE SCREEN so the memvar holding the snapshot of the current screen will be included in it. (In procedure Cleanup, we must consequently use RESTORE FROM <file> to restore the memvars in Oldmem.mem before issuing RESTORE SCREEN FROM oldscrn.)

Purging the Prior Environment and Displaying the Sign-On Message

Having saved the prior environment, we cannot purge all preexisting memory objects and begin reconfiguring FoxPro as required by our application. First, we use CLEAR to erase anything displayed in the FoxPro main window. Then CLEAR ALL is used to close all tables and erase all user-defined memory objects, including memvars, windows, menu bars, and popups. CLEAR ALL, however, does not purge macros from memory. We must use CLEAR MACROS to do this.

Saving Memory Objects to Memo Fields

The FoxPro SAVE and RESTORE commands, used to save and restore memvars, windows, and macro definitions, will make use of Memo fields instead of files. For example, to SAVE memvars to a Memo field, open a table that includes a Memo field, append a record, and execute SAVE TO MEMO <field>. FoxPro will save all memvar definitions to the Memo field. To restore the memvars, use RESTORE FROM MEMO <field>.

If you plan to use a table to store memory objects, you need only include one record in it, provided you place an appropriate number of Memo fields in it, since different Memo fields must be used for SAVE, SAVE WINDOWS, and SAVE MACROS. The better alternative, though, is to use only one Memo field in the table but to use different records to store output from each SAVE command you must issue. You can then use other fields to label the information, thus creating an object definition library that can be used not just to restore the prior environment but to restore whatever objects you choose to save in it.

Once we have cleared the decks, we can begin taking control of FoxPro for our application. To this end, we begin by hiding the Command window, activating the status bar, and displaying the system clock while continuing to record prior settings to memvars. (Since there is no SET command controlling the Command window, we must test for its presence on the screen with WVISIBLE().) Moreover, since procedure Setup still has plenty of work to do, this is a suitable time to display our application's sign-on message if we intend to use one. With the MBS, this is achieved by the last commands shown in Figure 8.1. We simply define a window, center it, and display our sign-on message in it, in this case using @ SAY to fill the window with a bitmap file. (See Figure 8.2.)

NOTE If you are creating an .exe program, the commands testing for and hiding the Command window should be removed since the Command window is automatically excluded from an executable program, as are the Debug and Trace windows.

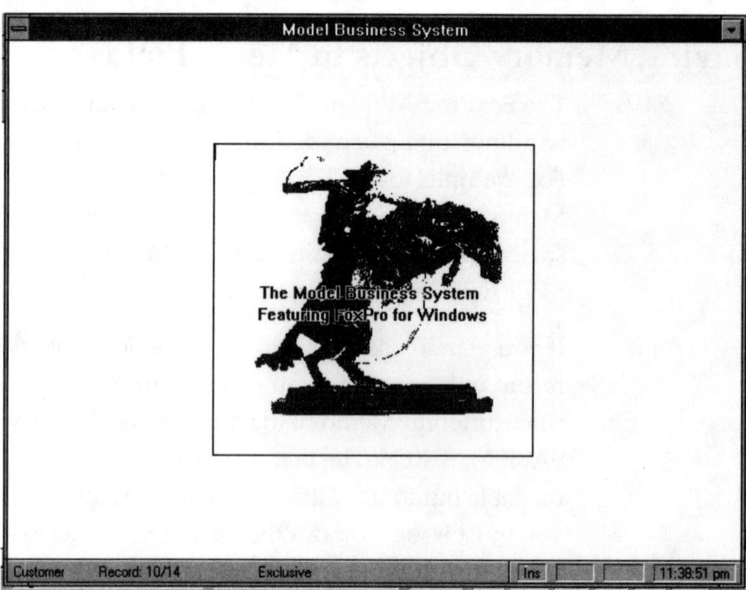

FIGURE 8.2:
An attractive sign-on message is easily created with the FoxPro Screen Builder.

Note that elaborate sign-on messages are easily created using the Screen Builder. With it you can readily draw and size a window and place whatever text you want in it. You can also include pictures drawn from bitmap files, assuming you create them in advance. When you finish, you have two choices. You can execute the sign-on message using the generated screen program, after including the special screen file #NOREAD directive to prevent the inclusion of READ in the screen program so the program displays the sign-on message and terminates, leaving the message on the screen. The other choice is to use the Clipboard to transfer only those commands required to execute the sign-on message to the main program. (Chapter 11 discusses screen file directives.)

The one concession we make to expediency in procedure Setup is the use of HIDE WINDOW ALL, which we issue before displaying our sign-on message. We must hide the Command window as we do so because FoxPro's system windows, including the desktop or main window, are not affected by SAVE and CLEAR ALL (or CLEAR WINDOWS). These commands affect only user-defined windows created with DEFINE WINDOW. The Command window, however, is not the only nonmodal FoxPro system window (or dialog) that can be present on the screen if the operator launches our application from the interactive mode. And while MBS, for example, makes use of the Calculator, Puzzle, and Calendar, making it unnecessary to remove them from the screen except for aesthetic reasons, the presence of the FoxPro View or Filer window can lead to problems since they will be perfectly functional. We get rid of them, one and all, with HIDE WINDOW ALL—in this case, without worrying about restoring them when our application terminates, supposing they are open when it begins. We go to this trouble only with the Command window.

Controlling the Desktop Window and System Menu

Before we place our sign-on message on the screen, there is also the issue of replacing the title displayed in the FoxPro main window (or desktop) with one more suited to our application and removing the current system menu from view. We change the title with MODIFY WINDOW SCREEN, a command about which we will have more to say when we return from procedure Setup to BigBiz.prg, where we will use MODIFY WINDOW SCREEN a second time to set the main window attributes and font required by our application. Here we use it only for cosmetic reasons.

Note that the current main window title and font can be referenced using the window title function, WTITLE(), and window font function, WFONT(), respectively, with an entry of "SCREEN". WTITLE("SCREEN") returns the title, while WFONT(1,"SCREEN") returns the current font. (With WFONT(), use 1 to return the name of the current font, 2 to return font size, or 3 to return style.) If we do not save these values here, it is because we will change other main window attributes, the settings of which cannot be referenced and saved to memvars. Since this will require us to restore the main window to its prior state manually unless we restore it to its default configuration, we might as well not bother with WTITLE() and WFONT(), though under other circumstances they may prove useful.

With respect to the current system menu, which we will soon replace with the MBS main menu, we can use SET("MENU") to determine its ON/OFF/AUTOMATIC setting, but we cannot save the menu itself to a memvar, file, or memo. Instead we use the command PUSH MENU _msysmenu to place a copy of the current system menu (which, not incidentally, always bears the name _msysmenu) in memory. We can then issue SET SYSMENU OFF to deactivate and remove it from the screen. Later on, in procedure Cleanup, we can restore this menu with POP MENU _msysmenu and then execute SET SYSMENU &oldmenu to reestablish its ON/OFF/AUTOMATIC setting. (We discuss these commands in greater detail in Chapter 9.)

Setting the Application's Environment

In the next set of commands included in procedure Setup, we open our application's procedure file, holding our application's error-handling routine along with other procedures vital to the system, and use ON ERROR <command> to make FoxPro execute it if and when an error occurs. Then we use SET PATH to show FoxPro the way to the directories holding the tables and other external files used by our application and use SET RESOURCE and SET HELP to open our resource and Help files.

```
* Establish MBS resources.
SET PROCEDURE TO bizlib
* Deactivate ON ERROR <command> during testing.
ON ERROR DO errorhndlr
SET PATH TO dbfs;dbfs\reports;\dbfs\labels;
oldres = SET("RESOURCE")
SET RESOURCE TO bigbiz
oldhelp = SET("HELP")
oldtopic = SET("TOPIC")
SET HELP TO mbshelp
SET HELP ON
```

NOTE Since the view file created earlier by procedure Setup saves the current file search path as well as the names of open resource, Help, and alternate (text output) files, we need not save this information to memvars. We must, however, save the prior ON/OFF settings of SET RESOURCE and SET HELP, as well as the name of the current help topic, supposing one was defined.

Next, after restoring whatever operator-defined macros are found in the system macro file (supposing MBS.fky has been created and is found on disk), we use SET MACKEY to enable operator use of the FoxPro Macro Key Definition dialog, which we therefore include in the application.

```
oldmackey = SET("MACKEY")
SET MACKEY TO "Shift+F10"
IF FILE("mbsmacs.fky")
    RESTORE MACROS FROM mbsmacs
ENDIF
```

Finally, after saving the setting of SET DELETED prior to setting it ON, as required by our application, we execute procedure Opendata, discussed in Chapter 6, to establish our default database view:

```
oldeleted = SET("DELETED")
SET DELETED ON
DO opendata
```

Note that we do not bother to supply FoxPro with the path name of our procedure file, Bizlib.prg, since it is included in the application. Nor do we include the path names of the directories holding our screen, .prg, bitmap, or menu files in our SET PATH command since all these files are included in the application. However, if you attempt to execute Bigbiz.prg in order to execute the application using the source code files instead of the .app file, the program will crash unless FoxPro is made aware of the directory locations of all source code files. The easiest way to do this is to add the directories to the file search path.

We now look more closely at some of the new facilities, though we reserve discussion of Help files until the end of the chapter.

Working without Procedure Files

The fact that procedure files are included in an .app file along with all the other programs calling the procedures and functions they contain makes their use in a FoxPro application *passé*. Since the Project Manager takes care to link together all procedures and functions found in any program or procedure file regardless of where the procedures and functions are found, all the procedures stored in a procedure file might just as well be placed in a single .prg file or even written as separate .prg files. We nonetheless make use of a procedure file in MBS as an organizational tool, useful for holding in one place those procedures and functions that are used over and over by other programs included in the application.

Using ON ERROR to Establish a Global Error-Handling Routine

If an error occurs during program execution, if it is available FoxPro opens the source code file containing the command resulting in an error (as described in Chapter 7) and offers the options Cancel, Suspend, and Ignore. While such behavior is appropriate while testing a program, the default FoxPro error dialog will not be helpful to the operator using the finished application. For this reason, when we finish our testing, we use ON ERROR <command> to make FoxPro execute a specific procedure when an error occurs.

In a stand-alone application like the MBS, the error-handling routine can be quite simple since we need use it only to execute QUIT—though it is best to first alert the operator that an error occurred and prepare the operator for the action, as is done in procedure Errorhndlr by placing a call to the MBS system alert procedure, which we looked at in Chapter 3.

```
PROCEDURE errorhndlr
DO alert WITH MESSAGE(),"Press any key to terminate program."
QUIT
```

For the first line of our two-line alert message, we tell procedure Alert to display the value of MESSAGE(), which returns a message indicating the nature of the error triggering our error-handling routine. Since procedure Alert uses WAIT to halt program execution after displaying its message, the moment the operator presses any key, program control returns to procedure Errorhndlr, which then executes the QUIT command, terminating FoxPro and our application with it.

If it is appropriate to return to the FoxPro interactive mode after an error, use CANCEL instead of QUIT. As an alternative, if the application uses a cleanup procedure, execute it before issuing CANCEL. This will help to straighten out the environment before returning to FoxPro unless the error also affects one of the commands in the cleanup procedure. Where this is a concern, use the PROGRAM() function, as described below, to pass to the error handler the name of the procedure in which the error has occurred. Then you can test to see if the error originates in the cleanup procedure and respond accordingly by issuing CANCEL without placing another call to the cleanup procedure.

In network applications, however, a more complex error-handling routine is usually used to deal with errors generated when an operator attempts to lock a record or file already locked by another operator. Whether or not such an action generates an error, or how many times FoxPro will retry the lock before the error is generated, will depend on the setting of SET REPROCESS, discussed in Chapter 3. Be that as it may, if an error-handling routine is to be employed to resolve conflicts, use the ERROR() function with IF to distinguish between errors arising from unsuccessful record and file locking and other types of errors. (ERROR() returns the current error number.) If the command resulting in the error should be retried, this can be done by issuing the RETRY command in the error-handling routine. It can also be ignored by issuing RETURN, which has the effect of returning program control to the next line of the program generating the error. Of course, CANCEL and QUIT can also be used to cancel the application or quit FoxPro. (See your FoxPro documentation for a complete list of error numbers and messages and their meanings.)

Operators should be instructed to document errors as best they can to help you diagnose and fix the problem. This is why we display MESSAGE() when an error occurs. More information about the error can also be displayed by using ERROR() to display the error number and/or by using PROGRAM() and LINENO() to display the name of the program being executed and the line number of the command generating the error. However, to make use of PROGRAM() and LINENO() you must pass them to the error handler as parameters—for example, with ON ERROR DO <procedure> WITH PROGRAM(), LINENO(). (ERROR() and MESSAGE() will hold onto the last error, but PROGRAM() and LINENO() will change when the error handler is executed.) Note that numeric arguments can be used with MESSAGE() and PROGRAM() to return additional information, though you must refer to your FoxPro documentation or Help file for more information about this. For examples of more complex error-handling routines, you can also examine the sample programs supplied with FoxPro.

Enabling the Use of Macros

Most operators will greatly benefit from being able to define their own macros for entering often-used strings with a single (combination) keystroke. For this reason, we enable access to the FoxPro Macro Key Definition dialog, shown open in Figure 8.3, by executing the command SET MACKEY TO "Shift+F10". (We use Shift+F10 simply because it is the FoxPro default for activating the dialog.) This will enable operators to record macros as they choose. Moreover, so these macros will not be erased when MBS terminates, we execute the command SAVE MACROS TO mbsmacs to save them to a macro file. If we test for the existence of Mbsmacs.fky before attempting to open it in procedure Setup with the FILE() existence function, it is because we do not include it with MBS. Instead, we allow our application to create it.

FIGURE 8.3:

Use SET MACKEY to make the FoxPro Macro Key Definition dialog available to the operator.

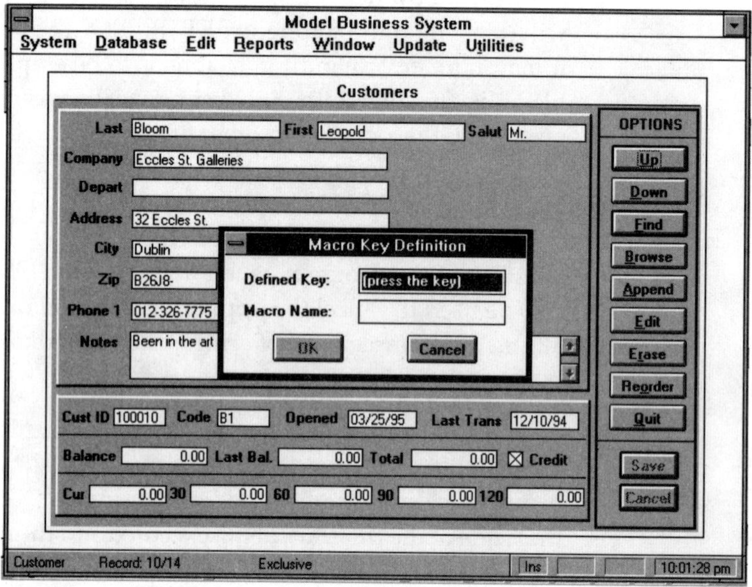

Of course, if we grant the operator the freedom to create and use macros, we must also provide cursory instructions regarding their use. We must also warn the operator against accidentally reassigning a keystroke used as one of our menu pad hot keys—or better yet, since the operator may want to assign his or her own menu pad hot keys using macros, explain how to restore the menu pad hot keys assigned by the application. This is done by simply redefining the macro and placing nothing in it. (The menu pad hot key established by the menu program does not change. Only a macro using the same key definition takes precedence over it.) Fortunately, Ctrl+Esc, accessing the Windows Task List, and the Esc key, the various functions of which we discuss later in this chapter, cannot be used as macro definition keys. There is no danger of the operator reprogramming these important keys.

WARNING

Be aware that many programmers will not enable operator definition and use of macros in their applications since there is always the possibility that accidental execution of a macro will have weird effects—or at least interfere with the current action in an undesirable way.

Other Pertinent SET Commands

In the final and lengthiest portion of procedure Setup we deal with all other environment settings that affect our application but can have no negative effect on our startup procedure. For the most part this means issuing more SET commands, which, for the sake of convenience, we execute in alphabetical order by parameter name:

```
* Establish other default environment settings.
oldansi = SET("ANSI")
SET ANSI OFF
oldauto = SET("AUTOSAVE")
SET AUTOSAVE ON
oldbell = SET("BELL")
SET BELL OFF
oldblock = SET("BLOCKSIZE")
SET BLOCKSIZE TO 64
SET BRSTATUS ON
oldcarry = SET("CARRY")
SET CARRY OFF
* Other set commands follow...
```

When a SET command doesn't affect the application or when we wish to make use of its current setting, we can obviously omit it. For example, in the above commands, we SET BELL OFF. This makes the setting of SET BELL TO, controlling bell tone pitch and duration, immaterial—as it may well be even if we SET BELL ON, supposing we wish to use the current tone setting. (With respect to SET BRSTATUS, which controls the appearance of the status bar during BROWSE, we need not trap its prior setting since it is stored in the view file created at the outset of procedure Setup to store information about the prior database environment.)

Other SET commands we do not trouble to use are SET PRINTER TO and SET COLOR, controlling the selected printer port and the color attributes of user-defined windows and menus, respectively, since we are content to make use of the current settings because they can be changed at any time through use of the Windows Print Manager and Control Panel.

TIP

When executing printed reports with REPORT FORM <file>, you can include the PROMPT option to display a print settings dialog before printing. Using the dialog, the operator can specify the number of copies and the page numbers to print, redirect print output to a file, and access the Windows Printer Setup dialog to modify or change the print driver and output device.

With respect to the use of colors, the fact that FoxPro adopts the Windows color scheme (unless another is selected in Config.fpw or set with SET COLOR OF SCHEME)—and, moreover, must use the Windows color scheme for various elements, including the system menu bar and the Command and View windows—makes it unnecessary and in most cases undesirable to trifle with color sets and schemes; most operators will appreciate being able to select and change window color schemes by themselves. (We will have more to say about screen colors in Chapter 11.)

As for the remaining SET commands appearing in procedure Setup, you are left to scout out the majority of them on your own with the aid of the FoxPro Help file. We make an exception, however, with SET DEBUG and SET ESCAPE. During system development you will want to work with SET DEBUG and SET ESCAPE ON so the Trace and Debug windows can be accessed (DEBUG) and pressing the Esc key (ESCAPE) will interrupt command execution and access a dialog allowing us to cancel, suspend, or resume the program. However, when you finish the system, you will want to change the settings of both commands to OFF.

NOTE

SET ESCAPE OFF does not disable the use of the Esc key during READ, APPEND, EDIT, and other commands enabling data entry. If you want to change or disable the function of Esc during data editing or elsewhere in your program, use ON ESCAPE <command> or ON KEY LABEL ESC <command>. Of course, during @ GET/READ a push button can be selected for automatic execution with Esc. (See Chapter 5.)

Terminating the Setup Procedure

We bring procedure Setup to a close by using SAVE TO <file> once again to save the memvars used to store the prior environment settings to a memory file. This gives us two memory files holding information that will be used by procedure

Cleanup. (The first holds settings saved to memvars before execution of CLEAR ALL at the outset of procedure Setup.) We then release the window displaying our sign-on message and return program control to Bigbiz. There is no need to erase the memvars created by procedure Setup since it is a nested procedure. As soon as it terminates, all memvars created in it (and not declared PUBLIC) are automatically released.

TIP

Though we do so, there is no real need to get rid of the window holding our sign-on message. We can leave it open in the main window for the duration of the application. Though the window will be listed on the Window pulldown, activating it can cause no harm.

Using ON KEY LABEL during Program Development

When procedure Setup terminates, program control returns to Bigbiz.prg (again, see Figure 8.1), where we use ON KEY LABEL F1 HELP to enable execution of the FoxPro system Help window. While the command might just as easily be executed in procedure Setup, where we direct FoxPro to use the MBS Help file, Mbshelp.dbf, we leave it in Bigbiz.prg, along with the three disabled ON KEY LABEL commands that appear below it, so that anyone reading the program will be immediately aware of which global interrupt programs are in effect.

As for the other ON KEY LABEL commands, they are *commented out*, which means they are rendered nonexecutable by a leading asterisk since they are needed only during system development. The first is used to execute Dimens.prg, which we discussed in Chapter 5. As you may recall, its function is to trap the coordinates of a BROWSE window and to use the coordinates to write a DEFINE WINDOW command suitable for controlling the BROWSE window's attributes. The other ON KEY LABEL commands, which are described in the next section, serve as panic buttons.

Placement of Commands in the Startup Program

There are other commands relegated to procedure Setup that might have been issued in Bigbiz along with ON KEY LABEL. ON ERROR, SET PATH, SET RESOURCE, and SET PROCEDURE are the most obvious candidates since they all indicate system resources or, in the case of SET PATH, the way to find to them. A glance at their settings tells us not so much where to find things but what there is to look for. Still, this is mentioned only to call attention to the fact that there is no set rule for determining which commands appear in the main program and which commands are relegated to procedure Setup, where one must go to greater effort to find them when opening Bigbiz.prg for edit.

Straightening Things Out after a Crash

During program testing, we work without an ON ERROR routine to control FoxPro's actions in the event of an error. This way, FoxPro will access the source code file, as described above, and allow us to RESUME, SUSPEND, or CANCEL the program. If we elect to CANCEL the program, we can then edit the source code file displayed by FoxPro. However, to make this option workable, since canceling the application throws us back in the interactive mode, we must see to it that we have a means of automatically restoring the environment to what it was before we launched our application. (The MBS resource file, for example, will still be open after we cancel the application. If we fail to SET RESOURCE TO DEFAULT to reopen Foxuser.dbf, FoxPro will continue to use our application's resource file as we work on our project, thereby filling it with records regarding objects not used by the application. And this will obviously create a nuisance.) Rather than executing all the commands from the Command window, we can simply take advantage of the procedure MBS itself uses to restore the environment since it is deliberately written to reference no values other than those it RESTOREs itself from the files created by procedure Setup. For this reason we use ON KEY LABEL Alt+F8 to execute procedure Cleanup, though we are careful to supply FoxPro with the name of the source code file in which the procedure is to be found since we intend to use the Alt+F9 hot key only after canceling the application. (We also supply Bigbiz.prg's path since the PRGS directory is not included in the application's file search path, assuming it is still set.)

NOTE

It is actually rare to cancel an application when an error occurs in order to make changes to source code files because the majority of an application's source code is usually found in screen programs. Since screen program source code is generated automatically on the basis of the contents of a screen design file, which is created and revised using the Screen Builder, changes to screen programs must be made to the screen design file, not to the source code file. (If you alter the source code file, the next time FoxPro regenerates the screen program using the screen design file, your changes will disappear.) When an error occurs in a screen program, however, it is often useful to suspend the program so as to better diagnose it. You can then choose to cancel the program just to return quickly to the interactive mode.

Using ON KEY LABEL to Access or Create Debugging Tools

ON KEY LABEL Alt+F9 SUSPEND is used if we want to suspend the application at any time and access the Command window to conduct further tests. Not every program error causes a crash, and those that don't are usually difficult to diagnose without testing the environment. Accessing the Command window while the application is suspended will not only allow us to test the environment as we choose; we can also change the values of memvars controlling the application and/or open the Trace and Debug windows with ACTIVATE WINDOW Trace and ACTIVATE WINDOW Debug, respectively, before setting the application in motion again with the RESUME command.

Of course, you can use ON KEY LABEL to add other routines that may be helpful to you during program development. For example, when testing window-level event handling in a new application, you may want immediate access to the value of WONTOP() or WREAD(). While these values can be reported through use of the Debug window, placing the additional window on the screen can confuse matters. To access the values of these and other window functions without using the Debug window, use ON KEY LABEL with WAIT WINDOW:

```
ON KEY LABEL Alt+F5 WAIT WINDOW "wontop is "+WONTOP()+ ;
    " wread is "+WREAD()
```

This will save you the trouble of activating and using the Debug or Command window just to test window status, which is sometimes altered by activating these FoxPro windows.

TIP

Many programmers like to use ON KEY LABEL with SET SYSMENU TO DEFAULT. If a crash occurs during testing and you must cancel the application, you may find yourself trapped in the interactive mode without access to the Command window or the FoxPro system menu. You'll be trapped like a rat in a trap, to quote the Three Stooges. This is why we execute it with ON KEY LABEL Alt+F6—that is, if procedure Cleanup, a more thorough tool for cleaning the stables, cannot be used.

Initializing Global Memvars

All programs belonging to the MBS are nested within Bigbiz.prg, so all memvars declared in Bigbiz.prg (but not in its procedures) will be globally available to all programs in the application without having to be declared PUBLIC. If the list of global memvars is not extensive, it is therefore best to initialize them in the main program, where anyone reading the program is certain to be struck by them. (Part of learning the system will involve learning their function.) The alternative is to initialize global memvars in procedure Setup after first declaring them PUBLIC since they will otherwise be erased when procedure Setup terminates. Anyone surveying the source code must then go looking for a list of the global memvars.

With respect to the memvars initialized in Bigbiz.prg, you will recognize only one of them at this point—memvar m.doit—though we have already noted the existence, if not the function, of memvar m.hide. As you will recall, memvar m.doit is set to .T. by all screen programs as a means of indicating when data entry is under way. It is used, in other words, as a means of controlling events. The other memvars, including m.hide, also serve to control window-level events. They are discussed in Chapter 10.

Using the Main FoxPro Window

With our environment fully set down to the last global memvar, we can now take full control of the FoxPro main window, changing its title, size, and attributes as we choose. We do this with the command MODIFY WINDOW SCREEN, which we already used in procedure Setup to render the main window a more fitting background for our sign-on window. Here, however, we must do more than supply the main window with a title; we must prepare the window to function properly as our application's window *within Windows*. In the case of MBS, we make our application's main or parent window function in Windows more or less like we make its child (READ) windows function with respect to each other:

```
MODIFY WINDOW SCREEN TITLE "Model Business System" ;
    NOCLOSE FLOAT NOGROW MINIMIZE NOZOOM ;
    FONT "FoxFont,7"
```

By using FLOAT (as opposed to NOFLOAT), we make it possible for the operator to drag the window about by the title bar. By using MINIMIZE, we make it possible to reduce the application window to an icon at the bottom of the Windows Program or File Manager, where we can click it to restore it. Though the operator is free to access the Windows Task List with Ctrl+Esc regardless of what we do, by using FLOAT and MINIMIZE we make it much easier for the operator to move back and forth between different applications.

On the other hand, unlike our READ windows, we prevent Close from appearing in the main window's control box by using NOCLOSE instead of CLOSE. While this is not essential (attempting to use Close when FoxPro is in a wait state under the control of READ will only generate the warning message "Cannot Quit FoxPro"), it does serve to remove the useless Close option from the main window control box. In any case, it is our intention to make the operator quit the application through use of the two system menu options devoted to this purpose: Quit to Windows and Quit to FoxPro.

We use NOGROW simply to remove the Size option from the window control box. Though we can alter the size and position of the main window by taking advantage of MODIFY WINDOWS FROM and TO or AT and SIZE <coordinates>, once the main window falls under program control through use of a Foundation READ, it can be neither sized nor maximized. (Using ZOOM will not enable you to maximize the window during a Foundation Read; nor will the control box display the Maximize option. At present FoxPro is sloppier when you use GROW since it will display

Size in the control box, but the option will have no effect.) My assumption is that these features will be enabled with future versions of FoxPro.

In any case, using NOCLOSE, FLOAT, NOGROW, and MINIMIZE, we end up with an application window that sports Move (FLOAT) and Minimize in the control box along with irrepressible Restore and Switch to options.

NOTE

An unpleasant side effect that goes with the loss of Maximize during Foundation Read is that when the Foundation Read is executed, the maximize button at the top right of the FoxPro window suddenly disappears, causing a momentary flash. For this reason we used NOZOOM with MODIFY WINDOW in procedure Setup to get rid of the maximize button from the start.

The other attribute we change with MODIFY WINDOW SCREEN is the screen font, which we set to "Foxfont,7", a monospace font. With respect to the MBS, however, this is just a formality since we specify fonts with the rest of our windows rather than allowing them to adapt the attributes of the window in which they are opened. (In the majority of cases this will be the main window.) Still, it is a good idea to set the main window's font to a known value since you may have occasion to make use of it.

NOTE

There is no compelling reason to issue MODIFY WINDOW SCREEN twice in a startup program. We might have changed the main window's attributes in procedure Setup the first time we issued the commands. However, my own preference is to leave the command actually controlling the main window's attributes in the main program so it will stand out.

Restoring the Main Window

If our application is to allow the operator to return to FoxPro, we must see to it that the FoxPro main window is returned to its default configuration. This is readily done by issuing MODIFY WINDOW SCREEN without any parameters. We use it in procedure Cleanup.

NOTE

Unlike user-defined windows created with DEFINE WINDOW, the FoxPro main window—or rather, its configuration—cannot be saved to memory with SAVE WINDOWS TO <file>. If and when you execute one application from within another, changing the main window as you go, upon returning to the calling application you must restore the main window to its prior configuration manually with MODIFY WINDOW SCREEN. (As previously mentioned, the main window title and font can nonetheless be trapped with WTITLE() and WFONT().)

Replacing the FoxPro System Menu

We now come to the second-to-last step in launching our application: replacing the FoxPro system menu with a system menu of our own devising. (As you may recall, we already saved a copy of the existing system menu to memory with PUSH MENU _msysmenu, while also turning it off, in procedure Setup.) Now we replace it by executing MBS.mpr, a menu program written with the aid of the FoxPro Menu Builder. Both are discussed in detail in the next chapter. We will say no more about MBS.mpr here except to remind those who are new to FoxPro that the MBS system menu, once activated with SET SYSMENU TO AUTOMATIC (a command issued in MBS.mpr), functions as the FoxPro system menu. Were we to suddenly cancel our application and return to the interactive mode—that is, without issuing SET SYSMENU TO DEFAULT (or POP MENU) first—FoxPro would go on using the MBS system menu, though only those options native to the default FoxPro system menu would be functional. Options that execute programs included in the application will obviously result in error since the application itself has terminated.

Placing FoxPro in a Wait State with Foundation Read

Leaving aside the warning message sent to the screen with procedure Alert if a month has passed since statements were last written, we next come to the command that places FoxPro in a wait state under program control. This again is our Foundation READ, which we use in FoxPro in the place of DO WHILE .T. to create an event loop, enabling the operator to execute one program after another, not just by using the MBS system menu, but by clicking or selecting open application (READ) windows (something we cannot make FoxPro do in the interactive mode).

We say no more about our Foundation READ until Chapter 10, where we review the event handler executed by its VALID clause whenever the operator executes or terminates a program. (Its function within the application is similar to that of the VALID clause of our control push button within our screen programs). But we must comment on the possibility of creating programs that do not make use of Foundation READ. Of course, take it away and the application terminates, returning FoxPro to the interactive mode, where our system menu will still be active, assuming we remove DO Cleanup (the procedure restoring the prior system menu) as well. While this is obviously undesirable with MBS and with any other application requiring an events loop, it nonetheless opens up the possibility of writing a menu program that is designed to reconfigure the FoxPro interactive mode by supplanting or altering the programs available in the system menu. I mention this possibility now so readers new to FoxPro will be aware of this alternative way of working with FoxPro. It is discussed further in the next chapter. Of course, in the case of an .exe file, omission of the Foundation READ will return the operator to the Windows Program Manager, not to the FoxPro interactive mode.

Cleaning Up the Environment When Returning to FoxPro

Procedure Cleanup is executed when the operator makes a menu selection or presses a hot key set with ON KEY LABEL, executing a command terminating our Foundation READ. (It will not be executed if the QUIT or CANCEL command is issued.) We will not say more about it now; we have already anticipated its every action and reviewed the majority of commands by which it achieves its end in our coverage of procedure Setup. It will be worth your while, though, to glance at the first screenful of commands listed in procedure Cleanup (see Figure 8.4) just to take note of the order in which they are issued. Of course, we must restore the memvars contained in the two memory files created by procedure Setup before we can reset any of the SET commands or RESTORE SCREEN. So too must we ERASE the various files created by procedure Setup after restoring the memory objects they

FIGURE 8.4:

Use a cleanup procedure to restore FoxPro to its prior environment when terminating your program.

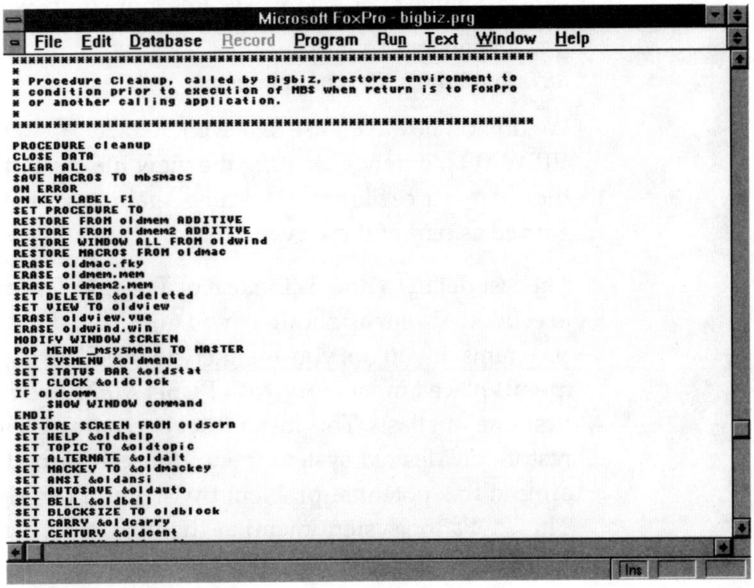

Microsoft FoxPro - bigbiz.prg

File Edit Database Record Program Run Text Window Help

```
****************************************************************
*
* Procedure Cleanup, called by Bigbiz, restores environment to
* condition prior to execution of MBS when return is to FoxPro
* or another calling application.
*
****************************************************************

PROCEDURE cleanup
CLOSE DATA
CLEAR ALL
SAVE MACROS TO mbsmacs
ON ERROR
ON KEY LABEL F1
SET PROCEDURE TO
RESTORE FROM oldmem ADDITIVE
RESTORE FROM oldmem2 ADDITIVE
RESTORE WINDOW ALL FROM oldwind
RESTORE MACROS FROM oldmac
ERASE oldmac.fky
ERASE oldmem.mem
ERASE oldmem2.mem
SET DELETED &oldeleted
SET VIEW TO oldview
ERASE oldview.vue
ERASE oldwind.win
MODIFY WINDOW SCREEN
POP MENU _msysmenu TO MASTER
SET SYSMENU &oldmenu
SET STATUS BAR &oldstat
SET CLOCK &oldclock
IF oldcomm
    SHOW WINDOW command
ENDIF
RESTORE SCREEN FROM oldscrn
SET HELP &oldhelp
SET TOPIC TO &oldtopic
SET ALTERNATE &oldalt
SET MACKEY TO &oldmackey
SET ANSI &oldansi
SET AUTOSAVE &oldauto
SET BELL &oldbell
SET BLOCKSIZE TO oldblock
SET CARRY &oldcarry
SET CENTURY &oldcent
```

Ins

contain, supposing we do not want to leave them on disk, where they will be overwritten each time our application starts.

The only command that doesn't participate in the cleanup operation is SAVE MACRO, which is used to save all current operator-defined macros to the MBS macro file so they can be restored by procedure Setup the next time the operator starts the application.

In the majority of instances we employ macro substitution to suppy FoxPro with SET command settings. This is when the memvar holds a command word (for example, ON or OFF) and not an expression. However, a good number of SET <parameter> TO commands expect expressions, like SET MARGIN TO and SET MEMOWIDTH TO, and you will receive an error if you use macro substitution to supply their values using the memvars created by the setup procedure. With respect to SET commands expecting the name of a file (or a null string), though we include none in procedure Cleanup, macro substitution is also avoided, but in this case because using a name expression will be faster. For instance, the following two commands do the same thing, but the second one, using parentheses to tell FoxPro to expect a name expression, executes more quickly:

```
SET RESOURCE TO &oldreso
SET RESOURCE TO (oldreso)
```

We do not, however, use SET RESOURCE TO in procedure Cleanup because SET VIEW TO oldview, executing the view file created in procedure Setup, will reopen the old resource file automatically. Again, resource, procedure and Help files are regarded as part of the view.

The last detail to note is the use of TO MASTER with POPUP MENU. During the execution of your application, you may have occasion to use several different menu programs. If you do, you are likely to use PUSH MENU more than once. However, menus placed in memory with PUSH MENU come out with POP on a last-one-in, first-one-out basis. This means that procedure Cleanup's POP command will fail to restore the desired system menu unless it is the first one in the stack. But we get around this potential problem by issuing POP MENU _msysmenu TO MASTER. This POPs the system menu at the bottom of the stack instead. It also clears the menu stack.

Using FoxPro Help Files

Creating an application Help facility is easy with FoxPro; you need do no more than replace the Help file FoxPro uses with a Help file of your own. As with FoxPro resource files, FoxPro .dbf-style Help files are simple tables with a specific structure. And while you can create a Help file manually, it will be far easier to USE FoxPro's default .dbf Help file, Foxhelp.dbf, and simply copy its structure:

```
USE \foxprow\foxhelp AGAIN
COPY STRUCTURE TO mbshelp
```

Once you have created your Help file, you can open it with USE and begin adding records to it, each record representing an item that will be listed in the Help table of contents. To make FoxPro use your Help file in place of its own, use the command SET HELP TO <file>. Once this is done, pressing function key F1, if it is enabled, or selecting Contents from the FoxPro Help pulldown accesses your Help file table of contents (assuming SET HELP is ON).

FoxPro .dbf Help files include three fields:

Field	Field Name	Type	Width
1	Topic	Character	30
2	Details	Memo	10
3	Class	Character	20

The Topic field is used to enter the Help item topic name as it will appear in the Help file table of contents. (See Figure 8.5.) The Details field contains the Help file entry that is displayed in the FoxPro Help window when the topic is selected. Because it is a Memo field, your entries can be as long or short as you care to make them. Class, which we do not make use of in the MBS, can be used to enter a code or keyword for each topic, making it possible to filter which topics appear in the Help table of contents when F1 or Help Contents is selected.

FIGURE 8.5:

Use the FoxPro Help facility in your application by replacing FoxPro's default .dbf Help file with one of your own.

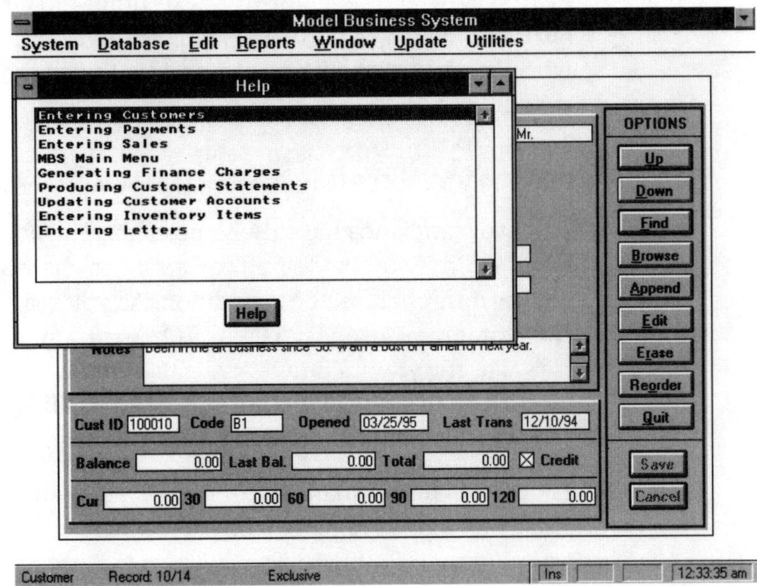

NOTE

If you have the FoxPro Distribution Kit, you can also create and use a Windows-style Help facility with your applications, though this takes more effort. (See your Distribution Kit documentation for instructions.)

To switch between FoxPro's .dbf- and Windows-style Help, use the command SET HELP TO <file>. SET HELP TO foxhelp.dbf establishes .dbf-style help, while SET HELP TO foxhelp.hlp enables Windows-style Help.

Controlling Use of Help during Program Execution

While your application is running, the Help facility can be enabled and disabled with SET HELP ON/OFF. When it is enabled, and assuming that ON KEY LABEL F1 has its default assignment of executing the HELP command, you can instruct FoxPro to display a particular Help file entry instead of the Help table of contents when the operator presses F1 by using the command SET TOPIC TO <expC> or <expL>.

```
SET TOPIC TO "MBS main menu"
SET TOPIC TO TOPIC = "MBS main menu"
```

The two commands have the same effect. The only difference is that the first supplies FoxPro with the desired topic using a character string, while the second designates it through use of a condition. As you may recall from Part I, the MBS data entry programs use SET TOPIC TO <expL> in their setup code to designate the Help file entry written to describe their usage. In the cleanup code, SET TOPIC is used again without supplying any topic to make FoxPro return to its normal practice of displaying the Help file table of contents when F1 is selected.

Though we do not make use of it in the MBS, the command SET HELPFILTER can also be employed to place a filter on which topics appear in the Help table of contents. If your Help file will contain a large number of records, SET HELPFILTER will prove quite useful. Use the Class field to provide each record in the Help file with a keyword or code that will allow it to be identified with other records dealing with a similar topic. Then SET HELPFILTER TO Class = <expC> to display only those topics with a specific keyword or code in the Class field in the Help table of contents.

TIP

When your Help file is engaged with SET HELP, its records will be listed in the Help table of contents in their physical order. An index tag cannot be used. However, you can rearrange the records in the table in a logical order according to the contents of the Topic or Class field by opening the table with USE and employing SORT or INDEX and COPY to create a sorted version of the table. Then use the sorted version of the table in place of the original Help file.

Help file topics can be as general or specific as you wish to make them. In a program like the MBS, it is generally sufficient to include one Help topic for each screen program. However, Help topics can be written simply to detail which entries an operator may make to a single input field. You can, after all, issue SET TOPIC in @ GET WHEN or use the VARREAD() or SYS(18) function, both of which return the name of the current @ GET object, with SET HELPFILTER or SET TOPIC to make FoxPro access a Help file entry devoted to a single @ GET object when the operator presses F1.

Another feature of FoxPro .dbf-style Help files is the use of *See Also* cross-references. When a Help file entry is selected, the See Also popup, shown in Figure 8.6, will be enabled if the specific Help file record displayed in the window includes one or more cross-reference topics at the end of its Memo field. Selecting a topic displayed in the popup will immediately display that topic in the Help window.

See Also cross-references are easily arranged. First, go to the end of the Details field of the Help file record requiring the cross-references and enter See Also: <topic list>, followed by a carriage return and a blank line, which is used to indicate the end of the cross-reference list. For example, the following line, entered at the end of the Entering Customers topic, will place the Entering Payments and Entering Sales topics in the See Also popup when the Entering Customers topic is displayed in the Help window:

```
See Also: Entering Payments, Entering Sales
```

Each cross-reference topic in the topic list must be separated by a comma. You can insert as many spaces as you want before or after each topic in the list, but remember to follow the last line in the topic list with a blank line so FoxPro will know where the topic list ends.

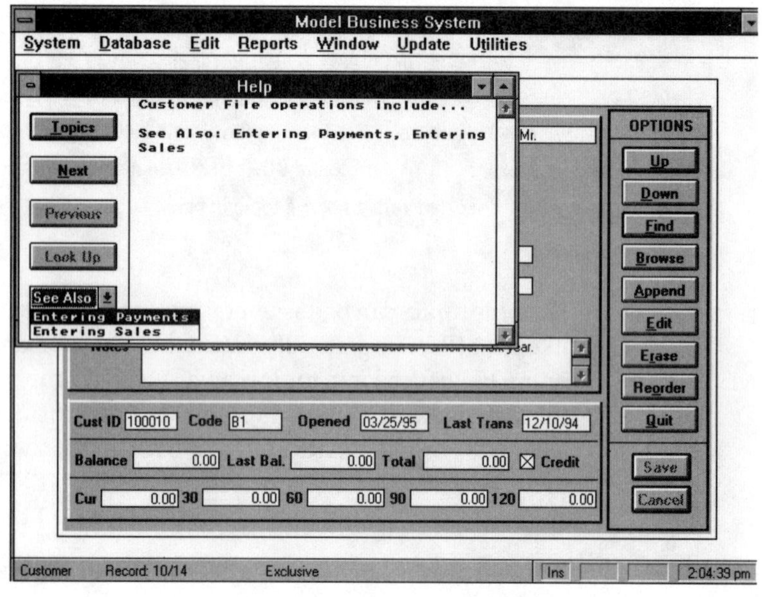

FIGURE 8.6:
See Also topic lists can be supplied with each Help file topic so the operator can quickly access Help file information from related topics.

NOTE

Though it is easy to regard the Help file as a secondary matter when developing your application, it is best to include it in the project from the start. This way, commands like SET TOPIC and SET HELPFILTER, if they are to be used, can be entered in your programs as you create them instead of being stuck in at the last minute. This will not require you to write the actual Help file entries, though you are advised to enter records for some or all of the topics so the Help facility can be tested.

Finally, bear in mind that all records in the FoxPro Help file are available to you and can be copied from Foxhelp.dbf into your own Help file, though you will need to ask Microsoft for permission to employ any text taken from the FoxPro Help file in applications you plan to distribute to others. For a listing of categories and codes used in Foxhelp.class, see the *FoxPro Language Reference* entry for SET HELPFILTER. To review all topics, press F1 when the FoxPro .dbf Help file is engaged to display all topics in the table of contents or open the file with USE and issue BROWSE to scan the table.

CHAPTER

NINE

Creating the Application System Menu

- Working with Quick Menu
- Defining menu pads and pulldown menus
- Menu program architecture
- Memo program definition commands
- Controlling and altering the system menu
- Controlling the interactive mode system menu
- Installing a security system

9

Creating a system menu for your application is quite easy with FoxPro's Menu Builder. This is because there's no program code to write, at least with respect to the menu itself. All we do is fill in the items we want listed in the system menu bar and associated pulldowns, indicate which command or action we want FoxPro to perform when each menu item is selected, and, optionally, select a shortcut key and message for each item. All the information defining a system menu is stored in a menu file—a FoxPro table with an .mnx extension and a corresponding memo file, which is assigned an .mnt extension. This makes it possible to modify a system menu over and over and even create different versions of the menu while working in the Menu Builder by using the File pulldown Save As option. Once you have created or modified a menu file, you can generate the program necessary to execute it by rebuilding your project or application (if the menu file is included in a project) or by selecting the Generate option on the Program pulldown (when the menu file is open in the Menu Builder). The resulting menu program is assigned an .mpr extension to denote its special function.

The process of creating a system menu is, moreover, rendered easier yet by the fact that FoxPro offers its own system menu, complete with all pulldowns, as a ready-made template with which to work. Since your own system menu, when executed, becomes the current FoxPro system menu, it can include all options available on the startup FoxPro system menu, which should be regarded only as the default configuration. If you start the Menu Builder, for example, by issuing CREATE or MODIFY MENU from the Command window and select the Quick Menu option from the Menu pulldown (which is available only when the Menu Builder is in use), FoxPro will immediately fill the Menu Design window with all the values used by the default FoxPro system menu, as shown in Figure 9.1. You can then delete the items that are inappropriate to your own application and add items of your own. Of course, you can also start from scratch, without the aid of Quick Menu; but if you intend to make use, for example, of the FoxPro desk accessories or include the FoxPro Window pulldown in your application, you will find it easier to get rid of unneeded menu pads, pulldowns, and pulldown menu options by highlighting them in the Menu Design window and pressing the Delete button than by adding the items you want one at a time to a new menu.

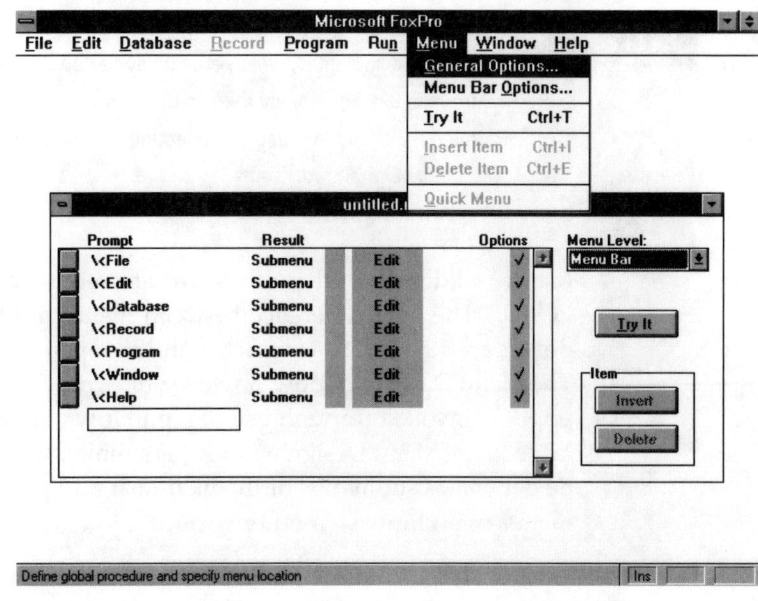

FIGURE 9.1:

Select Quick Menu to use the FoxPro system menu as a template for designing your own system menus.

System Menu Nomenclature in Brief

System menus are made up of a menu bar and attached menu pulldowns, though menu pulldowns are an optional feature. Menu pulldown options can also be defined to open popups, and popup options defined to open other popups, creating what is known as a cascading menu system.

Menu bar options are also known as *pads* since they are created with the DEFINE PAD command. Pulldown and popup options, for their part, are also known as *bars* since they are created with the DEFINE BAR command.

NOTE

Every pad and bar in the default FoxPro system menu has a specific pad or bar name. These names, which are somewhat cryptic, are to be distinguished from the prompts used to identify them in the menu. In fact, the prompts can be changed without altering the result of selecting the option. But the pad and bar names cannot be changed.

Menu pulldowns and popups are created with the same command: DEFINE POPUP. The only difference between menu pulldowns and popups is that pulldowns are attached to a menu bar and are opened when a menu pad is highlighted. The Menu Design window, however, does not distinguish between pulldowns and popups (invoked through use of a pulldown option) as such. They are both indicated in the Menu Design window as submenus, though pulldowns will obviously be defined as submenus of the menu bar and popups, if used, are defined as submenus of pulldowns or other popups.

When you start the Menu Builder, FoxPro sends the Menu Design window to the screen and adds the Menu pulldown to the system menu. The larger portion of the Menu Design window is devoted to a table in which FoxPro displays the items you add to your menu bar or to its attached pulldowns. At first, only the record representing menu bar pads appears in the table. To move to and display the record representing the items in a particular pulldown (once one or more pulldowns have been defined), highlight the menu pad that opens it and click the Edit button. This takes you to the item's submenu. To move back to the menu bar (or to any previous level in a cascading menu system with more than one level of submenus), use the Menu Level popup located at the top right of the Menu Design window.

Working from a Quick Menu

The Quick Menu option is available only as long as the Menu Design window is empty. Once entries are made to the Menu Design table, Quick Menu is disabled, and there is no other way of adding FoxPro menu pads or pulldowns to the Menu Design window automatically. For this reason, it is best to begin the process of menu creation by considering what FoxPro menu pads and pulldowns you'll need in your system menu. In the case of the MBS, for example, we must include the Edit pulldown so the operator will be able to use the Insert Object option to place pictures of inventory items created with other Windows programs into Inventry.dbf's General field. The Edit pulldown also provides access to the Windows Clipboard and a variety of text-editing tools, all of which will be useful when working with Memo or Character fields. We have every reason to make these facilities available to the operator.

Given our intention of making MBS function primarily as a nonmodal window application, we also have need of FoxPro's Window pulldown to supply the operator with a pick list of open windows, just as it does in the interactive mode. The facility to display the names of open windows is built directly into the Window submenu and will be extremely difficult to replicate by creating a popup of our own. On the other hand, several options on the Window pulldown, including Hide/Unhide, Clear, Command, and View, will not be desirable in our application's Window pulldown. We will therefore delete them all, with the exception of Cycle.

Finally, since we intend to make several of the FoxPro desk accessories available to the operator, we will want to include the FoxPro Help pulldown in our system menu. In addition to Help Contents, the pulldown includes the Calculator, Puzzle, and Calendar/Diary among its options. We will, however, delete the Filer and the other Help options since they are active only when Windows-style Help is employed.

NOTE

To delete a menu pad, just highlight its record in the Menu Definition table and select the Delete push button. If the pad has an assigned result, FoxPro will warn you that the result—for example, a submenu, command, or procedure (stored in the menu file)—must be deleted along with the pad and give you a chance to cancel the action. Menu pulldown (or popup) options are deleted in the same way.

After deleting the unneeded menu pads, we end up with a menu bar that includes only three pads, as shown in Figure 9.2. Our next step is to access the submenus used with the Window and Help pulldowns and remove the unneeded items. We leave only the Edit pulldown intact.

To access a submenu, the definitions of which are also stored in the menu file, just select the Edit push button. The Menu Design table will then list all the items included in the pulldown. Figure 9.3, for example, displays all the options included in the Window pulldown.

FIGURE 9.2:

To include FoxPro menu pads in your system menu, use Quick Menu, and then delete the pads you don't need.

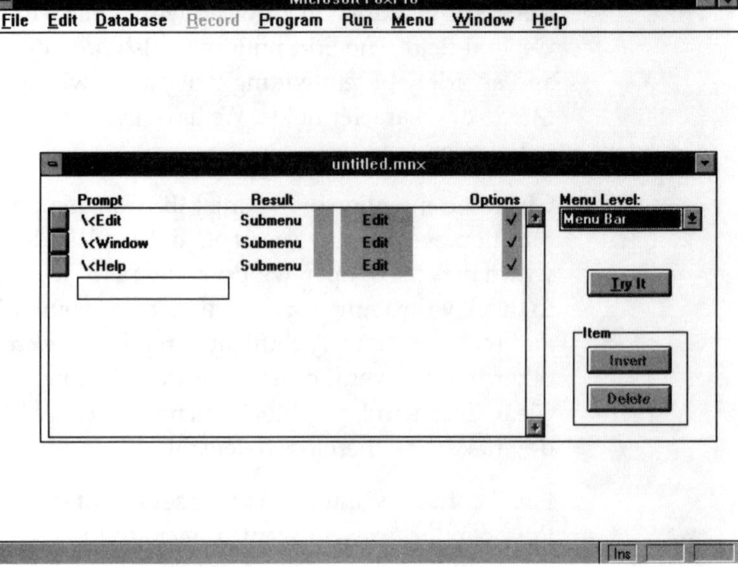

FIGURE 9.3:

The FoxPro Window pulldown options list special menu bar names as their result.

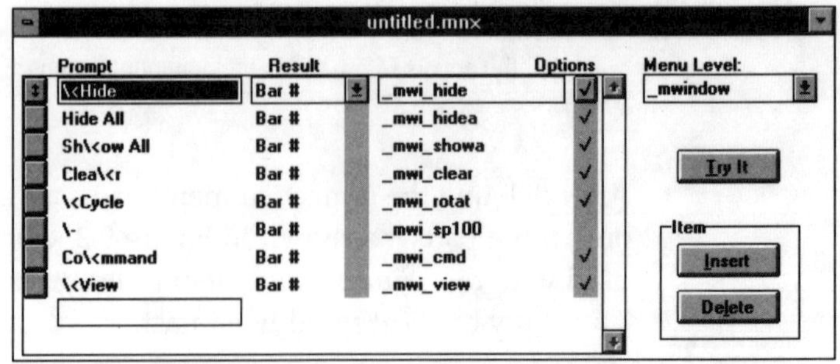

NOTE

Again, the Menu Level popup in the top-right corner of the window is the means by which you move from a submenu back to the higher menu. When you open a menu file, the popup displays Menu Bar since that is the current menu level. When you move to a submenu, the popup displays the prompt of the menu in the parent menu or the menu's name if it is one of FoxPro's system menu pulldowns.

Each of the pulldown menu options (or bars) includes a prompt and a result. In the case of the FoxPro menu pulldowns, however, the result is invariably Bar #. This is a special result option that points to one of FoxPro's pulldown menu bars, which must be identified by name in the dialog box just to the right of the Result popup. This, again, is one of the advantages of working with Quick Menu (or another menu template that includes the desired FoxPro menu pads and bars) since even the lines used to separate groups of related bars in a FoxPro pulldown have specific names.

Manual Entry of FoxPro Menu Bars and Pads

You can add FoxPro pulldown menu options to any submenu manually by selecting Bar # as the result and entering the name of the desired Foxpro pulldown menu bar. (All FoxPro system menu pad and bar names are listed in the Help file topic MENU—System Menu Names and in the *FoxPro Language Reference* under MENU. The SYS(2013) function also returns a list of all pad and bar names.)

FoxPro menu pads can also be placed manually in a menu bar. Just open the Prompt Options dialog by clicking the Options button to the right of the Result entry area, click the Pad Name check box, and enter the name of the desired menu pad, as shown in Figure 9.4. You can then create the submenu and add FoxPro pulldown menu bars as needed. (You may use whatever prompt you like for the pad; you are not limited to the prompts used by FoxPro.)

FIGURE 9.4:

Use the Pad Name dialog to place one of FoxPro's system menu pads in your menu bar.

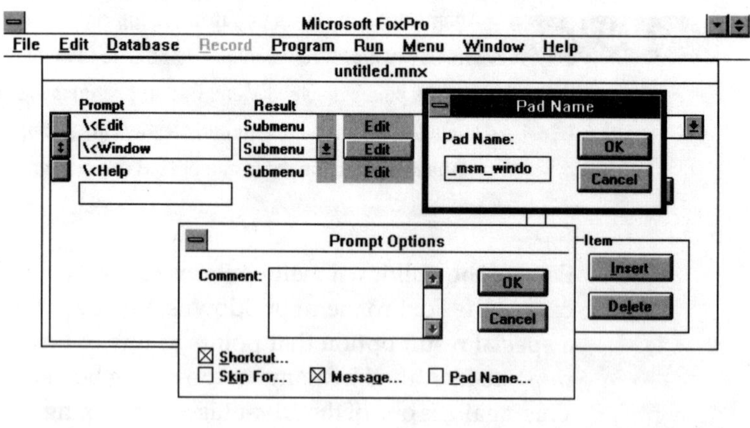

TIP

The Prompt Options dialog is the same whether you are defining menu pads or pulldown menu bars. The Pad Name option, however, will not appear when the dialog is accessed for defining pulldown menu bar options.

Modifying a FoxPro Pulldown

With respect to the Window pulldown, the only action we have to take involves deleting the unneeded options. With the Help pulldown, however, we have more work to do. We erase the FoxPro File pulldown and pad since all of its actions save one (Exit) are useless in our application. (We can also erase the Print Setup option, though the print setup dialog can be accessed when printing reports with REPORT FORM TO PRINT PROMPT. It is also available directly through Windows.) Having dispensed with the File pulldown, we need someplace to list our two Quit options. Moreover, since we remove two of the three Help pulldown options accessing Help file features, the menu pad prompt, Help, no longer suits the pulldown. We can take advantage of the situation by providing the Help pad with a different prompt

(System) without changing its pad name (_msm_systm). (System just happens to be the pad's default prompt in FoxPro for MS-DOS, as is suggested by the pad's name, which is the same in both versions of FoxPro.) We then move our new System pad into position as the first pad in our menu bar by dragging the position button to the left of the prompt with the mouse.

Entering Menu Pad and Bar Shortcut Keys

The one other thing we must do, before or after adding our System pulldown options for Quit, is to use the Prompt Options dialog to change the macro (shortcut key) and message used with the pad since they are no longer appropriate to its new function. To change the macro, we click the Shortcut check box to open the Key Definition dialog, shown in Figure 9.5, and enter Alt+S to change the (ON KEY) key label from Alt+H, its old setting, to Alt+S. (FoxPro will change the key text to Alt+S automatically when you close the dialog, so there no need to enter the key text.)

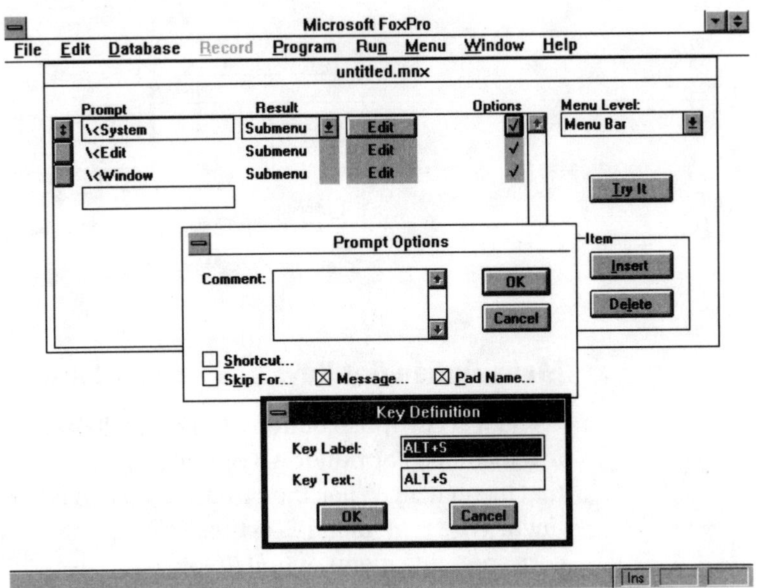

FIGURE 9.5: Shortcut keys (macros) can be defined for activating any menu pad or bar.

We change the message that will appear in the status bar when the pad is highlighted by selecting the Message check box. This accesses the Expression Builder, which we must use to enter our message as an <expC>. (See Figure 9.6.) If you enter a character string, be sure to use delimiters. Note the Verify button to the right of the expression entry box. If you select it after entering your expression, FoxPro will test your entry to make certain it is a valid expression.

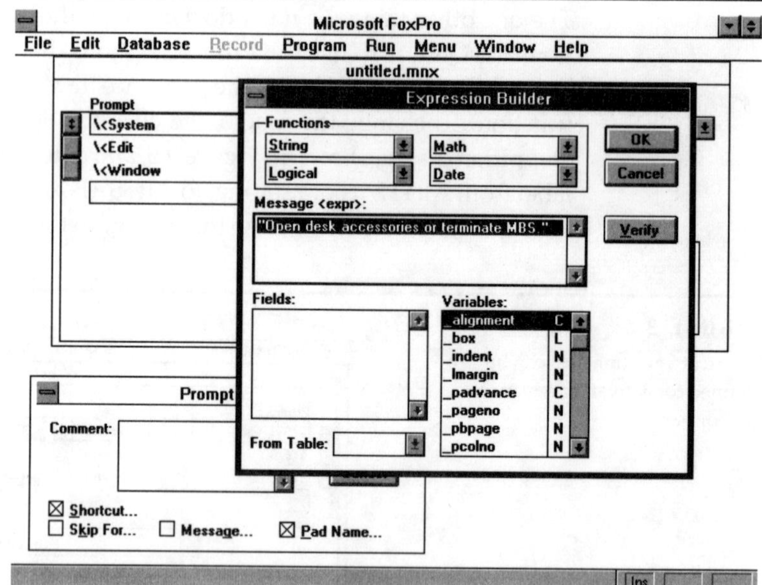

FIGURE 9.6:
Use the Prompt Options dialog to open the Expression Builder and enter a message that will be displayed when the menu option is highlighted.

Menu Option Hot Keys and Divider Lines

As with @ GET push buttons, the symbol \< can be placed in front of any character in a menu pad or pulldown option prompt to turn that character into a hot key for that menu item. When the prompt is displayed, the assigned hot key will be underlined. When the menu is active, selecting the hot key automatically executes the corresponding menu option. (Note that this is different from shortcut keys, which are used to activate/highlight menu options but not to select them. The operator may nonetheless use them together, entering a shortcut key immediately followed by a menu hot key to select and execute a menu option.)

You can place dividing lines between pulldown menu options by entering the symbol \– as the prompt of an otherwise blank pulldown menu option.

Entering Pulldown Menu Options

At this point, we can finish with our System pulldown by adding a divider line and our two Quit options at the bottom of the prompt list. However, in entering our Quit options, we must also specify a result through use of the Result popup shown open in Figure 9.7.

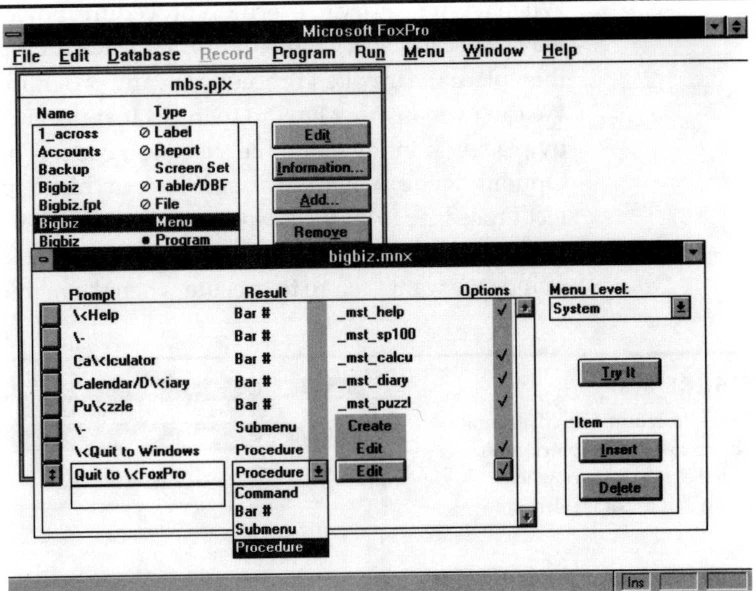

FIGURE 9.7:

Use the Result popup to select the action performed by a menu pad or pulldown option.

Under the circumstances the Bar # option is of no use to us here. Nor do we want FoxPro to open a submenu when the operator selects Quit to FoxPro, though we could create one if we wished. The two Result options that will serve our needs in this instance are Command and Procedure.

Entering Command and Procedure Results

Selecting the Command option from the Result popup enables the text entry box to the right, where we can enter the FoxPro command we want executed when the menu option is selected. Since the action we want to perform is Quit to FoxPro, we might achieve this end by simply entering the CANCEL command. However, this will be insufficient to our needs since the Quit to FoxPro option must trigger execution of procedure Cleanup at the end of our main program, Bigbiz.prg, as discussed in the Chapter 8. (If procedure Cleanup is not executed, our application will fail to restore the FoxPro environment to its prior condition before terminating.) The obvious alternative is to enter DO <procedure> as the command so FoxPro will execute a procedure containing the commands necessary to terminate our application's Foundation READ and, thus, execute procedure Cleanup before our application ends.

When it is necessary to execute a procedure, however, we can work in two different ways. We can select Command from the Result popup, enter DO <procedure>, and then place the invoked procedure in any program file belonging to the application. We can even instruct FoxPro to insert it at the end of the generated menu program by placing it in the menu file's cleanup code. (This can be done using the General Options dialog, which we discuss later in this chapter.) As an alternative, we can select Procedure from the Result popup and click the Create push button to the right of the popup. This opens a text-editing window in which we can enter the commands we want FoxPro to execute when the menu option is selected. Figure 9.8, for

FIGURE 9.8:

Select Procedure from the Result popup to enter the procedural code FoxPro executes when a menu pad or bar is selected.

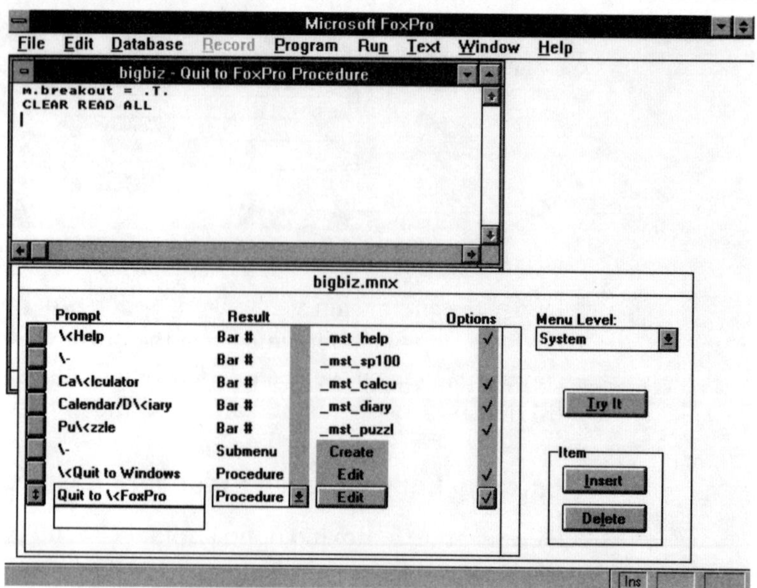

example, shows the two commands we use to terminate our Foundation READ. (We discuss their use in Chapter 10.)

FoxPro stores procedural code entered through use of the Procedure option directly in the menu (design) file. When the menu program is generated, FoxPro provides the procedure with a unique name and places it with comments identifying it with the menu pad or bar that invokes it at the end of the menu program's cleanup code. For this reason, you should not enter PROCEDURE <name> as the first line of the procedure. Use of RETURN is optional, though it is best left out.

NOTE

This is our first actual use of a code snippet, which is nothing more than a piece of program code, making up the text of a procedure or function, that we supply the Menu or Screen Builder for storage in a menu or screen (design) file and for automatic inclusion in the generated menu or screen program. It is because of the Menu and Screen Builder's capacity to handle customized code, entered as code snippets, that they can be used interactively to create menu and screen programs of any level of complexity.

For our Quit to Windows option, we employ the Result procedure shown in Figure 9.9. Of course, the essential command is QUIT. But since issuing QUIT will terminate the application without executing procedure Cleanup in Bigbiz.prg, it will leave the files created by procedure Setup to hold the prior environment settings on disk and will not update the MBS macros file. (See Chapter 8.) To avoid this, we insert the necessary commands in the code snippet before QUIT.

Again, when FoxPro generates the menu program, it will give both procedures unique names and place them in the menu program after the executable program. (Menu program architecture is discussed later in this chapter.)

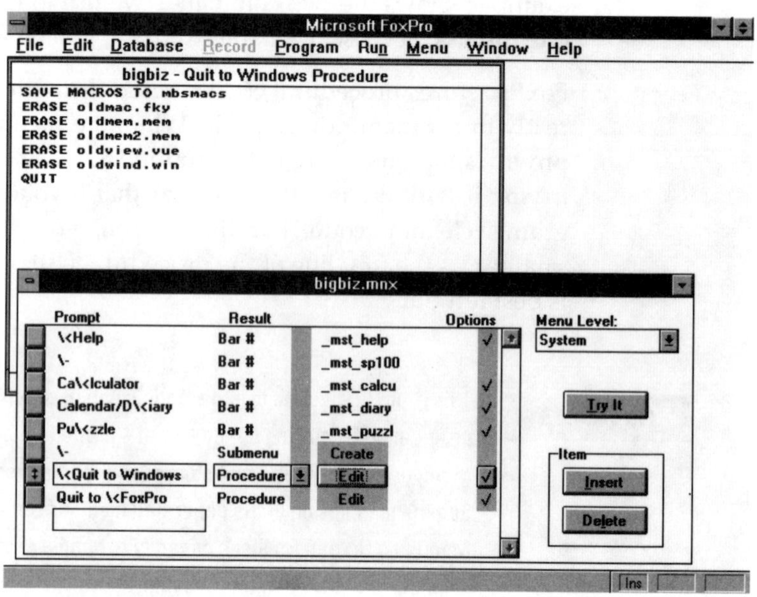

FIGURE 9.9:

The MBS Quit to Windows option erases temporary files and saves all currently defined macros to a disk file before issuing the QUIT command.

TIP

When you enter a code snippet in a text entry window opened by the Menu or Screen Builder, it is not necessary to close the window in order to continue working on the menu or screen file. In fact, if you leave them open, you can move from window to window as you choose, clipping and editing text as you go. When you close the Menu or Screen Design window, terminating work on a menu or screen file, FoxPro automatically closes the text entry windows associated with the file. Moreover, when you reopen the file to make modifications to the menu or screen file, FoxPro automatically reopens the text entry windows that you left open. They will be listed in the Window pulldown.

Using Skip For to Enable/Disable Menu Options

We are not yet done with our two Quit options; there are several situations in which we will want to prevent the operator from terminating MBS. As you may recall from Chapters 5 and 6, we use READ DEACTIVATE in our screen programs to prevent them from terminating when data editing is under way. We test for this condition using the global MBS memvar m.doit, which is set to .T. whenever an append or edit action is launched. However, if we issue QUIT or CLEAR READ ALL, FoxPro will not trouble with READ DEACTIVATE. For this reason, we must find some other way to prevent the operator from terminating the MBS with the Quit options when m.doit = .T.

There is also another situation in which we must prevent the operator from immediately terminating the MBS. As you may recall from Chapter 6, the Sales Entry/Edit program, Saletrns.spr, must execute its cleanup code in order to make final adjustments to the customer's account following the entry or edit of an invoice. It will therefore be inappropriate to allow the operator to use either of the Quit options until Saletrns.spr is terminated.

We can take care of both these situations by clicking the Options button for each item to access the Prompt Options dialog. We then click the Skip For check box to open the FoxPro Expression Builder and enter a logical condition. When the condition we enter is .T., FoxPro dims and disables the menu item. When it is .F., the item is enabled. Figure 9.10 shows the compound condition we use with the Skip For option for both our Quit items. The use of m.doit should require no explanation. The WREAD() function will return .T. when window Sale_trans is involved in the active

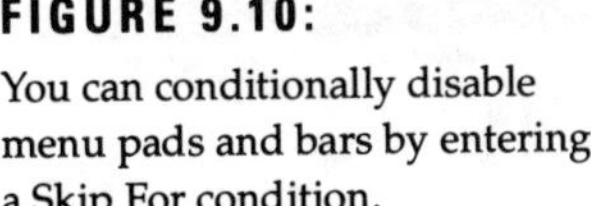

FIGURE 9.10:

You can conditionally disable menu pads and bars by entering a Skip For condition.

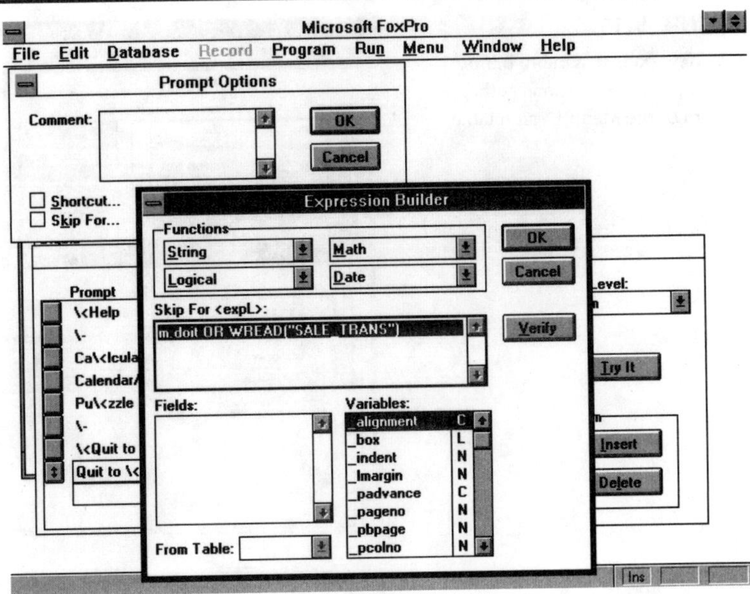

READ. We do not use WONTOP() since Sale_trans is not the only window used by Saletrns.spr. The program makes use of a BROWSE window as well. Additionally, the FoxPro desk accessories can be opened and used while Saletrns.spr is under way. WREAD() is therefore the tool of choice for use in this situation.

While the Expression Builder's Verify button can be used to determine if the entered expression is valid, it will not be useful unless the memvars and other variables included in the expression are current in FoxPro's memory. If they are not, FoxPro reports an error, though the expression may otherwise be valid.

Adding Menu Bar Pads and Pulldowns

To finish constructing the MBS menu, we must now add the menu pads and pulldowns executing our application programs. For example, to add our Database pulldown, we begin by entering \<Database in the empty prompt box at the bottom of the menu bar table, as shown in Figure 9.11.

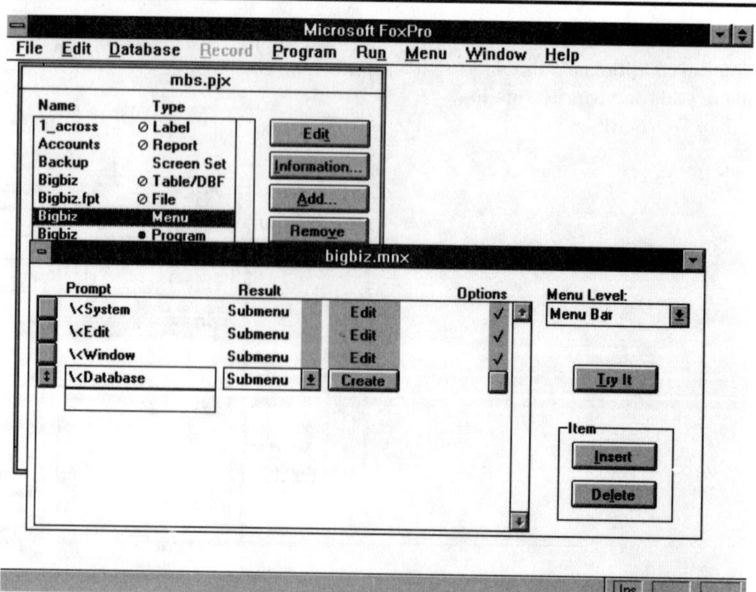

FIGURE 9.11: Add new pads to a menu bar by entering their definitions at the bottom of the Menu Design table.

Next, since Submenu is already selected as the default result, we click the Create button to open the Database submenu in the Menu Design window, where we must add our pulldown options one at a time. (The order in which we enter them makes no difference since we can reposition each option in the list by dragging the button to its left with the mouse.) As for the result of each option, that's simple. Since each of our Database options executes a screen program through use of procedure Dospr, as described in Chapter 6, in every case we select Command as the result and enter the appropriate command. For example, to execute Customer.spr, we use the command DO dospr WITH [customer.spr], to execute Payments.spr, we use the command DO dospr WITH [payments.spr], and so on. (Don't be thrown off by the use of the square brackets ([]). They are just one of the three sets of available character string delimiters. You can use single or double quotes instead.) We show the finished Database pulldown in Figure 9.12, though only the first portion of each command appears in the scrollable Command entry box.

The Prompt Options dialog is once again available to us for entering a message, shortcut key, and Skip For condition for each of our pulldown menu bars, though with respect to the MBS Database pulldown, we have no pressing need to employ these options.

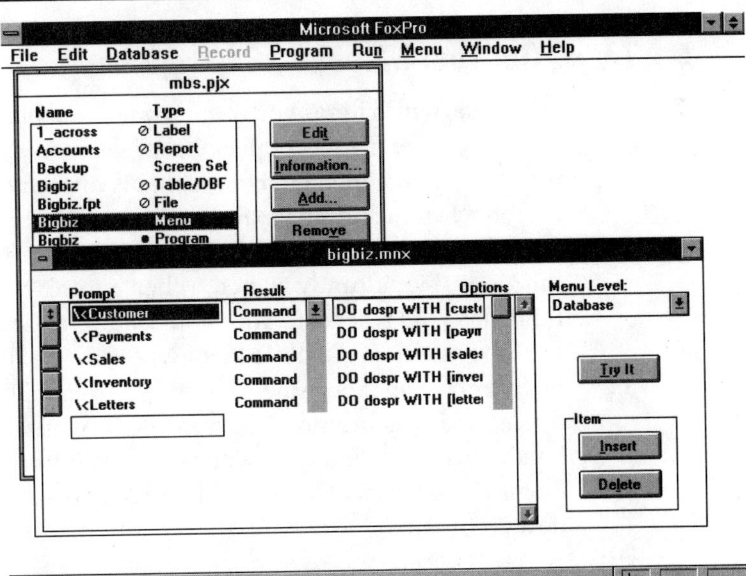

FIGURE 9.12:

Supply FoxPro with the command to be executed when a menu pad or pulldown menu bar is selected by entering it directly in the Command entry box.

TIP

Use the command WAIT WINDOW "Not implemented yet" as a pulldown menu option's result if you have yet to write the procedure or program the option must eventually execute. This way you can use the menu program to test whichever portion of the application has been finished, though no error is generated by a menu item that has no defined result.

When we finish with the pulldown, we use the Menu Level popup to return to the menu bar, where we can select the Prompt Options dialog to enter options for the Database pad, move back to the submenu to make changes, begin entering the next menu pad and pulldown, or use the mouse to drag the Database pad into its proper position between System and Edit.

NOTE

When entering pads to a menu bar it is unnecessary to use the Pad Name dialog to enter pad names. If you do not supply a pad name (not to be confused with the prompt used for the pad) FoxPro will make one up when it generates the menu program. It is the prompt that appears when the menu is activated.

Trying Out Your Menu

Of course, which items you use in your menu bar and pulldowns and how you arrange them are matters of personal preference, though you will certainly want the resulting system menu to be reasonably attractive and easy to use. A good rule of thumb when including FoxPro menu pads and pulldowns in your system menus is to keep them in their usual positions, at least relative to one another, unless their function is significantly altered. When adding pads of your own that have similar functions with respect to your application to those of a deleted pad in the default FoxPro system menu, place them where the FoxPro pads they replace would normally appear and reuse their prompt. (An example of this is the MBS Database pulldown, which is inserted between the System and Edit pads.) By emulating the FoxPro system menu, you will be relatively certain of producing a system menu that is consistent with the typical design of the system menus used with most Windows programs.

To help you determine the best arrangement for your menu, the Menu Builder will allow you to try it out without having to generate and run the actual menu program. Selecting the Try It push button, located in the Menu Design window, replaces the FoxPro system menu with a mock-up of the currently defined system menu and activates the Try It dialog, as shown in Figure 9.13. The system menu will be fully functional, but none of the commands and procedures it executes will be carried out. Instead, FoxPro displays the prompt and pad or bar name of each item as you select it in the Try It dialog window. When you are through checking out your menu, pressing the OK push button reactivates the FoxPro system menu and returns you to the Menu Definition window, where you can continue working on the menu.

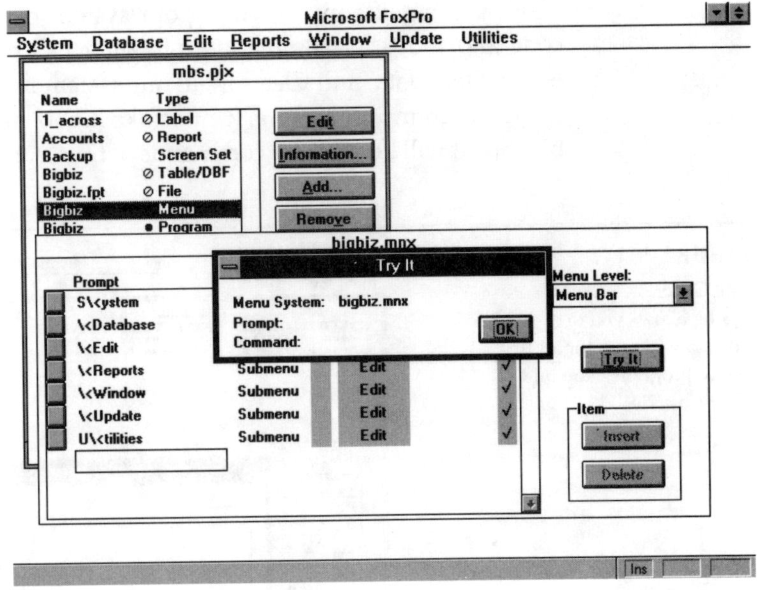

FIGURE 9.13: Use the Try It dialog to test a system menu without leaving the Menu Builder.

The Try It option enables you to shuffle items and divider lines in the system menu until you are satisfied with the current arrangement.

Menu Program Architecture

While the MBS menu program is specifically designed to do no more than execute the MBS system menu when called upon by the main program, menu programs are hardly limited to such a subordinate role. The General Options dialog, activated through the Menu pulldown, provides check boxes for activating text-editing windows in which you can enter menu program startup and cleanup code. (See Figure 9.14.)

If you enter setup and cleanup code to be executed immediately before and after the menu program replaces (or modifies) the FoxPro system menu, the menu program can be made to function as the main program in your application. To use the MBS as an example, we might place all commands in Bigbiz.prg preceding the command DO bigbiz.mpr, executing our system menu, in our system menu's setup code and move all commands following DO bigbiz.mpr, including procedures Setup, Opendata, and Cleanup, to our system menu's cleanup code. The resulting menu program will look very much like Bigbiz.prg, except that in place of DO bigbiz.mpr, it will hold all the commands defining and activating the system menu. As

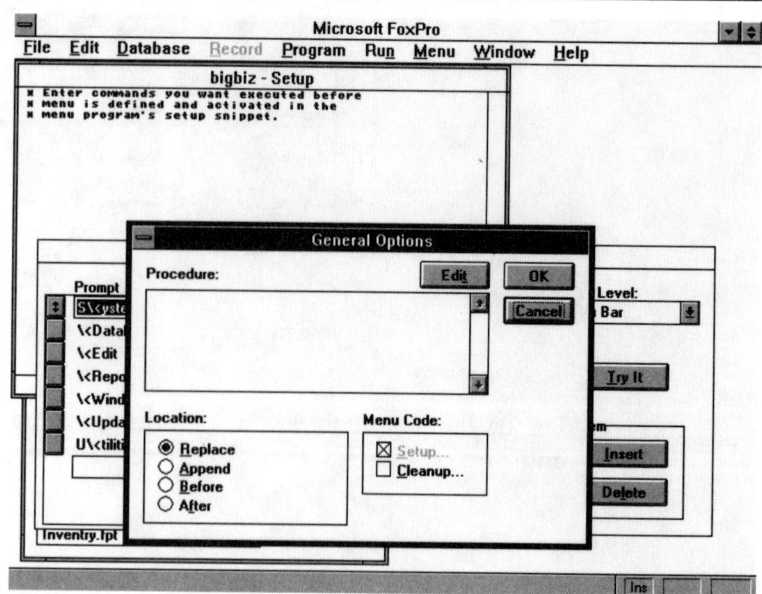

FIGURE 9.14: The General Options dialog allows you to open editing windows for adding menu program setup and cleanup code.

for the Result procedures we entered in text-editing windows for use upon selection of specific items, FoxPro places them after the commands and/or procedures we enter in the menu cleanup code window. The overall architecture of the menu program is therefore the same as any .prg program. The executable program comes first, followed by whichever procedures and functions are to be included in the menu program.

Menu Program Sections and Comments

The only unpleasant side effect of using the Menu and Screen Builders to generate programs is that program errors that turn up in menu and screen programs must be corrected not in the source code files—though that is where FoxPro locates the errors—but in the menu or screen files. (Obviously, if you make corrections to a menu program, they will be overwritten the next time you modify the system menu using the Menu Builder and regenerate the program.) We must therefore be able to trace any command appearing in a menu or screen program to a specific code snippet in the menu or screen (design) file. To help us do this, FoxPro places extensive comment lines in menu and screen programs, labeling each section of code so it can be easily identified with a specific snippet in the design file. For example, at the bottom of Bigbiz.mpr, we find the two procedures automatically generated by FoxPro to hold the Result procedures that must be executed upon selection of the System pulldown's Quit to FoxPro and Quit to Windows options. (See Figure 9.15.)

Even though we have allowed FoxPro to name the procedures for us, thereby making it potentially more difficult to locate the ON SELECTION BAR commands that execute them, the program comments tell us the exact function of each procedure and where we can find it when the menu file is opened with the Menu Builder.

NOTE

In the code snippet header, FoxPro indicates the name it has assigned the procedure when generating the program as well as the command that executes it in the system menu. The bar number indicates the order of the menu item in the pulldown menu.

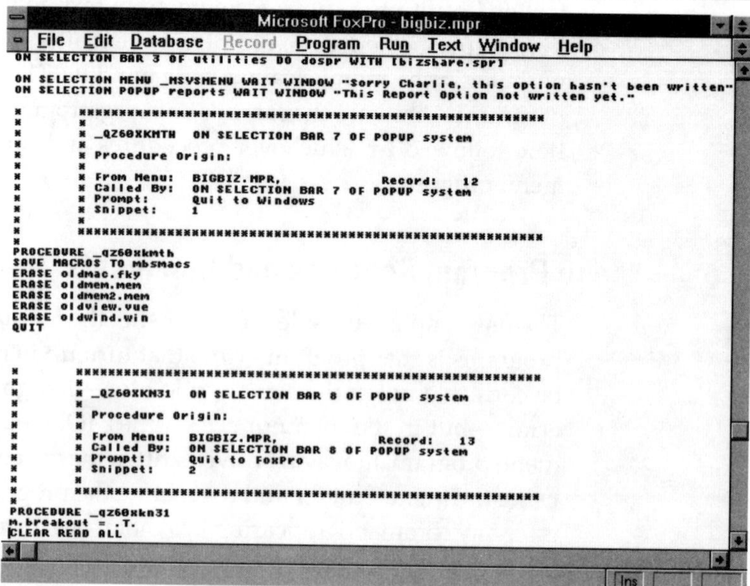

FIGURE 9.15:

Result procedures are placed at the end of the generated program along with program comments indicating their function.

Working with the Menu and Screen Builders

Unlike the editing of monolithic .prg files, in which sections of code are located by paging up and down in a text file or by using Find, the editing of menu (and screen) programs is managed through the use of multiple text entry windows in conjunction with a central menu (or screen) design window representing the program interface. The compositional method the Menu and Screen Builder propose is that used in filling out forms. It is faster, because menu and screen programs are reducible to forms. It is, moreover, better, because if you take full advantage of the Windows environment, you can move rapidly and intelligently from one section of the program to another, editing, copying, and pasting commands as you go. You can even work simultaneously on two or more menu, screen, and .prg files.

NOTE

As we will see in Chapter 11, the objects placed in the Screen Builder design window can be copied to the Clipboard and pasted, along with all code snippets associated with them, to the design window employed with another screen file. Unfortunately, menu items cannot be copied to the Clipboard in this way. You can, for example, copy and paste a prompt or a command or Result procedure—one at a time. But you cannot select the entire definition of a menu pad or pulldown menu bar, nor can you group and select items.

Using General Procedures

It is typical to assign each pad and pulldown menu bar in the system menu a specific result, but this is not necessary. If two or more options in a menu bar or pulldown must execute the same commands (or procedure), you can avoid entering the commands over and over for each item by creating and using general procedures.

NOTE

General procedures, if used, are executed upon selection of a menu item only if that menu item has no assigned result. You can, therefore, use general procedures with menus holding items with assigned results. The general procedure serves as a default result when no specific result is assigned.

Bear in mind that general procedures are menu specific. The general procedure entered in the General Options dialog's procedure box (see Figure 9.16) is used only upon selection of menu bar pads not assigned a specific result. It is not used with pulldown (submenu) bars that have no assigned result.

To enter a general procedure for execution by all submenu options assigned no result, we use the Menu Options dialog, shown in Figure 9.17. Use of the Menu Options dialog, however, is not limited to entry of a default result for all submenu items. When you are working with a specific submenu, the Menu Options dialog enables entry of a general procedure for that specific submenu. (A general procedure assigned to a specific submenu will take precedence over a general procedure assigned to the menu opening the submenu, just as specific results assigned any menu option will take precedence over any and all general procedures assigned to the menu on which it appears.)

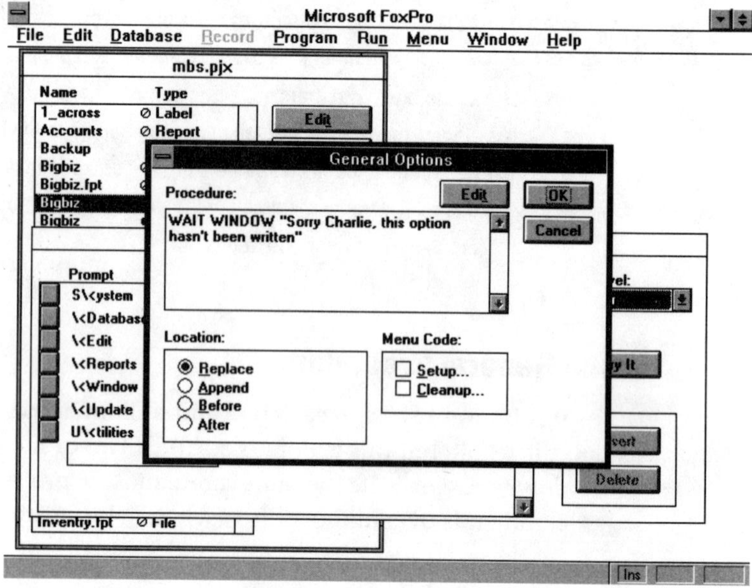

FIGURE 9.16: Menu pads not assigned a specific result will execute a general procedure, if one is entered.

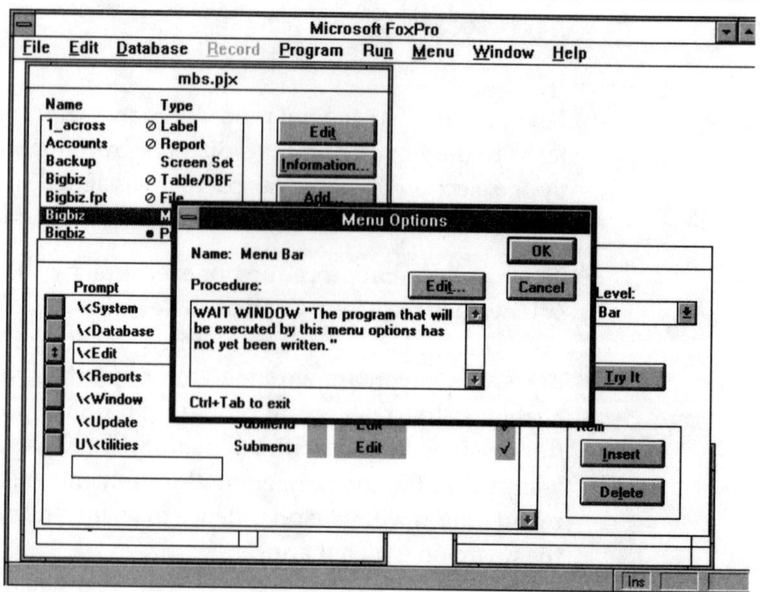

FIGURE 9.17: Use the Menu Options dialog to enter a general procedure for all submenu items.

General procedures are often used during program development to assign an innocuous action to menu pads and bars that must execute programs we have yet to write. In Figures 9.16 and 9.17, for example, we employ WAIT WINDOW with a suitable message so that selecting any menu pad or pulldown menu bar not yet assigned a specific result will trigger a message, reminding us of the work we have yet to do.

Still, general procedures are scarcely limited to such roles. Since the name and prompt (label) of a selected menu pad are returned by the PAD() and PROMPT() functions, respectively, you can use either of these functions with IF or DO CASE in the General Options general procedure to execute different actions for each menu pad. The same thing can be done in a general procedure used by a submenu since BAR() and PROMPT() can be used to return the number or prompt of the selected pulldown menu bar.

NOTE FoxPro offers a variety of other functions for returning information about a menu. It even includes commands and functions for marking and unmarking the prompts appearing in a menu with a check mark. (See your FoxPro documentation or Help file for more information about these options.)

FoxPro System Menus Up Close

Given the sophistication of the Menu Builder, one can create and use system menus of great complexity without knowledge of the commands FoxPro actually uses to generate a menu program. On the other hand, there are so many supplementary commands that can be usefully employed to control or alter the behavior of system menus that a cursory knowledge of the basic command set used to define them becomes indispensable for comprehending the options open to you.

To begin with, though you can create and use any number of different system menus in an application or even replace or modify the system menu employed in the interactive mode, there is only one system menu, _msysmenu. Though you can disable it during program execution with SET SYSMENU OFF or remove its current pads with SET SYSMENU TO, it is a permanent FoxPro feature. Moreover, _msysmenu has a default configuration that is always retrievable, regardless of what you do. The default configuration includes but is not limited to the set of menu pads and pulldowns supplied with Quick Menu. Though you replace or modify the current system menu, the default configuration can be immediately restored with SET SYSMENU TO DEFAULT.

Restoring the Default System Menu

There is one difficulty in using the term *default system menu* without further qualification. The fact is you can make whichever system menu is current the default system menu configuration by issuing the command SET SYSMENU SAVE. Once this is done, regardless of how you change the menu, the command SET SYSMENU TO DEFAULT restores the menu configuration you saved. Yet the startup FoxPro system menu can be restored at any time. If it is no longer the default system menu, we can still use the command SET SYSMENU NOSAVE and then SET SYSMENU TO DEFAULT to restore it as the default configuration. We therefore have two levels of default system menus between which we must distinguish: the default system menu, defined as that menu which will be restored by SET SYSMENU TO DEFAULT, and the startup FoxPro system menu, which we can restore with SET SYSMENU NOSAVE when it has been replaced as the default system menu.

The Menu Definition Commands

When it comes to the commands actually used to define our system menus, we find that system menus are generated with the same commands used to create user-defined menu bars, attached pulldowns, and stand-alone popups.

NOTE

While user-defined menu bars (so called because, unlike the system menu, they do not exist until we define them with DEFINE MENU) will rarely be used in a FoxPro program, we note their existence since they are available in all recent versions of Xbase. In this sense, system menus represent a special implementation of the older user-defined menu bars.

Three basic commands are used to define a user-defined (or nonsystem) menu bar. We show them below, though we omit many of their options, including those used to control the menu bar's position on the screen and the position of each pad in the menu bar. (Options used to control the position of the menu bar and its pads are, in any case, not used when defining system menus.)

```
DEFINE MENU <menu name>
DEFINE PAD <pad name> OF <menu name> [SKIP FOR <expL>] ;
    [KEY <key label>]
ON SELECTION PAD <pad name> OF <menu name> [<command>]
```

The first command declares the menu bar and assigns it a name. Unlike the other two commands, it is not used in creating system menus for the simple reason that the system menu _msysmenu is already defined. We do not define it; we replace or otherwise modify its pads, pulldown menus, and pulldown menu bars.

The second command, DEFINE PAD, is issued as many times as needed to define each of the pads included in a system or user-defined menu bar. The third command, ON SELECTION PAD, is susbequently used to assign a result for each menu pad. For example, when selection of the pad must activate a pulldown, the command ACTIVATE POPUP <popup name> is used to achieve this end. When the pad must execute a procedure, DO <procedure> is used instead.

NOTE

The SKIP FOR and KEY options of DEFINE PAD correspond to the Skip For and Shortcut key options entered for each pad using the Prompt Options dialog.

If a general procedure is entered for use with the menu bar, the command ON SELECTION MENU <menu name> [<command>] is used to define it.

Of course, when generating a system menu with Genmenu.prg, the FoxPro menu-generation program, FoxPro writes out each of the commands required to define the menu bar as specified by the instructions entered in the menu file. The amount of work this spares us is astronomical, as will be readily apparent from Figure 9.18, showing only the first portion of Bigbiz.mpr. In addition to the two SET SYSMENU commands, which we discuss in the following section, the screen in Figure 9.18 includes all commands defining the pads of our system menu bar and the first portion of the commands defining our System pulldown.

Though you may take note of the names FoxPro uses for the pads and the bars adapted from the default FoxPro system menu (they all begin with an underscore), it is unnecessary to learn them, at least as long as you work with Quick Menu or use another menu file containing the system pads and bars you require as a template. (Again, if you need to enter a system pad or bar name manually, you can look up its proper name in the FoxPro documentation or Help file.)

FIGURE 9.18: Using the instructions in a menu file, FoxPro generates the commands necessary to execute the menu automatically.

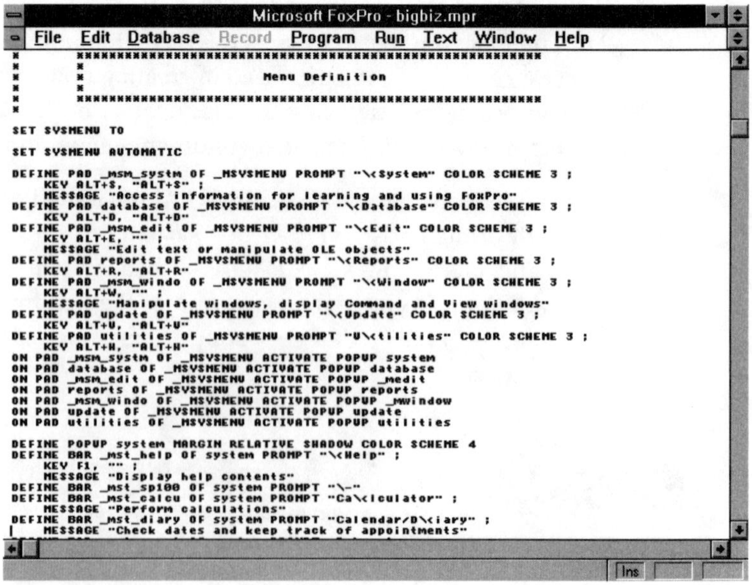

Microsoft FoxPro - bigbiz.mpr

File Edit Database Record Program Run Text Window Help

```
*       ************************************************************
*       *
*       *                    Menu Definition
*       *
*       ************************************************************
*

SET SYSMENU TO

SET SYSMENU AUTOMATIC

DEFINE PAD _msm_systm OF _MSYSMENU PROMPT "\<System" COLOR SCHEME 3 ;
    KEY ALT+S, "ALT+S" ;
    MESSAGE "Access information for learning and using FoxPro"
DEFINE PAD database OF _MSYSMENU PROMPT "\<Database" COLOR SCHEME 3 ;
    KEY ALT+D, "ALT+D"
DEFINE PAD _msm_edit OF _MSYSMENU PROMPT "\<Edit" COLOR SCHEME 3 ;
    KEY ALT+E, "" ;
    MESSAGE "Edit text or manipulate OLE objects"
DEFINE PAD reports OF _MSYSMENU PROMPT "\<Reports" COLOR SCHEME 3 ;
    KEY ALT+R, "ALT+R"
DEFINE PAD _msm_windo OF _MSYSMENU PROMPT "\<Window" COLOR SCHEME 3 ;
    KEY ALT+W, "" ;
    MESSAGE "Manipulate windows, display Command and View windows"
DEFINE PAD update OF _MSYSMENU PROMPT "\<Update" COLOR SCHEME 3 ;
    KEY ALT+U, "ALT+U"
DEFINE PAD utilities OF _MSYSMENU PROMPT "U\<tilities" COLOR SCHEME 3 ;
    KEY ALT+H, "ALT+H"
ON PAD _msm_systm OF _MSYSMENU ACTIVATE POPUP system
ON PAD database OF _MSYSMENU ACTIVATE POPUP database
ON PAD _msm_edit OF _MSYSMENU ACTIVATE POPUP _medit
ON PAD reports OF _MSYSMENU ACTIVATE POPUP reports
ON PAD _msm_windo OF _MSYSMENU ACTIVATE POPUP _mwindow
ON PAD update OF _MSYSMENU ACTIVATE POPUP update
ON PAD utilities OF _MSYSMENU ACTIVATE POPUP utilities

DEFINE POPUP system MARGIN RELATIVE SHADOW COLOR SCHEME 4
DEFINE BAR _mst_help OF system PROMPT "\<Help" ;
    KEY F1, "" ;
    MESSAGE "Display help contents"
DEFINE BAR _mst_sp100 OF system PROMPT "\-"
DEFINE BAR _mst_calcu OF system PROMPT "Ca\<lculator" ;
    MESSAGE "Perform calculations"
DEFINE BAR _mst_diary OF system PROMPT "Calendar/D\<iary" ;
    MESSAGE "Check dates and keep track of appointments"
```

Ins

The system menu pulldowns are each defined with the three basic commands that go into the creation of user-defined popup menus. Again, we omit a good number of their options.

```
DEFINE POPUP <menu name>
DEFINE BAR <expN>/<system bar name> OF <popup name> ;
    PROMPT <expC> [SKIP FOR <expL>] [KEY <key label>]
ON SELECTION BAR <expN> OF <popup name> [<command>]
```

The first command defines the popup and assigns it a name. The second is used as many times as needed to specify each of the bars appearing in the pulldown (or popup), while the third command is used to provide each of the bars with a result. Figure 9.19 shows the commands used in Bigbiz.mpr to define the System, Database, and _medit pulldowns, the last being the proper name of the FoxPro Edit pulldown. Here again, no row and column coordinates are needed to define the system menu pulldowns since FoxPro knows exactly where to place them in the system menu.

FIGURE 9.19:

System menu pulldowns and user-defined popups are created with the same commands.

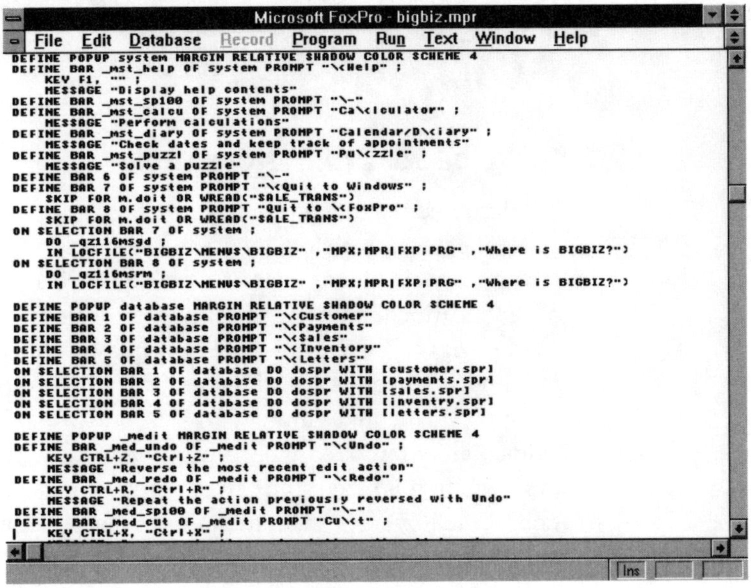

Microsoft FoxPro - bigbiz.mpr

File Edit Database Record Program Run Text Window Help

```
DEFINE POPUP system MARGIN RELATIVE SHADOW COLOR SCHEME 4
DEFINE BAR _mst_help OF system PROMPT "\<Help" ;
    KEY F1, "" ;
    MESSAGE "Display help contents"
DEFINE BAR _mst_sp100 OF system PROMPT "\-"
DEFINE BAR _mst_calcu OF system PROMPT "Ca\<lculator" ;
    MESSAGE "Perform calculations"
DEFINE BAR _mst_diary OF system PROMPT "Calendar/D\<iary" ;
    MESSAGE "Check dates and keep track of appointments"
DEFINE BAR _mst_puzzl OF system PROMPT "Pu\<zzle" ;
    MESSAGE "Solve a puzzle"
DEFINE BAR 6 OF system PROMPT "\-"
DEFINE BAR 7 OF system PROMPT "\<Quit to Windows" ;
    SKIP FOR m.doit OR WREAD("SALE_TRANS")
DEFINE BAR 8 OF system PROMPT "Quit to \<FoxPro" ;
    SKIP FOR m.doit OR WREAD("SALE_TRANS")
ON SELECTION BAR 7 OF system ;
    DO _qz116msgd ;
    IN LOCFILE("BIGBIZ\MENUS\BIGBIZ" ,"MPX;MPR|FXP;PRG" ,"Where is BIGBIZ?")
ON SELECTION BAR 8 OF system ;
    DO _qz116msrm ;
    IN LOCFILE("BIGBIZ\MENUS\BIGBIZ" ,"MPX;MPR|FXP;PRG" ,"Where is BIGBIZ?")

DEFINE POPUP database MARGIN RELATIVE SHADOW COLOR SCHEME 4
DEFINE BAR 1 OF database PROMPT "\<Customer"
DEFINE BAR 2 OF database PROMPT "\<Payments"
DEFINE BAR 3 OF database PROMPT "\<Sales"
DEFINE BAR 4 OF database PROMPT "\<Inventory"
DEFINE BAR 5 OF database PROMPT "\<Letters"
ON SELECTION BAR 1 OF database DO dospr WITH [customer.spr]
ON SELECTION BAR 2 OF database DO dospr WITH [payments.spr]
ON SELECTION BAR 3 OF database DO dospr WITH [sales.spr]
ON SELECTION BAR 4 OF database DO dospr WITH [inventry.spr]
ON SELECTION BAR 5 OF database DO dospr WITH [letters.spr]

DEFINE POPUP _medit MARGIN RELATIVE SHADOW COLOR SCHEME 4
DEFINE BAR _med_undo OF _medit PROMPT "\<Undo" ;
    KEY CTRL+Z, "Ctrl+Z" ;
    MESSAGE "Reverse the most recent edit action"
DEFINE BAR _med_redo OF _medit PROMPT "\<Redo" ;
    KEY CTRL+R, "Ctrl+R" ;
    MESSAGE "Repeat the action previously reversed with Undo"
DEFINE BAR _med_sp100 OF _medit PROMPT "\-"
DEFINE BAR _med_cut OF _medit PROMPT "Cu\<t" ;
    KEY CTRL+X, "Ctrl+X" ;
```

Ins

> **NOTE**
> When a general procedure is entered for use with all pulldown items not assigned a specific result with ON SELECT BAR, FoxPro uses the command ON SELECTION POPUP <command> to execute it.

Still, there is little reason to linger over these commands, owing to FoxPro's ability to generate them automatically on the basis of our entries to a menu file. However, since you may find occasion to create popups of your own, it is worth keeping these basic commands in mind.

> **TIP**
> User-defined popups, once defined, are activated with ACTIVATE POPUP <name> and are deactivated with DEACTIVATE POPUP. They are also released from memory with RELEASE POPUP. Nonsystem menu bars created with DEFINE MENU must be activated with ACTIVATE MENU <name>. They are deactivated and released from memory with DEACTIVATE MENU and RELEASE MENU, respectively. (For more information about user-defined menu bars and popups, refer to your FoxPro documentation or Help file.)

Modifying the FoxPro System Menu

We designed the MBS system menu, Bigbiz.mpr, with the intention of using it to replace the current system menu, but menu programs can be devised to modify the current system menu instead. We can, for example, create a menu program that adds additional menu pads (and associated pulldowns) to the current system menu. FoxPro provides ample examples of this practice. The Browse, Menu, Project, and Text menus are added to the FoxPro system menu only when you activate a BROWSE, menu definition, project, or text-editing window, respectively. They are immediately removed when you close or deactivate the window with which they are used. In this same spirit, menu programs can be designed to append pads to the end of the FoxPro system menu or to insert them before or after a specific FoxPro system menu pad.

The menu program's action with respect to the current system menu is determined through use of the General Options' embedded Location dialog, shown in Figure 9.20. Since the Replace radio button is selected by default, we need not bother with the dialog unless we intend to use the menu program to modify the current system menu. The function of the other three options should be plain enough. If we select Append, when we execute the resulting menu program, FoxPro adds the menu pads defined by our program to the end of the current system menu. Selecting Before or After, on the other hand, prompts FoxPro to display a popup listing the default FoxPro menu pads, as shown in Figure 9.20. Use the popup to select the system menu pad before or after which FoxPro should insert the menu pads defined in your menu program.

With respect to the menu program, choice of location is effected through use of SET SYSMENU and, with Before and After, additional options of DEFINE PAD. When Replace is selected as the location, FoxPro inserts the command SET SYSMENU TO before the commands defining the menu pads. (This is shown in Figure 9.18.) This has the effect of discarding all pads present in the current system menu, so the pads defined in the menu program will be loaded when _msysmenu is vacated.

It is the omission of this same command, SET SYSMENU TO, that allows FoxPro to add menu pads to the current system menu when Append, Before, or After is selected as the location. Since menu pads are added by default after the last pad in the current system menu, no further action is taken when Append is selected. With

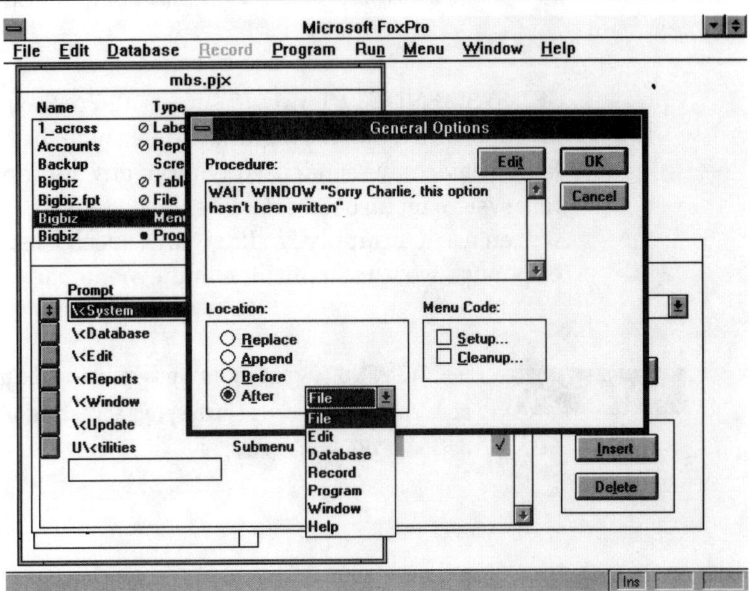

FIGURE 9.20:

The General Options' Location dialog is used to determine how the menu program affects the current system menu.

Before and After, however, FoxPro must use the corresponding BEFORE <pad name> or AFTER <pad name> option of the DEFINE PAD commands to execute your choice.

SET SYSMENU Options

As we saw above, the SET SYSMENU command is specially charged with controlling the action of the system menu. But it uses two different settings: one to control the menu's availability during program execution and another to control the actual content of the system menu.

During program execution, SET SYSMENU ON/OFF/AUTOMATIC is used to control the availability of the system menu. ON is not quite what you'd expect it to be. This is because, while SET SYSMENU ON makes the system menu available to the operator, it does not display it on the screen until the operator presses the Alt or F10 key or double-clicks the right mouse button. The AUTOMATIC setting, on the other hand, makes the menu available and also displays it on the screen. SET SYSMENU OFF does what it says; it turns the menu off.

NOTE SET SYSMENU OFF/ON/AUTOMATIC has no effect on the system menu in the interactive mode. In the interactive mode SET SYSMENU is always AUTOMATIC.

SET SYSMENU TO, however, affects all FoxPro modes. It is used alone or in conjunction with a menu program to determine the content of the system menu. Thus far we have only seen it used without any additional parameters to vacate the current system menu before loading the system menu with new menu pads. However, we can use it to supply FoxPro with a specific list of the default FoxPro menu pads or popups we want to include in the menu bar.

TIP SET SYSMENU TO <pad list> or <popup list> can be used in a menu program's setup code so the pads defined in the program can be added to a specific subset of the default FoxPro menu pads.

Another function of SET SYSMENU, mentioned earlier in this chapter, is its use in controlling the content and use of the default system menu, which can be restored at any time with the command SET SYSMENU TO DEFAULT. The actual content of the default system menu is determined through use of SET SYSMENU SAVE/NOSAVE. Again, SET SYSMENU SAVE saves the current system menu as the default, so it will be restored with SET SYSMENU TO DEFAULT. SET SYSMENU NOSAVE, on the other hand, overwrites the default system menu with the default FoxPro system menu. It can then be restored with SET SYSMENU TO DEFAULT.

TIP

As long as the system menu is active, during program execution FoxPro continues its practice of adding the Text pulldown (not included in the Quick Menu) to the system menu whenever a text-editing window is used in the program. If no other menu pads are present in the system menu, this may be unappealing. This is where SET SYSMENU ON may be of service since it can be used to keep the pad out of sight until the operator wants to use the pulldown.

Reactivating the System Menu during READ MODAL

In the MBS we make things easy on ourselves by using only one system menu. In part, this is one of the benefits of making the MBS data entry screen programs non-modal. Since we have no reason to prevent the operator from selecting one data entry program before manually terminating another, we have no compelling reason to deactivate the majority of our menu pads each time the operator selects a program. However, in applications that do not use an event handler (the focus of Chapter 10) to automatically terminate one screen program the moment the operator selects another, care must be taken to prevent the operator from surpassing the maximum READ level by executing one too many screen programs. This is usually achieved by using READ MODAL in the data entry programs to make them function like dialogs.

As you may recall, READ MODAL has two effects. It places all windows not specifically included in the READ out of bounds to the mouse or cursor so the operator cannot select them until the READ is terminated. It also disables all pulldown menu bars except those bars on the FoxPro Edit and Text pulldowns that are automatically activated whenever data entry to an @ GET input field or text-editing window is under way. The only major drawback to READ MODAL's behavior—it otherwise serves perfectly to make the operator finish with one screen program before selecting the next—is that it also places the pulldown menu bars activating the desk accessories, and the windows used by the desk accessories themselves, out of reach.

To overcome this problem, we do two things. First, we use READ's WITH <associated window list> clause to enter the names of the desk accessories (and other windows) to which we want access during the modal READ. For example, the command READ WITH Calculator, Calendar, Puzzle will include the three desk accessories that go by those names in the modal READ.

TIP

When using READ's WITH <associated window list> clause, it is unnecessary to include the MODAL keyword. It will be redundant since use of an associated window list implicitly assumes a modal READ.

Entry of an associated window list is handled automatically just before generation of a screen program using the Generate Screen or Edit Screen Set dialog. (The Generate Screen dialog is available from the Program pulldown when the Screen Builder is open, while the Edit Screen Set dialog is available through the Project Manager's Edit button when a screen file is highlighted in the project's file list.) We will see how to do this in Chapter 11, where we review the Generate Screen and Edit Screen Set dialog options.

However, after including our desk accessories in the READ as associated windows, we must still make them available to the operator by reactivating the disabled pulldown options. This is easily done by simply reexecuting the disabled menu at the outset of READ MODAL or READ WITH. To this end, we simply tuck the command required to activate our menu in READ's WHEN clause. This way it will be executed only once, the moment the READ is activated, and before the execution of READ ACTIVATE and READ SHOW if they are also used. Of course, which command or commands you use depend upon the status of the window you want to activate. For example, we can reactivate the default system menu by entering SET SYSMENU TO DEFAULT. On the other hand, we can reexecute the MBS system menu with DO Bigbiz.mpr. But given the fact that we can make Bigbiz.mpr the default system menu by issuing the command SET SYSMENU SAVE when it is active, if we take this step before launching the screen program (or execute the command in the screen program's setup code prior to READ), we can reactivate it with SET SYSMENU TO DEFAULT. (Remember, the default FoxPro system menu can be restored as the default system menu with SET SYSMENU NOSAVE.)

NOTE

When activating or reactivating the system menu with SET SYSMENU or DO <file.mpr>, you are not placing one menu on top of the other. You can, for example, issue the command SET SYSMENU TO DEFAULT or DO <file.mpr>, executing a menu program, over and over until you are blue in the face without running out of available memory, because each time you activate a system menu, you are activating the same menu, _msysmenu.

TIP

Though it is typical to reactivate the system menu during READ MODAL by reexecuting it in the READ WHEN clause of a screen program, alternative strategies abound. You can, for example, program a function key with ON KEY LABEL to execute SET SYSMENU TO DEFAULT or a menu program. (Function key F10 is a good selection since it normally has the function of accessing the system menu in Windows programs.) Function keys can also be programmed to issue specific commands opening desired windows. ON KEY LABEL F5 ACTIVATE WINDOW Calculator, for example, will activate the Calculator when function key F5 is pressed.

Still, having reactivated the system menu whole, we gain access to our desk accessories at the expense of making all other options on it available as well. For all practical purposes, we have undermined the positive effect and our reason for using READ MODAL. There are two obvious ways out of this dilemma. One is to use SET SKIP to deactivate those menu pads and pulldown options that are inappropriate to the current screen program. In the other, we supply the operator with another system menu, listing only those options that are appropriate during execution of the modal screen program. We review these two strategies in the following section.

Controlling and Altering System Menus

During program execution you can replace or modify the current system menu as you choose. The motive is simple: to make the current system menu fit the present application. There is one caveat: The lengths you go to and the means you employ to do it depend upon such immaterial things as deadlines and personal preferences; there are two components to the fit, and one of them is decidedly the aesthetic.

In the case of the MBS, we are deliberately laconic in our use of the system menu. The MBS main menu, after all, includes the Edit pulldown, though none of its options will be enabled until a data entry program is launched. Were we real sticklers for order, we might choose to leave the Edit pad out of Bigbiz.mpr (executing the MBS main menu) altogether and then add it to the system menu whenever one of the screen programs listed on the Database pulldown is executed. This would require us to do no more than create a menu file holding the Edit pulldown (and no other menu pads), select After Help as the location (see "Modifying the FoxPro System Menu" earlier in this chapter), and execute the resulting menu program in the READ WHEN clause of each of our data entry screen programs. The alternative is to replace the initial menu by executing a menu program that includes all options on the main menu as well as the Edit pulldown.

However, in altering or replacing the main menu with a menu specific to certain screen programs, we will always want to revert to the main menu upon termination of the screen program. You already know one way to do this.

```
* Commands placed in READ WHEN clause:
SET SYSMENU SAVE
DO <file.mpr>

* Command placed in screen program cleanup code:
SET SYSMENU TO DEFAULT
```

Here, we save the system menu current at the time the screen program is launched as the default system menu configuration, execute the screen program modifying or replacing the system menu, and, upon termination of the screen program, restore the default configuration.

As an alternative, you can use the PUSH MENU command to push the current system menu onto the stack—that is, into a special holding area in memory—so it can be restored, when the screen program terminates, with the POP MENU command.

```
* Commands placed in READ WHEN clause:
PUSH MENU _msysmenu
DO <file.mpr>

* Command placed in screen program cleanup code:
POP MENU _msysmenu
```

As you may recall from Chapter 8, we use this method in the main MBS program, Bigbiz.prg, to deal with the system menu current at the time MBS is executed. If we use this routine, we therefore place two versions of _msysmenu onto the stack. However, since POP MENU reactivates the last menu placed in the stack, it will restore the correct menu upon termination of the screen program.

However, quite aside from my laconic nature, I follow FoxPro's example in managing the Edit pulldown, making it available on the MBS main menu, for a good reason. Owing to the nonmodal organization that makes the MBS an event-driven rather than simply menu-driven application, the several screen programs with which the Edit pulldown is useful can be repeatedly reexecuted without returning to the main menu. Since we can terminate each screen program and leave its READ window open on the screen so the operator can reselect the window and reuse the program, pushing, changing, and popping the system menu for the sake of adding and removing the Edit menu will not only be more work than it's worth, it will also be aesthetically unappealing. In our nonmodal system, it will distract from the illusion of seamless movement from one window to another.

You will have a better motive for altering the system menu, however, when a menu pad is used with only one application program. This is how FoxPro itself behaves. The Menu pulldown, for example, is present only when the Menu Design window is active—that is, when the Menu Builder program is being run. We have no examples of this in the MBS since we have no pulldowns that are specific to a single application.

In contrast to nonmodal applications, however, applications that rely upon READ MODAL are, with few exceptions, menu and/or event-driven and, therefore, rigorously hierarchical in organization. Since we must always return to the main menu upon terminating a data entry program before we can launch another program, pushing, changing, and popping the main menu makes sense. We have no illusion to maintain of seamless movement between one application window and another. But with respect to modal screen programs, there is far more reason to change the system menu. During READ MODAL (as discussed in the previous section), operator access to most of the options on the application's main menu will be undesirable, supposing we have it in mind to reactivate the system menu at all. In any case, since the data entry screen programs in a modal version of the MBS would have use for only the System and Edit pulldowns, we would create an application-specific system menu for use with all screen programs launched by the Database pulldown holding only these two pulldowns and use either of the strategies mentioned above to arrange for their execution in each of our screen programs. This is the most acceptable way to handle the system menu when the majority of options available in an application's main menu must be disabled during execution of all data entry programs.

TIP

If you need a system menu that includes only a subset of the default FoxPro menu bars or popups, you can use SET SYSMENU TO <pad list> or TO <popup list> instead of creating a menu program to execute it.

Releasing System Menu Pads and Popups

Another way you can modify a system menu (or any menu bar or stand-alone popup) is by using the RELEASE command to discard some or all of its elements. Menu pads can be selectively removed from the current system menu with RELEASE PAD <pad name> OF <menu>. For example, to remove the Record and Edit pads from the default FoxPro system menu, we use the following commands:

```
RELEASE PAD _mrecord OF _msysmenu
RELEASE PAD _medit OF _msysmenu
```

To leave the pads in the menu bars but remove the popups they activate, we can use RELEASE POPUP <popup list> instead:

```
RELEASE POPUP _mrecord, _medit
```

TIP

If you must restore a popup, before releasing it use the command PUSH POPUP <popup name> to place a copy of it in the menu stack. POP POPUP <popup name> can subsequently be used to restore the popup to active duty.

We can also release specific bars from system menu pulldowns with RELEASE BAR <expN> OF <popup name>. For example, to remove the Customer bar from the

MBS Database pulldown, we issue the following command:

```
RELEASE BAR 1 OF database
```

Pulldown menu bars released in this way can be restored with the DEFINE BAR command, though in most instances it will be easier to PUSH and POP the entire popup.

TIP

Bear in mind that RELEASE will have additional functionality in menu programs since it can be used to remove unneeded elements from the current system menu before the menu program adds new pads and pulldowns. It can also be used in menu program cleanup code with IF/ENDIF to selectively remove elements from the new system menu's definition in keeping with the specific program invoking the menu program. In this way, a single menu program can be made to supply system menus with several different configurations.

Using SET SKIP OF to Enable/Disable Menus and Menu Options

Another important tool in the FoxPro arsenal of menu control commands is SET SKIP OF. In effect, SET SKIP OF works much like the Menu Builder's Skip For prompt option, which can be used to enter a SKIP clause for each pad or pulldown menu bar defined by the menu program. However, unlike Skip For, which makes the SKIP <expL> a permanent part of the menu option's definition, SET SKIP OF permits us to selectively enable/disable menu items on an *ad hoc* basis within any program. What's more, SET SKIP OF has options allowing you various levels of control over the system menu:

```
SET SKIP OF MENU _msysmenu <expL>
SET SKIP OF PAD <pad name> OF _msysmenu <expL>
SET SKIP OF POPUP <popup name> <expL>
SET SKIP OF BAR <expN> OF POPUP <popup name> <expL>
```

With the first command we can enable/disable the entire system menu at once, with the second we enable/disable a specific menu bar pad, with the third we enable/disable a specific pulldown (or popup), and with the fourth we can enable/disable specific pulldown (or popup) menu bars. As you may recall from Chapters 5 and 6, in the MBS we use SET SKIP OF BAR at the outset of Customer, Payments, and Sales.spr to disable the Database option used to launch each of these screen programs. This prevents the operator from wasting time by accidentally relaunching a screen program that is already in use. Since the MBS would automatically terminate the reselected program before executing it again, the command is not required to prevent recursive use of our screen programs, but it does make the Database pulldown easier to use.

NOTE

In citing the syntax of SET SKIP OF MENU and SET SKIP OF PAD above, I have stuck in _msysmenu as the menu bar name since our focus is on using these commands to control the system menu. The commands can be used to control any other (user-defined) menu bar simply by substitution of the menu name for _msysmenu. As their syntax implies, SET SKIP OF POPUP and BAR can also be used to control the action of any defined popup.

In a modal application, SET SKIP can also be used to disable menu options once a modal screen program has reexecuted the system menu, as previously described in this chapter. For example, in a modal version of the MBS, we might issue the following commands in Customer.spr's READ WHEN clause to reactivate the system menu while disabling all options that launch other screen programs:

```
DO bigbiz.mpr
SET SKIP OF PAD database OF _msysmenu .T.
SET SKIP OF PAD reports OF _msysmenu .T.
SET SKIP OF PAD update OF _msysmenu .T.
SET SKIP OF PAD utilities OF _msysmenu .T.
```

The four SET SKIP OF PAD commands tell FoxPro to disable the referenced menu pads in the current system menu, leaving only our System, Edit, and Window pulldowns active. To reenable the disabled pads, we just reexecute the same commands with an <exp> of .F.

TIP If you plan to use SET SKIP OF PAD to enable/disable menu pads, be certain to use the Pad Name dialog to supply your menu pads with easy-to-remember names. In Bigbiz.mpr, for example, each menu pad not taken from the FoxPro default system menu is assigned a pad name corresponding to its prompt. This is the easiest convention to follow. Bear in mind that if you do not supply pad names for the menu pads you add to the system menu, FoxPro will make up names for them. Since these names will change each time you regenerate the menu program, they will make it difficult to use SET SKIP OF PAD effectively.

Of course, with the large number of commands available to you for controlling the content of the system menu, how you go about enabling and disabling menu options is up to you. You can use Skip For or SET SKIP OF to enable or disable options on a system menu or use menu programs to actually add or remove options from the menu, while employing PUSH and POP or SET SYSMENU TO DEFAULT to restore the system menu to a previous configuration.

Altering the Interactive Mode System Menu

When FoxPro executes a menu program, it returns to the calling program or to the interactive mode (if there was no calling program) unless it comes upon a command in the menu program's cleanup code placing it in a wait state. (As mentioned earlier in this chapter, we can make the MBS menu program function as the application's main program by placing our Foundation READ in its cleanup code.) Supposing a menu program contains no such command and is executed from the Command window with DO <file.mpr>, this means that FoxPro returns to the interactive mode after executing the menu program's instructions. The menu then plays the role of the FoxPro interactive mode system menu until it is replaced or modified with another system menu or SET SYSMENU TO DEFAULT is used to restore the default system menu configuration.

There are two reasons for modifying the interactive mode system menu. One is to add customized programs to the development environment. The other is to make their applications executable by operators who are otherwise free to start their work from the FoxPro interactive mode. To do this, one need only execute a menu program automatically during FoxPro startup (see Chapter 8 for instructions) that adds an Application menu pad and pulldown, listing each of the available applications, to the system menu. DO <file.app> can naturally be used as the command result of each pulldown option to start the selected application.

Referencing Procedures in a Menu Program's Cleanup Code

Bear in mind that when you execute a menu program, when the menu program terminates, the procedures stored in its cleanup code can no longer be executed with DO <procedure> unless the menu program is included in an .app file and the application is still running. This is because FoxPro will have no way of knowing where to find the procedures once the menu program terminates. To avoid this problem, which is certain to arise when using a menu program to modify the interactive mode system menu, use DO <procedure> IN <file.mpr> whenever referencing procedures stored in the menu program's cleanup code.

Notably, when a command result is a procedure—that is, when we allow FoxPro to manage procedural code entered in a snippet as a menu option's result—FoxPro automatically takes care to reference the procedure with DO <procedure> IN <file.mpr>. Here we can simply cite the command FoxPro uses in Bigbiz.mpr to execute our Quit to Windows result procedure. (It also appears in Figure 9.19.) The essential command is

```
ON SELECTION BAR 7 OF system DO _qza1fktxb IN BIGBIZ.MPR
```

However, as an added measure of protection against errors that may arise if the terminated menu program no longer resides in the current file search path, FoxPro will automatically make use of the LOCFILE() function whenever referencing result procedures.

```
ON SELECTION BAR 7 OF system ;
    DO _qza1fktxb ;
    IN LOCFILE("BIGBIZ\MENUS\BIGBIZ" ,"MPX;MPR|FXP;PRG" , ;
    "Where is BIGBIZ?")
```

The function of LOCFILE() is simple, and you can use it as needed when referencing files of all types in your FoxPro applications or programs. The first <expC> included in the function is mandatory. It is used to pass FoxPro the name and full path of the file to search for. It may or may not include a file extension. The second

<expC> is optionally used, when the file extension may be in doubt, to supply FoxPro with a list of file extensions to try and the order in which to try them. (The backslash is used to separate extensions actually considered when searching for the file and the names of files that may appear by default in the Open dialog, as we explain in a moment.) If FoxPro is able to find the file in the default directory or file search path, LOCFILE() returns its name and location. If not, it activates the FoxPro Open File dialog and asks the operator to assist it in locating the right file. (The third <expC> provides FoxPro with the prompt to use when the Open dialog is employed. If a file extension list was entered, FoxPro uses it to control the list of files displayed in the Open dialog.)

.mpx is the extension FoxPro uses for the compiled object code versions of menu programs. .mpx is cited first in the LOCFILE() file extension list so that FoxPro will not trouble to recompile the source code file if the object code file already exists.

Including Security Levels in Your Application

Given the array of tools available for enabling and disabling system menu options, it is relatively easy to design and implement a security system in your application. The only question is what level of sophistication is required. To keep things simple, you can, for example, create a table named Password.dbf with two Character fields, one to hold available passwords (one of which must be entered by the operator upon starting the application to gain access to the system menu) and another to hold the access level (an integer 0–9, stored as a character string) that is provided an operator using a specific password.

Field Name	Type	Width
Password	Character	20
Access	Character	1

During application startup, we execute a small screen program allowing the operator to enter his or her password. If it exists, we store the value of Access to global memvar m.access and go on with the execution of the application. If the operator's entry cannot be found after permitting two or three tries, we use WAIT MESSAGE "Sorry Charlie" or some other message, perform whatever cleanup is required, and CANCEL or QUIT the application.

When an appropriate password is entered and m.access is initialized, we can subsequently use its value throughout the application to control which system menu options are available, though we can do this in two different ways. Assuming "9" represents the highest access level (and "0" the lowest), we can use a condition of m.access = "9" in the Skip For clause of menu items that should be accessible only to the system administrators. (The system administrator should naturally be given access to a screen program overseeing the update of Password.dbf records.) Using Skip For, other options can be made conditionally available to operators with an m.access >= <expC>. In the same fashion, m.access can also be used with SET SKIP OF during program execution to enable or disable menu options on the basis of the operator's access level.

However, another approach would be to use different system menus for operators with different access levels. For example, you can use m.access with IF or DO CASE at the outset of the application to determine which of several menu programs is executed as the application's main menu. This way, operators with low access levels needn't see the options that are unavailable to them.

The @ GET push button options used to control the action of the data entry program can be enabled or disabled using memvar m.access as well. This is most easily done by using IF m.access >= <expC> to control the action of SHOW GET ENABLE/DISABLE in the READ SHOW clause of the screen program. Access to @ GETs of all types can also be controlled by using m.access >= <expC> in the @ GET WHEN clause of specific input fields, popups, lists, and the like.

Using these methods, you should have no difficulty in arranging whatever level of security is required to control which actions can be taken by any operator logging into the application with a suitable password.

CHAPTER

TEN

Event Handling in a Windows Application

- Using Foundation READ in modal applications
- Using Foundation READ in nonmodal applications
- Controlling window events in a nonmodal application
- Managing system menu execution of screen programs
- Creating an event handler
- Using READ DEACTIVATE to best effect
- Using nonmodal and modal screen programs

In Chapters 3 through 6 of Part I, "Learning the Ropes," we examined the functions of the various READ clauses—CYCLE, MODAL, WHEN, ACTIVATE, SHOW, DEACTIVATE—used to control *intra-window* events during execution of a screen program. In Chapter 6, we also introduced the method, if not the means, by which FoxPro enables *extra-window* events, which allow an operator to click any open READ window or select it from the Window pulldown in order to reexecute the screen program that activates it. Now you will see how this is achieved through use of the Foundation READ, a screen execution routine, and an event handler executed through use of a Foundation READ's VALID clause.

Intra-window events must be properly staged to function correctly in response to extra-window events (such as operator selection of an inactive READ window). For a review of the basic intra-window events and how they are managed within a screen program through use of the READ clauses mentioned above and strategic composition of screen program cleanup code, see Chapter 6 before beginning this chapter. Here we consider the full range of window events that can be enabled in a Windows application all at once.

Using the Foundation READ

The last few chapters have gradually introduced you to the special form of the READ command used to keep FoxPro under program control during the execution of an application and to control window-level events. The Foundation or Getless READ is able to do this because, like the normal form of READ, it places FoxPro in a wait state, which also means FoxPro is ready for operator input of data or selection of any control key, hot key, or menu item that is designed to execute a command or program. But with the Foundation READ there is no data input to @ GETs.

Controlling Application Termination with Foundation READ

We use a Foundation READ at the outset of an application—in the case of the MBS, immediately after executing the MBS system menu—for two distinct, though related, reasons. The first, which is pertinent to both modal and nonmodal applications, is to prevent FoxPro from returning to the interactive mode. This function of the Foundation READ should not be underestimated. Since FoxPro's interactive mode facilities, including the Command window, can be hidden or deactivated and the system menu altered to place them out of reach of the operator, all the modal programs included in an application can be effectively executed from the interactive mode. The only caveat is that they cannot be bundled together in a single self-referencing .app file, as can be readily explained by taking another look at the MBS main program, Bigbiz.prg, though here we exclude all but the essential commands.

```
MODIFY WINDOW SCREEN TITLE "Model Business System" ;
    NOCLOSE FLOAT NOGROW MINIMIZE FONT "FoxFont,7"
DO bigbiz.mpr
READ VALID handler()
RETURN
```

Take away the getless READ and FoxPro returns to the interactive mode (or to Windows if the program is an .exe) after modifying the main window and system menu. As a result, when the operator selects a menu option executing DO <file> or DO <procedure>, FoxPro must find a stand-alone program or a procedure in an open procedure file with the correct file or procedure name or else fail to execute the command. Since MBS.app will have terminated, FoxPro can no longer look for any file, procedure, or function contained in it. To integrate all our programs into a single .app file rather than make them available as stand-alone screen, menu, and .prg files, which can be executed from the interactive mode, we must therefore use Foundation READ to keep our application file running.

Using the Foundation READ VALID Clause

To keep our application from terminating, however, it is not sufficient to use READ on its own. Just as @ GET/READ will terminate when the operator surpasses the last active @ GET unless READ CYCLE or some other READ clause is used to prevent this, Foundation READ will terminate when a subordinate (or nested) screen program terminates. As indicated in Chapter 8, we use READ's VALID clause to prevent this. READ's VALID clause is tested every time some event takes place or a command is issued instructing FoxPro to terminate READ. If the VALID clause returns a value of .T., the READ terminates; if it returns .F., the READ remains active. Where it is simply a matter of preventing Foundation READ from terminating—and we do not wish to use the VALID clause to control the automatic reexecution of specific programs, based upon which windows may remain open upon termination of a nested screen program—we can therefore keep our application running with either of these two VALID clauses:

```
READ VALID .F.

m.breakout = .F.
READ VALID m.breakout
```

Where the literal value of .F. is used, only two commands can terminate our application: CANCEL and QUIT. However, since both commands immediately terminate the application, they must prevent FoxPro from executing any commands in the main program placed after the Foundation READ. Where READ VALID .F. is used, it is therefore necessary to design a menu option that results in the execution of a procedure that takes care of whatever application cleanup duties must be performed before executing QUIT or CANCEL. The alternative, of course, is to control the value returned by the VALID clause with a global memvar that is initially set to a value of .F. before execution of the Foundation READ. With READ VALID m.breakout, we can make any event or command causing FoxPro to test the VALID clause terminate the READ by simply setting the value of m.breakout to .T. in advance.

Commands and Events Affecting Foundation READ

As previously stated, a Foundation READ, unprotected by VALID, will be terminated upon the termination of a nested program using @ GET/READ. However, like @ GET/READ, it will also be terminated by the CLEAR READ command or by any keystroke that doesn't execute a menu selection or hot-key (ON KEY LABEL) command or program.

It stands to reason that termination of a screen program (or READ command) launched by and returning program control to a nested screen program does not affect the Foundation READ. The Foundation READ is considered only when FoxPro returns to it. Since the parent-child metaphor is often used to describe the relation among nested READs, we can say that Foundation READ is affected only by termination of a *child* READ, not by termination of a *grandchild* READ. There is, however, one exception to this rule: Executing the command CLEAR READ ALL will cause FoxPro to automatically clear all active READs, including the Foundation READ. CLEAR READ ALL can therefore be used to terminate a child or grandchild READ (or screen program) and return program control to the Foundation READ, provided VALID is used in the Foundation READ to prevent it from terminating as well.

Testing the Behavior of Foundation READ

Since there is no occasion to use a Foundation READ without VALID, the real point of enumerating the commands and events that will terminate a Foundation READ is to get a clear idea of when our Foundation READ's VALID clause will be triggered. We can then use it since we choose to control when and how our application is terminated without recourse to CANCEL or QUIT and to conditionally determine what happens when a child READ terminates.

In this regard, those who are new to Foundation READ may find it useful to create and execute the following program. It is designed to illustrate the effects of various commands and events on the triggering of READ VALID.

```
ON KEY LABEL F3 DO gets
ON KEY LABEL F4 CLEAR READ
ON KEY LABEL F5 CLEAR READ ALL
ON KEY LABEL F6 m.breakout = .T.
ON KEY LABEL F7 CANCEL
ON KEY LABEL F8 DO dclear
m.breakout = .F.
READ VALID handler()

FUNCTION handler
WAIT WINDOW "In handler"
RETURN m.breakout

PROCEDURE gets
memvar = "    "
@ 10,2 GET memvar
READ
WAIT WINDOW "Child read cleared."

PROCEDURE dclear
m.breakout = .T.
CLEAR READ
```

In this case we use a UDF with READ VALID, though we do so only for the sake of executing the WAIT WINDOW command that will tell us when the VALID clause has been triggered. Other than that, the use of the UDF has the same effect as using READ VALID m.breakout since it is the value of the logical memvar m.breakout that determines whether or not the Foundation READ is terminated when the VALID clause is triggered.

> **TIP** When experimenting with Foundation READ or with the behavior and order of execution of READ clauses in screen programs, WAIT WINDOW is an indispensable tool. Stuck in the right places with an appropriate message, it can help you trace FoxPro's movement through a screen program or application without having to use the Trace and Debug windows. (Use of the Trace and Debug windows will sometimes alter FoxPro's execution of a program in ways that make it difficult to fully understand how a program will behave in their absence.)

As to the actual action of the program, execution of function keys F4 and F5, issuing CLEAR READ and CLEAR READ ALL, will trigger READ VALID but will not terminate it. However, if function key F5, changing the value of m.breakout to .T., is executed, while it does not trigger READ VALID, the next time F4 or F5 is used, the Foundation READ terminates and we end up back at the Command window. Essentially the same thing happens when we use F3 to execute the nested @ GET/READ. As soon as the nested READ terminates, the Foundation READ VALID is triggered. But the Foundation READ does not terminate unless we use F5 first to change the value of m.breakout to .T. Finally, function keys F7 and F8 both terminate the program, though F7 does so by issuing CANCEL, so READ VALID is never triggered, while F8 does so by changing m.breakout to .T. before issuing CLEAR READ.

> **TIP** If you're curious about the behavior of Foundation READ with respect to grandchild READs and the use of CLEAR READ and CLEAR READ ALL, just add another procedure calling a nested @ GET/READ to the program and execute it with ON KEY LABEL when the child READ issued by procedure Gets is active. Of course, the demonstration program can be altered in a variety of different ways to test other situations.

Foundation READ in Modal Applications

In applications that rely on the use of READ MODAL in all screen programs to prevent the operator from exceeding the maximum READ level of 5, Foundation READ is typically used only to prevent termination of the application when child screen programs are terminated. For this, a simple READ VALID clause using a literal value of .F. or a memvar preset to .F., as described above, will suffice to keep FoxPro under program control for the duration of the application. There is no need to employ a complex event handler to determine what action FoxPro should take upon termination of a child screen program since we want FoxPro to return to a wait state only so the operator can make another menu selection.

Controlling Window Events with Foundation READ

In nonmodal or largely nonmodal applications like the MBS, our intention is to make it possible for the operator to execute one screen program after another and to switch back and forth among them by clicking their associated READ windows, by selecting these windows from the Window pulldown, or by reselecting the system menu option that executes them in the first place. Of course, as you already know from Chapter 6, we are able to launch our child screen programs with such abandon, giving the operator the illusion that several window programs may be open and functioning at once, by using a little trick. On the one hand, we execute the screen programs listed on the system menu indirectly, through the use of a procedure that is designed to test the current READ level and, if the READ level is greater than 1 (indicating that a child program is already being run), to execute CLEAR READ before executing the newly selected screen program. Here we repeat the simplistic version of procedure Dospr presented in Chapter 6:

```
PROCEDURE dospr
PARAMETER m.sprtodo
IF RDLEVEL() >  1
    CLEAR READ
ENDIF
DO (m.sprtodo)
RETURN
```

On the other hand, we write our child screen programs so that when CLEAR READ is executed by procedure Dospr—and not by @ GET VALID in the screen program as a result of operator selection of a Quit push button—the current screen program terminates but leaves its associated READ window on the screen.

NOTE

Again, all system menu options executing screen programs use the result command DO Dospr WITH <screen program>. The WITH <screen program> parameter clearly serves to pass procedure Dospr the name of the screen program that must be executed. (For more on this aspect of procedure Dospr, see Chapter 6.)

What we failed to explain in Chapter 6 (and what plainly remains unexplained by the versions of procedure Dospr we have examined thus far) is how any READ window left on the screen, owing to the operator's execution of another screen program, can be automatically reanimated, via reexecution of the corresponding screen program, when the operator terminates the current screen program, clicks it with the mouse, selects it by name from the Window pulldown, or, in a word, takes any action that makes it WONTOP(). Without instructions to reexecute the screen program associated with the new WONTOP(), FoxPro can do no more than return to a wait state. The window will remain WONTOP(), but it will also remain dead on the screen. The solution to this problem, however, is not far to seek since every time a child READ (of our Foundation READ) is terminated, FoxPro will test the Foundation READ's VALID clause. We can therefore use it to supply FoxPro with the missing instructions.

System Menu Execution of Screen Programs as Window Events

Before examining the VALID clause used by MBS's Foundation READ, we must take care of another gross inadequacy of procedure Dospr as presented thus far in the text. The fact is that the CLEAR READ command issued in it will never be properly executed so as to terminate one screen program before procedure Dospr executes another. For those readers used to controlling program action with DO WHILE and EXIT, this will be somewhat difficult to grasp since the EXIT command immediately breaks the DO WHILE loop. Depending upon how it is issued, CLEAR READ may have no such immediate effect upon the current READ. To be exact, when CLEAR READ (or CLEAR READ ALL) is executed in procedure Dospr or anywhere else, FoxPro is obliged to execute whatever commands follow it in the procedure (or user-defined function). Only when the procedure actually terminates and FoxPro is able to return to the wait state administered by the READ that was current when CLEAR READ was issued can the CLEAR READ action be fulfilled.

Looking again at our half-baked version of procedure Dospr, we can now see why it can't fit the bill.

```
PROCEDURE dospr
PARAMETER m.sprtodo
IF RDLEVEL() >  1
    CLEAR READ
ENDIF
DO (m.sprtodo)
RETURN
```

Since the CLEAR READ command cannot be carried out until the procedure terminates, when we use procedure Dospr to execute a second screen program, FoxPro is compelled to launch the second screen program with DO (m.sprtodo) without deactivating the first screen program. The second screen program is thus launched as a grandchild screen program and RDLEVEL() is raised to 3. (Again, the CLEAR READ cannot be carried out at the new RDLEVEL() since it is addressed, in this example, to the child screen program at RDLEVEL() = "2".) The same thing will happen when the operator launches yet another screen program from the system menu. It is not until the screen program at the current RDLEVEL() is manually terminated that FoxPro will have a chance to return to the previous read levels and carry out as many CLEAR READs as will have stacked up in the process of executing the several screen programs. Needless to say, this is not what we want to happen. We must devise some means of separating the two actions presently combined in procedure Dospr so FoxPro can execute CLEAR READ and return to RDLEVEL() = 1 before actually launching a second screen program. That our Foundation READ VALID clause supplies us with a means of doing this is owing to the fact that in addition to terminating the current READ, CLEAR READ, returning FoxPro to RDLEVEL() = 1, the level of our Foundation READ when procedure Dospr terminates will also trigger READ VALID. To use a rough analogy, the Foundation READ's VALID clause plays the role in our application's main or parent window (the modified FoxPro main window) that the READ SHOW clause plays in our individual screen programs: It manages the events that are manipulable within RDLEVEL() = 1, the Foundation READ level of our application.

Here, then, is procedure Dospr in its final form, though we omit a few details, touched on in Chapter 6, that have no bearing on the procedure's triggering and use of READ VALID.

NOTE

Procedure Dospr is located in the MBS procedure file, Bizlib.prg, where it can be found along with the other procedures and functions discussed in the remainder of this chapter.

```
* Procedure Dospr oversees the execution of all screen programs
* selected from the system menu.
PROCEDURE dospr
PARAMETER m.sprtodo
IF RDLEVEL() > 1
    m.donext = m.sprtodo
    CLEAR READ
ELSE
    DO (m.sprtodo)
ENDIF
RETURN
```

Following the method employed in the FoxPro demonstration, nonmodal program, Ex2.app, we design procedure Dospr so it will execute the screen program passed it by name with DO Dospr WITH <screen file> only if no other screen program is active. However, when RDLEVEL() > 1, again indicating that a screen program (child READ) is already active, it issues CLEAR READ and takes no further action other than to pass the name of the next screen program to execute from memvar m.sprtodo to m.donext, a global MBS memvar. As a result, when procedure Dospr terminates, returning control to the READ at the current RDLEVEL(), 2, the READ will terminate (supposing that READ DEACTIVATE doesn't stop it), returning control to the Foundation READ and automatically executing READ VALID.

NOTE

Here again, it is worth emphasizing that we specifically design our nonmodal screen programs so that when they are terminated by any means other than operator selection of a Quit button or Close in the window control box, the program's READ window will not be released from memory and erased from the screen. (See Chapter 6 for an introductory discussion of how this is done using READ DEACTIVATE and the screen program's cleanup code. We expand on this topic later in this chapter.)

Note that in using a name expression with DO (m.sprtodo) to execute the screen program passed by name to procedure Dospr, we assume that no additional parameters must be passed to the called screen program with WITH <parameter> list. We call procedure Dospr with DO dospr WITH <screen program name>—for example, DO Dospr WITH [customer.spr]. However, if we need to execute Customer.spr or any other screen program with DO customer.spr WITH <parameters>, we must do this with macro substitution instead of a name expression. For example, if the menu option executes procedure Dospr with DO Dospr WITH [customer.spr WITH .F., "Up", 2], we must execute the screen program in procedure Dospr with DO &sprtodo. A name expression can be used only to indicate an object name. It cannot be used to pass parameters with WITH <parameter list> as well. The same thing applies to execution of screen programs in our event handler, as described below.

TIP

When procedure Dospr is executed when a child screen program is already active, we use it recursively. However, the moment procedure Dospr terminates and clears RDLEVEL() = 2, terminating the active screen program, FoxPro is able to terminate procedure Dospr as used to launch the first screen program. Again, once we reach the READ VALID event handler, procedure Dospr is no longer in the picture.

Creating an Event Handler for Nonmodal Applications

Turning our attention to the function we create to serve as our Foundation READ's VALID clause—this is our event handler—we can now make a quick study of its several functions. Like procedure Dospr, function Handler is stored in the MBS procedure file, Bizlib.prg.

```
FUNCTION handler
IF m.breakout
    RETURN .T.
ENDIF
IF NOT EMPTY(m.donext)
    m.currspr = m.donext
    m.donext = ""
    DO (m.currspr)
```

```
    RETURN .F.
ENDIF
DO CASE
CASE WONTOP() == ""
CASE WONTOP() = "CUSTOMER" AND NOT WMINIMUM("CUSTOMER")
    DO customer.spr
CASE WONTOP() = "PAYMENTS" AND NOT WMINIMUM("PAYMENTS")
    DO payments.spr
CASE WONTOP() = "SALES" AND NOT WMINIMUM("SALES")
    DO sales.spr
* Other cases listing other child screen program READ windows.
ENDCASE
RETURN .F.
```

At the outset of the MBS main program, Bigbiz.prg, we initialize the global memvar m.breakout to hold a value of .F. The only thing that sets it to .T. is the result procedure executed by the system menu option Quit to FoxPro, which, as you may recall, issues the following commands:

```
m.breakout = .T.
CLEAR READ ALL
```

CLEAR READ ALL terminates all child READs and then triggers the Foundation READ VALID handler(). Since m.breakout = .T., the IF statement at the beginning of function Handler will make the function RETURN .T., thereby terminating the application's Foundation READ. The main program therefore terminates after executing whatever commands follow the READ. (See Chapter 8 for a discussion of the MBS main program, Bigbiz.prg.) In the MBS, no other action is designed to trigger termination of the application in this way.

The second portion of function Handler is devoted to executing the screen program placed in global memvar m.donext by procedure Dospr when another screen program was being executed. We repeat the pertinent commands here:

```
IF NOT EMPTY(m.donext)
    m.currspr = m.donext
    m.donext = ""
    DO (m.currspr)
    RETURN .F.
ENDIF
```

Because memvar m.donext is altered to a null string after its value is passed to another memvar, the IF NOT EMPTY(m.donext) statement will be .T. only when function Handler is triggered by CLEAR READ in procedure Dospr (since procedure Dospr is the only program that places a value in m.donext); otherwise, the embedded commands are skipped. Of course, when the IF statement is .T., the command DO (m.currspr) executes the referenced screen program directly within our READ VALID. When the screen program terminates, function Handler moves on to the next line and returns .F., preventing the READ VALID from terminating the application. However, owing to the effect of the termination of the child screen program on Foundation READ immediately after RETURN .F. terminates function Handler (as executed by CLEAR READ in procedure Dospr), READ VALID is triggered yet again. The result should be obvious. Since the two IF statements discussed above will both be .F., FoxPro moves down to the following DO CASE in procedure Handler.

```
DO CASE
CASE WONTOP() == ""
CASE WONTOP() = "CUSTOMER" AND NOT WMINIMUM("CUSTOMER")
    DO customer.spr
CASE WONTOP() = "PAYMENTS" AND NOT WMINIMUM("PAYMENTS")
    DO payments.spr
CASE WONTOP() = "SALES" AND NOT WMINIMUM("SALES")
    DO sales.spr
* Other cases listing other child screen program READ windows.
ENDCASE
```

Here, everything is written out longhand. In a nutshell, we use WONTOP() to see if any of the READ windows used by our screen programs remains as the window on top (after termination of another screen program). If so, we use procedure Handler to reexecute the screen program associated with it. This is how an inactive READ window, left on the screen after the termination of the screen program with which it is used, is brought back to life. (We discuss the use of WMINIMUM() in a moment.)

Of course, if no CASE testing for a READ window WONTOP() is .T., function Handler terminates and RETURNs .F., thus keeping our application running at RDLEVEL() = 1. However, if a screen program is relaunched, once it terminates, function Handler will terminate with RETURN .F., only to be reexecuted once again by reason of the termination of the child screen program. If another inactive READ window is now WONTOP(), FoxPro will reexecute the corresponding screen program, and so on.

TIP

Because WONTOP() returns a null string when no window is open in the application main (parent) window, we use CASE WONTOP() == "" to prevent FoxPro from having to read through and evaluate all the following CASEs. Since no command is executed by the CASE, FoxPro simply jumps to the ENDCASE.

Using a Screen Program Window Name Schema

In the portion of function Handler devoted to reexecuting a screen program corresponding to WONTOP(), we must make use of a DO CASE structure owing to the occasional inconsistencies between the name of the main READ window used by a screen program and the screen program's name. For example, Saletrns.spr uses a READ window named Sale_trans. Such inconsistencies, when they arise in the MBS, are owing to my effort to keep the READ window names from becoming cryptic. They will, after all, be listed on the Window pulldown. They should therefore make the function of the window—or rather the function of the screen program that uses each window—as plain as possible. The simple fact is that DOS file name conventions must be followed in naming screen programs. But window names may

Making Your Own Window Pulldown

You can gain absolute control over the names displayed in your Window pulldown for each open window by creating a completely customized Window pulldown of your own. Change the pad name of the MBS Window pulldown so it no longer identifies FoxPro's _mwindow menu pad. (This inhibits the automatic display of window names.) Then, in the READ ACTIVATE clause of your nonmodal screen program, execute a routine that surveys the names of all currently open windows. Add a menu bar to the Window pulldown for each open window—for example, substituting window title for window name as the menu prompt—and issue, for each bar, an ON SELECTION BAR command designed to execute ACTIVATE WINDOW with the corresponding window's name when the menu bar is selected. (You must also see to it that menu bars are released from your Window pulldown whenever a window is released.)

be ten rather than eight characters in length, unlike the screen file names. I therefore took advantage of the two additional characters when I thought they'd help.

Many programmers will prefer to follow a strict convention in making READ window names correspond exactly to their screen program names. The reason for this is not far to seek: Working in this way will allow you to write more compact code. For example, supposing we followed such a convention, we could vastly simplify the coding of that portion of function Handler devoted to the reexecution of our screen programs on the basis of WONTOP().

```
IF NOT WONTOP() == "" AND NOT UPPER(WONTOP()) $ "CALCULATOR "+ ;
    "CALENDAR/DIARY PUZZLE HELP"
    m.dospr = WONTOP() +".spr"
    DO (m.dospr)
ENDIF
```

Indeed, this is much simpler and certainly requires much less writing. In fact, we can add additional screen programs to our application without having to add a single command to our event handler. Our event handler is ready for any screen program that uses the same name as its READ window.

In addition to making sure the embedded commands are not executed when no window is present on the screen, we must inhibit their execution when a desk accessory is on top or else run right into a program error since the desk accessories are not user-defined windows executed by screen programs. Of course, this rendering of the routine also assumes that no non-READ windows will be present on the screen when RDLEVEL() returns to 1. Assuming we change the names of the MBS READ windows so we can use the routine, this will be no problem since we do not leave such windows on the screen. Other programs, however, may need to do so. Additionally, applications that make use of a separately defined control push button window with most screen programs will often leave it up to the event handler to determine whether the Control window (actually a second READ window) should be removed from the screen. In these cases, you must add the names of windows that may remain on the screen but have no corresponding screen program to the list of desk accessory window names in the IF statement. This way, FoxPro will take no further action when they are WONTOP().

Still, if you don't mind displaying slightly bizarre window names on the Window pulldown, another, more complex convention can be followed that will greatly enhance your control over window events. Specific letters can be inserted in front of all user-defined window names to denote their function. This is suggested by

Yair Alan Griver in *The FoxPro 2.6 Codebook* (SYBEX, 1994). You can, for example, use an arbitrary *WR* as the first two letters of all main READ window names that have a corresponding screen program, a *WB* as the first two letters of BROWSE windows, and so on. From the standpoint of the programmer such window-naming conventions will provide a program with useful information. With respect to the relaunching of screen programs by an event handler on the basis of WONTOP()—though this is only one small example of what can be done—we can simply check the first two letters of WONTOP() to see if a screen program can be executed.

```
IF NOT WONTOP() == "" AND UPPER(WONTOP()) = "WR"
    m.dospr = WONTOP() +".spr"
    DO (m.dospr)
ENDIF
```

There is no need to provide FoxPro with a list of windows that should be excluded from consideration.

Though I will go no further in exploring the possibilities open to you in arranging more complex window events by taking advantage of window/screen program name schemas, it is well to consider what is to be gained, simply in terms of simplifying program code, by using one. In applications in which you must juggle user-defined windows on the basis of their functions and perhaps even identify two or more windows with a specific screen program (and with each other), a window-naming schema like that described above may well supply you with the key to doing what you want with relative ease.

NOTE

The drawback of window-naming schemas that use prefixes to identify windows by type or function is that they are bound to make the FoxPro Window pulldown less appealing, owing to its display of the prefixed window names. Mr. Griver, for example, gets around this problem by creating a customized Window pulldown that displays window titles instead of names.

Quick Survey of Window-Level Events

The utility of the event handler is best appreciated from afar—that is, from the perspective of the operator who has opened several screen programs at once. The Window pulldown lists all windows executed with the current screen program, open desk accessories, and inactive (main) READ windows belonging to screen programs that have, in fact, been terminated. The operator can choose any of them as WONTOP() by using the pulldown, the mouse, or Ctrl+F1 (Cycle).

Of course, in changing WONTOP() (assuming the operator is moving from the current READ window to another window), the operator triggers the READ DEACTIVATE clause employed in all MBS nonmodal screen programs, where we can test to see what has happened and exert control over what happens. After all, if a desk accessory or BROWSE window used by the current screen program has been made WONTOP(), there is no compelling reason to terminate the READ; in fact, we should avoid doing so. These windows are intended to be simultaneously available with the current READ window or windows. On the other hand, if an inactive READ window belonging to a previously launched screen program has been selected, and provided no action was taking place that must be completed before the current screen program can be terminated (for example, data editing), we will want to allow the current READ to terminate, leaving the current READ window on the screen though it is no longer WONTOP(). In the MBS screen programs we take care of this last-minute matter in the screen program's cleanup code, which typically tests to see if the operator selected the screen program's Quit push button or Close in the window control box. In both cases, this sets the value of memvar m.but1, used in all MBS screen programs with control push buttons, to "Quit," though this is done manually in READ DEACTIVATE when the operator uses Close. (We return to this in a moment.) Since Quit and Close are the only actions that signal the operator's decision to terminate a program—as opposed to simply interrupting it to work with another—we release the current READ window only if Quit or Close was selected.

```
* Payments.spr cleanup code.
SELECT customer
IF but1 = "Quit"
    RELEASE WINDOW "Payments"
ENDIF
RELEASE WINDOW "Payment List"
RELEASE WINDOW "Sale List"
SET SKIP OF BAR 2 OF Database .F.
SET TOPIC TO
```

The termination of the screen program takes FoxPro back to function Handler, which terminates with RETURN .F. (with respect to its use in executing the screen program that has just terminated), only to be reinvoked as a result of the termination of the child READ. Thus, the event handler finds out which READ window is now WONTOP() and reexecutes the program that brings it back to life.

Handling of Non-READ Windows

When it comes to managing window-level events, the use of BROWSE windows in nonmodal screen programs poses certain difficulties that must be addressed. This is because READ DEACTIVATE—our means of monitoring the environment during the current child READ—is triggered only when the operator leaves the current READ window. Were an operator to move to a BROWSE window used with one screen program (an action that would be allowed without terminating the current READ) and subsequently to an inactive READ window (or any other window) belonging to another screen program, the action would fail to trigger READ DEACTIVATE. The current screen program fails to terminate, even though it is no longer WONTOP().

Releasing BROWSE Windows

Because moving from one BROWSE window to another cannot trigger READ DEACTIVATE, leaving them on the screen when they are not required by the current screen program can only lead to confusion for the operator, who may justifiably expect immediate use of all windows normally employed with the selected BROWSE. We therefore typically release BROWSE windows upon termination of the screen programs with which they are used. Note, however, that there is nothing to prevent us from testing to see if a specific BROWSE window has been selected in our event handler and using this information to reexecute the correct screen program. The difficulty is in getting FoxPro back to the event handler. (The same thing holds true when MODIFY FILE or MODIFY MEMO is used to open text-editing windows with a screen program.)

The same problem comes up if the operator moves from the current READ window to a desk accessory. Surely, the action should not terminate the screen program. Thus, we rig READ DEACTIVATE to allow the action without terminating the READ. But subsequent operator selection of another inactive READ window is beyond the ken of our program. It will not trigger READ DEACTIVATE.

To get around this problem we must make do with available tools. Since READ DEACTIVATE is our only means of controlling events, we must use it the moment the operator leaves the READ window for one of these ancillary windows to disable operator selection of any window belonging to a terminated screen program until the operator returns to the current READ window and READ DEACTIVATE becomes available again. (Of course, we can use READ ACTIVATE to reenable whichever events we have disabled with READ DEACTIVATE since ACTIVATE will be triggered the moment the READ window is reselected as WONTOP().) In effect, we must make our nonmodal program behave like a modal screen program with associated windows and a reactivated system menu, containing only those options pertinent to the current action, when the operator strays from the current READ.

Before showing how this is done in the READ DEACTIVATE clause of all MBS nonmodal screen programs, there is one other side effect of using desk accessories and BROWSE windows of which you should be aware. Simply stated, FoxPro cannot execute the CLEAR READ command when a BROWSE window or desk accessory is WONTOP(). The wait state these facilities use is not controlled by the current READ. For this reason, menu selection of any screen program while a BROWSE window or desk accessory is WONTOP() gets temporarily hung up. For example, if we launch Payments.spr, which uses two BROWSE windows, and move to one of the BROWSE windows before selecting Customer from the Database pulldown, FoxPro will execute procedure DO Dospr with the command DO Dospr WITH [customer.spr]. But when procedure DO Dospr issues CLEAR READ, FoxPro must come to a halt since it does not have access to the READ it must clear. In one sense, such behavior is not so objectionable since the moment the operator moves back to the READ window, the event will go through. But the momentary hangup can lead to confusion. The operator may, for example, select other menu options in the hope of getting something to work. For this reason, when the operator moves from a READ window to a BROWSE or desk accessory, we will have good cause to momentarily disable the system pulldowns that execute other screen programs.

NOTE

There is an alternative approach. Before execution of CLEAR READ in procedure Dospr, we can test to make sure WONTOP() is the current READ window, the name of which is available to use through WREAD(). If it is not, and no condition exists that would otherwise prevent us from launching the new screen program, we can simply use ACTIVATE WINDOW WREAD() to reactivate it. CLEAR READ will then have the desired effect.

Creating a Protected Window Mode

Turning our attention to the READ DEACTIVATE clause of our nonmodal screen programs, we can mimic a modal environment when the operator moves off the READ window to activate a BROWSE window or one of the disk accessories by first using IF with WONTOP() to see if selection of such a window is responsible for triggering READ DEACTIVATE. Since some but not all of the MBS screen programs make use of BROWSE windows, we can make things easy on ourselves by using a memvar, m.dothers (short for *the other windows*), which we initialize in the setup code of each screen program to hold the names of whichever BROWSE windows are used by the program. (When no BROWSE windows are used, we initialize it to hold a null string.)

```
IF UPPER(WONTOP()) $ "CALCULATOR CALENDAR/DIARY PUZZLE HELP " ;
    + m.dothers
    DO hide WITH dwindow,dothers
    RETURN .F.
ENDIF
```

Thus, if the operator triggers READ DEACTIVATE through selection of one of the listed windows, including those indicated by the value of m.dothers, the DEACTIVATE clause ultimately RETURNs .F., preventing the screen program from terminating. But before doing so, it also executes procedure Hide, which performs the various actions necessary to prevent the operator from selecting an inactive READ window belonging to a terminated screen program or from trying to launch another screen program through use of the system menu. The command DO Hide passes two parameters: m.dothers, holding the names of any BROWSE windows (or other non-READ windows) used by the current screen program, and m.dwindow, which we also initialize in the screen program startup code to hold the name of our main READ window. We now show the text of procedure Hide, which is placed in the MBS procedure file, Bizlib.prg, where it will be accessible to the READ DEACTIVATE clauses of all our screen programs. Though we discuss its action immediately below, glance over it and see if you can understand what it does on your own.

```
* Procedure Hide simulates a modal environment when the operator
* leaves a screen program's READ window.
PROCEDURE hide
PARAMETER dwindow,dothers
m.hide = .T.
dhidden = ""
nohide = dwindow + "  " + dothers + " CALCULATOR "+ ;
    "CALENDAR/DIARY PUZZLE HELP "
FOR m.count = 0 TO WCHILD("")
    winame = UPPER(WCHILD("",m.count))
    IF NOT EMPTY(winame) AND WVISIBLE(winame) ;
        AND NOT winame $ nohide
        HIDE WINDOW (winame)
        dhidden = dhidden + winame + ","
    ENDIF
ENDFOR
IF LEN(dhidden) > 0
    dhidden = SUBSTR(dhidden,1,LEN(dhidden)-1)
ENDIF
WAIT WINDOW "Hide has "+dhidden
SET SKIP OF PAD database OF _msysmenu .T.
SET SKIP OF PAD reports OF _msysmenu .T.
SET SKIP OF PAD _msm_windo OF _msysmenu .T.
SET SKIP OF PAD update OF _msysmenu .T.
SET SKIP OF PAD utilities OF _msysmenu .T.
RETURN
```

In regard to the last portion of the procedure, we use SET SKIP OF PAD to disable the MBS menu pads and, as well, the associated pulldowns that can be used to launch other screen programs. The list of disabled pads naturally includes the Window pulldown, which will list all open windows (except the desk accessories), whether or not they are hidden.

For the rest, though the strategy employed by procedure Hide should be straightforward enough, the commands it uses to carry it out warrant explanation. Ultimately, the idea of procedure Hide is to use the command HIDE WINDOW <window name> to make FoxPro remove any and all READ windows not belonging to the current screen program from the main window until the user reactivates the current READ window. To orchestrate the full action properly, we must take the action that must be performed in READ ACTIVATE—namely, showing the hidden windows once again and reactivating the system menu pads—into account. To this end, in procedure Hide we make use of two MBS global memvars, m.hide and m.dhidden. The first holds a logical value that is set to .T. only when procedure Hidden has been executed. The second, m.dhidden, is reinitialized by procedure Hide to hold a list of any and all windows that have been hidden (but not released) through the action of HIDE WINDOW. The text of the portion of our READ ACTIVATE clause devoted to reversing the action of procedure Hide is simple enough.

```
IF m.hide
    DO unhide
ENDIF
```

As with procedure Hide, we write procedure Unhide as a separate procedure and place it in the MBS procedure file, Bizlib.prg, where it will be accessible to the READ ACTIVATE clauses of all our screen programs.

```
PROCEDURE unhide
m.hide = .F.
IF NOT EMPTY(dhidden)
    SHOW WINDOW &dhidden BOTTOM
    m.dhidden = ""
ENDIF
SET SKIP OF PAD database OF _msysmenu .F.
SET SKIP OF PAD reports OF _msysmenu .F.
SET SKIP OF PAD _msm_windo OF _msysmenu .F.
SET SKIP OF PAD update OF _msysmenu .F.
SET SKIP OF PAD utilities OF _msysmenu .F.
RETURN
```

In contrast to procedure Hide, procedure Unhide is quite simple. It resets the global memvar m.hide, indicating that procedure Hide has been executed, to .F. so another action retriggering READ ACTIVATE will not execute procedure Unhide again. It then tests memvar m.dhidden to see if procedure Hide actually hid any windows. If m.dhidden is NOT EMPTY(), the SHOW WINDOW command is issued to make the hidden windows listed by m.dhidden visible once again. The keyword BOTTOM is used to prevent any of the windows referenced by m.dhidden from being restored on top of the windows already visible on the screen.

NOTE

In addition to its role in unhiding windows, SHOW WINDOW can be used simply to change the front-to-back order of windows on the screen. Use the keywords TOP, BOTTOM, and SAME to show the referenced windows on top of other windows, behind other windows, or in the same order they previously occupied relative to other windows, respectively.

Unhiding Windows with BROWSE Windows on the Screen

One of the unfortunate side effects of using SHOW WINDOW BOTTOM instead of SAME is that it doesn't preserve the front-to-back order of the windows it unhides with respect to each other. SAME will take care of this, though at this writing it ignores whatever BROWSE windows are visible on the screen. BROWSE windows used with the current screen set end up on the bottom. And while this can be quickly corrected by using SHOW WINDOW, the overall effect is distracting. The BROWSE windows disappear only to reappear with a flash. For this reason, and noting that any open window can be selected with the Window pulldown regardless of its front to back order on the screen, I opted to restore the hidden windows with SHOW WINDOW BOTTOM to avoid having to deal with the BROWSE windows. However, there are situations in which preserving the front-to-back order of windows unhidden with SHOW WINDOW can be an important consideration. This is not true, in my opinion, with the screen programs included in the MBS.

Going back to procedure Hide, we can quickly make sense of its action. Initiated by the command DO hide WITH dwindow,dothers, executed in the READ DEACTIVATE clause of our screen programs when the operator activates a non-READ window (BROWSE, MODIFY COMMAND, MODIFY MEMO, MODIFY FILE) or a desk accessory, procedure Hide begins by placing the passed parameters in memvars, using the same memvar names.

```
PARAMETER dwindow,dothers
```

This is actually unnecessary since procedure Hide does not change the values of m.dwindow or m.dother, which are readily available to procedure Hide, since it is a nested procedure. The PARAMETER command, however, will help to remind us of the crucial values that are being passed.

Next we set m.hide to .T. so procedure Unhide will be executed when the operator moves back to the deactivated READ window and set m.dhidden to a null string so we can begin using it to store the names of whichever windows are actually hidden.

```
m.hide = .T.
dhidden = ""
```

We also use the content of m.dwindow, holding the name of the current READ window, and m.dothers, holding the name of non-READ windows belonging to the current screen program, to compile a list of windows that should not be hidden. In addition, we throw the names of all desk accessories into memvar m.nohide, making it a complete list of all windows that may be safely displayed on the screen when we lose control of window events following operator activation of a non-READ window.

```
nohide = dwindow + " " + dothers + " CALCULATOR "+ ;
    "CALENDAR/DIARY PUZZLE HELP "
```

In the next, crucial portion of procedure Hide, we use FOR ENDFOR to make FoxPro reel through a list of all windows present on the screen. The WCHILD() function that we discuss immediately below is used to control the number of repetitions of FOR/ENDFOR and to supply FoxPro with the names of all open windows one at a time, according to the current value of m.count, which is initially set to 0.

```
FOR m.count = 0 TO WCHILD("")
    winame = UPPER(WCHILD("",m.count))
    IF NOT EMPTY(winame) AND WVISIBLE(winame) ;
        AND NOT winame $ nohide
        HIDE WINDOW (winame)
        dhidden = dhidden + winame + ","
    ENDIF
ENDFOR
```

The first instance of WCHILD() in the routine gives us the total number of windows open within the main FoxPro window, which can be referenced with a null string or by title. WCHILD(<expC>), to be more explicit, returns the number of windows open within the indicated parent window.

NOTE

Though we do not do this in the MBS, windows can be opened within a user-defined window, making them child windows of the window in which they are opened instead of child windows belonging to the main FoxPro window. Use the IN WINDOW <window name> or WINDOW <window name> option of FoxPro commands defining or opening a window—for example, DEFINE WINDOW, BROWSE, MODIFY MEMO, and so on—to make a window a child of a user-defined window. Note also that the name of any child window's parent window can be referenced with the WPARENT(<child window name>) function.

Our second use of WCHILD() makes use of its full syntax, WCHILD (<expC>,<expN>). When a number is supplied, the function returns the name of the child window appearing *n*th in *back-to-front* order in the designated parent window, the number 0 being used to indicate the child window at the very bottom. Thus, using FOR/ENDFOR, we can repeat the embedded commands once for every child window while using WCHILD("",<expN>) to supply the routine with the names of each child window in its given order, though we pass the value to memvar m.winame so FoxPro won't have to evaluate the function several times.

```
winame = UPPER(WCHILD("",m.count))
IF NOT EMPTY(winame) AND WVISIBLE(winame) ;
    AND NOT winame $ nohide
    HIDE WINDOW (winame)
    dhidden = dhidden + winame + ","
ENDIF
```

In each repetition we use IF to determine if the child window presently under consideration should be hidden with HIDE WINDOW and its name added to the hidden window name list stored in m.dhidden. Here we test several things. As a precaution, we make sure that m.winame doesn't contain a null string; we also use WVISIBLE() so FoxPro will not waste its time with a window that is already hidden and, moreover, add the hidden window's name to the list of windows that should be unhidden when procedure Unhide is used later on. The last IF condition, NOT winame $ nohide, is used to make sure that FoxPro does not hide the windows listed by name in m.nohide. (As you will recall, m.nohide is initialized before FOR/ENDFOR to hold the names of the windows we want excluded from the HIDE WINDOW action.)

When FOR/ENDFOR terminates, we have but one more action to take. Since window names added to m.dhidden are deliberately followed by a comma in order to form a window name list acceptable to the SHOW WINDOW command in READ DEACTIVATE, if any window names were actually added to m.dhidden, the comma at the end of the window name list must be removed or it will cause an error. We therefore use SUBSTR() and LEN() together to remove it before procedure Hide moves on to its last duty of disabling the system menu pads that are inappropriate to the protected window mode we create to control things while the operator is away from the current screen program's READ window or windows.

```
IF LEN(dhidden) > 0
    dhidden = SUBSTR(dhidden,1,LEN(dhidden)-1)
ENDIF
SET SKIP OF PAD database OF _msysmenu .F.
SET SKIP OF PAD reports OF _msysmenu .F.
SET SKIP OF PAD _msm_windo OF _msysmenu .F.
SET SKIP OF PAD update OF _msysmenu .F.
SET SKIP OF PAD utilities OF _msysmenu .F.
RETURN
```

Once procedure Hide has performed its action, the operator can do what he or she pleases with the available windows and menu options. We have thus moved from the vast freedom of nonmodal READ to emulation of READ MODAL with an associated window list and a reactivated but pared-down system menu. When the operator returns to the READ window, which is required to continue with data entry or to terminate the program, the triggering of READ ACTIVATE restores the nonmodal environment.

NOTE

A second place in which we make use of procedures Hide and Unhide in the MBS is when the operator selects the Browse push button while using any of the screen programs listed on the Database pulldown. Opening and activating the additional BROWSE window has the same effect as moving to any other BROWSE window used with a nonmodal screen program. We must therefore use the same or similar measures to prevent the operator from trying to execute events that we cannot in fact stage through the auspices of READ DEACTIVATE.

Working with Minimized Windows

When defining your screen programs' READ windows with the Screen Builder, you can choose to allow the operator to mimimize them. Choosing the Mimimize option in the Screen Builder's Window Style dialog, which we discuss in the next chapter, makes the Minimize option available in the window's control box. Figure 10.1 shows the effects of minimizing all the Database pulldown screen programs' READ windows. Since we do not supply our own icons when defining the READ windows (though this can be done by using the Window Style Icon File dialog), FoxPro uses its own icon as a default.

FIGURE 10.1:
With the MBS you can minimize the screen program's main READ windows.

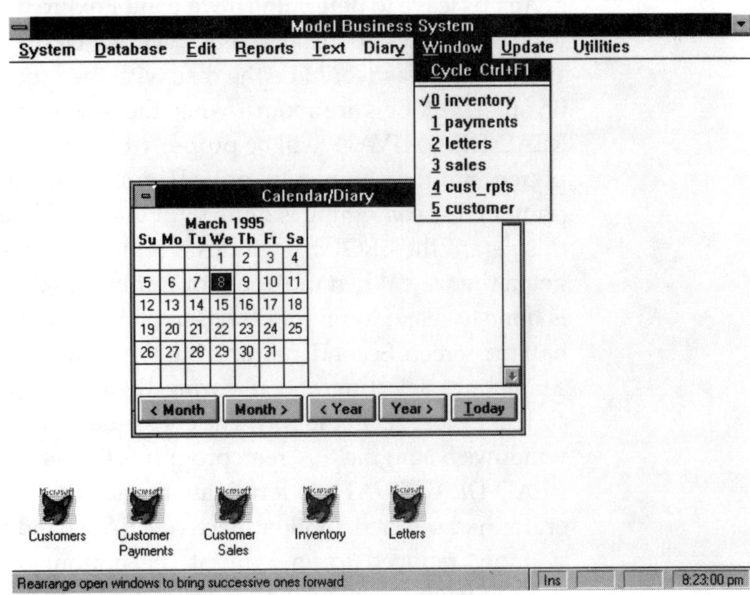

As Figure 10.1 indicates, all minimized windows are still listed on the Window pulldown. Each screen program can be restarted by clicking the corresponding icon and selecting Restore from the icon (window) control box, by double-clicking the icon, by selecting the window from the Window pulldown, or by relaunching the program with the Database pulldown.

However, while the use of minimizable windows would seem desirable in an application, there are a few idiosyncrasies to minimizing windows that you (and ultimately the operator) will have to get used to. The problem is that minimizing the current READ window does not trigger READ DEACTIVATE unless another window becomes WONTOP() as a result. For example, Customer.spr uses only one window. For this reason, when the Customers window is minimized and no other windows—for example, desk accessories or inactivated READ windows belonging to terminated programs (or their icons)—are present on the screen, the READ window is minimized to an icon without triggering READ DEACTIVATE. On the other hand, when Payments.spr is running and its READ window is minimized, the first BROWSE window becomes WONTOP(), triggering READ DEACTIVATE and thus giving us leave to determine if we want FoxPro to take some specific action. This in itself constitutes no real problem since even if the minimized READ window is still WONTOP()—as would be the case with the minimized Customers window when no other windows are about—when the operator launches another screen program, READ DEACTIVATE will be properly triggered and events will be executed as expected. But then, minimizing the Payments window would seem to be beside the point unless something is done with the two Payments.spr BROWSE windows. In this regard the BROWSE windows represent a double problem. First, they simply get in the way. When the operator minimizes the READ window, presumably this is done to make room for other screen programs. The BROWSE windows take up half the screen. Second, minimizing them along with the READ window makes no sense since selecting and restoring them cannot retrigger READ ACTIVATE. In sum, they just get in the way. The consequence is simple. When we minimize READ windows belonging to screen programs that also use non-READ windows, we use READ DEACTIVATE to terminate the screen program the same way as if the operator had selected another inactive READ window. We therefore leave the READ window, reduced to an icon, at the bottom of the screen while releasing the BROWSE windows. As for our single-window screen programs like Customer and Inventry.spr, we write their DEACTIVATE clauses to have the same effect, though it will not be triggered until the operator opens another window. (We will examine the full READ DEACTIVATE clauses used by the MBS nonmodal screen programs in a moment. I only want to make you aware of the *last* issue they must deal with.)

Another problem related to the use of minimize with our READ windows is when and how they will be reactivated once they are reduced to icons. Since a window reduced to an icon can still become WONTOP(), if a screen program is terminated leaving an icon WONTOP(), our READ VALID event handler, function Handler, will seek to execute the corresponding screen program unless we stop it. This is problematic to say the least, especially since we may have BROWSE windows to contend with. Certainly, we do not want the BROWSE windows reactivated while the READ window remains an icon. Nor is it clear that we want the program reexecuted at all—that is, automatically, since we must assume the operator reduced the READ window to an icon to put it to one side until it is time to manually restore it. The best policy is therefore to inhibit the execution of the screen program in READ VALID Handler() if WONTOP() is minimized. We have already shown how this is done in the portion of function Handler devoted to reexecuting the programs associated with an inactive READ window when it becomes WONTOP(), though it will be helpful to take another look at a few of the pertinent commands.

```
DO CASE
CASE WONTOP() == ""
CASE WONTOP() = "CUSTOMER" AND NOT WMINIMUM("CUSTOMER")
    DO customer.spr
CASE WONTOP() = "PAYMENTS" AND NOT WMINIMUM("PAYMENTS")
    DO payments.spr
CASE WONTOP() = "SALES" AND NOT WMINIMUM("SALES")
    DO sales.spr
* Other cases listing other child screen program READ windows.
ENDCASE
```

Not only do we test for WONTOP(), but we use the WMINIMUM() function to test to see if the window is minimized. If it is, we take no action. When the operator wants to work with the window, double-clicking the icon or using Restore will be sufficient to restore the window to its full size and retrigger function Handler so it can launch the correct program.

Unfortunately, this is not the end of the issues that must be considered when working with minimizable READ windows. For once we have minimized a READ window, if the operator reexecutes the screen program with which it is used from the system menu (rather than selecting the window from the Window pulldown), the screen program will not automatically restore the window to its normal dimensions unless we provide FoxPro with specific instructions for doing so. This, however, is handled easily enough by placing the following commands in the READ ACTIVATE clause of the screen program:

```
IF WMINIMUM("PAYMENTS")
    ZOOM WINDOW payments NORM
ENDIF
```

NOTE

Screen programs designed with the Screen Builder and generated automatically by FoxPro are designed to be responsive to the preexisting window and database environment. In this case, if a READ window used in a screen program is already WONTOP(), FoxPro does not issue ACTIVATE WINDOW to make it WONTOP(). Thus, if the READ window is WONTOP() and WMINIMUM() when the screen program is launched, FoxPro activates the READ associated with the minimized window without restoring the window to its normal dimensions.

The routine tests to see if the READ window is minimized. If it is, the ZOOM WINDOW command is used to restore it to its normal (defined) size.

TIP

The ZOOM WINDOW command has several different options. Use MIN to minimize the referenced window, MAX to maximize it, and NORM to restore it to its predefined, normal size. AT and SIZE options are also available for repositioning and resizing the window.

Another problem that surfaces when using minimizable READ windows has to do with use of the window (or icon) control box to close the window. As you may recall, while the screen program is active, Close triggers READ DEACTIVATE. We can thus take steps to terminate the screen program in the same way we do when the operator selects the Quit push button. We RELEASE the READ window along with all other windows specifically used by the screen program. However, once the window is minimized and the screen program terminated to make way for another, the Close option in the minimized window's control box cannot have the same function since selecting it cannot trigger READ DEACTIVATE. The consequence is that selecting Close does not RELEASE the window; it hides the window. With respect to the MBS, this has no adverse effect, but it does lead to an inconsistency since the window will still be listed in the Window pulldown.

While there are several ways around this problem, I have not used any of them in the MBS, in part because I expect to see changes in FoxPro's management of minimizable windows. However, one work-around would be to test for leftover hidden and minimized child windows in the event handler and to RELEASE them when found. (The portion of procedure Hide devoted to testing all open child windows will provide you with a model for doing this.) The downside is that using such a routine will necessarily slow the action of the event handler since it must be executed whenever the Foundation READ VALID is triggered and WCHILD("") > 1, whether or not any minimized and hidden windows are present. The other, more obvious option, in light of the several issues that must be dealt with in order to make the READ windows minimizable, is to forego use of minimizable windows altogether. In most applications this will be perfectly reasonable—unless, of course, your application must show others how to work with minimizable windows. Again, with respect to MBS's behavior, the only untoward effect of the operator's using Close with a minimized READ window (when the screen program has actually been terminated) is that instead of being RELEASEd—the effect of Close when the screen program is active—the window will continue to be listed in the Window pulldown, where it can be selected and reexecuted. If you find the inconsistency unacceptable, you can do away with it as suggested above.

NOTE

Windows hidden as a result of using Close to close a minimized window after the corresponding screen program has terminated will not have an adverse effect on the proper functioning of procedure Hide and procedure Unhide, used to create a protected window mode when the operator leaves the current READ window for a desk accessory or non-READ window belonging to the current screen program. This is because procedure Hide will hide only windows that are WVISIBLE(), and only windows it hides are added to the list of windows that should be redisplayed by procedure Unhide with the SHOW WINDOW command.

Using READ DEACTIVATE to Best Effect

In our discussion of window events, we have kept returning to READ DEACTIVATE since it is the primary means of controlling window events during execution of a screen program. Triggered when the operator changes WONTOP(), leaving an active READ window, it is used in the MBS screen programs to determine how and under what circumstances the screen program (READ) should be terminated. If data entry or edit is under way, as signified throughout the MBS by the value of global memvar m.doit being set to .T., we use it to block the termination of the

READ and to conditionally determine whether the newly selected window can be left WONTOP(). (For example, if the selected window is a BROWSE window used by the screen program of one of the desk accessories, we can allow the selection as long as we defend against the operator's moving from the new WONTOP() to an inactive READ window not belonging to the current screen program, as described above.)

However, having now reviewed all the various functions ascribed to READ DEACTIVATE, including the imperfect role it plays when the READ window is minimized (again, this is because minimizing a window does not in itself trigger READ DEACTIVATE), we can view READ DEACTIVATE one last time for the sake of summarizing its action as it is used in the MBS nonmodal screen programs. In this regard, if you open one of the MBS screen programs listed on the Database pull-down with the Screen Builder and look at the code snippets entered for their READ DEACTIVATE clauses, you will find they contain only one command. Here, for example, are the code snippets used with the READ DEACTIVATE employed with Customer and Payments.spr:

```
* Customer.spr READ DEACTIVATE clause.
RETURN stop("CUSTOMER","")

* Payments.spr READ DEACTIVATE clause.
RETURN stop("PAYMENTS","PAYMENT LIST, SALE LIST")
```

In both cases, we use the READ DEACTIVATE clause to return the logical value generated by a user-defined function, function Stop, in which we consolidate all routines hitherto presented as falling under the auspices of READ DEACTIVATE. Of course, we can use a single UDF to perform all the actions associated with READ DEACTIVATE for all our nonmodal screen programs (with the exception of Letters.spr, which uses two READ windows) instead of writing out the clause once for each program, owing to our use of global memvars such a m.doit and m.but1. Again, m.doit is used to indicate when data edit is under way with all screen programs, while m.but1 is used with a value of "Quit" to indicate when the operator has selected the Quit push button—a consistent feature of all screen programs. (As you will recall from our earlier discussions of READ DEACTIVATE, when READ DEACTIVATE is triggered by operator selection of Close from the window control box, we manually set the value of m.but1 to "Quit" before returning .T., so that in terminating the screen program, FoxPro will release the READ window when it executes the screen cleanup code, just as it does when the operator actually selects the Quit push button. See Chapter 6.)

In fact, so standard are the functions that must be performed by READ DEACTIVATE that they can be reduced, as we have done in the MBS, to a single function, provided we supply it with whatever information it needs that is specific to each screen program. As the two commands cited above indicate, what function Stop needs to know (in addition to the setting of m.doit and m.but1, which are already available to it as a nested function) is the name of the current READ window and the names of all non-READ windows that are used by the current screen program. Here then is the text of function Stop, which we discuss below:

```
FUNCTION stop
PARAMETERS dwindow,dothers
* READ window has been closed.
IF NOT WVISIBLE(dwindow) AND NOT m.doit
    m.but1 = "Quit"
    RETURN .T.
ENDIF
* Read window minimized.
IF WMINIMUM(dwindow) AND NOT m.doit
    RETURN .T.
ENDIF
* Desk accessory or non-READ window selected.
IF UPPER(WONTOP()) $ "CALCULATOR CALENDAR/DIARY PUZZLE HELP " ;
    + dothers
    DO hide WITH dwindow,dothers
    RETURN .F.
 ENDIF
* Editing action in process.
IF m.doit
    DO alert WITH "Cannot change windows until editing "+ ;
    "is over.", "Press any key to continue."
    IF NOT dothers == ""
        SHOW WINDOW &dothers TOP
    ENDIF
    ACTIVATE WINDOW (dwindow)
    IF WMINIMUM(dwindow)
        ZOOM WINDOW (dwindow) NORM
    ENDIF
    RETURN .F.
ENDIF
RETURN .T.
```

We have already discussed all the functions of READ DEACTIVATE, here consolidated in function Stop, so you should be able to make sense of its every action. Since each IF statement included in the function is designed to execute RETURN with .T.

or .F., thereby instructing FoxPro, on return to the READ VALIDATE clause of the calling screen program, to terminate or not terminate the READ, respectively, the overall function is designed to work by process of elimination.

The first condition for which we test is whether the operator has closed the window using the Close option in the READ window's control box. If so, the READ window, the name of which is passed to function Stop through memvar m.dwindow, will be hidden or, in FoxPro's terms, NOT WVISIBLE(). If this is the case, we want to terminate the READ just as though the operator had used the Quit push button. This we accomplish by setting m.but1 = "Quit" so that upon reaching the screen program's cleanup code, FoxPro will execute the commands triggered by IF m.but1 = "Quit". However, as our IF statement indicates, there is one situation in which we will not want FoxPro to take this action: when record append or editing is under way as indicated in all MBS screen programs by m.doit = .T. IF m.doit = .T., FoxPro obviously bypasses the IF, even if the READ window is NOT WVISIBLE().

Next we check to see if the READ window has been minimized using WMINIMUM(), though, as you may recall, minimizing the READ window will not of itself trigger READ DEACTIVATE unless another window is present and unhidden on the screen. (Again, if no other window is open on the screen, WONTOP() does not change if the window is minimized.) Be that as it may, when READ DEACTIVATE is triggered owing to immediate or subsequent change of WONTOP()—or through the operator's execution of another screen program—if the READ WINDOW is WMINIMUM() and data append or edit is not under way, we RETURN .T. without, in this case, touching the value of m.but1 (which will not be "Quit" since the Quit button executes CLEAR READ, thereby bypassing READ DEACTIVATE) so FoxPro will terminate the READ without releasing the minimized READ window. (Again, this last action—releasing or not releasing the READ window—is controlled in screen program cleanup code with IF m.but1 = "Quit", as discussed in Chapter 6.)

The next issue we address is whether the operator has triggered READ DEACTIVATE by selecting one of the desk accessories or one of the non-READ windows included in the current screen program. (Remember, changing WONTOP() when the READ window is current triggers READ DEACTIVATE.) As discussed earlier in this chapter, we can safely allow this event without terminating the READ (we RETURN .F. to stop it) and do so whether or not data editing is under way, provided we place FoxPro in a protected window mode so the operator has no choice but to ultimately return to the READ window before executing another screen program in any of the normal ways. Thus, we first test to see if the new WONTOP() is a desk accessory or one of the screen program's non-READ windows, the names of which are passed to function Stop through memvar m.dothers. If it is, we execute procedure Hide, discussed in depth earlier in this chapter, to hide inactive READ windows belonging to other screen programs, if any are still open on the screen, and disable menu options executing other screen programs before returning .F. so the READ remains in effect. (Again, when the operator reselects the READ window, the READ ACTIVATE clause is used to return our window environment to its normal, nonmodal state.)

Now we come to the last issue that prevents us from allowing whatever action has triggered READ DEACTIVATE to terminate the READ—without our having to do anything at all. However, IF m.doit = .T., meaning that data edit is under way (and, owing to the prior IF, that the operator has not selected a window that can be safely used in protected mode when editing is under way), we must absolutely prohibit termination of the READ; otherwise, the data being entered will be lost when the screen program terminates. However, it is not enough just to RETURN .F. since the READ window may no longer be WONTOP(), much less WVISIBLE(). Indeed, the operator may have already closed (hidden) it using the window control box. The READ window may also have been minimized—an unsuitable state for terminating data entry (though we might leave the operator to restore it). Another consideration is the state of non-READ windows used by the screen program. If WONTOP() is changed, they may now be covered by the new WONTOP() even though we don't allow the window to stay on top. (Placing the READ window back on top will not automatically place the non-READ windows back on top with it.)

Taking another look at the last portion of procedure Stop, we can now make sense of all its actions and the order in which it executes each.

```
IF m.doit
    DO alert WITH "Cannot change windows until editing "+ ;
    "is over.", "Press any key to continue."
    IF NOT dothers == ""
        SHOW WINDOW &dothers TOP
    ENDIF
    ACTIVATE WINDOW (dwindow)
    IF WMINIMUM(dwindow)
         ZOOM WINDOW (dwindow) NORM
    ENDIF
    RETURN .F.
ENDIF
```

If editing is under way (and the operator has not moved to one of the permitted windows, specified in the prior IF statement), we begin by using procedure Alert to inform the operator that the action taken, triggering READ DEACTIVATE, will not be allowed and why. In countermanding the action (which, remember, has already been taken) we begin by restoring all non-READ windows used by the screen program and passed function Stop through memvar m.dothers to the foreground with SHOW WINDOW TOP—that is, assuming m.dothers does not contain a null string indicating that no such non-READ windows are being used. Again, we do this in case our BROWSE and/or other non-READ windows have been covered by whatever window the operator may have placed WONTOP().

NOTE

Since memvar m.dothers can contain a list of window names separated by commas (a window name list) and not the name of a single window, we do not reference it in the SHOW WINDOW command as a name expression (dothers). If it contains a list, the list must be supplied using macro substitution (&dothers). We are also deliberate in not using the memvar prefix with macro substitution; we do not use &m.dothers. As explained in Part I, entering &m.dothers will tell FoxPro to look for a memvar named *m* and to add to its expanded value the letters *dothers*, owing to the use of the period in macro substitution to denote continuation.

In the next step, we reactivate the READ window, placing it back on top. This is crucial since we must reinstate it as WONTOP() so the operator can immediately finish editing the record and then go ahead and take the action we have disallowed. Of course, since the ACTIVATE WINDOW command will not reopen a minimized window automatically and since we intend to restore the READ window for edit, if it is minimized we end by using ZOOM WINDOW NORM before executing RETURN .F. to prevent the READ from terminating.

Clearly, if FoxPro reaches the end of function Stop, READ DEACTIVATE has been triggered by an allowed event requiring no intervention in READ DEACTIVATE. We therefore RETURN .T. at the end of the function to terminate the screen program. The Foundation READ VALID event handler will control what happens next.

Alternative Ways of Writing the DEACTIVATE Clause

While the actions taken by procedure Stop, used as the READ DEACTIVATE clause of all MBS nonmodal screen programs (again, with one exception), will be standard to all FoxPro applications using nonmodal screen programs, the order in which they are taken can vary. In particular, many programmers will begin the DEACTIVATE clause, whether it is executed through a nested function or not, by testing to see if data editing was under way when READ DEACTIVATE was triggered. If so, they disallow the action and RETURN .F. before considering anything else. While this simplifies the logic of the IF statements used in READ DEACTIVATE, there are also specific situations that may require you to work in this way. The advantage of writing the DEACTIVATE clause as we have in procedure Stop is that it enables the operator to access desk accessories and non-READ (in the case of MBS, BROWSE) windows used by the screen program, even when data entry is under way. (We simply place MBS in what I have called a protected window mode using procedure Hide.) However, in more complex programs than MBS, data entry can also be enabled in BROWSE windows, and this may be contraindicated until data entry in the READ window is finished. Moreover, movement of the record pointer in a BROWSE window may lead to problems if the READ window holds memvars representing a record in the BROWSE table. (As you may recall from Chapter 6, this is a danger we must deal with in Saletrns.spr, where the operator can BROWSE sale items while in the middle of editing a specific sale item in the READ window. For the GATHER or REPLACE command to update the right record, we must always check the record number before executing the action in order to guard against the possibility that the record pointer has been moved.) In any case, if the screen programs in your application will include numerous BROWSE windows, you may want to disallow operator movement to any non-READ window or desk accessory—the action that places READ DEACTIVATE out of immediate reach—until the data entry/edit action is over, without qualification.

READ DEACTIVATE with Two or More READ Windows

The second alternative rendering of READ DEACTIVATE has to do with the handling of more than one READ window in a screen program. This is characteristic of screen programs that make use of a separate Control Push Button window, though much more complex screen programs can be devised using multiple READ windows, which can be layered on the screen. The one example of this we include in the MBS is Letters.spr, overseeing the entry and edit of letters placed in Letter.dbf. (Its function is to supply form letters used by the letter-printing program accessed through the Customer Database option on the Reports pulldown.) We show the screen used by Letters.spr once again in Figure 10.2.

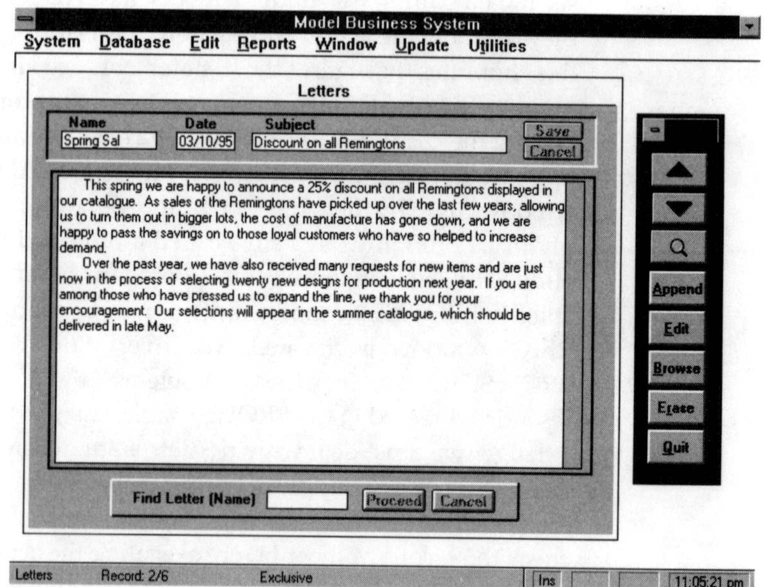

FIGURE 10.2:
Letters.spr uses two READ windows.

While we will see how to create screen programs with two or more READ windows in Chapter 11, we need only mention at this point that while the @ GETs in both windows are controlled by the same READ, movement from one READ window to the other will nonetheless trigger READ DEACTIVATE. Clearly, such movement should not be allowed to terminate the READ in the DEACTIVATE clause. Still, with respect to the DEACTIVATE clause we use to handle the situation, how it is written must depend not only upon what you want to enable the operator to do with the separate push button control window, but also upon how and the extent to which you use a separate control window in your screen programs. When separate Control Push Button windows are used, they are normally designed with a high degree of standardization. In fact, in most cases only one standard set of push buttons will be employed. When a specific screen program has need of other options, the additional push buttons are placed directly in the main (or data entry) READ window. Now, where a standard set of push buttons is used in most or all screen programs, it is hardly necessary to remove it from the screen when another screen program using it is executed. When this is the case, the DEACTIVATE clause, working in conjunction with the screen program cleanup code, must see to it that the Control Push Button window always remains open on the screen upon termination of the screen program. What this means, in turn, is that responsibility devolves upon the Foundation READ VALID clause to determine whether or not the window should actually be released and erased from the screen.

NOTE

Bear in mind, if you don't understand this already, that every screen program using the Control Push Button window will reexecute it. The overall action will be no different than when the operator selects an inactive READ window while working with another screen program. By leaving the Control Push Button window on the screen, we simply provide the illusion that the window is independent of the various screen programs that must reexecute it in order to use it and is a standard, separate component of the larger application. This, however, does not require us to always leave it in the same place. The READ ACTIVATE or WHEN clause can be used to reposition it with MOVE or ZOOM WINDOW.

The situation becomes a bit more complex when a standard set of push buttons is used but the window displaying them has more than one configuration—for example, one displaying them in a vertical column, as in Letters.spr, and another displaying them horizontally. Where this is the case, however, it is probably best and easiest just to release the Control Push Button window upon termination of each screen program, though you can of course go to pains to make the Foundation READ event handler test to see if the Control Push Button window still open on the screen is appropriate to the screen program it must launch next.

The other determinant in how you manage a Control Push Button window is, again, what you want the operator to be able to do with the window—a decision you must make when defining it with the Screen Builder's Window Type dialog. Shall the operator be allowed to minimize or close it? Certainly the operator should be able to move it; otherwise, we tend to diminish its potential functionality. For most applications, it will be sufficient to define the window as FLOAT NOCLOSE

NOMINIMIZE so the operator can move it but cannot close or minimize it. (Again, the DEFINE WINDOW keywords NOCLOSE and NOMINIMIZE prevent the Close and Minimize options from appearing in the window control box.) If this is how the window is defined (noting that its attributes do not affect which attributes you can use with the other READ windows), the Control Push Button window can be managed in the READ DEACTIVATE and ACTIVATE clauses in much the same fashion as we handle BROWSE windows in the MBS screen programs that use them, provided we don't place responsibility on the Foundation READ event handler to determine if and when the Control Push Button window is to be removed from the screen.

Looking at the DEACTIVATE clause used with Letters.spr, where the Control window is defined with FLOAT NOCLOSE NOMINIMIZE, we can see that there is not much to change in the writing of the DEACTIVATE clause—though here we reference our windows by name rather than with memvars.

```
IF UPPER(WONTOP()) $ "LETTERS CONTROL" AND WVISIBLE("LETTERS") ;
    AND NOT WMINIMUM("LETTERS")
    RETURN .F.
ENDIF
IF NOT WVISIBLE("LETTERS") AND NOT m.doit
    m.but2 = "Quit"
    RETURN .T.
ENDIF
IF WMINIMUM("LETTERS") AND NOT m.doit
    RETURN .T.
ENDIF
IF UPPER(WONTOP()) $ "CALCULATOR CALENDAR/DIARY PUZZLE HELP"
    DO hide WITH "LETTERS","CONTROL"
    RETURN .F.
ENDIF
IF m.doit
    DO alert WITH "Cannot change windows until editing "+ ;
        "is over.", "Press any key to continue."
    SHOW WINDOW control TOP
    ACTIVATE WINDOW letters
    IF WMINIMUM("LETTERS")
        ZOOM WINDOW letters NORM
        ENDIF
    RETURN .F.
ENDIF
RETURN .T.
```

The only key difference between the DEACTIVATE clause used with Letters.spr and function Stop, used with all MBS single READ window screen programs, is the first IF, which will be repeatedly executed whenever the operator switches between the two READ windows or when an action is taken in either window that sends the cursor to the other. Since either READ window can be safely activated without putting us out of touch with READ DEACTIVATE—in this, the Control window is very different from using a BROWSE, since deactivating it triggers READ DEACTIVATE—there is no need to put FoxPro in a protected window mode when WONTOP() changes from the Letters to Control window or back again.

However, before issuing RETURN .F., we must check to make sure that the Letters window has not been closed or minimized. (While we do not permit this with the Control window, we still enable these actions with the Letters window.) If either of these things has happened, we move on to the following IFs to determine what action will be taken. If the main (Letters) READ window has been closed or minimized, we allow the READ to terminate, provided that m.doit does not indicate that data edit is under way. (When the main READ window is closed and NOT m.doit, we change the value of m.but2 instead of m.but1 since the Control window actually includes two sets of push buttons, m.but1 and m.but2. It is m.but2, however, that is used when the Quit push button is selected.) This covers the only real differences between Letters.spr's READ DEACTIVATE clause and function Stop. Note, however, that while this DEACTIVATE clause is hard coded, using actual window names, it could be easily rewritten as procedure Stop2 and used with the DEACTIVATE clause of all screen programs using a Control window, though we must pass the procedure the names of more than one READ window along with the list of non-READ windows used by any given screen program.

Of course, if you allow the Control window to be closed or minimized (though I believe few programmers do this), you will have to write a more complex READ DEACTIVATE clause to supply FoxPro with instructions on how to behave when the Control window is closed or minimized. More instructions must also be added if release of the Control window is to be handled by the Foundation READ event handler. Again, with Letters.spr, we treat the Control window just as we treat our BROWSE windows upon screen program termination. We release it.

Mixing Nonmodal and Modal Screen Programs

As you are aware, the MBS includes both nonmodal and modal screen programs. The screen programs listed on the Database and Reports pulldowns are all nonmodal and can be launched one after the other in all the ways we described in detail in Chapter 6. The screen programs executed from the Update and Utilities pulldowns, however, make use of READ MODAL for several reasons. To begin with, the actions they execute are not ones that may be repeated over and over again. During a single session, they will be, at most, used once. Moreover, programs like Backup MBS Data Files or Update MBS Index Tags, both listed on the Utilities pulldown, will require use of all tables in a way that will be difficult to coordinate with the requirements of the nonmodal screen programs. Programs on the Update pulldown are no different. In any case, we would be ill-advised to allow the operator to leave such windows as that used by Generate Finance Charges floating about inactive on the screen since a few mistaken keystrokes or mouse moves could accidentally execute it when there is no real reason to do so.

Still, in writing the modal screen programs that will be used in an application that includes nonmodal screen programs, you must do more than simply add them to the system menu and execute them in the same way you execute the nonmodal programs—that is (in the case of the MBS), through the use of procedure Dospr. You must also decide whether modal screen programs that will completely alter the default database view—or run best if they are allowed to—should also go to the effort of restoring the prior database view to such an extent that it is reasonable or possible to leave inactive nonmodal READ windows on the screen.

In the case of most MBS modal screen programs, restoring the prior environment to such an extent is more work than it is worth. True, CREATE and RESTORE VIEW are available for resetting the default database view. We can also reexecute procedure Opendata in the main program, Bigbiz.prg. But if we leave inactive nonmodal READ windows about, the operator will also expect our program to return to a specific customer, sale, letter, and so on. This can be done, but why bother? In any case, to get around this difficulty, we work as follows. In the setup code of each modal READ program that must have free play with our tables—that is, before defining or activating the new READ window—we test the environment with IF NOT WONTOP() == "" to see if there are any open windows already present on the screen. If such windows are present, we use procedure Question to inform the operator that the selected program cannot be run without closing all open windows. They can then choose to proceed with or cancel the action. If they elect to proceed, we use CLEAR WINDOWS to remove all open windows before continuing with the program. If they cancel the program, we simply issue RETURN to terminate the program before it has altered the environment. Program control then returns to the Foundation READ VALID clause, where our event handler determines what happens next.

Final Comments on Event Handling in FoxPro Applications

We still have several chapters ahead of us, in Parts III and IV, where we examine the actual use of the Screen Builder and Report and Label Writers in creating the MBS screen programs controlling data entry and the production of reports. But in coming to the end of this chapter we have covered those aspects of FoxPro programming that are most difficult for would-be developers to master. You now know the fundamentals that go into writing fairly sophisticated windows applications, but it is important to remember that the programming style used in the MBS screen programs is somewhat limited with respect to what can actually be done—and deliberately so. In a Windows environment using a graphical interface there are many different programming styles that can be used. And while all involve varying use of tools, the majority of which you are already familiar with, to some extent we have gone no further than to examine their basic uses.

Regarding the demonstration programs supplied by Microsoft with FoxPro, while their event handlers will be no more complex than that employed by MBS (after all, the MBS follows their example, albeit with many variations), the MBS screen programs themselves are generally simpler than the FoxPro demonstration screen programs. This was necessary to ensure intelligibility when introducing the already complex within-window events that are overseen by READ's various clauses. However, now that you are at home with Foundation READs, event handlers, screen programs, and the various READ clauses and their functions, it is necessary to take another look at the FoxPro demonstration programs in order to observe how more elaborate screen programs than those offered by the MBS can be designed. You will then be in a position to choose your own style or vary it according to what works best with any given application, given what the application must accomplish and the amount of time you have to work on it.

NOTE

In Chapter 11 we outline an alternative programming style that many programmers find more useful when working with screen sets that include a separately defined Control Push Button window, though the style used by the MBS single READ window screen programs discussed in Part I will still suffice, with one modification.

PART 

Using the Screen Builder

CHAPTER

ELEVEN

Working with the Screen Builder

- Overview of the Screen Builder
- Selecting and manipulating objects
- Using the Screen Layout dialog
- Screen program architecture
- Adding and defining objects
- Generating the screen program
- Generating screen programs with multiple screen sets

The FoxPro built-in Screen Builder is a remarkable tool, though there are several factors that can make it difficult to master. First, the Screen Builder is used not just to design screens but to create entire screen programs, based upon organizational principles largely determined by the action of @ GET and READ and their many clauses. Second, unlike the process of system menu creation, there is no strict one-to-one relation between the screen design (.scx) files created with the Screen Builder and the generated (.spr) screen program. With a menu, we design a system menu and then generate the menu program, and that's that. With the Screen Builder, we can design one or more screen files, each defining one screen set, and then use the Edit Screen Set (or Generate Screen) dialog to instruct FoxPro to generate a screen program that combines the screen sets in a single program, as is done in the MBS with Letters.spr. (See Figure 11.1.)

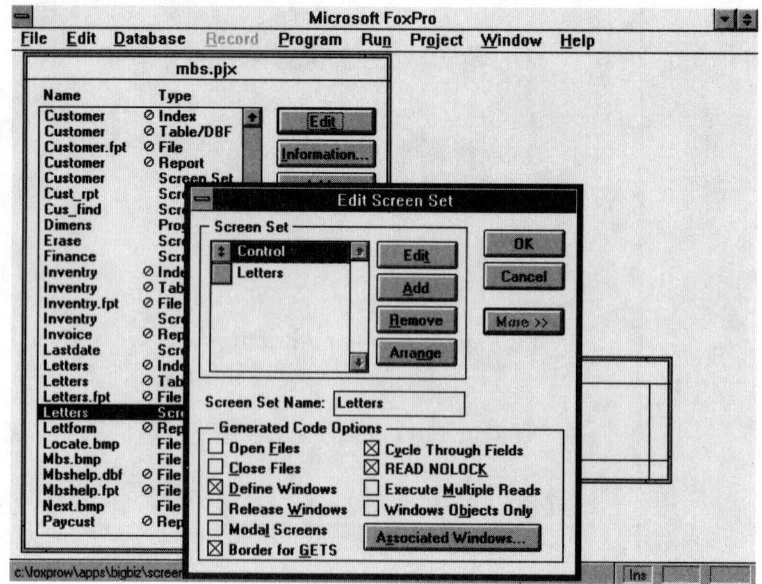

FIGURE 11.1:

Use the Edit Screen Set (or Generate Screen) dialog before generating a screen program to include one or more screen sets in the program.

Screens and Screen Sets

Screen files created with the Screen Builder will include one READ window. But they may also include instructions for using other non-READ windows, as is the case with Payments.scx, used to generate Payments.spr. For this reason, we refer to a screen file as defining a *screen set* rather than a READ window or screen program.

Third, there is the matter of how the screen program, or rather the screen set(s) it oversees, fits into the larger application environment. One look at the Edit Screen Set dialog's More options, also shown in Figure 11.1, is enough to discourage most novices. Indeed, despite the use of smooth dialog boxes and the like, to use the Screen Builder with any degree of sophistication you must already know what a screen program does and how every major command in it behaves.

The process of learning how to use the Screen Builder is vastly simplified if you do, in fact, know everything or nearly everything about the operation of screen programs in advance. Then using the Screen Builder becomes a routine affair. You just lay out the screen, fill in the required code snippets, and, after saving the screen file, fill in the Generate options and get FoxPro to trot out the finished screen program. All you need to know about the Screen Builder's interface is how its dialogs and tools are used to create screen programs quickly and easily to your own specifications.

Assuming you have already learned the ropes by reading Chapters 3 through 6 and Chapter 10, you are more than ready to take this approach to the Screen Builder. You already know the various READ clauses that must be used to control intra- and extra-window events. You are, moreover, aware of window attributes, such as MOVE, CLOSE, and MINIMIZE, and how they affect window events in larger applications. As for screen program architecture and the commands that bring them to life, only the former requires further explanation. For the rest, there is the matter of learning how to use the Screen Builder's window and layout editor to best effect.

We now begin filling in the blanks by reviewing the construction and generation of several MBS screen programs, beginning in this chapter with Customer.scx. This is the program used to generate Customer.spr, which oversees data entry and display of records in Customer.dbf (described in Chapter 3). Later in this chapter, we examine Payments.scx, used to generate Payments.spr, a screen program with two BROWSE windows, and Control and Letters.sdx, used to generate Letters.spr, a screen program with two READ windows. However, since our use of these screen files is intended to serve as a scaffold for demonstrating how the Screen Builder, screen files, and screen programs work, we will provide more details about these important FoxPro facilities as needed.

NOTE As with menu and project files, the screen files FoxPro uses to store information entered with the Screen Builder are FoxPro tables with a special structure and an .scx extension. (Memo field data is stored in a file with an .sct extension.) You will normally have no reason to open and manipulate a screen file, though advanced programmers will sometimes do this to make global changes to code snippets, for example through use of REPLACE. (See your FoxPro documentation for a list and description of screen file fields.)

Overview of the Screen Builder

When activated through the use of CREATE/MODIFY SCREEN in the Command window (or through selection of the Screen radio button when using the New File dialog), the Screen Builder opens the screen design window shown in Figure 11.2. It also adds the Object and Screen pulldowns to the FoxPro system menu.

NOTE As with the Menu and Project Manager, the screen design window will bear the title of the screen file being created or modified. When a screen file is being created, it bears the title Untitled.scx unless the Screen Builder was initiated, for example, with CREATE/MODIFY SCREEN and a file name was supplied. If the screen file is Untitled.scx, FoxPro will request a specific file name when you select Save As or Close from the File pulldown. (Save is disabled until the file is assigned a name other than Untitled.scx.)

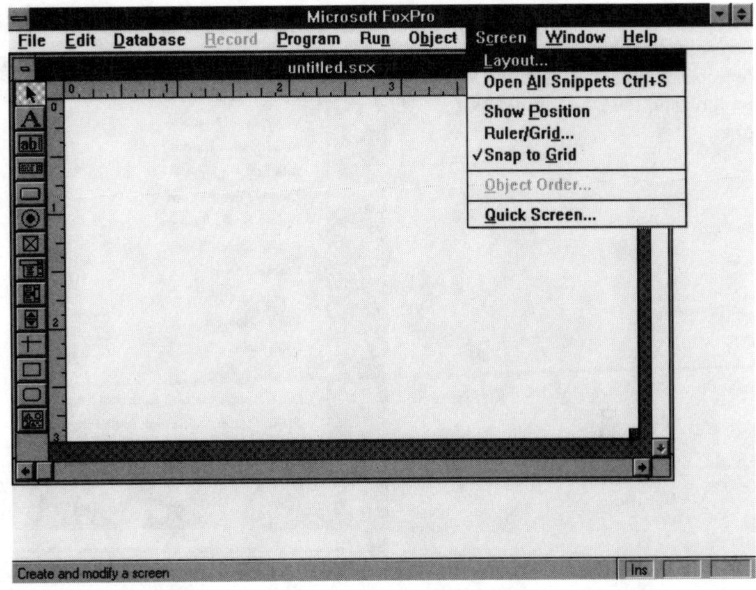

FIGURE 11.2:

When you start the Screen Builder, FoxPro opens a screen design window and adds the Object and Screen pulldowns to the system menu.

The screen design window is occupied by the WYSIWYG (what-you-see-is-what-you-get) layout editor, which includes an input screen bordered by a ruler on top and at the left, indicating input screen coordinates, and a toolbox. The toolbox provides a push button menu of @ SAY or @ GET objects we may place in the input screen. Each object is represented in the toolbox by an appropriate icon, which we refer to as a tool.

In Figure 11.3 I have placed text in the input screen next to each tool describing that tool's usage. Then, after selecting the last text object with the mouse, I opened the Object menu, which is described shortly. The one tool that has no description in Figure 11.3 is the selection pointer at the top of the toolbox. It is used to unselect an action initiated by clicking another tool or to unselect objects in the input screen previously selected with the mouse.

Bear in mind that clicking a tool will activate the mouse for placing only one object in the input screen. However, if you double-click a tool—it darkens quite noticeably when selected in this way—you can enter as many objects as you like before clicking the selection pointer at the top of the toolbox to unselect the tool.

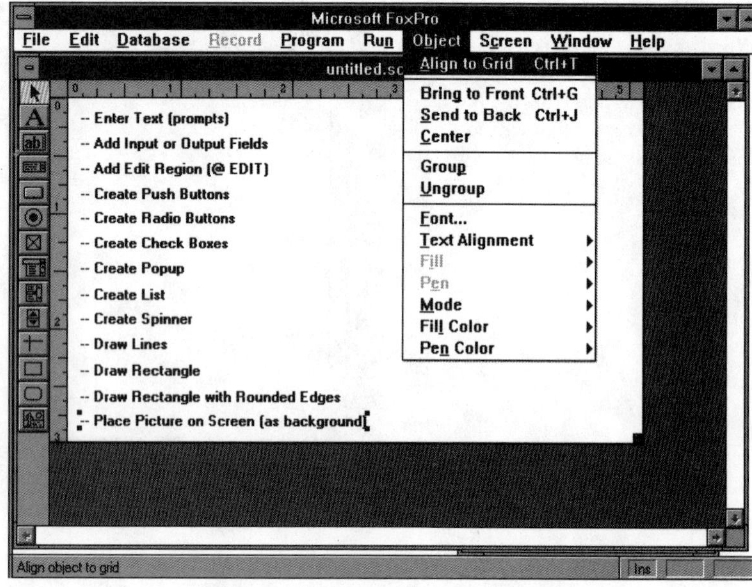

FIGURE 11.3:
Screen design window with text objects labeling buttons in the toolbox and the Object pulldown open

TIP

If you forget the function of a tool, just point to it with the mouse and hold down the left button. FoxPro will provide more information about the tool in the message line.

To place an object in the input screen, click the desired tool, move the mouse pointer to the appropriate position in the input screen, and click again. In the case of input/output fields, this opens the Field dialog, which we then use to specify an input or output field and to define @ GET or @ SAY clauses as needed. When we finish defining the object, FoxPro places it in the input screen, where we may move and size it as we please. @ GET push buttons, radio buttons, check boxes, and @ EDIT Character or Memo field editing regions are all handled in a similar fashion, though each uses a specific dialog. We will look at several of these dialogs as we use them to re-create the MBS screen files.

Positioning and Sizing the Input Screen Window

When you place objects in the input screen, they must always be entered in that portion of the input screen occupied by the mock (or model) READ window, which is anchored at coordinates 0,0 of the input screen. The mock window is readily sized by dragging on its bottom-right corner, though its size can also be adjusted with the Layout dialog, which we discuss later in this chapter. (When the mock READ window is made wider or longer than the input screen, the editor activates the scroll bars on the input screen's right and bottom borders so you can pan vertically or horizontally in the window.) Note that we do not position the window in the input screen—and to this extent, the layout editor is not quite WYSIWYG. Nor does the Screen Builder have a Try It option, as does the Menu Builder. Instead, we determine the position of the READ window when it is actually executed by a screen program using the Layout dialog, though we may also set the window's position before generating the screen program with the Generate Screen or Edit Screen Set's Arrange dialog.

Screen Programs with No Window or No Read

Note that while we must always work with a mock READ window when creating a screen file, it is not necessary to include the window in the actual screen program. In the Edit Screen Set dialog in Figure 11.1, you can see the Define Windows check box. If you uncheck this box, when FoxPro generates the screen program it will not include commands defining or activating the READ window specified in the corresponding screen file. This feature allows you to create screen programs that direct objects to an already active window or, more typically, to the FoxPro main window.

As mentioned in Chapter 8, we can also create screen programs that direct objects to a window but do not execute the READ command. This is done by placing the special screen file directive #NOREAD in the screen file's setup code. (We discuss #NOREAD and other screen file directives later in this chapter.) This feature allows us to use screen programs that immediately terminate after displaying objects in the active window—or in the FoxPro main window if the program doesn't define a window and no other user-defined window is active.

Owing to the various ways you can manipulate FoxPro's usage of a window and the READ command in a screen program, it is best to regard the creation of screen programs that use READ windows only as the Screen Builder's usual function.

The Object and Screen Pulldowns in Brief

As previously mentioned, whenever the screen design window is activated, the system menu is modified to include the Object and Screen pulldowns. The Object pulldown, shown in Figure 11.3, is used to change the color of objects, the thickness and color of lines and perimeter lines of boxes, the font used by text, @ SAY output fields, @ GET input fields, and @ GET controls using text prompts. It also allows us to select or unselect groups of @ GETs so we can change the attributes of several objects at once. (Groups of objects can also be selected with the mouse, as described later in this chapter.) All options used to alter object attributes open dialogs for selecting the desired attribute. We will encounter several of them when re-creating Customer.scx.

NOTE

Object pulldown options are enabled only when an object that can be altered is selected.

The Screen pulldown, shown open in Figure 11.2, contains options to

- Define the attributes, position, and size of the input screen's mock READ window
- Open text-editing windows for entering code snippets defining READ clauses and screen program setup and cleanup code
- Alter the appearance and behavior of the layout editor
- Adjust the order in which @ GETs placed in the mock READ window will be executed by the screen program
- Execute Quick Screen, when it is available

We discuss each of these options as we use them in re-creating our MBS screen programs.

Using the Clipboard with the Screen Builder

One of the virtues of the Screen Builder is the capacity to copy objects—complete with their full definitions and any associated @ GET or @ SAY clause code snippets—from one screen design window into another using the Clipboard.

> **NOTE**
>
> Though copied objects will always be pasted at the top of the mock READ window, you need not move objects already in the window out of the way. This is because pasted objects are automatically selected so you can immediately reposition them in the window as a group. However, objects can overlap one another in the window without loss of the ability to select and move any one of them, though you may need to alter their front-to-back order in the window to select an object covered by other objects.)

We will use this feature later on to select and copy objects in Customer.scx, including its push buttons, to the Clipboard in order to paste them into Payments.scx. You can also use this feature to get around the restriction on the use of Quick Screen. For example, you can issue CREATE SCREEN to open another screen design window and use Quick Screen to place objects in it. You can then use the Clipboard to transfer those objects or a selected group of objects to any other screen design window, whether or not its mock READ window already holds objects.

Setting Up and Saving the Environment

To make your work easier, the Screen Builder provides pick lists of fields in open tables. Quick Screen, for example, either makes use of all fields of the current table by default or provides a pick list of all fields of the current table along with a popup listing all available (open) tables. (The popup can be used to select another table, thereby changing the fields displayed in the field pick list.) The input field tool provides a similar pick list, though use of the list is optional since any variable name—even that belonging to a nonexistent field or memvar—can be entered as the input field name without error. However, when FoxPro has direct access to the table fields you place in the mock READ window (just as it must when you execute the finished screen program), it will be able to help you size the fields in the window and will also be able to verify any expressions included in the screen file that reference them.

Moreover, to make revising your screen files easier, the Screen pulldown Layout dialog includes a nested Environment dialog. The Environment dialog, which presents a simple set of push buttons, allows you to instruct FoxPro to save the environment—or rather, instructions specifying the current environment—in the screen file. This way, when you call the screen file for edit, for example, with MODIFY SCREEN, FoxPro can immediately replicate the environment it uses.

NOTE

Since Save Environment is the default environment setting, you need not use the Environment dialog unless you want to clear the environment instructions.

TIP

The Restore environment button is included in the Environment dialog in case you change the table view while editing a screen file and then wish to restore the environment. (Since you may open more than one screen file for edit at a time, Restore can be used to restore the environment used with a screen file when you reselect the window in which it is open.)

Screen Programs That Establish Their Own View

In the case of the MBS, we work with an application-level default table view, as explained in Chapter 6. All the tables required by our screen programs are already open and available for use before any screen program is executed. This, however, need not be the case. FoxPro can also use the environment instructions saved in a screen file when you generate a screen program to place commands in the screen program's setup code to replicate the view. (This includes setting all index tags and reestablishing any and all SET RELATIONs.) In Figure 11.1, note the Open Files and Close Files check boxes. (They are initially checked by default.) If the Open Files check box is checked, FoxPro restores the environment required by the screen file in the screen program. If the box is left unchecked, FoxPro does not place commands opening tables included in the screen file's environment in the screen program.

NOTE

Opening tables in a screen program does not otherwise affect the environment current when the screen program is executed. The screen program will not close other open tables, nor will it attempt to reopen a table if it is already open.

The Close Files check box can be checked to make the screen program close whatever tables it opens—and no others.

Clearly, if you save screen file environment instructions, you can use the Open Files and Close Files check boxes to create screen programs that are self sufficient with respect to the tables they use. This is preferable in smaller applications or in applications that do not use default views. It is also indicated when producing standalone screen programs. Because screen programs, in addition to opening and closing tables, will execute any FoxPro commands you care to place in a screen file's setup and cleanup snippets, you can, moreover, create screen programs that are self sufficient in every way.

Opening Tables While in the Screen Builder

Because the screen design window is nonmodal, you can open and close tables and otherwise alter the environment while the Screen Builder is active through use of the Command window or the Open or View dialog. There is no need to open all tables holding fields referenced in a screen file in advance, but doing so will often make your work more orderly and prevent you from having to cancel one or more Screen Builder dialogs in order to return to the design window to open a table. Whether or not you save the environment—or choose the Environment dialog to clear all environment instructions—will depend upon whether or not the screen program must open tables, in which case saving the environment is a necessity, or upon how much is to be gained by having FoxPro restore the environment each time you modify the screen file.

In the case of MBS screen files, we always save the environment of screen files used to execute data entry programs, though we do so for the sake of convenience when editing the screen files. Again, since we make use of an application-level default table view, we have no need to open or close files when we generate our screen programs. Opening files will be a waste of time since the tables will already be open when the screen programs are executed; and closing tables will be disastrous since doing so will alter the table view expected by all other programs in the system.

We begin the process of creating Customer.scx by opening Customer.dbf and Bizshare.dbf, the two tables referenced by Customer.scx, though only fields from Customer.scx are displayed in Customer.spr's READ window. (See Chapter 3 for a discussion of Bizshare.dbf's role in supplying Customer.spr with the last assigned Custno.) Since Customer.spr will function with Customer.dbf, we make it the currently selected table and then initiate creation of Customer.scx by executing CREATE SCREEN in the Command window or by selecting Screen when using the New File dialog.

Starting Out with Quick Screen

Like the Menu Builder, the FoxPro Screen Builder has a Quick Screen option that will immediately place all the fields of the current table—or a selection of its fields—in the mock READ window, provided the window is large enough to accommodate them all. What doesn't fit is simply left out. As with Quick Menu, the Quick Screen option is available only when the input screen is empty. This means that if we intend to use it, at least in the most convenient way, we must do so at the start.

Since our intention in creating Customer.scx is to represent all Customer.dbf fields in the READ window, we can put Quick Screen to good use. But before executing it, we must enlarge the READ window so it will accommodate Customer.dbf's many fields. Again, we do this by dragging the window's bottom-right corner with the mouse.

Note that when placing objects in the READ window, Quick Screen observes the window's current default settings for font and style. Initially, these will correspond to the Windows defaults—usually MS Sans Serif 8, Regular, for input fields and Bold for all prompt text. If you do not want to use the defaults, you can save yourself the trouble of manually changing the font and style of objects after Quick Screen has already placed them in the window by moving to the Layout dialog first and using the nested Font dialog to change the default font and style. The READ window's default settings for font and style are also used when you employ tools to add input and output fields and text to the window.

The availability of Quick Screen provides two alternative ways of proceeding in designing your data entry screen programs. As with Customer.scx (the creation of which we continue below, after examining several issues bearing on the Screen Builder's use of the current table environment), we can start with Quick Screen and then add, delete, modify, move, size, and replace text, input fields, controls, graphical objects, and the like as we go, using the toolbox, mouse, and system menu. Or we can start with an empty window and rely upon the toolbox and/or the Clipboard to place our objects on the screen. The easiest way in any instance will depend upon what's faster.

Using the Quick Screen Dialog

Selecting Quick Screen from the Screen pulldown opens the dialog shown in Figure 11.4. It attests to the sophistication of the Screen Builder. First of all, we can choose between two different formats using the picture buttons at the top of the dialog, the first specifying the use of multiple columns of fields and the second a single column of fields. Also, we can use the check boxes to determine whether FoxPro adds field name titles (@ SAY prompts) to the window for each field it adds.

NOTE

If no table is current when you select Quick Screen, FoxPro will automatically access the Open Files dialog so you can open the desired table. Unlike the input/output field tool, Quick Screen can do nothing without an open table.

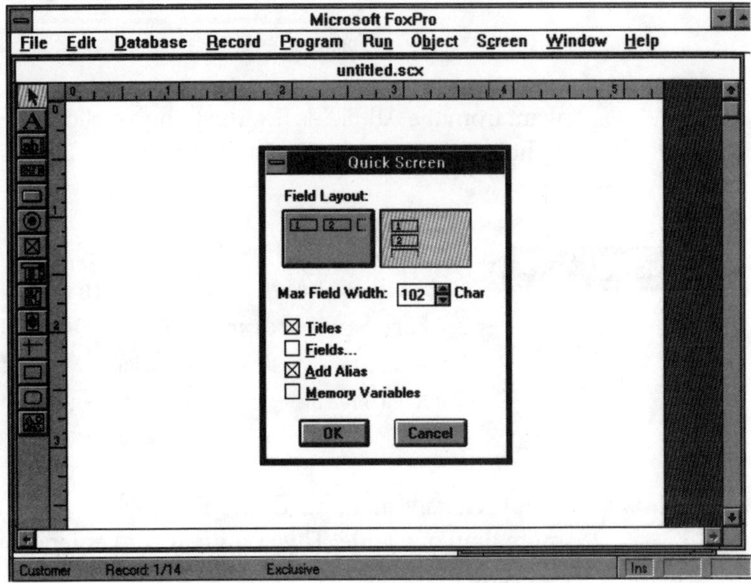

FIGURE 11.4: Use the Quick Screen dialog to place input fields (or memvars) and titles in the screen layout for any or all fields of open tables.

Moreover, unlike Quick Menu, Quick Screen doesn't put us in an all-or-none situation with respect to our selection of fields. All fields of the currently selected table is only the default Quick Screen setting. We can, for example, click the Fields check box to access the Field Picker dialog, shown in Figure 11.5, and choose the fields we

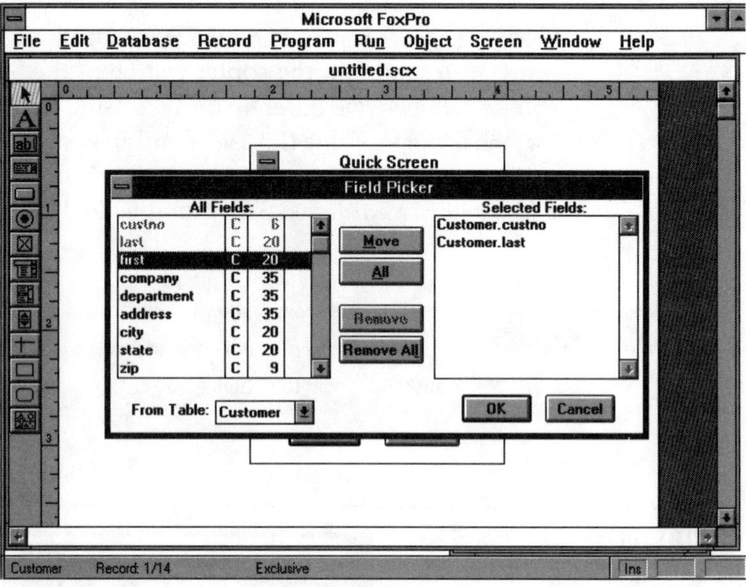

FIGURE 11.5: Use the Field Picker dialog to select the fields Quick Screen places in the screen design from one or more open tables.

want from the All Fields list. (Just double-click a desired field or click it once to highlight it and then press the Move button to place its name in the Selected Fields list.)

> **NOTE** The one failing of the Field Picker is that you cannot change the order of fields in the Selected Fields list. The order in which you choose them is the order in which Quick Screen will place and order them in the READ window. However, there's little reason to worry about order since all fields can be easily repositioned and reordered once they are placed in the input screen.

As previously mentioned, the Field Picker can also be used to select fields from more than one table. This is a great convenience when designing input screens for data entry and display of records in a multi-table view. However, to take advantage of this feature you must open all the tables from which you want to choose fields before selecting Quick Screen.

When more than one table is open, the Field Picker's From Field popup lists all available (open) tables. Select a different table from the popup, and FoxPro selects it as the current file and places its fields in the All Fields list. They can then be added to the Selected Fields list. To make Quick Screen select input fields for all fields listed in the Selected Fields list rather than all fields of the current table, just quit the Field Picker with OK instead of Cancel.

NOTE

The Selected Fields list always includes alias prefixes. This, however, has no bearing on Quick Screen's use of alias prefixes with the @ GET fields it places in the input screen; it only enables Quick Screen to find each field so it can properly size the input fields, whether or not it names their alias.

Use the Quick Screen Titles check box to instruct FoxPro to place field name prompts in the mock READ window just to the left of each input field. Titles are text objects, no different than those you enter manually using the text tool. In the screen program they turn up as @ SAY commands. Since you can add, alter, move, or delete text objects to your heart's content, you can use the Titles option even if you must change a good number of the titles. Like all fields of the current file, Titles is a Quick Screen default.

NOTE

Because FoxPro displays the name of each input field placed in the READ window directly in the object, there is no need for titles to keep track of which input field is which. This is readily apparent when you look at the screen.

The Add Alias check box, also checked by default, controls whether or not table fields placed in the READ window will be referenced in the screen program using alias names. This is required when the screen program must reference fields in unselected tables in a multi-table view but is unnecessary when only the current table is used.

Finally, we come to the Memory Variables check box, which is used to instruct FoxPro to substitute memvars for the selected Quick Screen fields by prefixing each field name with the m. memvar prefix. This way we can more easily create screen programs that keep table fields at arm's length from the operator by enabling data entry to sets of memvars instead. This last feature fits in precisely with the strategy we followed in designing the MBS screen programs, as discussed in Chapters 3 through 6. And it is clearly present in Quick Screen for the purpose of supporting screen programs relying on SCATTER and GATHER MEMVAR to shuttle data between the input field memvars and the data fields they represent.

The maximum display size, displayed in the spinner above and to the right of the Quick Screen check boxes, indicates the maximum number of characters in the currently selected font that will fit in one row of the mock READ window. This number can be decreased to reduce the default sizes assigned input fields (which use maximum display size only when their width is greater than or equal to it), but you cannot increase it without first increasing the width of the mock READ window. It is most typical to arrange input fields in a single column when executing Quick Screen, emulating the default table field format used with APPEND and EDIT/CHANGE, so the maximum display size need be of no concern as long as it is ample to accommodate the largest selected field, optionally accompanied on the left by a field name title and a delimiting space.

However, if you want Quick Screen to arrange the input fields and their titles, if chosen, in multiple columns, be aware that the number of columns FoxPro uses will depend upon how many columns of the maximum display size will fit in the mock READ window as currently drawn in the input screen. If there is insufficient space for more than one column, FoxPro uses only one column, just as though the multiple-column format had not been selected. If there's enough room for two, it arranges the fields in two columns, placing the first field in the first column, the second in the second column, the third in the first column, and so on. If you want multiple columns, you must therefore pay more attention to the maximum display size figure—though there is nothing to prevent you from arranging input fields into columns after Quick Screen has already placed them in the READ window.

With respect to the use of Quick Screen in creating Customer.scx, we select the picture button specifying a single-column format, ignore the Fields dialog (since we want all fields of the current table), and select the Titles and Memory Variables check boxes. We then press OK to produce the Quick Screen shown in Figure 11.6.

We now turn our attention to moving, sizing, and rearranging the objects until we find what we believe to be the best arrangement. We may at any time add new objects—for example, the two sets of push buttons required by Customer.scx—or begin entering the @ GET clauses used by the input fields, as described in Chapter 3.

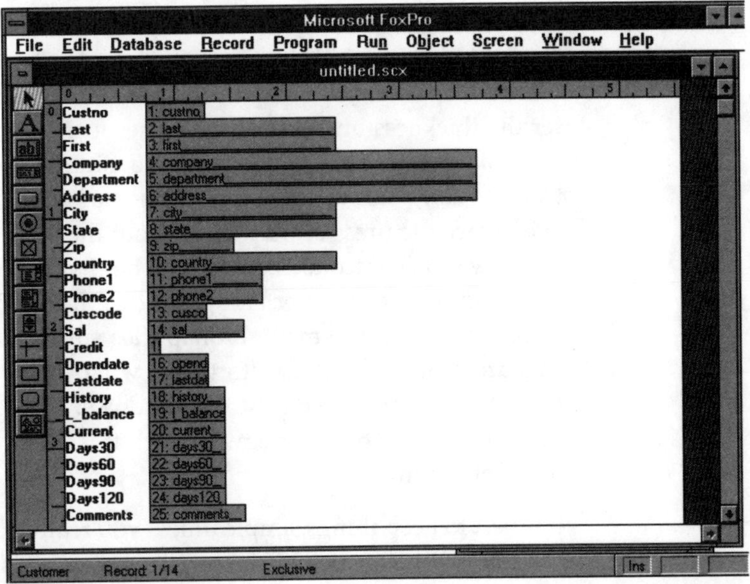

FIGURE 11.6: We begin the creation of Customer.scx by using Quick Screen to place titles and input fields in the screen design window for all fields of Customer.dbf.

But it is usually best to think about the position and sizes of objects first since finding the best arrangement for input fields may take some experimentation. As long as you don't perform other work, if you are dissatisfied with what you have done you can easily start again from scratch by choosing Select All from the Edit pull-down and pressing the Del key to erase all objects from the window before trying Quick Screen again.

Designing the READ Window

When it comes to designing the READ windows that will be used to oversee data entry to the key tables in an application, every freedom (even ones you probably cannot imagine) is yours. The mouse can be used to drag any object anywhere in the window. Once selected with the mouse, input fields can be sized and their font, fill, and pen color changed. You can even use a different font and style for every data value displayed on the screen, though doing so can make the screen display harder to read.

Text objects can be just as rigorously exercised. Changing their font and pen color can have dramatic effects. Moreover, when you use the toolbox, graphical objects can be placed in the window to set off other objects. With respect to rectangles, which we draw on the screen with the mouse, we can give them distinct fill colors and alter the thickness and color of the lines forming their borders. The thickness and color of lines can also be altered. Quite aside from the more pragmatic array of controls we can place in the window, each of which has its aesthetic appeal, we can even place pictures (bitmap files) about the screen, sizing them as we please. The window's background color, too, can be changed. You can select a picture (bitmap) file to serve as wallpaper background. You can even employ a map of the world, included among the many bitmap files supplied by Microsoft with FoxPro, as a backdrop for the worldly efforts that will take place as data is input to the @ GETs that sit on top of it in your READ windows. And you can use the map to wallpaper the main application window, though it is likely to clutter the display and make data fields harder to read.

It is best to keep things simple unless you really have something to gain by executing fancy displays. In a business environment it is good to be smart, but smartness must be applied to the end of making things easy on the operator.

In the MBS, we keep things simple by adopting the standard layout, font, and color schema that is readily apparent in the Customers window. Following the Windows defaults, font is uniformly MS Sans Serif, 8, Regular, for all data values and, with few exceptions, Bold for all text objects and push button labels. Owing to the use of MS Sans Serif, a proportional font that makes good use of available space without being too small to be easily legible, our READ window will be wide enough, for example, to display the input fields for name—Last, First, and Sal (salutation)—on the same row and still leave room on the right for a set of control push buttons, provided we reduce the default size Quick Screen assigns the input fields, as we can without running into difficulties. (See Figure 11.7.)

However, to help highlight the data in the READ window, we change the READ window's background color to light gray, the fill color of all input fields to white, and separate all input fields so that each is distinctly set off against the gray background.

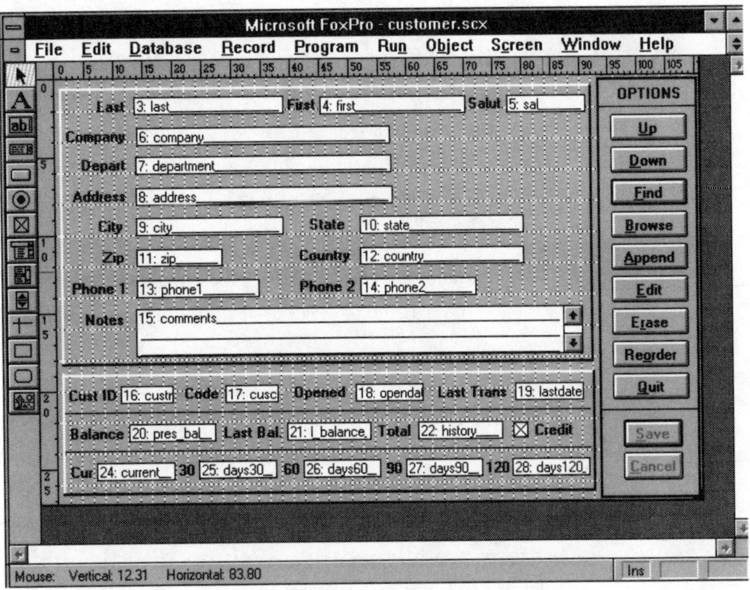

FIGURE 11.7:

Since we use a proportional font with Customer.scx's input fields, we can reduce the size of most character input fields to create a more attractive form.

NOTE

Input field borders are specified not through use of the Screen Builder but, prior to generation of the screen program, by checking the Generate Screen or Edit Screen Set More dialog's Borders check box. (Again, see Figure 11.1.) We use Borders with all MBS screen programs to place the thin black borders around each input field.

The data values displayed in the Customers window fall into two sets, one devoted to name and address and personal information, the other devoted to account information. Moreover, we render the overall display easier to read by placing the two sets of values in distinct panels, which are formed not with rectangle objects as such but with distinct line objects that are arrayed to form rectangles. Within each panel, input fields are arranged in hierarchical or logical order. In the case of account data, they are also further subdivided in the panel according to function, using lines with less thickness than those used to form the panel.

TIP

We use lines instead of rectangle objects to form panels since we can choose a different pen color and thickness for each line. This is how the 3-D effect is achieved. (Rectangle objects use only one pen color.) For example, in the Customers window two of the intersecting lines (used to form a rectangle) are assigned the color black, while the opposite lines use a pen color of white. Bear in mind, however, that rectangles formed in this way cannot be assigned a distinct fill (background) color because they are not true rectangle objects. It is nonetheless possible to place line objects on top of a rectangle to create 3-D panels with fill colors.

Another characteristic feature of the MBS data entry screen programs, with the exception of Letters.spr, is the use of two standard sets of push buttons set directly in the READ window, one to control screen program action and another to save or cancel an append or edit action. When space permits, the Save and Cancel push buttons are aligned in a column directly underneath the control push buttons, which are vertically arranged and set off in a rectangle to the right of the READ window. This is our basic design.

In the following sections, we show how to achieve these basic effects. In so doing, we touch upon the great range of options open to you when designing your own input screens. Again, the order in which you proceed in designing your READ windows is not set in stone. Most actions can be taken in any order, and in many cases you will find it necessary to make repeated adjustments to the size and position of objects. This is to be expected. We nonetheless present the operations required to create the Customers window, starting out from the Quick Screen shown in Figure 11.6, in separate sections to facilitate discussion.

Selecting Window Background Color

To change the READ window's background, select the Screen Layout dialog from the Screen pulldown and click the Color button. This opens the Screen Color dialog shown in Figure 11.8, though, rendered in grayscale, the screen shot scarcely indicates the available colors displayed in the rectangular Background color boxes.

Note that the default screen color is Automatic, as indicated in Figure 11.8 by the heavy selection border around the Automatic color box. The Automatic setting instructs FoxPro to use the current Windows color setting for window background

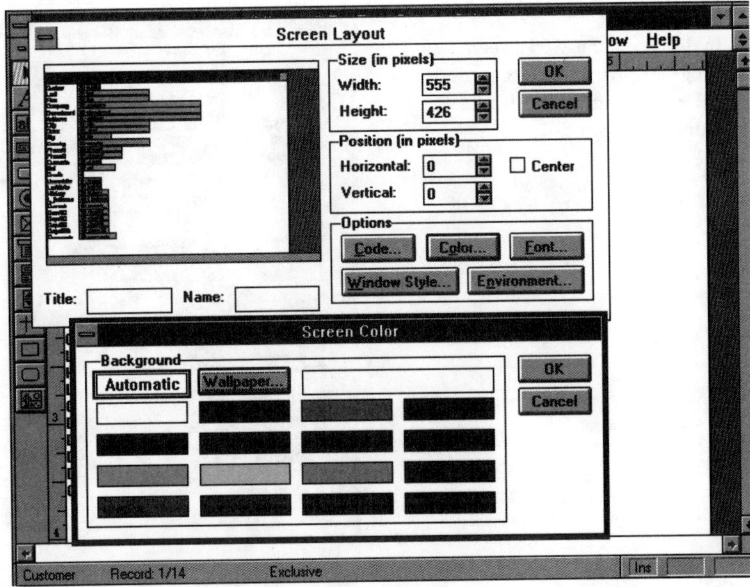

FIGURE 11.8: Use the Screen Color dialog to select a background color or wallpaper for the READ window.

color. If you don't have a particular color schema in mind for your application's main screen programs, it is best to stick with Automatic. This way, window color can be selected or altered later using the Windows Color dialog.

NOTE The MBS dialogs, unlike the nonmodal (main) READ windows, use the automatic settings not just for window color but also for input field fill and pen color.

However, following the color scheme selected for the MBS main READ windows, we click light gray to select it and then press OK twice—once to close the Screen Color dialog and again to close the Layout dialog. Our READ window background color will now be the same as the default (Automatic) input field fill color—light gray—as shown in Figure 11.9.

Using a Wallpaper Background

Though we do not do this in the MBS, you can select and use a bitmap file to supply the READ window with a background color pattern or picture through use of the

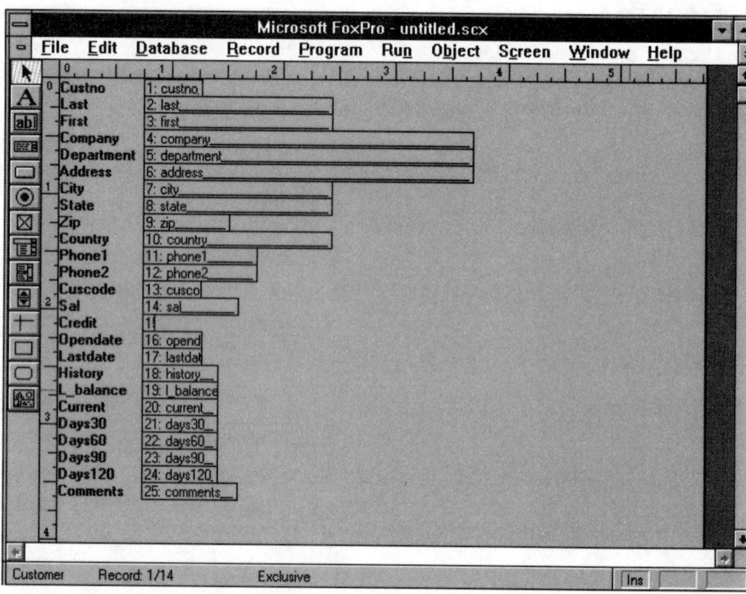

FIGURE 11.9:

In designing the MBS screen programs, we use a background color of light gray for all data entry READ windows.

Screen Color dialog's nested Wallpaper dialog. We might, for example, use the Wallpaper dialog to select and open the bitmap file, MBS.bmp, employed in the MBS sign-on message, as a background for our READ window. To save space, we show the effects of this selection in Figure 11.10 with the Wallpaper dialog still on the screen.

The size of each sheet of wallpaper is determined by the size in pixels of the bitmap file. Since MBS.bmp is smaller than the READ window, FoxPro must use several sheets to cover the window. You can alter the size of the wallpaper by modifying the size of the bitmap file, though this cannot be done directly in the Screen Builder. (The Screen Builder will size and clip pictures or General fields placed in the READ window, but not wallpaper.) You must rescale the bitmap file with the Windows Paintbrush program or with some other bitmap utility. For these reasons, wallpaper bitmaps using color patterns are generally easier to handle.

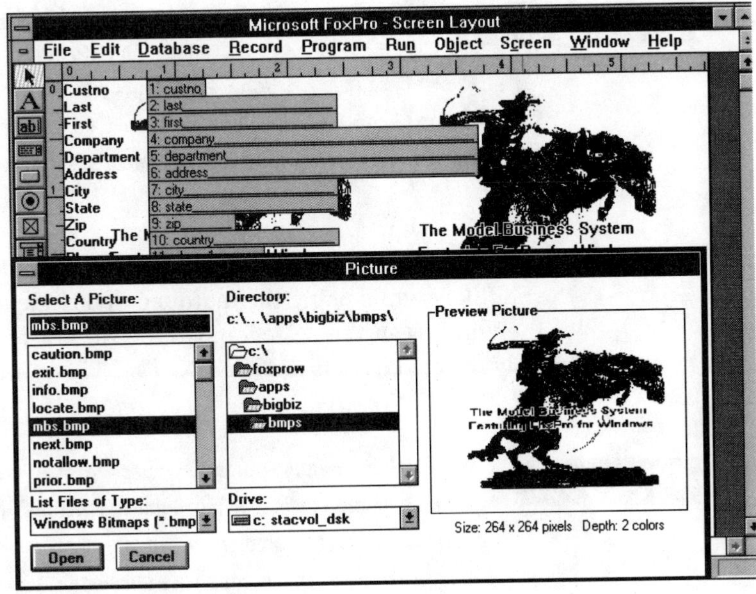

FIGURE 11.10:

Use the Wallpaper dialog, accessed through the Screen Color dialog, to select a bitmap file as a wallpaper window background.

Selecting and Manipulating Objects

To manipulate an object you must first select it by clicking it with the mouse. (Selection handles will appear at the corners of the object and around its sides.) Several objects can be selected at once by holding down the Shift key and clicking each object in turn. (To unselect one of several objects, Shift-click it again.)

Groups of adjacent objects can be more readily selected by drawing a box around them with the selection marquee. Position the mouse outside an object in one corner of the area where the objects to be selected are arranged. Press and hold down the mouse button while drawing the mouse to a position outside (or on) the object in the opposite corner of the rectangle. (The mouse pointer assumes the shape of a hand with a pointing finger, and a rectangular box formed with a dotted line appears to indicate the region included in the selection.) When you release the mouse button, the selection marquee disappears, leaving all objects placed within it—and all those across which its dotted line passed—selected.

NOTE

Use of the selection marque must be initiated while the mouse is not pointing to a specific object because pressing the mouse button when the mouse is pointing to an object signals FoxPro to select that object only. However, the selection made with the marquee can be completed with the mouse positioned directly on an object because FoxPro knows what action is intended.

The selection marquee can also be used to select additional objects. Just hold down the Shift key while using the marquee to include additional objects in other areas of the window in the selection. (If you do not hold down the Shift key, the previously selected objects are released.)

NOTE

The selection marquee can also be used to invert the selection of objects in any given region of the window. If you hold down the Shift key while using the marquee, when you complete the action, all objects previously selected in the region covered by the marquee are unselected, while those objects previously unselected are selected.

Any and all selected objects are released by clicking outside any selected object or by clicking the mouse pointer in the toolbox.

TIP

To select all objects present in the READ window at once, use the Edit pulldown's Select All option.

Grouping and Ungrouping Objects

When several objects are selected, you can use the Object pulldown's Group option to formalize their selection as a group and to reorder the input field objects so they will be executed in the screen program in the order in which they were selected before use of the Group option. (The order of the first object selected for inclusion in the group remains unchanged. The other objects are reassigned order numbers that follow it.)

NOTE

The reordering of input fields in a group should not be regarded as final. The Screen pulldown Object Order dialog is usually used before finishing a screen set to establish the final order. In general, the use of Group to reorder objects just helps to make the final reordering of objects easier.

Once objects are included in a group, unselecting them with the mouse does not disrupt their group relation. If you subsequently select any of the objects included in the group with the mouse, FoxPro selects the entire group. Again, to break the group relation so the fields can be moved, sized, or assigned different attributes individually, select the group and use the Object pulldown's Ungroup option.

Selecting Object Attributes

To change the fill color of our input fields to white so they will stand out clearly against the gray background, we choose the Object pulldown's Fill Color dialog after using the selection marquee as described above to select all input fields but no titles (text objects) for manipulation. Figure 11.11 shows the result of this selection with the Fill Color dialog still open on the screen.

The Fill Color dialog is also available, when a rectangle is the selected object, for choosing a distinct color for the object's background. With respect to the finished Customers window, the only rectangle on the screen is that used to set off our two sets of push buttons. When developing the MBS, I initially selected the rectangle and used dark green as a fill color. The use of grayscale screen shots in this book required me to return the fill color to its default Automatic setting, though the green panel will make the READ window more appealing.

TIP

When specifying a fill color for rectangles, objects appearing within the rectangle may disappear from view in the window. They are covered by the opaque fill color of the rectangle. To make them reappear, select the rectangle and use the Object pulldown's Send to Back option to place the rectangle behind the other objects. They will then reappear in the window. (The Object pulldown's Send to Back and Send to Front options control the order in which the @ commands executing each object are executed in the finished screen program.)

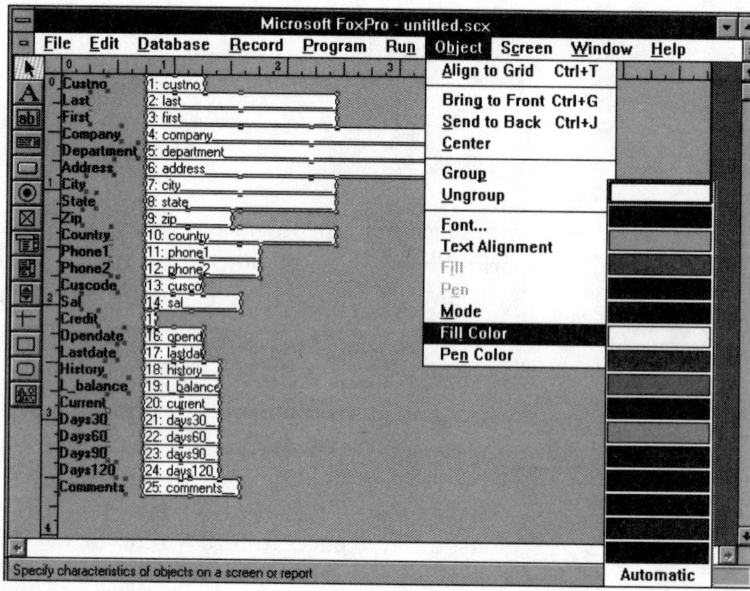

FIGURE 11.11:
The Fill Color dialog, selected from the Object pulldown, can be used to pick a distinct fill color for the selected objects. Here, white is selected as the fill color of all input fields.

Though we do not use it in the Customers window, the Pen Color dialog is similarly used to control the color of lines, rectangle borders, and text, including that of the data values displayed in input fields.

NOTE

Like the Screen Color dialog, both the Fill Color and Pen Color dialogs (the latter used to control the color of lines and text) include an Automatic option. This is the default selection. It instructs FoxPro to use the Windows default color setting for fill or pen color.

Other object attributes that are subject to change include text and input field font, the fill pattern of rectangles, the pen thickness of lines and boxes, and the alignment and spacing (text alignment) of text objects. We will have occasion to use some of the Object pulldown dialogs controlling these attributes, but in general it is best for you to experiment with them on your own; hands-on instructions are likely to be more tedious than what they explain.

NOTE

Text alignment options—Center, Left and Right Justify, Single, 1 1/2, and Double Space—are available only when a text object is selected. Center, Left and Right Justify, moreover, will have a noticeable effect only when the text object is wider than the characters displayed, owing to the use of spaces. Spacing options, for their part, are useful only when a text object includes one or more Returns, continuing the object on subsequent rows immediately beneath the first, in a column.

Still, it is worth remarking that the Text Alignment option can be gainfully employed, for example, with an enlarged, bold, or italicized font and a distinct pen and/or fill color to place headings or titles for groups of input fields in prominent display in the window. However, if you just need to center a text object in the window, the Object pulldown's Center option will do this automatically. It can also be used to center any other selected object in the window.

Selecting Mode

Another Object pulldown option we do not make use of in the MBS is Object Mode. Object Mode can be Opaque, the default setting, or Transparent. If you select Transparent, whatever objects are beneath the selected object will be visible. This is often employed, when displaying several objects on top of a rectangle with a distinct fill color, to use that color as the objects' background without having to define a fill color for each object. It can also be used to make objects use the screen's color or wallpaper as their background.

Positioning and Sizing Objects

Having established our basic color scheme for the Customers window, as shown in Figure 11.11, we can begin the process of moving the Quick Screen input fields and titles, where the latter correspond to our needs, into position. When the field name title is unsuited for use in the final screen, we just click it to select it and then press the Del key to erase it. Titles, as text objects, can also be edited by selecting them with the text tool.

TIP Objects erased from the input screen can be recovered with the Edit pulldown's Undo Edit option. Redo Edit is also available.

To begin arranging our input fields, we will need to open up free space at the top of the window. This is easily done by selecting all objects at once with the selection marquee, as described above, or with the Edit pulldown's Select All option and then using the mouse to drag the objects down and to the right in the READ window—though the READ window must of course be large enough to do this.

TIP While the arrow keys can also be used to move selected objects in the window, use of these keys is normally reserved for making final position adjustments. This is because each press of an arrow key moves the selected objects only 1 pixel in the indicated direction at a time.

Once we have freed up space at the top of the window and cleared the selection by clicking the mouse outside the selected objects or by clicking the mouse pointer in the Toolbox, we can begin using the mouse to drag our input fields and titles into place (or out of the way) as suggested in Figure 11.12.

Note that when several objects are selected, moving any one of them moves them all without affecting unselected objects. To move an individual object you must either unselect the others or unselect all objects and reselect the one you want to move. If the objects are grouped through use of the Object pulldown's Group option, you must ungroup the objects before you can select them on an individual basis.

Sizing Input Fields with Proportional Fonts

As should be clear from Figure 11.12, the input fields representing m.last, m.first, m.salut, m.company, and m.department—all of which display text in the selected font identifying them by object order and name—take up far more space than they are allowed in the finished Customers window. We can reduce the size of these input fields without fear of making them too small for the data values they must display; double-click the text tool and type in strings of numbers just above the input

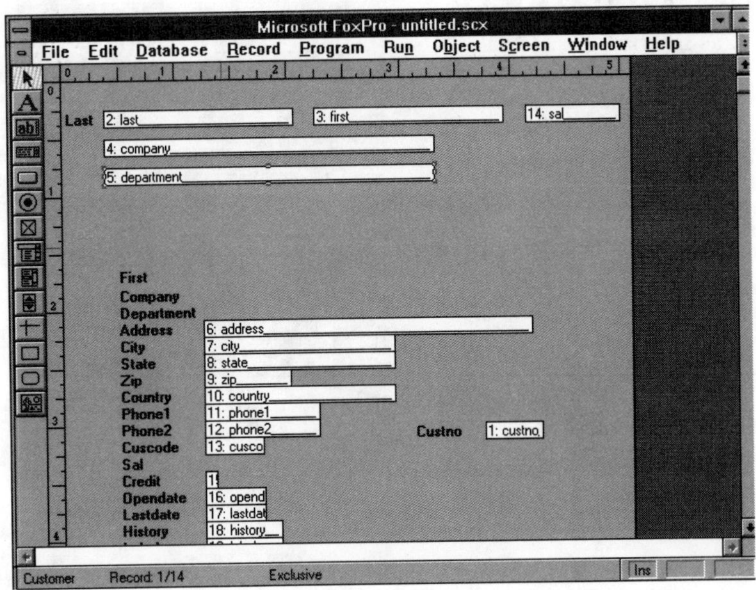

FIGURE 11.12:
After executing Quick Screen, we move all input fields and titles down in the window and then use the mouse to reposition them as we want.

fields, indicating the typical width (in characters) of the table fields they represent. This has been done in Figure 11.13. As you may recall, the width of Customer.last is 20, while the width of Customer.company is 35.

The reason for the disparity is simple. The size requirements of different characters in a proportional font, and especially of upper- and lowercase letters, vary so tremendously that a field sized to accommodate all uppercase *W*'s—one of the largest characters in any proportional font—will be three times larger (to make a guess) than will be required by character data using only lowercase letters. Of course, if you use a monospace font, the size of input fields (unless you have reason to change this) will be exactly right for any and all data entries, be they in upper- or lowercase characters. But when using proportional fonts, size becomes an issue; reserving space for a string of uppercase *W*'s will waste a great deal of space in the window, when name, address, and the like will include only a few uppercase characters. Since FoxPro automatically makes input fields displaying character or memo data horizontally scrollable, we are free to reduce their size to correspond to the data values we actually expect them to display. If and when a data value is too large for the display, the operator can scroll in the input field (or Edit region) to view what FoxPro can't display.

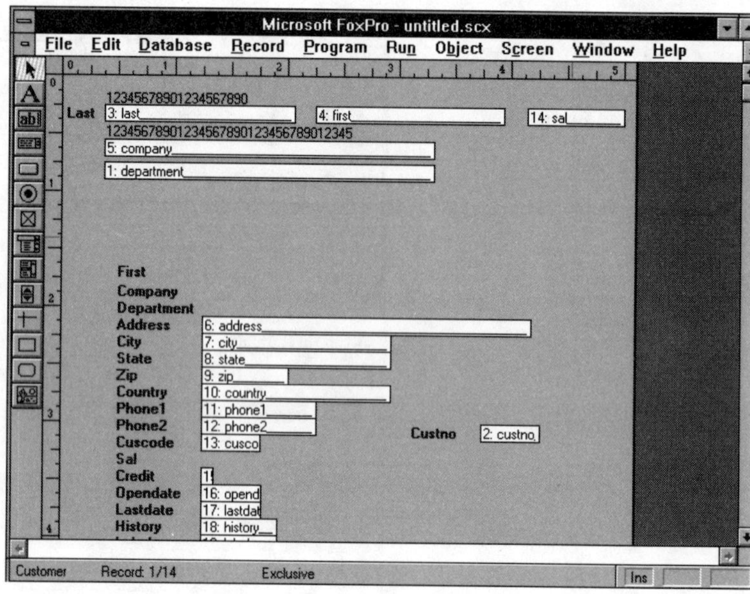

FIGURE 11.13:

As an aid in sizing input fields using a proportional font, place a text object formed with as many characters as must be displayed in each input field above or below the input field.

When we execute Quick Screen (without so reducing the maximum field size as to prevent FoxPro from assigning default sizes to input fields) or use the input field tool, FoxPro determines input field size by multiplying each table field's width by the average size of characters in the font, calculated in pixels. That the set of uppercase characters is included in the calculation is what makes the default field sizes generally larger than they need be. Thus, when we begin arranging our input fields on the screen, we reduce the sizes of Character and Memo fields when we have something to gain by it—or just to prevent the input fields from appearing disproportionately large with respect to the data that will be entered or displayed in them. In the case of the Customers window, for example, we manage to arrange the input fields for m.last, m.first, and m.salut, along with their titles, in a single row at the top of the window—and still leave room for the push buttons—by reducing their size.

TIP

If you assign input fields the same fill color as the selected screen color (or make them transparent) and do not select the Border check box when generating the screen color, the size of the input fields will not be apparent to the operator until they are selected with the cursor. This is useful if you want to disguise input field sizes so the data they display will not be set off from other objects in the window, including the titles.

Sizing of input fields and, indeed, of all objects is remarkably easy. When you click an input field or drag it with the mouse, selection markers, also known as handles, appear at each of its corners and on all sides, as shown in Figure 11.12, where the input field for m.department is selected. Once the field is selected, you can drag the corner handles to increase or reduce the field's size or drag the handles on its top or bottom to increase or decrease the number of rows it occupies. The sizing of graphical objects and even of pictures is handled in exactly the same way.

NOTE

The size of objects can also be increased or decreased a pixel at a time with Shift+→ and Shift+←, respectively, though this method is generally used only when making final adjustments.

Sizing Numeric and Date Input Fields

When a proportional font is used, FoxPro generally makes input fields displaying numeric and date values larger than necessary as well. However, greater care must be taken when reducing their display size; FoxPro will display a series of asterisks in an input field when it is too small to display a numeric value. This is intended to prevent the operator from mistaking what appears as the entire value. With respect to dates, no such measures are taken, but it will be a great inconvenience if the operator must move to a Date field and scroll within it to learn the date. In contrast, the *Inc.* or *Co.* at the end of a Company field is likely to have less significance than the last bytes of a date.

TIP

A good way to estimate the size requirements of Numeric and Date fields when a proportional font is used is to place a string of *6*s, formed with as many characters as the width of the table field, just over the input field. Since *6* will be the largest numeric character in the font, this will keep you from accidentally making the input fields too small.

Using Snap to Grid

When you begin using the Screen Builder, the Snap to Grid option, available on the Screen pulldown, is selected. FoxPro detects the position of each object placed in the READ window through use of a grid, the row and column coordinates of which are measured in units of pixels. (The number of pixels in each row or column unit normally corresponds to the selected ruler setting, which we describe in a moment, though the units can be manually set.) The function of Snap to Grid is simple. When you move objects with the mouse instead of moving them pixel by pixel, FoxPro actually moves them from grid coordinate to grid coordinate. For the most part this is useful when you need to position objects on the same row or in a column because FoxPro snaps each moved object into position in the grid. However, such action can also get in the way of placing objects exactly where you want them. When this is the case, you can unselect Snap to Grid using the Screen pulldown or select and move the object with the arrow keys, which always move selected objects 1 pixel at a time in the indicated direction.

Orienting Objects with Show Position

When you are making final adjustments to object positions, it is often helpful to select the Screen pulldown's Show Position option. When this option is selected, the FoxPro message line reports the mouse position or the top, bottom, left, and right position of a selected object in the grid. For example, with Show Position in effect, objects that must be aligned in a column can be selected one by one and moved pixel by pixel with the ← and → keys until they all share the same starting (left) position. Objects that must be aligned on the same row can be positioned in much the same fashion by using the ↑ and ↓ keys to move them a pixel at a time until they share the same top or bottom position. Moreover, if the row spacing you want cannot be achieved with Snap to Grid owing, for example, to the use of graphical objects to display groups of objects in panels, you can rely upon the figures displayed in the message line for the selected object's top or bottom position to achieve consistent spacing between objects on different rows.

WARNING

Do not become overly concerned with the grid and object positions. Along with the ruler, these are intended (and should be used as) aids in making final adjustments. For the most part, you should lay out your screens in proper WYSIWYG fashion by placing objects where they look best. When you finish, you can check actual positions as needed to place objects in perfect alignment relative to one another.

Using the Ruler/Grid Dialog

Selecting the Ruler/Grid option from the Screen pulldown opens the dialog shown in Figure 11.14. The radio buttons in the embedded Ruler dialog are used to select the units represented in the ruler at the top and left of the input screen or to remove the ruler from the input screen altogether. (The default ruler setting is inches.)

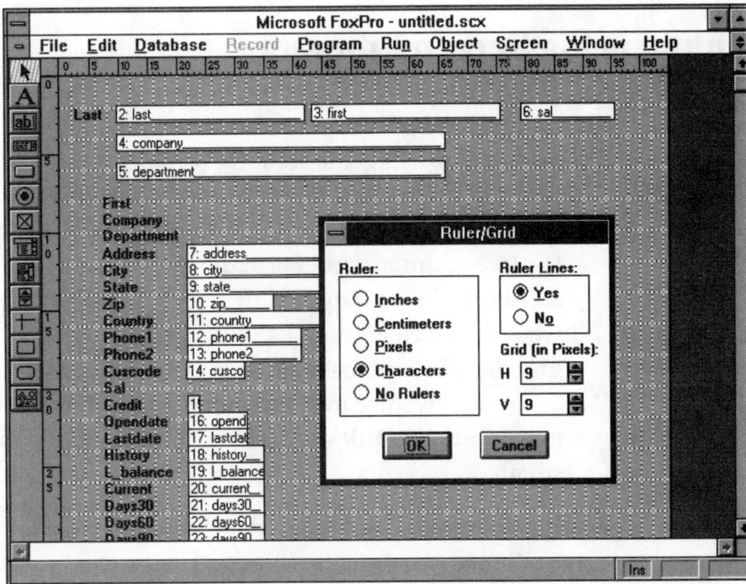

FIGURE 11.14:

Use the Ruler/Grid dialog to control ruler and grid settings and to display ruler lines directly in the input screen.

The default ruler setting is inches, but it is often convenient to change this, for example, to characters, to help you judge spacing better. However, when you are using a proportional font, this is more helpful in determining available rows than columns in the window.

As a further aid, you can select the Yes radio button in the Ruler Lines dialog to display ruler lines in the input screen. Figure 11.14, for example, shows the effect of selecting ruler lines when Characters is the ruler setting. This will help in rapidly positioning and aligning objects with the mouse.

The embedded Grid dialog uses two spinners for setting horizontal (H) and vertical (V) grid units in pixels. These settings, though affected by the ruler setting, do not pertain directly to the ruler lines but rather to the operation of Snap to Grid, described above. For example, when we select a ruler setting of Characters, FoxPro automatically adjusts the grid settings to represent the average number of pixels required for a character in the selected font. If we then move objects with the mouse when Snap to Grid is in effect, FoxPro actually moves the objects as many pixels at a time in the indicated direction as specified by the horizontal and vertical grid settings. Using the spinners, you can adjust the grid settings as you like.

Filling in the Screen Program

In developing Customer.scx we begin with Quick Screen simply because it will be faster than using the toolbox to place titles and input fields representing Customer.dbf's fields in the READ window one by one. However, whether or not you work with Quick Screen, the time will come when you must begin using the toolbox to place additional objects in the READ window. For example, having dragged and sized the objects supplied by Quick Screen as required to approximate the design we aim at (see Figure 11.15), we must now add our two sets of push buttons, the graphical objects that help to make the window more attractive, and the read-only input field we use to represent the customer's present balance. We must also add new input field titles where the field name titles supplied by Quick Screen are unsuitable.

In addition to completing the window layout—a process that will involve making continual adjustments—we must begin to concern ourselves more directly with the various components of the larger screen program in which the READ window is

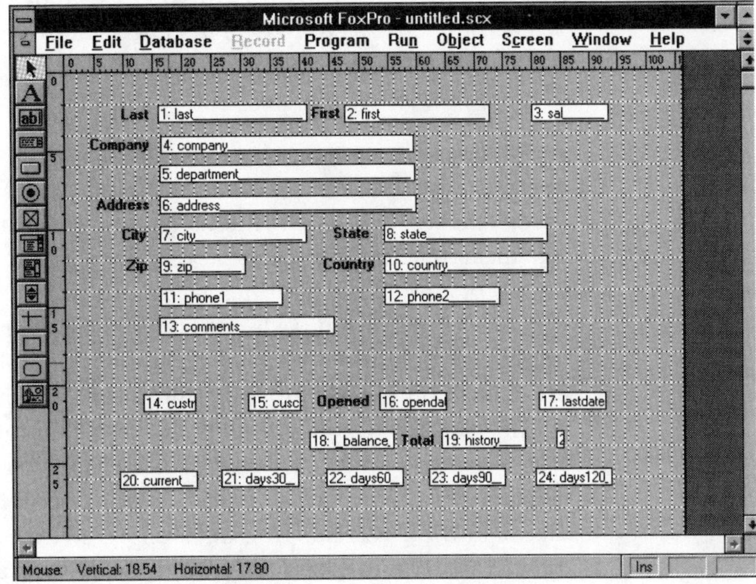

FIGURE 11.15:
Once you have moved and sized the objects placed in the window with Quick Screen, you can begin adding additional objects and controls using the toolbox.

used. Not only must we enter all the code snippets employed in the screen program's READ clauses, but also the setup and cleanup code. All these code snippets are stored in Customer.scx and rolled out by Genscrn.prg when it writes the finished screen program. There is also the small matter of double-clicking each of our input fields one by one so we can modify their definitions as needed with the Field dialog, discussed in Chapter 3. It is through the Field dialog, after all, that we must enter the @ GET WHEN clauses we use to make operator access to our input fields conditional on the value of the global memvar m.doit or to render input fields read-only by assigning them a WHEN clause of .F. The Field dialog must, moreover, be used to enter whatever display formats are required. @ GET VALID, RANGE, MESSAGE, and ERROR clauses may also be required, and these, too, are entered through the Field dialog.

Despite all the work that remains to be done, there's no need to despair. Everything can be done semi-automatically through the use of dialogs; and when we're done, not only will we have a complete data entry program, we will also have a template for creating more quickly the READ windows used by Payments.spr, Sales.spr, and, indeed, all READ windows that use a design similar to the one for Customer.spr. Anytime we need to create a screen program that uses control and Save and Cancel push buttons directly in the main READ window, we can open Customer.scx in the Screen Builder, use Save As in the File pulldown to create and open a copy of the screen design file under another name, and, after deleting all the objects that are not needed, fill in those that are, while modifying the various code snippets.

As an alternative, we can start our other screen design files with Quick Screen and, after opening Customer.scx in a second screen design window, use the Clipboard to copy and paste its push buttons, complete with all related @ GET clauses, directly into the new screen files. This is possible because of the way FoxPro stores the definitions of all @ GET input fields and controls in the screen file. Since we use the Clipboard to copy and paste objects, FoxPro copies the screen file records, containing the full definitions of those objects—that is, all the data we enter through the Field, Push Button, Popup, List, and Check Box dialogs—into the new screen file. All READ clauses and code snippets are also fair game for the Clipboard. We can therefore move rapidly from one screen program to the next, provided we have a reasonably clear plan of action and, with respect to the larger application, a good idea of how each screen program is expected to behave in our application environment. If we lack this perspective or fail to develop it quickly while creating our first screen programs, we will end up wasting time revising our screen program setup and cleanup code as well as our READ ACTIVATE and DEACTIVATE clauses.

However, since we already have a clear conception of the work to be done and, moreover, have examined in detail the code snippets we use to bring Customer.spr and our other screen programs to life, we can quickly and confidently complete Customer.scx, troubling only to show how everything is entered.

WARNING

Never go too far in developing a screen program without using the File pulldown's Save option to save current screen file instructions to disk. A lot of work goes into creating a screen program and you will not want to lose a sizable chunk of it due to a power outage. Also, if you want to experiment wildly with design changes, it is best to try them out on a copy of the screen program by using the File pulldown's Save As option. If the experiment doesn't pan out, you can abandon the copy, return to the original file, and try again.

Using the Screen Layout Dialog

Before proceeding further, it is best to use the Screen pulldown's Layout option to open the Screen Layout dialog and take a look at our READ window (in its present state of development) as it would appear if activated in the FoxPro main window. This is indicated by the Screen Layout dialog's Preview window, which displays a scaled model of our READ window as it would appear if activated in the main window using its current size and position. (See Figure 11.16.)

FIGURE 11.16:

Use the Screen Layout dialog to position and size the READ window, to define all window attributes, and to enter screen program code.

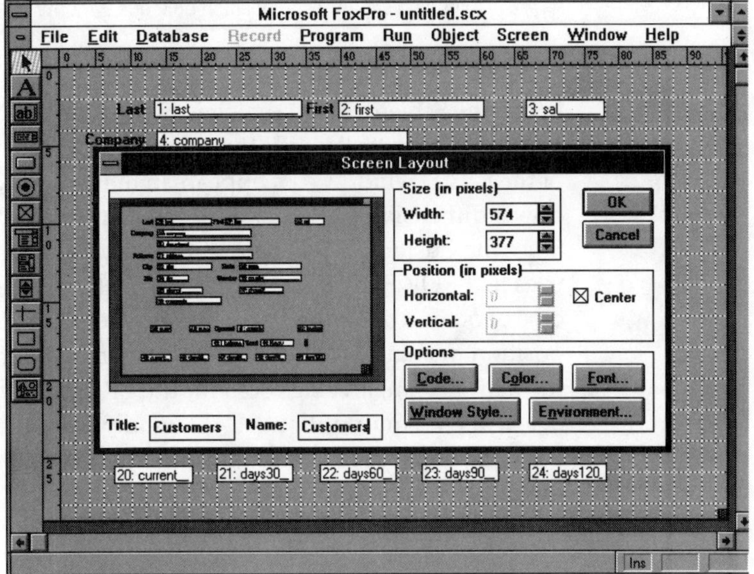

At the end of the development process, we will refer to the Screen Layout dialog to make final adjustments to our window's position and size. However, at this point we need only make sure that our current window layout leaves sufficient room for our control push buttons and that, as far as we can tell, the finished window can be comfortably centered in the main window above the status bar. Remember, the screen design window is not truly WYSIWYG with respect to the mock READ window's appearance in the main window. When you are working with large READ windows, it is easy to misjudge the window's dimensions just enough to force you to revise it when you think you're done. And this can be more work than you want if the field layout must be radically altered to reduce the window's size.

NOTE

While window size is determined once and for all by the Size settings displayed in the screen layout (they are recorded in the .scx file), window position, also recorded in the .scx file, can be altered through use of the Arrange dialog just before generation of the screen program. (When creating screen programs based upon two or more screen sets, we must rely on the Arrange dialog to help us select the best layout for our multiple READ window. This is too difficult to do when you can examine the position only one window at a time.)

When the Screen Layout dialog is first opened, spinner figures for the window position will be set to 0, while those for window size will correspond to the actual size of the READ window as it appears in the screen design window. To check our window's dimensions, we first click the Center check box, as shown in Figure 11.16. Since the Customers window will occupy the main window by itself (Customer.spr uses no BROWSE windows), this will be the window's final position setting. In the case of other READ windows, like Payments and Sales, however, we must set their position manually so they will be properly centered (horizontally) near the top of the main screen, leaving room for the BROWSE windows we display immediately below them. You position READ windows by dragging the scaled window's title bar or by using the Horizontal and Vertical Position spinners, though you can also directly overwrite the figures.

TIP

When positioning or sizing a window using the spinners, you can generally ignore the pixel figures as indicators of window position or size. This is because the scaled window's position and size are automatically adjusted as the settings are changed. We can see the results. The figures are also automatically adjusted when we use the mouse to change the scaled window's position or size.

Once we have positioned the window by choosing the Center check box, we can adjust the size of the window as needed to determine if our current layout corresponds to our expectation. The window's size can be adjusted by dragging the lower-right corner of the scaled window or by manipulating the Size spinners.

For now, our intention is only to make certain we are on the right track with our window layout before investing more work in the screen file. If the layout is not turning out as we expect, we can still start again with Quick Screen, after selecting and deleting all the objects in the window, to try something quite different, supposing we want to begin anew with input fields arrayed in their default sizes.

Defining the READ Window

At this point, entering the window title and name in the Screen Layout dialog boxes supplied for this purpose is a mundane matter. You can do it at any time, and as you may imagine, this won't be the last time we have to access the Screen Layout dialog in the process of whipping Customer.scx into shape. The name and title are to be slipped into the DEFINE WINDOW <name> TITLE <title> command that Genscrn.prg will spew out into Customer.spr when we generate the screen program. In fact, a large number of dialogs accessed through the Screen Layout dialog, not to mention its own Name, Title, Size, and Position dialogs, are devoted to gathering up the parameters FoxPro places in the DEFINE WINDOW command. The other dialogs are devoted to the related matter of entering the code snippets that will make the whole thing run. We will return to this more exciting matter in a moment. But first, let's finish with DEFINE WINDOW.

Note that it is not necessary to enter a window name in the Screen Layout dialog unless you must specifically reference the window by name elsewhere in the screen program. If you leave the Name entry box blank, Genscrn.prg makes up a unique name for the window when it executes the screen program. However, since most of our screen programs—and certainly Customer.spr—must include DEACTIVATE and ACTIVATE clauses that identify the READ window by name, we supply each of our READ windows with a specific name as well as a title.

TIP

The #WNAME <string> directive can be used, at the outset of a screen file's setup code, to make Genscrn.prg substitute the unique name it assigns the READ window for <string> when transferring the program code stored in the screen file to the screen program. This feature is useful to advanced users.

Supplying Window Titles through Use of Memvars

With respect to window title entry, there is one special Screen Builder feature worth noting. FoxPro dialogs, for example, often go by several different titles, each indicating a slightly different use or function. Thus, the dialog may appear in several different contexts without confusing the operator as to its function. In the MBS, we follow this practice in creating Cus_find.spr, the nested modal screen program called by Customer, Payments, and Sales.spr to locate customers, reorder the Customer table or, in the case of Customer.spr, initiate the Append customer action.

To display the correct title in window Cus_find and to pass Cus_find.spr a parameter that can be used with IF or DO CASE to control the screen program's execution of the selected routine, we execute each call to Cus_find.spr with DO Cus_find WITH <parameter>.

```
DO Cus_find.spr WITH "Locate Customer"
DO Cus_find.spr WITH "Reorder Customers"
DO Cus_find.spr WITH "Append Customer"
```

However, while picking up the passed parameter in Cus_find.spr and using it to control program action may be no problem—we just stick in the command PARAMETERS m.title as the first executable command in Cus_find.spr's setup code—how do we tell FoxPro to use the value of memvar m.title (or any other memvar) as the window title when executing DEFINE WINDOW TITLE, since we must always enter the window title in the Layout dialog? (The Title dialog expects a literal window name. So how do we signal Genscrn.prg, the screen generation program, that our entry for Title in Cus_find.scx, the screen design file, is a memvar and not a literal window title?)

The answer to this question is simple. FoxPro supplies a special directive, used only in screen files, for providing Genscrn.prg with instructions regarding how it is to read the entry we make to the Title dialog (or to the Format dialog, used when entering @ GET field formats, for example, with the Field dialog).

```
#ITSEXPRESSION ~
PARAMETER m.title
```

By placing the #ITSEXPRESSION <symbol> directive at the outset of our screen program setup code, which we will see how to do in a moment, we signal Genscrn.prg, when it creates Cus_find.spr, that we prefix any dialog entry we intend it to regard as a memvar with the single character symbol ~ (tilde). As a result, we can enter ~m.title in Cus_find.scx's Screen Layout dialog for Title and expect the

DEFINE WINDOW TITLE <title> command Genscrn.prg placed in Cus_find.spr to read *m.title* and not *"m.title"*.

Of course, once we establish the tilde—or any other character—as a symbol for "this is a memvar and not a literal entry," we can also use it to prefix the names of memvars in other screen file dialogs. As noted above, it is especially useful for supplying different PICTURE clauses for use with any @ GET. This is done by entering the name of a memvar holding the desired picture format in the Field Format dialog, preceded by the #ITSEXPRESSION symbol. The only limitation on this practice is that once the @ GET command is executed using the format specified by the memvar's current value, changing the memvar's value after the fact won't alter the format, even if you execute SHOW GET/S, since it is the @ GET command that executes the format.

WARNING

When Genscrn.prg creates a screen program, the screen setup code we enter in the screen design file is normally inserted after several code segments automatically generated by Genscrn.prg. To tell Genscrn.prg that our PARAMETER command must appear as the first line in the screen program, we must also make use of another screen file directive, #SECTION 1/2, when entering our setup code. We return to this issue later in this chapter, when we discuss entry of screen program setup code.

Specifying Window Style

In the Screen Layout dialog, we select the Window Style button to open the Window Style dialog, shown in Figure 11.17. This is where we specify the use of DEFINE WINDOW keywords controlling how the window can be manipulated by the operator (that is, which options will appear in the window control box), what kind of border the window will use, and, optionally, which icon will be used to represent the window when it is minimized, assuming the Miminize check box is selected. (By default, FoxPro uses its own icon for every minimized window.)

To help you make selections that are consistent with Windows guidelines, the Window Style dialog makes use of a Type popup, which includes five window type options—Desktop, User, System, Dialog, and Alert—several of which correspond to specific roles the window (and the corresponding screen program) may play in an application. (The default type is User.)

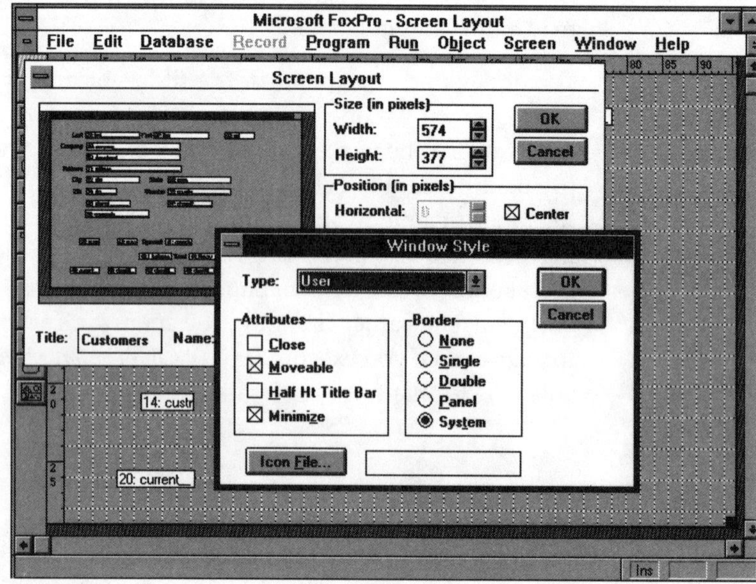

FIGURE 11.17:

Use the Window Style dialog to select the attributes of the READ window and which options will be available in the window control box.

In each case, selecting a window type also selects the default configuration—Attributes and Border—normally used when a READ window is employed, for example, as a dialog or an alert window. When Dialog is selected as the type, the Move and Close Attribute check boxes, corresponding to the DEFINE WINDOW CLOSE and FLOAT keywords, are checked, along with the Double (line) Border check box, corresponding to the DOUBLE keyword. The Attribute and Border dialogs are simultaneously disabled to encourage you to use these specific settings, conforming with Windows guidelines, when defining your own dialogs. The configuration used with alert windows is also written in stone. The Movable and Double check boxes are selected and the dialogs are disabled. The system window type, which we use with all MBS nonmodal READ windows, is used to mimic the attributes (Move, Close, and Minimize) and border (System) of FoxPro system windows. Again, selecting System disables the Attribute and Border dialogs to encourage you to stick to conventions.

Selection of User and Desktop Type windows, however, works slightly differently. In the case of a User window, Movable and Minimize Attributes and System Border are selected as defaults, but the dialogs remain active, so you can select whatever attributes or border you like. With Desktop, on the other hand, Single Border is selected and the Border dialog is disabled, while the Attributes dialog remains enabled with the exception of the Half Ht Title Bar option, which cannot be used in a window serving as the application's desktop or main window.

Coordinating Window Style Selection with Screen Program Action

With respect to the MBS, we stick primarily to system windows and dialog boxes, using the former with our nonmodal screen programs and the latter with the screen programs that must function as dialogs and are, therefore, executed with READ MODAL. (See Chapter 6 for a discussion of READ MODAL and modal and nonmodal screen programs.) Of course, in selecting System, thus placing the Close and Minimize options in the READ window control box, we must be prepared to write code snippets and a Foundation READ event handler (discussed in Chapter 10) to control program action when the operator clicks either of these window control options.

NOTE

Selecting Close does not terminate READ—it only hides the READ window—though it will also trigger READ DEACTIVATE if a deactivate clause has been written. Minimize also has its peculiarities, as described in Chapter 10. It minimizes the READ window but does not terminate the READ, nor will it trigger READ DEACTIVATE, even when a deactivate clause has been entered, unless the minimize action results in a change of WONTOP().

Selection of window type is therefore incumbent not just upon the function of the READ window but also upon how you intend to manage the window events that you invariably enable or disable through selection of window attributes and/or use or non-use of READ MODAL. Of course, you must plan for this. If you define your dialogs so they can be closed, you must be prepared to enter a READ DEACTIVATE clause to allow operator selection of the Close option in the window control box to terminate the READ (and the screen program). This is how Close is handled with MBS dialogs. On the other hand, if you want to make your data entry READ windows minimizable and, moreover, enable operator use of the Window pulldown as a means of switching between screen programs, you must be prepared to use READ DEACTIVATE in conjunction with screen program cleanup code, as described in

Chapter 6, to terminate a screen program while leaving its READ window or icon on the screen. You must also make use of Foundation READ with an event handler capable of reexecuting each screen program when the operator reselects its READ window or icon as WONTOP(), as described in Chapter 10.

NOTE

As you can see in the Edit Screen Set dialog in Figure 11.1, selection of the READ MODAL keyword is made just before generating the screen program by selecting the Modal Screens check box. We do not select or enter MODAL in the screen design file. At the bottom of the Edit Screen Set dialog in Figure 11.1 you will also see the Associated Windows push button. This is used to open a dialog for entering an associated window list—that is, the names of windows that an operator may still access during a modal READ. (We discuss the Edit Screen Set and Generate Screen dialogs at greater length later in this chapter.)

Bear in mind that in designing the MBS my purpose has been to present you with an application that illustrates the full range of options open to you and to provide you with the programming routines necessary to implement dialog boxes that can be closed and system (data entry) windows that can be closed and minimized. But it is not necessary to follow my lead. You can, for example, keep things simple by selecting User as the type of all your windows in order to exclude the Close option from your dialogs and the Close and Minimize options from the screen programs you use for data entry, in both cases sticking to READ MODAL and forcing the operator to terminate every screen program through use of a control push button. If you work in this way, you will have no need of a sophisticated Foundation READ event handler; the Foundation READ VALID clause can be handled with a memvar holding a logical value. (Again, see Chapter 10.) And though you end up with an application with a good deal less pizzazz, it is an open question as to whether operators will actually miss the special features of nonmodal applications, especially if you use an associated window list to give them access to BROWSE windows and FoxPro desk accessories when they prove useful. (We give explicit instructions on how to do this when discussing Payments.scx in the next chapter.)

Again, in the case of Customer.scx, we respond to the Window Style dialog by selecting System from the Type popup to select the Close, Minimize, and Float attribute options and a System border.

NOTE

The Icon dialog you use to select the .ico file works exactly like the Picture dialog employed to select a wallpaper window background. All that is required is an appropriate .ico file. FoxPro does the rest.

Selecting Window Font

As previously mentioned, the Screen Layout's nested Font dialog, shown in Figure 11.18, is used to establish the default font and style employed by Quick Screen and the toolbox when they are used to place text and input fields in a READ window. The window-level font and style can be changed during the screen design process so that multiple objects can be entered using a specific font and style. This is often faster than using the Object pulldown Font dialog to change font, font size, and/or style after the objects are already placed in the READ window.

Still, whatever font and style settings are saved to the screen design file will find their way into the DEFINE WINDOW FONT and SIZE clauses Genscrn.prg writes for the READ window. In most cases, this will have no bearing on screen program execution since all objects placed in the READ window through use of the Screen

FIGURE 11.18:

The Font dialog, when accessed through the Screen Layout dialog, is used to establish the READ window font and style as well as the default font and style settings used by Quick Screen and the toolbox.

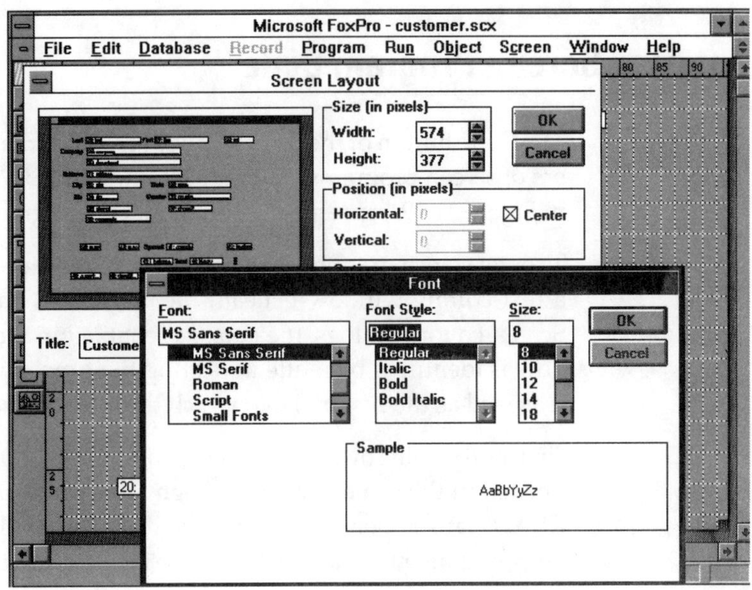

Builder's input screen will have their own font and style clauses. However, there are a variety of objects, including popups (executed with ACTIVATE POPUP), BROWSE windows, and other child windows, that will adapt the active window's font and style unless they are provided with specific settings. It is therefore best to save the screen file with font, font size, and font style set to standard values. If we leave ours set to the defaults for input fields, this will have the additional benefit of providing us with the settings we are most likely to use when modifying our screen files, or at least with foreknowledge of which settings are in effect.

NOTE

When we used Quick Screen with Customer.scx above, we knowingly employed the Windows defaults for font and style—MS Sans Serif, 8, Regular. This resulted in input fields with the default font and style, but with titles in bold, also the Windows default. However, once we begin entering text objects with the text tool, they will be entered with the default style of Regular unless we change the default style to Bold before clicking the text tool. Since our next step in developing Customer.scx will be to add and/or edit the existing titles with the text tool, we might just as well choose to establish Bold as the default style before leaving the Font dialog.

Entering Screen Program Code

The Code button of the Screen Layout dialog is the key to opening up the true powers of screen programs. Each push button listed in the Screen Code dialog, shown in Figure 11.19, represents an optional code segment of the screen file.

To enter screen program setup code, we select the Screen Setup Code button to open a text-editing window beneath the dialog. When we close the Screen Code and Screen Layout dialogs, the cursor is enabled in the text-editing window. This window is identified by a title indicating the function of the program code entered in it as well as the screen file to which the code belongs.

Text entry windows for screen program cleanup code and READ clauses are opened in the same fashion, though selection of any button initializing entry of a READ clause opens a further nested dialog, as shown in Figure 11.20. The Code Snippet dialog for each READ clause includes a set of radio buttons used to indicate

FIGURE 11.19:

The Screen Code dialog, accessed through the Screen Layout dialog, is used to open text-editing windows for entry of screen program setup and cleanup code and READ clause code snippets.

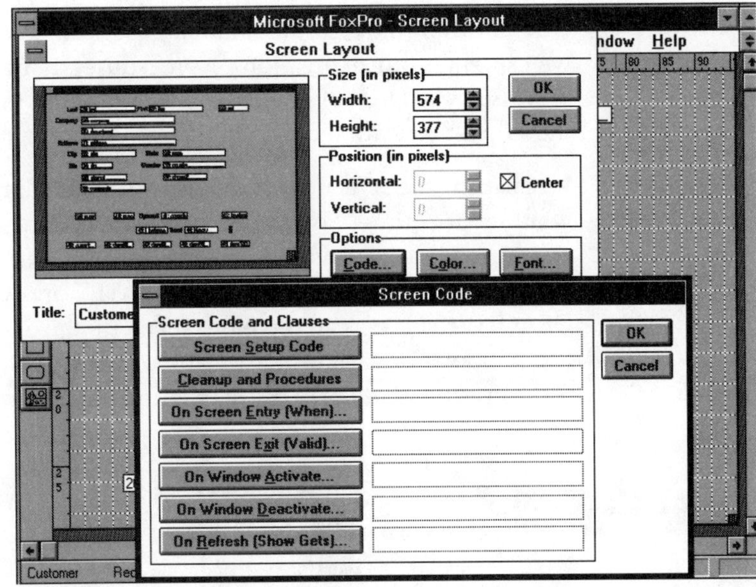

FIGURE 11.20:

Code Snippet dialogs are used for entering READ clause expressions or procedural code, though an Edit button is available for opening a sizable text-editing window for entry of procedural code.

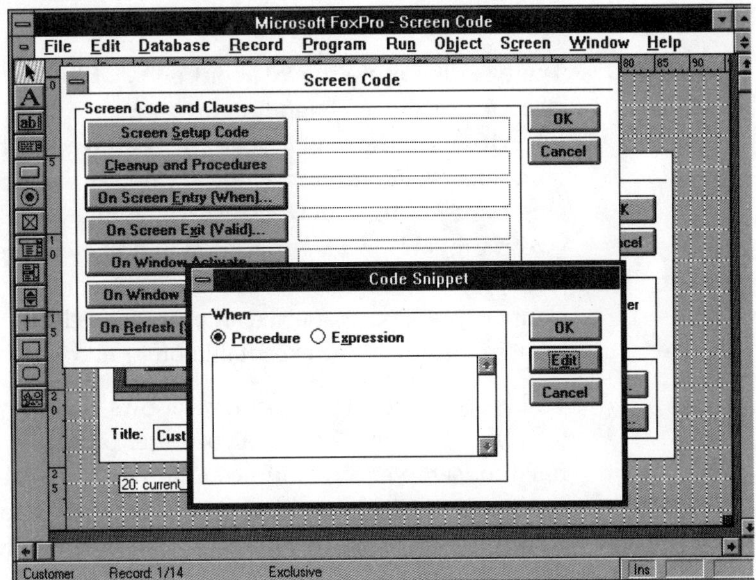

if the entered code snippet will be a logical expession or a procedure (actually, a UDF returning a logical value). Using the editing region in the Code Snippet dialog, we can enter our expression or procedure, though procedures of any length are more easily entered by selecting the Edit button to open a text-editing window for the snippet beneath the dialogs.

When using the Screen Code dialog, you are not limited to opening one text-editing window at a time. For example, with Customer.scx, we must enter setup and cleanup code as well as code snippets for On Refresh—Show Gets (READ SHOW), On Window Activate (READ ACTIVATE), and On Window Deactivate (READ DEACTIVATE). We can therefore speed up the development process by opening a text window for each of these clauses at once, before exiting the Screen Code and Screen Layout dialogs to begin entering our program code.

TIP

As you may have guessed, code snippets and screen program setup and cleanup code are stored in screen file Memo fields. The more you conceive of your work in entering and working with code snippets as a process of data entry to a standard form, the easier your work will be. It is a matter of getting used to working with the Screen Builder as a screen program text editor.

There is little more to say about entry of logical expressions for use with READ clauses; the screen generation program simply slips them in the READ command when it creates the screen program. Bear in mind, however, that you can supply the name of a UDF returning a logical value as the expression. This is often done when entering a DEACTIVATE clause specifying a UDF that is used by more than one screen program in an application and is therefore stored as an independent program or placed in a procedure file. You can also store a UDF referenced by a READ clause expression in the screen program's cleanup code after any commands you want to include in the executable program.

With respect to the text-editing windows, however, there is much to say about how to work with them. For once you enter program code in any of the windows supplied for setup and cleanup code or READ clause procedures, the window is immediately available without your having to reopen it (as you may) through the Screen Layout and Code dialogs. The Screen pulldown option Open All Snippets reopens text-editing windows for all snippets stored in the screen file. These also include code snippets supplied for use with @ GET clauses.

> **NOTE**
>
> Don't close Code Snippet windows to return to the main screen design window unless you want to remove the Code Snippet windows from the Window pulldown list. That way, you can return to any Code Snippet window without having to reopen it with the Screen Layout Code dialog or the Screen pulldown's Open All Snippets option. (When you save or close the screen file, all entries to Code Snippet windows will be automatically saved.)

When all snippets are opened, you can move to any one of them by clicking it, if it is accessible, or by selecting its name from the Window pulldown. Working in this way, you will find it remarkably easy to move from one code segment of the screen program to another (and back to the screen design window, which is indicated by the screen file's name), making changes and clipping and pasting commands as you go.

> **TIP**
>
> When you enter program code in a text-editing window or Code Snippet dialog, program code on contiguous lines can be selected with the keyboard (using the Shift and arrow keys) or with the mouse and then dragged and dropped or copied to another position in the window using the mouse. (To copy the selected code instead of dropping it, hold down the Shift key before dragging the code with the mouse.)

The only hazard that comes with working on screen files that include a good number of snippets is that the Window pulldown can list the names of no more than ten windows. When more windows are available, the last bar in the Window pulldown indicates More Windows and is used to open a dialog listing the names of all open windows. (See Figure 11.21.) This is tiresome to use. However, if you need to work on only a few code snippets, you can select the Close All Snippets option, available on the Screen pulldown only when all snippets are open, to close all the editing windows used by the current screen file. You can then selectively reopen the windows holding the snippets you want to address using the Screen Code dialog, thereby avoiding having to search the More Windows list for the snippet or code segment you want.

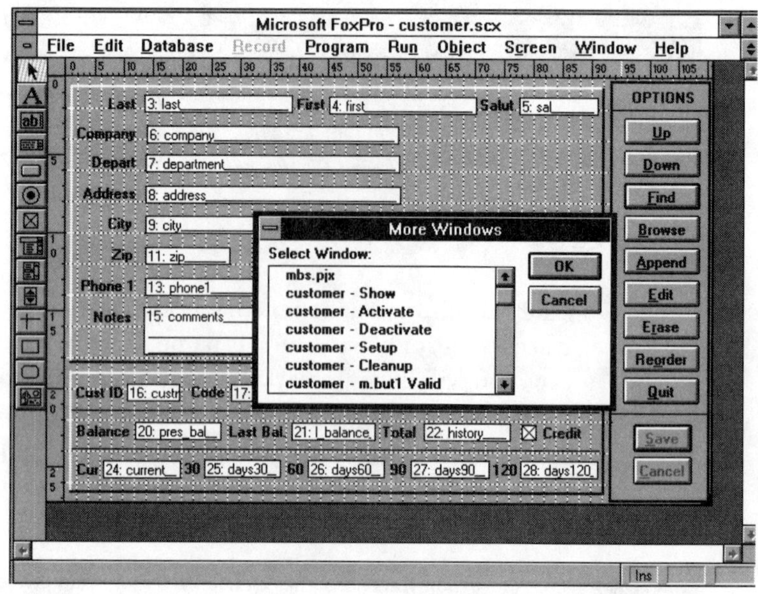

FIGURE 11.21: When more windows are open than can be displayed in the Window pulldown, select the pulldown's More Windows option to pick the desired window from a scrollable list.

Because you are still working in the FoxPro interactive mode, the Command window can be selected from the Window pulldown and brought foward at any time to alter the environment you are working in or to enter or test commands. As previously mentioned, more than one screen file can be opened at a time, allowing you to copy and paste program code as well as screen objects and their related code snippets from one screen file to another. Moreover, when you access the Screen Builder through the Project Manager, the Project window can also be selected and reactivated with the Window pulldown, enabling you to automatically open and edit any other program, menu, or screen file listed in the project file.

TIP

Output from FoxPro commands directed to the main window will not be visible if one or more windows are open. To view the main window without closing other windows or altering their front-to-back positions, press and hold down the Ctrl, Alt, and Shift keys together. FoxPro removes the windows so you can view the main screen. When you release the keys, all windows are restored to their proper order.

Code Snippet Names and Use of RETURN

As mentioned in Part I, Genscrn.prg, the FoxPro screen generation program, assigns unique function names for the procedural code we enter in code snippets for use in any READ clause. We therefore omit the FUNCTION <name> command in entering READ clause code snippets. Since use of RETURN at the end of a procedure or UDF is optional—FoxPro assumes RETURN .T. if no RETURN command is found—we generally omit entering RETURN at the end of our READ clause snippets unless RETURN .F. is required.

Screen Program Architecture

Screen program architecture is relatively straightforward, though you need to be sensitive to Genscrn.prg's placement of automatically generated code segments, some of which are optional, in the screen program in order to shape a screen program to your needs.

Genscrn.prg starts the screen program by using the information stored in the Project (or Generate) Options dialog to create a program header. By default, Genscrn.prg then adds a few lines of code to the screen program controlling environment parameters that are crucial to the smooth functioning of every screen program (produced by Genscrn). It also saves their prior settings, along with the alias name of the current table, to memvars. (See Figure 11.22.) The SET READBORDER ON command, however, is inserted at our request. In all MBS screen programs, we want borders placed around our input fields. We achieve this by selecting the Border for GETS check box in the Generate Screen or Edit Screen Set dialog before generating each screen program. This is why Genscrn.prg places SET READBORDER ON in the environment code section of Customer.spr. (Ignore the #REGION 0 directive for now. We discuss region directives later in this chapter.)

Next, supposing we saved the table environment with Customer.scx and, before generating Customer.spr, selected the Open Files check box in the Generate Screen or Edit Screen Set dialog, Genscrn.prg inserts commands reestablishing the table view, as shown in Figure 11.23.

FIGURE 11.22:

Screen programs begin with a file header and environment setup code.

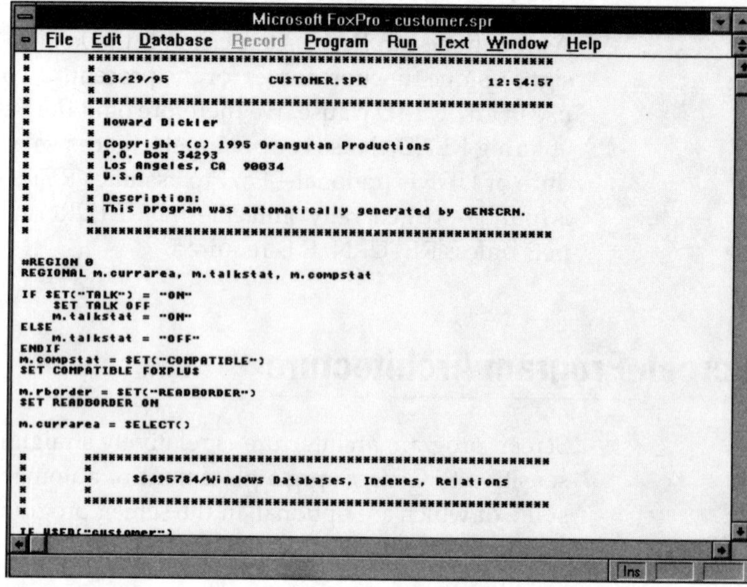

FIGURE 11.23:

If you select the Open Files option before generating a screen program, Genscrn.prg restores the screen file's environment in the screen program.

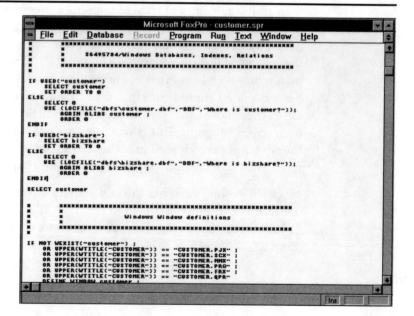

```
Microsoft FoxPro - customer.spr
File  Edit  Database  Record  Program  Run  Text  Window  Help
*       ***********************************************************
*       *
*       *       S6495784/Windows Databases, Indexes, Relations
*       *
*       ***********************************************************
*

IF USED("customer")
    SELECT customer
    SET ORDER TO 0
ELSE
    SELECT 0
    USE (LOCFILE("dbfs\customer.dbf","DBF","Where is customer?"));
        AGAIN ALIAS customer ;
        ORDER 0
ENDIF

IF USED("bizshare")
    SELECT bizshare
    SET ORDER TO 0
ELSE
    SELECT 0
    USE (LOCFILE("dbfs\bizshare.dbf","DBF","Where is bizshare?"));
        AGAIN ALIAS bizshare ;
        ORDER 0
ENDIF

SELECT customer

*       ***********************************************************
*       *
*       *                Windows Window definitions
*       *
*       ***********************************************************
*

IF NOT WEXIST("customer") ;
    OR UPPER(WTITLE("CUSTOMER")) == "CUSTOMER.PJX" ;
    OR UPPER(WTITLE("CUSTOMER")) == "CUSTOMER.SCX" ;
    OR UPPER(WTITLE("CUSTOMER")) == "CUSTOMER.MNX" ;
    OR UPPER(WTITLE("CUSTOMER")) == "CUSTOMER.PRG" ;
    OR UPPER(WTITLE("CUSTOMER")) == "CUSTOMER.FRX" ;
    OR UPPER(WTITLE("CUSTOMER")) == "CUSTOMER.QPR"
Ins
```

As previously noted, the commands used to open tables are written to disrupt an existing table view as little as possible. Before opening tables, the screen program executes SELECT 0 so no open table will be closed by the action. (SELECT 0 selects an unused work area.) Moreover, if the tables referenced by the screen program are already open, the screen program simply takes them over for the duration. As the Open Files code segment header indicates, the screen program limits itself to opening tables, resetting indexes, reestablishing SET RELATIONs, and selecting the current table, as indicated by the environment information saved in the screen file.

In the MBS, where we make use of an application-level default view, the Open Files code segment is not needed, and we generate our screen files without selecting the Open Files check box in the Generate Screen or Edit Screen Set dialog. I show the commands opening the tables used by Customer.spr in Figure 11.23 only so you'll know what to expect when you direct Genscrn.prg to Open Files.

Following the commands opening tables (if they are used), Genscrn.prg places the commands defining the READ window as specified through our use of the Screen Layout dialog. (See Figure 11.24.) Like the Open Files code segment (heading: Windows Databases), the Window Definition code segment (heading: Windows windows)

FIGURE 11.24:

Genscrn.prg places the Screen Program code segment defining the READ window after commands opening files and just before our screen file setup code.

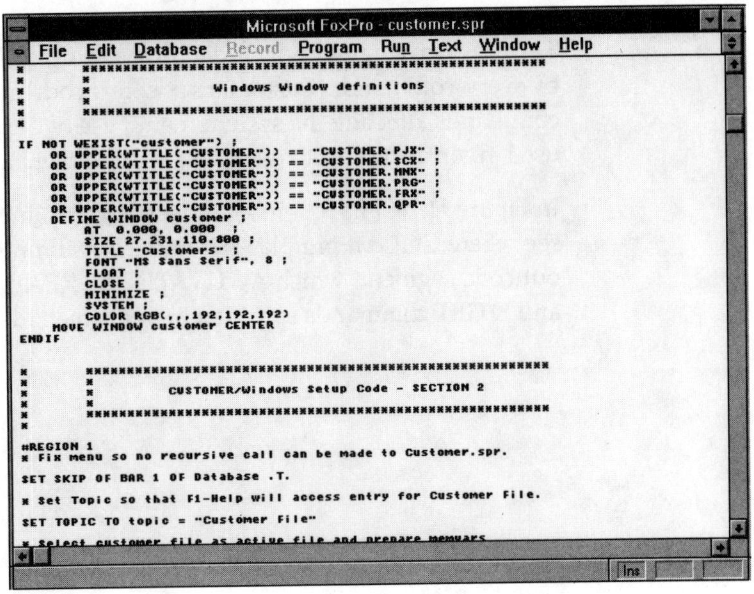

```
Microsoft FoxPro - customer.spr
File  Edit  Database  Record  Program  Run  Text  Window  Help
*       ****************************************************
*       *
*       *               Windows Window definitions
*       *
*       ****************************************************
*

IF NOT WEXIST("customer") ;
   OR UPPER(WTITLE("CUSTOMER")) == "CUSTOMER.PJX" ;
   OR UPPER(WTITLE("CUSTOMER")) == "CUSTOMER.SCX" ;
   OR UPPER(WTITLE("CUSTOMER")) == "CUSTOMER.MNX" ;
   OR UPPER(WTITLE("CUSTOMER")) == "CUSTOMER.PRG" ;
   OR UPPER(WTITLE("CUSTOMER")) == "CUSTOMER.FRX" ;
   OR UPPER(WTITLE("CUSTOMER")) == "CUSTOMER.QPR"
   DEFINE WINDOW customer ;
      AT  0.000, 0.000  ;
      SIZE 27.231,110.800 ;
      TITLE "Customers" ;
      FONT "MS Sans Serif", 8 ;
      FLOAT ;
      CLOSE ;
      MINIMIZE ;
      SYSTEM ;
      COLOR RGB(,,,192,192,192)
   MOVE WINDOW customer CENTER
ENDIF


*       ****************************************************
*       *
*       *          CUSTOMER/Windows Setup Code - SECTION 2
*       *
*       ****************************************************
*

#REGION 1
* Fix menu so no recursive call can be made to Customer.spr.

SET SKIP OF BAR 1 OF Database .T.

* Set Topic so that F1-Help will access entry for Customer File.

SET TOPIC TO topic = "Customer File"

* Select customer file as active file and prepare memvars
```

is also optional. It is included in the screen program only if we check the Define Windows check box in the Generate Screen or Edit Screen Set dialog before generating the screen program.

Note that the commands used to define and position windows are embedded within an IF statement to prevent FoxPro from redefining the READ window if it is already present in memory. (The length of the IF statement is owing to the necessity of ruling out project, screen, report, and other FoxPro windows displaying files with a root name that matches the name supplied for the READ window.) This is typical behavior and is certainly required to prevent FoxPro from doing anything with the Customers window (to refer to it by title) if it is already displayed on the screen. (In our nonmodal application, the operator can click an inactive READ window left on the screen after termination of the screen program in order to restart the screen program that uses the selected window. If the operator moved the READ window, we do not want FoxPro, for example, to move the window from its current position.)

As Figure 11.24 indicates, it is only after the Define Windows code segment—or more precisely, after the Environment code segment and the Open Files and Define Window code segments, if they are used—that Genscrn.prg inserts our setup code into the screen program (assuming we have entered setup code in the screen file). Figure 11.25 shows the setup code entered in the Customer.scx Setup Code window. The program comments included in the setup code will remind you of the function of every command. (Customer.scx setup code is discussed in Chapter 3, and the commands affecting the system menu, use of the Help file, and resetting memvars used in conjunction with the MBS event handler are discussed in Chapters 6 and 10.)

In Figure 11.26, I have removed the comment lines from the setup code so you can see where Genscrn.prg places it in the screen program: just before the Screen Layout code segment, which ACTIVATEs the READ window and executes all @ SAY and @ GET commands specified in our screen file layout.

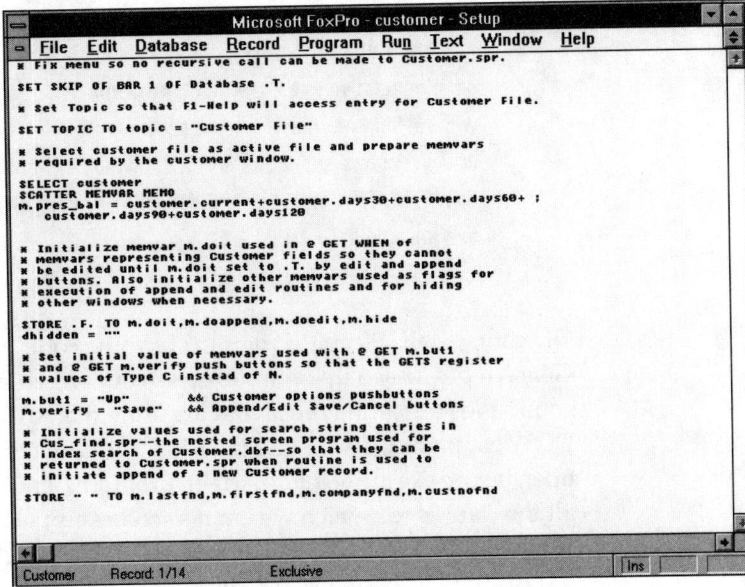

Microsoft FoxPro - customer - Setup
File Edit Database Record Program Run Text Window Help
* Fix menu so no recursive call can be made to Customer.spr.
SET SKIP OF BAR 1 OF Database .T.
* Set Topic so that F1-Help will access entry for Customer File.
SET TOPIC TO topic = "Customer File"
* Select customer file as active file and prepare memvars
* required by the customer window.
SELECT customer
SCATTER MEMVAR MEMO
m.pres_bal = customer.current+customer.days30+customer.days60+ ;
customer.days90+customer.days120
* Initialize memvar m.doit used in @ GET WHEN of
* memvars representing Customer fields so they cannot
* be edited until m.doit set to .T. by edit and append
* buttons. Also initialize other memvars used as flags for
* execution of append and edit routines and for hiding
* other windows when necessary.
STORE .F. TO m.doit,m.doappend,m.doedit,m.hide
dhidden = ""
* Set initial value of memvars used with @ GET m.but1
* and @ GET m.verify push buttons so that the GETS register
* values of Type C instead of N.
m.but1 = "Up" && Customer options pushbuttons
m.verify = "Save" && Append/Edit Save/Cancel buttons
* Initialize values used for search string entries in
* Cus_find.spr--the nested screen program used for
* index search of Customer.dbf--so that they can be
* returned to Customer.spr when routine is used to
* initiate append of a new Customer record.
STORE " " TO m.lastfnd,m.firstfnd,m.companyfnd,m.custnofnd
Customer
Record: 1/14
Exclusive
Ins

FIGURE 11.25:

We use the screen file Setup Code window to enter commands we want executed in the screen program before FoxPro executes the screen layout.

FIGURE 11.26:

Genscrn.prg places Screen Layout code in the screen program immediately after our setup code.

```
Microsoft FoxPro - customer.spr
File  Edit  Database  Record  Program  Run  Text  Window  Help
*        *******************************************************
*        *
*        *            CUSTOMER/Windows Setup Code - SECTION 2
*        *
*        *******************************************************
*

#REGION 1
SET SKIP OF BAR 1 OF Database .T.
SET TOPIC TO topic = "Customer File"
SELECT customer
SCATTER MEMVAR MEMO
m.pres_bal = customer.current+customer.days30+customer.days60+ ;
    customer.days90+customer.days120
STORE .F. TO m.doit,m.doappend,m.doedit,m.hide
dhidden = ""
m.but1 = "Up"
m.verify = "Save"
STORE " " TO m.lastfnd,m.firstfnd,m.companyfnd,m.custnofnd

*        *******************************************************
*        *
*        *              CUSTOMER/Windows Screen Layout
*        *
*        *******************************************************
*

#REGION 1
IF WVISIBLE("customer")
    ACTIVATE WINDOW customer SAME
ELSE
    ACTIVATE WINDOW customer NOSHOW
ENDIF
@ 0.154,93.200 TO 27.154,110.600 ;
    PATTERN 1 ;
    PEN 2, 8
@ 1.231,7.200 SAY "Last"  ;
    FONT "MS Sans Serif", 8 ;
    STYLE "BT"
@ 1.231,39.600 SAY "First"  ;
    FONT "MS Sans Serif", 8 ;
    STYLE "BT"
@ 3.154,1.800 SAY "Company"  ;
    FONT "MS Sans Serif", 8 ;
Customer        Record: 1/14        Exclusive        Ins
```

NOTE

In activating the READ window, the screen program first checks to see if the window is already open on the screen. If it is, it is activated without changing its position relative to other windows that may be open. If it is not, it is activated without being displayed on the screen. After all @ SAY and @ GETs are executed and just before executing READ, the window is brought to the front and/or displayed. This tends to reduce flashing as FoxPro prepares the window for execution with READ.

Of course, all Screen Program Layout code is automatically generated by Genscrn.prg, based upon the objects in our screen file layout. The @ SAY and @ GET commands executing the layout are immediately followed by an ACTIVATE WINDOW command, displaying the READ window or bringing it to the front (if it was open before execution of the screen program), and a READ command that includes all the clauses for which we entered code snippets as well as keywords (for example, MODAL and CYCLE) selected by means of a check box in the Generate Screen or Edit Screen Set dialog before generating the screen program. (We show this portion of Customer.spr in a moment.)

Following the READ command, Genscrn.prg inserts commands releasing the windows defined in the Define Windows code segment—that is, if the Release Windows check box is selected in the Generate Screen or Edit Screen Set dialog. Next it closes the tables it opened in the Open Files code segment (if the Close Files check box was selected before executing the screen program) and, using the memvars it initialized in the Environment code segment at the beginning of the screen program, reselects the work area that was current before the screen program was executed and restores SET READBORDER, SET TALK, and SET COMPATIBLE to their prior settings. (See Figure 11.27.) Only after finishing with these environment commands does Genscrn.prg place our screen file cleanup code in the screen program. It is important to note that in the executable program, though not necessarily in the .spr file, our cleanup code comes last.

As a rule, MBS screen programs never close tables since doing so would disrupt our application-level default view. (This is discussed in Chapter 6.) When we generate our screen program, we leave the Open and Close Files check boxes unchecked.

FIGURE 11.27:

When Genscrn.prg writes the READ command, it automatically includes clauses for all expressions and procedures entered in screen file READ clause code snippets.

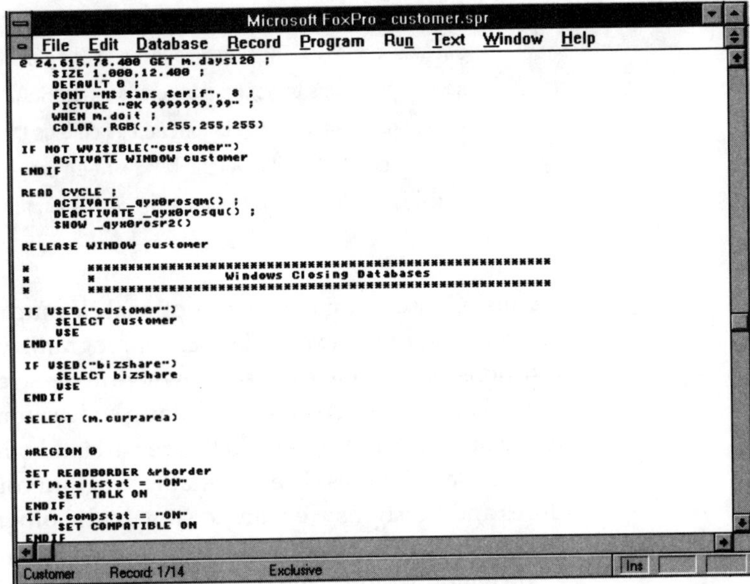

If we need to alter the view, we do this in the setup and cleanup code. (The Open and Close Files generate options are most useful in stand-alone screen programs. When you use an application-level default view, Close Files gets in the way and Open Files is, at best, redundant.) Moreover, while we select the Define Windows check box prior to generating all MBS screen programs (so Genscrn.prg will write the commands defining our READ windows), when generating Customer.spr and our other nonmodal screen programs we do not select the Release Windows check box. This is because we do not want the READ window released when READ terminates because the operator has started another screen program. In our nonmodal application, READ windows used during data entry are removed from the screen only when the operator selects the Quit push button or selects Close from the window control box. (This is discussed in Chapter 6.) We must take care of this ourselves in the cleanup code in addition to executing any other commands required to straighten our application environment.

NOTE

Unless you have an event handler to manage the reexecution of screen programs based upon WONTOP(), as discussed in Chapter 10, you will typically want your screen programs to define and release their READ windows. This is also true of screen programs written to function as dialogs through use of READ MODAL or an associated window list. All the MBS screen programs listed on the Update and Utitlities pulldowns, for example, are written in this way.

Because Genscrn.prg places the optional cleanup code we enter in the screen file at the very end of the executable screen program, we can include any procedures or functions we may have use of elsewhere in the screen program in our cleanup code, immediately after any and all cleanup code commands we want to include in the executable screen program. In this regard (and others), screen program structure is the same as .prg files. The executable program comes first, followed by any procedures and functions we want to store in the program file, usually for use by commands in the executable program. For programmers, the screen file's Cleanup Code window represents the end of the .spr file.

There is also the small matter of the many code snippets we may enter in the screen file for use, as UDFs given unique names by Genscrn.prg, in the READ and @ GET clauses. In some cases (for example, READ SHOW) Genscrn.prg will write a UDF even if we supply no procedural code since it must itself use READ SHOW to refresh any @ SAY output fields that have been included in the screen layout. In any case, Genscrn.prg places any and all procedural code entered as READ and @ GET clause code snippets immediately after the executable screen program or after the cleanup code we ourselves enter. (Our cleanup code comes first, so we can add commands to the end of the executable program.) This is apparent in Figure 11.28, which shows Customer.spr's cleanup code section the way it actually appears when we leave the Generate Screen or Edit Screen Set dialog's Close Files and Release Windows check boxes unselected. Note that our cleanup code is immediately followed in the screen program by the first of many UDFs Genscrn.prg writes for the code snippets entered in the screen file for our READ and @ GET clauses. As the code section header indicates, the function appearing in Figure 11.28 is the VALID clause code snippet entered for use with @ GET m.but1, our control push buttons. Of course, only the first few lines of the snippet, the complete code of which we discussed in Chapter 3, appear in the screen shot. This is only the first of six UDFs Genscrn.prg places in the screen program as we enter VALID clause procedures in the screen file for two other @ GETs and code snippet procedures for READ ACTIVATE, DEACTIVATE, and SHOW. All these Genscrn.prg-generated functions appear at the end of Customer.spr, where FoxPro can find them when executing the screen program.

FIGURE 11.28:

Genscrn.prg inserts all automatically generated procedural code in the screen program after the cleanup code.

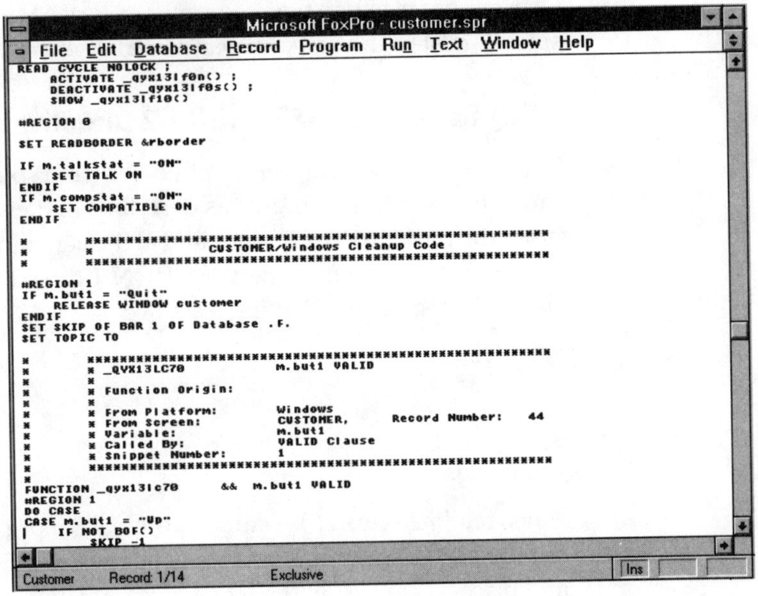

Microsoft FoxPro - customer.spr

File Edit Database Record Program Run Text Window Help

```
READ CYCLE NOLOCK ;
    ACTIVATE _qyx131f0n() ;
    DEACTIVATE _qyx131f0s() ;
    SHOW _qyx131f10()

#REGION 0

SET READBORDER &rborder

IF m.talkstat = "ON"
    SET TALK ON
ENDIF
IF m.compstat = "ON"
    SET COMPATIBLE ON
ENDIF

*       ***********************************************************
*       *                 CUSTOMER/Windows Cleanup Code
*       ***********************************************************

#REGION 1
IF m.but1 = "Quit"
    RELEASE WINDOW customer
ENDIF
SET SKIP OF BAR 1 OF Database .F.
SET TOPIC TO

*       ***********************************************************
*       * _QVX13LC70                  m.but1 VALID
*       *
*       * Function Origin:
*       *
*       * From Platform:              Windows
*       * From Screen:                CUSTOMER,     Record Number:   44
*       * Variable:                   m.but1
*       * Called By:                  VALID Clause
*       * Snippet Number:             1
*       ***********************************************************
*
FUNCTION _qyx131c70     &&  m.but1 VALID
#REGION 1
DO CASE
CASE m.but1 = "Up"
    IF NOT BOF()
        SKIP -1
```

Customer Record: 1/14 Exclusive Ins

We have reviewed the basic structure of screen programs—at least those based upon a single screen set—and explained the function of a good number of the Generate Screen and Edit Screen Set dialog check boxes in controlling Genscrn.prg's action. We must now consider some of the ways we can further manipulate Genscrn.prg's action through the use of additional screen file directives.

Entering Screen Program Setup Code

In terms of code segments, Genscrn.prg places our screen file setup code fourth in the screen program by default—after Environment, Table, and Window Definition code (the second and third segments being optional) and just before the commands executing our screen layout. Because most setup code is usually devoted to initializing memvars, many of which may derive their values from table fields, this is the most opportune arrangement, supposing the screen program is to open files. It may also be necessary to execute commands manipulating the position and size of the

READ window, depending upon what other windows are detected on the screen. You will want to do this after the screen program has defined the window.

But there are several instances in which you will want to place commands deliberately at the very outset of the screen program, ahead of any and all commands Genscrn.prg places in the program. The PARAMETERS command is a case in point since it must be the first command line in the executable program to work correctly.

Using Setup Code #SECTION 1/2 Directives

In the case of a screen program like Cus_find.spr, which receives its window title through a passed parameter, as described earlier in this chapter, it is necessary to insert the PARAMETERS command at the very outset of the screen program. We do this by using the screen file #SECTION 1 directive. In fact, screen file setup code should be regarded as having a syntax:

```
#SECTION 1
<commands>

#SECTION 2
<commands>
```

When reading screen file setup code, Genscrn.prg takes all commands entered under the #SECTION 1 directive—and before the #SECTION 2 directive, if it is used—and places them first in the screen program, immediately after the screen program file header. #SECTION 2 code is inserted in the default setup code position. (The #SECTION 2 directive need only be used when #SECTION 1 is used, to direct commands to the default setup code location.) In the screen program Genscrn.prg always labels the code placed in either location. Figure 11.26, for example, shows Customer.scx setup code labeled as Windows Setup Code — Section 2. Since we use no #SECTION directives in entering Customer.scx setup code, it ends up in the default setup code location in the screen program.

In contrast, with Cus_find.scx, we use #SECTION 1 and #SECTION 2 directives, as shown in Figure 11.29, to place the PARAMETERS command first in the screen program and to place the other setup commands in the default setup code location. Figure 11.30 shows the first portion of Cus_find.spr, with the PARAMETERS command clearly placed in the desired position. (Had we placed other commands in #SECTION 1 following PARAMETERS they would, unlike the PARAMETERS command, appear under the Section 1 header. PARAMETERS appears to be placed first for emphasis.)

FIGURE 11.29:

Use the #SECTION 1 directive to insert setup code at the beginning of a screen program.

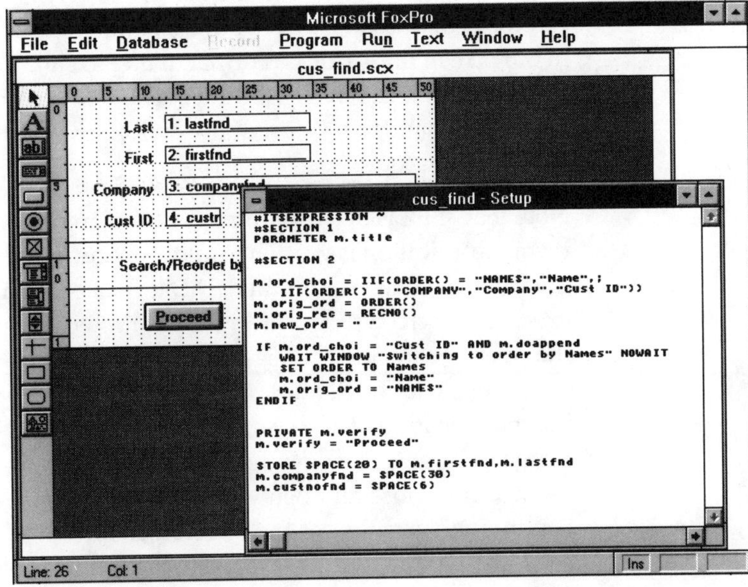

FIGURE 11.30:

To insert a PARAMETERS command first in a screen program, place it below the #SECTION 1 directive in the screen file setup code.

Microsoft FoxPro - cus_find.spr

File Edit Database Record Program Run Text Window Help

```
*       ********************************************************
*       *
*       * 03/01/95            CUS_FIND.SPR              16:50:01
*       *
*       ********************************************************
*       *
*       * Howard Dickler
*       *
*       * Copyright (c) 1995 Orangutan Productions
*       * P.O. Box 34293
*       * Los Angeles, CA  90034
*       * U.S.A
*       *
*       * Description:
*       * This program was automatically generated by GENSCRN.
*       *
*       ********************************************************

PARAMETERS m.title

*       ********************************************************
*       *
*       *        CUS_FIND/Windows Setup Code - SECTION 1
*       *
*       ********************************************************
*

#REGION 1


#REGION 0
REGIONAL m.currarea, m.talkstat, m.compstat

IF SET("TALK") = "ON"
    SET TALK OFF
    m.talkstat = "ON"
ELSE
    m.talkstat = "OFF"
ENDIF
m.compstat = SET("COMPATIBLE")
SET COMPATIBLE FOXPLUS

m.rborder = SET("READBORDER")
SET READBORDER ON
```

Ins

Figure 11.29 also illustrates the use of the #ITSEXPRESSION <symbol> screen file directive, discussed earlier in this chapter, to establish the tilde as the sign we use in our screen file's Title or Format dialog to signal our use of a memvar rather than a literal value. All screen file directives are best placed in the setup code prior to any setup commands so Genscrn.prg will know of their existence before generating any program code.

Note that #SECTION 1 setup code is also an opportune place to check RDLEVEL( ) if your application is written to allow execution of screen programs that might otherwise exceed the maximum READ level. For example, if RDLEVEL() is too high to execute the screen program and/or its nested screen programs safely, you can warn the operator to close other windows before reexecuting the screen program and then execute RETURN to cancel the program before it has taken any action requiring the execution of any cleanup code. #SECTION 1 can also be used, as it is by the screen programs listed on the MBS Utilities pulldown, to test the window environment and to close all open windows, conditional upon operator approval, before continuing execution of the selected action. (If the operator doesn't want to proceed, we execute RETURN to delay the action and return the operator to the screen program represented by the window WONTOP().

Screen Program #REGION Directives

As you have probably noted, Genscrn.prg sprinkles our screen programs with #REGION directives. Their function is easily explained. There is always the danger that the memvar names Genscrn.prg uses in automatically generated setup code will conflict with the names of variables we use in our screen program or the larger application. Genscrn.prg gets around this problem by declaring these memvars regional before initializing them. The pertinent commands are

```
#REGION 0
REGIONAL m.currarea, m.talkstat, m.compstat
```

Later on, in Customer.spr, when Genscrn.prg writes the commands using these memvars to restore the environment, it will use the #REGION 0 directive again so FoxPro will ignore memvars that have the same names but are not made regional to #REGION 0.

Moreover, by preceding all screen program code segments originating from Customer.scx with #REGION 1, Genscrn.prg allows us to use memvars with the same names as those declared REGIONAL in #REGION 0 without thinking about it. The assignment of #REGION 1 directives to all Customer.scx code segments also allows us to knowingly declare regional memvars of our own in our screen file setup code. Doing so, however, would be useless in Customer.scx since Genscrn.prg combines it with no other screen files (sets) in producing Customer.spr. But this is not so, for example, in Control.scx and Letters.scx, which we combine when generating Letters.spr. This is because Genscrn.prg uses different #REGION assignments for all the code segments belonging to each screen file included in the screen program. Were we concerned that memvars used in one screen file might conflict with the memvars used in other, we could get around the problem in advance by declaring the memvars regional in each of the screen files.

Still, regional variables are an esoteric feature of FoxPro programming and need only be resorted to if and when you begin creating multiple screen set programs as a matter of course. I make note of #REGION directives and the REGIONAL command so you'll know what's going on in your screen program when FoxPro changes from region to region—and how to take advantage of this to avoid or resolve memvar name conflicts among screen files included in the same screen program without having to change the names of the memvars in your screen files.

NOTE Bear in mind that #REGION directives and the REGIONAL command are executed by FoxPro during program execution. Genscrn.prg inserts them in the screen program. This is different from the screen file directives, #SECTION 1/2, #ITSEXPRESSION, #WNAME, and those discussed in the next section. These are directives we place in our screen file to provide Genscrn.prg with special instructions when it creates our screen program. They do not appear in the screen program.

Additional Screen File Directives and READ Clauses

There are several other screen directives we can place in our setup code to control Genscrn.prg's action when it creates our screen program. (The #SECTION 1/2, #ITSEXPRESSION, and #WNAME directives were discussed earlier in this chapter.)

Placed in the setup code, the #NOREAD directive instructs Genscrn.prg to place no READ command in the screen program. The availability of the #NOREAD clause makes it possible to use screen programs to create fancy screen displays, including sign-on messages.

TIP

To suppress all commands in the screen program except the @ SAY, @ GET, @ EDIT, and #REGION commands, place #NOREAD PLAIN in the setup code.

The #READCLAUSES and #WCLAUSES directives allow us to supply the READ and DEFINE WINDOW commands, respectively, generated by Genscrn.prg with clauses that are not available through the Screen Builder or the Generate Screen or Edit Screen Set dialog.

```
#READCLAUSES OBJECT 5 TIMEOUT 30
#WCLAUSES IN WINDOW frame
```

Placed in Customer.scx setup code, the #READCLAUSES directive instructs Genscrn.prg to add the OBJECT <expN> and TIMEOUT <expN> clauses to the READ command. The OBJECT clause supplies FoxPro with the object number of the @ GET you want selected as the current cursor object when READ is initiated. TIMEOUT directs FoxPro to terminate the READ after <expN> seconds have elapsed without operator input. Another useful READ clause is COLOR, which can be used to assign a specific color to the current @ GET input field. SAVE and NOMOUSE are also available. SAVE is used to prevent @ GET and @ EDIT objects from being cleared upon termination of the READ; the objects can then be reactivated through reexecution of the READ command. NOMOUSE can be used to prevent objects from being selected with the mouse.

The #WCLAUSES directive directs Genscrn.prg to add the clause IN WINDOW frame to the DEFINE WINDOW command it writes for the READ window. When the screen program is executed, the clause will instruct FoxPro to define the READ window as a child window of a window named "frame". This is how we can create screen programs that execute within other windows. (See your FoxPro documentation or Help file for information about other available DEFINE WINDOW clauses.)

When executing your screen program, you may want FoxPro to define the READ window whether or not it is already present in memory. (As you may recall, Genscrn.prg uses an IF statement to prevent execution of the DEFINE WINDOW command if the READ window—or, more precisely, a window with the same name as the screen program's READ window—is already defined.) To make Genscrn.prg suppress the IF statement in the screen program so DEFINE WINDOW will always be executed, place the #REDEFINE directive in your screen file setup code.

Finally, there are two other directives worth noting, though they function quite differently from those we have already discussed. The #INSERT <file> directive can be used anywhere in a screen file to direct Genscrn.prg to find the indicated <file> and insert its contents in the screen program at that point. The designated file must be a text file containing FoxPro commands. (Genscrn.prg looks for the file first in the current directory and then along the set FoxPro and DOS path.) This will allow you to store often-used screen program routines in external files and to insert them in your screen programs automatically instead of copying their text into the screen file with the Clipboard.

The #NAME <snippet name> clause can be used as the first line in any code snippet to provide Genscrn.prg with the name it must use for the FUNCTION it writes for the code snippet. For example, we might force Genscrn.prg to name Customer.spr's READ SHOW clause FUNCTION cust_show by entering #NAME cust_show as the first line in Customer.scx's SHOW (Refresh Gets) code snippet.

NOTE The #INSERT and #NAME directives can also be used in menu files created with the Menu Builder to insert files and to provide names to UDFs written by Genmenu.prg when it executes a menu program.

Adding and Defining Objects

Having completed our discussion of screen program architecture, including the use of the Generate Screen and Edit Screen Set dialogs and screen file directives to control the screen program generation process, we can now turn our attention to finishing Customer.scx.

Working with Text Objects

Since we need to replace and add several titles to the screen layout, all using the same font and style, we return to the input screen from the Screen Layout dialog, having selected MS Sans Serif, 8, Bold (the font and style we use with our titles) as the default window font and style. (This simply saves us the trouble of selecting a font and/or style for objects after adding them to the READ window.) Next we double-click the text tool to keep it selected until we click the selection pointer tool.

This way we can enter and/or edit as many text objects as we like. (When selected with a single click, the text tool is disabled the moment we finish working on a text object.)

When you select the text tool, the mouse pointer assumes the shape of a small I-beam. This is the insertion marker. Using the mouse, move the insertion marker into position in the READ window and click once to activate the cursor at that position for text entry. When you finish entering the text (usually an input field title), click the mouse outside the text object to terminate use of the text tool (if it was selected with a single click) or move the mouse into position for entry of the next text object (if the text tool was selected with a double-click). Then click the mouse to begin entering the next text object.

The size of text objects is determined by the text (including blanks) you place in them. Of course, when a proportional font is used, changing font size and style will automatically change the size of a text object. As previously noted, text objects may occupy several rows in a column. Just press Enter to move the cursor to the next screen row, directly beneath the previous row of the text object. (If you need to position text in different rows of a single text object, insert spaces as needed.)

TIP

All text objects can be dragged into position, so if you must enter several titles at once, it is usually easier to enter them one by one in a vacant area of the READ window and then drag them into position. This way you can be done with the text tool before having to concern yourself with the positioning of the text objects and the possible repositioning and sizing of the other objects that appear next to them.

Editing text objects is just as easy. You activate the text tool, move the insertion marker into position in the text object you want to alter, and click the mouse. (The arrow keys and mouse can be used to reposition the insertion marker in the object.) When the cursor is activated you can insert or delete any characters or move the cursor to the end of the object and begin adding new text.

When the text tool is not active, clicking a text object selects it for repositioning (but not sizing) with the mouse or arrow keys and as the object of actions taken with the Object pulldown (which we can use to change the font, pen color, and fill color of text objects, as described earlier in this chapter). Genscrn.prg refers to all this information when it adds an @ SAY command to the screen program for each text object in the screen file. Here are the lines Genscrn.prg places in Customer.spr for several titles:

```
@ 1.231,7.200 SAY "Last"  ;
   FONT "MS Sans Serif", 8 ;
   STYLE "BT"
@ 1.231,39.600 SAY "First"  ;
   FONT "MS Sans Serif", 8 ;
   STYLE "BT"
@ 1.231,70.800 SAY "Salut"  ;
   FONT "MS Sans Serif", 8 ;
   STYLE "BT"
```

The only thing remarkable about the @ SAY commands Genscrn.prg generates for our titles is the row and column coordinates Genscrn.prg assigns them. The row and column coordinates are determined by the READ window's default font. Fractions are typical since we are not obliged to place objects at specific row and column coordinates in the READ window. We position objects by sight and leave Genscrn.prg to calculate the precise position for us.

When selected individually or along with other objects in the READ window, a text object can be deleted with the Del key, cut or copied with the Edit pulldown, repositioned with the mouse or arrow keys, and manipulated as described above using the Object pulldown.

TIP

Though we do not show it, double-clicking a text object opens a Comments dialog in which you can insert comments about the object. Comments are not placed in the screen program, but they are stored in the screen file as part of the object's definition. Use comments to remind yourself (or another programmer) of a text object's meaning or function.

By double-clicking the text tool we can quickly add the remaining text objects we need to Customer.scx and drag them into position, as shown in Figure 11.31. We can do this all at once because we already know which text objects we require. This may not be the case when you are actually creating a new screen file. You are more likely to reselect the text tool several times, especially if you experiment with text objects that use different fonts, styles, pens, or fill colors.

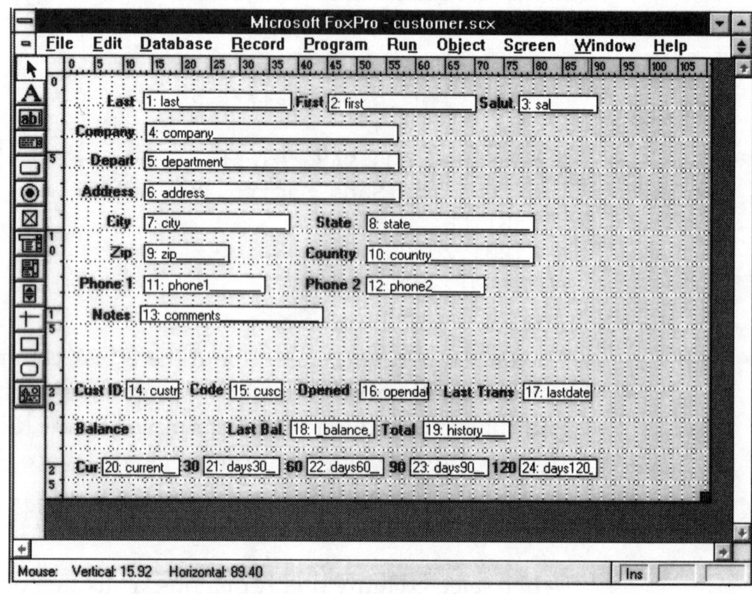

FIGURE 11.31: After executing Quick Screen, we arrange Customer.scx's input fields as desired. After deleting inappropriate field name titles, we double-click the text tool to add input field titles of our own.

Working with Input/Output Fields

With respect to input fields, which Genscrn.prg executes as @ GET commands, Quick Screen suffices to place all but one of our input fields in the Customers window. We will want to use an @ GET check box for entry and display of Customer.credit (a logical field indicating customer credit status) instead of an input field. (We come back to this in a moment.) We must also determine how we want to display the customer's current balance, which, as you may recall, is calculated on the fly by summing the customer's debt-aging fields, Current through Days120. We have two choices. We can create an @ SAY output field and supply Genscrn.prg with the calculation that must be performed so it can take care of everything automatically. Alternatively, we can initialize a memvar of our own and display it in an @ GET input field while making its value read-only. The former method is easier but does not work well aesthetically if the output field must be displayed along with @ GET input fields with borders. We therefore make use of an input field to display the present balance.

Still, before creating m.pres_bal and an input field to display it, we have other, more tedious matters to attend to. As discussed in Chapter 3, we must make the input field for m.custno read-only and make access to all other input fields conditional on the value of m.doit, which is set to .T. only when data entry is enabled. To add these expressions to the @GET WHEN clauses of our input fields, we must double-click each of them in turn to access their definitions for modification in the Field dialog and then click the When button to open a Code Snippet dialog, as shown in Figure 11.32. As in the Code Snippet dialogs used for entry of READ clauses, we can choose between entering a logical expression and entering procedural code. We can also select the Edit button to open a text-editing window, which will become available through the Window pulldown when all code snippets are open. (If we want to edit the procedure, we need not access it again through the Code Snippet dialog.) However, our WHEN clauses require only an expression, so we leave the Expression radio button checked (as it is by default) and simply enter the expression—in this case, m.doit—before selecting OK to close the dialog.

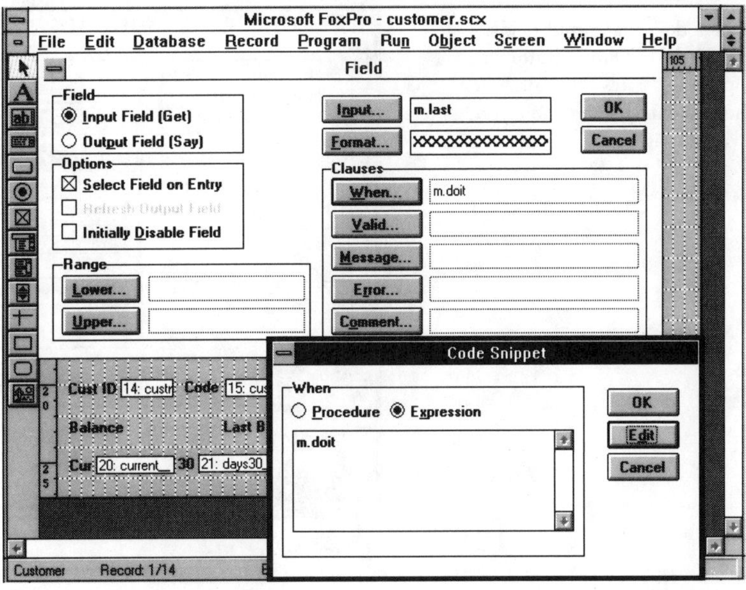

FIGURE 11.32: Use Code Snippet dialogs to enter @GET clauses.

The other attributes of the Field dialog were discussed in Part I. Note that if you need to enter the same procedural code or complex expression over and over to many input field clauses, you can use the Clipboard to assist you. Also bear in mind that you may enter the name of a memvar as the format if you precede the memvar name with the symbol used with #ITSEXPRESSION in the screen file setup code.

You can then use the memvar in the screen program to supply the input field with the correct picture format.

We now return to the issue of the field that must display the customer's current balance. Were we to use an output field, we would click the input/output field tool, move the mouse pointer (which assumes the shape of a cross hair) to the desired position (though this need not be exact since we can drag the field later), and click the mouse button to open the Field dialog. Next we click the Output Field (Say) radio button and make the entries shown in Figure 11.33. Though we can enter the output expression directly in the Field dialog, we can also click the Output button to open the Expression Builder and enter the expression there, as in Figure 11.33. The expression can be verified as long as Customer.dbf is the current table.

FIGURE 11.33:

When defining output fields, you can click the Output button to open the Expression Builder for help in entering the value you want to display.

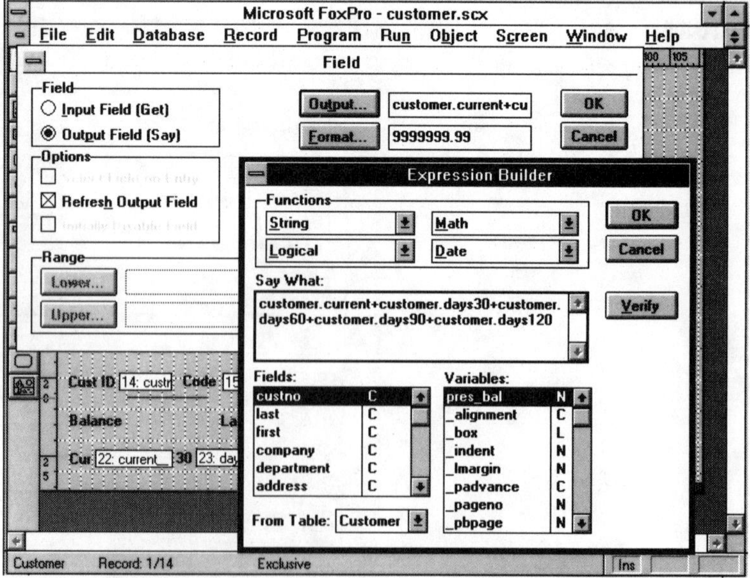

Once we click OK in the Field dialog we are returned to the READ window, where we must size the output field as needed. With respect to the attributes of the output field—font, pen, and fill color and size—it can be treated the same way as text objects. It is, after all, an @ SAY. With respect to FoxPro's handling of the output field during screen program execution, we select the Refresh Output Field check box.

Doing so tells Genscrn.prg to recalculate and redisplay the output field in the screen program's READ SHOW clause.

NOTE

If we create a READ SHOW clause of our own, when Genscrn.prg creates a screen program that includes output fields that must be refreshed, it places the commands updating and redisplaying the output field after whatever code we have placed in READ SHOW. For this reason, you must be careful to code your READ SHOW clause, when output fields are used, so FoxPro will have a chance to refresh the output fields as needed.

However, since we use an @ GET input field to display the customer's present balance, when we access the Field dialog we leave the Input Field (get) radio button selected and define the input field as shown in Figure 11.34. We can enter the name of the memvar we intend to use to hold the customer's present balance directly in the Field dialog. Alternatively, if the memvar has been defined using the Command window, we can click the Input button to select the memvar by name from the list of variables provided by the Choose Field/Variable dialog, also shown in Figure 11.24.

FIGURE 11.34:

Input fields can be used to display the results of calculations stored in a memvar. To make an input field read-only, enter a WHEN expression of .F.

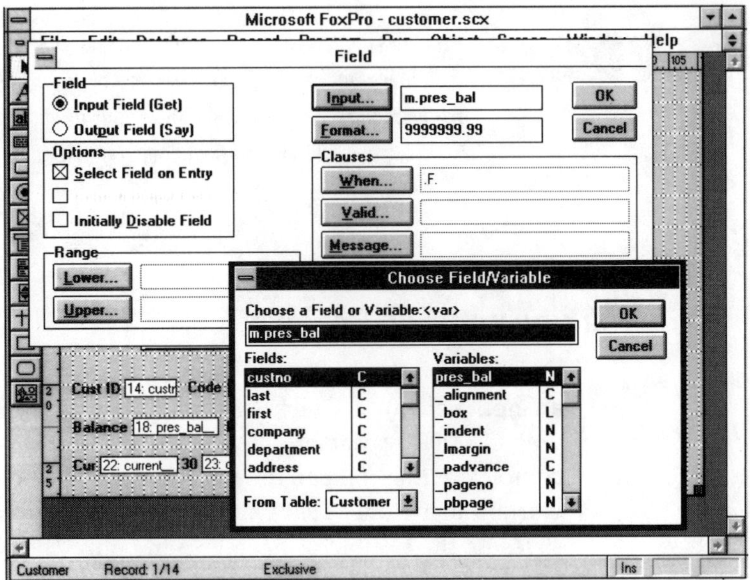

When we finish defining the input field, we are returned to the READ window, where we must size and position the new input field as needed. (Because it is based on a memvar and not on a field, the Screen Builder gives it an initial size equivalent to one character in the default font. You must increase the size of memvar input fields not derived from table fields through use of Quick Screen on your own.)

Having chosen to display the customer's present balance using an input field, we must not only initialize the memvar in the screen program's setup code, we must refresh the value ourselves in READ SHOW. Genscrn.prg cannot do this for us. For this reason, we can return to the Screen Layout dialog's nested Code dialog and open text-editing windows for setup and cleanup code and for the READ clauses we are likely to use. We can then begin entering program code as needed to fill out the program, even as we begin adding our controls. The command defining m.pres_bal by summing the customer's debt-aging fields, for example, must be placed in the setup code and in READ SHOW. (Actually, m.pres_bal need only be initialized in the setup code. The actual calculation, however, must appear in the SHOW clause. But m.pres_bal is only one of many memvars we must prepare before execution of READ SHOW, and READ SHOW has many other commands to execute as well. (Full Customer.scx setup code is displayed in Figure 11.25. For a detailed discussion of READ SHOW and the other significant program routines used in Customer.spr, refer to Chapter 3.)

TIP

When the mouse pointer assumes the shape of a cross hair for initializing the entry of an object in the READ window, the actual beginning position of the object, once placed in the window, will not be directly under the cross hair but rather in the quadrant to the lower right of center. (I mention this because it seems to go against intuition.)

Working with Edit Regions

Quick Screen knows that our Comments field is a Memo field, so instead of creating an input field for it, Quick Screen defines it as an edit region. An edit region, created with @ EDIT <variable>, allows us to create a vertically scrollable editing window, complete with scoll bar, for any Memo field or character variable large enough to warrant using one. That Quick Screen makes m.comments an edit region simply saves us the trouble of having to initialize the edit region ourselves, though we must size it. (Given the size Quick Screen assigns an edit region, we can easily mistake it for an input field.) This changes, however, after we size the edit region with the mouse, access the Edit Region dialog (after double-clicking the edit region), and select the Scroll Bar check box. (See Figure 11.35.)

FIGURE 11.35:

Use the Edit Region dialog to define a vertically scrollable region for entry and display of Memo field data.

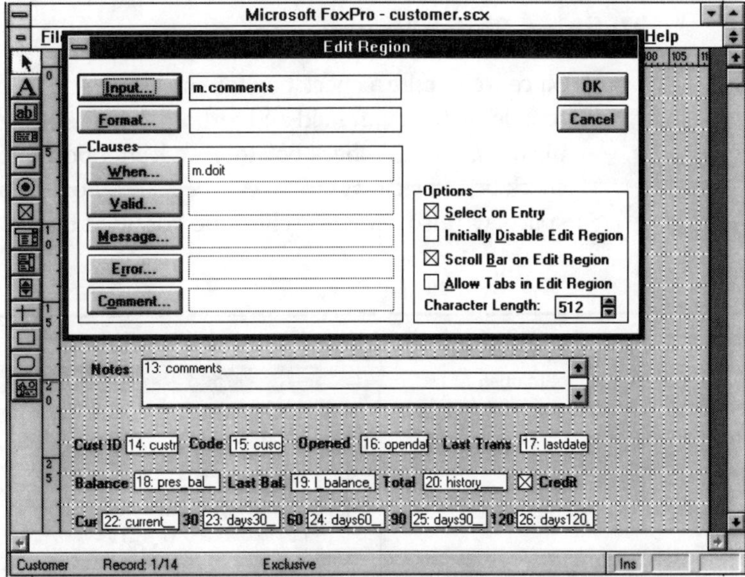

You must select the Allow Tabs in Edit Region check box if you want to enable operator use of the Tab key in the edit region. (Otherwise, Tab moves the cursor to the next object.) We do not use this feature here, but when we do employ it in Letters.spr, where tab stops can be entered into the text of a letter stored in Letters.dbf, we place the message "Press Ctrl+Tab to Exit" next to the edit region. This is how the operator must leave an edit region when Allow Tabs is selected, though it in no way prevents the operator from leaving the edit region with the mouse. We can also control how much text can be entered in the edit region by using the Character Length spinner. We use it here to limit the operator to entry of 512 characters of comments. This is intended to encourage economic use of the field. The other edit region options are self explanatory.

WARNING

The character-length spinner used to control how much text can be entered in an @ EDIT region has a maximum setting of 999. If you want no limit to the amount of text that can be entered in the region, you must leave the spinner's value set to 0.

Defining Check Boxes

Since we require a check box for entry and display of the customer's credit status, we first delete the input field and text object Quick Screen places in the READ window for m.credit, click the check box tool, and, after positioning the mouse where we want the check box, click again to access the Check Box dialog shown in Figure 11.36. To save space, we also show the check box defined by the dialog entries in the figure.

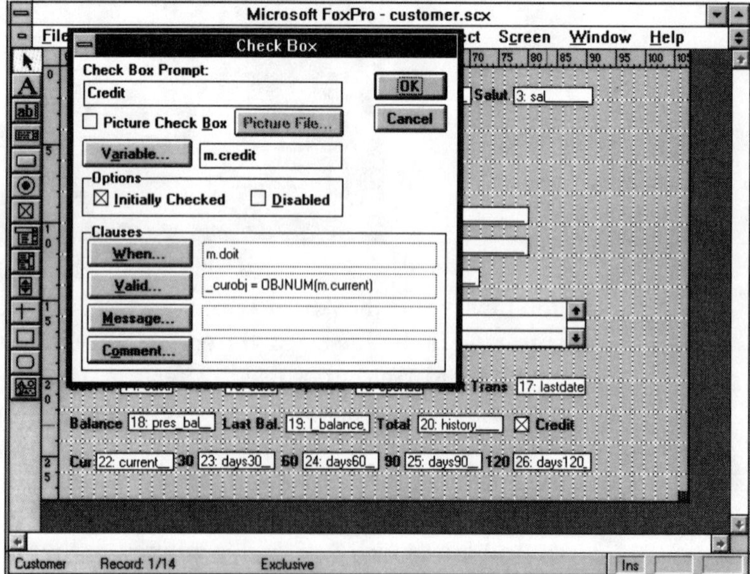

FIGURE 11.36: Use the check box tool to open the Check Box dialog and define an @ GET check box.

In defining the check box—which, as you may recall, FoxPro creates with an @ GET command, using a special PICTURE format—we enter the prompt we want displayed to the right of the check box and enter the name of the variable that will represent the checked or unchecked status of the check box with a logical .T. or .F.

(or numeric value of 1 or 0), respectively, for checked and unchecked. Since we use the check box to represent the status of a logical field, we can use it without alteration to display and oversee data entry to the memvar the SCATTER MEMVAR command (used to initialize memvars for display in the rest of our input fields) will automatically create for Customer.credit. We therefore name the variable m.credit. To force FoxPro to use logical values instead of the numbers 1 and 0 to represent the checked or unchecked status of the check box—the check box uses numeric values by default—we need only initialize m.credit as a logical variable in the screen file setup code. But this will be taken care of automatically by SCATTER MEMVAR, which we place in the setup code and in READ SHOW to update all memvars representing the current customer's fields.

The Initially Checked Options check box is selected in Figure 11.36, though it will only affect the check box status and the value of m.credit during the data append routine that is initiated after execution of SCATTER MEMVAR MEMO BLANK. This is because in the normal run of things, m.credit will represent the value of Customer.credit in an existing record. In selecting the Initially Checked check box we therefore assign new customers a default credit status of .T.

In accordance with our strategy of using memvar m.doit to enable/disable operator access to all data entry fields, not just input fields, we place m.doit in the check box's WHEN clause and leave the Disabled check box unchecked, so the check box will not appear dimmed on the screen when the window is first activated.

NOTE

Though m.current follows the check box in order of execution in the screen program, during testing FoxPro showed a penchant for skipping from the check box to the Save and Cancel push buttons, which are enabled during data entry or edit. To curb FoxPro's behavior in responding to operator use of the Tab key, I included the VALID clause shown in Figure 11.36, which does no more than make m.current the current READ object when the operator leaves the check box with Tab; it has no other function. It has no effect, for example, on the value of the memvar m.credit.

Once we finish with the dialog, FoxPro returns us to the READ window and displays the new check box. We can adjust its position, and even adjust its size, though this must be done by changing its font. (Check boxes are not sizable with the arrow keys or mouse.) We can also double-click the check box to regain the Check Box dialog and change the check box's definition in any way we choose.

Creating Picture Check Boxes

Instead of displaying a text prompt and an actual check box, we can create @ GET check boxes using pictures stored in bitmap files. For example, at the bottom right of Figure 11.37 you can see the picture check box produced by using the Picture dialog (accessed by selecting the Check Box dialog's Picture check box and Picture File button) to open Caution.bmp as the check box picture.

FIGURE 11.37:

You can represent a check box with a picture by opening the Picture Check Box dialog and opening a bitmap file.

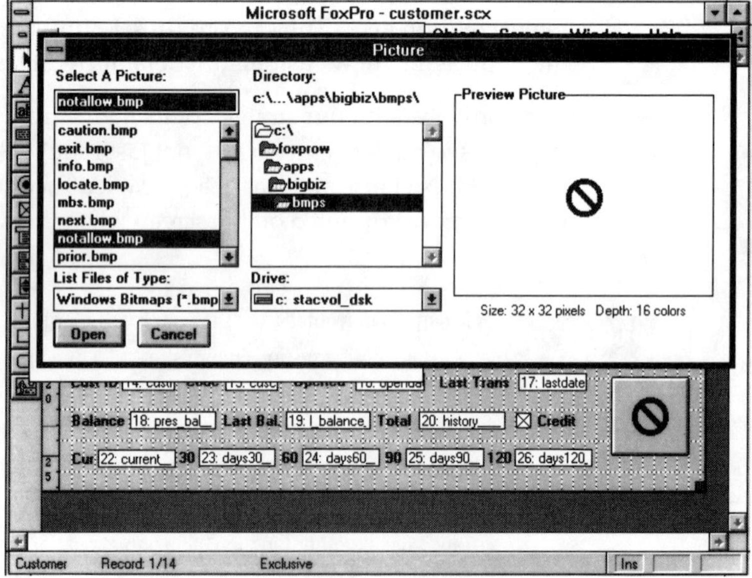

> **NOTE**
>
> Picture check boxes, which look a lot like buttons, have three display states—up, down, and dim—corresponding to checked, unchecked, and disabled, respectively. FoxPro automatically controls the picture's appearance in accordance with the check box's current value and status, though you can override the default appearance of the check box by using a picture mask (a monochrome bitmap file with an .msk extension) to control the background color of the check box. (See your FoxPro documentation or Help file for more information on how to do this.)

Unlike text prompt check boxes, picture check boxes can be sized, though the picture you use cannot be scaled, clipped, or edited. In other words, though you can increase or decrease the size of the square defining the boundaries of the check box, the picture itself retains its original size in pixels, as indicated in the Picture View box. (You cannot, however, make the size of the picture check box smaller than that of the actual picture.) The same thing holds true when using pictures to define radio and push buttons.

> **NOTE**
>
> Unlike picture check boxes, you can scale pictures displayed in a window using the picture tool. However, like check boxes, pictures used with @ GET push buttons and radio buttons cannot be scaled, though the buttons themselves can be sized.

Clearly, picture check boxes can serve just as well as prompt check boxes in representing logical table fields. They are, moreover, quite useful, as are prompt check boxes, for triggering program action. FoxPro dialogs, for example, often make use of prompt check boxes for executing nested dialogs or for registering operator selection of multiple dialog options, each of which is represented by a single check box. You can use prompt and picture check boxes for the same purpose.

Creating Push Buttons

The last objects we must place in Customer.scx are our two sets of @ GET push buttons. We discussed the creation and use of push buttons extensively in Chapter 3, so here we simply review the steps for placing our menu control push buttons in the READ window. After selecting the push button tool and moving the mouse pointer into position, we click the mouse to open the Push Button dialog and define one or more push buttons. Figure 11.38 shows the definition of m.but1, our control push buttons, with the resulting set of buttons displayed on the screen. (They are not yet sized.)

FIGURE 11.38:

Use the push button tool to place a push button or set of push buttons in the READ window.

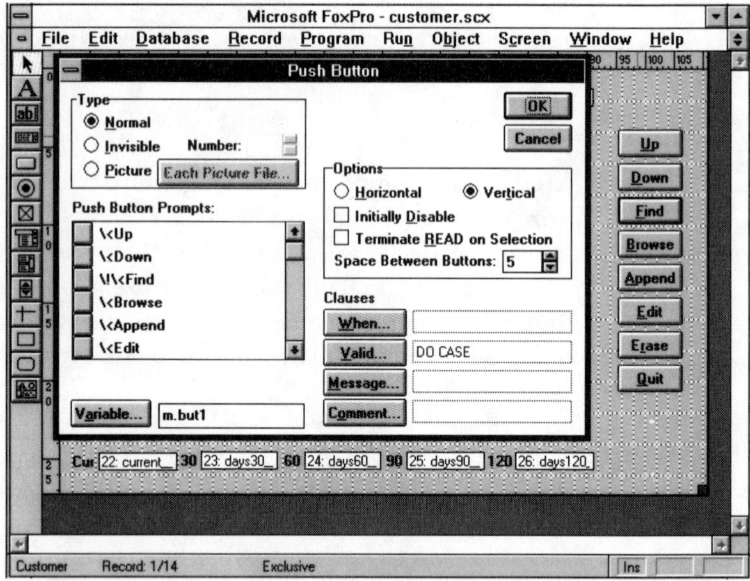

As the Push Button Type dialog indicates, we can choose among three types of push button: normal (that is, push buttons that use the text prompts we enter in the Push Button Prompts list), invisible, and picture. Regardless of the type, operator selection of an activated push button—which may include one or more push buttons as determined by the prompts or files entered in the Prompt list or by the number in the spinner when the Invisible radio button is selected—returns a numeric value to the memvar we enter as the @ GET variable corresponding to the order 1, 2, 3, and so on, of the selected button. Numeric values must be used with picture and invisible push buttons, but when using normal push buttons we may return the prompt label used by the selected push button to the @ GET variable, usually a memvar, by initializing the memvar as a character string in our screen file setup code. Thus, we include the command m.but1 = "Up" in Customer.scx's setup code. Again, when creating a set of push buttons as we do here with @ GET m.but1, when the push button is activated the first button will be automatically highlighted, even when we assign the @ GET variable a default value corresponding to another button. (The memvar, however, will retain the assigned default as long as the push buttons are not used.)

Also, as described in Chapter 4, when defining normal push buttons using text prompts, we can include the symbols \< before whatever character in a prompt we want to assign the function of serving as the button's hot key when the @ GET push button is the current cursor object. The symbols \! can also be placed in a text prompt to make FoxPro select the corresponding button when the operator presses Ctrl+W or Ctrl+Enter. The symbols \? can be used to make FoxPro select a button when the operator presses the Esc key.

Of course, in the case of Customer.scx, we use @ GET m.but1 to control screen program action through use of a VALID clause containing a DO CASE structure. In the DO CASE structure (discussed in in Chapter 3; see Figure 3.3), we use the returned value of m.but1 to launch each of the subroutines indicated by the button labels. Because we leave the Push Button dialog's Terminate READ on Selection check box unselected and because READ CYCLE is used in the screen program, the operator can use the push buttons over and over, repeatedly reusing any of the listed actions, until selection of the Quit push button executes the CLEAR READ command or until the operator takes some action—for example, clicking Close in the window control box or selecting another window—that terminates the READ through triggering of READ DEACTIVATE (discussed in Chapters 6 and 10).

There is no great secret to the arranging, positioning, and sizing of push buttons. Vertical or horizontal arrangement is determined through use of radio buttons in the Push Button Options dialog. The number of spaces (calculated in terms of the window font) FoxPro inserts between buttons in a set of push buttons is determined by the Space Between Buttons spinner. (The default value is 4, though it is typical to return to the Push Button dialog to change this while making adjustments to the size and position of the buttons.) The buttons themselves are positioned and sized like any other object, but bear in mind that an @ GET push button with multiple buttons still represents a single object. When you click any of the buttons (when the object is displayed in the screen design window), the Screen Builder selects the entire object. When you drag the object, all the buttons included in the object move as one. And when you size one of the buttons, the Screen Builder sizes them all, though it will not allow you to make the buttons smaller than the largest prompt or picture displayed by any given button. The same thing is true of @ GET radio buttons.

Use of Pictures in Buttons

The creation of push buttons using pictures is readily illustrated by the push button control window defined in Control.scx. This is the screen file we combine with Letters.scx to create Letters.spr, the MBS screen program that uses two READ windows. Because picture and text prompt buttons cannot be used in the same @ GET push button, we must use two different sets of push buttons in designing Control.scx. The first, @ GET m.but1, defines the three picture buttons at the top of the window. (See Figure 11.39.) Positioned just below it is @ GET m.but2, a set of normal push buttons that use text prompts. (We arrange and size the second set of push buttons so that, positioned just below the picture buttons, the two @ GET push buttons will appear to form a single set of push buttons. And since the two commands are issued in their order of appearance in the window, they will, moreover, appear to behave in that way, as a single set, since use of the ↑ and ↓ keys will move the cursor to highlight any button in the column.)

FIGURE 11.39:

To create picture buttons, select the Push Button dialog's Picture radio button and then press the Each Picture File button to open the Picture dialog and select the bitmap file to use with each button.

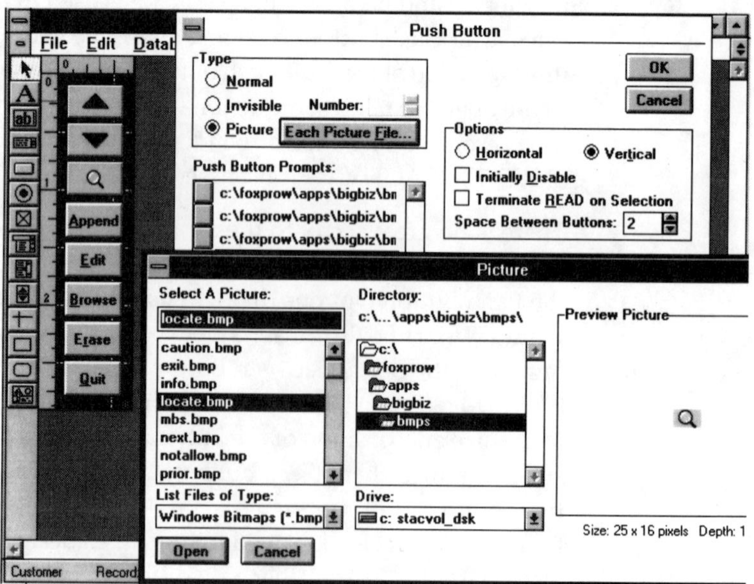

When using picture buttons, you must plan to make use of an @ GET memvar that returns a numeric value indicating which button the operator has selected. Thus the DO CASE structure we place in @ GET m.but1 VALID to control program action when the operator selects one of the picture buttons will use CASE m.but1 = 1, for example, to test for operator selection of the first picture button, which uses Prior.bmp, containing a small up arrow. CASE m.but1 = 3 tests for operator selection of the third picture button, which uses Locate.bmp, containing the small looking-glass. This is the bitmap file that has been opened in the Picture dialog shown in Figure 11.39.

TIP

Microsoft supplies a veritable cornucopia of useful bitmap files with FoxPro, in addition to those used by the FoxPro demonstration programs. They are stored in \foxprow\goodies\goodies.pak. See the file Readme.txt, found in the \foxprow\goodies directory, for information on how to unpack the bitmap files stored in Goodies.pak.

Note that each of the two sets of push buttons used in Control.scx employs its own VALID clause to register operator selection of one of its buttons. This is necessary because the VALID clause of one @ GET will not automatically be triggered by selection of a button in another @ GET—though this could be manually arranged through use of the KEYBOARD command in the VALID clause of the second @ GET. There's just no point in doing it; it is easier to enter a VALID clause for each of the two @ GET push buttons.

Taken together, the two sets of push buttons included in Control.scx do no more than the single set of control push buttons (@ GET m.but1) we use in Customer.scx. With respect to text prompt and picture push buttons, you may even choose to use a distinct @ GET—and an appropriate VALID clause—for every control button you require. This will give you much greater control over their arrangement in a READ window, when such control is required, and make them easier to address with SHOW GET. (See Chapter 3 for a discussion of the use of SHOW GET to enable/disable specific buttons in a set of push buttons defined with a single @ GET.)

Invisible Push Buttons

It has been suggested that the creators of FoxPro included invisible push buttons in FoxPro as a practical joke. Invisible buttons, though visible and sizable in the Screen Builder, are, in fact, invisible in the READ window—that is, until a button becomes the current cursor object. When that happens the button's outline is made apparent by the dotted line FoxPro uses to highlight the selected button. This, however, may make them useful; scalable pictures, created with the picture tool, may be placed on top of them, allowing you to form scalable picture buttons. Invisible buttons are sometimes used to launch a "credits" screen to show who wrote a program. An invisible button can also be used if it becomes necessary to activate a window when all other objects in the window are disabled. We see an example of this at the end of this chapter.

Customer.scx's second set of push buttons, @ GET m.verify, oversees the Save/Cancel append and edit operations through the use of VALID. Like the control push buttons, they are normal and do not terminate READ on selection. If you already have experience with the Screen Builder, you know how to enter them and how to open and enter their VALID code snippets. If you are new to the Screen Builder, it is time to start experimenting with it to find out how to do these things. With a tool as complex as the Screen Builder, there is no substitute for experience.

Using Radio Buttons, Popups, and Lists

In regard to @ GET radio buttons and @ GET popups, radio buttons function very much like push buttons, and we have already enountered both types of popups—list and array—in Chapters 4 and 5. Along with @ GET lists (and push buttons), radio buttons and popups are used when the operator must select one of several options. With radio buttons, we display the available options in the window all at once, using either a text prompt or pictures; with a popup, we display only the default popup item and leave the operator to open the popup to select a different item.

The MBS Customer Database Reports window, for example, shown in Figure 11.40, uses two sets of radio buttons—one to select the desired order of report output and

FIGURE 11.40:

The Customer Reports window uses radio buttons, a popup, and two scrollable lists to enable operator specification of report parameters.

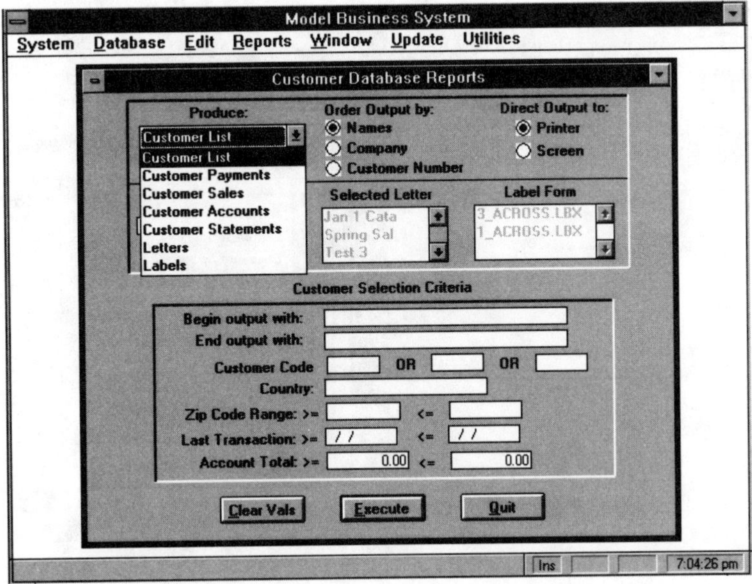

the other to select between output devices. The Customer Database Reports window also uses a list popup to provide the operator with a menu of available reports and two scrollable lists produced with @ GET List. One of the @ GET lists enables operator selection of a letter stored in Letters.dbf when Letters has been selected from the Report popup. The other @ GET list enables operator selection of a Label form file when Labels has been selected from the Report popup.

Chapters 12 and 13 examine what goes on behind the scenes in Cust_rpts.spr, the screen program that uses the Customer Report window. But with respect to the preparation of data for output and the execution of the Report and Label form files it references, we can use Cust_rpts.spr now to provide examples of the @ GET objects being discussed.

Again, the popup used by the Customer Reports window is a simple list popup, like that used by Cus_find.spr to provide the operator with a list of available index tags. You can see the definition of the popup in Figure 11.41.

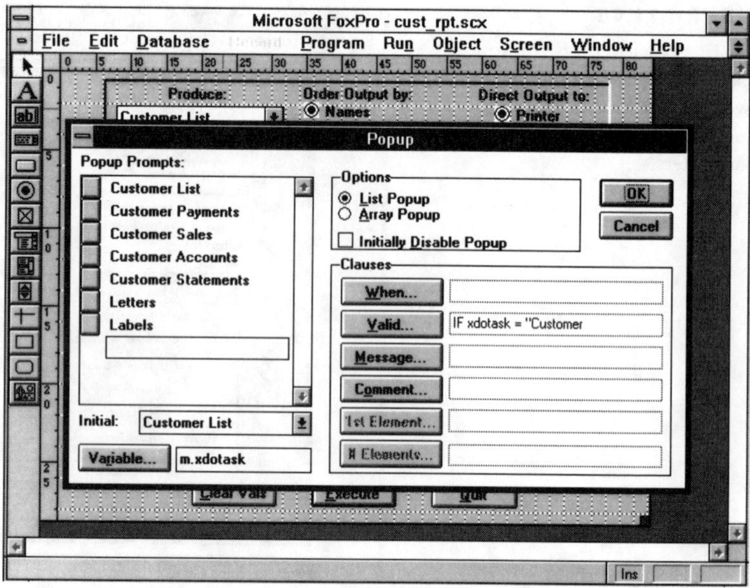

FIGURE 11.41:
The Customer Reports window uses a single @ GET popup to provide the operator with a list of available reports.

The only item of note about the popup that lists available reports is its VALID clause. Though it may initialize default transaction dates (when Customer Statements is selected), its primary function is to execute SHOW GETS. Specifically, it reexecutes READ SHOW, which uses the value of m.xdotask (initially set to Customer List) to selectively enable/disable the transaction input fields or one of the @ GET lists, depending upon which report option has been selected. This is handled with DO CASE and SHOW GET ENABLE/DISABLE. (See Chapter 3 for a discussion of the use of SHOW GET in the READ SHOW clause of a screen program to selectively enable/disable @ GET objects.)

NOTE

In Cust_rpt.scx we use an *x* as a prefix for all memvars representing input fields and @ GET controls so they can be stored to a memory file for later reactivation with the SAVE command. We discuss this feature of Cus_rpt.scx in Chapter 12.

Because the Selected Letter and Label Form lists (to identify them by the text objects placed just above them) are not used when Customer List is the selected popup option and because Customer List is m.xdotask's default value (as determined by a memvar initialization command in the setup code), both lists will be initially disabled. Figure 11.42, for example, shows the List dialog used to create the Selected Letter list. We initially disable the list by selecting the Initially Disable List check box. More important, we select the From Field radio button to enable the entry of an expression designating the items to be displayed in the list. (Clicking the Field button opens the Expression Builder for help in doing this.) In this case, because we want the list to display the names of available letters listed in alias Lettpic (Letters.dbf), we enter lettpic.name. This creates a scrollable list of the values in the Name field of all records in lettpic.

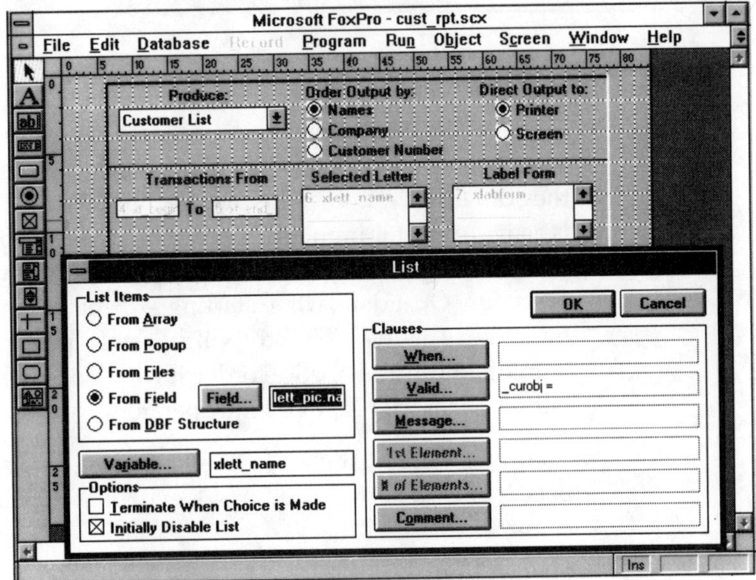

FIGURE 11.42:

Use the List dialog to define a scrollable list of field values stored in a table.

When the operator selects an item located in the scrollable field value list, the item's prompt—in this case, the name of the desired letter—is stored in memvar xlett_name. We can subsequently use this value to position FoxPro to the desired letter in any copy of Letters.dbf that happens to be open, though selecting the name of the desired letter from the list also makes it the current record in the table used to provide the list—alias lettpic. (The Memo field containing the text of the desired letter is therefore immediately available to us.) The VALID clause, only part of which appears in Figure 11.42, is used only to move the cursor to a specific object after the operator has made a selection.

NOTE

The various types of scrollable lists are roughly the same as the various types of popups that can be created with DEFINE POPUP. For example, we might use DEFINE POPUP PROMPT FIELDS lettpic.name to create a popup menu displaying the same items as the @ GET list defined in Figure 11.42. (See Chapter 6 for a discussion of how to create a popup displaying field values from a table.) In general, however, it is best to work with scrollable lists whenever the list will fit comfortably in the READ window.

Once placed in the READ window, scrollable lists can be sized both vertically and horizontally, though they must occupy at least three rows in order to display the scroll bar. Space permitting, it is often desirable to stretch (size) them vertically so they can display more items at once. But this is not necessary because when the list is active, operator input of a keyboard character will instantly display the first item in the list beginning with that character, if one is available. (We open alias lettpic in procedure Opendata, when starting MBS, using an index tag organizing its records by name. This way FoxPro will not only present the list of values taken from lettpic.name in alphabetical order, it will also be able to move to any item beginning with the character input by the operator.)

The other @ GET list used in Cust_rpt.scx takes its items from an array named Labels. It is created in procedure Opendata at the outset of MBS with the following commands:

```
PUBLIC ARRAY labels[1]
=ADIR(labels,"dbfs\labels\*.lbx")
```

The first command declares array Labels public so it will not be erased when the procedure terminates. The second command executes the FoxPro ADIR(<array name>, <filespec>) function to create an array that lists directory information about all files conforming to the entered file specification. The <filespec> we use indicates all .lbx (Label form) files in directory dbfs\labels, where we store all MBS label files. While the ADIR() function creates a two-dimensional array listing a variety of information about each .lbx file, what's important in this case is that the first column of the array will hold the file names of all our .lbx files. This is the column an @ GET list FROM

Array will automatically use for the values it displays from a two-dimensional array unless the 1st Element option in the List dialog is used to begin the list with an element found in another column of the array. (See Figure 11.43.) Since the list defaults to element 1, which is always found in the first column of the array, we need not trouble to enter 1 as the first element. Moreover, since we want to display all elements listed in the array's first column, we make no use of the # of Elements option to limit the number of elements displayed from the selected column, beginning with the first element. The default value for # of Elements is all elements in the selected column.

FIGURE 11.43:

Scrollable lists can be created to list the values of all array elements found in a one-dimensional array or in any column of a two-dimensional array.

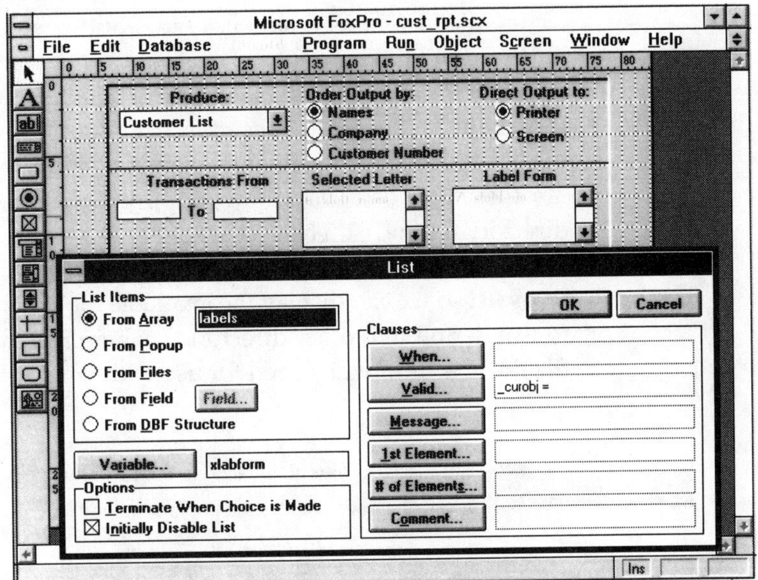

NOTE

The optional 1st Element and # of Elements clauses, used with array lists, are supplied through the entry of numeric expressions or procedural code snippets returning a numeric value. (Genscrn.prg writes out UDFs for procedural code entered into snippets, just as it does for code snippets supplied for the clauses of all other @ GETs.) Using procedural code, you can conditionally determine which elements should be displayed in the list when it is executed with @ GET.

When the operator selects one of the items displayed in the list of array elements, FoxPro stores the element—the name of the desired label file—in memvar m.xlabform. When executing the LABEL FORM command, we can then supply the name of the desired label form using a name expression (xlabform).

NOTE As with @ GET push buttons, the variable used in an @ GET list must be initialized as a character string to return list item names instead of numbers.

As an alternative, we might execute the scrollable list of available .lbx files by selecting the List Items From Files radio button and then entering dbfs\labels*.lbx in the From Files entry box. This of course is easier since it does not require us to initialize or load an array listing the available label files. On the other hand, lists formed using the From Files <filespec> option always include items at the top of the list enabling the operator to change the directory in which FoxPro looks for the .lbx files it will list. The path we supply in the <filespec> serves only as the default directory for the list. This feature of file lists is often desirable, but in the case of the MBS we expect all .lbx files to be placed in a specific directory. We therefore use an array list so we can display the available file names without enabling the operator to wander off into other directories, where FoxPro could possibly turn up an .lbx file not specifically designed for use with our Customer table.

NOTE The two label files included with the MBS have file names that were devised to inform the operator of the label format they use: 1_across or 3_across.lbx. The first is designed to output labels in a single column and the second to output labels in three columns.

One of the nice features provided by file lists (or array lists created with the aid of ADIR( )) is that the list is open ended. You can, for example, create additional .lbx files for use with the MBS Customer table. If you place the new files in directory dbfs\labels, Cust_rpt.spr will automatically display their names in the Label form list and use them to produce labels when selected.

Finally, returning to the two sets of radio buttons used in Cust_rpt.scx, their function is unremarkable. Figure 11.44, for example, shows the Radio Button dialog used to define the three radio buttons provided at the top of the Customer Reports window for operator selection of Customer table output order. The selections correspond to the three major Customer table index tags.

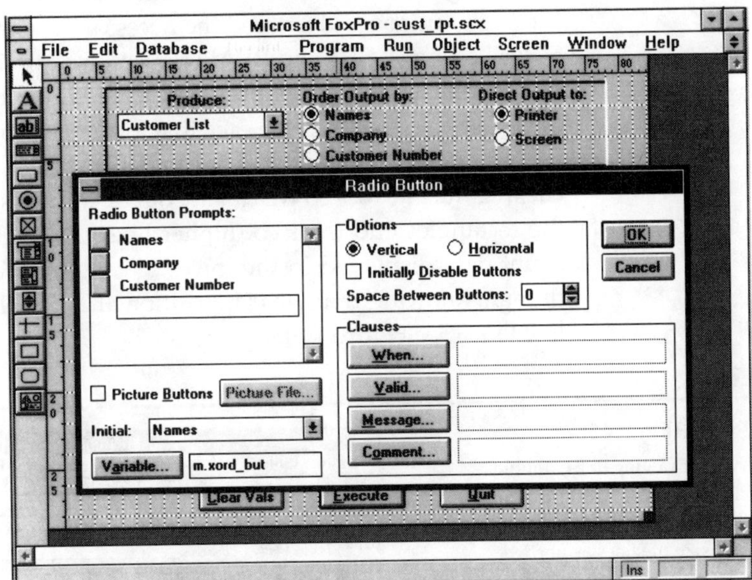

FIGURE 11.44:
Radio buttons provide an ideal tool when the operator must choose one of several set options.

Like push buttons, radio buttons can use text prompts or pictures and can be arranged vertically or horizontally. They also return a numeric value corresponding to the order of the selected radio button included in the set unless the variable assigned to trap the operator's selection—in this case xord_but, short for *order button*—is initialized to hold a character string before execution of the @ GET radio buttons. In the case of @ GET xord_but, we initialize the memvar in the screen file's setup code to hold a character value. When the operator makes a selection, FoxPro automatically stores the prompt used by the selected radio button to xord_but. Later on in the screen program, we can reference this value when arranging the order of records selected from the Customer database for output in the selected report. (This takes place after the operator selects the Execute push button located at the bottom of the Customer Reports window—a matter we look into in the following chapters.) We do not look at the other set of radio buttons used in Cust_rpt.scx to trap the operator's selection of output device because @ GET m.out_but works exactly like @ GET m.ord_but; it only uses a different variable to store the operator's selection and different text prompts.

Adding Graphical Objects

Returning to the creation of Customer.scx at this point, assuming we have added the push buttons and entered the necessary code snippets for startup and cleanup as well as our @ GET and READ clauses, we can finish off the screen file by adding our graphical objects. As previously noted, the two 3-D boxes are formed using lines, not box objects. Since each line forming our rectangles is an individual object, we can choose a distinct pen thickness and color for it. We thus begin by double-clicking the line tool so we can lay out all ten lines at once—the eight lines forming the rectangles and the two thinner lines that further subdivide the customer account data displayed in the lower rectangles. We do so in the roughest fashion, though, knowing that we can position and size them after terminating use of the line tool. (See Figure 11.45.)

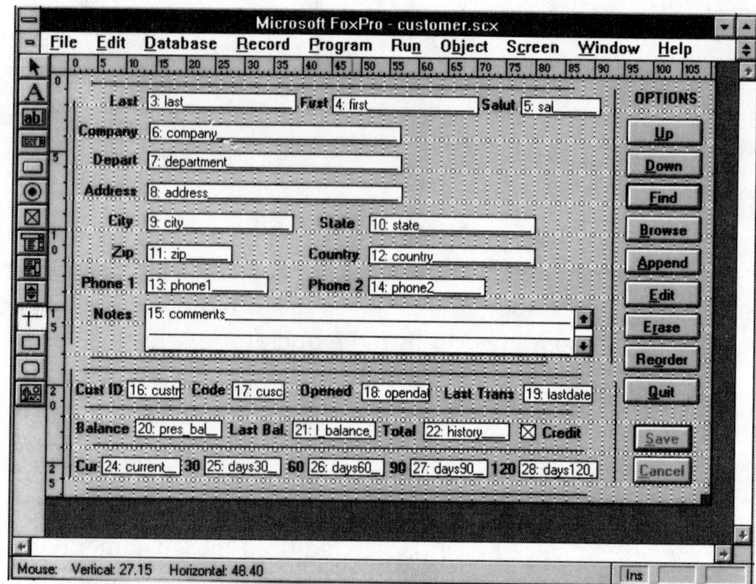

FIGURE 11.45:

When drawing lines, double-click the line object and draw the lines all at once. Then position and size the lines as needed.

All lines drawn with the line tool are vertical or horizontal. You click and hold down the mouse button where you want the line to begin and then extend the line that is anchored at that position with the mouse. Release the mouse button and the line is defined. You can change its length and starting position, but you cannot change its horizontal or vertical orientation. (If you want to get rid of a line, just re-select it by clicking it with the mouse and press the Del key.)

Once we have our lines in the window, we can move them into position and lengthen or shorten them. Note that while the mouse is quite helpful for dragging lines or setting their initial length, ultimately you will want to make final position and length adjustments using the arrow and Shift-arrow keys. We are dealing with lines, and they do need to be aligned exactly with each other, down to the last pixel.

The next step is to select the lines requiring a specific pen thickness other than the default setting of 1 point and to use the Pen option available on the Object pull-down to change their thickness as desired. (See Figure 11.46.)

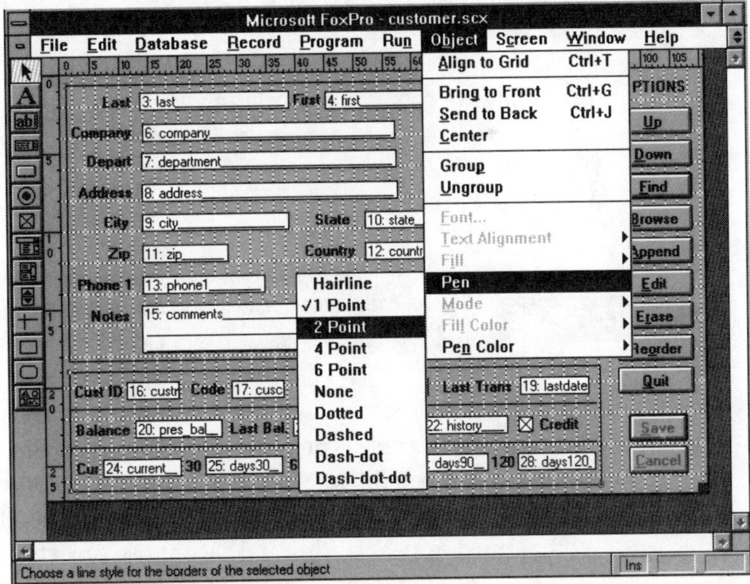

FIGURE 11.46:

Use the Pen option on the Object pulldown to change the pen thickness of lines or rectangles.

Adjusting pen thickness of lines is best done in batch; otherwise it becomes tedious. Since we make the eight lines forming our rectangles 2 points in thickness, we select them all with Shift-click before accessing the Pen dialog. We can then reassign their thicknesses all at once. (The two other lines are assigned the hairline thickness setting.)

With respect to line color, FoxPro makes them black by default. This is suitable for our needs, except for the four lines we must change to white in order to give our rectangles their 3-D appearance. We therefore select them and use the Pen Color dialog to change their color to white.

TIP

Rectangles formed with lines can have no fill color since they are not objects; the lines that form them are. If you want a rectangle so formed as to have a 3-D appearance and a fill color, you can do this by using the rectangle tool to draw a rectangle coinciding with the one formed by the lines. After giving the rectangle the desired color and assigning it no border (a pen thickness option), use the Object pulldown's Send to Back option to position the rectangle under the lines forming the 3-D box.

Finally we come to the rectangle we place underneath our push buttons. To create it we click on the rectangle tool, move the mouse pointer to where we want one corner, and then drag the mouse to the diagonally opposite corner. We release the mouse button to finish the rectangle. (See Figure 11.47.)

NOTE

The rounded rectangle tool works in exactly the same fashion. Double-click the rectangle once it is drawn to activate a dialog allowing you to change its curvature.

Once the rectangle is on the screen you can size and position it like any other object, change the pen thickness or pen color of the border (or use no border), and change its fill color. Note that when you create a rectangle, it may cover the other objects that must appear within it. Place those objects on top of the rectangle by selecting the rectangle and using the Object pulldown's Send to Back option. This places

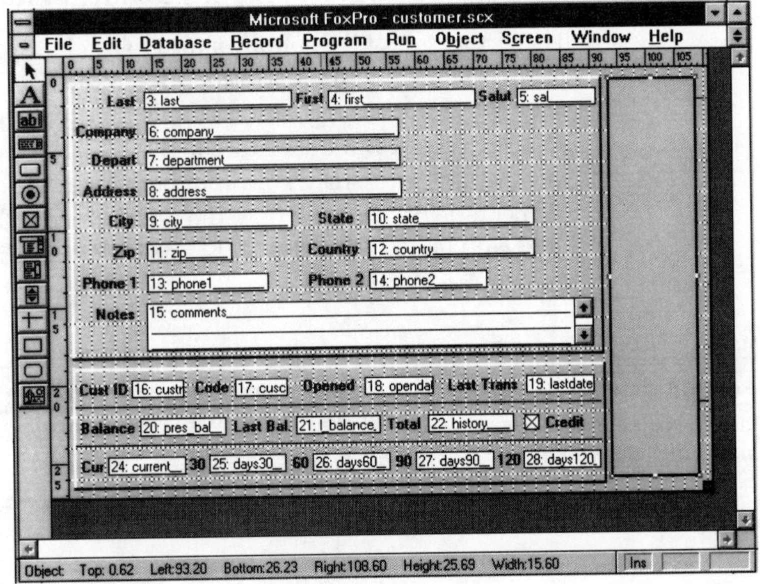

FIGURE 11.47:

When drawing rectangles, the Screen Builder places them on top of other objects. Use Send to Back to change their position so the other objects will appear on top.

the rectangle underneath the other objects. (Note that the front-to-back order of overlapping text and graphical objects in the Screen Layout window determines Genscrn.prg's ordering of the @ SAY commands that execute the objects in the screen program. The objects are executed beginning with the one at the very back.)

After finishing with the rectangle and drawing the two lines we place within it (to set off the Options text object from the push buttons and to separate the control push buttons from the Save and Cancel push buttons), we are done with Customer.scx. We can now use the Object Order dialog, available from the Screen pulldown, to make sure all our @ GET objects are in the correct order. We can then generate the screen program and do one of two things. We can try it out on a standalone basis using the Generate Screen dialog, provided we allow Customer.spr to open and close files, or we can add Customer.scx to the MBS project, select the generate options we require with the Edit Screen Set dialog, and allow the Project Manager to generate the screen program when we rebuild the project or build the application. (We will have more to say about the Object Order, Generate Screen, and Edit Screen Set dialogs after examining the two remaining Screen Builder tools used to create picture objects and spinners.)

Adding Pictures and Displaying General Fields

The picture tool at the bottom of the toolbox has two functions. It can be used to add pictures stored in bitmap or icon files to the READ window for use as part of the window's static design. You might do this, for example, to add a company logo to an entry screen. But the picture tool is also used to display General fields holding pictures in the READ window. In both cases the display is managed with @ SAY. (General fields are not sent to the screen or edited with @ GET, as we explain in a moment.) Figure 11.48 shows the Screen Picture dialog, used in Inventry.scx to define the @ SAY picture object that displays the pictures of inventory items.

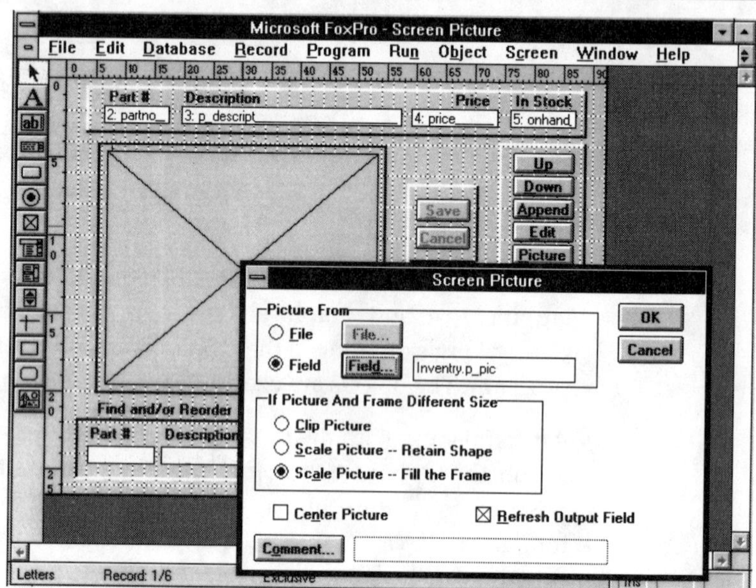

FIGURE 11.48:

Use the picture tool to place static pictures or to display pictures stored in General fields in the READ window.

When the picture definition is finished, FoxPro returns us to the screen layout, where we must use the mouse to position and size the frame in which the picture is to be displayed. The action is the same as drawing a rectangle, though the Screen Builder places diagonal lines across the picture frame to distinguish it from a rectangle object. (To supply the picture frame with a border, as we do in Inventry.scx, use the rectangle tool to draw a box around it.)

We use the the Picture dialog to select the bitmap file or General field we want to display within the picture frame. Unlike selecting a picture to use as window wallpaper, however, here we can instruct FoxPro to scale the picture so it fills the frame, to scale it as best as possible to fill the frame while retaining its shape, or to clip the picture, displaying only the portion of it that fits the frame. (We select the radio button to scale the picture to fill the frame, so we have no need of the Center picture check box, which can be used to center pictures that are smaller than the frame.)

We must also select the Refresh Output Field check box. This instructs Genscrn.prg, when executing Inventry.spr, to place commands automatically updating the picture display at the very end of the screen program's READ SHOW clause.

```
@ 4.615,7.000 SAY Inventry.p_pic ;
    SIZE 15.000,46.600 ;
    STRETCH ;
    STYLE ""
```

Owing to this command, FoxPro is able to update the picture displayed in the READ window as we move from record to record in the Inventory table. Again, bear in mind that commands refreshing output fields are placed at the end of READ SHOW. For this reason, if you enter a READ SHOW clause in the screen file, be careful not to place RETURN at the end of it. If you do, FoxPro will never get to the commands it inserts in READ SHOW after your snippet to refresh the picture display. (Of course, the Refresh Output Field option is not required when displaying a static picture in the window. It is used only to update the display of General fields, though it might also be used to change a picture drawn from an external file, based upon a conditional statement.)

Updating General Fields Holding Pictures

In Inventry.spr, we enter or change the picture stored in the General field of a table by adding a button labeled Picture to the main set of control push buttons and executing the command MODIFY GENERAL p_pic, referencing the General field displayed in the READ window's output field. This opens a window displaying the current General field picture, as shown in Figure 11.49, and enables the Edit pull-down Insert Object dialog. (See Figure 11.49.)

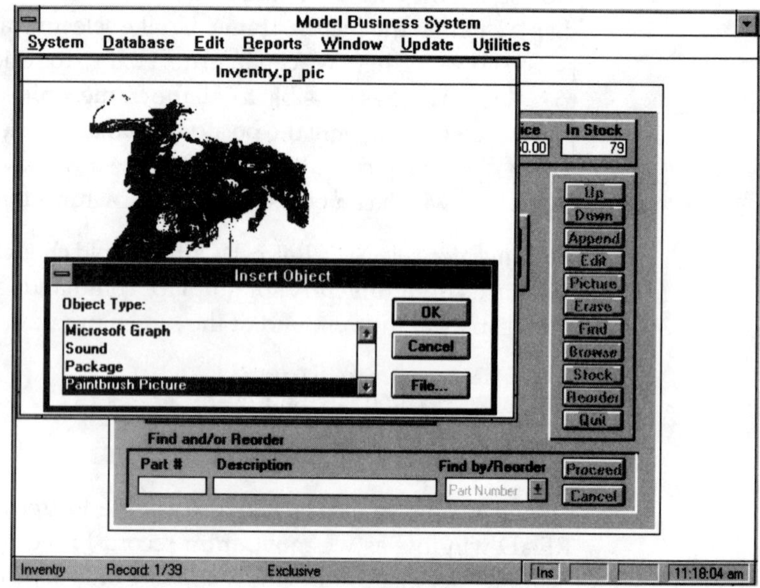

FIGURE 11.49:

Use the command MODIFY GENERAL <field> to display the current General field object in a window and activate the Insert Object dialog in the Edit pulldown.

To insert a picture or modify the displayed picture, the operator selects the Insert Object option from the Edit pulldown. From here, the operator can start any of the Windows applications available for creating or editing a picture (or other OLE object). For example, the operator might select the Paintbrush picture to start the Windows Paintbrush program, create or modify a picture, and copy it to the Clipboard. Then, after exiting the Paintbrush program and returning to FoxPro, the operator can paste the picture into the General field from the Clipboard.

If the desired picture (or other OLE object) already exists, the operator can instead pick the File button from the Insert Object dialog to open the Insert Object From File dialog. (See Figure 11.50.) The operator can then insert a picture automatically in the General field of the current record by simply selecting the desired picture file from the file list.

Note that objects inserted in a General field using the Insert Object dialog will first exist as linked objects. This means that the object itself is not stored in the General field. Instead, the General field holds a pointer instructing FoxPro how to find and display the correct object (file). The object (file) can then be edited or otherwise changed by the program used to create it, and the edited version of the file will

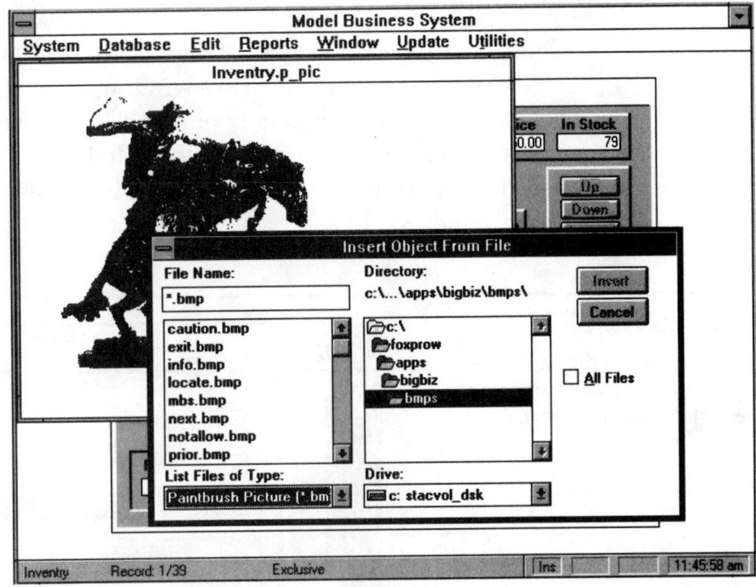

FIGURE 11.50:

Insert the image contained in an existing picture file in a General field of the current record by selecting it from the Insert Object From File dialog.

appear automatically when we display its image through the General field. (Note that if the file is erased, the object will no longer be available for display in the General field.) We can, however, place a static image of the object in the General field by using the Edit pulldown's Convert to Static option when the object is displayed in the General field window. This places a complete copy of the object in the General field. And while the object (file) can then be erased without affecting the object in the General field, editing the object, for example, with the Paintbrush program will have no effect on the static General field object. (Static objects cannot be edited. If you want to alter an object that has been converted to a static object, you must replace it.)

We have only scratched the surface of a complex topic. In addition to pictures, General fields can hold graphs and sound bytes. And there is much to learn about OLE (object linking and embedding) if you plan to make serious use of it in your applications. For more information about OLE, refer to the FoxPro for Windows *Developer's Guide* as well as your Microsoft Windows *User's Guide*.

Adding Spinners

Though we do not make use of them in the MBS, spinners just like the ones used in FoxPro dialogs can be placed in a window, allowing the operator to select a numeric value by entering it manually or by clicking the up or down spinner arrow to increase or decrease the displayed value. In Figure 11.51, we show the Spinner dialog used to define the spinner that appears in the otherwise empty screen layout in the background.

FIGURE 11.51:

Use the Spinner dialog to define a spinner to assist the operator in entering a numeric value.

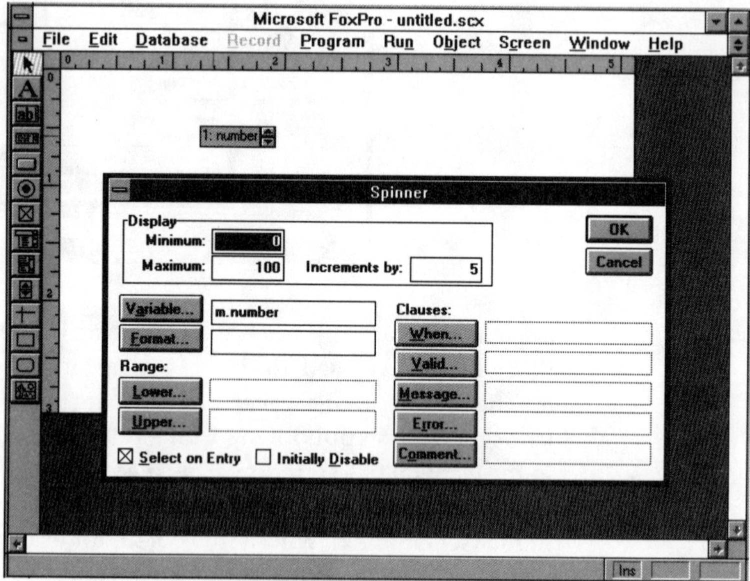

Spinners are created like all other @ GET objects. Click the spinner tool, position the mouse in the READ window where you want the spinner positioned, and click again to open the Spinner dialog. In Figure 11.51, we define a spinner that will display and spin the numbers 0 (the entered minimum) through 100 (the entered maximum), though the operator will be able to overwrite the displayed value with a value outside the range set with Minimum and Maximum. If you want to reject manual entries outside the actual spin range, you can use the Lower and Upper Range options for this purpose, though this can also be done using a VALID clause.

The Increments value is used to determine the value by which the number displayed in the spinner will be increased or decreased through operator use of the spinner's up and down arrows. (The default value is 1.)

Spinners are useful for making data entry to a numeric table field holding values that must fall within a range. (Negative numbers can be entered as the minimum and maximum if you choose, and decimals can be used.) Spinners are also useful for entering integer values to memvars employed to control program action in some way—for example, to specify the number of copies of a printed report or the number of records to be added to a table at once. When activated, the spinner displays the current value of the variable. This value is retained until the operator changes it through use of the spinner.

Spinners are positioned and sized like all other @ GET objects. (Increasing the vertical size of a spinner also increases the size of the up and down spinners.)

Using the Object Order Dialog

When creating a screen file, we do not concern ourselves with the final ordering of the @ GET objects we place in the READ window, though this will ultimately determine the order in which each @ GET is executed by the screen program. The order in which they are executed determines the order in which each @ GET will be activated when the operator presses the Tab, Shift+Tab, or Enter key.

Initially, the Screen Builder assigns each @ GET object a number corresponding to the order in which it was entered in the screen layout; and to make things easier on us, it displays the object's order number in front of the object's variable name. Still, the reason we do not trouble with object order while defining, manipulating, and sizing our @ GETs is that we can do it most easily with the Object Order dialog, accessed from the Screen pulldown, once we are satisfied with the layout of all objects. (See Figure 11.52.)

With a screen layout like that used with Customer.scx, we expect the operator to enter data starting with the first input field at the top left of the form and ending with the last input field at the bottom right. We can therefore approximate this order instantly by selecting the By Row push button. All the @ GET variables listed in the Object Order list will be instantly reshuffled and their order numbers reassigned to correspond to this selection. (When arranging input fields in columns, use the By

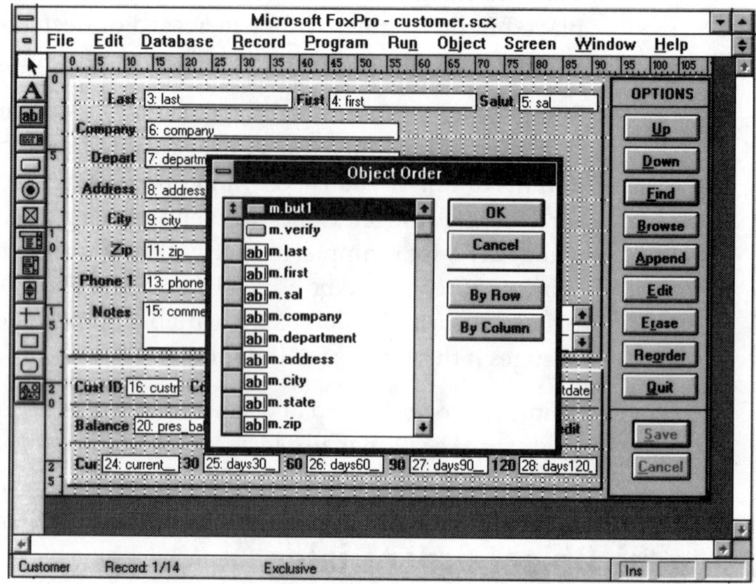

FIGURE 11.52:

The execution order of @ GETs in a screen program can be arranged semi-automatically at the end of the screen design process using the Object Order dialog.

Column push button to reorder the objects according to their position in each column, beginning with the leftmost column.)

TIP

Always work with Snap to Grid set on to ensure that the Object Order By Row and By Column buttons reorder all @ GETs as you expect. The slightest disparity of row coordinates between two objects that appear on the same row in the screen layout will affect how the Screen Builder reorders the objects when you use By Row. If the first object is positioned just a fraction of a row below the row coordinate of the second object, it will appear after the second object in the Object Order list.

However, after using By Row to quickly place our @ GETs in order, we can make further adjustments by dragging objects directly in the Object Order list. For example, to make our control push buttons the first @ GET executed in the screen program, we locate its prompt in the list and drag the button to its immediate left with the mouse until the object appears at the top of the list. We do the same thing with @ GET m.verify, representing our Save and Cancel push buttons, to make it the second object. (Again, we place the push button objects at the top of the list so they will be redrawn first when the Customers window is reactivated. This also makes @ GET m.but1, our control push buttons, the first cursor object when READ is activated, though the use of WHEN m.doit with all @ GET input fields and the initial disabling of the Save and Cancel push buttons would force this to happen anyway, regardless of @ GET m.but1's order.)

TIP

Be sure to look over the order of all objects in the Object Order list before finishing with a screen file. This will save you the trouble of having to modify a screen file and regenerate a screen program just because a single @ GET is out of place.

Generating the Screen Program

As you know, screen programs can be generated in two different ways. If you are designing a screen program for execution on a stand-alone basis, you can access the Generate Screen dialog from the Program pulldown while the Screen Builder is active. FoxPro automatically lists the open screen file at the top of the Screen Set list and enters the screen file's name in the Output File entry box, though it gives the output file name an .spr extension. This is the name Genscrn.prg will assign to the generated screen program. You can change it if you like. (By default, Genscrn.prg places the screen program in the default directory.)

In Figure 11.53 we show the Generate Screen dialog as it would appear when opened with Customer.scx in the active screen design window, after the More button has been selected to show the Generated Code option check boxes. (The majority of these were discussed earlier in this chapter.)

Supposing that Customer.scx included no commands referencing procedures and functions found in other MBS program files—Function Stop, for example, used in the DEACTIVATE clause of all MBS nonmodal screen programs, is stored in Bizlib.prg—we might generate Customer.spr for execution on a stand-alone basis by allowing the screen program to open and close files. More generally, we would accept the default Generated Code settings, shown in Figure 11.53, as is, though we might consider checking the Modal Screen check box to make the screen program behaves like a dialog through the use of READ MODAL.

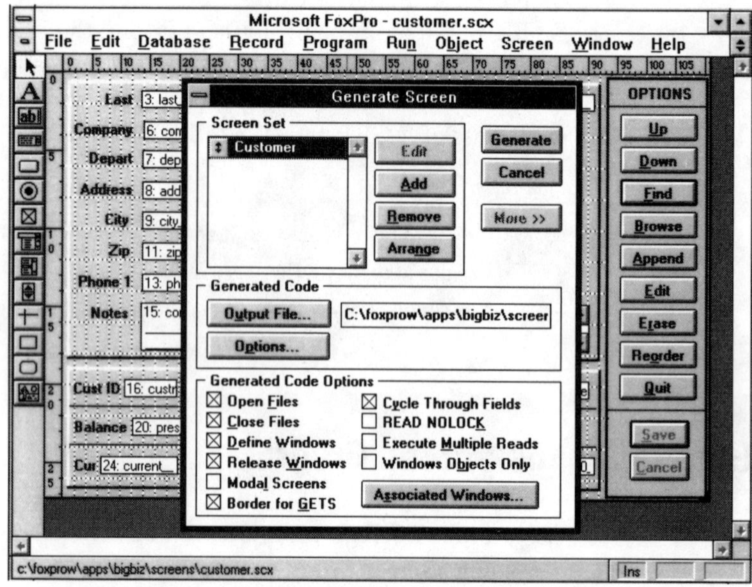

FIGURE 11.53: Access the Generate Screen dialog from the Program pulldown to generate a screen program based upon the open screen file.

Another check box we might select is Window Objects Only. This tells Genscrn.prg to exclude certain commands enabling the screen program to operate on platforms other than FoxPro for Windows. Using the READ NOLOCK check box will have no effect here since Customer.scx references table fields indirectly through the use of memvars. However, when you create screen programs that directly reference table fields with @ GET and must operate in a network environment, you can use READ NOLOCK to make Genscrn.prg include the NOLOCK keyword in the READ command. This is normally done when you include record-locking routines of your own in the screen program. Table records must, in any case, be locked before their fields can be updated. Unless you intend to oversee record locking yourself, do not check the READ NOLOCK check box. (We discuss the Multiple READ check box below, when we examine how to generate screen programs using multiple screen sets.)

Using an Associated Window List with Modal Screen Programs

When designing modal screen programs you can select the Associated Windows button at the bottom of the Generate Screen or Edit Screen Set dialog to provide Genscrn.prg with a list of windows the operator may activate during a modal READ. This is crucial when creating modal screen programs that include several non-READ windows activated through commands placed in a screen file's setup code or READ WHEN or ACTIVATE clause; otherwise, FoxPro will prevent the operator from selecting them. As you will recall, during READ MODAL only the READ windows belonging to the screen sets listed in the Generate Screen or Edit Screen Set list will be automatically available to the operator. To make other windows available during the READ, we must enter them by name or title in the Associated Windows dialog list. Figure 11.54, for example, shows the associated window list we would use in a modal version of Payments.spr.

Since Payments.spr is designed to use two BROWSE windows along with the Customer Payments window, defined in Payments.scx—one to display customer payments, the other to display customer sales—we include them at the top of the list,

FIGURE 11.54:

To make BROWSE and other non-READ windows, including the FoxPro desk accessories, available to the operator in a modal screen program, list their names or titles in the Associated Windows dialog.

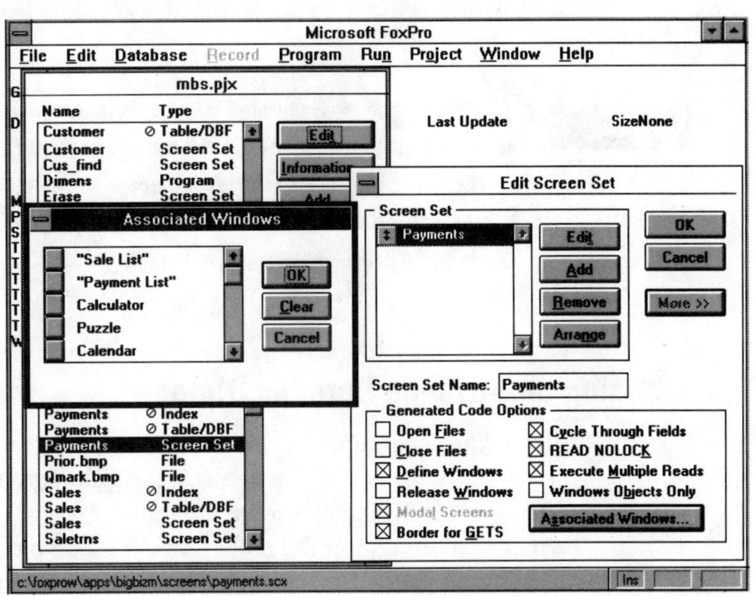

though the ordering of the windows in the list really makes no difference. We also want to make the Calculator, Calendar/Diary, and Puzzle available to the operator during execution of Payments.spr, so we include their names in the list. When Genscrn.prg produces the screen program, the READ command it produces will include a WITH <associated window> clause listing all five windows.

```
READ CYCLE MODAL ;
    WITH "Sale List", "Payment List", Calculator, ;
    Puzzle, Calendar
```

Again, you can enter windows in the list using their window names or titles, though window titles must be entered as delimited character expressions. For this reason, we enter the titles of the two BROWSE windows in quotes in the Associated Windows dialog so Genscrn.prg will list them as character expressions in the WITH clause. With respect to the desk accessories, their window names and titles are the same, except in the case of the Calendar/Diary. Its window name is Calendar. If we wanted to reference it by title instead of name, as was done above, we would have to enter Calendar/Diary in quotes. Otherwise FoxPro would not be able to identify the window during screen program execution. (For an in-depth discussion of Payments.spr and how to include BROWSE and other non-READ windows in your applications, see Chapter 5. For a discussion of how to reactivate the system menu during execution of READ MODAL so the operator can, for example, select desk accessories included in an Associated Window list, see Chapter 9.)

NOTE

When using the Generate Screen or Edit Screen Set dialog, FoxPro selects and disables the Modal Read check box upon entry of an Associated Windows list. READ MODAL is assumed. In generating Payments.spr we do not include an Associated Windows list since the screen program is designed to operate in a nonmodal fashion, as explained in Chapters 5, 6, and 10.)

Using the Arrange Screens Dialog

Just before generating the screen program, you can alter the position of the Customers window, as set in Customer.scx, by clicking the Arrange button. This opens the Arrange Screens dialog shown in Figure 11.55, where you can reposition the READ window by dragging the scaled model's title bar or by using the Horizontal and Vertical spinners or the Center check box. The window position controls work the

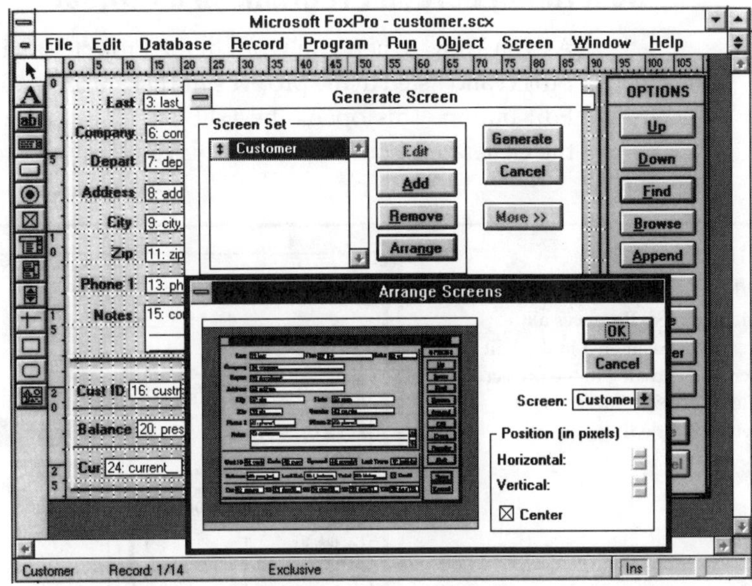

FIGURE 11.55:

Just before generating a screen program, you can reposition the READ windows using the Arrange Screens dialog.

same as those in the Screen Layout dialog, discussed earlier in this chapter. Bear in mind, however, that changing a READ window's position with the Arrange Screen dialog does not affect the window's position settings in the screen file; it only alters the READ window's position in the generated screen program.

In fact, once we generate the .spr program using the Generate Screen dialog's Generate button, all instructions entered with the dialog to guide Genscrn.prg in its work are thrown out. What if we generate Customer.spr and then execute it from the Command window with DO Customer.spr, only to discover one or two errors? When we next open the Generate Screen dialog to produce the corrected screen program, we will be compelled to select all nondefault Generated Code options over again; FoxPro does not retain them in the screen file. This is one of the advantages of working with a project file. When you enter Generate Code options through the Project Manager's Edit Screen Set dialog, FoxPro saves the settings in the Project file. You do not have to reenter them. (We will return to the Arrange Screens dialog later in this chapter, when we discuss the creation of screen programs based upon multiple screen sets.)

Generating Screen Programs in a Project

As you know, when you work in the Project Manager all screen files included in a project and listed in the project's file list are immediately available for edit using the Edit button. This opens the Edit Screen Set dialog, shown in Figure 11.56 with the Generated Code options displayed through use of the More button.

FIGURE 11.56:

When working in the Project Manager, FoxPro saves all instructions entered in the Edit Screen Set dialog to the project file record for the screen set selected for edit.

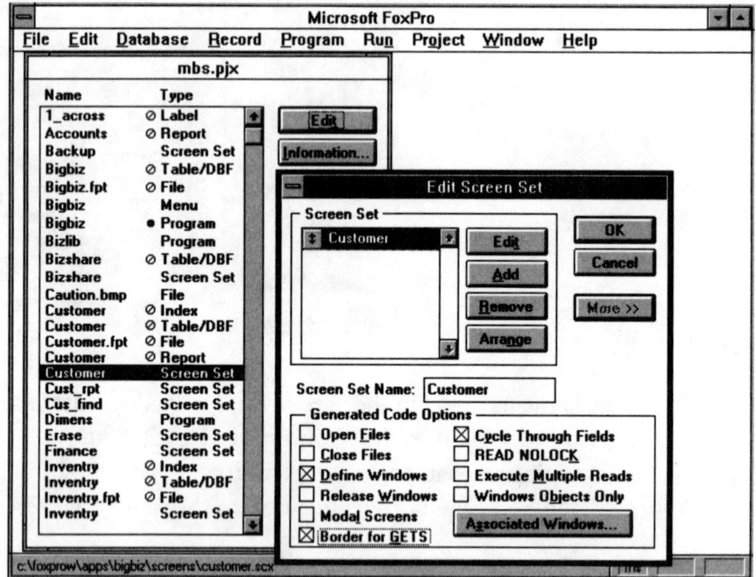

In this figure we see the actual settings used in generating Customer.spr. (The Arrange Screens dialog is not used, to allow Genscrn.prg to arrange the window using the screen file setting of Center.) Since the MBS startup program establishes the database environment Customer.spr is to employ without changing, we unselect the Open Files and Close Files check boxes. We also uncheck Release Windows since Customer.spr's cleanup code is designed to conditionally release the READ window only when the operator terminates the READ by selecting the Quit push button or by selecting Close from the window control box. Actual termination of the READ, though, is accomplished through the READ DEACTIVATE clause. (Remember, Close does not in itself terminate READ; it only hides the READ window, as explained in Chapter 6.)

Of course, if we actually want to edit Customer.scx, we can do so now by selecting the Edit button in the Edit Screen Set dialog. Still, the great benefit is that all instructions entered with the Edit Screen Set dialog are saved in the project file record for the screen set. As long as you modify and generate the screen file and program through the Project Manager, you don't need to reenter them. However, the Generate option is not available from the Edit Screen Set dialog. To generate the .spr program using the instructions stored in the project file, you must rebuild the project or build the application, as described in Chapter 7.

It is worth remembering that in developing the MBS, we have no special interest in Customer.spr except as an aid in program debugging. This is because our goal is to produce an .app file. (The .spr file is required only as part of the .app file generation process and need not be present on disk for the .app to be executed.) On the other hand, owing to the Project Manager's ability to hold onto the Edit Screen Set instructions, one can well imagine including screen files in a project just for the sake of regenerating stand-alone .spr files after modifying one or more screen files. (If you rebuild the project, the Project Manager regenerates all screen programs that are out of date but does not build an .app file.)

Generating Screen Programs with Multiple Screen Sets

The reason the Generate Screen and Edit Screen Set dialogs cannot store or take their settings from a particular screen file is that they are designed to oversee Genscrn.prg's production of screen programs that can include two or more screen sets (files), each defining a window with @ GET objects. In the Screen Builder, the object of our labor is a specific screen file. In the Generate Screen and Edit Screen Set dialogs, the object is the screen program; the settings we enter in them direct Genscnr.prg's action (opening or closing files or defining and releasing windows) in generating a screen program based on the instructions found in each screen file listed by root name in the Screen Set list.

Here, Letters.spr, the MBS screen program that uses two screen files, is our example. The Edit Screen Set dialog shown in Figure 11.57 is opened by selecting the Letters screen set for edit when MBS.pjx is open in the Project Manager.

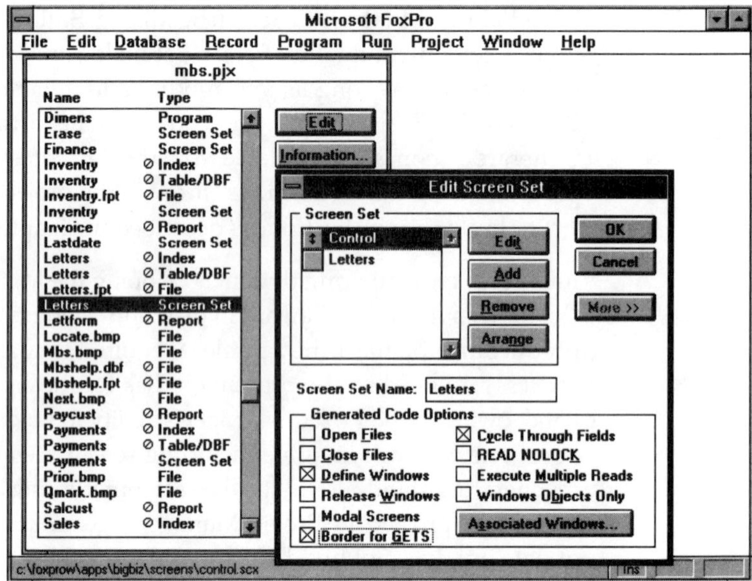

FIGURE 11.57:
Screen programs based on more than one screen set (file) are generated by placing the names of all screen files that must be included in the program in the Generate Screen or Edit Screen Set list.

At first, after Letters.scx was added to the project, only the Letters screen set was listed in the Edit Screen Set dialog. To include the screen set holding the control push button window, defined in Customer.scx, in the screen program, we select the dialog's Add button. This opens the Add Screen dialog shown in Figure 11.58. We use this to select the screen file we want to add to the screen program, though the dialog's New button can be used to activate the Screen Builder in order to create the desired screen file.

Once we have added all the screen sets that must be included in the screen program to the Edit Screen Set dialog, we can turn our attention to their order of execution in the screen program, as well as to the arrangement of the windows they define on the screen. When we click the Arrange button, the Arrange Screens dialog's window will display scaled models of all windows defined by the screen files included in the Screen Set list; they are also listed by name in the Screen popup, which is shown open in Figure 11.59. We can now move them into position as we want by selecting and dragging them with the mouse or by using the position spinners or Center check box to alter the position of the currently selected window. (Separate position settings are maintained for each window.)

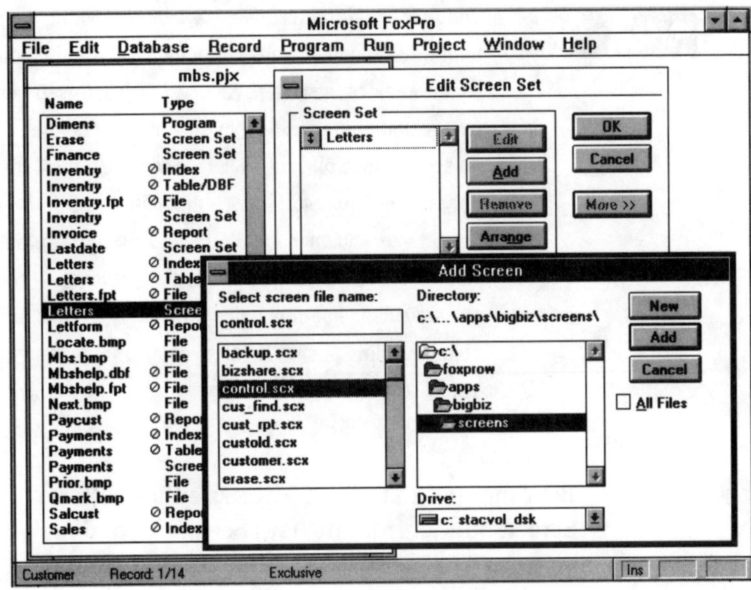

FIGURE 11.58:

Use the Add Screen dialog to select the screen sets you want to add to the Generate Screen or Edit Screen Set list for inclusion in a screen program.

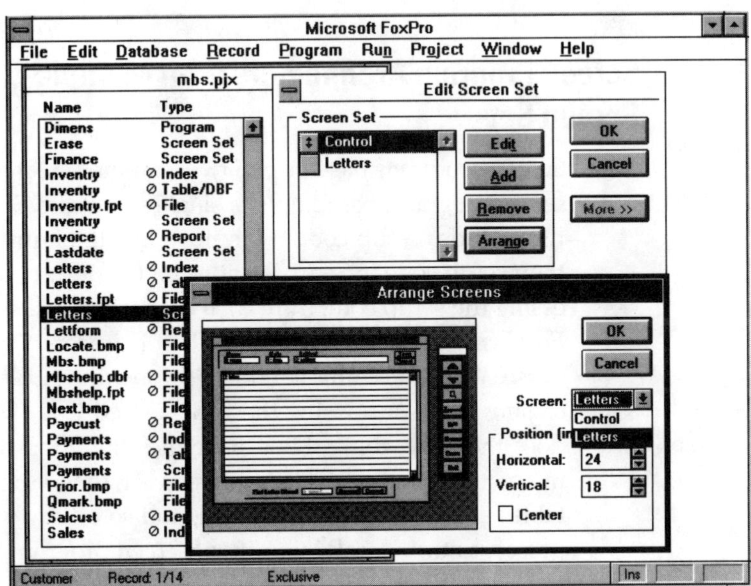

FIGURE 11.59:

Arranging multiple READ windows in a screen program is easy using the Arrange Screens dialog.

NOTE

The Arrange Screens dialog's window showing the scaled models of Letters.spr's two READ windows does not work as well as it should. In fact, to place the Control window next to the Letters window in the screen program as suggested in Figure 11.59, we must actually position it horizontally at column 640 with the spinner. When we do so, the Control window disappears from the Arrange window's display area because 640 exceeds its width. (With the Control window's current horizontal position, as shown in the figure, when we execute the screen program the Control window will appear on top of the Letters window—not next to it as it should.) Since you may also experience this problem when arranging screen sets, be ready to adjust window positions using the spinners—and dead reckoning, based upon actual results.

Bear in mind that we can access either Letters.scx or Control.scx for edit with the Screen Builder from the Edit Screen Set dialog. We simply double-click the desired screen set or highlight it and press the Edit button. This makes it relatively easy to modify any and all screen files employed within a screen program in one session. With respect to the open project, moreover, it is only necessary to include one of the screen files since the project file record for that screen set will include the entire Edit Screen Set list as well as instructions as to the directory location of each screen file.

Screen Program Architecture with Multiple Screen Sets

Screen programs based upon two or more screen files use the same architecture as screen programs based upon a single screen file. Supposing each contributing screen file includes setup code (with no #SECTION directive), Genscrn.prg combines all their setup code in Setup Section 2 of the designated output file. It does so by processing the setup code from each of the screen files listed in the Generate Screen or Edit Screen Set dialog in their order of appearance in the Screen Set list. This makes sense. When defining windows or opening files—or when closing windows and closing files—supposing these Generated Code options are selected, Genscrn.prg does the same thing. First, it defines the window or opens the tables following instructions in the first listed screen set, then it defines the window and opens the tables as specified in the second, and so on. By working in this way, Genscrn.prg preserves the overall integrity of screen program architecture, as described earlier in this chapter. Figure 11.60, for example, shows part of the screen layout code segment Genscrn.prg executes for Letters.spr. In it, you will note the commands executing the objects included in the Control window followed by those executing the objects belonging to the Letters window. This, of course, corresponds to the position of Control.scx and Letters.scx in the Edit Screen Set dialog, shown earlier in Figure 11.57. When the one READ command used by the screen program is executed, the READ window defined first in the screen program will be made WONTOP( ) unless this is altered through use of READ WHEN, ACTIVATE, or SHOW, the code for which Genscrn.prg takes from all screen files including such clauses.

FIGURE 11.60:

When creating screen programs based on multiple screen files, Genscrn.prg activates and executes the objects in each READ window according to the order of the corresponding screen file in the Generate Screen or Edit Screen Set list.

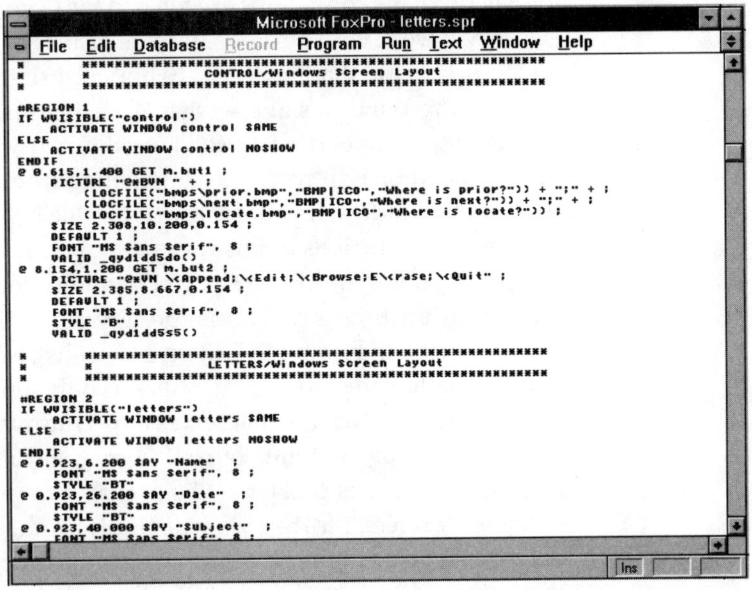

Microsoft FoxPro - letters.spr

File Edit Database Record Program Run Text Window Help

```
*       **********************************************************
*       *                 CONTROL/Windows Screen Layout
*       **********************************************************

#REGION 1
IF WVISIBLE("control")
    ACTIVATE WINDOW control SAME
ELSE
    ACTIVATE WINDOW control NOSHOW
ENDIF
@ 0.615,1.400 GET m.but1 ;
    PICTURE "@*BVN " + ;
        (LOCFILE("bmps\prior.bmp","BMP|ICO","Where is prior?")) + ";" + ;
        (LOCFILE("bmps\next.bmp","BMP|ICO","Where is next?")) + ";" + ;
        (LOCFILE("bmps\locate.bmp","BMP|ICO","Where is locate?")) ;
    SIZE 2.308,10.200,0.154 ;
    DEFAULT 1 ;
    FONT "MS Sans Serif", 8 ;
    VALID _qyd1dd5do()
@ 8.154,1.200 GET m.but2 ;
    PICTURE "@*VN \<Append;\<Edit;\<Browse;E\<rase;\<Quit" ;
    SIZE 2.385,8.667,0.154 ;
    DEFAULT 1 ;
    FONT "MS Sans Serif", 8 ;
    STYLE "B" ;
    VALID _qyd1dd5s5()

*       **********************************************************
*       *                 LETTERS/Windows Screen Layout
*       **********************************************************

#REGION 2
IF WVISIBLE("letters")
    ACTIVATE WINDOW letters SAME
ELSE
    ACTIVATE WINDOW letters NOSHOW
ENDIF
@ 0.923,6.200 SAY "Name"  ;
    FONT "MS Sans Serif", 8 ;
    STYLE "BT"
@ 0.923,26.200 SAY "Date"  ;
    FONT "MS Sans Serif", 8 ;
    STYLE "BT"
@ 0.923,40.000 SAY "Subject"  ;
    FONT "MS Sans Serif", 8 ;
```

Ins

Genscrn.prg combines the setup and cleanup code, as well as the code snippets for READ clauses, of all screen files in generating each of the screen program's code segments. While this is a fairly easy convention to work with, it does have its pitfalls. For example, if two screen files include READ ACTIVATE clauses, we must be certain that actions taken by the commands in the ACTIVATE code snippet of the first screen file do not prevent FoxPro from executing commands taken from the second screen file—unless that ought to happen. If setup and/or cleanup code is supplied from more than one screen file, we must be certain that setup and cleanup code are written to avoid conflicts. For the most part, this is easily done by choosing a main window (or screen file), just as you would choose the main program in starting a project. In the case of Letters.spr, we choose Letters.scx. In it, we place all screen program code that pertains to the general action of the screen program and to the specific operation of all objects defined in Letters.scx. The only code included in Control.scx is that specifically related to the initialization of the memvars it uses, the @ GET VALID clauses required by its two push buttons, and a cleanup code command releasing its window.

When it comes to using a separately defined control push button window, like that supplied by Customer.scx, there are added advantages to working in this way. Actions like Up, Down, Find, Append, and so on, can all be written in a generic fashion, such that the commands executed in the Control window's push button VALID clause will work with whatever table is displayed in the main READ window. This assumes, though, that the READ SHOW clause supplied by the main screen file is written to respond to signals—that is, changes in the values of specific memvars, like m.doit, m.append, and m.edit, used in the MBS to signal the launching of the data Append or Edit routines—originating from operator selection of buttons in the Control window. If you create a screen file holding all instructions for a Control window that functions in this way, not only can you use it over and over in every screen program requiring a Control window, you can also substitute the Control window at any time, say, with a more advanced model by simply removing the old Control screen file from the Edit Screen Set list, adding the new screen file, and regenerating the screen program. Still, this only illustrates a general rule that can be applied to any screen file that serves a specific role in a screen program. There is no need, for example, to limit yourself to one control push button window when several different sets of tools must be available to the operator. If your windows are opaque, the screen files can be strategically arranged and ordered in the Edit Screen Set list so that one or more windows (say, those holding secondary controls) are initially opened underneath other READ windows. (They can also be hidden or minimized through use of READ WHEN or ACTIVATE.) When they are needed, the operator can simply select them by name from the Window pulldown, cycle to them if they are not hidden, or maximize them if they are initially minimized. There is no end of things you can arrange through the intelligent combination of screen files. Using a single control push button window along with a main READ window is only the simplest example of FoxPro's potential.

There are a couple of things to look out for in creating screen programs based on multiple screen files. First, if values used by commands entered in more than one contributing screen file must be passed to the screen program with the PARAMETERS command, it will not do to place a PARAMETERS command (along with the #SECTION 1 directive) in the setup code of more than one of the screen files. This, again, is why we select a main screen file. Other screen files can contribute #SECTION 1 or #SECTION 2 setup code; that makes no difference. But you must be prepared to trap the parameters passed by DO <.spr> WITH <parameters> with one PARAMETERS command.

The second issue pertains to the management of memory variables. As noted earlier in this chapter, Genscrn.prg uses #REGION directives to place the commands originating from different screen files, as well as the commands it automatically generates, for example, as environment setup and cleanup code, in different memory areas. Figure 11.61, for example, shows Letters.spr's cleanup code, which is executed when the READ command used to activate all @ GET objects in all READ windows is terminated. It begins with #REGION 0, where Genscnr.prg places automatically generated environment commands referencing the memvars it declared REGIONAL in the #REGION 0 setup code it includes by default in all screen programs. It then executes the one cleanup command supplied by Control.scx, RELEASE WINDOW control, in #REGION 1 and finishes with cleanup code supplied by Letters.scx in #REGION 2.

FIGURE 11.61:

When executing screen programs based on more than one screen file, Genscrn.prg executes the commands originating from different screen sets in different #REGIONs.

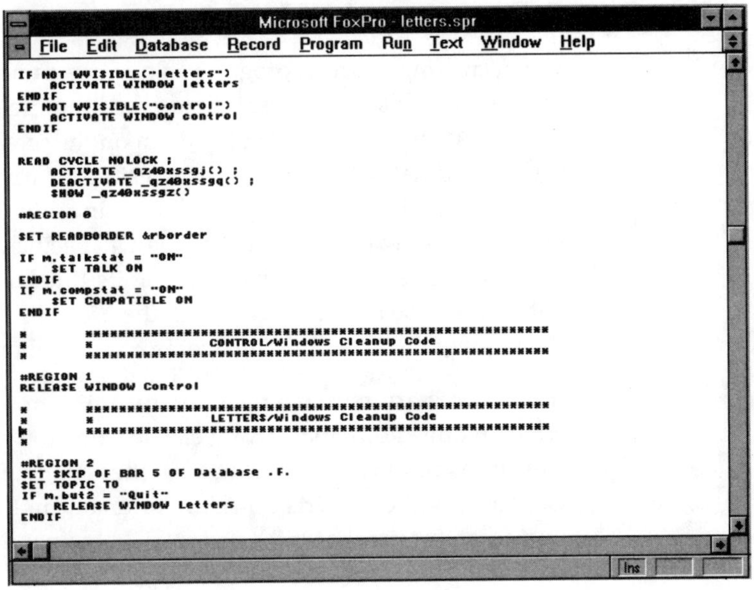

Microsoft FoxPro - letters.spr

File Edit Database Record Program Run Text Window Help

```
IF NOT WVISIBLE("letters")
    ACTIVATE WINDOW letters
ENDIF
IF NOT WVISIBLE("control")
    ACTIVATE WINDOW control
ENDIF

READ CYCLE NOLOCK ;
    ACTIVATE _qz40xssgj() ;
    DEACTIVATE _qz40xssgq() ;
    SHOW _qz40xssgz()

#REGION 0

SET READBORDER &rborder

IF m.talkstat = "ON"
    SET TALK ON
ENDIF
IF m.compstat = "ON"
    SET COMPATIBLE ON
ENDIF

*       ********************************************************
*       *                  CONTROL/Windows Cleanup Code
*       ********************************************************

#REGION 1
RELEASE WINDOW Control

*       ********************************************************
*       *                  LETTERS/Windows Cleanup Code
*       ********************************************************
*

#REGION 2
SET SKIP OF BAR 5 OF Database .F.
SET TOPIC TO
IF m.but2 = "Quit"
    RELEASE WINDOW Letters
ENDIF
```

Ins

With respect to Letters.spr, the effect of Genscrn.prg's use of #REGION directives is nil. None of the memvars used by Control.scx or Letters.spr are declared regional with the REGIONAL command, described earlier in this chapter. Nor do their names conflict with one another or with the names of the REGIONAL memvars Genscrn.prg creates in #REGION 0 setup code so it can restore certain SET environment parameters. They are therefore available in all regions of the screen program.

However, you may run into situations in which the names of memvars used by @ GET objects in one screen file conflict with the names of memvars used in another. You can get around this problem by declaring the memvars REGIONAL in each screen file. FoxPro will then maintain all of them in memory by providing them with unique names and will make them available under their original names whenever it is executing commands in the #REGION to which they individually belong.

NOTE

FoxPro keeps track of declared regional memvars with conflicting names by extending their names to a full ten characters with underscores, followed by their region number. This keeps them out of the way when FoxPro is executing commands belonging to a different region.

Screen Programs with Multiple Pages

When creating a screen program to oversee data entry to tables with an excessive number of fields, you can subdivide the input fields and use two or more overlapping READ windows to display them on the screen. Give the READ windows the same coordinates and window dimensions to arrange them as pages, or better yet, arrange them in cascading order so that, in addition to cycling through them or using the Window pulldown to move to a specific window (page), the operator can select any given window by selecting its title bar. Windows holding subordinate data can also be minimized through the use of READ WHEN or ACTIVATE to keep them out of the way until the operator selects them.

If it is necessary to move the operator through several windows of data, each of which requires different READ clauses, this too can be managed by selecting the Execute Multiple Reads check box in the Generate Screen or Edit Screen Set dialog. Genscrn.prg then inserts a READ command in the screen program's layout code immediately after the @ SAY and @ GET commands used with each READ window.

Using the various READ clauses and #READCLAUSES in the screen file setup code, you can obtain a variety of different effects. Bear in mind, however, that though the screen program will define all windows at once, operator use of the windows must be sequential (unless READ SAVE is used) so the @ GETs appearing in each READ window will be reactivated by the READ command used with the following window.

We make no use of these features in the MBS, even though we might, for example, arrange data entry to Customer.dbf using two windows (pages) and a control push button window as well. But you are now aware of the various options open to you in constructing screen programs based upon multiple screen sets so you will be able to use them when you run into a programming problem that requires their use.

Using One Screen File to Create Another

When designing Customer.scx, my intention was to establish the typical format that would be used by all other MBS data entry screen programs. Since Payments.spr, Sales.spr, Saletrns.spr, and Inventry.spr all use a similar configuration, the creation of the single screen files on which they are based could in each case be initiated with a copy of Customer.scx. This made their development much faster, as is readily illustrated by taking a look at Payments.scx. (See Figure 11.62.)

Starting with a copy of Customer.scx, renamed to Payments.scx with the File pull-down's Save As option, we can use the selection marquee to get rid of input fields not required in the Customer Payments window. Since Payments.scx must perform updates to records in Payments.dbf, we make the input fields displaying parent record data from Customer.dbf read-only by altering their WHEN condition from m.doit to .F. Memvar m.doit, however, is used again in Payments.scx, as it is in all MBS screen programs, to control execution of the data Append and Edit routines. More important, we simply reuse the same set of menu control and Save and Cancel push buttons, though we alter, add, or remove items in the @ GET control push buttons and edit the code snippets taken over from Customer.scx as needed.

The Clipboard can be used to transfer screen objects along with all their clauses from one screen file to another, so you can also scavenge objects from other screen

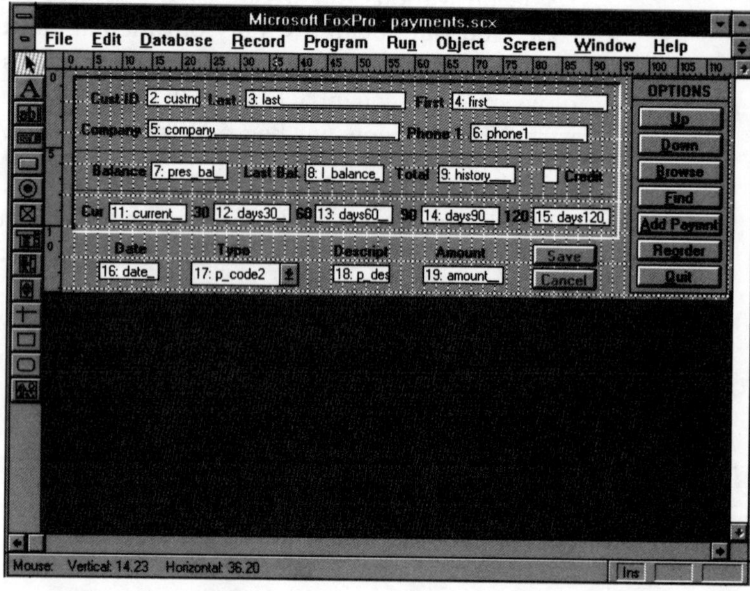

FIGURE 11.62:
Since Payments.scx includes many of the input fields as well as both sets of push buttons used by Customer.scx, we begin its creation by using a copy of Customer.scx.

files. Just select the desired objects with the selection marquee and use the Edit pull-down's Copy option to copy them to the Clipboard. You can then paste them into any screen file, as described earlier in this chapter. Of course, once you have a fair number of screen files on hand, screen file creation becomes more a matter of copying and pasting than creating. Remember, too, that all screen file code snippets are also open game to the Clipboard and can be transferred from one screen file into the Code Snippet window of another.

Controlling Operator Access to @ GETs and @ EDITs in Screen Programs

If you plan to make use of a control push button window in your data entry screen programs, instead of including control push buttons directly in the main READ window you must slightly alter the programming style used by all MBS single READ window screen programs. As you may recall, when executing Customer.spr we use the logical memvar m.doit in the WHEN clause of all input fields to prevent the cursor from entering them until the operator presses the Edit or Add push button. Because m.doit is set to .F. and the Save and Cancel push buttons are disabled when Customer.spr is first executed—and remain so except during execution of the Add and Edit routines—the operator is limited to use of the control push buttons at all other times.

While this strategy works fine with all single READ window screen programs, as soon as you remove the control push buttons to a separate READ window you will find yourself in trouble. Since all @ GET objects in the main READ window (or windows) are out of bounds to the mouse or cursor until the Add or Edit routine is launched, the main READ window cannot itself be brought forward as the active window. (The push buttons in the control push button window are the only addressable objects, so FoxPro will insist upon keeping it WONTOP( ).) What this means is simple: Because you cannot bring the main READ window forward, you cannot open and use the options displayed in its window control box to close or minimize it, thus, given the way the MBS nonmodal screen programs are written, terminating the screen program.

There are many ways to get around this problem. The first, actually used by Letters.spr—the MBS screen program that uses the separate control push button window—is to place a *dummy object* (namely, an invisible push button) sized down to nothing in the Letters.scx READ window. Then position the dummy object in a corner of the window so that the light dotted line will be more difficult to see when the push button is highlighted. Because we assign the invisible push button a WHEN condition of NOT m.doit, the button can be activated except when the Add or Edit routine is launched and m.doit is set to .T. As a result of its placement in the READ window, the operator can activate the Letters window and get at the window control box without even knowing that the invisible push button is activated. Since @ GET m.dummy, the invisible push button, does absolutely nothing, use of it will only send the cursor to the next active @ GET—the control push buttons in the Control window. This seems to be a good work-around to this problem, but there are others worth noting.

Instead of using a dummy object, you can remove the WHEN m.doit clause from one or more of the input fields in the main READ window. While this introduces an irregularity to the program, in certain instances it may not be objectionable. For example, in the case of Letters.spr, it is reasonable to allow the operator to access the @ EDIT region we use to display letter text. By removing the WHEN m.doit clause from @ EDIT but leaving it in place with the other input fields, we allow the operator to do this—and also allow the main READ window to be brought forward at any time so the window control box can be used. However, if we allow the operator to enter the edit region (or any other input field) without having first selected the Add or Edit push button, we must also make certain the operator is aware that any changes made to the current letter will not be saved. (Since we display memvars in the window and not actual table fields, changing the values held in the memvars will have no effect unless GATHER MEMVAR or some other command is used to transfer their values to a table.) This is the work of the Add and Edit routines. Unless the Edit button is selected first, changes to the current record will never be recorded to disk. This can lead to confusion and to loss of work. If you use this method, at the very least you must place a message on the screen to remind the operator that changes will not be saved without the use of the Edit button.

The demonstration programs supplied by Microsoft with FoxPro, the majority of which use a separate control push button window, address the problem of making the main READ window accessible at all times in a slightly different way. With the exception of objects displaying read-only values, all input fields and edit regions are made universally accessible to the operator. Besides making it possible to activate the main READ window at any time, this has the advantage of allowing the operator to select and scroll in any input field or edit region whatsoever. The strategy, therefore, has value even when working with screen programs with single READ windows. Of course, this allows the operator to make changes to memvars representing the values in the current table record without first selecting the Edit button—the dilemma we encountered above. However, in the FoxPro demonstration programs, such as Organize.app, this problem is easily managed, though at the expense of adding tons of VALID clause code snippets to the screen file so that any change made to an input field or editing region will automatically trigger the Edit routine. We might, for example, convert Customer.scx so Customer.spr will behave in this way by removing the WHEN m.doit (expression) from every @ GET and @ EDIT in the Customers window and adding the following VALID clause. (Here we show the VALID clause we would use for @ GET m.last.)

```
* VALID clause for @ GET m.last
IF m.last <> customer.last
    STORE .T. TO m.doit, m.doedit
    SHOW GET m.but1 DISABLE
    SHOW GET m.verify ENABLE
ENDIF
```

If the operator makes any change to m.last, whether deliberately or accidentally, the VALID clause sees to it that the Edit routine is launched by resetting the values of m.doit and m.doedit (controlling program action), disabling the control push buttons, and enabling the Save and Cancel push buttons—just as is done in READ SHOW when the Edit button is selected. (We test for a change to the memvar by comparing its value with that of the table field it represents.)

Of course, if the operator scrolls in the input field and then leaves it without making changes, the edit action is not launched. If the operator makes an accidental entry while scrolling in the input field, the changes can be abandoned through use of the Cancel button. In any case, owing to the disabling of the control push buttons and to m.doit's effect on window events, the operator will not be able to move to any other record or quit the screen program without first using the Save or Cancel button. (As you will note in running the FoxPro demonstration programs, the enabling of the Save and Cancel buttons—and the disabling of the control push buttons—when you change an input field value is quite pronounced. There can be no mistaking a screen program's entry into an edit mode.)

If you determine to adopt this approach to managing operator access to and use of input fields and edit regions, you can shorten the code snippets used in the VALID clauses of your @ GETs and @ EDITs as follows:

```
* VALID clause for @ GET m.last
IF NOT mdoit AND m.last <> customer.last
    DO doedit
ENDIF

* Procedure doedit is placed in cleanup code of screen program.
PROCEDURE doedit
STORE .T. TO m.doit, m.doedit
SHOW GET m.but1 DISABLE
SHOW GET m.verify ENABLE
```

Place the commands enabling the Edit routine in a separate procedure in the screen file's cleanup code. This way it does not have to be entered over and over—a tedious task even with the aid of the Clipboard. In the VALID clause of your @ GETs and @ EDITs, place the DO Doedit command, triggering initiation of the edit mode, in an IF statement that is designed to execute it only if the edit (or add) action is not already under way (we use NOT m.doit for this purpose) and then only if the value of the memvar has been changed. There's no reason to waste time reexecuting the procedure each time a data value is changed.

Whether it is better to follow the method used in the FoxPro demonstration programs, allowing cursor address to all input fields at all times, or to stick to that used in the MBS, disallowing cursor address of input fields except when the edit or append action is under way, depends on your own requirements. If your READ windows will make heavy use of edit regions or input fields that must be scrolled by the operator to view important data, it seems best to allow the cursor to address the edit regions and input fields at all times. The operator is bound to get used to the idea of being careful not to make unintended entries or to immediately press the Cancel button after so doing. If, on the other hand, your application will make limited use of edit regions and all input fields are sufficiently sized to make operator scrolling unnecessary as a means of displaying data, it seems best to keep the operator out of trouble by preventing the cursor from entering input fields until the Edit button is selected. This works unless you constantly need to scroll through edit regions or input fields just to view data. The best plan is to try out both methods as an operator and see which you'd prefer. You can do this by running MBS.app and then switching to the FoxPro Organize.app. The MBS screen programs are easily adapted to this alternative method of controlling operator access to input fields and edit regions.

PART IV

Executing Reports

CHAPTER

TWELVE

Creating Report Programs

- The MBS Customer database reports
- Creating a report program interface
- Using SELECT to prepare report data
- Using SELECT with multiple source tables
- Preparing record filters and order directives

Creating reports or labels with FoxPro is easy. We use the built-in Report Writer, which is much simpler to master than the Screen Writer, to create a Report or Label form suitable to our needs. We then establish the required table view and execute the REPORT FORM or LABEL FORM <file> command—with or without supplying additional record filters. In this regard, it is important to remember that both REPORT FORM and LABEL FORM are sequential commands. We use them just like we use LIST and DISPLAY. The difference is that with LABEL FORM and REPORT FORM, instead of a feeble FIELDS list, we supply FoxPro with an elaborate data format, including headers, footers, data groupings, and the like.

Still, two major issues arise as soon as we move to integrate reports in a system. First, we must consider the user interface, which also means considering what control the operator will be able to exert over data output. Second, and before creating the required Report and Label forms, we must decide how to prepare the data for report output. Given the availability of SQL-SELECT and Rushmore optimization, there are no less than four ways to establish table views suitable for report output. You can

- Use the standard Xbase tools (SET ORDER, SET RELATION, SET FILTER, and WHILE and FOR <condition>)
- Modify your use of these tools to take advantage of Rushmore optimization
- Use SQL-SELECT to produce a temporary (or permanent) table that holds all the data required for any given report
- Combine the use of SQL-SELECT with the standard Xbase tools

In the following pages, we attempt to cover the basic issues involved in executing reports and labels in an event-driven DBMS by reviewing the construction of Cust_rpt.spr, the screen program executing all Customer database reports. In so doing, our coverage of SQL-SELECT will be limited to its use in preparing data for the Customer database reports. The end of the chapter focuses on additional functions of SQL-SELECT and reviews some of the other MBS screen programs producing reports. Discussion of the Report Writer, used to create the Report and Label forms executed by Cust_rpt.spr and all other MBS programs executing screen and printed reports, follows in Chapter 13.

The MBS Customer Database Reports Window

In the MBS, all Customer database reports listed in the Customer Database Reports window are executed through the use of SQL-SELECT in conjunction with REPORT and/or LABEL FORM. Report and label parameters are established through operator use of the Customer Database Reports window, shown in Figure 12.1. The SELECT and REPORT and LABEL FORM commands executing the action are embedded in the @ GET push button VALID clause. Since Cust_rpt.spr, the screen program overseeing the window, does not terminate upon execution of any given report, the operator can continue using the window over and over to produce different reports, using the same or different filter conditions and record order.

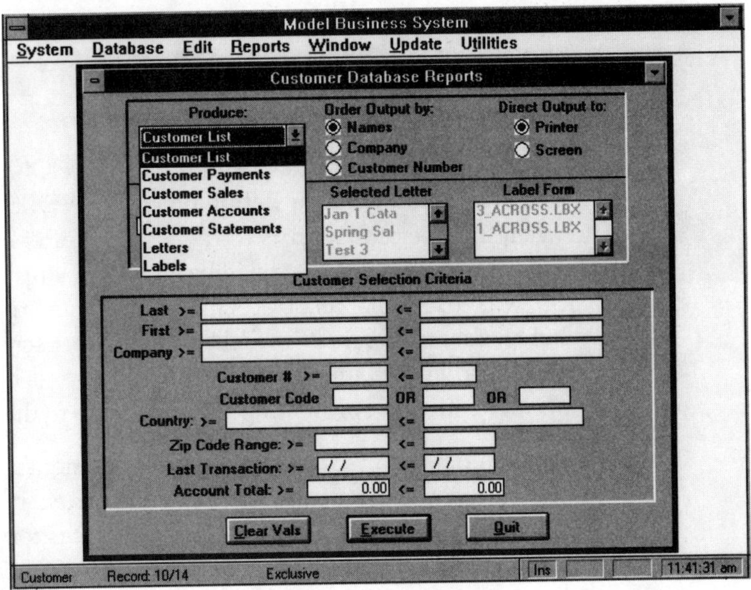

FIGURE 12.1:

The Customer Database Reports window handles operator specification and execution of all reports and labels drawing data from the Customer database.

The organization of Cust_rpt.spr, which is based upon a single screen file, Cust_rpt.scx, makes common sense. To make the screen program function in non-modal fashion (though we could just as easily write it to a function as a dialog), we enter #SECTION 1 setup code in Customer.scx to test for the prior existence of window Cust_rpts (the Customer Database Reports window), as shown in Figure 12.2.

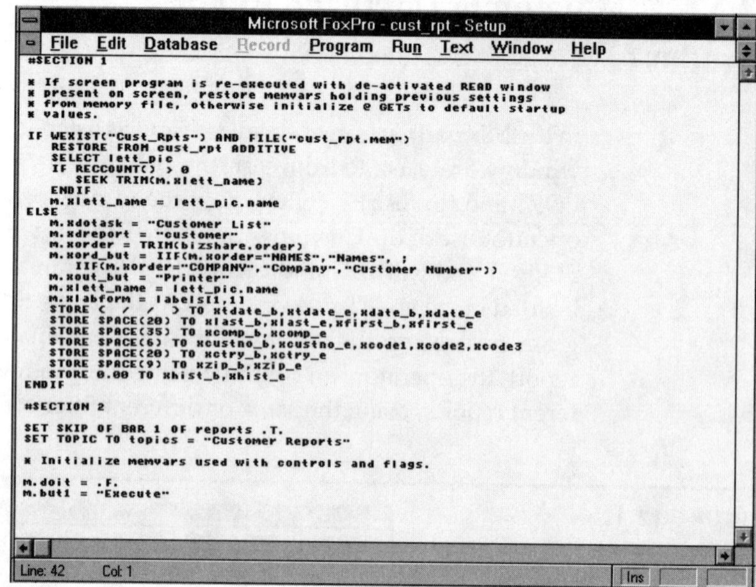


```
#SECTION 1

* If screen program is re-executed with de-activated READ window
* present on screen, restore memvars holding previous settings
* from memory file, otherwise initialize @ GETs to default startup
* values.

IF WEXIST("Cust_Rpts") AND FILE("cust_rpt.mem")
   RESTORE FROM cust_rpt ADDITIVE
   SELECT lett_pic
   IF RECCOUNT() > 0
      SEEK TRIM(m.xlett_name)
   ENDIF
   m.xlett_name = lett_pic.name
ELSE
   m.xdotask = "Customer List"
   m.xdreport = "customer"
   m.xorder = TRIM(bizshare.order)
   m.xord_but = IIF(m.xorder="NAMES","Names", ;
      IIF(m.xorder="COMPANY","Company","Customer Number"))
   m.xout_but = "Printer"
   m.xlett_name = lett_pic.name
   m.xlabform = labels[1,1]
   STORE {  /  /  } TO xtdate_b,xtdate_e,xdate_b,xdate_e
   STORE SPACE(20) TO xlast_b,xlast_e,xfirst_b,xfirst_e
   STORE SPACE(35) TO xcomp_b,xcomp_e
   STORE SPACE(6) TO xcustno_b,xcustno_e,xcode1,xcode2,xcode3
   STORE SPACE(20) TO xctry_b,xctry_e
   STORE SPACE(9) TO xzip_b,xzip_e
   STORE 0.00 TO xhist_b,xhist_e
ENDIF

#SECTION 2

SET SKIP OF BAR 1 OF reports .T.
SET TOPIC TO topics = "Customer Reports"

* Initialize memvars used with controls and flags.

m.doit = .F.
m.but1 = "Execute"
```

FIGURE 12.2:

Section 1 setup code is used in Cust_rpt.scx to test for the prior existence of the READ window and, when the window exists, to restore input field values from a memory file.

(As you will recall from Chapter 11, #SECTION 1 setup code is executed before screen program window definition code.) WEXIST("Cust_Rpts") will be true only when the operator returns to the window after switching to another screen program. So that the operator will be able to pick up work exactly where he or she left off, we see to it that all objects in window Cust_rpts are restored to the values they held before the operator switched to the other screen program. If the window does not already exist—meaning that Cust_rpt.spr is being executed from scratch—we set all memvars representing @ GET objects to their startup default values.

As should be clear, execution of the IF statement in the Section 1 setup code also assumes prior existence of memory file Cust_rpt.mem. This is created in the Cust_rpt.scx cleanup code when the READ is terminated without operator selection of the Quit push button or the Close option in the window control box, thus leaving window Cust_rpts inactive on the screen.

```
* Cust_rpt.scx cleanup code leaves the window on the screen and
* saves all memvars prefixed with x to a memory file when the
* operator leaves window without use of Quit or Close. Otherwise
* window is released and memory file used with screen program is
* erased if found on disk.
```

```
IF m.but1 = "Quit"
    RELEASE WINDOW cust_rpts
    IF FILE("cust_rpt.mem")
        ERASE cust_rpt.mem
    ENDIF
ELSE
    SAVE ALL LIKE "x*" TO cust_rpt
ENDIF
SET SKIP OF BAR 1 OF reports .F.
SET TOPIC TO
```

We prefix all memvars used in the screen layout with *x* by design. This makes it easy to address them as a group with the SAVE command. Of course, referring back to the Section 1 setup code, we use the RESTORE command with the ADDITIVE keyword so memvars are restored from the memory file without affecting other memvars.

Section 2 setup code (again, see Figure 12.2) is not nearly as dramatic. We simply deactivate the menu option executing Cust_rpt.spr; set the help topic; initialize memvar m.but1, used by our control push buttons; and reset the global memvar m.doit to .F. (Actually, we do not need to reset m.doit because it must already be set to .F. before a screen program can be launched. With respect to Cust_rpt.spr, m.doit, moreover, has no real role to play since we edit no table data. m.doit, however, is referenced by the READ DEACTIVATE clause, which executes function Stop, discussed in Chapter 10.) Clearly, the Section 2 setup code could have just as easily been placed in Section 1, but not vice versa. The test for the window, after all, must come before the screen program defines window Cust_rpts.

Enabling Operator Entry of Record Filters

The function of the many memvars we initialize in the setup code should be fairly obvious from Cust_rpt.scx's screen layout, shown in Figure 12.3. The input fields listed in the Customer Selection Criteria region of the window are used for operator entry of optional record filters. If no entries are made, all records in the Customer database view required for the selected report are included in report output. On the other hand, wherever the operator chooses to make entries, we use them to form record filters, which we later use with SQL-SELECT when preparing report data. (As you will see, the filters could just as easily be used with SET FILTER or in the FOR <condition> clause of the REPORT or LABEL FORM command.)

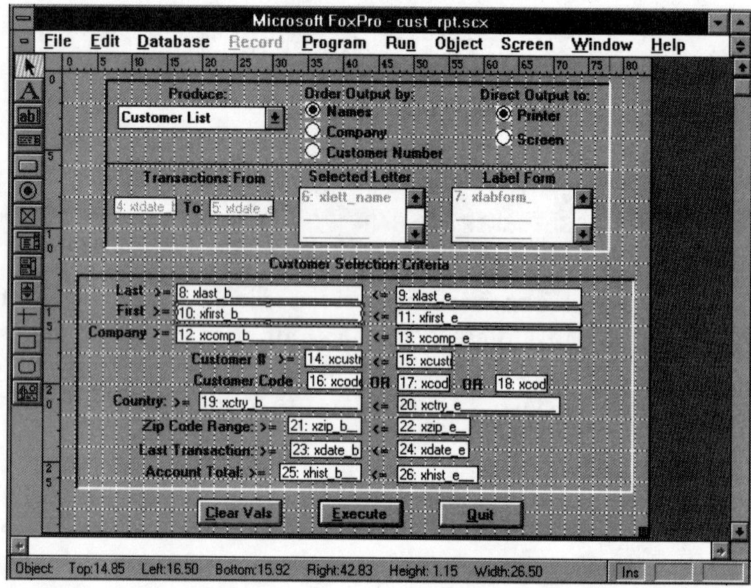

FIGURE 12.3:
The screen layout used with the Customer Database Reports window (Cust_rpt.scx) includes input fields for operator entry of record filters and radio buttons and lists for selecting other report parameters.

Though this need not be the case, we limit the operator to entry of optimizable conditions that Rushmore and SQL-SELECT can immediately evaluate through the use of existing Customer.dbf index tags. When creating the filters based upon the operator's entries to the customer selection criteria input fields, we therefore manipulate the values in order to form fully optimizable filters. For example, xcomp_b and xcomp_e, representing Customer.company *begin* and *end* positions, can be evaluated through use of index tag Company (key expression: UPPER(company)). If the operator makes entries to both input fields, we can use the values to form the following filter:

```
UPPER(company) >= xcomp_b AND UPPER(company) <= xcomp_e
```

NOTE

The SQL-SELECT command's WHERE <condition> clause accepts filters written with the same syntax used in forming standard Xbase filters, though, as you will see later in this chapter, there are minor differences that must be observed. SQL-SELECT, moreover, provides an alternative set of operators in keeping with SQL syntax.

Since index tag Company uses only uppercase characters, we format @ GET m.xcomp_b and m.xcomp_e to force operator entry of alphabetic characters to uppercase. Thus we need not use UPPER() with m.xcomp_b and m.xcomp_e in forming the filter. Moreover, with @ GET m.xcomp_e, we use a Lower Range expression of m.xcomp_b to prevent the operator from accidentally entering a filter that will exclude all customer records from the view. We do the same things with the input fields for m.xlast_e, m.xcustno_e, m.xctry_e, m.xzip_e, and so on, with the _e suffix representing ending position. Lower Range is specified with the memvar of the same name but bearing the _b suffix, indicating the begin position. (The memvars, of course, correspond to the Customer table fields Customer.last, Customer.custno, Customer.country, and Customer.zip, respectively.)

Operator entries for memvars m.xlast_b and m.xfirst_b and m.xlast_e and m.xfirst_e must be properly entered and concatenated in order to be used in an optimizable filter that takes advantage of index tag names (key expression: UPPER(last + first)). Thus we must do more than force to uppercase the operator's entries to these input fields. When the cursor is active in m.xfirst_b or m.xfirst_e, we must also use @ GET MESSAGE to warn the operator to make no first-name entries unless complete last names have been entered to m.xlast_b or m.xlast_e. We must also see to it that the width of the Customer.last field is preserved in m.xlast_b and m.xlast_e whenever first-name entries are used. We do this by predefining memvars m.xlast_b and m.xlast_e to have a width of 20, corresponding to Customer.last. Then, when the operator makes an entry to m.xlast_b or to m.xlast_b and m.xfirst_b, we can write the filter as follows:

```
UPPER(last + first) >= TRIM(xlast_b + xfirst_b)
```

It makes no difference whether or not the operator makes a first-name entry as long as he or she enters a complete last name when doing so. (See Chapter 4 for more information on Customer table index tags and how to enter search strings and optimizable filters that take advantage of them.)

Unlike the other customer selection criteria input fields, m.xcode1, m.xcode2, and m.xcode3, which are to be used in forming filters based upon the Customer.cuscode field, will be used with the equal (=) operator. If the operator makes entries to all three input fields, we write the filter as follows:

```
(cuscode = xcode1 OR cuscode = xcode2 OR cuscode = xcode3)
```

This is intended to allow the operator to specify customers assigned any of three customer codes. However, since the operator may not need to use all three input fields, we use WHEN clauses with m.xcode2 and m.xcode3 so the cursor will skip them WHEN EMPTY(m.xcode1) and WHEN EMPTY(m.xcode2), respectively. (For a discussion of Customer.cuscode, see Chapter 2.)

Again, the values entered in the customer selection criteria fields are left unchanged after execution of a report, so the operator can, for example, print letters to a selection of customers and immediately thereafter print mailing labels for the same customers without having to reenter the selection criteria. To blank out all selection criteria input fields at once, the operator can select the Clear Vals push button. The push button VALID clause begins with the following commands:

```
IF m.but1 = "Quit"
    CLEAR READ
    RETURN
ENDIF
IF m.but1 = "Clear Vals"
    STORE SPACE(20) TO xlast_b,xlast_e,xfirst_b,xfirst_e
    STORE SPACE(35) TO xcomp_b,xcomp_e
    STORE SPACE(6) TO xcustno_b,xcustno_e,xcode1,xcode2,xcode3
    * Commands reinitializing other memvars omitted.
    SHOW GETS ONLY
    _curobj = OBJNUM(m.xlast_b)
    RETURN
ENDIF
```

The commands listed under IF m.but1 = "Clear Vals" reinitialize the customer selection criteria memvars to empty values. We then issue SHOW GETS ONLY to refresh the input fields without executing the READ SHOW clause. (This is prevented by use of ONLY, though executing the SHOW clause, which we discuss in a moment, will not adversely affect the program.). Next we select @ GET m.xlast_b, the first of the customer selection criteria input fields, as the current cursor object and issue RETURN (.T.) to terminate the VALID clause and send the cursor on its way.

TIP

Individual customers can be easily selected by using the same begin and end values in the input fields supplied for forming filters with index tag Names, Company, or Custno. Since the filters are fully optimizable, this will work almost as quickly as locating a customer with the SEEK command.

Enabling *Ad Hoc* Queries with SELECT or SET FILTER

In the MBS, we limit what filters can be entered, but this need not be the case. We might, for example, add a picture check box or button to the Customer Reports window that allows the operator to open the Expression Builder, shown in Figure 12.4.

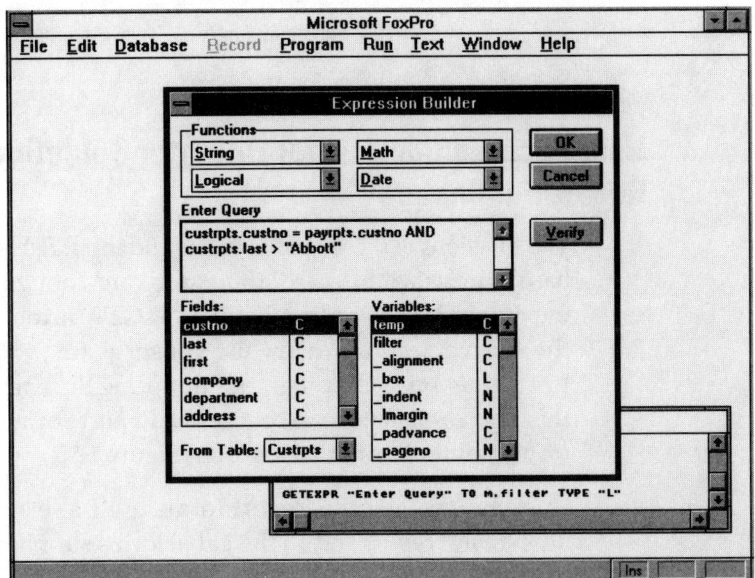

FIGURE 12.4:

If your system must allow operators to make *ad hoc* queries, you can let them access and use the Expression Builder to enter record filters.

By executing the GETEXPR command, shown at the bottom of Figure 12.4, we place the prompt "Enter Query" just above the Expression Builder's editing window. By using TYPE "L", we instruct FoxPro to make sure the operator's entry is a valid expression of type L, as is necessary when building a record filter. The TO m.filter simply instructs FoxPro to place the operator's entry into memvar m.filter when the operator closes the Expression Builder. The filter contained in m.filter can then be executed through the use of macro substitution with SET FILTER TO <condition>, FOR <condition>, or SELECT WHERE <condition>.

The downside to including the Expression Builder in the MBS or any other system is that the operator will require additional training in how to write filters using FoxPro expressions. This is much more complicated than plugging last- and first-name entries into input fields and becomes more complicated yet if the Expression Builder is to be used with SELECT WHERE to build multi-file queries.

TIP

If you plan to run your system under FoxPro rather than as a stand-alone .exe, you can also provide the operator with direct access to FoxPro's RQBE window by executing the command CREATE QUERY, but your clients will require a good deal of hands-on training to master RQBE's full potential.

Using Screen Controls for Operator Selection of Report Parameters

The functions of the @ GET controls and input fields at the top of the Customer Database Reports window are straightforward enough, though a few details are worth mentioning. The Produce popup—@ GET m.xdotask—is obviously used to select the desired report. When Cust_rpt.spr is first executed, m.xdotask = "Customer List". Later on in the program, supposing the operator presses the Execute button, this will result in the execution of Report form Customer.frx. We show sample printed output from this report in Figure 12.5.

Customer.frx, like the Report forms used to execute the Customer Accounts (or debt-aging) report and all the Label forms supplied with MBS, reference data from Customer.dbf only. This is also essentially true of Report form Lettform.frx, used to execute mass personalized form letters. Figure 12.6 shows a sample letter.

Lettform.frx, which we examine more closely in Chapter 13, takes the text of the letter from the Memo field of the letter selected by name from Letters.dbf (alias lett_pic) through operator use of the Selected Letter list (@ GET m.xlett_name). It also takes the business return address and phone number from the Bizline1-Bizline5 and Bizphone fields of Bizshare.dbf's single record. However, the REPORT FORM command executing Lettform.frx never moves the record pointer in either of these tables. Only the customer name and address lines and salutation change as the REPORT FORM command moves through the selected records in the Customer

FIGURE 12.5:

Sample output from Report form Customer.frx, executing the Customer List report

04/02/95 **CUSTOMER LIST** **Page 1**

Name/Cust #	Company/Department	Address	Country	Phone	Credit	Open/Total
Bloom, Mr. Leopold 100010	Eccles St. Galleries	32 Eccles St. Dublin, B26J8	IRELAND	012-326-7775 012-326-7743	Y	03/25/95 2,420.00
Borgesius, Dr. Katje 100001	The White Visitation Entertainment & Therapy	34012 Pennsylvania Ave. Washington, DC 02043-2222	USA	204-333-3333 204-555-5555	Y	01/03/86 34,055.00
Boylan, Mr. Blazes 100011	Boilin' Art Enterprises Ltd.	56 Horse Trader Lane Trenton, NJ 04102	USA	208-345-2245 208-345-2246	Y	03/25/95 10,000.00
Cunningham, Mr. Martin 100014		11245 Wilshire Blvd. Los Angeles, CA 90045	USA	310-345-6789 310-345-6790	Y	03/25/95 20,000.00
Dingham, Mr. Pat 100013	Charon's Place Gallery	32 Charon's Place Atlantic City, NJ 32145	USA	402-556-7655 402-556-7655	Y	03/25/95 50,000.00
Fahringer, Mr. Sam 100006	Zen Art Objects	2343 Small Cart Way St, Louis, MO 63122	USA	314-567-5677 314-567-5678	Y	02/03/89 9,420.00
K., Mr. Joseph 100008	Big Brother's Fine Art & Sculptures	5634 Kendall Square Boston, MA 06860	USA	617-322-4532 617-454-6755	N	01/14/87 5,000.00
McDowell, Ms. Gerty 100012	McDowell Studio	32450 Broadway New York, NY 10034	USA	212-345-6788 212-345-6789	Y	03/25/95 5,000.00
Pokler, Mr. Franz 100005	Goteppe Art Studios	Serecebey Yok. 61-63 Besiktas, Istanbul D1011	TURKEY	011-233-3223 - -	Y	06/11/89 10,400.00
Prentice, Mr. Pirate 100007	Counterforce Ltd.	789 Mole St. #2 London, England B0456J2	UNITED	01222333-456 012223334578	Y	03/12/87 4,500.00
Rathenau, Mr. Walter 100009	I.G. Art Exchange	117820 Wilshire Blvd. Los Angeles, CA 90036-2246	USA	213-757-4566 213-757-4566	Y	03/04/95 17,105.00
Samsa, Mr. Gregor 100004	Samsa Culture Clinic	3454 Soho St. New York City, NY 10002334	USA	212-222-2222 212-344-6555	Y	02/01/90 10,000.00
Slothrop, Mr. Hogan 100002	Aloha Novelties Acquisitions Dept.	30333 Kalihi Honolulu, HI 96060	USA	808-333-3445 - -	Y	02/16/93 13,165.00
Tripping, Ms. Geli 100003	Just Say NO2 Procurement	344 Hugo St. Victoria, BC GH3344	CANADA	209-333-3333 - -	Y	02/12/89 6,500.00

table. (We could just as easily close Bizshare.dbf and Letters.dbf before executing letters, provided we transfer the letter text and return address data to memvars and change Lettform.frx to reference them instead of the table fields.) Lettform.frx, in other words, is not a true multi-table report since the tables it references are not linked or joined in any way. Lettform.frx, like Customer.frx, Accounts.frx, 1_across.lbx, and 3_across.lbx, is a *flat-file report,* which simply means it needs to process records in only one table.

FIGURE 12.6:

Report form Lettform.frx produces mass personalized form letters for all selected customers, using a letter selected from Letters.dbf.

```
Howard Dickler
PO Box 34293
Los Angeles, CA 90034
310-204-2780
April 2, 1995

Dr. Katje Borgesius
The White Visitation
Entertainment & Therapy
34012 Pennsylvania Ave.
Washington, DC 02043-2222
USA

Dear Dr. Borgesius,

    This spring we are happy to announce a 25% discount on all
Remingtons displayed in our catalogue.  As sales of the Remingtons
have picked up over the last few years, allowing us to turn them out
in bigger lots, the cost of manufacture has gone down, and we are
happy to pass the savings on to those loyal customers who have so
helped to increase demand.
    Over the past year, we have also received many requests for new
items and are just now in the process of selecting twenty new designs
for production next year.  If you are among those who have pressed us
to expand the line, we thank you for your encouragement.  Our
selections will appear in the summer catalogue, which should be
delivered in late May.

Sincerely,


Howard Dickler
Programmer in Chief
```

The Customer Sales, Customer Payments, and Customer Statements reports, however, are all multi-table reports because they must include transaction data taken from Sales.dbf and/or Payments.dbf, in addition to Customer table data. Figure 12.7, for example, shows sample output from Salcust.frx, the Customer Sales Report form. This is a simple Group report. Each customer is listed separately along with records of his or her invoices.

Of course, in the case of customer statements, we must include only those transaction records found in Sales and Payments.dbf that fall in the current billing period. Quite aside from linking or joining the tables with Customer.dbf, we must, in other words, filter records in the child tables on the basis of Payments.date and Sales.date. In producing the customer payments and customer sales, it will often be desirable to filter transaction records as well, in order to review customer sales and payments falling within any given period—though this is clearly optional. In the case of these three reports, we must therefore have a means of entering a date range filter to be applied to transaction records supplied by Sales and/or Payments.dbf.

FIGURE 12.7:

The Customer Sales report, Salcust.frx, is a simple Group report, listing each customer in Customer.dbf along with his or her records in Sales.dbf.

```
04/02/95                              Customer Sales                              Page - 1

           Date        Sale #        PO #              Type                    Amount
100010     Bloom, Leopold              Eccles St. Galleries                   012-326-7775
           03/26/95    100043                          Cash                    880.00
           03/26/95    100044                          Cash                  1,210.00
           04/02/95    100045                          Cash                    330.00
           Cash:          2,420.00  Charges:                   Totals:       2,420.00
100001     Borgesius, Katje            The White Visitation                   204-333-3333
           03/04/95    100005       KBCSH001           Cash                  1,045.00
           03/04/95    100004       KBCH0001           Charge                3,410.00
           03/04/95    100012       KBCH0004           Charge               15,290.00
           03/04/95    100006       KBCG0002           Charge                1,870.00
           03/04/95    100007       KBCH0003           Charge                5,940.00
           Cash:          1,045.00  Charges:       26,510.00  Totals:       27,555.00
100006     Fahringer, Sam              Zen Art Objects                        314-567-5677
           03/05/95    100013       FH000001           Charge                5,940.00
           03/05/95    100014       FH00002            Charge                1,980.00
           Cash:                    Charges:        7,920.00  Totals:        7,920.00
100005     Pokler, Franz               Goteppe Art Studios                    011-233-3223
           03/04/95    100011                          Cash                  4,400.00
           Cash:          4,400.00  Charges:                   Totals:       4,400.00
100009     Rathenau, Walter            I.G. Art Exchange                      213-757-4566
           03/04/95    100010       RATHCHG1           Charge               17,105.00
           Cash:                    Charges:       17,105.00  Totals:       17,105.00
100002     Slothrop, Hogan             Aloha Novelties                        808-333-3445
           03/04/95    100009       SLCHG002           Charge                1,375.00
           03/04/95    100008       SLCH0001           Charge                6,490.00
           Cash:                    Charges:        7,865.00  Totals:        7,865.00
```

To take care of the different requirements of the reports listed in the Produce report popup, we include two input fields and two @ GET lists in the second row of objects in the Customer Database Reports window. The @ GET input fields m.xtdate_b and m.xtdate_e are used for operator input of transaction date begin and end range; the Selected Letter list, @ GET m.xlett_name, is used for operator selection of a letter by name from Letters.dbf (alias lett_pic); and the Label Form list, @ GET m.xlabform, is used for operator selection of a specific .lbx file from the DBFS\LABELS subdirectory. Again, any .lbx file included in DBFS\LABELS will appear in the Label Form list. (See Chapter 11 for a discussion of these two @ GET array lists.) However, these objects, unlike the customer selection criteria input fields, are useful only with specific Produce popup selections. We therefore conditionally enable/disable them according to the value of m.xdotask, the memvar holding the selected popup value, through the use of Cust_rpt.scx's READ SHOW clause. (See Figure 12.8.)

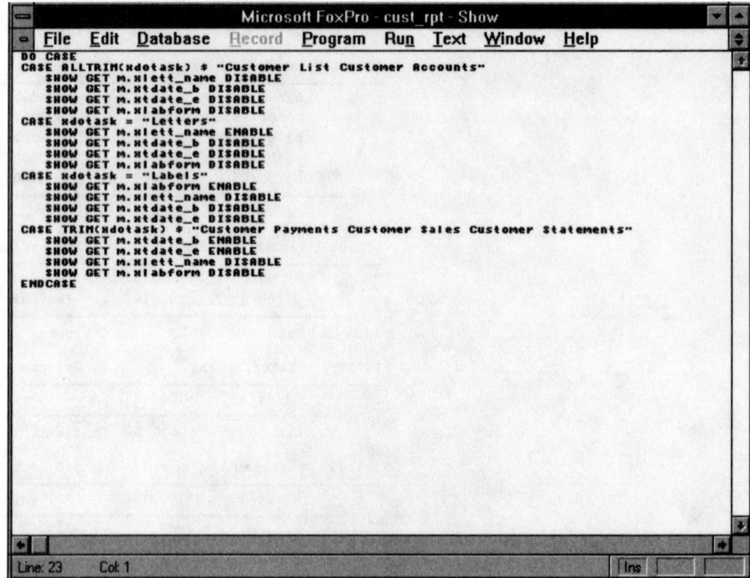

FIGURE 12.8:
The Customer Database Reports window's READ SHOW clause is used to conditionally enable/disable objects used with specific reports listed in the Produce report popup.

When Cust_rpt.spr is executed for the first time, we arbitrarily set the value of m.xdotask to "Customer List" in the screen program setup code. Since the SHOW clause is automatically executed the moment READ is activated, the input fields for Transactions From and To and the Selected Letter and Label Form lists will be initially disabled. However, upon operator use of the Produce report popup, we execute the VALID clause shown in Figure 12.9.

If Customer Statements is selected from the Produce report popup, the popup's VALID clause changes the values of m.xtdate_b and m.xtdate_e to represent the current billing period. m.xtdate_b is updated to hold Bizshare.lastdate, representing the date on which monthly customer statements were last printed (and the customer account fields updated); m.xtdate_e is updated to hold today's date as

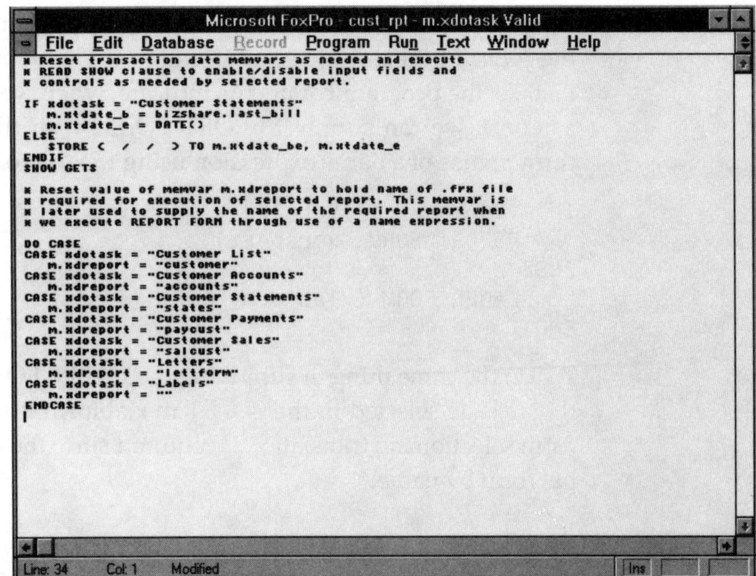

FIGURE 12.9:

After the operator selects a report from the Produce report popup, we use the popup's VALID clause to reexecute Cust_rpt.spr's READ SHOW clause.

indicated by DATE(), the current system date. Again, m.xtdate_b and m.xtdate_e control which payments and sales records will be detailed in customer statements. They must therefore represent the period covered by the statements about to be printed. When Customer Statements is not the selected report, however, we reset m.xtdate_b and m.xtdate_e to empty values; the use of a transaction date filter is optional with the Customer Sales and Payments reports. (The input fields are ignored by the other reports.)

Immediately after dealing with the transaction date memvars, we issue SHOW GETS, not just to refresh the objects on the screen (only m.xtdate_b and m.xtdate_e actually require refreshing), but to trigger execution of the READ SHOW clause. Working in this way, we can conditionally enable/disable the objects in question without having to repeat the required SHOW GET commands directly in the popup VALID clause. We simply reuse the SHOW clause (shown in Figure 12.7).

The last portion of the @ GET popup VALID clause uses the prompt returned by m.xdotask in a DO CASE structure to provide memvar m.xdreport with the name of the Report form (.frx) file corresponding to the operator's selection. (Note that when the screen program is first executed, m.xdreport is arbitrarily set to *customer*, the name of the .frx file corresponding to the popup's default prompt, Customer List. As the program comments indicate, when we finally get around to executing a report, we can supply REPORT FORM with the name of the required report through use of a name expression using m.xdreport.

```
IF m.xdotask <> "Labels"
    REPORT FORM (xdreport)
ELSE
    LABEL FORM (xlabform)
ENDIF
```

We do the same thing in supplying the LABEL FORM command with the name of the .lbx file selected in the @ GET m.xlabform list. However, in the case of Label form selection, no translation is required since the operator actually selects the Label form by name.

TIP

When it comes to providing the operator with a popup or list of available Report or Label forms, using a data dictionary will help cut program code to a minimum and make for a more flexible programming environment. For example, a table can be used to hold prompts for display in a popup or list in one field and the actual names of the corresponding reports in another. After the operator makes a selection, the popup or list VALID clause can be used to look up the actual name of the form corresponding to the selected prompt.

As for the two sets of radio buttons at the top of the Customer Database Reports window, these are functional with all customer reports. Note that we initialize them in the setup code as character variables so they will return the prompt used with the selected button instead of a numeric value.

We use the Order Output By radio buttons, @ GET m.xord_but (short for order button), so the operator can arrange report records in one of three orders corresponding to the three main Customer table index tags. This is somewhat limiting, in part because we have several other index tags available for instantly ordering customer records. The operator may, for example, want to output report records in order by zip code or country. This might be arranged by replacing the radio buttons, which provide limited space for display of options, with an array or list popup like the one used by Cus_find.spr, but listing all available Customer table index tags. Still, there is no reason to stop there since index tags can be created on the fly for any fields or combination of fields in the report table using the INDEX command or SQL-SELECT's ORDER BY clause. The only limitations on this practice are related to actual need and the processing time required to achieve the desired order without the aid of an index tag. (We will have more to say about this and about extending the filtering capacities of report programs later in this chapter.)

The Direct Output To radio buttons, @ GET m.xout_but, are of course used to provide the operator with a choice of output device. Here we include only Screen and Printer since the REPORT FORM TO <file> option for sending reports to a disk file, available with FoxPro for DOS, is nonfunctional in FoxPro for Windows unless the report is a character-mode report imported from FoxPro for DOS. (You can, however, direct report output to a file using the Print dialog, discussed below.) Naturally, we use the value of m.xout_but later in the program to control the action of REPORT and LABEL FORM. This is done with the following commands:

```
IF m.xdotask <> "Labels"
    IF xout_but = "Printer"
        REPORT FORM (xdreport) TO PRINTER PROMPT NOCONSOLE
    ELSE
        REPORT FORM (xdreport) PREVIEW
    ENDIF
ELSE
    IF xout_but = "Printer"
            LABEL FORM (xlabform) TO PRINTER PROMPT NOCONSOLE
    ELSE
             LABEL FORM (xlabform) PREVIEW
    ENDIF
ENDIF
```

Further compression of program code is possible, provided we use macro substitution to supply REPORT and LABEL FORM with the necessary keywords.

```
m.keywords = IIF(m.out_but="Screen","PREVIEW", ;
    "TO PRINTER PROMPT NOCONSOLE")
IF m.xdotask <> "Labels"
    REPORT FORM (xdreport) &keywords
ELSE
    LABEL FORM (xlabform) &keywords
ENDIF
```

However, you will be going too far if you try to input the LABEL and REPORT commands themselves with macro substitution since this cannot be supported in an .exe application without using special directives and, in any case, will make the program code more difficult to read.

With respect to the REPORT and LABEL FORM commands cited above, when we use the TO PRINTER keyword to direct output to the printer, we also include NOCONSOLE to inhibit simultaneous report output to the screen and PROMPT to invoke the Print dialog before initiating output to the Windows print manager. (See Figure 12.10.)

FIGURE 12.10:

When directing output to the printer with REPORT and LABEL FORM, use the PROMPT option to enable operator use of the Print dialog.

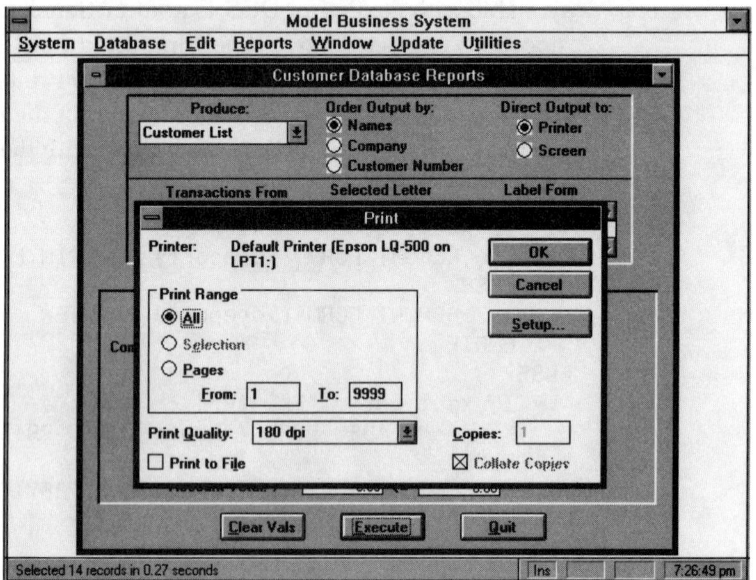

Using the Windows Print dialog, the operator may select the number of copies for the report; pinpoint specific pages, if, for example, several pages of a longer report require reprinting; change the print driver and port and the print quality; and so on. From a programming perspective, this dialog also supplies an automatic means of verifying report execution, making it unnecessary to include a program routine for this purpose or use the PRINTSTATUS() function to test the availability of the print driver. The Windows Print Manager automatically takes care of these things.

An additional feature of the Windows Print dialog is the ability to direct report or label output to a disk file, using the Print to File dialog. However, to take advantage of this option, you must define a special print driver that directs output to a file in advance, using the Windows Print Manager. (See your FoxPro and Windows documentation for more information about directing report output to a disk file.)

More interesting is the way FoxPro for Windows allows us to handle report output to the screen. The REPORT and LABEL FORM PREVIEW keyword instructs FoxPro to direct output to the Page Preview window, which is also available when designing reports and labels with the Report Writer, for previewing the results of the report layout. Figure 12.11 shows a page of the Customer Sales report in the Page Preview window.

FIGURE 12.11:

When directing report output to the screen, you can take advantage of the Page Preview window by using the REPORT and LABEL FORM PREVIEW option.

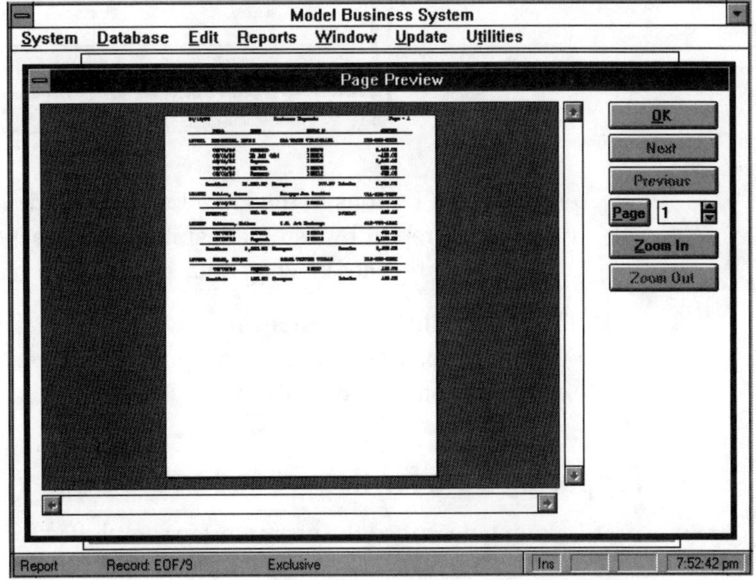

When the Page Preview window first appears on the screen, the first page of the report is displayed in miniature. To enlarge the data in any region of the page to make it legible, move the mouse pointer (which takes on the shape of a small looking glass) to the desired position and click—or select the Zoom In button. You can then navigate in the page using the window scroll bars. Figure 12.12 shows a zoomed-in view of the Customer Sales report.

FIGURE 12.12:

When using the Page Preview window, you can zoom in on the data in any page of a report.

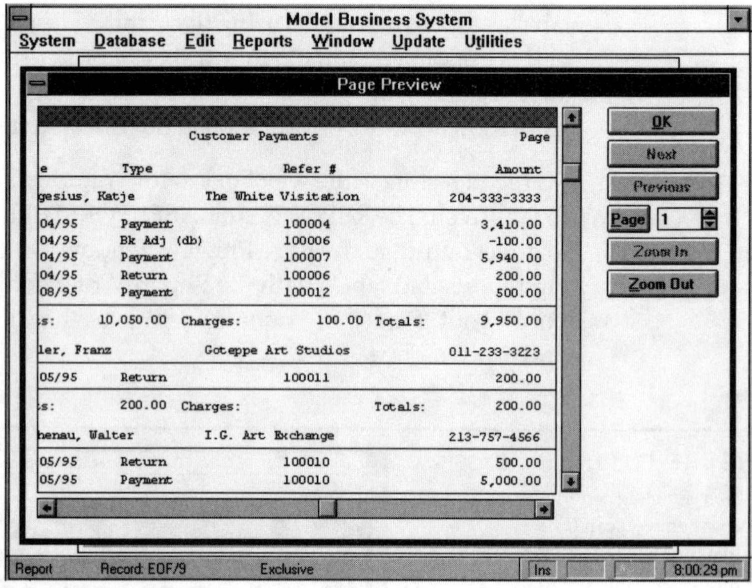

As the push buttons in the Page Preview window indicate, you can move to any page in the report by using the spinners or the Next and Previous buttons. When the operator finishes viewing data, the OK button is used to deactivate the window.

The availability of the Page Preview window makes it unnecessary to struggle with other ways of directing report output to the screen. Note that the Page Preview window functions as a modal dialog.

Preparing Data for Report and Label Output

Having described the user interface employed for operator execution of Customer database reports, we can now turn our attention to what happens when the operator selects the Execute push button to execute a Customer database report. Here we return to the @GET push button VALID clause, the first portion of which (pertaining to commands executed when the operator selects Clear Vals or Quit) we have already discussed.

```
IF m.but1 = "Quit"
    CLEAR READ
    RETURN
ENDIF
IF m.but1 = "Clear Vals"
    * Commands reinitializing memvars omitted here.
    RETURN
ENDIF
DO CASE
CASE m.xdotask = "Customer Statements"
    IF EMPTY(m.xtdate_b) OR EMPTY(m.xtdate_e)
        DO alert WITH ;
            "Transaction date range must be entered to "+ ;
            "produce", "statements. Press any key to continue."
        _curobj = OBJNUM(m.xtdate_b)
        RETURN
    ENDIF
CASE m.xdotask = "Letters"
    IF EMPTY(m.xlett_name)
        * Commands executing procedure Alert omitted.
        RETURN
CASE m.xdotask = "Labels"
    IF EMPTY(m.xlabform)
        * Commands executing procedure Alert omitted.
        RETURN
    ENDIF
ENDCASE
```

When the operator selects the Execute push button, we first make sure the operator has made entries to the transaction date range memvars if Customer Statements has been selected. If Letters or Labels has been selected instead, we must check to make sure an existing letter in Letters.dbf or a Label form has been selected from the @ GET lists. If these requirements are not met, we use procedure Alert to warn the operator of the problem, use _CUROBJ to send the cursor back to the GET object or objects requiring the operator's attention, and execute RETURN to break off further execution of the VALID clause.

However, if these criteria are met—or if the selected report is not Customer Statements, Letters, or Labels—we now move on to execute the user-defined function Maketabl, stored in Cust_rpt.scx's cleanup code, to prepare data for report output with the following commands:

```
IF NOT maketabl()
    DO alert WITH "sorry, no records in your selection.", ;
```

```
        "Press any key to continue."
    _curobj = OBJNUM(xord_but)
    RETURN
ENDIF
* Commands executing desired Report or Label form.
```

Function Maketabl is designed to execute the commands required to prepare data for the specified report and to return a value of .T. if the result table holds records (RECCOUNT() > 0). When this is the case, when program control returns to the VALID clause, FoxPro jumps past the ENDIF and executes the desired Report or Label form. On the other hand, if the result table does not hold records, function Maketabl erases the empty structure and returns a value of .F. The operator is therefore warned of the problem before being sent back to the Customer Database Reports window, where the report parameters can be changed.

Assembling the Database View with SELECT

As previously mentioned, in preparing the Customer database view for production of all Customer Database reports, we make exclusive use of the SELECT command. It is generally fastest and easiest to use, provided it is used to produce temporary tables stored in *cursors*—that is, tables stored in memory rather than in disk files, although SELECT will produce both. However, whether or not it is used to create cursors or disk files, SELECT has additional advantages. For example, in the case of our Customer Sales and Payments reports, we draw data for our report from two tables. When we use SELECT to prepare the data for these reports, all data from the source files is consolidated in the result table. This reduces what would be a multi-table report into a flat-file (single-table) report. This makes it somewhat easier to create the report with the Report Writer since we do not have to make use of alias names in specifying any report fields. All fields referenced in the report will be present in the current table.

Another advantage of SELECT is that Rushmore optimization is automatically used whenever possible in producing the result table. Nor is SQL-SELECT limited to use of available index tags when it evaluates filters or establishes record orders.

SELECT is built to think on its feet. When given an optimizable or partially optimizable filter, it automatically takes advantage of index tags available with the referenced source tables. (This includes all index tags in structural index files as well as index tags in other open compound index files.) However, if a useful index tag is not available, SELECT will also create a temporary index on the fly if doing so will speed up the action. This makes SELECT especially useful if you use the Expression Builder or some other means to enable operator execution of *ad hoc* queries.

Still, this is not to say that SELECT is faster or easier to use in all cases than the normal Xbase tools, especially when Rushmore is immediately available or when a combination of SET RELATION, SEEK, and WHILE will suffice to instantly establish a multi-table view. SELECT does after all create a result table and this can require additional processing time, especially when the result table is so sizable that FoxPro must place it on disk rather than create it in memory. There are also memory restraints to consider. SELECT places temporary tables (cursors) in the SORTWORK or TMPFILES drive, provided either a SORTWORK or TMPFILES drive has been defined in Config.fpw. If you want to create cursors that reside in memory as opposed to being stored on disk, your designated SORTWORK or TMPFILES drive must, moreover, be a virtual RAM disk drive, initialized during computer startup. If it is not, the result tables, though defined as cursors, will be physically stored on disk, thus slowing result table creation.

With respect to the MBS, I have used SELECT to prepare data for all reports (with the exception of the invoice-printing program, discussed in Chapter 6) in part to showcase this important command and also for the sake of being as consistent as possible in writing the screen programs listed on the Reports pulldown. However, for the sake of a balanced presentation, I also review the traditional Xbase tools required to prepare data for each reports, after showing how it is done with SELECT. More important, in preparing the filters that will be used to execute each SELECT command, I have stayed as close as possible to standard Xbase syntax, even though it forms a subset of SQL-SELECT syntax. This is intended to make it as easy as possible to replace the SELECT command used to prepare data for each report with its Xbase equivalent, whether because you prefer to work with traditional Xbase tools or because, with or without the aid of Rushmore, outputting report data directly from tables will be more economical either in terms of processing time or in terms of available memory and disk space.

Using SELECT with a Single-Source Table

For those who are new to SQL-SELECT, the best way to regard it is as a mini-program. When using it to prepare a cursor based upon data taken from a single table, we use the following basic syntax:

```
SELECT <field list or * for all> ;
    FROM <source table or alias> [<local alias>] ;
    INTO CURSOR <alias> ;
    WHERE <filters>
    ORDER BY <field list>
```

On the surface, this seems simple enough, but there are many details worth noting. First, the FROM table need not be open—unless you intend to reference it by an alias different from its root name. As long as the source table is in the defined path, SELECT will find and open it. (We discuss the use of the optional local alias in a moment.) Note also that SELECT clauses preceded by keywords can be entered in any order. Many programmers, for example, put the INTO or TO clause designating the output table last.

Entering the SELECT Field List

The field list determines which fields (or columns) are included in the result table as well as their order of appearance. Field list entry is mandatory, though you can use a single asterisk (*) to include all fields of the source file. Note that SELECT's field list, unlike SET FIELDS', is really an expression list, and you can play around with it as such. Calculated fields, defined using all FoxPro functions and operators, for example, can be included in a SELECT field list. To give a calculated field a name or assign a field from the source table a different name in the result table, use the formula <exp> AS <c-string>, where <c-string> is a character string, entered with or without delimiters, supplying the desired field name. All three of these SELECT commands have the same effect.

```
SELECT last+first AS "Name" FROM customer
SELECT last+first AS Name FROM customer
memvar = "Name"
SELECT last+first AS &memvar FROM customer
```

Note that source file fields can be referenced by alias in all SELECT clauses, though this is obviously more helpful when there are two or more source tables.

```
SELECT customer.last + customer.first AS "Name" ;
    FROM customer WHERE customer.last > "Bloom"
```

However, SELECT's FROM <table> option permits the assignment of a *local alias*—that is, an alias to be used only during execution of SELECT.

```
SELECT a.last + a.first AS "Name" ;
    FROM customer a WHERE a.last > "Bloom"
```

By inserting the letter *a* immediately after the name of the source table, we establish *a* as Customer's local alias and then use it to keep the alias references short—though once we assign the local alias, we cannot use the source table's normal alias (in this case, Customer) in the SELECT command. Again, this will only be helpful when using multiple-source tables, where use of alias prefixes is mandatory to identify fields. It is optional when referencing a single-source table.

Using SELECT to Perform Calculations

Though we do not use it for this purpose in the MBS, SELECT is quite useful for tabulating data. It provides a ready alternative to the use of the SUM, COUNT, AVERAGE, and CALCULATE commands.

```
SELECT COUNT(custno), SUM(amount), AVG(amount) ;
    FROM sales INTO CURSOR values
```

This command queries the Sales table and produces a result table named Values. Notably, the result table has only a single record with three fields named Cnt, Sum_amount, and Avg_amount. (In the absence of assigned column names, FoxPro does its best to provide the fields with intelligible field name labels.) Still, the point is that use of aggregate functions designed to summarize data, including SUM(), COUNT(), AVG(), MIN(), and MAX(), change SELECT's function. Instead of producing a table with one record for each source record included in the command, SELECT produces only one record containing the results. (If fields or calculated fields designating literal values—that is, non-summary fields—are included in the field list along with summary fields, the result table cites the value only of the field or calculated field for the last record processed in the source file. For all practical purposes, their values will be meaningless.)

Since SELECT output can be sent to a cursor or to an array (see below), this provides us, for example, with an excellent means of instantly recalculating customer account (or debt-aging) field values for any customer.

```
memvar = customer.custno
SELECT SUM(amount) FROM sales ;
    INTO ARRAY current ;
    WHERE sales.date >= DATE()-30 ;
    AND sales.custno = memvar
```

This command returns the total of the customer's sales for the current period to array element Current[1,1] by summing all sales with a date falling in the last 30 days. The command can be repeated with different WHERE <conditions> in order to provide us with figures for the other debt-aging fields. Note that we must supply the desired customer's Custno through a memvar or literal value. (Using Customer.custno would indicate a join condition, as described later in this chapter.)

The following command gives us the figure for sales in the previous period:

```
memvar = customer.custno
SELECT SUM(amount) AS FROM sales ;
    INTO ARRAY days30 ;
    WHERE sales.date >= DATE()-60 AND sales.date < DATE-30 ;
    AND sales.custno = memvar
```

Assuming we provide SELECT with the index tags it needs to perform these calculations with customer sales and payments, so that SELECT wastes no time creating them on the fly, we could depend upon it to supply debt-aging information whenever such information is required in the system. There would be no need to store it in Customer table fields.

TIP

You can also produce result tables that summarize data in groups of source table records by using SELECT's GROUP BY <field list> option. This creates a result table similar to that produced by the Xbase TOTAL command, though SELECT allows the use of all aggregate functions—for example, SUM(), AVG(), MIN(), and MAX(). The GROUP BY field list is used to designate the field or fields of the result table holding the values that must be used in identifying groups of related records. All source table records with the same value in the GROUP BY field(s) are presented in one record in the result table. Numeric fields display the sum of values of all records in each group unless aggregate functions are explicitly used to return other values, while fields of other types will hold the values of the last record in each group. The HAVING <filter> clause can also be used to filter records in each group. (See your FoxPro documentation for more information about the use of GROUP BY and HAVING.)

SELECT Output Options

When we use INTO CURSOR <alias>, the cursor SELECT creates functions like any other table, though it is immediately erased the moment we close it. While it is in memory, we can index it, reference it, BROWSE it, and link it to other tables, including other cursors, as we choose. We will see an example of such manipulation when we use SELECT to prepare data for statement printing. However, the cursor is read-only. If you want to create a permanent table, use INTO DBF <file> or INTO TABLE <file> instead of INTO CURSOR <alias>. This creates a normal .dbf file on disk. As mentioned above, TO ARRAY <array> is also available for sending output to an array. This is often used for instantly preparing an array for use in an @ GET popup or list.

TIP

SELECT results are directed by default to a BROWSE window unless INTO is used to direct results to an ARRAY <array name>, CURSOR <alias>, or DBF <file>. However, intead of using INTO, you can also employ TO FILE, TO PRINTER, or TO SCREEN to send the results to an ASCII file or to direct it to the printer or main window. When using TO FILE or TO PRINTER, use NOCONSOLE to suppress output to the main FoxPro window and PLAIN to suppress field headings. (See your FoxPro documentation for more information about these SELECT command output options.)

As previously mentioned, FoxPro places cursors in the SORTWORK or TMPFILES drive if either of these facilities is defined in Config.fpw. To create cursors in memory instead of in temporary disk files, use a RAM disk for SORTWORK or TMPFILES. (See your FoxPro documentation for more information about SORTWORK and TMPFILES and your Windows documentation for more information about creating a RAM disk.)

Another thing to bear in mind is that each cursor will support a compound index (.cdx) file. Moreover, if you create only one index tag for the cursor, the structural compound index will be automatically erased when you close the cursor. This saves you the trouble of having to erase it yourself.

NOTE

When directing SELECT command results to a BROWSE window, use SELECT's PREFERENCE <expC> option to save the BROWSE window attributes and format to the open resource file for subsequent use with SELECT or BROWSE PREFERENCE. (See Chapter 5 for a discussion of resource files and BROWSE PREFERENCE.) Like BROWSE, SELECT includes a NOWAIT option for executing the result table in BROWSE without halting program execution.

Eliminating Duplicate Records in the Result Table

Not included in the SELECT command's simplified syntax as presented above are the keywords ALL and DISTINCT. Inserted immediately after the SELECT command and before the field list, the keyword DISTINCT instructs SELECT to eliminate duplicate records (records having the same values in all fields included in the

SELECT field list) from the result table. The keyword ALL, on the other hand, instructs SELECT to include all records even if they are duplicates. The keyword ALL, however, need not be entered since it specifies the default result.

Entering Record Filters with SELECT WHERE

Moving on to SELECT's WHERE clause, when dealing with a single source table, this functions just like SET FILTER TO <condition>. Here we can make use of all Xbase relational and logical operators to form filter conditions to our heart's content. In other words, this is where we will apply the optional filters entered by the operator through use of the Customer Database Reports window's customer selection criteria input fields, though we must first write the filters, based upon the operator's entries, before plugging them into SELECT WHERE using macro substitution.

```
m.filter = UPPER(last + first) >= xlast_b AND ;
   UPPER(last + first) <= xlast_b
SELECT * FROM customer TO CURSOR temp WHERE &filter
```

Again, this is no different from passing filters to SET FILTER with macro substitution.

```
USE customer
SET FILTER TO &filter
```

This accomplishes the same thing, though without creating a temporary table. Since index tag Names can be used by Rushmore in executing the Xbase filter, there is no advantage in this case to using SELECT. It is when a potentially optimizable filter cannot be referred to an available index tag—or when a specific record order is required and filters must also be used—that SELECT will generally do better than the comparable Xbase commands. (As you will recall from Chapter 4, a controlling index used to establish record order will slow Rushmore's execution of record filters with SET FILTER or FOR <condition>.) The only exception to this rule is when SEEK and WHILE <condition>, and optionally FOR <condition>, can be used together to pinpoint groups of records using a controlling index. This is the method employed in Saletrns.spr for preparing data for invoice printing, as discussed in Chapter 6. Though use of WHILE <condition> automatically deactivates Rushmore, we have no need of it since SEEK and WHILE <condition> are sufficient to filter out sales belonging to other customers.

Still, there are several special functions, some of which correspond to available Xbase functions, that can be used in forming SELECT WHERE filters. For example, when filtering records on the basis of a range of values, we can use SQL's BETWEEN <value> AND <value> operator.

```
m.xhist_b = 100
m.xhist_e = 1000
SELECT...WHERE customer.history BETWEEN m.xhist_b AND m.xhist_e
SELECT...WHERE customer.history NOT BETWEEN m.xhist_b ;
   AND m.xhist_e
```

The NOT logical operator in the second command is used, just as it is used in Xbase filters and conditions, to reverse the result of the logical expression.

To test for the existence of one value in a list of other values, we can use the SQL IN operator:

```
m.code1 = "A1"
m.code2 = "B2"
m.code3 = "A3"
SELECT...WHERE customer.cuscode IN (m.code1, m.code2, m.code3)
SELECT...WHERE customer.cuscode NOT IN (m.code1, m.code2, m.code3)
```

And to perform pattern search, we can use LIKE:

```
m.string = "__AT%"
SELECT...WHERE customer.cuscode LIKE m.string
SELECT...WHERE customer.cuscode NOT LIKE m.string
```

When using LIKE, we can employ the underscore (_)and the percent (%) sign as wildcard symbols to mask individual characters and all remaining characters in the string, respectively.

Of course, each of the special SQL operators used here has a corresponding Xbase function, though there are slight differences in syntax, as indicated by the following commands:

```
SELECT...WHERE BETWEEN(customer.history, xhist_b, xhist_e)
SELECT...WHERE customer.cuscode INLIST(code1, code2, code3)
SELECT...WHERE LIKE(m.string,customer.cuscode)
```

Note that when using the Xbase LIKE() function, instead of using underscores and the percent sign to mask individual or all remaining characters in a string, we use the Xbase wildcard symbols, the question mark (?) and the asterisk (*).

An additional feature of SELECT's WHERE clause is the ability to filter records on the basis of the results of a subquery performed with SELECT. For example, if we want a list of customers who do not have sales on file in Sales.dbf, we can use the following subquery:

```
SELECT * FROM customer WHERE NOT EXISTS ;
    (SELECT * FROM sales WHERE customer.custno = sales.custno)
```

Leaving aside SELECT's creation of a temporary cursor, this is functionally equivalent to either of the following sets of Xbase commands:

```
USE customer
USE sales ORDER sales IN 0    && Sales index key: custno+saleno
SET FILTER TO NOT SEEK(custno,"sales")

USE customer
USE sales ORDER sales IN 0
SET RELATION TO custno INTO sales
SET FILTER TO NOT FOUND("sales")
```

In all three cases, we create a table (or table view) that lists only those customers who do not have sales on file in Sales.dbf, though we may do the opposite by simply removing the NOT operator.

To be explicit, when SELECT reads through the source (Customer) table, the EXISTS operator returns a logical True whenever the subquery (SELECT) includes a record. We test for the existence or nonexistence of a record and not of a specific value or values in the subquery table. We may, however, achieve the same thing by including a subquery in SQL's IN() operator.

```
SELECT * FROM customer WHERE custno NOT IN ;
    (SELECT custno FROM sales)
```

Here the subquery is used to supply the list of values in which Customer.custno must not be found for a source table record to be included in the result table. Again, remove NOT to reverse the meaning of the filter.

TIP

Additional subquery filters can be created using ALL(), ANY(), or SOME(), all of which use the same syntax as IN(subquery): <field> <comparison operator> SQL operator(subquery). See your FoxPro documentation for examples of how to use these special SQL operators.

Ordering Records in the SELECT Result Table

The SELECT command's ORDER BY <field list> is used to order the records in the result table. Note that like the SORT command—and unlike INDEX—the ORDER BY clause takes a field list.

```
SELECT customer.last, customer.first, customer.company ;
    FROM customer ;
    INTO CURSOR temp ;
    ORDER BY customer.last, customer.first
```

This places the records in the result table Temp in ascending order by last and first names. Moreover, like SORT ON <field list>, we may use ASC or DESC to indicate ascending or descending alphabetical order for each field included in the ORDER BY list. ASC is naturally the default order. Also be aware that, like SORT ON <field list>, Xbase functions cannot be used in the ORDER BY <field list>. You are limited to the names of existing source table fields.

Note that the ORDER BY <field list> can also be entered by using integers to indicate columns (fields) in the SELECT <field list>. For example, we can rewrite the above ORDER BY clause as follows:

```
ORDER BY 1, 2
```

Here the 1 points SELECT to the first column in the field list, Customer.last, while 2 points SELECT to Customer.first, the second field in the field list. While this method is not especially fruitful here (though it is shorter than writing out the field names), it does supply a means of ordering records according to the values of calculated fields placed in a field list.

TIP

Since the ORDER BY clause refers to expressions in the SELECT field (or expression) list, you can employ functions in the ORDER BY clause if and when the functions are used in the field list. For example, if UPPER(last) is the first field in the SELECT field list, ORDER BY 1 will order records in the result table using UPPER(last) as the order expression.

Establishing a Table View for MBS Single-Table Reports

At this point, we can look at the commands actually used in Cust_rpt.spr for preparing Customer table data for production of the Customer List and Customer

Accounts reports, as well as Letters and Labels. Note that in order to keep unindexed copies of source files on hand for exclusive use by SELECT when preparing report tables, we open an additional copy of Customer.dbf in procedure Opendata (Bigbiz.prg) under the alias name Custrpts. Here is the command used to prepare records for the Customer List report:

```
SELECT custno,last,first,company,department,address, ;
    city,state,zip,country,phone1,phone2, ;
    cuscode,sal,credit,opendate,lastdate,history ;
    FROM custrpts ;
    INTO CURSOR Report ;
    &filter ;
    ORDER BY &sel_order
```

The field list includes all fields required by Customer.frx, the Customer List report. As with all result tables produced by Cust_rpt.spr, we use a cursor named Report. This is arbitrary and is intended to give us a known name for our result table. Later in the program, after the report has been completed, we use the command USE IN Report to close and automatically erase the cursor. The line &filter uses macro substitution not only to enter the WHERE <condition> filter but to input the WHERE keyword as well. After all, if no filter is required, the WHERE keyword, followed by no filter, will result in an error. (We will see how suitable filters are pieced together on the basis of operator entries to the customer selection criteria input fields in a moment.)

As for the ORDER BY clause, we also provide the required field list through macro substitution, after preparing m.sel_order to hold a value corresponding to the operator's selection from the Order By radio buttons, @ GET m.ord_but.

The SELECT commands used for preparing the other flat-file Customer table reports differ only in terms of field list. (See Figure 12.13.) True, we might combine all the SELECT commands shown in Figure 12.13, either by using a field list suitable to all flat-file reports or by entering the required field list with macro substitution. I have written out each command separately to keep things simple, on the one hand, and on the other, to be as economical as possible with regard to the use of available space on my virtual drive used by TMPFILES.

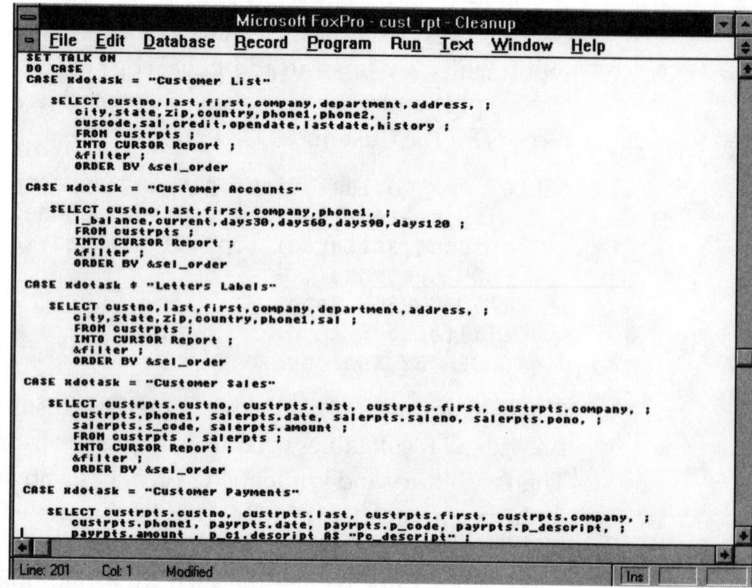

FIGURE 12.13:

When executing SQL-SELECT to prepare data for report output, we input filter conditions and record order directives using macro substitution.

With respect to the production of letters, Letters.frx, the Form Letter report, also assumes that Letters.dbf, alias Lett_pic, is open in another work area and that the letter chosen for the text of the form letter is current in it—though this happens automatically as a result of the operator's use of the @ GET m.lettform list, which references Lett_pic.name.

In all cases, the SELECT command used to establish the result table used by our flat-file reports can be just as easily established with the following commands:

```
SELECT custrpts
SET ORDER TO &sel_order
SET FILTER TO &filter
```

Of course, SET ORDER's syntax is different from SELECT ORDER BY <field list>, so we must prepare the value of m.sel_order in a slightly different way. We must name an existing index tag rather than names of result or source table fields in a list. However, assuming we prepare SELECT WHERE <condition> filters sticking to Xbase syntax, the only change we must make to the value of m.filter—that is, when the operator has actually specified a filter—is to remove the WHERE keyword. Otherwise the filters will work just as well with SET FILTER as they will with SELECT WHERE.

Note that instead of using SET FILTER TO, we can execute our filters with the aid of Rushmore by placing them directly in the REPORT FORM command.

```
m.filter = "FOR UPPER(company) >= comp_b AND "+ ;
   = "history >= hist_b"
REPORT FORM (xdreport) &filter
```

This will work just as quickly.

Using SELECT with Multiple-Source Tables

When preparing data for printing multi-table reports with SELECT, the general strategy is to reduce the source tables to a single result table or flat file. This has the advantage, noted earlier, of making it unnecessary to use alias names to identify table fields in the Report form executing the report. The Report form can therefore be used to output data from any current table with the right fields without having to manipulate the table's alias to make it conform to the expectations of the Report form. The action used to achieve these results is an *inner join*, executed by virtue of a join condition entered in SELECT's WHERE clause. The basic formula is

```
SELECT <alias.field1>[, <alias.field2>...] ;
    FROM <source table1> [<local alias>] ;
        [,<source table2> [<local alias>]] ;
    INTO CURSOR <alias> ;
    WHERE <join condition> AND/OR <filters>
    ORDER BY <alias field and/or column order list>
```

All we do is list the source tables in the FROM clause and specify the appropriate join condition in WHERE. Here, for example, is the basic command we issue in Cust_rpt.spr to prepare data for production of the Customer Sales report. (Note that alias Custrpts is a copy of Customer.dbf and alias Salerpts is a copy of Sales.dbf, both of which are held open in a nonindexed state for exclusive use by SELECT in preparing Customer Database reports.)

```
SELECT custrpts.custno, custrpts.last, custrpts.first, ;
    custrpts.company, custrpts.phone1, salerpts.date, ;
    salerpts.saleno, salerpts.pono, salerpts.s_code, ;
    salerpts.amount ;
    FROM custrpts , salerpts ;
    INTO CURSOR Report ;
    WHERE custrpts.custno = salerpts.custno ;
    ORDER BY &sel_order
```

Though we supply other filters to the WHERE clause as needed, the use of custrpts.custno = salerpts.custno is mandatory. Without it SELECT produces a result table joining record information from every record in the first source table with every record in the second listed source table. (We get a file with a number of records equal to RECCOUNT("custrpts") * RECCOUNT("salerpts").) This is hardly what we desire. We want a result table that joins record information in the Customer table with record information in the Sales table only where there is a match between Custrpts.custno and Salerpts.custno.

Here are the commensurate Xbase commands used to achieve this view, though in multi-table, rather than flat-file, format:

```
* Custrpts and Salerpts are already open.
SELECT salerpts
SET ORDER TO sales IN salrpts  && key exp: custno + saleno
SELECT custrpt
SET RELATION TO custno INTO salerpts
SET SKIP TO salerpts
SET ORDER TO (sel_order)
SET FILTER TO FOUND("salerpts")
```

Since this roughly corresponds to our normal use of the Customer and Sales tables in the MBS default table view—though we use different alias names here—there is no need to comment on the effects of these commands. However, the use of SET FILTER TO FOUND() is worthy of note since it is required to filter our records in Custrpts that have no child records in Salerpts. SET RELATION does not, after all, produce an inner join—or any join at all. It links tables in terms of parent-child relations. (In a join, there is no parent or child. All tables referenced in a join have equal status, as in the Xbase JOIN command.) Since SET RELATION includes one record in the view for every parent record, even if the parent record has no corresponding child records, we must filter out childless parent records if we want to remove them from the view. Moreover, we must use SET SKIP if we want to include one record in the view for every child record having a parent record since SET RELATION does not do this of its own accord. With SET RELATION, in other words, SET SKIP and SET FILTER are the means of emulating the effects of SELECT—in this case, an inner join.

TIP

An inner join is one that excludes records from any source file with no matching records in the other source files. The virtual join created with SET RELATION and SET SKIP, which includes parent records with no children, is referred to as an outer join. This is difficult but not impossible to effect with SELECT since it requires the use of UNION SELECT and a WHERE NOT EXIST (subquery).

To join data from more than two source files with SELECT, we just extend the source table list and add the necessary <join condition> to the WHERE clause using the logical operator AND. The SELECT command used to prepare data for the Customer Payments report gives us a good example of this since we will want to include the full payment descriptions, stored in lookup file P_codes, in the report output. (The copy of P_codes.dbf held open for use in reports is arbitrarily assigned the name P_c1. For a review of the function and uses of P_codes.dbf, see Chapter 5.) In this case, however, we precede the SELECT command with the Xbase commands that would be used to achieve the required view.

```
* Custrpts and Salerpts and P_c1 are already open.
SET ORDER TO p_code IN p_c1
SELECT payrpts
SET RELATION TO p_code INTO p_c1
SET ORDER TO payments  && key expression: custno
SELECT custrpts
SET RELATION TO custno INTO payrpts
SET SKIP TO payrpts
SET ORDER TO (sel_order)
SET FILTER TO FOUND("payrpts")
```

Here we have a chain of tables. The Customer table is linked as a parent into the Payments table, while the Payments table is linked as a parent into the P_code table. With respect to the relation between the Customer and Payments tables, we use SET SKIP and SET FILTER to emulate an inner join, just as we do in preparing data for the Customer Sales report. Because it is used as a lookup file, we do not include P_codes in the SET SKIP command since it should have only one record corresponding to a parent record in the Payments table. And if it had more, we would not want to include additional records in the resulting view in any case; it would falsify the data. (It would report duplicate payments.) Nor do we want to filter the resulting view with FOUND("p_codes"). Given the action of SET RELATION, this would just waste time since each Payments.p_code will be listed in the

P_codes lookup file. (And if for some reason a payment were recorded without a P_code, we would certainly want to see it since the lack of P_code makes the payment record defective. It must be fixed.) Still, this is one of the conveniences and advantages of SET RELATION over SELECT in forming multi-table views. It is, in fact, more flexible than SELECT, which is most readily used to execute inner joins. Still, it is an inner join that is required for production of the Customer Payments report, so we achieve our end with the SELECT command.

```
SELECT custrpts.custno, custrpts.last, custrpts.first, ;
    custrpts.company, custrpts.phone1, payrpts.date, ;
    payrpts.p_code, payrpts.p_descript, ;
    payrpts.amount , p_c1.descript AS "Pc_descript" ;
    FROM custrpts , payrpts , p_c1 ;
    INTO CURSOR Report ;
    WHERE custrpts.custno = payrpts.custno AND ;
        pay_rpts.p_code = p_c1.p_code ;
    ORDER BY &sel_order
```

Again, we use the logical operator AND when entering more than one join condition to make the join conditions cumulative in effect. Each record in the result table must satisfy both. This gives us a record in the result table for every record in the Customer table with a matching record in the Payments table that has a matching record in the P_codes table. (However, since this is a join, we can also state the result in two other ways. For example, the resulting table includes one record for every record in the P_codes table that matches a record in the Payments table that also matches a record in the Customer table.) This is the nature of an inner join executed with SELECT.

In preparing our table for production of the Customer Sales and Customer Payments reports, if the operator enters customer selection criteria, we will want to add additional filters to the WHERE clauses. Moreover, both reports allow the entry of transaction dates, which can be used to filter which payments or sales are to be included in the report by date range. These filters, however, are easily added on to the join conditions shown above with the logical operator AND or OR. The ordering of the filters and join conditions in the SELECT WHERE clause makes no difference. The only important thing to remember is that a join condition must be preceded by AND when it does not appear first in the WHERE clause, while normal record filters can be preceded by AND or OR. In Cust_rpt.spr, we therefore add the join conditions as needed to the memvars we create to store optional filter conditions when they are entered and insert them, along with the WHERE clause, in each SELECT command through the use of macro substitution, as shown in Figure 12.14.

FIGURE 12.14:

When creating multi-file result tables with SELECT, you must list the source tables in the FROM clause and provide a join condition in the WHERE clause.

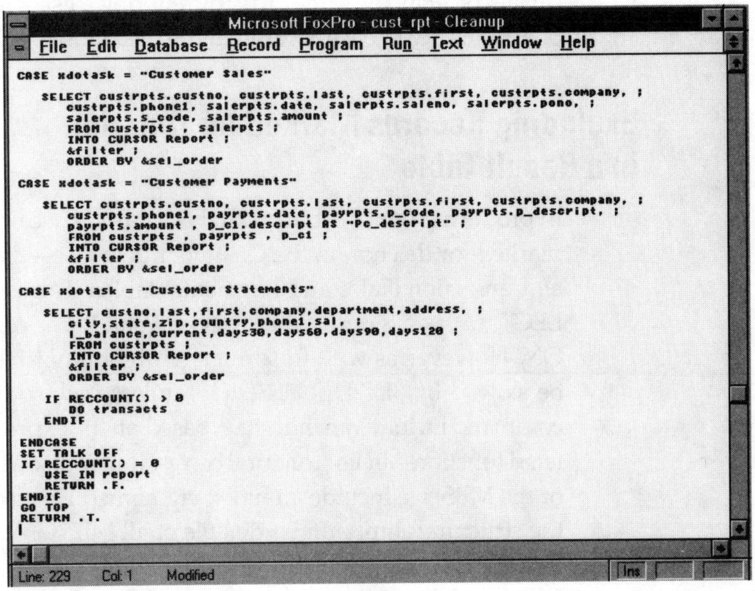

Note that when entering the SELECT commands used to prepare data for the Customer Sales and Customer Payments reports, we might use local aliases to shorten entry of alias names in the SELECT command clauses.

```
SELECT a.custno, a.last, a.first, a.company, a.phone1, ;
    b.date, b.p_code, b.p_descript, b.amount , ;
    c.descript AS "Pc_descript"
    FROM custrpts a, payrpts b, p_c1 c;
    INTO CURSOR Report ;
    WHERE a.custno = b.custno AND b.p_code = c.p_code ;
    ORDER BY a.last, a.first, b.date
```

In this case we rewrite the command used to prepare data for the Customer Payments report using the local alias names *a*, *b*, and *c*, for Custrpts, Payrpts, and P_c1, respectively. By declaring the local aliases in the FROM clause, we make it possible to use them in all other SELECT command clauses in place of the source tables' longer Xbase alias names. (Use of a local alias does not change the source table's Xbase alias. The local alias is only observed by SELECT.)

With respect to the above command's ORDER BY clause, we write out the field list only to provide a concrete example. (ORDER BY clauses are supplied in Cust_rpt.spr through macro substitution.) Here again, we refer to fields by local alias, though we can also specify the same order by entering a list of integers corresponding to the order of appearance of each column in the result table. This would be ORDER BY 2, 3, 6.

Excluding Records Marked for Deletion in a Result Table

In producing our Customer Database reports, we naturally want to exclude all records marked for deletion in the Customer database—that is, in the Customer table and in all transaction (Sales and Payments) tables. This is readily done when executing SELECT, just as it is done when executing all Xbase commands, by using SET DELETED ON. However, as with Rushmore (with optimizable Xbase commands), SELECT will be slowed by SET DELETED ON unless each source table included in the SELECT command includes an index tag, based on the expression DELETED()—the FoxPro deleted function—in its structural compound index, as described in Chapter 4. In the case of the MBS, we include an index tag named Deleted (key expression: DELETED()) in the structural compound index file of all MBS tables referenced with SELECT or with Xbase sequential commands, so the SET DELETED action can be properly optimized. It's a good idea for you to do the same thing in your own systems.

Whether or not you created index tags based on DELETED() for your tables, you can issue SELECT with SET DELETED OFF and still filter out records marked for deletion from a single source file with WHERE NOT DELETED(). This will be optimized if the index tag is readily available, though SELECT may generate it on the fly if doing so will speed command action.

WARNING

When entering filters with SELECT WHERE, avoid Xbase functions that must designate a source table (alias) if the result table is based on more than one source table. The fact is that SELECT does not generally refer to source tables by alias (or local alias) when processing data from multiple-source tables but often makes up its own aliases as it goes along. Xbase functions that require entry of an alias will therefore not function as expected. With respect to the WHERE NOT DELETED() condition, which can be used to filter out records marked for deletion in a SELECT result table, the filter will work correctly only when the SELECT command has just one source table.

Using SELECT UNION to Combine Two Result Tables

Another facility of SELECT is the ability to combine—to append rather than join—the result tables of two SELECT commands while ordering all records in the final result table at once. This is done by using SELECT...UNION SELECT. The basic syntax is

```
SELECT [ALL/DISTINCT] <alias.field1>[, <alias.field2>...] ;
    FROM <source table1> [<local alias>] ;
        [,<source table2> [<local alias>]] ;
    INTO CURSOR <alias> ;
    WHERE <join condition> AND/OR <filters> ;
    UNION [ALL]
    SELECT [DISTINCT/ALL] <alias.field1>[, <alias.field2>...] ;
        FROM <source table1> [<local alias>] ;
            [,<source table2> [<local alias>]] ;
        WHERE <join condition> AND/OR <filters>
        ORDER BY <column order list>
```

Though the size of the beast is enough to give one pause, there's really not that much to master. Each SELECT command should be conceived of as producing a separate result table; UNION simply tells FoxPro to append the records produced by the second SELECT command to the result table produced by the first. Three things, however, must be kept in mind. First, the type and width of the fields of the two result tables must match exactly on a field-by-field basis for UNION to work correctly. (The field names need not be the same.) Second, if a record order is required for the result table, which receives its name or destination in the first SELECT command, the ORDER BY directive must appear after the UNION SELECT command. It must also be specified using integers to represent the column order of the fields to be used to establish record order. Third, when combining the results of the two SELECT commands, the UNION action automatically eliminates duplicate records from the final result table. To prevent this from happening—to include all records from both SELECT commands in the final result table—use UNION ALL.

A good example of the use of UNION SELECT is provided by the SELECT command used to prepare transaction data for printing customer statements. (See Figure 12.15.) We use the first SELECT command to create a result table that includes all records from Salerpts that belong to the current billing period and all fields (or expressions) necessary to accommodate Sales and Payments table records in the same result table. Sales table data goes into result table fields Report2.custno, Report2.date, Report2.saleno, Report2.pono, and Report2.samount. As the UNION SELECT command indicates, Report2.custno and Report2.date are also used by Payrpts.custno and Payrpts.date. (This makes it possible to order the final result table on the basis of Report2.custno, providing us with a means of joining it with Customer table data, whether through use of additional SELECT commands or SET RELATION.) The UNION SELECT command then adds all records to Report2 from Payrpts that belong to the current billing period. Note that the empty fields we insert in each SELECT command must be defined to have the same width, type, and name as the corresponding fields in the other SELECT command. Otherwise, the command will produce an error.

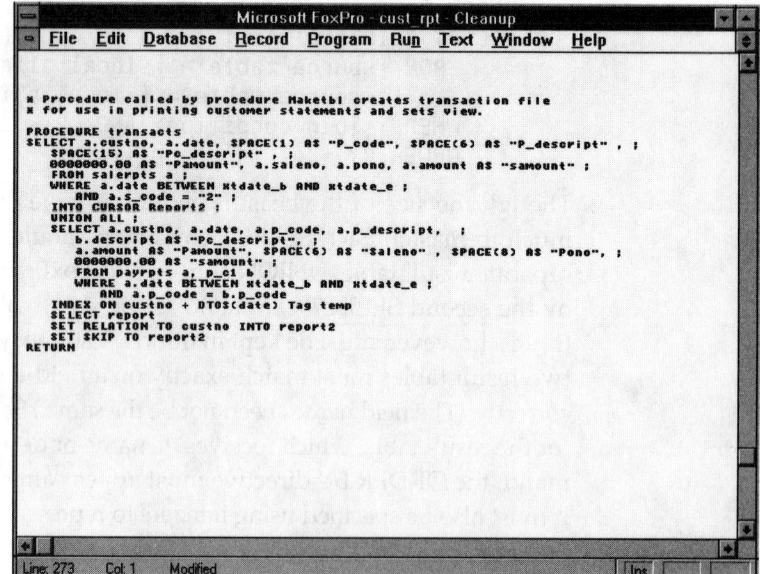

FIGURE 12.15: When using UNION SELECT to combine the results of two SELECT commands in a single result table, we must make the field lists of both SELECT commands match exactly—even by adding empty fields to each field list.

As the UNION SELECT command indicates, when creating the second result table we also use a join condition to include payment descriptions held in lookup file P_codes (alias P_c1) in the final result table. In specifying the result table field names, we also make use of AS <field name> to rename Salerpts.amount as Report2.samount and Payrpts.amount as Report2.pamount. Though this need not be done, it prevents us from having to make extensive use of IIF() in Report form States.frx to distinguish the meaning of a value found in an Amount field holding both sales and payment amounts.

Having combined our sales and payments for the current billing period, we can now complete the view required for statement printing by bringing the Customer table into the act.

There are several objections to making further use of SELECT to combine Customer table records with the records in result table Report2, which we may treat like any other (read-only) .dbf file as long as it is open. The problem is that we are likely to have many customers on file in the Customer table with active accounts but who have no transactions in the current billing period. (We must remind them to pay their bills by sending them another, even if it includes no new sales and payments.) This, of course, is the sort of thing that SET RELATION is good at but that SELECT can handle only with difficulty. We must first use SELECT to join records in the Customer table with records in Report2 on the basis of matching Custno. However, the inner join naturally filters out Customer table records representing active accounts with no current transactions. To include these records in the result table, we must use SELECT UNION once again and use NOT IN (subquery), referencing Report2, to specify those customers (by Custno) who are not included in the other (second) SELECT command. (The use of the condition custrpts.l_balance <> 0.00 before custrpts.custno NOT IN (subquery) in the first SELECT command's WHERE clause serves to specify those customers with active accounts but no current transactions.)

```
SELECT ;
    <field list with needed Custrpts and Report2 fields> ;
    FROM custrpts ;
    INTO CURSOR final
    WHERE custrpts.l_balance <> 0.00 AND ;
        custrpts.custno NOT IN ;
        (SELECT report2.custno FROM report2) ;
    UNION ALL ;
    SELECT <same field list> ;
        FROM custrpts, report2 ;
        WHERE custrpts.custno = report2.custno ;
        ORDER BY &sel_order
```

The difficulties of proceeding in this way are many, even excluding the one-time chore of writing out the field list. An incredible amount of processing is required to achieve the desired result table. In fact, we perform the same tasks with the Customer table twice over, though each of the SELECT commands interprets the results differently. Moreover, if the operator is allowed to enter additional filters—customer selection criteria—we will be forced to include all filters in both WHERE clauses or execute yet another SELECT command to dispense with them. The strategy is not only too complicated, it is also uneconomical in terms of processing time and memory use.

The easy solution is to use a separate SELECT command to create a result table that includes all Customer records requiring a statement, without referring to Report2 at all, and to subsequently resort to standard Xbase tools to take care of the relation between the two SELECT result tables. Without citing the field list, here is the basic command we use to create our parent Customer result table:

```
SELECT <custrpts field list> ;
    FROM custrpts
    INTO CURSOR report
    WHERE ABS(current) + ABS(l_balance) <> 0.00
    ORDER BY &sel_order
```

The SELECT command uses the same syntax we employ for preparing data for production of the Customer List or Customer Accounts reports. It is a flat file. And while we must include the WHERE condition shown above to filter out any and all customer records representing inactive accounts—again, all active accounts will have a positive or negative amount in current and/or l_balance (the balance forward field)—there is nothing to prevent us from adding to the end of the filter whatever customer selection criteria filters the operator enters.

Once we have created result table Report, holding all Customer records requiring statements, and table Report2, combining all sales and payments that must be detailed in customer statements, we can easily complete the view by using INDEX and SET RELATION to establish the desired parent-child relation between the two tables. Figure 12.16 shows the entire sequence used to prepare data for production of MBS statements.

We first use the SELECT command just discussed to create our filtered and ordered Customer table (alias Report). If the table is not empty (RECCOUNT() > 0), we place a call to procedure Transact, which executes the SELECT UNION command required to create table Report2, holding all transaction records that must be detailed in customer statements. Note that if we do not use an ORDER BY clause in creating Report2, it is because we require an actual index tag to link Report2 to Report with SET RELATION. (ORDER BY physically sorts the records in the result table, like the SORT command. It does not index the table.) In executing the INDEX command, we include DTOS(date) in the key expression so each customer's transactions will be output in date order—though the suborder by Report2.Date could

FIGURE 12.16:

In preparing data for production of customer statements, we use standard Xbase tools to manipulate result tables produced with the SELECT command.

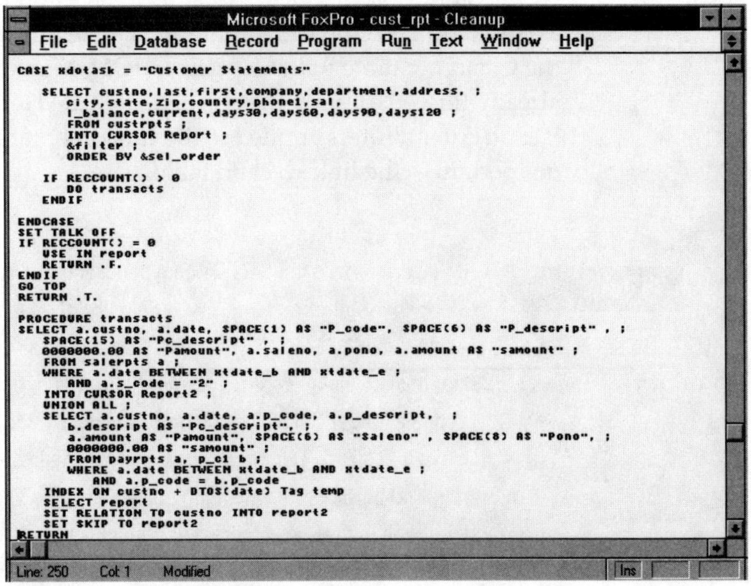
Microsoft FoxPro - cust_rpt - Cleanup
File Edit Database Record Program Run Text Window Help
CASE xdotask = "Customer Statements"
SELECT custno,last,first,company,department,address, ;
city,state,zip,country,phone1,sal, ;
l_balance,current,days30,days60,days90,days120 ;
FROM custrpts ;
INTO CURSOR Report ;
&filter ;
ORDER BY &sel_order
IF RECCOUNT() > 0
DO transacts
ENDIF
ENDCASE
SET TALK OFF
IF RECCOUNT() = 0
USE IN report
RETURN .F.
ENDIF
GO TOP
RETURN .T.
PROCEDURE transacts
SELECT a.custno, a.date, SPACE(1) AS "P_code", SPACE(6) AS "P_descript" , ;
SPACE(15) AS "Pc_descript" , ;
0000000.00 AS "Pamount", a.saleno, a.pono, a.amount AS "samount" ;
FROM salerpts a ;
WHERE a.date BETWEEN xtdate_b AND xtdate_e ;
AND a.s_code = "2" ;
INTO CURSOR Report2 ;
UNION ALL ;
SELECT a.custno, a.date, a.p_code, a.p_descript, ;
b.descript AS "Pc_descript", ;
a.amount AS "Pamount", SPACE(6) AS "Saleno" , SPACE(8) AS "Pono", ;
0000000.00 AS "samount" ;
FROM payrpts a, p_c1 b ;
WHERE a.date BETWEEN xtdate_b AND xtdate_e ;
AND a.p_code = b.p_code
INDEX ON custno + DTOS(date) Tag temp
SELECT report
SET RELATION TO custno INTO report2
SET SKIP TO report2
RETURN
Line: 250 Col: 1 Modified
Ins

also have been achieved using the SELECT command's ORDER BY directive, owing to the INDEX command's preservation of the relative order of records with the same index keys. Finally, after indexing Report2, using an index tag so FoxPro will erase it automatically when we close the result table, we use SET RELATION and SET SKIP TO report2 to establish the desired view. Once we issue GO TOP in Report, we are ready to roll; all parent records in Report are already properly ordered and filtered in keeping with the operator's instructions. By combining the power of SQL-SELECT and the greater flexibility of SET RELATION with respect to multitable handling, we thus establish the desired view, more quickly and efficiently than we can using SELECT or standard Xbase tools on their own.

Establishing the same view using standard Xbase tools is relatively simple, though we can begin more quickly by using another SQL command, CREATE TABLE, to create an empty table with a structure suitable to accommodate records from Sales.dbf and Payments.dbf. Then we use APPEND FROM FOR <condition> to place all sales and payments belonging to the current period in the empty transaction table. (Note that to use APPEND FROM successfully, the transaction table must include fields with exactly the same names as the FROM tables. We cannot change FROM file field names as we can with SELECT unless we use REPLACE instead of

APPEND FROM to transfer data to transaction table fields with different names. This will be a bit slower.) After indexing the new transaction table, we can link it to the Customer table with SET RELATION. Moreover, because our transactions are already filtered, despite the use of SET RELATION, we can optimize customer selection criteria filters applied to the Customer table with SET FILTER since they do not pertain to the linked, child table.

TIP

If you are new to the SELECT command, you are likely to make many errors when entering lengthy commands with complex clauses before you become fully accustomed to SELECT command syntax. Syntax errors, however, can be difficult to diagnose since FoxPro does not report the actual clause causing the error. To debug a longer SELECT command, execute it in an independent .prg file. This will make it easier to edit and retest than working in the Command window since all required parameters, including those entered with macro substitution, can also be initialized in the mini-program. If problems persist, strip out optional clauses one by one until the command works; then begin adding them until you discover the clause containing the error.

Preparing Filters and Record Order

Having reviewed the SELECT (and Xbase) commands used to prepare data for production of Customer database reports, we can now conclude our discussion of Custrpt.spr by examining how we piece together the record filters and order directives we supply SELECT through the use of macro substitution.

To begin with, when the operator selects the Execute button and the @ GET push button VALID clause executes function Maketabl, as described earlier in this chapter, the first thing we do in function Maketabl is to copy memvars holding customer selection criteria data into a second set of memvars, prefixed with *z* for the sake of convenience. (See Figure 12.17.) The fact is we will need to TRIM() the character memvars in order to use them in filters; but we must also preserve the memvars' originally assigned widths so we can continue to use them as @ GET input fields without having to reset their widths. This is best done by manipulating the values in a second set of memvars and leaving the memvars used in the input fields alone.

FIGURE 12.17:

When preparing filters, we begin by passing values from the memvars used with customer selection criteria input fields to a second set of memvars, which we then use in forming the filters.

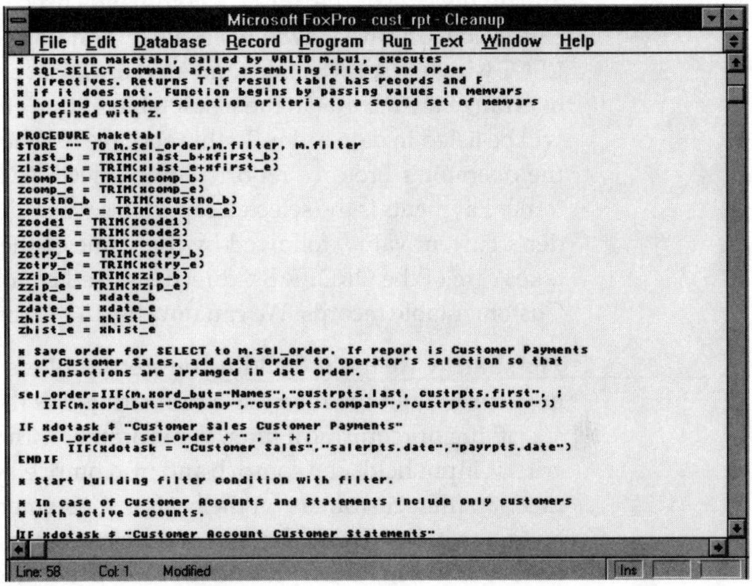

Microsoft FoxPro - cust_rpt - Cleanup

File Edit Database Record Program Run Text Window Help

```
* Function maketabl, called by VALID m.bu1, executes
* SQL-SELECT command after assembling filters and order
* directives. Returns T if result table has records and F
* if it does not. Function begins by passing values in memvars
* holding customer selection criteria to a second set of memvars
* prefixed with z.

PROCEDURE maketabl
STORE "" TO m.sel_order,m.filter, m.filter
zlast_b = TRIM(xlast_b+xfirst_b)
zlast_e = TRIM(xlast_e+xfirst_e)
zcomp_b = TRIM(xcomp_b)
zcomp_e = TRIM(xcomp_e)
zcustno_b = TRIM(xcustno_b)
zcustno_e = TRIM(xcustno_e)
zcode1 = TRIM(xcode1)
zcode2 = TRIM(xcode2)
zcode3 = TRIM(xcode3)
zctry_b = TRIM(xctry_b)
zctry_e = TRIM(xctry_e)
zzip_b = TRIM(xzip_b)
zzip_e = TRIM(xzip_e)
zdate_b = xdate_b
zdate_e = xdate_e
zhist_b = xhist_b
zhist_e = xhist_e

* Save order for SELECT to m.sel_order. If report is Customer Payments
* or Customer Sales, add date order to operator's selection so that
* transactions are arramged in date order.

sel_order=IIF(m.xord_but="Names","custrpts.last, custrpts.first", ;
   IIF(m.xord_but="Company","custrpts.company","custrpts.custno"))

IF xdotask $ "Customer Sales Customer Payments"
   sel_order = sel_order + " , " + ;
      IIF(xdotask = "Customer Sales","salerpts.date","payrpts.date")
ENDIF

* Start building filter condition with filter.

* In case of Customer Accounts and Statements include only customers
* with active accounts.

IF xdotask $ "Customer Account Customer Statements"
```

Line: 58 Col: 1 Modified Ins

However, before creating our filters—a long and tedious task—we dispense with the required SELECT ORDER BY directives, just to get them out of the way. By testing the value of m.xord_but, holding the operator's selection of the three available Customer table orders, we initialize m.sel_order to hold a string ordering the SELECT result table by columns Custrpts.last and Custrpts.first, if order by names is selected; Custrpts.company, if order by company is selected; and Custrpts.custno, if order by customer number is selected. The command used to do this, also shown in Figure 12.17, should require no explanation; it is essentially the same as that used in Cus_find.spr to change Customer table index order according to operator use of the Order By popup. (See Chapter 4.) The only difference here is that the strings we store to m.sel_order are designed for use with SELECT ORDER BY and must designate fields (or the order of fields) in the result table instead of the names of Customer.dbf index tags. Of course, in inputting the ORDER BY directive, we must use macro substitution. We cannot use a name expression to input a field list. SET ORDER TO, on the other hand, will accept a memvar, a name expression, or macro substitution.

Still, in the case of the SELECT commands used to prepare data for the Customer Sales and Customer Payments reports (done, as you will recall, through use of SELECT with two source tables and a WHERE join condition), we must also take steps to arrange the records in the result table so that each customer's sales or payments will be listed in date order. To this end, we refer to the value of m.xdotask, holding the operator's Produce report popup selection, to see if Customer Sales or Customer Payments is the selected report. If so, we add a comma to the end of m.sel_order's current value, followed by the name of the correct Date field column. This takes care of the ORDER BY directives used by all SELECT commands processing Customer table records. We can now begin building our filters.

The strategy we use in building our record filters is as follows. First we initialize a memvar to hold the filters as a null string. We then begin testing every condition specifying or requiring a filter. For example, with respect to the customer selection criteria input fields m.xcomp_b and m.xcomp_e, which the operator may use separately to filter customers on the basis of Customer.company field values, we begin by testing for entered values, though we do so using the memvars into which we have passed m.xcomp_b and m.xcomp_e's trimmed values: m.zcomp_b and m.zcomp_e.

```
IF NOT EMPTY(zcomp_b)
    m.filter = m.filter +  ;
        "UPPER(custrpts.company) >= zcomp_b AND "
ENDIF
IF NOT EMPTY(zcomp_e)
    m.filter = m.filter + ;
        "UPPER(custrpts.company) <= zcomp_e AND "
ENDIF
```

Working in this way we gradually build our filter, always being careful to insert the string AND (plus a space) at the end of each addition to m.filter. Where no value has been entered to a customer selection criteria input field, no filter is added. Here are the commands used to enter optional filters based on Custno:

```
IF NOT EMPTY(zcustno_b)
    m.filter = m.filter + "custrpts.custno >= zcustno_b AND "
ENDIF
IF NOT EMPTY(zlast_e)
    m.filter = m.filter + "custrpts.custno <= zcustno_e AND "
ENDIF
```

This should be straightforward enough, though we must be careful to make sure we write our filters so they can be optimized with the aid of an existing Customer table index tag when one is available. Thus, when forming the filter for Custrpts.company, we use UPPER() since index tag Company used a key expression of UPPER(company). This ensures maximum speed of execution since SELECT will have no cause to create a temporary index tag to execute the filter.

Two further things are required. When we finish placing all filters in m.filter (assuming any filter has been placed in it at all), we must strip off the AND at the end of the last filter. This is readily done by using LEFT() and LEN() together, as long as we have been consistent in placing AND at the end of each filter with a trailing blank.

```
IF NOT EMPTY(m.filter)
    m.filter = LEFT(m.filter,LEN(m.filter)-5)
ENDIF
```

If a filter has been placed in m.filter, the LEFT() function returns the value of m.filter, reduced 5 characters in length. This takes off the AND inserted at the end of the last filter actually added to m.filter. Then we can finish our preparation of m.filter by inserting the WHERE keyword in front of all filters (again, provided m.filter holds any filters).

```
IF NOT EMPTY(m.filter)
    m.filter1 = "WHERE " + m.filter
ENDIF
```

We can now execute our filters in each and every SELECT command used to process Customer (alias Custrpts) records by inserting &filter in the command.

```
SELECT <field list> ;
    FROM custrpts ;
    INTO CURSOR report ;
    &filter ;
    ORDER BY &sel_order
```

Since m.filter holds the WHERE keyword when it is needed—or otherwise holds a null string—no error will occur, for example, if no filters have actually been entered. &filter will have no effect on the command when it generates a null string or, for that matter, a string of blanks. However, if we placed WHERE in the SELECT command and then input a null or blank string with &filter, this would cause an error. We therefore include the WHERE keyword in the memvar delivering the filter. (We do not do this with ORDER BY since m.sel_order will always hold a value indicating record order.)

TIP

In the past, we would be concerned about the overall length of m.filter exceeding 256 bytes (the maximum width of a Character field). However, with FoxPro 2.6 for Windows character memvars can be up to 2048 bytes. This gives us more than enough room for storing all our filters in m.filter.

As one look at Figure 12.18, showing the first portion of commands placing filters in m.filter, will reveal, writing the program code necessary to input filters is, at best, a tedious process. Advanced developers, however, will simplify the task, at least in the long run, by writing a procedure that is designed to build filters on the basis of passed parameters.

```
PROCEDURE Genfltr
PARAMETER m.expr, m.op, m.value, m.memname
STORE &memname + "[" + m.expr + " " + m.op + " " + ;
    m.value + " AND ]" TO &memname
RETURN
```

FIGURE 12.18: Multiple filters can be stored in a memvar for subsequent use in SELECT WHERE or SET FILTER with macro substitution.

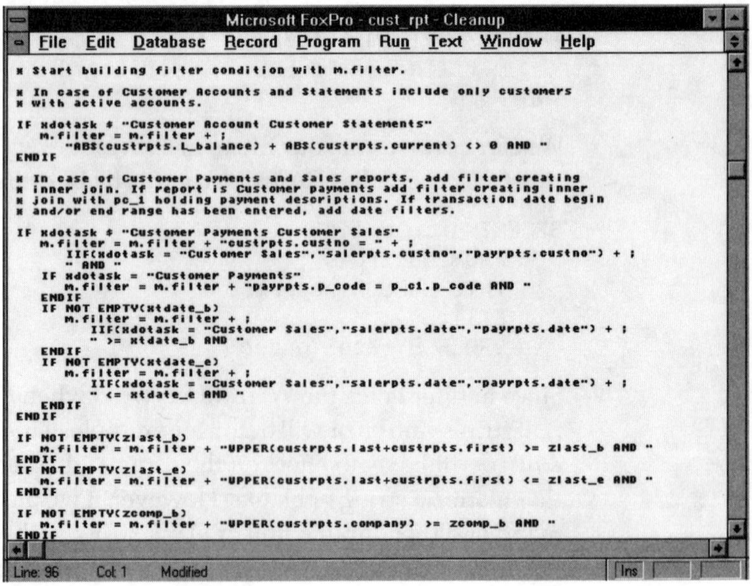

```
Microsoft FoxPro - cust_rpt - Cleanup
File  Edit  Database  Record  Program  Run  Text  Window  Help

* Start building filter condition with m.filter.

* In case of Customer Accounts and Statements include only customers
* with active accounts.

IF xdotask $ "Customer Account Customer Statements"
   m.filter = m.filter + ;
      "ABS(custrpts.L_balance) + ABS(custrpts.current) <> 0 AND "
ENDIF

* In case of Customer Payments and Sales reports, add filter creating
* inner join. If report is Customer payments add filter creating inner
* join with pc_1 holding payment descriptions. If transaction date begin
* and/or end range has been entered, add date filters.

IF xdotask $ "Customer Payments Customer Sales"
   m.filter = m.filter + "custrpts.custno = " + ;
      IIF(xdotask = "Customer Sales","salerpts.custno","payrpts.custno") + ;
      " AND "
   IF xdotask = "Customer Payments"
      m.filter = m.filter + "payrpts.p_code = p_c1.p_code AND "
   ENDIF
   IF NOT EMPTY(xtdate_b)
      m.filter = m.filter + ;
         IIF(xdotask = "Customer Sales","salerpts.date","payrpts.date") + ;
         " >= xtdate_b AND "
   ENDIF
   IF NOT EMPTY(xtdate_e)
      m.filter = m.filter + ;
         IIF(xdotask = "Customer Sales","salerpts.date","payrpts.date") + ;
         " <= xtdate_e AND "
   ENDIF
ENDIF

IF NOT EMPTY(zlast_b)
   m.filter = m.filter + "UPPER(custrpts.last+custrpts.first) >= zlast_b AND "
ENDIF
IF NOT EMPTY(zlast_e)
   m.filter = m.filter + "UPPER(custrpts.last+custrpts.first) <= zlast_e AND "
ENDIF

IF NOT EMPTY(zcomp_b)
   m.filter = m.filter + "UPPER(custrpts.company) >= zcomp_b AND "
ENDIF
Line: 96     Col: 1     Modified                              Ins
```

For example, procedure Genfltr, shown above, can be used to add filters to a memvar, the name of which is passed to the procedure through parameter memname.

```
IF NOT EMPTY(m.comp_b)
    DO genfltr WITH "UPPER(custrpts.company)", ">=", "comp_b", ;
        "filter"
ENDIF
```

With the above DO command, we place a call to procedure Getfltr, which will add the necessary filter involving m.comp_b to the end of m.filter. Using such a procedure will help to simplify your program code and make filter creation easier. (I do not use this method in Cust_rpt.spr because it doesn't make the process of filter creation using memvars easier to explain.)

Referring again to Figure 12.18, note that we begin the process of adding filters to m.filter with filters that are mandatory to specific reports. In the case of Customer Sales and Customer Payments reports, after all, we must enter the condition SELECT must use when joining records in the Customer and Sales or Payments tables. When executing Customer Payments, moreover, we must also join data from the payment codes lookup table P_c1. Also peculiar to the Customer Sales and Customer Payments reports is the possible operator entry of transaction date filters with m.xtdate_b and m.xtdate_e. Filters based upon entries to these input fields must also be included. (In producing customer statements, the transaction date filter is mandatory. We therefore enter it directly in the SELECT command used to produce the transaction result table.) With respect to the Customer Accounts and Customer Statement reports, we also include the filter ABS(current) + ABS(l.balance) <> 0.00 so as to exclude all customer records with inactive accounts from our result tables. The rest of the filters generated in function Maketabl are based upon operator entries to the customer selection criteria input fields and can be used with all customer database reports.

After assembling required filters in m.filter, we SET TALK ON and use DO CASE to execute the SELECT command(s) required to prepare data for the selected report, as described earlier in this chapter. (We also SET TALK ON so FoxPro will report the number of records SELECT places in the result table and the time it takes to create the table. This is for informational purposes only.) After the result table is formed, we conclude function Maketabl with the following commands. If the result table is empty—RECCOUNT() = 0—we close and simultaneously erase it with USE IN report and RETURN .F. to indicate what has happened.

```
SET TALK OFF
IF RECCOUNT() = 0
    USE IN report
    RETURN .F.
ENDIF
GO TOP
RETURN .T.
```

On the other hand, if the result table is not empty, we GO TOP to position FoxPro to the first record in the result table and RETURN .T.—though the RETURN command is optional in this position—to indicate that the result table is ready for execution of the report. Once program control is returned to the @ GET push button VALID clause, the final portion of which is shown in Figure 12.19, we use the value returned by function Maketabl to determine whether or not a report should be printed.

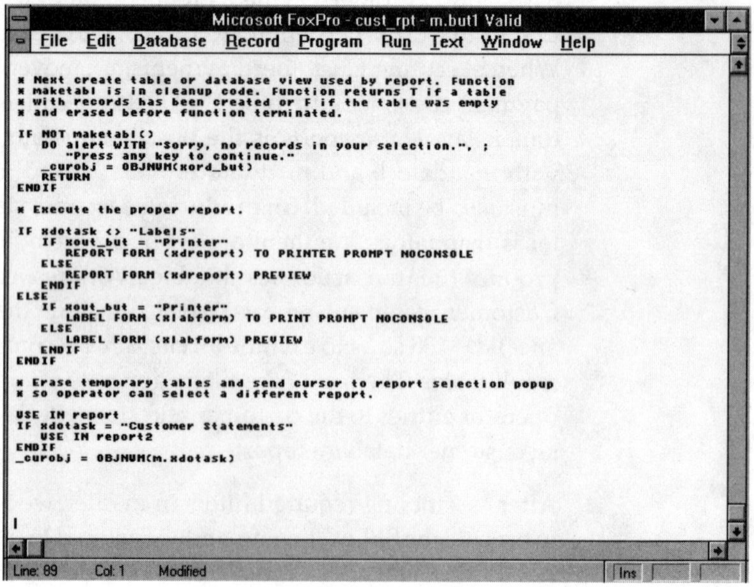

FIGURE 12.19: After executing the required REPORT or LABEL FORM using a name expression, we close and automatically erase the cursors used to prepare report data.

If the result table was empty (and erased), we warn the operator of the problem and send the cursor back to the Order By radio buttons in case the operator wants to begin assembling the table view differently. On the other hand, if the result table includes records, we proceed to execute the REPORT FORM or LABEL FORM command as required by operator selection of the report and output device. When the REPORT or LABEL FORM command terminates, we USE IN report—and IN Report2, if Customer Statements was the action—to close and automatically erase the temporary cursors. Again, if Customer Statements was the action, we do not need to erase the index tag used to order cursor Report2 since FoxPro erases it automatically. We then return the operator to @GET m.xdotask—the Produce report popup— so the operator can choose another report, using the same or other filters and report parameters.

The MBS Inventory and Letter Report Programs

The Inventory Report and Letter Report programs, Inv_rpt.spr and Lett_rpt.spr, are much simpler than Cust_rpt.spr since they include no popup enabling selection of multiple reports and allow the use of a minimal number of filters. For example, the Inventory Report window, shown in Figure 12.20, permits operator selection only of one of two record orders and the entry of filters based upon part numbers and part descriptions.

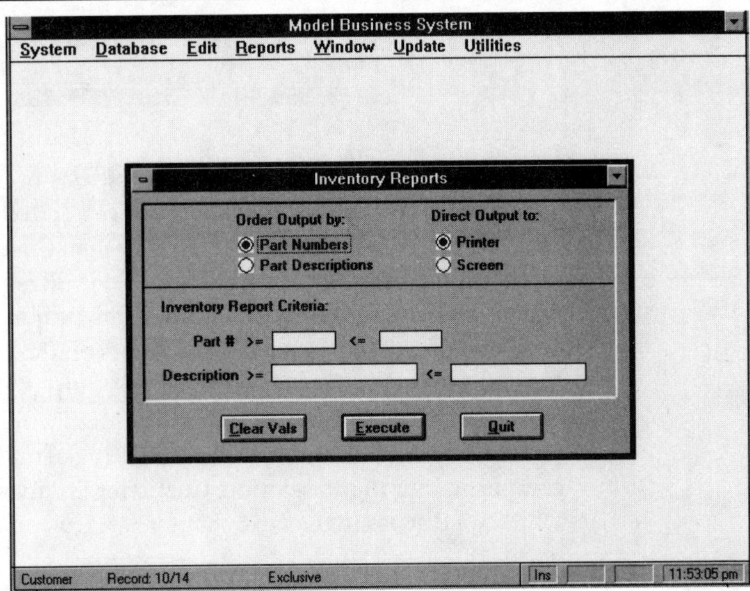

FIGURE 12.20:
The Inventory Reports window uses the same interface as the Customer Database Reports window but makes use of only one Report form.

Since the Inventory Reports window is executed by a nonmodal screen program, it can be quite useful during sales invoice entry for examining the inventory/price list in detail. Figure 12.21, for example, shows a screen shot of output from Report form Inventry.frx, directed to the Page Preview window.

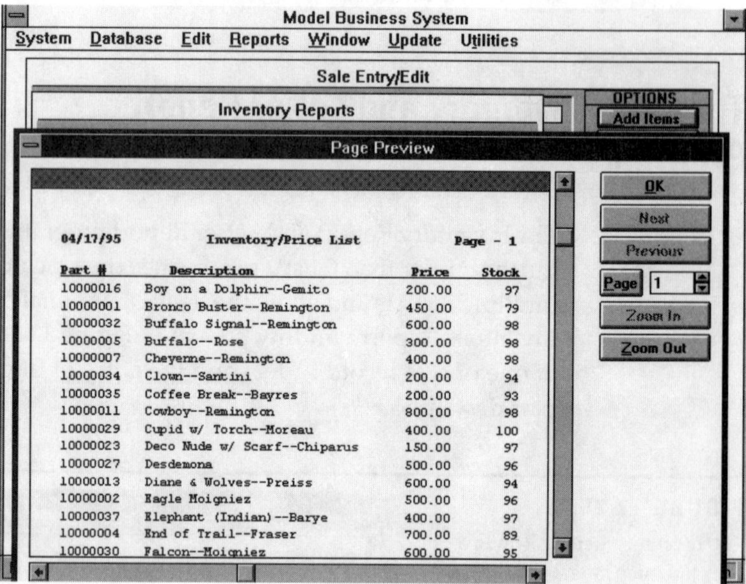

FIGURE 12.21:

Because the Inventory Reports program is written as a nonmodal screen program, the operator can examine the inventory/price list on the screen while entering a new sale invoice.

Still, in creating Inv_rpt.spr and Lett_rpt.spr, not only do we use the same standard interface as employed in Cust_rpt.spr, we also follow the same basic programming strategy. Since they are both far simpler than Cust_rpt.spr, there is no need to comment further on them. You will be able to understand their coding without any difficulty when you open and examine them. Bear in mind, however, that Lett_rpt.spr does no more than output a list of letters on file in Letters.dbf (alias Lettrpts). Letters.frx, the Report form used to format output, does not at present include letter text, though this facility can be easily added. It only includes letter date, name, and subject. Remember, too, that actual printing of mass personalized form letters is accomplished through use of the Customer Database Reports window. Lettform.frx, which we discuss in the next chapter, is a Customer table report.

CHAPTER

THIRTEEN

Using the Report Writer

- Creating Label forms
- Defining label and report expressions
- Creating Report forms
- Creating simple group reports
- Producing form letters
- Using report variables
- Creating multi-page forms for invoice and statement printing

13

The FoxPro built-in Report Writer is used to create the Report and Label form files used by the REPORT and LABEL FORM commands, respectively, when directing formatted output to the screen or printer. As explained in Chapter 12, it is best to conceive of the REPORT and LABEL FORM commands as what they are—sequential commands no different, for example, from LIST or DISPLAY, but deriving their more complex data formatting instructions from a report (.frx) or label (.lbx) file.

NOTE While report and label layout instructions are saved in tables, just like screens and menus, they are not used to generate programs. Instead, they are interpreted directly by the REPORT FORM and LABEL FORM commands.

Though the configuration and use of the Report Writer differ according to whether it is used to produce a Label form or Report form, the basic operations are the same. This presentation begins with the creation of Label forms since the formats used to produce mailing labels are generally quite simple in comparison to those used to produce customized reports. This will give us a chance to survey the Report Writer's basic features before confronting its full powers.

NOTE Creation of Label forms is not exclusively limited to the production of labels of various dimensions. Page and column headers and footers can be placed in a label format and the Label form used in place of a report. Similarly, a Report form can be designed and used to print labels, even on a laser printer, since FoxPro 2.6 supports the use of multicolumn reports.

Creating Label Forms

To create a Label form, we initiate the Report Writer in the Command window with CREATE/MODIFY LABEL; to create a Report form, we use CREATE/MODIFY REPORT instead. (You can also select the Label or Report radio button in the New File dialog.) The difference is in how the Report Writer prepares for execution of the form. For example, when we initiate creation of a Label form before accessing the label design window, the Report Writer presents us with the New Label dialog, shown in Figure 13.1. We use the dialog's pick list to select the label layout corresponding to the label stock we intend to use in printing labels.

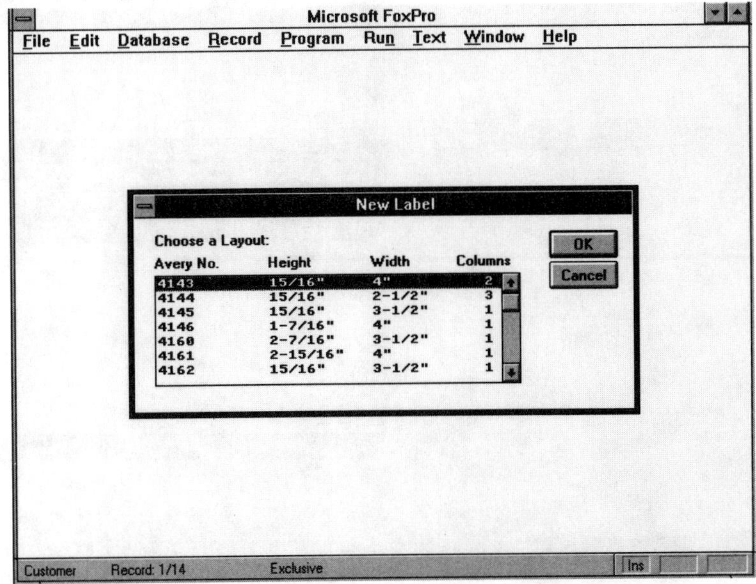

FIGURE 13.1: Before creating a Label form, you must select the label layout from the New Label dialog's pick list.

NOTE The New Label dialog used to select label layout dimensions is available only before accessing the label design window when creating a new Label form. It is not available for changing label dimensions once the design window has appeared, though label dimensions can be changed manually.

Once we select the label layout, the Report Writer takes us to the label design window, which it configures according to the dimensions of the selected layout, as shown in Figure 13.2, and adds the Report pulldown to the system menu. Using the toolbox at the left of the design window, which offers a subset of objects available in the Screen Builder, we can add text, output fields—known within the Report Writer as *report expressions*—graphical objects, and pictures to the label layout. (The report expression tool—the third picture button in the toolbox—uses the same icon as the Screen Builder's input/output field tool.)

FIGURE 13.2:
The Report Writer configures the label design window to correspond to the dimensions of the layout selected with the New Label dialog.

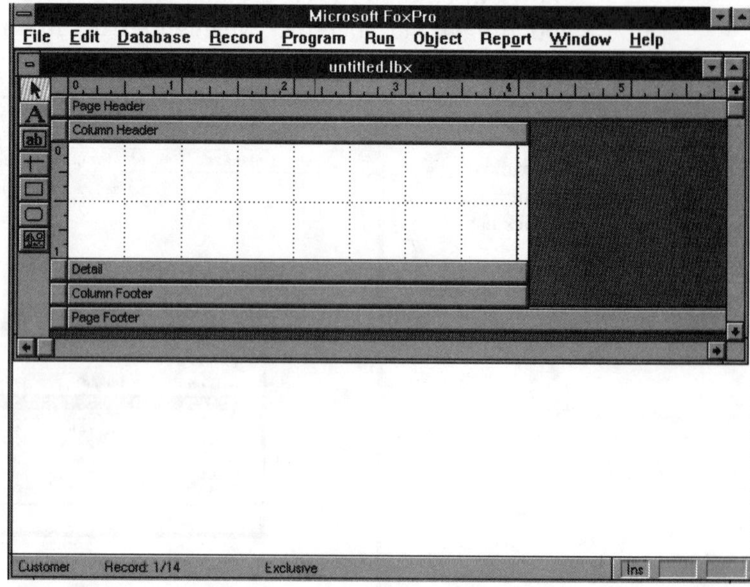

NOTE

This chapter often refers to report expressions as report or label fields to better denote their function in a form. We deliberately avoid using the word *column* in connection with report expressions (or fields) because report columns have a specific meaning in the Report Writer, as explained later in this chapter.

With respect to the production of mailing labels, the Detail band, which appears above the gray bar labeled *Detail* in Figure 13.2, is the only portion of the label layout we use. Whatever report expressions (or other objects) we place in the Detail band will be printed once, exactly as formatted, by the LABEL FORM command for every table record it processes. For example, in the case of 3_across.lbx, supplied with the MBS, we use the Detail band layout shown in Figure 13.3. Here, the label dimensions correspond to Avery # 4144, each label having a height of $15/16$ inches and a width of $2^1/2$ inches. Using the report expression tool and a font of Courier New, 10, Regular, we have room for five rows of data in the Detail band. By selecting a smaller font, we could probably squeeze in a sixth, though we want to avoid making the print too small to be easily read. (Of course, the number of characters that will fit in each row of a label, assuming we use the entire row for a report expression, will also depend on font size and style.)

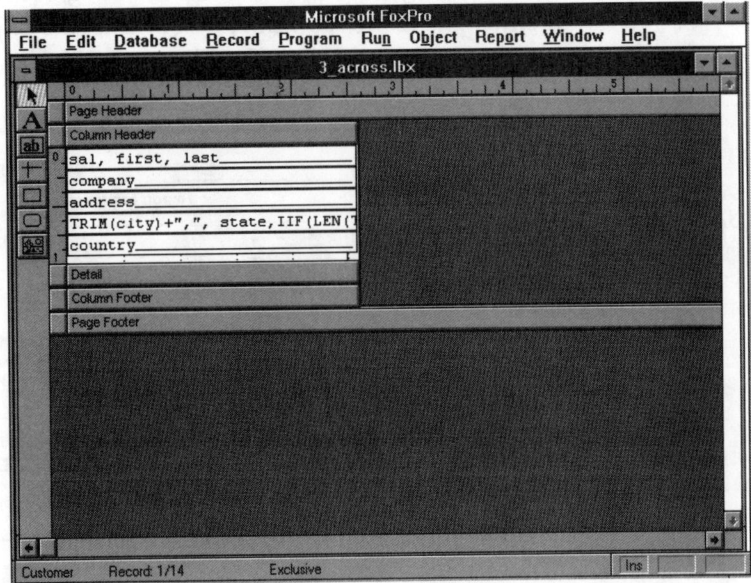

FIGURE 13.3: To create the MBS Label form 3_across.lbx, we simply add report expressions to the label layout in the order we want them printed.

Resource File Label Formats

The list of available label layouts displayed in the New Label dialog is taken from the current FoxPro resource file, which also stores the instructions the Report Writer uses to configure the design window properly. If you suddenly find that the New Label layout list is empty, you have probably closed Foxuser.dbf, the default FoxPro resource file, or changed to a resource file not containing the label format records. Since all label layouts have a resource file ID of LABELLYT, you can append them to any resource file with the command APPEND FROM foxuser FOR ID = "LABELLYT". (For a discussion of FoxPro resource files, see Chapter 5.)

Defining Report Expressions

The definitions of the report expressions are handled through use of the Report Expression dialog, which functions much like the Screen Builder's Field dialog, though it is specially tailored for defining output fields for use in a Report or Label form. In using the Report Expression dialog, we can enter the report expression directly in the Expression entry box or click the Expression button to access the Expression Builder for help. (See Figure 13.4.)

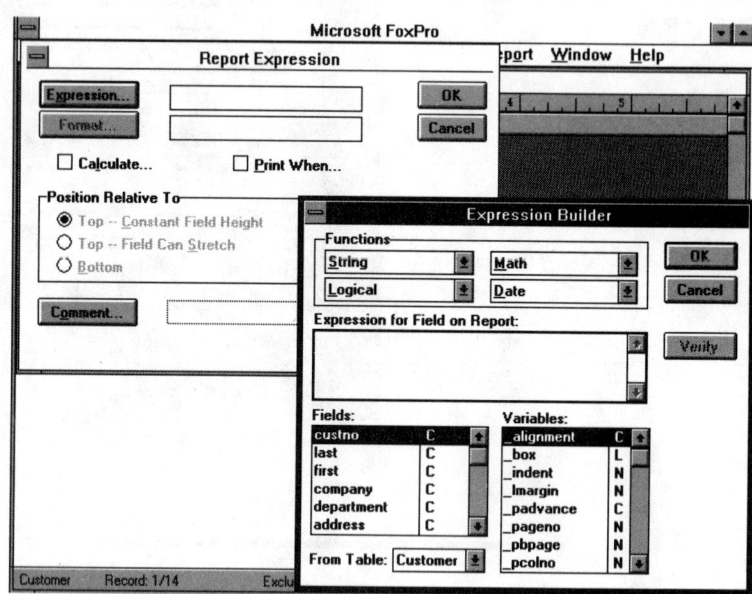

FIGURE 13.4: When using the Report Expression dialog to define report or label fields, select the Expression button to open the Expression Builder.

In preparing a Label form for use with our Customer table, we use five report expressions, one for each row of the label. Sticking to standard Xbase expressions, we can define them as follows:

```
ALLTRIM(TRIM(sal) + " " + TRIM(first)+ " " + last)
company
address
TRIM(city) + ", " + TRIM(state) + "  "+ zip
country
```

Once they are entered in the Detail band, we select, position, and size each of the label fields so they will use the full width of the band. (Label offset is best achieved through use of the Page Layout dialog, which we discuss in a moment. We do not enter an offset by positioning the label fields in the layout.)

Note that in entering the report expressions, we use no alias names, so the label form can be executed with any table holding the referenced fields. (As you will recall from Chapter 12, we use the SELECT command to build a result table holding only those Customer table records and fields required for execution of labels.) The entry process itself, moreover, requires no table to be open, though the Report Writer can size report expressions referencing table fields only if the fields are available in the current table or an unselected table identified by alias. Use of the Page Preview window to check the label layout also requires an open table with the referenced fields since it executes an implicit LABEL FORM command using the PREVIEW option. (If a table is not open when Page Preview is selected, the File Open dialog is automatically initiated so a table can be opened.)

TIP

Like the Screen Builder, the Report Writer operates in the interactive mode. We can open and close tables as we choose, using the Open File or View dialog or the Command window. We can also save instructions specifying the current environment to the .lbx or .frx file, using the Page Layout's Environment dialog, discussed later in this chapter.

Using Comma-Delimited Expression Lists

As an alternative to using Xbase expressions for each of our report expressions, we can use comma-delimited expression lists, which the Report Writer interprets in a special way. Here are the actual report expressions used in 1_across and 3_across.lbx, though we simplify the expression referencing Customer.zip:

```
sal, first, last
company
address
TRIM(city) + ",", state, zip
country
```

In executing a report expression holding a comma-delimited expression list, FoxPro ignores empty expressions. It prints only those expressions that have values for the current record, and it inserts a single space between them. Thus, the report expression sal, first, last suffices to output customer salutation (Mr., Ms., Dr., and so on), followed by Customer.first and Customer.last in the correct format, while also making all necessary adjustments when any of the referenced fields are empty. We do not need to use character concatenation and ALLTRIM(), LTRIM(), or TRIM() to prevent output from an empty field (in this case, Customer.sal and/or Customer.first) from adversely affecting the label format. We do, however, make use of TRIM() and character concatenation in the fourth row of the label in order to insert a single comma after Customer.city. Since we do not expect the City field of any Customer table record to be empty, we need not make any effort to suppress the comma when City is empty, though we can easily do this by using IIF():

```
IIF(EMPTY(city),"",TRIM(city)+","), state, zip
```

Another adjustment we actually make is to output from Customer.zip:

```
IIF(LEN(TRIM(zip))<>9, zip, TRANSFORM(zip,"@R 99999-9999"))
```

This expression tests the width of Customer.zip and—to reverse the logic of the condition—if the width is nine, uses the TRANSFORM() function to insert a single hyphen between the fifth and sixth characters, in keeping with the format of U.S. zip codes.

Note that one of the great advantages of using comma-delimited expression lists in a report expression is that expressions of any data type can be included in the list. There is no need to convert data in order to include expressions of different types in a single report or label field.

```
last, DATE(), days30, credit
```

This is a perfectly valid report expression, though it includes data of four different types.

WARNING

The Expression Builder does not at present recognize the validity of comma-delimited report expressions. If you enter one in the Expression Builder and click the Verify button, FoxPro will flag a syntax error, though it will not prevent you from using the expression. If the report expression includes an actual syntax error, this will turn up when you test the Label form with the Page Preview dialog.

Note that when defining report fields, you can also use semicolons in place of commas in an expression list to direct output of the expression(s) following a semicolon to the next available row of the report—provided the report expression is allowed to stretch. This feature, however, is not available when defining label fields since all label fields must use a constant field height. (This is controlled by the Position Relative To radio buttons in the Report Expression dialog. Again, see Figure 13.4.) When a label is being designed, Constant Field Height is selected and the radio buttons disabled. We will have more to say about the Position Relative To settings when we discuss Report forms.

TIP

Using the Object pulldown, you can select the font, pen color, fill color, and pen (thickness) of any report expression or other object included in a Label or Report form. Since the Object pulldown has the same function in the Report Writer as in the Screen Builder, we do not discuss it further in this chapter. (See Chapter 12 for a discussion of Object pulldown options.)

Suppressing Blank Lines

Of course, when printing mailing labels, we will want FoxPro to suppress any blank lines that might otherwise appear embedded in a label. For example, if a Customer table record has no Company entry, we will want FoxPro to move up output from the following label fields so the address will appear directly beneath the customer's name. We achieve this effect by selecting the Report Expression dialog's Print When check box when defining all but the last label field. This opens the Print When dialog, shown in Figure 13.5, which we use to select the Remove Line If Blank check box.

The Print Only When Expression Is True check box can also be selected to open the Expression Builder and enter a condition controlling FoxPro's execution of a report expression. For example, if the business using the MBS is in the U.S., we can conditionally suppress printing the country in the last line of labels addressing customers in the U.S. by using the expression country <> "USA". This, however, does not suppress a blank line left by a conditionally suppressed report expression that does not appear at the bottom of the label. To do this, you must select the Remove Line If Blank check box as well.

FIGURE 13.5:

To prevent blank lines from appearing in the middle of a label when a report expression returns an empty value, use the Print When dialog to select Remove Line If Blank.

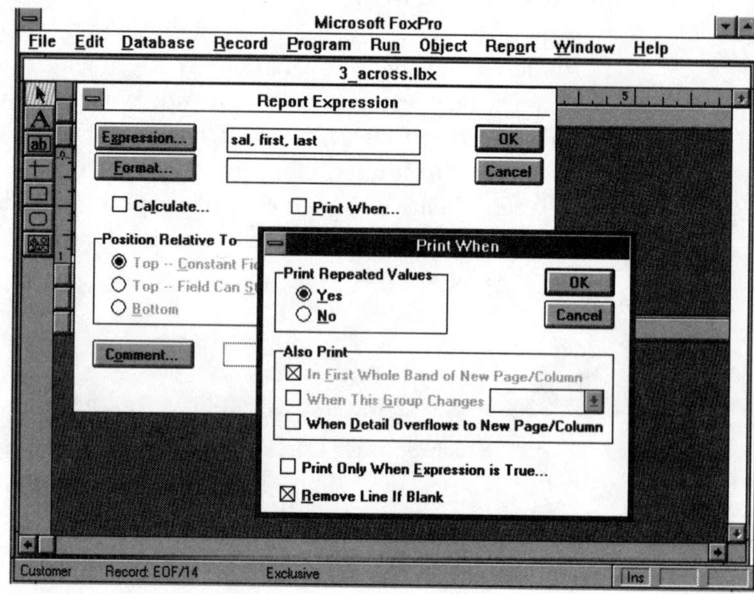

Inserting Text, Graphical, and Picture Objects

The process of inserting text, graphical, and picture objects in a Label (or Report) form is exactly the same as placing them in a screen layout. With respect to label production, with a much larger label stock and a good laser printer, we can generate fancy labels, placing a company logo and return address at the top of a label, followed by addressee information. (See Figure 13.6.)

We use text objects for the return address in Figure 13.6, though we might also reference the return address from Bizshare.dbf, the MBS system value file, as we do when executing customer invoices, statements, and letters, as discussed later in this chapter.

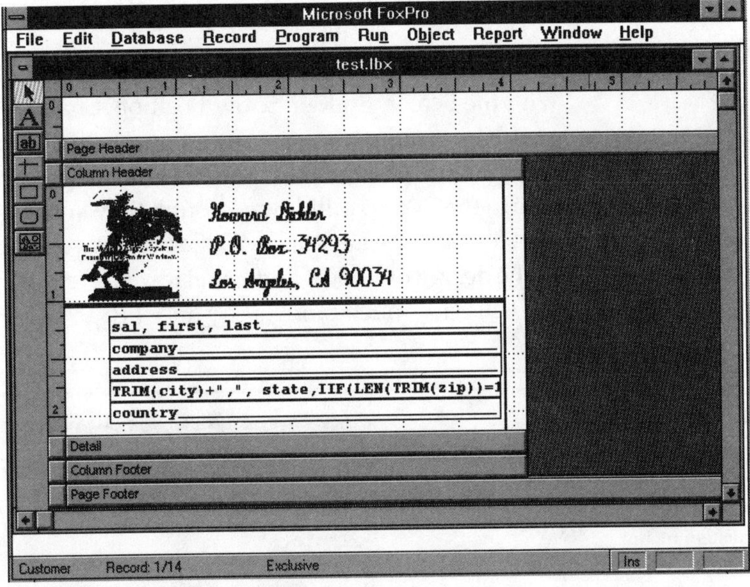

FIGURE 13.6:
Picture and text objects can be placed in a Label form, for example, to include a company logo and return address in the form.

TIP

Though execution of a Label form with the LABEL FORM command assumes an open table, it is not really necessary to reference any table fields in a Label (or Report) form. You can create a Label form that includes only text, graphical, and picture objects, if you so choose, and execute LABEL FORM to print the static label once for every record in the table. (Control over how many labels are executed can also be exerted through operator use of the Copies spinner in the Windows Print dialog if LABEL FORM TO PRINTER is executed with the PROMPT option.)

Using the Clipboard to Copy Label Fields

All objects in a Label or Report form can be copied to the Clipboard and pasted into another label or report. This makes it easy to create several different Label forms of different dimensions that use the same report expressions. Just open the Label form holding the desired report expressions, select them with the mouse marquee (or use Select All on the Edit pulldown), and copy them to the Clipboard. You can then paste them into any other label (or report) design window, regardless of its selected dimensions.

Using the Report Menu

The Report pulldown, shown open in Figure 13.7, has many options in common with the Screen Builder. Show Position, Snap to Grid, Ruler/Grid, and Quick Report have exactly the same functions as the corresponding options on the Screen pulldown. The Title/Summary, Data Grouping, and Variables options are all specific to the Report pulldown, though they are best described in connection with Report forms. Page Layout and Page Preview, on the other hand, are equally pertinent to the design of Report and Label forms. We therefore introduce them here, though we will have much more to say about Page Layout later in this chapter.

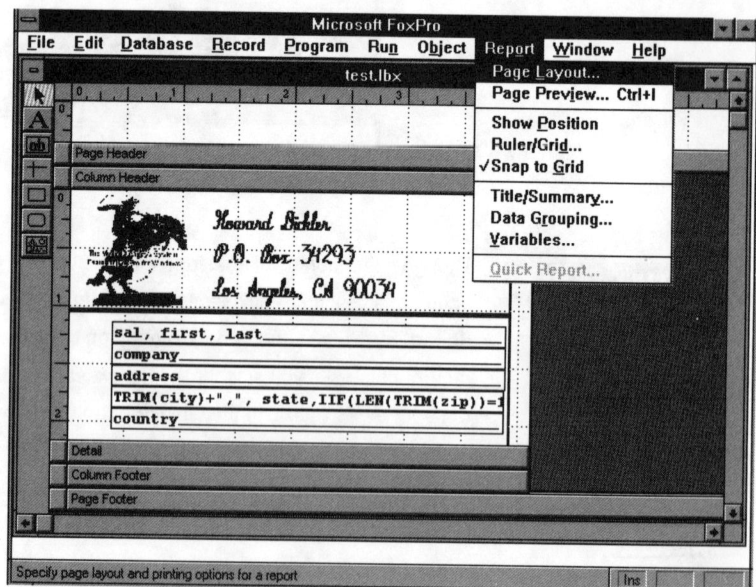

FIGURE 13.7:
When a label or report design window is active, FoxPro adds the Report pulldown to the system menu.

Using the Page Layout Dialog

Similiar in function to the Screen Layout dialog, the Page Layout dialog provides a graphical representation of the current label layout as it would appear on the printed page. Figure 13.8, for example, shows the label layout of 3_across.lbx.

FIGURE 13.8:

The Page Layout dialog shows a graphical image of the current Label or Report form.

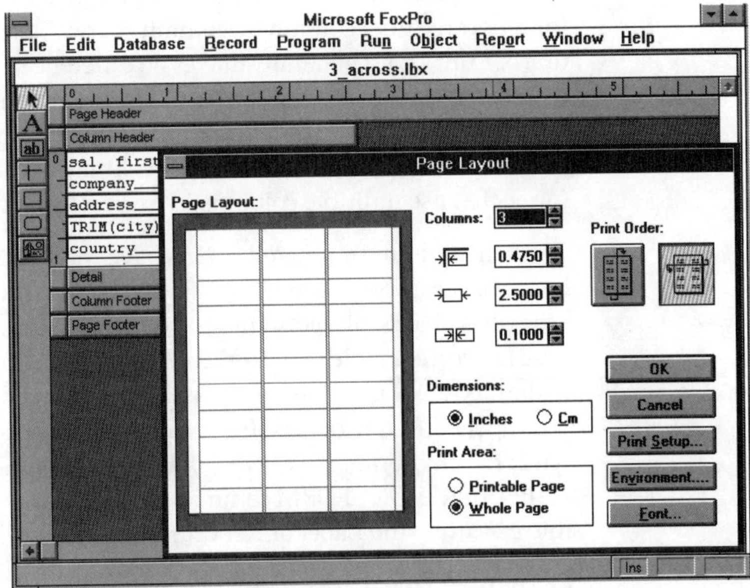

When designing a Label form, we do not want to touch the Page Layout settings controlling the number of report columns, the report column width, and the width of the margin between report columns because these are automatically set to correspond with the selected label layout. Only the left-hand column margin, represented by the second of the four column spinners, need be adjusted to obtain the correct left-hand offset. (Use the Dimensions radio buttons to display label layout dimensions in inches or centimeters.)

The Page Layout's Print Area radio buttons are used to select between directing output to the whole page or to the printable page as defined by the print driver current at the time the LABEL (or REPORT) FORM command is executed. When you design labels, Whole Page is selected by default so that the actual edges of the page will serve as the minimum margins of the form. When you design reports, on the other hand, Printable Page is selected as the default. The report or label is then executed within the margins established by the current print driver. (When Printable Page is selected, the printable page as defined by the current print driver is highlighted in the Page Layout area of the Page Layout dialog. There may be no noticeable difference if the current print driver is set to use the whole page.)

The Print Order picture radio buttons allow us to choose between printing labels (or report records) column by column or row by row. When you print labels, selection of Print Order generally makes no difference, though you may prefer one order over the other. However, if the Label form is to be used as a report and must include figures at the bottom of each column summarizing data appearing in that column, you will want to order record output column by column. (This is also true of Report forms that use multiple columns.) We give an example of this in a moment.

The Font and Environment buttons have the same functions they do in the Screen Layout dialog. Font is used to set the default font used by report expressions and text, as well as objects placed in the layout with Quick Report. Environment is used to save the current table environment, including all controlling indexes and relations, in the .lbx or .frx file. If this is done, the environment is automatically restored when you open the .lbx or .frx file to modify the Label or Report form. Moreover, when the environment is saved, you can use the ENVIRONMENT keyword in the LABEL or REPORT FORM command to force FoxPro to restore the environment before executing the Label or Report form.

Of course, in the MBS we do not use the ENVIRONMENT option with LABEL or REPORT FORM since we must do much more than open tables and set relations to prepare data for our reports and labels. (See Chapter 12.) However, in the case of all flat-file Report and Label forms based upon the Customer table, we nonetheless save the environment with the Customer table open so fields referenced by the forms will be available and we can make free use of the Page Preview window. Again, since alias names are not used in the report expressions, it will make no difference which table is current when we execute these forms with REPORT and LABEL FORM, as long as the fields they reference are available in the current table. (We will have more to say about the table view when we discuss the creation of the MBS Report forms that reference data from two or more tables.)

NOTE

When you save a Report or Label form, FoxPro asks if you want to save the current environment instructions in the .frx or .lbx file if this has not been done manually with the Environment dialog or if the table environment has changed since that time.

The Print Setup button is used to access the Windows Print Setup dialog. While we can use it, for example, to change the paper size and printer orientation, we rarely change these settings when creating Label forms. This is because page size and print orientation are set as required by the selected label layout. In any case, printer setup instructions regarding paper size, source, printer orientation, and selected print driver are stored in an .frx or .lbx file and are used to reset current print setup values whenever the form is opened for edit or executed with REPORT or LABEL FORM. (We say more about paper size and printer orientation when we discuss Report forms.)

Using Page Preview to Examine the Layout

Once you have completed a label or report layout, select the Page Preview option from the Report pulldown to examine the result. As previously mentioned, selecting Page Preview executes LABEL or REPORT FORM PREVIEW using the current label or report layout. For example, with 3_across.lbx open in the Report Writer and the Customer table open in the current work area, selecting Page Preview executes 3_across.lbx in the Page Preview window, as shown in Figure 13.9. This allows us

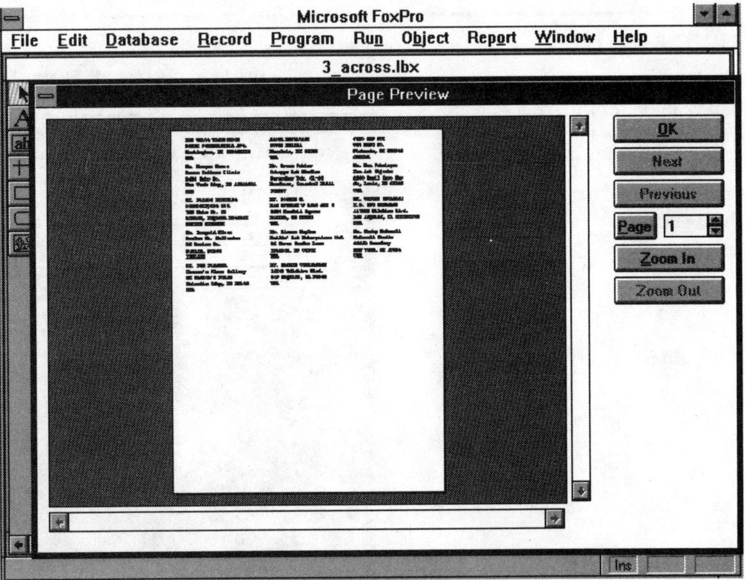

FIGURE 13.9: Use the Page Preview window to check the result of a Label or Report form layout without closing the Report Writer.

to check the position of all items in the form and modify its layout as needed without leaving the Report Writer.

NOTE If you select Page Preview and no table is current, the Report Writer activates the Open File dialog so you can select and open a table.

Using Page and Column Headers and Footers

As previously mentioned, Label forms can be readily modified to produce reports. The Page Header and Page Footer bands, for example, normally closed during label layout design, can be opened and their height adjusted by using the drag buttons just to the left of their title bars. You can also double-click the drag button to open the band dimension dialog, shown in Figure 13.10, to set the band height more precisely using a spinner.

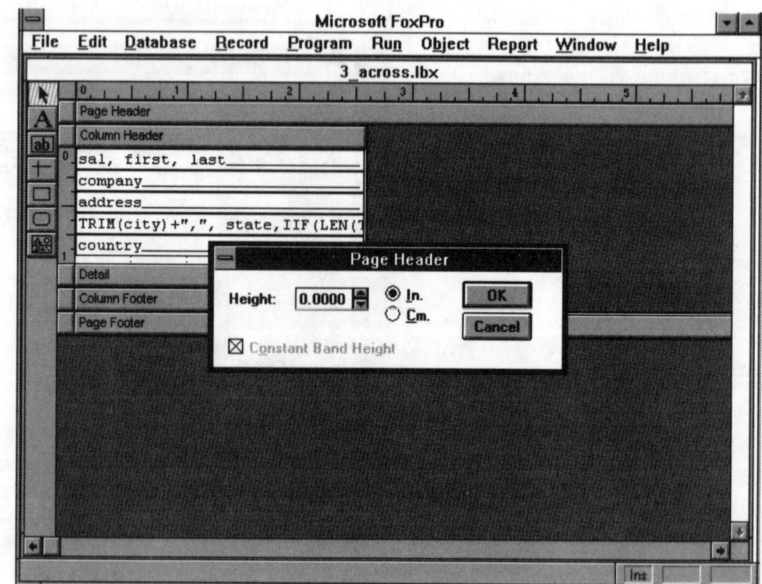

FIGURE 13.10: The height of each label or report band can be set with precision by double-clicking the button to the left of the band's title bar. This opens the band height dialog for that band.

In both Label and Report forms, the Page Header and Page Footer bands are used to set the top and bottom margins used by the form. This is why they are generally not used when designing Label forms for printing on label stock. However, as you will discover, many of the label layout options available in the New Label dialog actually require a top margin. When this is the case, the Page Header band will be opened with the correct setting. The height of the page header should not be changed; if it is, label output will not begin at the correct position on the label stock.

NOTE

When you design Label forms, all bands are designed to use a constant band height. This is why the Constant Band Height check box in Figure 13.10 is selected and disabled. The check box is enabled only when you are defining a Report form. (When the check box is unselected, the band can stretch. We return to this topic when discussing Report forms.)

When you design Label or Report forms that use two or more report columns, a Column Header and a Column Footer band appear directly above and below the Detail band. Figure 13.11 shows a Label form with text objects placed in the Page

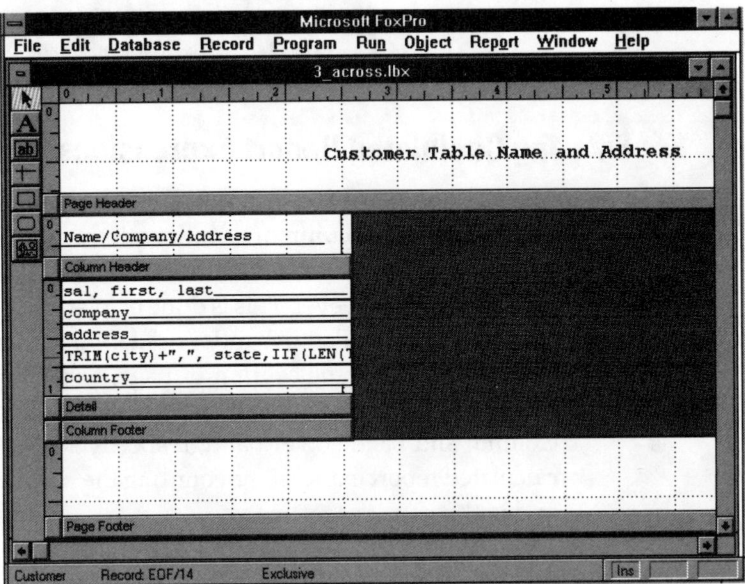

FIGURE 13.11:

Page and column headers and footers can be placed in a Label form to turn it into a report.

Header and Column Header bands. The Page footer band has also been opened to create a bottom margin for the form. In Figure 13.12, we see the result of this label layout in the Page Preview window. Note that the text and graphical (line) objects placed in the Column Header band are used above every column in the report.

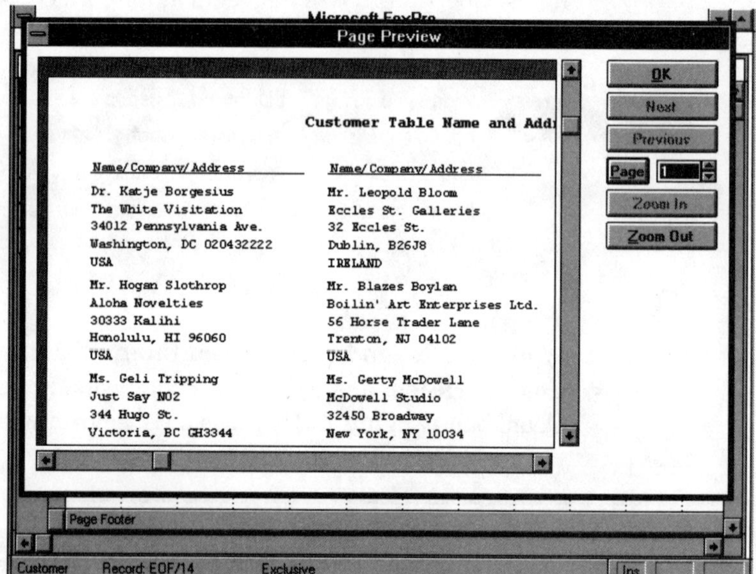

FIGURE 13.12: The column header entered in a multi-column Report or Label form is repeated just above the record's output in each report or label column.

Entering Caclulated Report Expressions

The Column Footer band can be used to count or otherwise summarize data appearing in each column of a multi-column Report or Label form, while the Page Footer band can be used to count or summarize the data appearing on each page of any form whatsoever. This is done by placing calculated report expressions in the Column and Page Footer bands and defining the report expressions so they will be reset at the end of the column or page, respectively. By way of demonstration, in Figure 13.13 we insert the text objects Column Total and Page Total in a Label form's Column and Page Footer band, respectively. Following the text objects, we insert calculated report expressions counting the number of records output in the column and in the page, respectively.

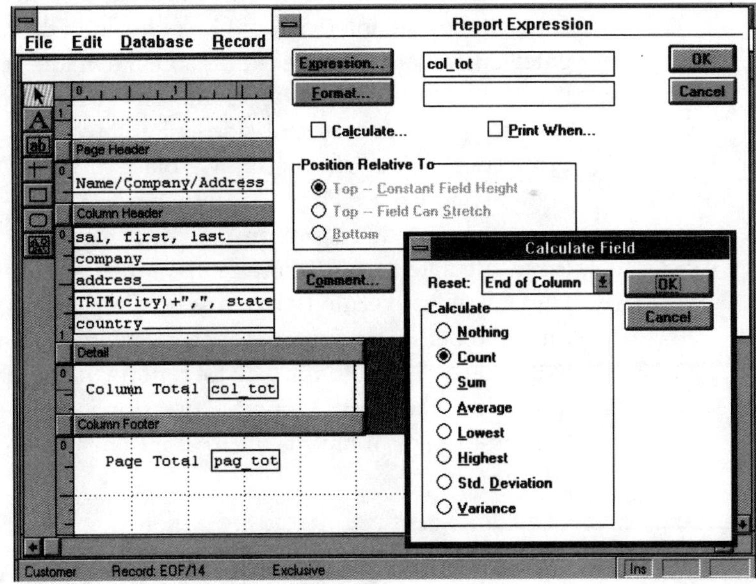

FIGURE 13.13: Calculated report expressions can be used in a column or page footer to count or summarize data appearing in a column or page of any Report or Label form.

To define a calculated report expression, we enter the expression that is to serve as the basis of the calculation in the Report Expression dialog. We then select the Calculate check box to open the Calculate Field dialog, where we select the kind of calculation we want to make and the way it is to be handled in the report. Except for the reset option, defining a calculated report expression is much like executing the CALCULATE command in the report and outputting the result where you position the expression in the layout. For example, suppose we wanted to sum the current debts of all customers output on the page. Assuming the Customer.current field is included in the view, we would enter Current as the expression, select Sum as the calculation, and select End of Page as the reset interval. By placing the calculated report expression in the Page Footer band, we make FoxPro output the result of the calculation for all records processed by the LABEL or REPORT FORM command in producing the page, before resetting the sum to 0 in preparation for the next page.

The method of entry of calculated report expressions is the same except when using Count. In the case of Count, the expression you enter is unimportant. It can even be the name of a variable you make up on the fly. This is because, regardless of what you enter as the expression, FoxPro counts the number of label or report records executed in the reset interval. Count will function the same, in other words, whether we enter Customer.last as the expression or a made-up memvar name like Col_tot. Figure 13.13, for example, shows the Report Expression and Calculate Field dialogs used to define report expression Col_tot, which we use to count the number of records reported in each column. We place it in the Column Footer band. In the Page Footer band we use Pag_tot, another calculated report expression, which we set to count the records output on the page. Figure 13.14 shows the result of entering these calculated report expressions in the Page Preview window. Since the Column Footer band is executed as soon as FoxPro finishes with the records in a specific column and before FoxPro resets any calculated report expressions that must be reset to 0 at the end-of-column, Col_tot reports the number of records output in each column. Since the Pag_tot report expression is defined just like Col_tot but is reset at the end-of-page, it reports the total number of records output on the page.

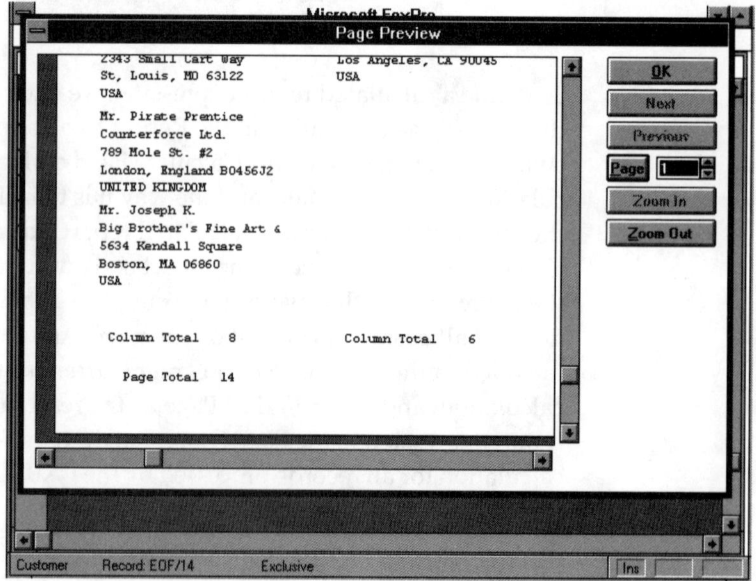

FIGURE 13.14:

Enter calculated report expressions in a column footer to summarize data in a report or label column or in the page footer to summarize data output on the page.

TIP

> To use calculated report expressions effectively in a Column Footer band, the Print Order by column picture button must be selected in the Page Layout dialog. If this is not done and FoxPro prints records row by row across the label or report columns as it moves down the page, when it reaches the Column Footer band the calculated report expressions will hold the results for all records on the page. Only by selecting Print Order by column is the column footer executed once after each column of records is processed—and before FoxPro gets busy with the next.

Figures 13.13 and 13.14 are intended only to illustrate how calculated report expressions and other objects can be gainfully employed in the Column Footer and Page Footer bands. We discuss calculated report expressions in greater depth later in this chapter, when reviewing the MBS reports that use them.

Band and Expression/Object Execution Order

When FoxPro executes each page of a form, it processes each of the bands included in the layout in top-to-bottom order, beginning with the Page Header band if it is open. Report expressions and objects in a band are processed in order according to their row and column position in the band. Only the Detail band (and Group bands, if used) can be executed more than once on a given page. It is executed once for every report or label record that can be output on the page, given the margin settings and the space requirements of the other bands. This becomes especially important when defining calculated report expressions. We can, for example, place a calculated report expression in a Page Header band. However, since FoxPro executes it before processing any records, it cannot be used to summarize data appearing on the page. Only a report expression appearing in a band following the Detail band can perform calculations based on records output on the page. We will have more to say about this when we discuss the MBS group reports.

Creating Report Forms

Turning now to the creation of Report forms, we begin by examining the Report Writer's default configuration when initiated for creation of a new report. Here, the layout editor begins with open Page Header and Page Footer bands. Their use in reports is not only assumed, it is required for defining top and bottom page margins. When we access the Page Preview window, blank space appears at the top and bottom of the page because the Page Header and Page Footer bands include blank lines at the top and bottom, respectively. Of course, in addition to using them in defining top and bottom margins, we make use of them for entering whatever text and/or report expressions we want to appear in them, though we must still leave blank space for the margins.

Figure 13.15, for example, shows the leftmost portion of Customer.frx, used to produce the MBS Customer list. In the Page Header band, we use the DATE() function as a report expression to output the date and a text object in bold style as a title. (Off the screen to the right we also use _PAGENO, the FoxPro system variable returning the Report or Label form page number, in a report expression to output the page number.) Since report detail will appear immediately under output from the Page Header band, we also use it to include report expression headings in the report. Under the text objects used as report field headings, we also include a line object to set off the headings from the report data. A small amount of blank space is left between the line and the bottom of the Page Header band to push output from the first report record down slightly. The Page Preview window in Figure 13.16 shows the result of the layout.

Bear in mind that Customer.frx's Detail band includes only one report column, though it is defined to use the full width of the page. This is the layout editor's default setting when creating a Report form. As a consequence, Column Header and Column Footer bands do not appear in the layout; Page Header and Page Footer bands suffice for supplying a column header and footer for fields laid out in a single report column.

Still, Customer.frx's use of a single report column does not mean we cannot arrange the data in our report in columnar fashion. This is easily done by positioning and sizing report expressions in the Detail band. However, were less room required for output of Customer table data, we could just as easily access the Page Layout dialog, shown in Figure 13.17, and change the Columns setting as needed.

FIGURE 13.15:

The Customer List report, Customer.frx, uses the Page Header band to set the top margin and to input page heading and report field titles.

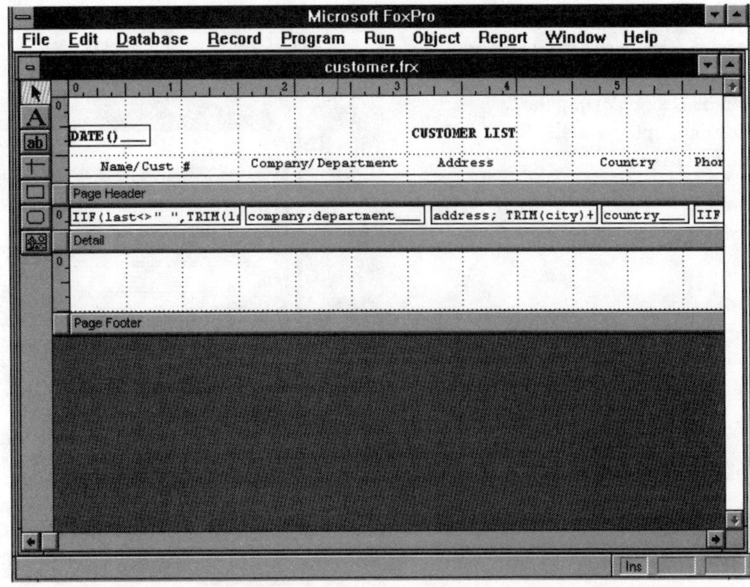

FIGURE 13.16:

In designing the Customer list we use the Page Header band to supply report expression headings.

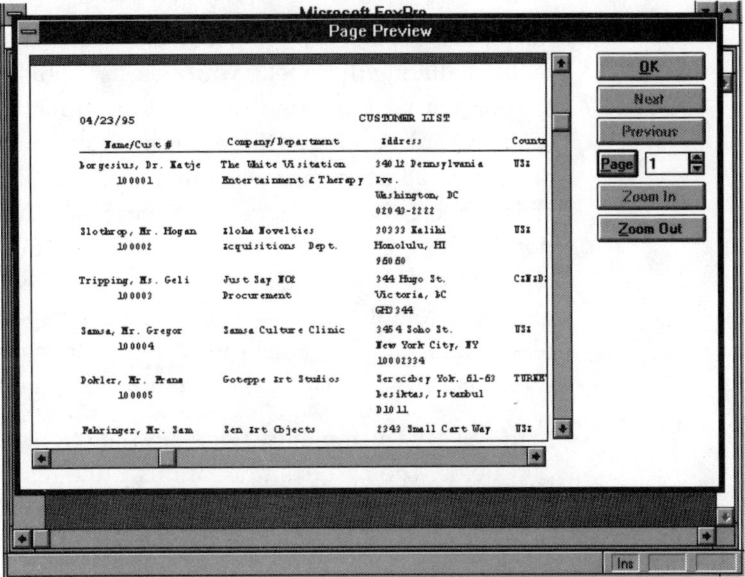

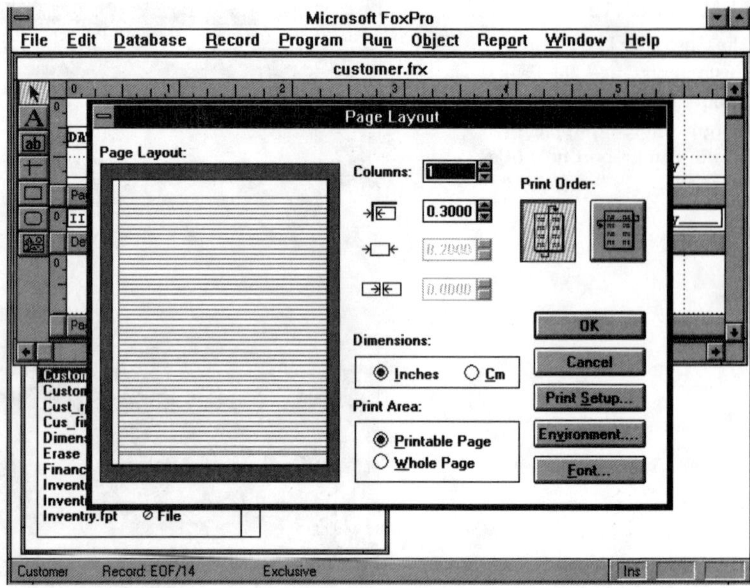

FIGURE 13.17:
Report forms use a single report column by default, though this can be changed using the Columns spinner in the Page Layout dialog.

Stacking Data in a Report Expression

In contrast to label design, where we cannot change the height of the Detail band without altering the label layout selected with the New Label dialog, in designing a report we need not concern ourselves with how many rows are required by each report record. As long as there is a clear division between one report record and the next, each can use a variable number of lines, though it is best to use as few as possible so more report records can appear on a single page. Naturally, the easiest reports to design, at least with regard to the Detail band, are those that can output all report record data using a single row in the Detail band. Things become considerably more complex, at least from a design perspective, when more data must be displayed than will fit on one row. We must then make use of more than one row for each report record. There are several ways to go about doing this.

In the case of Customer.frx, we stack data from related Customer table fields in report fields. The best example of this is the report expression used to output customer address data. In Figure 13.18, we show the Report Expression dialog used to define it, with the Expression Builder open to display the entire expression.

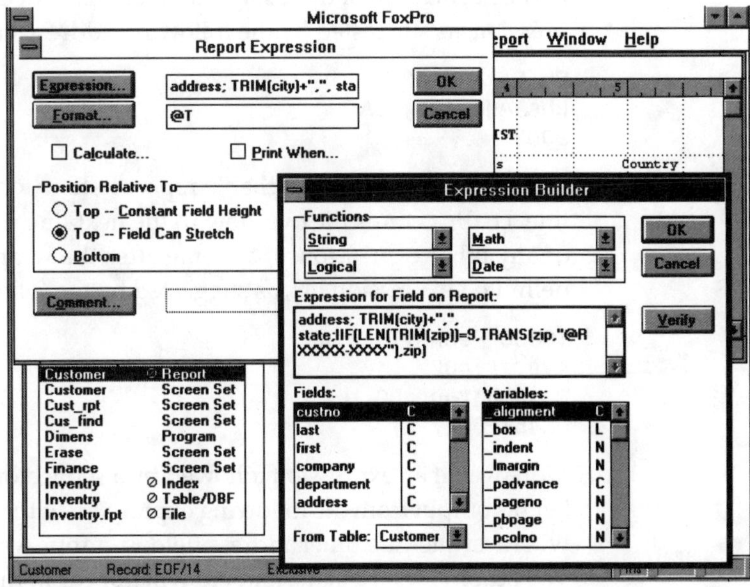

FIGURE 13.18:

Use a semicolon-delimited expression list to stack data in a single report field.

A close look at the report expression shows the use of a comma- and semicolon-delimited expression list. Leaving out the IIF(), LEN(), and TRIM() used to insert a hyphen in the zip code entry when it is exactly 9 bytes in length makes the report expression easier to read.

```
address; TRIM(city) +",", state; zip
```

As you will recall from our discussion of the report expressions used in the MBS Label forms, the comma instructs FoxPro to trim the delimited expressions and to insert one intervening space between them. Using a semicolon instead instructs FoxPro to trim the preceding expression and begin the output of following expressions on the next available line, preserving the report expression's columnar position and size. We therefore arrange output of the address in a single report field using several lines, assuming the report expression is defined to stretch through selection of the Position Relative To Top—Field Can Stretch radio button. (See Figure 13.18.) Because Constant Field Height is the default, we must select the Field Can Stretch radio button; otherwise FoxPro can use only one line for the report expression, whether or not it includes semicolon-delimited expressions. (They will be suppressed.)

In the normal run of things, we therefore use three lines for output of the report expression, as suggested by the following address, though this can and will vary.

```
PO Box 34293
Los Angeles, CA
90034
```

If an expression in a stretchable report field is too big to be output using a single line, FoxPro wraps the overflow to the next line. FoxPro also maintains the format of any other expressions that come after the wrapped expression in a semicolon-delimited expression list, as suggested by the following example output:

```
13456 Pennsylvania
Ave. # 402
Washington, DC
03456-6677
```

Moreover, if an expression followed by a semicolon is empty, FoxPro ignores it and begins output from the following expression without moving to the next line. Thus, wherever the Customer.address field is empty, we get two lines of output instead. The output for city, state, and zip will appear in the first line of the report field.

Referring again to the semicolon-delimited expression list used to define the address report field, note that by inserting a comma after the city field in the second line, we inadvertently force FoxPro to output the comma even when the city and state fields of a record are blank. We can suppress the comma as well by making its output conditional on NOT EMPTY(city) with IIF().

```
IIF(NOT EMPTY(city),TRIM(city)+",","")
```

This way the report line outputting city and state can be suppressed if both fields are empty. The comma we insert after the city cannot get in the way.

TIP When a complex expression must be used over and over in a report, you can enter it once in a report variable. If the same expression is needed in two or more reports, you can create and use a UDF instead.

Figure 13.19 shows sample output from Customer.frx. One look at it will show you the extent to which we use semicolon-delimited expression lists to stack items in its report fields.

FIGURE 13.19:

Semicolon-delimited expression lists are used to stack data in Customer.frx's report fields.

04/02/95 **CUSTOMER LIST** **Page 1**

Name/Cust #	Company/Department	Address	Country	Phone	Credit	Open/Total
Bloom, Mr. Leopold 100010	Eccles St. Galleries	32 Eccles St. Dublin, B26J8	IRELAND	012-326-7775 012-326-7743	Y	03/25/95 2,420.00
Borgesius, Dr. Katje 100001	The White Visitation Entertainment & Therapy	34012 Pennsylvania Ave. Washington, DC 02043-2222	USA	204-333-3333 204-555-5555	Y	01/03/86 34,055.00
Boylan, Mr. Blazes 100011	Boilin' Art Enterprises Ltd.	56 Horse Trader Lane Trenton, NJ 04102	USA	208-345-2245 208-345-2246	Y	03/25/95 10,000.00
Cunningham, Mr. Martin 100014		11245 Wilshire Blvd. Los Angeles, CA 90045	USA	310-345-6789 310-345-6790	Y	03/25/95 20,000.00
Dingham, Mr. Pat 100013	Charon's Place Gallery	32 Charon's Place Atlantic City, NJ 32145	USA	402-556-7655 402-556-7655	Y	03/25/95 50,000.00
Fahringer, Mr. Sam 100006	Zen Art Objects	2343 Small Cart Way St, Louis, MO 63122	USA	314-567-5677 314-567-5678	Y	02/03/89 9,420.00
K., Mr. Joseph 100008	Big Brother's Fine Art & Sculptures	5634 Kendall Square Boston, MA 06860	USA	617-322-4532 617-454-6755	N	01/14/87 5,000.00
McDowell, Ms. Gerty 100012	McDowell Studio	32450 Broadway New York, NY 10034	USA	212-345-6788 212-345-6789	Y	03/25/95 5,000.00
Pokler, Mr. Franz 100005	Goteppe Art Studios	Serecebey Yok. 61-63 Besiktas, Istanbul D1011	TURKEY	011-233-3223 - -	Y	06/11/89 10,400.00
Prentice, Mr. Pirate 100007	Counterforce Ltd.	789 Mole St. #2 London, England B0456J2	UNITED	01222333-456 012223334578	Y	03/12/87 4,500.00
Rathenau, Mr. Walter 100009	I.G. Art Exchange	117820 Wilshire Blvd. Los Angeles, CA 90036-2246	USA	213-757-4566 213-757-4566	Y	03/04/95 17,105.00
Samsa, Mr. Gregor 100004	Samsa Culture Clinic	3454 Soho St. New York City, NY 10002334	USA	212-222-2222 212-344-6555	Y	02/01/90 10,000.00
Slothrop, Mr. Hogan 100002	Aloha Novelties Acquisitions Dept.	30333 Kalihi Honolulu, HI 96060	USA	808-333-3445 - -	Y	02/16/93 13,165.00
Tripping, Ms. Geli 100003	Just Say NO2 Procurement	344 Hugo St. Victoria, BC GH3344	CANADA	209-333-3333 - -	Y	02/12/89 6,500.00

Note that when stacking items in a report field, we are not obliged to begin output of an expression following a semicolon in the report field's first column. In other words, data need not be left justified in the report field. We can insert spaces as needed in front of any expression to indent it. We do this, for example, in Customer.frx's first report expression, used to output customer name and customer number in a single report field.

```
IIF(last<>" ",TRIM(last)+",",""),sal,first; "      "+custno
```

Assuming Customer.last is not blank, the expression places the customer's name on one line and the customer's number on the next, indented six spaces. (The report expression is naturally defined to stretch from the top.) We make output of the comma following Customer.last conditional on Customer.last not being blank so that Customer.custno will be output in the report record's first line, correctly indented, when Customer.last, Customer.sal, and Customer.first are empty. Again, we use IIF() to prevent a literal comma—in this case, inserted after Customer.last—from getting in the way when it is not needed.

Of course, instead of using semicolon-delimited expression lists to stack items in a single report field defined to stretch, you can employ separate report expressions placed on different lines. Figure 13.20 shows the address report expression discussed above, reentered using these three report expressions:

```
address
TRIM(city) +",", state
IIF(LEN(TRIM(zip))=9,TRANS(zip,"@R XXXXX-XXXX",zip))
```

And though we position and size the report expressions so they appear to form a single field, this is hardly necessary, as shown by the two report expressions used to handle output of customer name and customer number in Figure 13.20.

Note that this will be the desired method of stacking data in a report field when the data in an expression must be given a specific format using picture symbols or functions or when each expression must be output on a specific line of the report record, at least relative to any report expressions appearing above it.

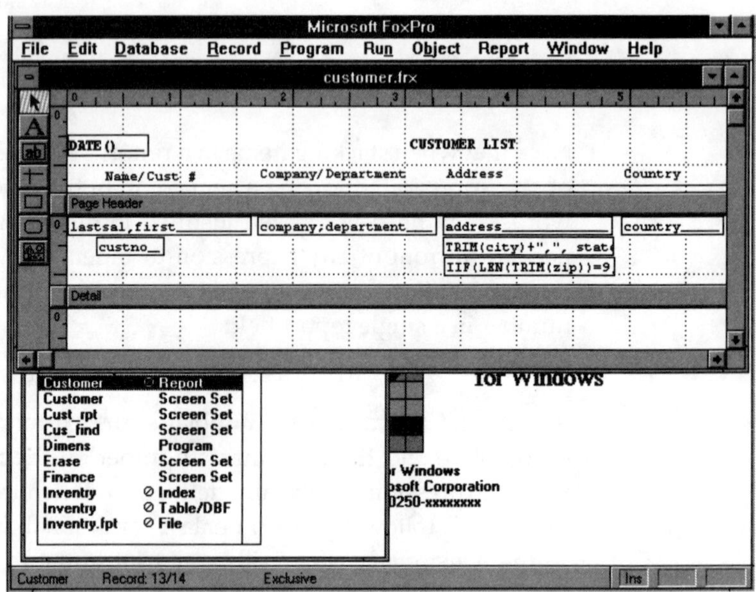

FIGURE 13.20:

Stack data in report records by placing report expressions on several lines in the Detail band.

NOTE

To use format (@ SAY PICTURE) symbols or functions to format a specific expression included in an expression list, we must use the TRANSFORM() function. This is because a format entered directly in the Report Expression dialog affects every expression in a semicolon-delimited expression list the same way. (Only expressions separated by a comma are unaffected by the use of template symbols, though format functions also affect them.)

Thus, when it is necessary to stack output from several different Numeric fields in a single column, we generally use distinct report expressions. (Since the line position of stacked numeric expressions is usually relied on to identify each expression and we want to avoid any wrapping of overflow—numeric fields should be sized to accommodate the largest output—we make such fields a constant height.)

The only disadvantage to stacking multiple report expressions on several rows is that you lose the capacity to remove the blank left by an empty expression if the report expression appears on the same row as other report expressions that are not blank.

NOTE

While the Print When dialog can be used with each report expression to suppress output when the line is blank, this cannot have the desired effect if other (horizontally adjacent) report expressions or objects must be output on the same report line. The entire line must be blank for FoxPro to suppress the output. This is one advantage of using semicolon-delimited expression lists in report expressions defined to stretch. If an expression is blank, FoxPro can output the expression that follows in its place. (FoxPro is not concerned with other report expressions appearing on the same line.)

Controlling Report Expressions That Stretch

When stacking multiple report expressions in any report band, care must be taken to ensure that a report expression defined to stretch does not overwrite objects or report expressions appearing below it in the same band. Referring back to the three report expressions used in Figure 13.20 to lay out the customer address fields, let's suppose we define the first, representing Customer.address, to stretch from the top. When overflow from Customer.address must be wrapped to the next row, it will overwrite the data output from the report expressions below it—that is, if they use the default Position Relative To setting of Top—Constant Field Height. (Again, when Top—Constant Field Height is used, the report expression cannot wrap, nor can it be moved down as needed to make way for data output by a stretch report field above it.) To assure that FoxPro will position output correctly from the two report expressions below Customer.address when a stretch occurs, we must use the Report Expression dialog to position them relative to the bottom of the Detail band or, alternatively, to position them relative to Top—Field Can Stretch. (We can also define the second report expression to stretch while positioning the third relative to the bottom.) The point is that when we place objects and report expressions in any band that includes one or more stretch fields, we must be careful to set their positions so that FoxPro will not overwrite them when a stretch occurs.

Stretch and Constant Height Bands

Unlike Label form bands, which are always of constant height, all report bands, with the notable exception of Page Footer and Column Footer, can be defined to stretch. In fact, Page Header and Detail bands are defined to stretch by default, though the setting can be changed by using the band height dialog. (See Figure 13.21.) Selecting the Constant Band Height check box makes the band a constant height; unselecting it allows the band to stretch. (As you may recall, the band height dialog is opened by double-clicking the drag button to the left of the band's title bar in the layout window. The dialog receives its name from the selected band. Again, the spinner can be used to set the band height with precision.) Group Header and Group Footer bands, discussed later in this chapter, are both defined to stretch by default.

Starting Out with a Quick Report

Quick Report is functionally equivalent to the Screen Builder's Quick Screen dialog. The Quick Report dialog is also virtually the same. (See Figure 13.22.) It even accesses the Field Picker for selecting any or all fields in open tables for inclusion in the Quick Report. The only Quick Screen option not available in Quick Report is the check box used to create fields using memvars.

FIGURE 13.21:

By default, the Constant Band Height check box is unselected with Page Header and Detail report bands so FoxPro can stretch the bands.

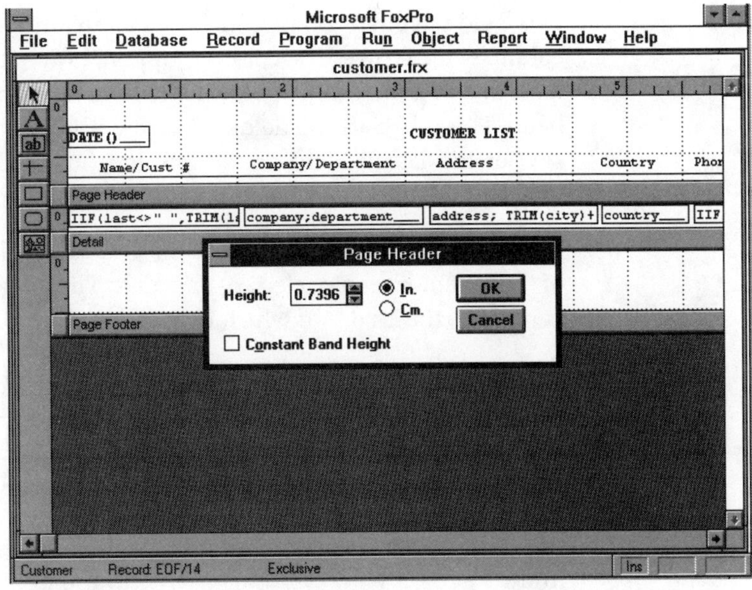

FIGURE 13.22:

Use the Quick Report dialog to place all selected table fields and corresponding field titles in the report layout.

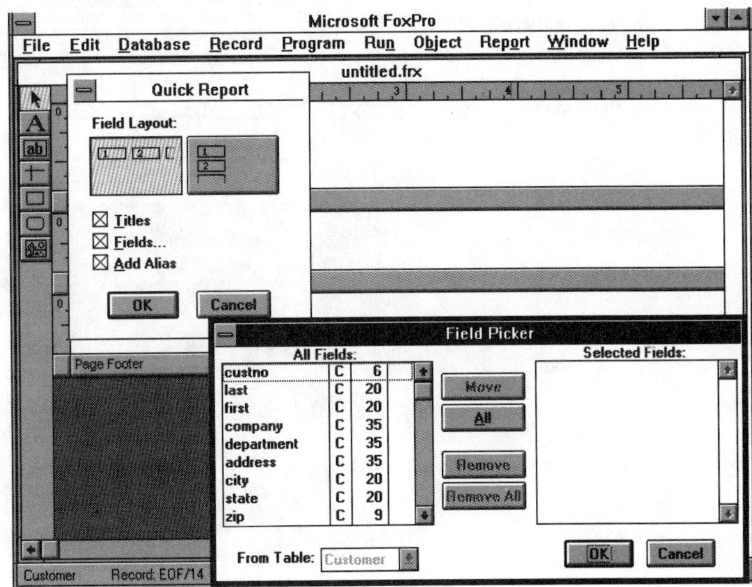

There are two ways to make use of Quick Report, basically corresponding to the two Field Layout options. Using the picture buttons, we can lay out report fields in columns or in rows. The columns option, however, is useful only when the source table or tables include just a few fields, which can be laid out in one row in the Detail band. This is because all fields selected with Quick Report but not fitting on the first row of the Detail band are simply left out of the Quick Report. (They are not wrapped around or stacked on additional rows in the Detail band.)

Figure 13.23, for example, shows the Quick Report layout produced with all fields of the Inventory table selected—no alias. This gives us a jump start in designing Inventry.frx, the layout of which is shown in Figure 13.24.

With respect to the Detail band, the only real difference between Inventry.frx and the initial Quick Report is the sizing of the report fields, which are reduced in Inventry.frx to allow all report fields to be displayed at once in the Page Preview window (when zoomed in). (As the ruler at the top of the layout editor indicates, they take up only five inches on the page.) The main benefit we gain from this is that it makes the report easier to read. Figure 13.25, for example, shows the Quick Report in the Page Preview window. Owing to the default sizing of the report fields by

FIGURE 13.23:

The Quick Report produced with all fields of the Inventory table provides a good starting point for producing the MBS Inventory report.

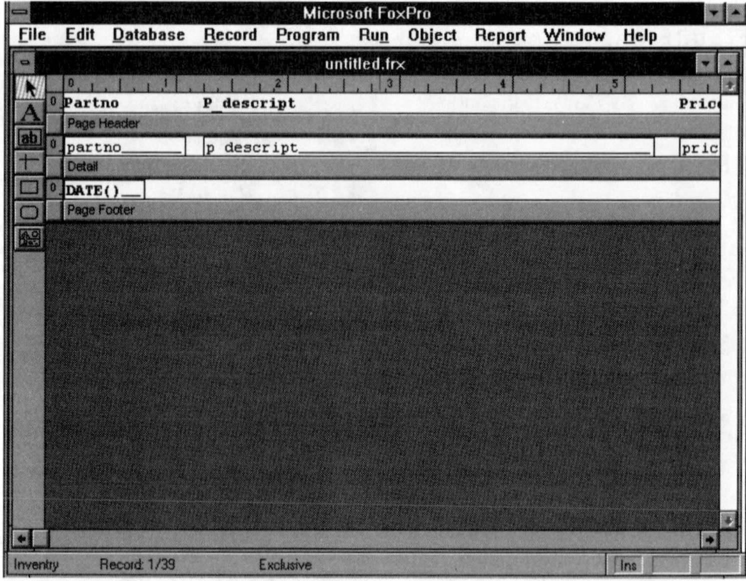

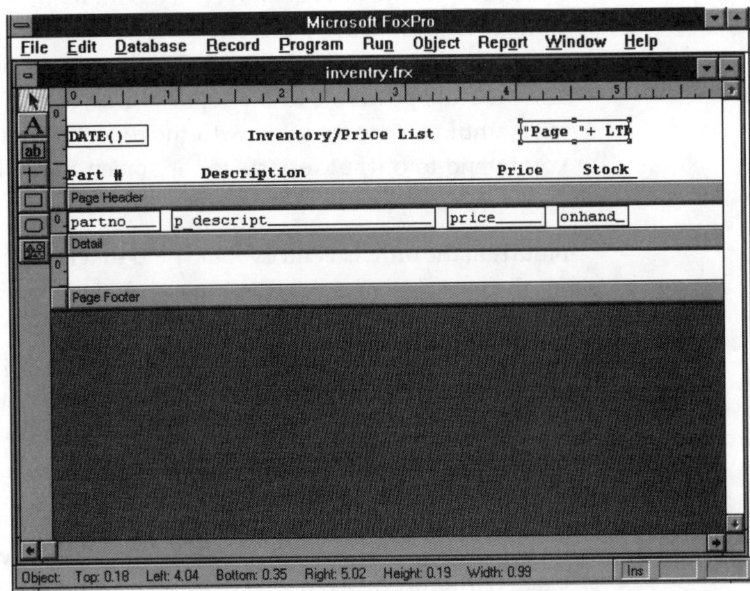

FIGURE 13.24:

Inventry.frx, the MBS Inventory Report form, was designed by adding test objects to the Page Header band and sizing and repositioning Quick Report fields.

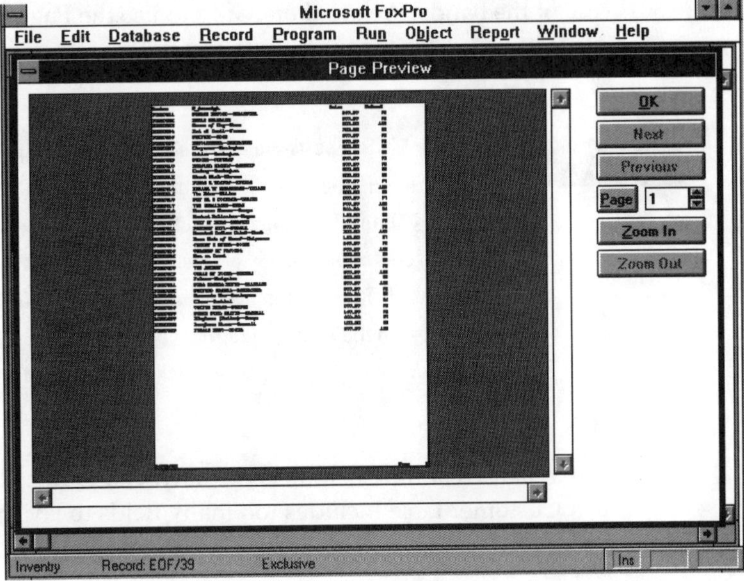

FIGURE 13.25:

Quick Report fields are often much larger than required for actual data output and unless reduced can make report records difficult to scan.

Quick Screen, the data displayed is too far apart to be easily read without inserting a line in the Detail band directly beneath the report fields to set off the data belonging to each report record with a line. Still, the easier solution is to reduce the sizes and alter the positions of the report fields, and to use Page Preview to test the results, until you are satisfied with the report format. This is also the best solution if you intend to output reports to the screen in the Page Preview window with REPORT FORM PREVIEW, as we do in the MBS.

Note that the only Inventory table field that is really subject to overflow is that used for the part description. This is no problem. We simply modify the report expression P_descript to stretch so that instead of P_descript values that may overflow the report field being truncated, overflow will be wrapped to the next report row. (The alternative is to leave the report field set to constant height and allow FoxPro to truncate whatever part of the part description cannot be output in one line of the report field.)

The only other changes to the Quick Report are superficial. After expanding the Page Header band, we use the text tool to change the Quick Report field titles as needed to supply each report field with a suitable title. We also insert a line beneath the field titles to set them off at the top of each page from the report records that appear directly beneath them. We then drag the DATE() and _PAGENO from the Page Footer band to the Page Header band, add a page title, and adjust the heights of the bands. We are then ready to use the Page Layout dialog to set the left-hand margin, check the result in the Page Preview window, and save the new report.

NOTE

In the MBS reports we use the expression "Page "+LTRIM(STR(_PAGENO)) in the Page Header band to output page numbers immediately after the character string "Page ". Owing to numeric templates, converting an <expN> to a character string usually produces a string that begins with several blank spaces. We use LTRIM() to remove them. However, if you must always align the page number in the same place, you can output _PAGENO as a separate report expression—the same way Quick Report does it.

When creating Customer.scx, however, Quick Report is not as useful since the Customer table includes too many fields to lay them out in columns. Still, we can gain some benefit from Quick Report by selecting Field Layout by rows to place all the Customer table fields, preceded by field name titles, in the Detail band. (See Figure 13.26.) Though we still have a long way to go in designing Customer.frx—most report expressions must be rewritten as stretch fields outputting comma- and semicolon-delimited expressions—this at least gives us something to work with. We can drag report fields into their approximate positions before redefining and sizing them and drag the usable field name titles into the Page Header band. Whatever we don't need, we erase. (Again, the process of selecting, sizing, and positioning objects in the report design window is the same as when working in the Screen Builder. See Chapter 11 for a discussion of these operations.)

Report Layout Design Considerations

Using the Print Setup dialog, accessed through the Page Layout dialog, we can select between portrait and landscape orientation, as you can see in Figure 13.27.

FIGURE 13.26:

In designing the Customer List report, we use Quick Report to place all Customer table fields in the layout, even though we must subsequently reposition them in columns.

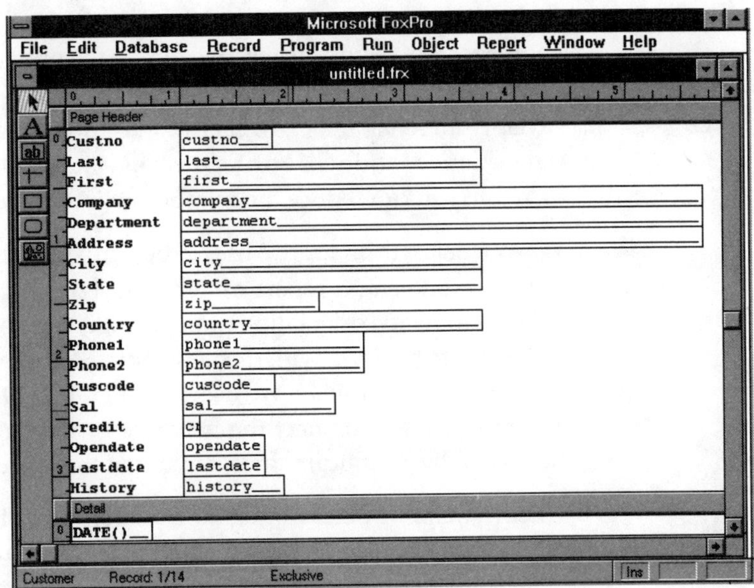

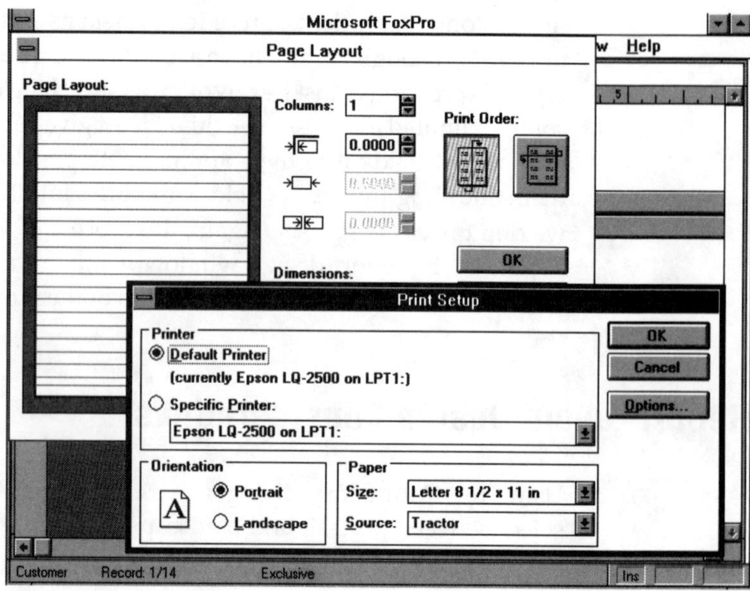

FIGURE 13.27: Use the Print Setup dialog to change the page size or printer orientation used in a report.

(In landscape orientation, the printed page is turned on its side. When the selected page size is 8½ by 11 inches, this means we print a page that is 11 inches wide and 8½ inches in height.) Using the Page Size dialog, we can also select from among several different page sizes. Each of these options affects report design by changing the maximum width of our report bands. Using landscape instead of portrait orientation, you can reduce the number of lines required for each report record.

When we start the Report Writer to design a Report form, it configures the page layout for producing a report on 8½- by 11-inch pages using portrait orientation. When we change orientation or paper size, the Report Writer reconfigures the layout editor to conform with the new settings. These settings, moreover, are stored in the .frx file so that when we execute REPORT FORM, FoxPro will print the pages correctly. They also affect the behavior of the Page Preview window and are reflected in the graphical representation of the layout in the Page Layout dialog.

Another variable determining the available space in a layout is the selected font. As we increase the size of the font, we decrease the number of characters that can be printed on each report row. With this in mind, we can create the largest report, in terms of the number of characters output to each report row, by using landscape orientation, the largest possible page size, and a miniscule font.

What works best for a given report will often be determined by experimentation. The font should not be so decreased in size that it renders the report difficult to read, unless the reduction in the number of pages required for normal execution of the report (as it will actually be used) compensates for the difficulty. In this regard, note that changing the page orientation to landscape does not necessarily reduce the number of report records that can be placed on a page. It can actually increase the number of records instead, as long as the font size is not increased to take advantage of the larger amount of space on each report row.

As to which font you should use, the Report Writer begins with a default font selection of TrueType Courier New, 10, Regular. (Quick Report uses this for report fields and titles, though it uses the Bold style with the field name titles as well as the DATE() and _PAGENO report expressions it places in the Page Footer.) Use of a TrueType font is indicated for most report objects since these fonts are designed to maintain the position of objects formatted with blank spaces. Changing report fields to a proportional font, as opposed to a TrueType or monospace font, will usually result in reports that do not maintain data in straight columns.

With respect to the MBS reports, in an effort to keep things simple, I stuck to the default font selection, though I reduced the font used in the Customer List and Customer Account reports so as to be able to create them using portrait orientation. As to the use of font styles, Regular was used with all report Detail bands and in other report bands, as well as in the page header. (In some reports a bold page header seems to work for the header and report field titles; in others it seems out of place.) Still, if you have occasion to use or revise any of the MBS Report forms, changing the font, font size, and/or style of any objects is quite easy. Use the selection marquee or Shift+Click to select all the objects that require a specific font setting, and then use the Object pulldown's Font option to make the required changes to all the objects at once. (You can also use the Edit pulldown's Select All option to select all text and report fields in the layout at once.) Again, the font used by Quick Report and by the text and report expression tools is determined by the settings of the Font dialog, accessed through the Page Layout dialog.

Creating Group Reports

In the Customer List, Customer Accounts, and Inventory List reports, each report record stands alone. However, in producing the Customer Sales and Payments reports, we are obliged to print report records for each sale or payment on file for each customer and, moreover, to group in one place all sales and payments for each customer. To achieve this effect we must do two things. First, we must open the Data Grouping dialog using the Report pulldown and, after selecting the Add button, enter an expression in the Group Info dialog's Group entry box that will enable FoxPro to determine when it has come upon a new group of records while executing the REPORT FORM command. (See Figure 13.28.) Customer.custno provides us with a ready means of identifying records belonging to specific customers. We therefore select Custno as the Group expression.

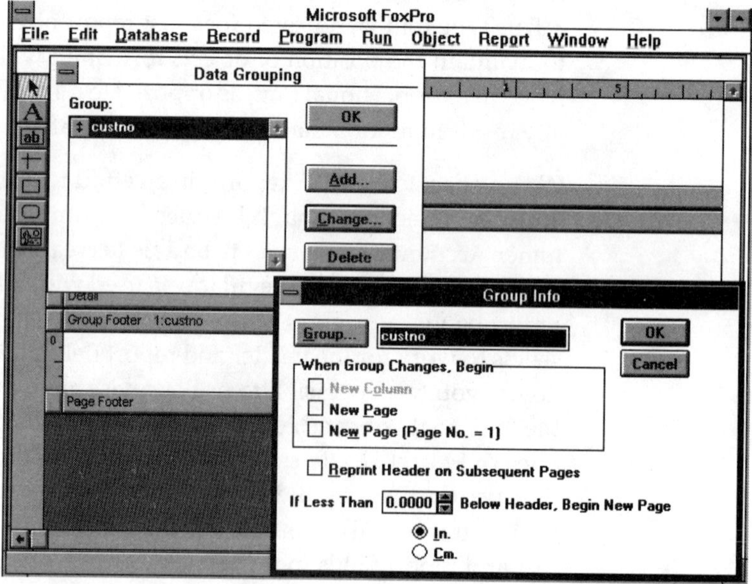

FIGURE 13.28: Use the Data Grouping dialog to enter the expression FoxPro must use in grouping report records in the Detail band.

Once we establish the data grouping, FoxPro adds a Group Header and Group Footer band just above and below the Detail band. Unlike what you see in Figure 13.29, showing Salcust.frx, executing the Customer Sales report, the Group Header and Group Footer bands will be initially closed. Their use is, in fact,

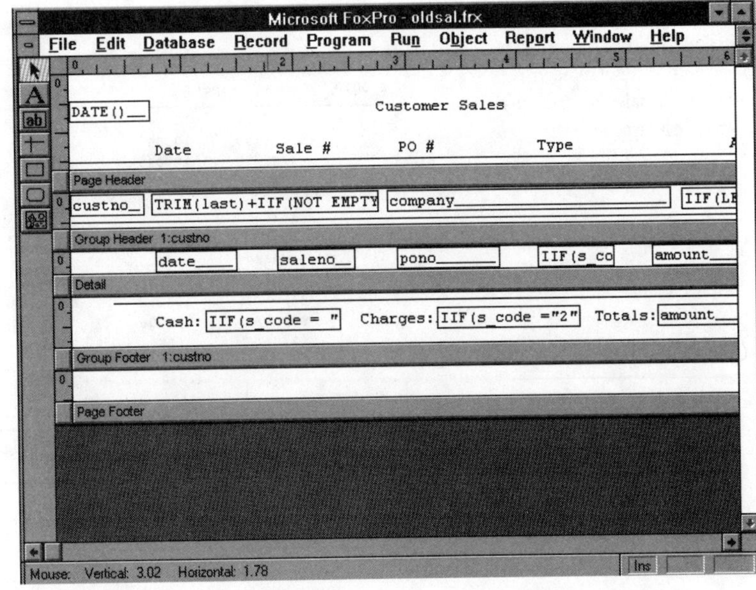

FIGURE 13.29:

In the Customer Sales report, Salcust.frx, we use the Group Header band to identify the customer, the Detail band to output the customer's sales, and the Group Footer band to present summary calculations about the customer's sales.

optional, though the Group Header band provides the best means of identifying groups of records and the Group Footer provides the only available means of presenting summary calculations based on records in each group, though running totals can also be calculated and printed in the Detail band.

FoxPro's execution of a Report form containing a defined data grouping works as follows. First, FoxPro prints the page header if one is entered. Next, coming to the Group Header band, FoxPro evaluates the group expression and stores the result to memory. It then prints out the Group Header band and begins printing report records according to the Detail band layout. It continues printing report records, one for each record in the current table, all the while checking for a change in the value of the Group expression. When the Group expression changes, it executes the Group Footer band and then executes the Group Header band for the next group of records, as indicated by the new value of the group expression. FoxPro keeps working in this way until it comes to the end of the page, at which point it executes the Page Footer band and begins with the next page, starting with the page header. Figure 13.30 shows sample output from Salcust.frx.

FIGURE 13.30:

The Customer Sales report is designed to display each customer's sales records as a distinct group.

```
04/02/95                          Customer Sales                         Page - 1
          Date         Sale #       PO #          Type                   Amount
100010    Bloom, Leopold            Eccles St. Galleries             012-326-7775
          03/26/95     100043                     Cash                     880.00
          03/26/95     100044                     Cash                   1,210.00
          04/02/95     100045                     Cash                     330.00
          Cash:          2,420.00  Charges:.                Totals:      2,420.00
100001    Borgesius, Katje          The White Visitation             204-333-3333
          03/04/95     100005       KBCSH001      Cash                   1,045.00
          03/04/95     100004       KBCH0001      Charge                 3,410.00
          03/04/95     100012       KBCH0004      Charge                15,290.00
          03/04/95     100006       KBCG0002      Charge                 1,870.00
          03/04/95     100007       KBCH0003      Charge                 5,940.00
          Cash:          1,045.00  Charges:.      26,510.00 Totals:     27,555.00
100006    Fahringer, Sam            Zen Art Objects                  314-567-5677
          03/05/95     100013       FH000001      Charge                 5,940.00
          03/05/95     100014       FH00002       Charge                 1,980.00
          Cash:                    Charges:.       7,920.00 Totals:      7,920.00
100005    Pokler, Franz             Goteppe Art Studios              011-233-3223
          03/04/95     100011                     Cash                   4,400.00
          Cash:          4,400.00  Charges:.                Totals:      4,400.00
100009    Rathenau, Walter          I.G. Art Exchange                213-757-4566
          03/04/95     100010       RATHCHG1      Charge                17,105.00
          Cash:                    Charges:.      17,105.00 Totals:     17,105.00
100002    Slothrop, Hogan           Aloha Novelties                  808-333-3445
          03/04/95     100009       SLCHG002      Charge                 1,375.00
          03/04/95     100008       SLCH0001      Charge                 6,490.00
          Cash:                    Charges:.       7,865.00 Totals:      7,865.00
```

By default, FoxPro includes as many groups as it can the same page. Also by default, if group detail records must be continued on the next page, it does not repeat the group header on the next page. These and other aspects of FoxPro's execution of group reports can be changed using the Group Info dialog, shown in Figure 13.28, or with the Group Header and Group Footer band height dialogs, which include much the same options. Select the New Page check box to force FoxPro to move to a new page before starting a new group, and New Page (Page No. = 1) if you want to reset _PAGENO to 1 for the first page of each new group. Select Reprint Header on Subsequent Pages if you want the group header reprinted at the top of every page holding detail records belonging to a group printed on the previous page. To prevent a group header from being printed at the bottom of a page when no room remains for any detail records, use the Less Than spinner to enter the height of the Detail band. That way, if not enough room remains for a detail record, FoxPro will go to the next page before printing the group header.

With respect to the Customer Sales and Customer Payments reports, the default Group Info settings are satisfactory. FoxPro prints as many groups as it can on each page and does not repeat the group header of a group carried over to a second or third page. Only with Invoice.frx, States.frx, and Lettform.frx, executing sale invoices, customer statements, and mass personalized form letters, respectively, do we instruct FoxPro to begin each group on a new page—Page No. = 1, to be exact.

Establishing the View for a Multi-Table Group Report

Of course, execution of a group report assumes that FoxPro will encounter all records belonging to each group as defined in the report in order in the current table. Remember, REPORT FORM is a sequential command and reads through and processes the records in the current table or multi-table view in order. Still, supposing we used SET RELATION to establish the report view, the proper arrangement of records is easily managed with the following commands:

```
USE customer
USE sales ORDER saleno IN 0  && saleno: custno+saleno
SET RELATION TO custno INTO sales
SET SKIP TO sales
SET FILTER TO FOUND()
```

This creates a view that includes one record for every Sales table record that can be matched with a Customer table record on the basis of shared Custno. Moreover, the records in the view are arranged so that FoxPro encounters all sales belonging to each customer in sequence—and according to the arrangement of records in the Customer table. Owing to the effect of SET RELATION, we can arrange the Customer table any way we want with an index tag without adversely affecting FoxPro's access to each customer's records in the Sales table.

However, while we might create Salcust.frx with this view, provided we reference all Sales.dbf fields in the Report form using alias names, as you know from Chapter 12, this is not how we prepare data for execution of the Customer Sales report. We use SELECT to create a result table that actually joins the data in the two tables.

```
SELECT a.custno, a.last, a.first, a.company, a.phone1, ;
    b.date, b.saleno, b.pono, b.s_code, b.amount ;
    FROM customer a, sales b ;
    INTO CURSOR Report ;
    WHERE a.custno = b.custno
```

Here I have simplified the SELECT command actually used in Cust_rpt.spr, though in so doing I have cited the one command placed in Salcust.prg during MBS development to immediately establish the environment required for working on Salcust.frx. The environment settings stored with a Report form cannot, after all, reproduce a SELECT result table. It is limited to restoring views with USE, SET ORDER, SET RELATION, and SET SKIP. However, with the SELECT command in Salcust.prg, the command DO salcust, executed from the command window, suffices to restore the view required by the report.

TIP

Whenever designing multi-table reports that will process data from result tables produced with SELECT, place the SELECT command in a .prg file and restore the environment required to modify or execute the report by executing the .prg file. A .qpr (Query Program) can also be created with RQBE to execute the SELECT command.

Of course, the advantage of designing Salcust.frx using the result table produced with SELECT, rather than working with the multi-table view produced with SET RELATION, is that we do not have to reckon with alias names with SELECT. This is even more significant in the case of the Customer Payments report, Paycust.frx, which draws on data from three tables. (We will say more about creating Report forms that reference fields from two or more tables using alias names when we discuss the Report forms used to produce customer invoices, statements, and mass personalized form letters.)

Using Group Header and Footer Bands

Group Header and Group Footer bands are typically used to introduce the new report group and to summarize report data belonging to the group, respectively. In the case of Salcust.frx, we use the Group Header band to print out cursory information about the customer: customer number, name, company, and phone number. Note that at the time FoxPro executes the Group Header band, it has no idea how many sales must be printed for the customer, nor is it able to present any data summarizing that customer's sales. It has only come to the first of any number of records for that customer and must perform all calculations as it processes those records in sequential order. However, since each report record includes Customer table data identifying each customer, we can save much space in the Detail band if we report whatever data is required from the Customer table in the Group Header band, thereby reserving all space in the Detail band for printing the customer's sales. We use the group footer to output summary information about the customer's sales.

TIP

Often the limitations of a Report or Label form can be overcome through the use of user-defined functions. If you want to output summary information about a group, for example, in the Group Header band, you can design a UDF that scans the records in the current group in order to make a calculation before returning the record pointer to the first record in the group. Referenced in the Group Header band, the UDF will return the correct group figure. Report variables can also be used to provide a UDF with a means of passing several values back to a report. We see an example of this at the end of the chapter.

Performing Calculations in the Footer Band

With respect to Salcust.frx's Group Footer band, we use three calculated report expressions to output totals for customer cash sales, customer charges, and a grand total. As you may recall from Chapter 6, Sales.dbf's S_code (or sales code) field uses a 1 to indicate cash sales and a 2 to indicate charges. Sales.amount holds the amount of each sale. We can therefore calculate the three totals by placing calculated report expressions in the Group Footer band that use the following definitions:

Function	Expression	Calculate	Reset
Sum cash sales	IIF(s_code="1", amount,0.00)	Sum	Custno (end of group)
Sum charges	IIF(s_code="2", amount,0.00)	Sum	Custno (end of group)
Total sales	Amount	Sum	Custno (end of group)

The important thing about the two calculated report expressions for summing cash and charge sales is the use of IIF() to return the sale amount or 0.00 as appropriate for each report record. IIF() is our means of conditionally controlling FoxPro's update of any calculated report expression.

NOTE Once we add data groups to a report, the Reset popups used with the Report Expression's Calculate dialog and the Variable Definition dialog, discussed below, list the group expressions. To reset the calculation at the end of the group—after execution of the Group Footer band, if it is included—select the group expression from the popup.

Using Report Variables

In situations where the same calculated report expression must be used more than once in the same report, rather than defining the same expression multiple times, you can define it once using a report variable instead. Then, wherever the calculation is required, you can reference the report (memory) variable by name instead of having to reenter the same expression for the *n*th time.

Report variables are added, edited, or deleted from a Report or Label form by selecting the Variables option from the Report pulldown. The Report Variables dialog, shown in Figure 13.31, presents a list of defined report variables. (Initially it is empty.) To create a report variable, select the Add button to open the Variable Definition dialog, where we make up a name for the report memvar and enter the value (expression) it is intended to hold. If the variable is to maintain its initial value, changed, if at all, by the expression entered as the value to store, we leave the Nothing radio button selected so no calculation will be performed. To create a variable that is updated exactly like a calculated report expression, we select whichever Calculate radio button is indicated. When defining calculated variables, we must also use the Reset popup to determine when it will be reset to 0—or to whatever initial value we choose to enter in the dialog.

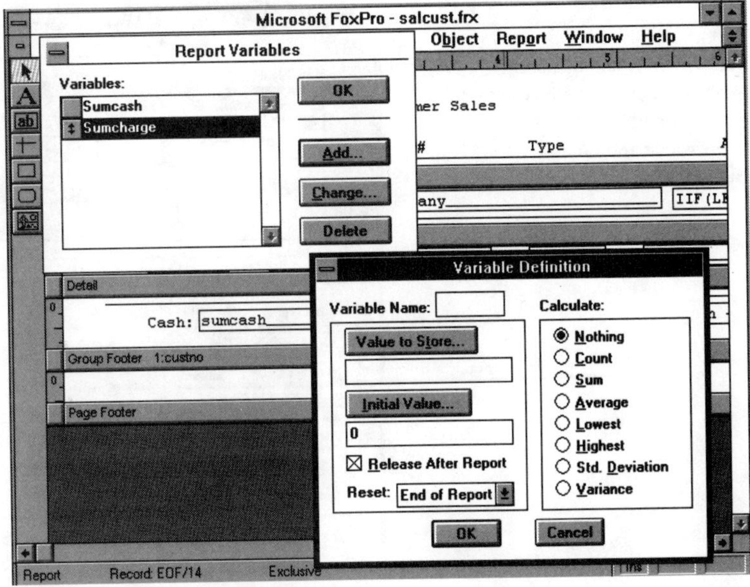

FIGURE 13.31:

When creating a Report or Label form you can initialize report variables to maintain values and calculations used in the form.

NOTE

By default, report variables are erased from memory when the REPORT or LABEL FORM command terminates. However, if you have further use of the values in one or more report variables, just unselect the Release After Report check box.

Using the Customer Sales report as an example, we can use two calculated variables to track the sum of customer cash and charge sales. Figure 13.32, for example, shows the definition of report variable sumcash, used to calculate the sum of all cash sales in the current report group.

Once we create the variables sumcash and sumcharge (sumcharge being used to calculate the total of customer charges), we gain free access to the two figures without having to recalculate them whenever they are needed. To report the total customer cash and charge sales in the Group Footer band, instead of using calculated report expressions, we use a static report expression referencing one or the other variable by name. As for the grand total, we do not require another calculated variable or calculated report expression since we can simply add the

FIGURE 13.32:

Report variables can be used to perform calculations using expressions. The results can then be employed in report expressions and other calculations.

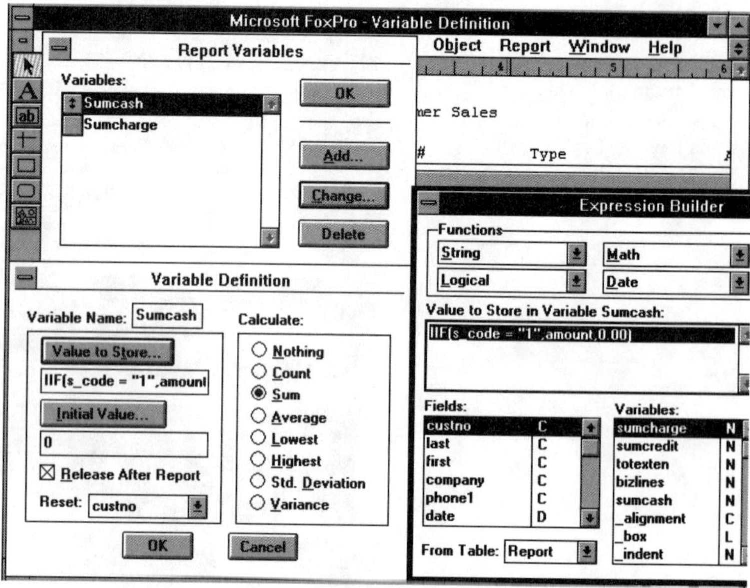

values of the two variables with the report expression sumcash + sumcharge. Similarly, if we require the figures in other calculations, we do not need to recalculate them; they are already available. (As shown in Figure 13.32, once variables are added to the report, FoxPro displays their names in the list of available variables in the Expression Builder, so we can readily use them in forming other report expressions and variables.)

WARNING

FoxPro updates calculated report variables in the order in which they are listed in the Report Variables dialog. Their order thus becomes quite important when an expression in one variable references another variable by name. In such instances, the variable being referenced must appear earlier in the Report Variable list. Otherwise its value will be referenced before it has been updated to reflect the current report record.

Using Nested Data Groups

When designing reports (or Label forms to be used as reports), more than one level of data grouping can be used. Indeed, you can create as many levels as you like. For example, if we order the table used by Salcust.frx by Custno and by S_code, thus arranging all sales for each customer so those representing cash sales (S_code = "1") appear first, followed by those representing customer charges, we can then revise Salcust.frx to subgroup sales for each customer using S_code. To do this we simply add S_code to the Group list in the Data Grouping dialog, shown open in Figure 13.33. This opens additional Group Header and Footer bands for use with the subgroup.

FIGURE 13.33:

Using the Data Grouping dialog, you can specify several levels of data grouping in a Report or Label form.

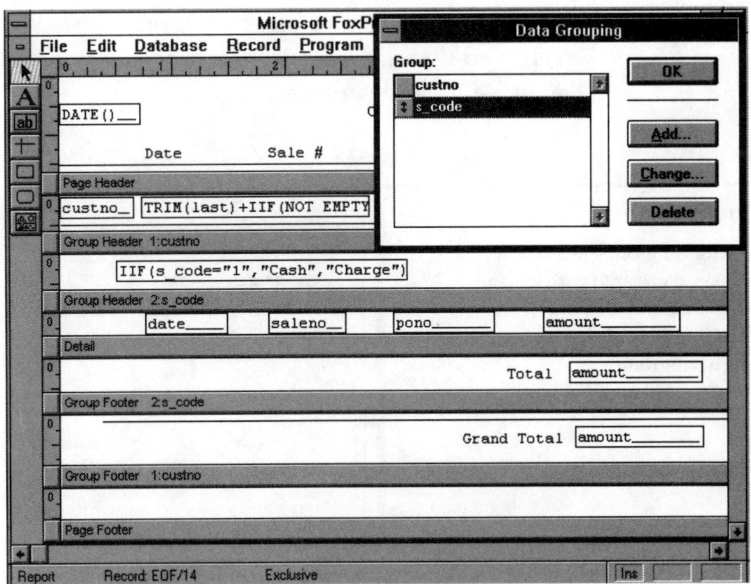

NOTE

In specifying multiple data groups, be sure to list each group in order of decreasing importance. The main grouping must be listed first, followed by the subgroup, followed by the sub-subgroup, and so on. Listing the groups out of order will prevent the report from processing data correctly.

As you will note in the report layout shown in Figure 13.33, we use Group Header 2 S_code to output "Cash" or "Charge", depending upon the current value of S_code, by using IIF() in a report expression. In Group Footer 2 S_code, we use Amount in a calculated report expression to total the subgroup records. (We choose S_code as the reset value.) In the Group Footer 1 Custno band, we again use Amount in a calculated report expression to total all records appearing in all subgroups. (We choose Custno as the reset value.) In Figure 13.34 we show the result of the layout in the Page Preview window. While the use of the subgroup obviously makes the report longer, owing to the space requirements of the additional group header and footer, it does make the report easier to read. Subgroups and sub-subgroups are especially useful when multiple calculations must be performed on records at different group levels; it enables us to avoid having to play around with IIF() to distinguish among detail records on the basis of expressions. With subgroups the same effect is achieved through the selection of the reset value when defining calculated report expressions and variables.

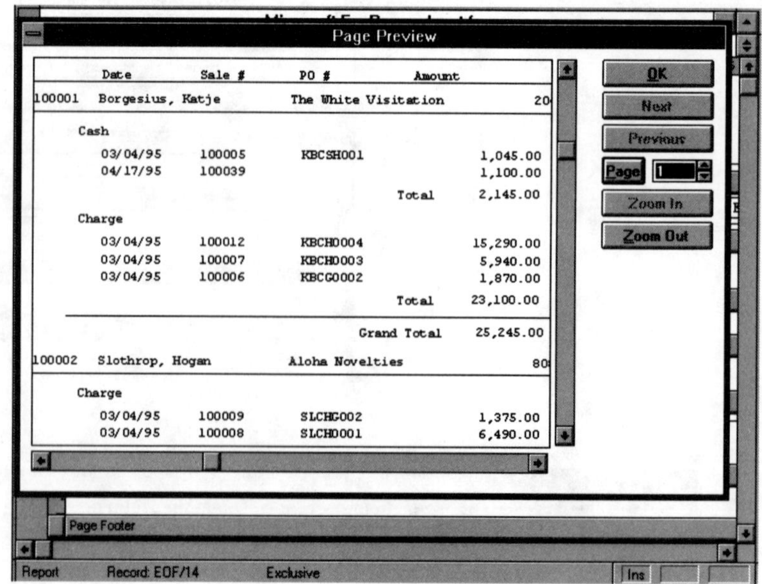

FIGURE 13.34:

Using subgroups in a report makes it easier to perform and display the results of calculations based on records belonging to each subgroup.

Producing Form Letters

Lettform.frx, the MBS Report form used for producing mass personalized form letters, is actually quite simple in design. (See Figure 13.35.) We define it as a group report, using Custno again as the group expression, primarily to take advantage of the Group Header band option, enabling us to begin each new group on the next page and to reset _PAGENO to 1.

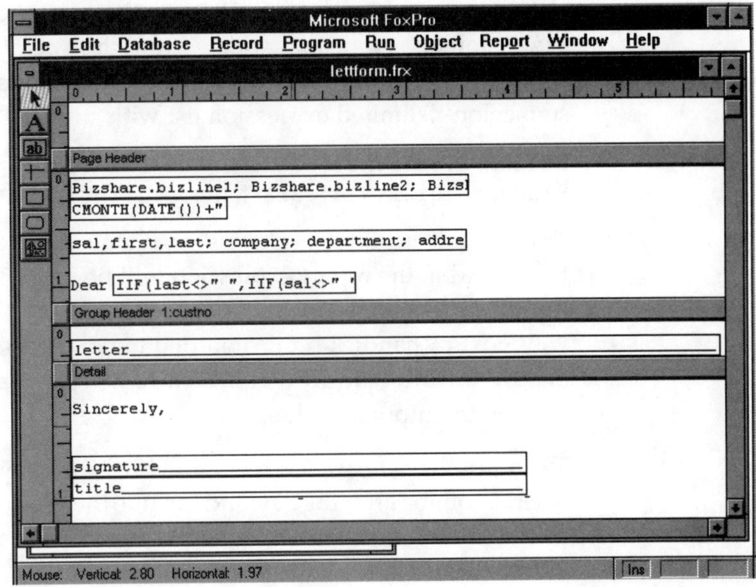

FIGURE 13.35:

Because the same letter (detail) must be printed for every customer, when designing a form letter we use a group report and print the letterhead in the Group Header band.

Since it is our intention to print one letter for each customer in the selected view, using the letter stored in the Memo field of the record current in Letters.dbf and drawing return address data, title, and signature from the MBS system values table, we can set the environment for the report as follows:

```
USE customer
USE letters ALIAS lett_pic IN 0
USE bizshare IN 0
```

We USE letters ALIAS lett_pic since lett_pic is the alias name given the copy of Letters.dbf used in Cust_rpt.spr's letter pick list. (See Chapter 11.) Since the SELECT result table used in Cust_rpt.spr to supply customer data is selected as the current table during execution of the Report form, we can open the Customer table to design the report without assigning it the alias name used by the SELECT result table. Unlike Letters (alias lett_pic) and Bizshare, we reference its fields without using alias names.

Managing Output of the Letterhead

With respect to the report layout, we use the Page Header band to establish the top margin. In the Grouper Header band we stack the report expressions required to output the return address and phone; the current date, with the month spelled out; the customer's name and address; and the opening salutation. The report expression used to output the return address and phone, accessed from Bizshare, uses a semicolon-delimited expression list with stretch.

```
Bizshare.bizline1; Bizshare.bizline2; Bizshare.bizline3;
Bizshare.bizline4; Bizshare.bizline5; Bizshare.bizphone
```

This way, if no return address or phone number has actually been entered in Bizshare.dbf, the report expression will be null. The date output by the following report expression will be the first printed line on the page. Moreover, owing to the way FoxPro handles semicolon-delimited expressions, if any of the fields referenced from Bizshare are blank, FoxPro will suppress the line that would otherwise be used to output its value.

To output the date, we use the following expression in order to spell out the month, insert a comma after the day, and include the century when outputting the year. (We do not place semicolons at the end of each line so as to present the expression as it would appear in the Expression Builder.)

```
CMONTH(DATE())+" "+
ALLTRIM(STR(DAY(DATE())))+", "+
STR(YEAR(DATE()),4)
```

Since this is tedious to enter, if you must output the date in this format in many reports included in a system, you are advised to transfer the expression to a UDF so it can be used whenever needed to return the full date.

```
FUNCTION ddate
RETURN CMONTH(DATE())+" "+ ;
    ALLTRIM(STR(DAY(DATE())))+", "+ ;
    STR(YEAR(DATE()),4)
```

Were we to add this function to the system procedure file—or to any other program included in the MBS project—we could use the report expression Ddate() to output the date instead of writing out the expression in full.

As to the customer address, we again use a stretch report expression with a semicolon- and comma-delimited expression list. (Here again, we present the expression as it would appear in the Expression Builder. The semicolons are part of the expression.)

```
sal,first,last; company; department; address;
TRIM(city)+",",state,
IIF(LEN(TRIM(zip))=9,TRANS(zip,"@R XXXXX-XXXX"),zip) ;
country
```

This should require no explanation, owing to our previous discussion of the stretch report expression included in the Customer List report, Customer.frx.

Still, bear in mind that when we place a stretch report expression above other report expressions in the same band, all report expressions below it must also stretch or be overwritten by the stretch report expression if it stretches down to their position in the band. The only exception to this rule is report expressions (of constant height) and text objects that are positioned relative to the bottom since FoxPro can handle their output correctly even when they are preceded by report expressions that stretch.

TIP

Because rectangles and vertical lines can be defined to stretch, you can use them to surround or delimit report expressions that stretch. Only horizontal lines and text objects are limited to top or bottom orientation.

With respect to the opening salutation, we follow the text object "Dear " with a complex report expression formed with IIF() to output the best name we can come up with given available data, followed by a comma.

```
IIF(last<>" ",IIF(sal<>" ",TRIM(sal)+" "+TRIM(last),
    "Mr/s. "+TRIM(last)),
    "Sir or Madam")+","
```

If the Last field is not blank, we use it with Sal—if Sal is not blank. If Sal is blank but Last is not, we use Last with Mr/s. instead. Finally, if Last is blank, we output "Sir or Madam". While this is as unpleasant to write as it is to explain, it is nonetheless necessary. We may, after all, need to output letters to companies listed in the Customer table that include no name entries. (If a first name should be used in the opening salutation if it is present in the record, you must add yet another IIF() to control its use.)

Orienting Text Objects in Bands with Stretch Report Fields

Since the text object and the report expression forming the salutation appear on the last printed line in the band—or at least after all stretch report expressions—we can position them relative to the bottom so FoxPro will print them in the correct position regardless of the number of lines used above them for the report fields that stretch. We would, however, run into difficulties with the text object if the report expression used to output the name required stretching. This is because text objects must be oriented at the top or bottom. As it is, we must double-click the text object (Dear) in order to open the Text dialog, shown in Figure 13.36, and select Position Relative to Bottom because Top is the default orientation.

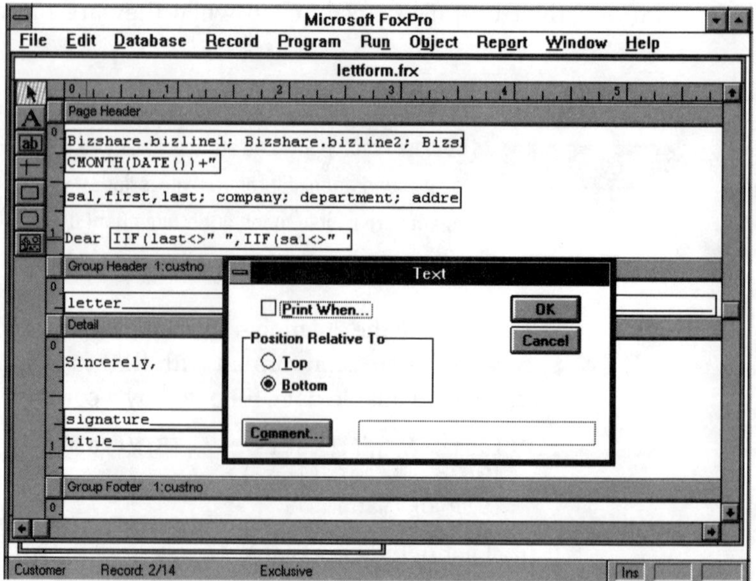

FIGURE 13.36:
Double-click a text object to open the Text dialog and change the selected text object's top/bottom orientation in the band.

Note that we use the stretch report expressions to output the return and customer addresses as a matter of convenience. The alternative is to use separate report expressions for each line of address data and to use the Print When dialog to remove each line when it is blank. (We will have more to say about positioning objects in stretch bands and the use of the Print When dialog when we discuss the Report forms producing invoices and customer statements.)

Controlling Printing of Objects in Header Bands

If we use the Group Header band for output of the letterhead and salutation, this too is a matter of convenience. Since we must prepare to print letters of more than one page, we must take care that the letterhead and salutation are not repeated after the first page. By placing the letterhead in the Group Header band, we can take care of this by simply unselecting the Reprint Header on Subsequent Pages check box in the Group Info or Group Band dialog. (See Figure 13.37)

However, we can place the entire letterhead and the opening salutation in the Page Header band and still achieve the same effect, provided we continue to use the Group Info dialog to move FoxPro to a new page and reset the page number to 1

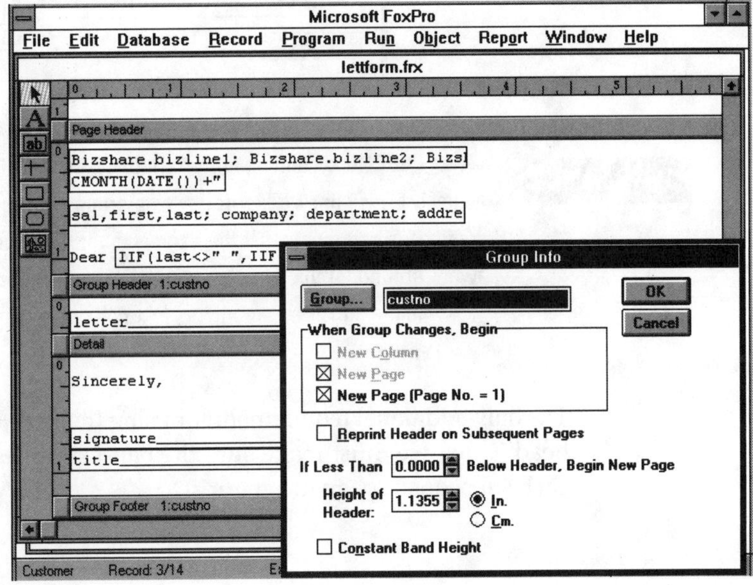

FIGURE 13.37: To print the letterhead on only the first page of a multi-page letter, we unselect the Reprint Header on Subsequent Pages check box in the Group Info dialog.

when the group changes. This is because we can use the Report Expression Print When dialog as needed to make the output of each object in the page header conditional on the expression _PAGENO = 1. (See Figure 13.38.)

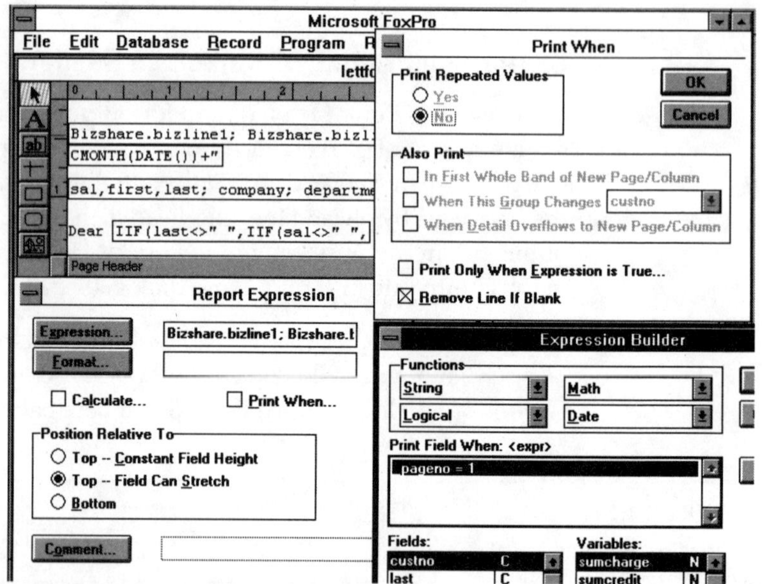

FIGURE 13.38: Printing of objects in the Page Header band of Report forms can be made conditional on the page number through use of the Print When dialog.

WARNING

The _PAGENO system memory variable, indicating Report and Label form page numbers, may not work corectly with group reports that begin new groups on a new page and must reset the page number to 1 for each new group. We discuss a work-around for this problem at the end of this chapter. In the meantime, we assume the correct resetting of _PAGENO when used this way.

The only additional requirement for using the Page Header band to output the letterhead is that we must make sure the band supplies an appropriate top margin for each subsequent page in a letter.

You can place a different page header on alternating pages and/or on the first and all subsequent pages of any report by entering all required objects in the Page Header band and making their output conditional on the current _PAGENO through use of each object's Print When dialog.

Output of the Letter Text and Closing Salutation

Output of the actual letter text in the Detail band is completely routine. We simply reference the Memo field of the Letter table in a report expression, define the report expression to stretch and to overflow onto subsequent pages, and set the width of the letter by sizing the report expression in the Detail band. (See Figure 13.39.)

FIGURE 13.39:

To output form letter text in the Detail band, reference the Letter table Memo field in a report expression defined to stretch and overflow on subsequent pages.

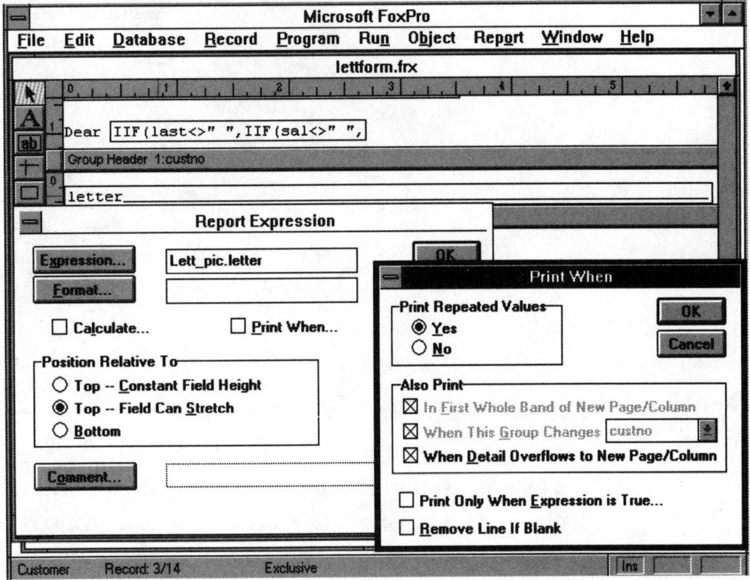

As to the closing salutation, we must place it in the Group Footer band, not the Page Footer band, so it will be output immediately after the letter text and not offset to the bottom of the page as defined by the Page Footer band. The overall results of the layout are indicated in Figure 13.40 by a letter output to the Page Preview window, zoomed out.

FIGURE 13.40:

Use the Page Preview window to check the position and alignment of objects in a form letter.

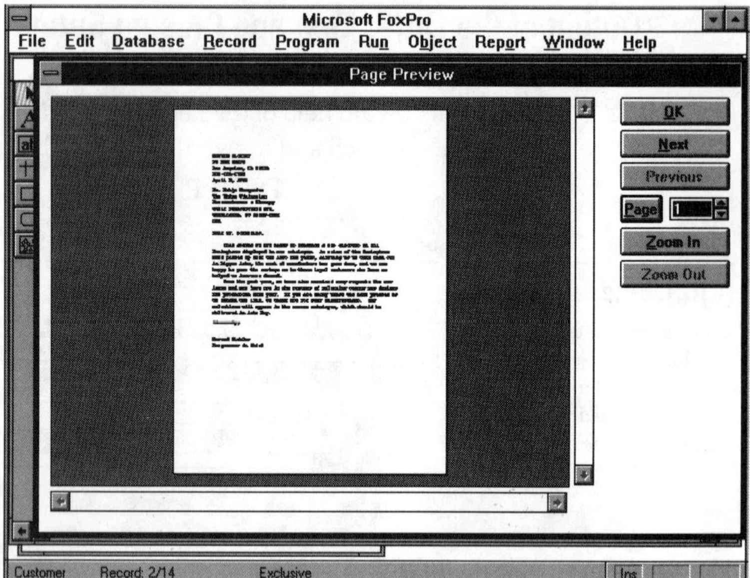

Producing Invoices and Statements

The MBS Report forms used to print invoices and customer statements combine the elements of a form letter with those of a group report presenting customer transactions and summary calculations. The Customer Statements Report form, States.frx, uses Custno as its group expression, while the Customer Invoice Report form, Invoice.frx, uses Custno + Saleno since it must produce a different invoice for each customer sale.

Controlling the Header in Multi-Page Forms

With respect to their Group Band definitions, States.frx and Invoice.frx work the same way. Both reports move FoxPro to a new page and reset the page number to 1 when the group expression changes. Both reports also repeat the Group Header band on subsequent pages, though in the case of States.frx, we use a conditional statement to control the printing of the customer's balance forward on the second and following pages of customer statements running over one page. Our reason for working in this way should be apparent from Figure 13.41, showing output from a sample MBS statement.

The balance-forward figure appearing just above the statement detail, listing customer sales and payments over the current period, has no place on the second or third page of any statement since it represents the beginning of the running figures for customer balance, maintained in the rightmost column of the Detail band. As

FIGURE 13.41:

Report form States.frx, used to print customer statements, is a group report designed to move FoxPro to a new page and reset the page number to 1 when the group expression (Custno) changes.

04/04/95 Customer Statement Page - 1

Howard Dickler
PO Box 34293
Los Angeles, CA 90034
310-204-2780

Statement for: 100001
Dr. Katje Borgesius
The White Visitation
Entertainment & Therapy
34012 Pennsylvania Ave.
Washington, DC 02043-2222
USA
204-333-3333

Date	Invoice	Charge	Credit	Type	Balance
				Balance Forward:	0.00
03/04/95	100006	1,870.00		Sale	1,870.00
03/04/95	100007	5,940.00		Sale	7,810.00
03/04/95	100012	15,290.00		Sale	23,100.00
03/04/95	100004	3,410.00		Sale	26,510.00
03/04/95	100004		3,410.00	Payment	23,100.00
03/04/95	100007		5,940.00	Payment	17,160.00
03/04/95	100012		10,000.00	Payment	7,160.00
03/04/95	100006		200.00	Return	6,960.00
03/04/95	100012		450.00	Return	6,510.00
03/04/95	100006	100.00		Bk Adj (db)	6,610.00
03/08/95	100012		500.00	Payment	6,110.00
	Totals:	26,610.00	20,500.00		

Current	30 Days	60 Days	90 Days	120 Days+
6,110.00				
		Please Remit Present Balance of:		$6,110.00

shown in Figure 13.42, the report expression outputting L_balance (representing the customer's last balance) and the text object used to label the "Balance Forward" are both included in the Group Header band.

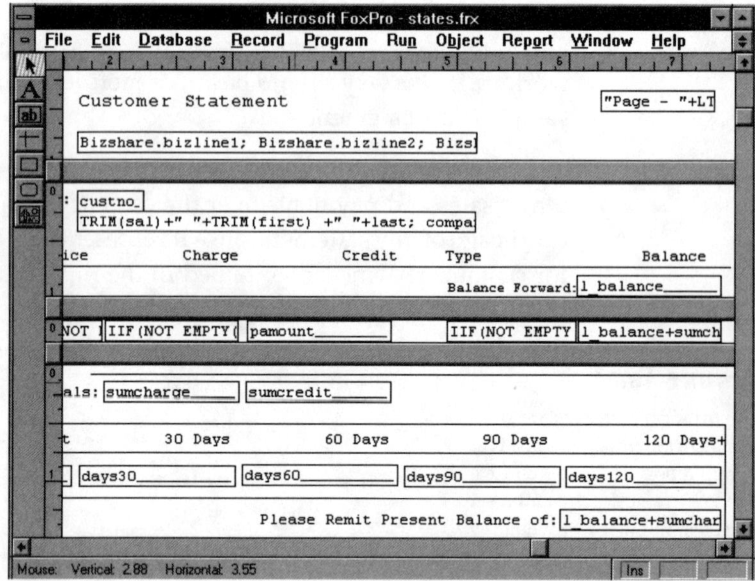

FIGURE 13.42:
Report layout of States.frx, used to produce customer statements, outputs the balance forward at the bottom of the Group Header band only of page 1 of a statement.

To exclude the balance-forward figure and its accompanying text object from the Group Header band of the second and following pages of a customer statement, we make their printing conditional on the expression _PAGENO = 1, which we enter through their respective Print When dialogs. Figure 13.43 shows the Expression Builder open for entry of the condition controlling the printing of L_balance.

Of course, this is small potatoes in comparison with what you can or may be expected to do when designing multi-page forms. It may be necessary to use an entirely different header on different pages. We might, for example, make output of all objects already present in States.frx's page and group headers conditional on _PAGENO = 1 and then overlay them in the bands with a second set of objects to be printed when _PAGENO > 1. The modulus function can be used to print objects on all odd- or even-numbered pages. The expression MOD(_PAGENO, 2) = 0 will

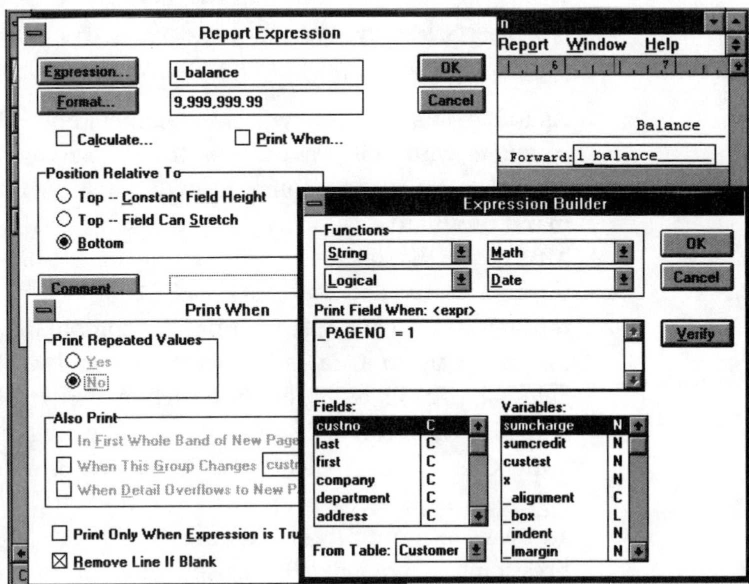

FIGURE 13.43:

The printing of any object in a Report form can be made conditional on an expression entered through the object's Print When dialog.

be true only when _PAGENO can be divided by 2 without any remainder. Change the equal sign to not equal (<>) and you have the expression for enabling output to odd-numbered pages. Compound expressions can be used to achieve a variety of different effects.

WARNING

As previously mentioned, the _PAGENO system variable may not keep track of the correct page number during execution of a group report that begins each new group on a new page and resets the page number to 1. If this is the case with your copy of FoxPro, you can get around this problem using the work-around provided at the end of this chapter.

With respect to work space, in entering the heading of a multi-page form like States.frx or Invoice.frx, we are free to use the Page Header and Group Header bands as we choose. (Since the group on the page does not change, the page header and group header amount to the same thing, though their order of output is set.) Take advantage of this state of affairs if it is necessary to mix text objects with stretch report fields in the page heading. Using the page header and group header, in other words, we have two tops and two bottoms to work with in fixing the positions of text objects, so they will not be overwritten or surpassed by output from stretch report expressions appearing in previous lines of the same band.

As to the data we display in the statement and invoice headers, as in the printing of letters with Lettform.frx, we draw the return address from Bizshare.dbf. All other data in States.frx comes from the Customer table by way of the SELECT command result table report, discussed in Chapter 12. Invoice.frx, however, is the one MBS report that takes its data from the main MBS tables, as organized and filtered through the use of SET RELATION, SET SKIP, and SET FILTER. Since each invoice represents not just a customer but the combination of a customer and a particular invoice—Custno + Saleno—report header data derives from the Customer and Sales tables as linked through the action of SET RELATION TO custno INTO Sales and SET SKIP TO Sales. On the top line of our invoices, we print the Customer.Custno, Sales.Saleno, and Sales.Pono (purchase order number), as shown in Figure 13.44. Directly below we print the return address and customer name and address, both output with report expressions based on semicolon-delimited expression lists much like those used with Lettform.frx.

FIGURE 13.44:

The Page Header and Group Header bands of Invoice.frx, used to print MBS sales invoices, output data from the Customer and Sales tables, while invoice detail is taken from the Sales Detail and Inventory tables.

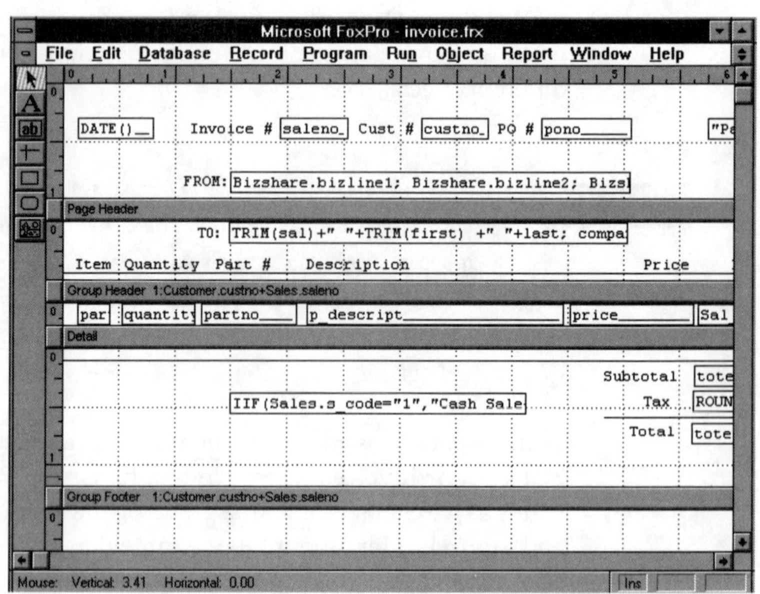

At this point, the use of text objects to provide the report fields included in the Detail band with titles probably seems incidental. Bear in mind, however, that it is often easier to enter all such titles using a single text object with blank spaces to separate each report field title from the next. This gets rid of the trouble of having to select and vertically align each text object separately; though placed in one text object, all titles must share the same font and style.

The Invoice Detail and Group Footer Bands

As you may recall from Chapter 6, where we laid out the multi-table view used in printing customer invoices, Invoice.frx detail is taken from the Sales Detail table, Sal_Det.dbf, and from the Inventory table (alias Invsales), which is used exclusively as a lookup file for input of sale item prices and part descriptions. Figure 13.45 shows a sample MBS invoice.

The report expressions used in Invoice.frx's Detail band are shown below, though only the first requires further discussion.

FIGURE 13.45:

In MBS sale invoices, report detail is taken from the Sales Detail table, while the Inventory table is used as a lookup file to supply part prices and character descriptions.

```
04/04/95    Invoice # 100012   Cust # 100001   PO # KBCH0004           Page - 1

            FROM: Howard Dickler
                  PO Box 34293
                  Los Angeles, CA 90034
                  310-204-2780
              TO: Dr. Katje Borgesius
                  The White Visitation
                  Entertainment & Therapy
                  34012 Pennsylvania Ave.
                  Washington DC 02043-222
                  USA
                  204-333-3333
```

Item	Quantity	Part #	Description	Price	Extension
1	6	10000001	Bronco Buster--Remington	450.00	2,700.00
2	3	10000004	End of Trail--Fraser	700.00	2,100.00
3	3	10000006	Rattlesnake--Remington	400.00	1,200.00
4	5	10000009	Salome--Foretay	300.00	1,500.00
5	3	10000013	Diane & Wolves--Preiss	600.00	1,800.00
6	4	10000021	Panther Girl--Bassin	500.00	2,000.00
7	2	10000027	Desdemona	500.00	1,000.00
8	2	10000030	Falcon--Moigniez	600.00	1,200.00
9	2	10000034	Clown--Santini	200.00	400.00
				Subtotal	13,900.00
			CHARGED to Customer Account	Tax	1,390.00
				Total	$15,290.00

Report Expression	Function
Invsales.Partno	Count items in invoice
Sal_det.Quantity	Quantity of item
Invsales.P_descript	Part description
Invsales.Price	Item price
Sal_det.Quantity*Invsales.Price	Total cost of item

Report expression Invsales.Partno is defined as a calculated report expression. Since the selected calculation is Count, it really doesn't make any difference which report expression we actually use. The count of any report expression will always be the same; the only variable is the selected reset interval. Because we want to use the expression to tally the number of items in each invoice, we select the group expression Customer.Custno+Sales.Saleno from the Calculate dialog's Reset popup. This resets the count to 0 when FoxPro finishes with the last record in each group (though not before the Group Footer band is executed). As to the other expressions, we have seen them all in Chapter 6, where we used them during the process of sale item entry. Since each field must be found in tables open in unselected work areas, we reference them using alias prefixes. Otherwise FoxPro will not be able to find them.

As to Invoice.frx's Group Footer band, we use it to print the subtotal, tax, and invoice total, as well as a character string labeling the invoice as a cash or charge, depending on the value in the Sales.S_code field. (Again, a value of 1 is used to indicate a cash sale, and 2 is used to indicate a charge.)

Report Expression	Function
Totexten	Subtotal
ROUND(totexten*Bizshare.taxrat,2)	Tax
totexten+ROUND(totexten*Bizshare.taxrat,2)	Total
IIF(Sales.s_code="1","Cash Sale--PAID", ; "CHARGED to Customer Account")	Cash or charge label

The only thing missing is where we get Totexten, the variable providing the total cost of all items in the sale. This is immediately available to us in the Group Footer band through use of a report variable that sums the expression Sal_det.Quantity* Invsales.Price for all report records—and is reset (after execution of the Group Footer band) when the group changes. Figure 13.46 shows the definition of report variable Totexten (short for *total extension*).

FIGURE 13.46:

When printing invoices, we use a report variable to sum the total cost of all items included in a sale.

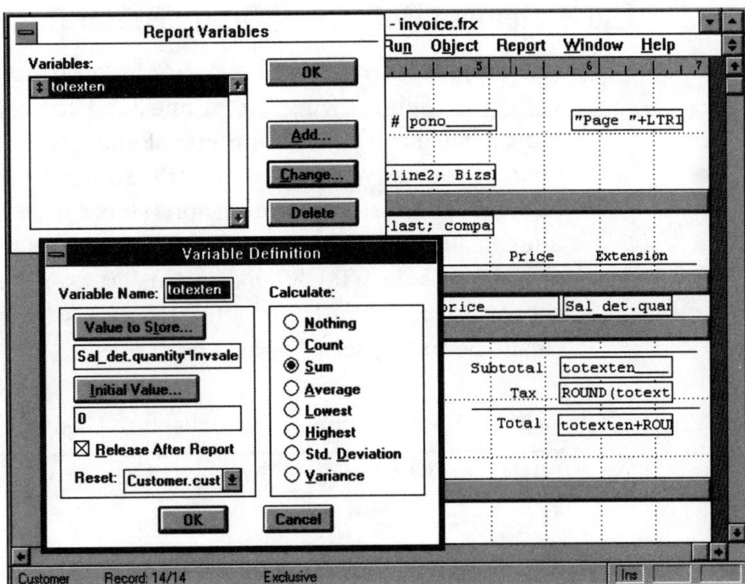

In the group footer, we report the invoice subtotal by including report variable Totexten in a report expression. Then, using the figure for tax rate, referenced from Bizshare.taxrat, the system values table, we calculate tax, using the ROUND() function to round the result, and then add Totexten to the tax calculation to return the invoice grand total in the last report expression.

NOTE

Report variables included in a Report or Label form are not only automatically initialized when the report is executed with the REPORT FORM command, they are also immediately initialized each time the Report form is opened in the Report Writer for modification. This way they can be used in report expressions entered with the Expression Builder and verified without error.

The Statement Detail and Group Footer Bands

The expressions used in States.frx's Detail band are a bit more complex than Invoice.frx's. This is owing, on the one hand, to the necessity of registering and summing detail records representing customer credits and debits differently and, on the other, to the native complexity of the source table, Report2, in which we combine all records of customer transactions stored in Sales.dbf and Payments.dbf that require inclusion in the statements. Here it is best to review the cursor's structure as created by SELECT UNION, in Cust_rpt.spr, before execution of States.frx. We show its structure in Table 13.1. For a discussion of the SELECT command used to create the cursor, see Chapter 12.

TABLE 13.1: Structure of Cursor Report2, Used in Statement Production

Field	Field Name	Type	Width	Dec	Function
1	Custno	C	6		Customer number
2	Date	D	8		Transaction date
3	P_code	C	1		Payment code 0-9
4	P_descript	C	6		Payment (sale) reference
5	Pc_descrip	C	15		Payment type description
6	Pamount	N	10	2	Payment amount
7	Saleno	C	6		Sales reference
8	Pono	C	8		Purchase order
9	Samount	N	10	2	Sale amount

In outputting statement detail, we begin easily enough with a report expression using Report2.date. The next report expression outputs the sales number. However, this is not as easy as entering Report2.saleno since the Payment table's P_descript field (represented here by Report2.P_descript) will generally be used to relate payments (or other transactions recorded in Payments.dbf) to sales by Saleno. If the report record represents a payment and not a sale (originating in Sales.dbf), we will want to output Report2.P_descript as the report record's sale number, in place of Saleno, which will, in any case, be empty. Our second report expression, titled in the header as Invoice (see Figure 13.44), must therefore look for a value in one table field and, if the field is empty, output the value in another field. This is achieved through the use of IIF().

```
IIF(NOT EMPTY(report2.saleno),report2.saleno,report2.p_descript)
```

Since only one of the fields can hold a value in any given record, there can be no conflicts. The complex expression, moreover, might be avoided by combining Sales.Saleno and Payments.P_descript in the same field when executing SELECT UNION. However, doing so would make it more difficult to move P_descript if it is adapted for a different use in the system.

The next expression, entering a customer charge, is no less complex. If the transaction record represents a sale, we output the value in Samount. However, if it doesn't represent a sale, it may represent a transaction stored in Payments.dbf. Since Payments table records can store customer charges—and will if P_code >= "5", according to the payment codes schema discussed in Chapter 5—if the record does not represent a customer sale, we must test P_code to see if the record is nonetheless a charge with P_code >= "5". If it is, we must output it in the Charge column. We handle this with the following expression:

```
IIF(NOT EMPTY(report2.saleno),report2.samount, ;
    IIF(Report2.p_code>="5",report2.pamount,0.00)
```

Output of Pamount, representing Payments.amount, we handle slightly differently. True, we must not enter the amount in the customer Credit column unless P_code < "5"; but we don't have to look to another field for the value to output if Pamount should not be used. We therefore define the report expression to use Report2.pamount but use the Print When dialog to make output of Pamount conditional on the expression Report2.P_code < "5".

Note that when outputting charge and credit amounts with the report expressions just described, we use the format @Z 9,999,999.99. Figure 13.47, for example, shows the Format dialog used with report expression Pamount. The @Z function is input through selection of the Blank If Zero check box. This ensures that 0.00 will not be output when the field is empty. The template symbol 9 allows for any number or a – (minus) sign, while the commas are placed where we want FoxPro to insert them, if and when the number is large enough to use them. You can use any of the other options available in the Format dialog to alter the way in which the amount is displayed.

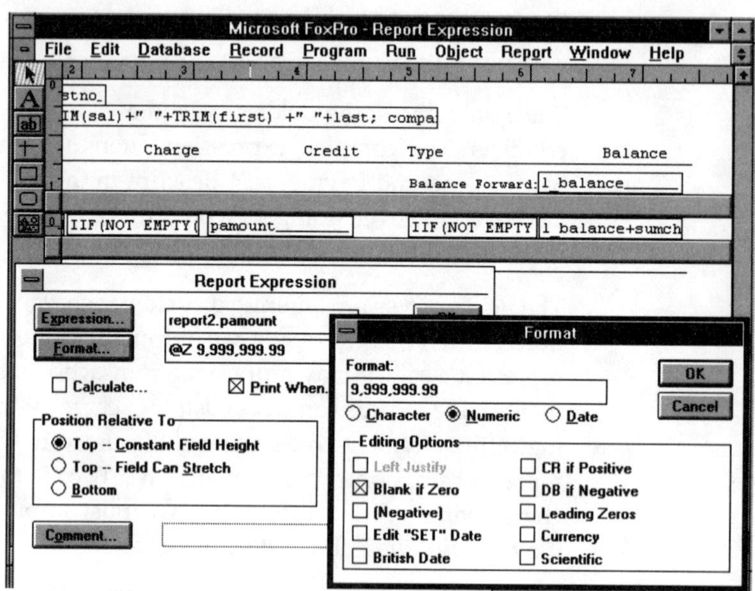

FIGURE 13.47:

In defining report expressions outputting or summing transaction amounts, we use the Format dialog to insert commas as needed in the numeric display and to output blanks instead of zeros if the amount field—here, Report2.pamount—is empty.

In outputting the transaction type in our statements, we must once again use IIF(), this time to output the string "Sale" if Report2.saleno is not blank. (This identifies the record as deriving from Sales.dbf.) However, if the transaction record originates from Payments.dbf, then we must output Report2.Pc_descrip, holding the full payment type description, originating from P_codes.dbf. (See Chapter 5 for a description of P_codes.dbf.) Still, in comparison with the other report expressions we have seen, this is relatively easy.

```
IIF(NOT EMPTY(report2.saleno),"Sale",report2.pc_descript)
```

Here again, we might have avoided using IIF() in the report expression had we written the SELECT UNION command used to create cursor Report2 slightly differently. (Instead of placing blanks in Pc_descript when placing sales records in Report2, we could have supplied the string "Sale".)

Finally, we come to the report expression outputting running figures for the customer balance as credits and charges are deducted or added to the balance-forward figure supplied by L_balance. Owing to the complexities involved in determining when a record in Report2 represents a credit or a debit, maintaining the running figure for the customer balance will be much easier if we have immediate access to report variables that do nothing but sum credits and charges for each customer (group), using the same expressions we employed above to control output from Samount and Pamount to the report columns for Credits and Charges. Figure 13.48, for example, shows the Report Variables dialog used to define report variable Sumcharge, used to sum the values in Samount and in Pamount when the Pamount represents customer charges.

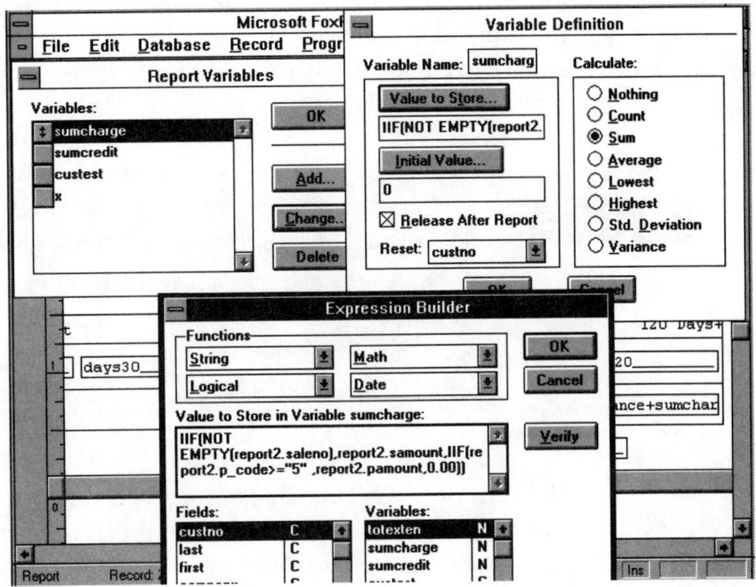

FIGURE 13.48: When printing customer statements with States.frx, we use report variables to sum customer charges from sales and from transactions entered in the Payments table representing customer debits resulting from finance charges, bookkeeping errors, and the like.

In defining Sumcharge, we select the Sum radio button to indicate the kind of calculation we want to make and enter 0 as the value Sumcharge must be reset to when the group (Report.Custno) changes. The variable expression instructs FoxPro to use Report2.samount in the sum when Report2.saleno is not empty and to use Pamount when Report2.saleno is empty and P_code >= "5"—meaning that Pamount represents a customer debit.

Report variable Sumcredit is the same as Sumcharge except for its expression, which simply tests to make sure that P_code < "5".

```
IIF(report2.p_code<"5", report2.pamount,0.00)
```

If it is, meaning that Pamount represents a customer credit, we allow FoxPro to add Pamount to Sumcredit. If it is not, we update Sumcredit with 0, so the variable's value remains unchanged.

With report variables Sumcharge and Sumcredit at hand, we can provide a running figure for customer balance in the Detail band by using the report expression L_balance + Sumcharge – Sumcredit. Moreover, turning our attention to States.frx's Group Footer band, Sumcharge and Sumcredit supply us with ready figures for outputting separate totals for customer charges and credits just below the report columns used to detail the individual charges and credits. We also reuse the expression L_balance + Sumcharge – Sumcredit at the bottom right of the rectangle used to set off customer account (debt-aging) data, where we output the present customer balance.

NOTE

When FoxPro updates report variables, it processes them in order according to their position in the report variable list. This is important when the expression used in one report variable references the value of another report variable. When this is the case, and assuming the referenced report variable must be updated before being used in the second report variable, you must be certain to position the variable being referenced above the report variable using it in the report variable list.

The other objects in States.frx's Group Footer band offer no challenges. We simply use a rectangle, two line objects, and text objects to set off and label the values present in the customer account (debt-aging) fields, drawn from the Customer table, or output blanks when they are 0. However, since the data available in executing Statements provides us with two ways of calculating Customer Present Balance—we can sum the debt-aging fields or use L_balance + Sumcharge – Sumcredit—we have a means of detecting customer statements in which the figures in the customer account fields do not jibe with L_balance plus all current customer debits minus all customer credits as represented by the transaction records. We take advantage of this state of affairs by placing a report field at the very bottom of the Group Footer band that outputs the string "*****DEFECTIVE STATEMENT******" when the two sums are not equal. (See Figure 13.49.) Output of the string is controlled through the use of the Print When dialog.

FIGURE 13.49:

When printing customer statements, if the customer's balance as calculated through the sum of the account fields is not equal to the balance as calculated through the sum of L_balance plus all charges and minus all credits, we flag the statement as defective.

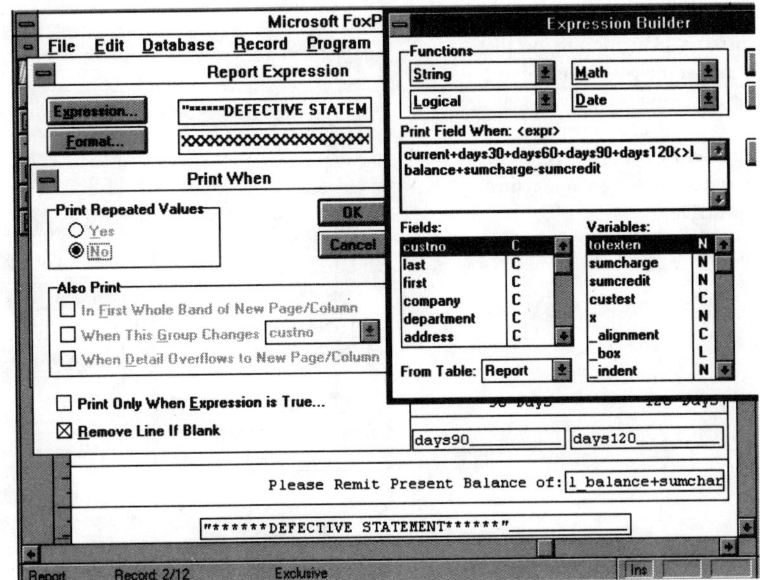

Correcting _PAGENO with Group Reports (New Page = 1)

When developing the MBS group reports, which must begin a new group on a new page and reset _PAGENO to 1, you may discover that _PAGENO does not work as expected, regardless of where you output it in the report. For example, when executing States.frx, after printing the first customer statement, the pages of which will be numbered correctly, the next customer statement will begin on page 2, not on page 1 as expected. If you find this happens with your reports, you can use the following work-around.

First, create a report variable that will hold a page number of your own making. In States.frx (and in Invoice.frx as it actually appears on disk), we use a variable named X, which calculates Nothing, holds an initial value of 0, is always updated with its own value, and is reset at the end of the report. Its definition is shown in Figure 13.50. During the execution of the report, memvar X, which will hold our customized page number, changes only when we change it.

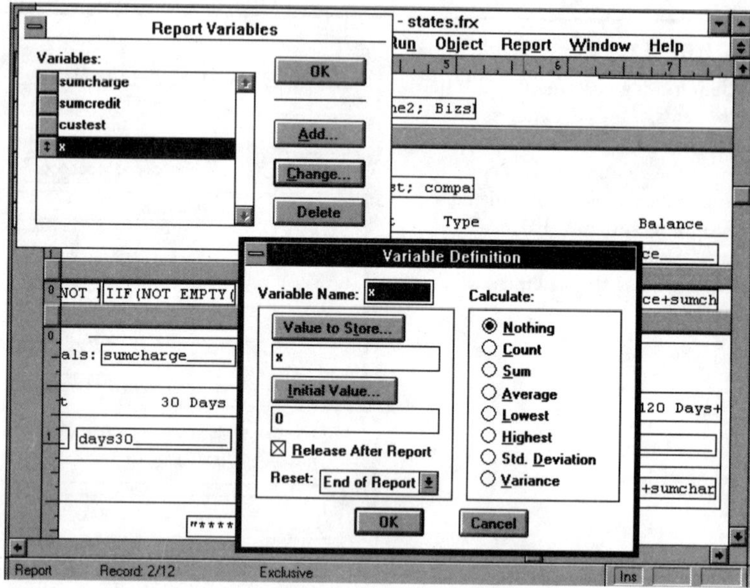

FIGURE 13.50: To report the page number correctly in a group report that must set the page number to 1 for each new group, you may need to calculate the page number by using a report variable to hold a value returned by a UDF.

The second thing we need is a report variable that will indicate when the group has changed. In States.frx and Invoice.frx, this is handled by report variable Custest, which calculates Nothing, is initially set to a value of "Z" (a value held by no Custno), is updated by FoxPro with the current value of Custno, and is reset at the end of each group. Its definition is shown in Figure 13.51.

The important thing about report variable Custest is that FoxPro will not actually update it to hold the new group expression until it begins output of the objects in the new group's Detail band. In other words, when FoxPro executes the page header and group header for the first page of a new customer statement, the value of Custno <> Custest. This is important because if _PAGENO does not function correctly, we must create an alternative means of conditionally controlling the output

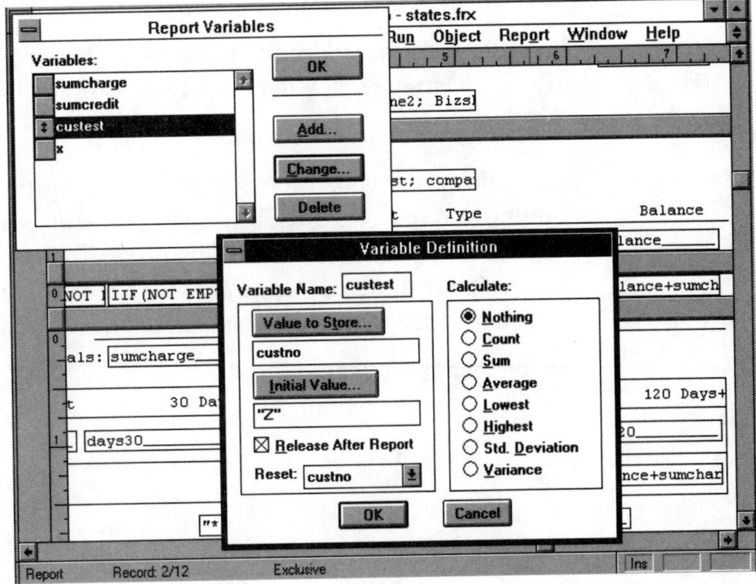

FIGURE 13.51:

In States.frx, we use report variable Custest to store the current group expression.

of objects in the page header and group header when the group changes and _PAGENO should properly be set to 1. Owing to the timing of FoxPro's update of report variables relative to its execution of page headers and group headers, the expression Custno <> custest gives us that means. (The second and following pages of any customer statement can be detected with Custno = Custest.)

As for obtaining the correct _PAGENO when _PAGENO fails, we use a UDF, stored in Bizlib.prg, the MBS procedure file, to update the value of report variable X, presented above, to hold the correct page number. Here is a version of function Mypageno, hard-coded for use with States.frx. We explain its operation in a moment.

```
FUNCTION mypageno
DO CASE
CASE _PAGENO = 1
    x = 1
CASE custno <> custest AND _PAGENO = 2
    x = 1
CASE custno = custest AND _PAGENO = 2
    x = 2
CASE custno = custest
    x = x + 1
```

```
ENDCASE
RETURN x
```

In States.frx's Page Header band, we reference function Mypageno in place of _PAGENO in the following report expression to output the page number:

```
"Page " + LTRIM(STR(mypageno()))
```

The action of function Mypageno is actually quite simple once you understand the conundrum it solves. Ideally, we should be able to update the value of memvar X relying only on the expression Custno <> Custest since we can rely upon this same expression in the Group and Page Header bands to conditionally control object output on the first page of a customer statement. We use it to detect page 1.

```
IF custno <> custest
    x = 1
ELSE
    x = x + 1
ENDIF
RETURN x
```

In fact, this does not work. X will also be set to 1 on the second page of a multi-page customer statement, for reasons that defy my own comprehension. The order in which FoxPro updates report variables reset when the group changes may be to blame and is probably responsible also for the difficulty with _PAGENO when new groups must be started on New Page = 1.

The work-around I finally arrived at involves using the way _PAGENO actually behaves when new groups must be started on a new page to correct the results of Custno <> Custest when the page number must be set to 1 and 2. (After page 2, the expression Custno = Custest works to increment X properly.) Though _PAGENO works incorrectly, it is nonetheless consistent in its results. The first customer statement will always have the correct page numbering with _PAGENO, regardless of how many pages it involves. The second and following customer statements will always begin with _PAGENO = 2. If you now look over function Mypageno's DO CASE structure, you may perceive its underlying logic. The only time _PAGENO = 1 will be with the first page of the first customer statement. We therefore set X to 1. Page number 1 is also indicated when _PAGENO = 2 and Custno <> Custest. Page number should be 2 only when Custno = Custest and _PAGENO = 2. Under all other circumstances, Custno = Custest can be used to update X with X + 1. Again, this work-around is entirely mechanical in its operation; it is designed to take advantage of the incorrect but consistent behavior of _PAGENO to correct the simpler work-around where it goes wrong.

Still, to make function Mypageno useful for inputting the correct page number with all group reports that must reset the page number to 1 when the group changes, we must revise it to handle any group expression.

```
FUNCTION mypageno
PARAMETER m.group,m.currgroup
DO CASE
CASE _pageno = 1
    x = 1
CASE m.group <> m.currgroup AND _pageno = 2
    x = 1
CASE m.group = m.currgroup AND _pageno = 2
    x = 2
CASE m.group = m.currgroup
    x = x + 1
ENDCASE
RETURN x
```

In a nutshell, we rewrite function Mypageno so we can pass it the current value of the group expression used by the current report as well as the current value of whatever report variable is employed in the report to track the current group. In States.frx this is variable Custest. (The function also assumes that report variable X is defined.) When we use function Mypageno in States.frx to input the correct page number, we must therefore provide it with the required parameters.

```
mpageno(<group expression>,<report variable with current group>)
```

We achieve this with mpageno(custno, custest). Function Mypageno then uses the values passed it in conducting its own tests with m.group and m.currgroup.

In the case of Invoice.frx, where the group expression is Customer.Custno + Sales.Saleno and we again use a report variable named Custest to track the current group, we reference the function instead with mpageno(Customer.Custno + Sales.Saleno, Custest). The names of the fields and/or memvars used to pass function Mypageno the values it requires are not important. The function only uses their values; it doesn't change them. It doesn't need to know their names.

WARNING While function Mypageno will work correctly to supply the correct page number in a group report designed to begin new groups on a fresh page and reset _PAGENO to 1, the report variable it uses to return the correct page number (memvar X) cannot be used to conditionally control output of other objects in the Page Header band. It just doesn't work. It can, however, be used reliably for this purpose in the Group Header band, though you are better off using the report variable used to track the current group since, with respect to indicating the first and subsequent pages (but not page numbers) of such a group report, it will always give correct results. For example, in States.frx's page header and group header, we can use Custno <> Custest to indicate a new group (page = 1) and Custno = Custest to indicate when we are on subsequent pages of a multi-page statement.

Restoring the Report Table View with a .prg File

As previously mentioned, Report forms can only save and restore environments constructed with normal Xbase tools. It cannot execute SELECT to restore a result table. You will therefore make report development much easier, when report data must be prepared with SELECT and more than one source table is involved, if you create a small .prg file that can be executed to instantly restore the report environment whenever you need to modify or test the report. (Again, you can also use a .qrp file produced with RQBE.)

In the MBS PRGS directory you will find Salcust.prg, Paycust.prg, and States.prg. Executing any of these programs, which are not included in the MBS project or application file, from the MBS home directory will immediately establish the table environment required by the Report form (.frx) of the corresponding name in the MBS DBFS\REPORTS subdirectory. Each program begins with the command CLEAR ALL to close all open tables and clear all memory objects. This is followed by SET PATH TO dbfs, which provides FoxPro with the path from the MBS home directory to the tables referenced in the SELECT command (or commands) that are then executed to establish the required report view. Note that we make them executable from the MBS home directory (through use of the SET PATH command) so they can be executed from the Command window when the MBS project is open in the Project Manager. This gives us immediate access to each Report form in the system through use of the file list and Edit button. The SELECT commands that appear in these .prg files—they are all simplified versions of the SELECT commands issued in Cust_rpt.spr before the execution of REPORT FORM—were discussed in Chapter 12. These additional .prg files are provided in case you need to modify the Customer Sales, Customer Payments, or Customer Statements Report form. While they can all be called for edit, like any other Report form, without any tables open, having the required tables open and properly ordered will enable you to verify all expressions entered in the Expression Builder, make use of table field pick lists and popups, and use the Page Preview window to examine the results, all without error.

Some Words of Encouragement

You are now ready to do pretty much anything you want in creating a DBMS that takes full advantage of FoxPro for Windows' programming language. You know the tools—indeed, two types of tools, including the set of FoxPro commands and functions that make everything happen and the FoxPro power tools (the Project Manager, Screen Builder, Menu Builder, and Report Writer) that make everything easy to put together. You also know your way around the Model Business System, which you can now explore and use as you choose. Moreover, owing to your familiarity with the FoxPro power tools and program architecture, you are prepared to open any FoxPro project in the Project Manager and make sense of what appears before you. This is important; it makes all the demonstration programs provided by Microsoft with FoxPro for Windows available for your inspection. After all, if you cannot find your way around the screen files included in a screen program—and this means knowing the functions of all pertinent READ clauses, not to mention how the commands typically used in them work—FoxPro projects and applications created by others will remain a closed book. For you, the book has been opened and you can begin to follow the examples provided by the MBS, the Microsoft demonstration programs, and any other FoxPro projects that come your way in building an event-driven DBMS, operable in a Windows environment, that meets your own specifications.

Good luck and good programming!

APPENDICES

APPENDIX

A

MBS Installation and File Listings

This appendix provides instructions for installing the Model Business System (MBS) on your computer. The complete process involves two steps, owing to the necessity of building MBS.app, the application file executing the MBS, using the FoxPro Project Manager after copying all files on the MBS distribution disk to the MBS's new home directory on your hard disk. Following the installation instructions, we provide a list of all files included on the distribution disk along with brief descriptions of their functions in the MBS.

Note that the files on the distribution disk are arranged in a directory tree that matches the one required by the MBS when installed on your hard disk. Since no files on the distribution disk are compressed, the installation can be performed manually with the DOS XCOPY command, provided that the /s switch is used to include subdirectories and all subdirectory files in the copy. This, in fact, is how the MBS installation program, Install.bat, works. Individual files on the distribution disk can also be manipulated in any way you choose with DOS, FoxPro, or the File Manager. I do not, however, recommend working with the MBS project or building the MBS application directly on the distribution disk; it is too small to accommodate the MBS application file and copies of all screen program source code files in addition to the files already present on it.

WARNING

Before installing the MBS on your hard disk, make a backup copy of the distribution disk. This can be done with the DOS DISKCOPY command. If you want to place the backup on a disk with a different format, use XCOPY with the subdirectory (/s) switch.

Installing the MBS

To install the MBS on your computer using the MBS installation (DOS batch file) program, Install.bat, follow these steps:

1. Access the DOS prompt in any way you choose.

Any current directory will do, though I recommend taking all actions from the root directory.

2. Use the DOS MD (or MKDIR) command to create a new home directory for the MBS.

This is the directory the MBS project will be copied into, along with its many subdirectories. (The MBS directory tree is discussed in Chapter 7, though you can use the DOS TREE command to view it directly on the distribution disk if you are interested.)

The MBS home directory can be placed anywhere in your hard disk's directory tree. You can even use an existing directory, though I recommend keeping the MBS and its files away from other work. The best course, in any case, will be to use the home directory I employed in developing it—\FOXPROW\APPS\BIGBIZ—assuming \FOXPROW is your FoxPro for Windows home directory. (If it is not, just place APPS\BIGBIZ in the directory you are using.)

Working from the root directory of your hard disk—and assuming you have yet to create an APPS directory to hold your own applications, as recommended in the *FoxPro for Windows Developer's Guide*—use the following command to create it:

```
MD \FOXPROW\APPS
```

Now create subdirectory BIGBIZ to serve as the MBS home directory:

```
MD \FOXPROW\APPS\BIGBIZ
```

3. Once you have created the MBS home directory, place the distribution disk in your floppy disk drive and make that drive the current disk drive.

NOTE

The following instructions assume that disk drive A is the floppy disk drive you will use and disk drive C is your hard disk. Change the instructions as needed to conform with your computer's configuration.

4. Now, execute Install.bat, while passing it the drive and full path name of the MBS home directory.

If you will use \FOXPROW\APPS\BIGBIZ as recommended, enter the following command:

```
A> INSTALL C:\FOXPROW\APPS\BIGBIZ
```

Before copying any files, the installation program checks to make sure the indicated directory exists. If it does not, Install.bat terminates with a warning message. If the directory exists, Install.bat begins copying all files on the MBS distribution disk to your hard disk, using that directory as the MBS home directory. (Subdirectories are automatically created as needed.)

When the MBS installation program terminates, all files on the distribution disk will be present on your hard disk. You can log back to your hard drive and, after removing the distribution disk and putting it away, start (or switch to) FoxPro for Windows in order to rebuild MBS.app, the MBS application file, and regenerate all screen and menu program source code files. This way, you can run the MBS and also examine screen and menu program source code files as you wish, while making your way through the *Programmer's Guide*. We describe how to do this next.

Building and Executing the MBS Application

To build the MBS application and regenerate all screen and menu program source code files, start (or switch to) FoxPro for Windows and proceed as follows:

1. Issue the command SET DEFAULT TO <directory> in the Command window to select the MBS home directory as the default directory. IF \FOXPROW is the current directory and \FOXPROW\APPS\BIGBIZ is the MBS home directory, you can select the MBS home directory using a relative path name.

   ```
   SET DEFAULT TO APPS\BIGBIZ
   ```

2. Open the MBS project file, MBS.pjx, in the FoxPro Project Manager.

   ```
   MODIFY PROJECT mbs
   ```

3. If you have placed MBS in a directory other than \FOXPROW\APPS\BIGBIZ, before opening the MBS project file FoxPro will ask you to verify that the current directory should be made the MBS home directory. (See Figure A.1.) Select the Yes button.

4. When the MBS project is opened in the Project Manager, select the Build button to open the Build Option dialog. It is shown open in Figure A.2. (Unless the FoxPro Distribution Kit is installed on your computer, the Build Executable radio button will be disabled in the dialog.) To build MBS.app, select the Build Application radio button and the Rebuild All check box as indicated in Figure A.2. Then select the OK button to proceed.

5. If you have changed the MBS home directory, you will be asked if you want to save changes to the MBS project. Select the Yes button.

6. The Save As dialog shown in Figure A.3 will now appear on the screen. The MBS home directory is highlighted in the directory list and MBS.app, the default name FoxPro uses for the MBS project, appears in the Application Filename entry box. (If \FOXPROW\APPS\BIGBIZ is your MBS home directory, it will be highlighted in the directory list. In Figure A.3, we use \PG_MBS instead.) Regardless of which directory you are using as the MBS home directory, just select the Build button to build MBS.app.

FIGURE A.1:

If you install the MBS in a directory other than \FOXPROW\APPS\BIGBIZ, FoxPro asks you to verify that the current directory should be used as the project's new home directory. Just say Yes.

FIGURE A.2:
Use the Build dialog to build the MBS application so you can execute the application in FoxPro.

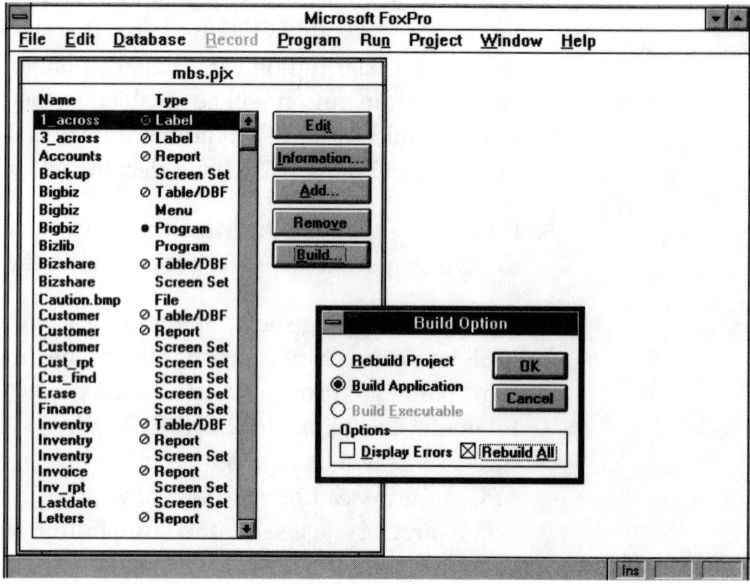

FIGURE A.3:
When the Save As dialog appears, select the Build button to build MBS.app in the MBS home directory.

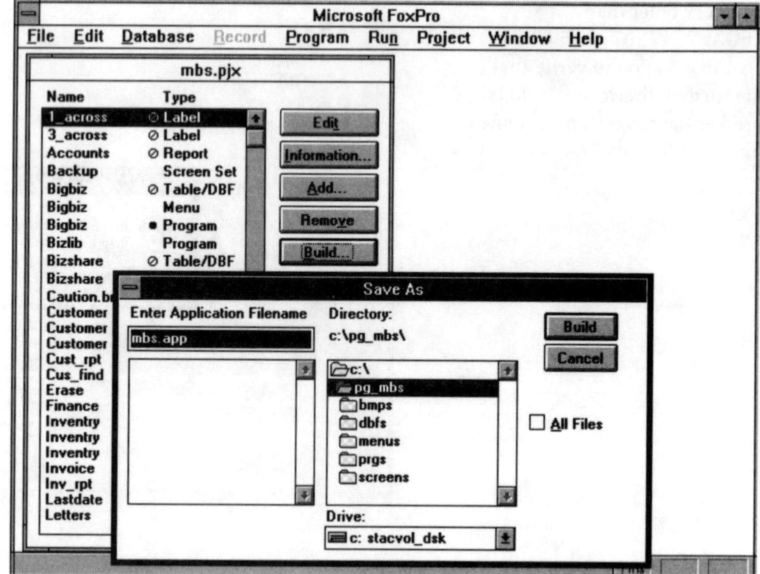

NOTE

If you are already familiar with the Project Manager, note that the Project Options dialog specifies that all screen and menu program source code files must be saved in the same directory used by the corresponding screen or menu (design) files. You may change this and other project options as you choose.

When the build action is completed, you are returned to the Project Manager's main window. If you know how to use the Project Manager, you can continue to use it to examine the MBS project. If you are not yet familar with the Project Manager, see Chapter 7, where you can examine the MBS project file as we discuss the operation and use of the FoxPro Project Manager. In the meantime you can explore the MBS by running it.

7. Close the Project Manager like any other FoxPro system window. Select Close from the File pulldown or from the window control box.

Executing the MBS

To execute the MBS, use SET DEFAULT to select the MBS home directory if it is not already the current directory. Then enter the command DO mbs in the Command window—or select Do from the Program pulldown to open the Do dialog, select MBS.app from the program list, and select the Do button.

Once the MBS is fully activated, you can begin using the MBS system menu to tour the system as you choose. As mentioned in the Introduction, I have left some test data in the Customer, Inventory, Letters, and system values tables to enable you to experiment with the MBS without having to waste time entering test data of your own. (Sale invoices cannot be entered unless records are present in the Inventory table.)

Suppressing the Startup Warning Message

When you first execute the MBS, you are likely to be greeted by an alert window warning you that a month has passed since customer statements were last printed. If this happens, press any key or press the mouse button to remove the window and activate the MBS system menu. Of course, as long as you use the MBS on a test basis, the warning message serves no useful purpose, though a single keystroke or click of the mouse button removes it. To prevent it from reappearing, select the Change Date of Last Billing option from the MBS Update pulldown. This opens the dialog shown in Figure A.4.

FIGURE A.4:

Select the Change Date of Last Billing option from the Update pulldown to store the current system date as the date of last billing. This will keep the message warning that statements must be printed from appearing on the screen when you start the MBS.

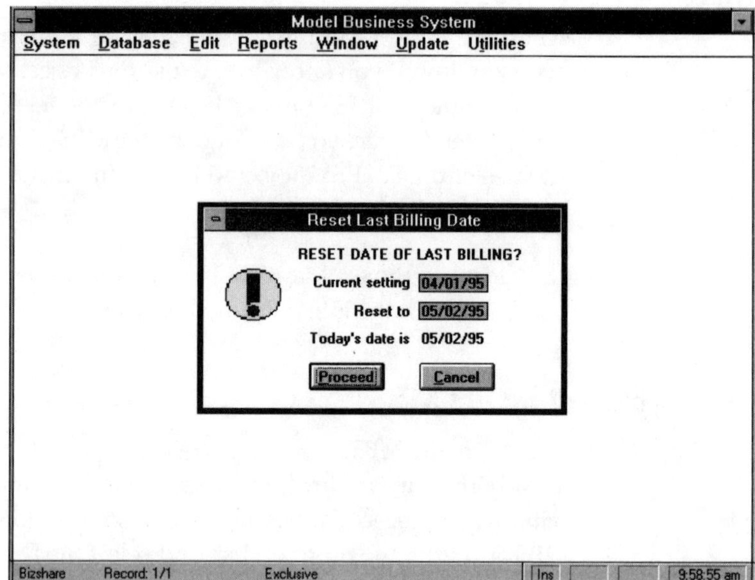

Select the dialog's Proceed button to save your current system date as the date statements were last printed. This will serve to suppress the warning message until the first day of the next month, when you can reuse the dialog or deactivate the warning by removing or commenting out the command lines in Bigbiz.prg, the MBS main program, that trigger it.

Starting and Using the MBS in Earnest

Since it is likely that many readers looking for a small accounts receivable system may find the MBS useful as is, I have included a special program file, Startup.prg, in the MBS \PRGS subdirectory. Startup.prg is designed to purge automatically all test data from the MBS tables. Startup.prg must be executed from the MBS home directory. To use it, issue the following command in the Command window:

```
DO prgs\startup
```

As a safeguard, Startup.prg asks you to confirm that you want to erase all test data. If you confirm the action, Startup.prg then erases all data found in the MBS tables with the ZAP command. There is, however, one exception. The single record in Bizshare.dbf (the MBS system values table, introduced in Chapter 2) is not erased. The data fields used to hold the last Custno (customer number), Saleno (sales invoice number), and Partno (inventory part number) assigned by the MBS are set to their proper startup values of 100000, 100000, and 10000000, respectively. All other fields in Bizshare.dbf, with the exception of Bizshare.order, used to set the default Customer table order, are left empty. Of course, you can modify Startup.prg's action as you choose by opening it with MODIFY COMMAND prgs\startup. You are hardly compelled to use it or any other program provided on the distribution disk as is.

NOTE

If you plan to use the MBS to produce customer statements, be sure to use the Change Date of Last Billing option on the Update pulldown to store the date you begin using the system as the date of last billing. (The date of last billing is also used by the MBS as the date the new current billing period begins.) MBS statement-printing protocol is discussed in Chapters 2, 5, and 6.)

MBS File Listings

In this section, we include a list of all files found on the MBS distribution disk and a brief description of their functions in the MBS system. As an additional aid, index tags and index tag key expressions are listed under the tables with which they are used. To find more information about any of these files, refer to the index.

> **NOTE**
> For the sake of being complete, I have included the MBS application file, MBS.app, in the listings, though it is not actually included on the MBS distribution disk. It must be rebuilt through use of the Project Manager as described earlier in this appendix. On the other hand, I omit mention of Install.bat, the DOS batch file used to oversee MBS installation. When you build the MBS application file, screen and menu program source code files using the extensions .spr and .mpr will appear in the directories holding the screen and menu design files on which they are based. These source code files are not present on the distribution disk. Other files automatically created by the MBS are mentioned at the end of this section.

Project files stored in the MBS home directory:

Mbs.pjx/pjt	MBS project file (Use this project to generate the executable MBS application file, MBS.app.)

Application files stored in the MBS home directory:

MBS.app	MBS application file

Program (.prg) files stored in directory PRGS:

Program (.prg) files included in MBS.pjx and MBS.app:

Bigbiz.prg	MBS main program file
Bizlib.prg	MBS procedure file
Tablefix.prg	Reindex and Pack tables program

Program files included on disk but excluded from MBS.pjx and MBS.app:

Dimens.prg	Developer's tool used to dimension BROWSE windows
Invoice.prg	Sets environment for modification of Invoice.frx

Paycust.prg	Sets environment for modification of Paycust.frx
Salcust.prg	Sets environment for modification of Salcust.frx
Startup.prg	Purges MBS tables of test data
States.prg	Sets environment for modification of States.frx

Menu files stored in directory MENUS:

Bigbiz.mnx/mnt	MBS system menu file

Screen files stored in directory SCREENS:

Backup.scx/sct	Backup tables program
Bizshare.scx/sct	MBS system value data entry program
Control.scx/sct	Push button control window used in Letters.spr
Cus_find.scx/sct	Customer lookup and reorder dialog
Cust_rpt.scx/sct	Customer database reports window
Customer.scx/sct	Customer table data entry program
Erase.scx/sct	Global delete record dialog
Finance.scx/sct	Finance charge generation dialog
Inv_rpt.scx/sct	Inventory table reports window
Inventry.scx/sct	Inventory table data entry program
Lastdate.scx/sct	Change date of Last Billing dialog
Lett_rpt.scx/sct	Letter table reports window
Letters.scx/sct	Letter table data entry program (used with Control.scx in creating Letters.spr)
Payments.scx/sct	Payments table data entry program
Sales.scx/sct	Sales data entry program (calls Saletrns.spr)
Saletrns.scx/sct	Sales transaction data entry program
Update.scx/sct	Update customer accounts dialog

Tables, memo files, structural index files, and index tags stored in directory DBFS:

Bigbiz.dbf/fpt	MBS resource table/memo
Bizshare.dbf	MBS system value table
Customer.dbf /fpt/cdx	Customer table/memo/structural index
Tag: Company	Key: UPPER(company)
Custno	Custno
Names	UPPER(Last+First)
Deleted	DELETED()
Country	UPPER(Country)
Zip	Zip
History	History
Lastdate	Lastdate
Inventry.dbf /fpt/cdx	Inventory table/general/structural index
Tag: Partno	Key: Partno
P_descript	UPPER(P_descript)
Deleted	DELETED()
Letters.dbf /fpt/cdx	Letters table/memo/structural index
Tag: Name	Key: UPPER(Name)
Deleted	DELETED()
Mbshelp.dbf/fpt	MBS help table/memo
P_codes.dbf/cdx	Payment codes table/structural index
Tag: P_code	Key: P_code
Descript	Descript
Payments.dbf/cdx	Payments table/structural index
Tag: Payments	Key: Custno

Deleted	DELETED()
Date	Date
Sal_det.dbf/cdx	Sales detail table/structural index
Tag: Sal_det	Key: Saleno+Partno
Sales.dbf/cdx	Sales (summary) table/structural index
Tag: Sales	Key: Custno+Saleno
Deleted	DELETED()
Date	Date

Report forms stored in directory DBFS\REPORTS:

Accounts.frx/frt	Customer accounts (debt aging)
Customer.frx/frt	Customer list
Inventry.frx/frt	Inventory list
Invoice.frx/frt	Sales invoice
Letters.frx/frt	Letter table list
Lettform.frx/frt	Form letter generator
Paycust.frx/frt	Customer payments
Salcust.frx/frt	Customer sales
States.frx/frt	Customer statements

Label forms stored in directory DBFS\LABELS:

1_across.lbx/lbt	1-across label format
3_across.lbx/lbt	3-across label format

Bitmap (.bmp) files stored in directory BMPS:

Caution.bmp	Exclamation point referenced in Update.scx and Generate.scx
Locate.bmp	Looking glass referenced in Control.scx
MBS.bmp	MBS sign-on message referenced by Bigbiz.prg
Next.bmp	Down arrow referenced in Control.scx
Prior.bmp	Up arrow referenced in Control.scx
Qmark.bmp	Question mark referenced by function Question in Bizlib.prg
Stopsign.bmp	Stop sign referenced by procedure Alert in Bizlib.prg

NOTE

The MBS generates several files on its own that are not included in the above listings. These include several memory (.mem) files and Mbsmacs.fky, the MBS macro file, used to store operator-entered macros. Only Mbsmacs.fky will remain on disk upon termination of the MBS application. The .mem files are automatically erased, assuming the MBS terminates normally. In any case, these .mem files will not get in the way; the MBS will simply overwrite them as needed.

APPENDIX

B

Using the FoxPro Distribution Kit to Create .exe Programs

Now that you are developing your own programs, your next question should be, How do I get this out to the users? This question has two components: compiling the program to protect the source code and figuring out how to split up the files on floppy disks. The other consideration when distributing an executable version of your FoxPro applications is that your client does not need FoxPro for Windows to use your custom program.

The FoxPro Distribution Kit for Windows 2.6 addresses these points specifically and provides several other indispensable Windows tools as well. The Distribution Kit, or DK, can create a Windows-executable program from your original FoxPro source, whether it is in the form of .prg or .pjx files.

Once you have created your executable file, the DK can use the SetupWizard (Setup.app in your FoxPro directory) to compress all files in your development directory and then split them into files that exactly fill floppy disks of the size you specify. These include an installation program the intended end users can run to install the program and its associated files on their machines.

Installing the Distribution Kit

The FoxPro Distribution Kit for Windows programs and supporting files requires you to already have the FoxPro for Windows program installed on your computer. The installation starts like most other Windows installations: Select Run from the File menu in the Windows Program Manager and enter the floppy disk designator and SETUP in the dialog (or click Browse to select the drive and SETUP program).

The first of two dialogs asks for the name of the drive and directory where you wish to install the Distribution Kit. (See Figure B.1.) The Setup.app file is placed in this directory and a subdirectory named DKSETUP is created under it. It is recommended that this directory be the FoxPro for Windows directory. If you choose to install in a different directory, make sure the DOS PATH and your FoxPro path reflect the new directory.

In this dialog you can also select the Program group where the DK supporting program icons will be placed. These supporting programs include the Hotspot Editor, the Knowledge Base articles, and the Windows Style Guide. The Knowledge Base files contain current suggestions and help for creating Windows applications using software packages other than just Microsoft FoxPro.

FIGURE B.1:
Select Installation Directory and Group dialog

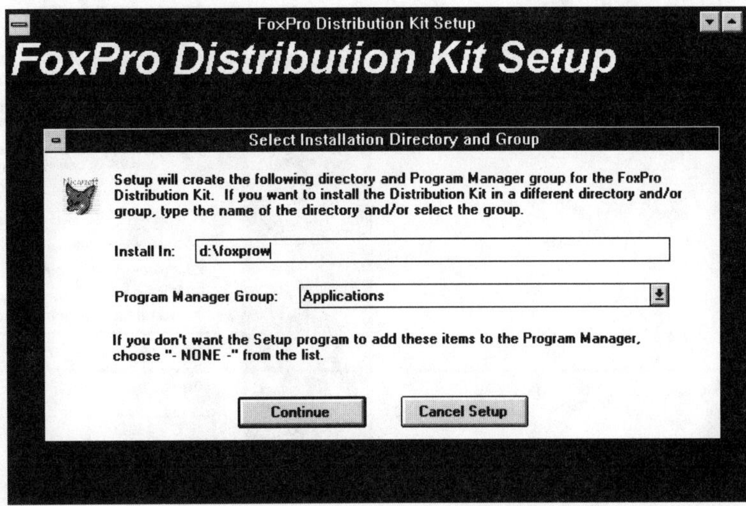

The Interface Design Guide, along with the Knowledge Base articles, is an invaluable tool for designing effective Windows applications. The Interface Design Guide provides tips and guidelines for creating graphical user interface (GUI) type displays and menu systems. Another good source for design specifications for GUI designs is the Apple Human Interface Guidelines.

The Hotspot Editor is a tool provided with the Distribution Kit for Windows to aid in creating hypergraphics used in Windows-style Help systems. The bitmap graphics can have several hotspots or hypergraphics attached to each graphic. They are enabled in the Help program.

In the second dialog, shown in Figure B.2, you select the DK files you want to set up on your system. If you have limited space on your system, you may not want to install the Windows Help Compiler, Windows Style Guide, or Knowledge Base articles.

FIGURE B.2:
FoxPro Distribution Kit Setup Options dialog

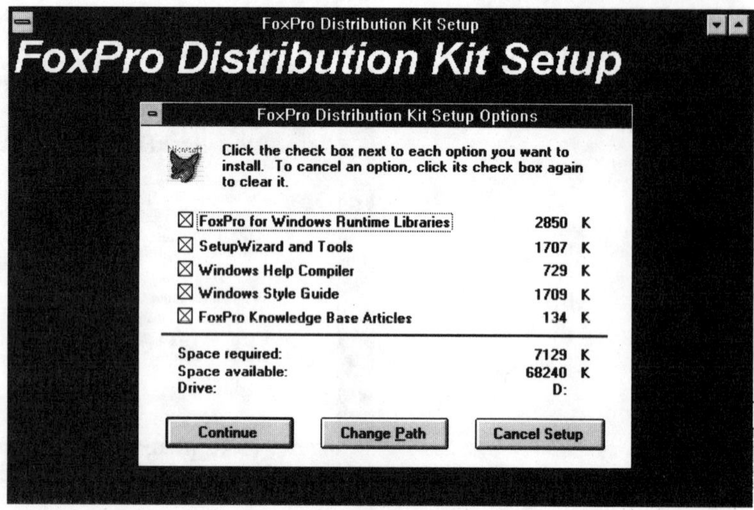

NOTE Hard drive space must be your first consideration before using the SetupWizard to compress and split up your program and other files for distribution. As when using the SORT command, you should have approximately three times as much space available as the space used by the files to be compressed.

Once you have specified the files to install, the installation routine prompts you for the appropriate disks as it copies the DK files. (By the way, the Distribution Kit for Windows installation was created by Microsoft using the SetupWizard application.)

The Executable Program File

When you have finished adding all the required files for your project, you are ready to create your executable program. The steps for creating an executable program from your source code were discussed in Chapter 7, where we looked at the Project Manager. At that time, before you installed the Distribution Kit software, the Build Executable selection was grayed out. When you go to the Project Manager after installing the DK, you will see that Build Executable is enabled. To compile/build your application into an .exe file, click Build Executable and then select OK.

The FoxPro Distribution Kit for Windows creates Compact .exe programs that are distributed with the version-specific Extended Support Library (.esl) file. The DK reads the list of program, menu, screen, and other required files needed in the application and links them together in one executable program.

Once you have created your executable application, there are several files you may need to include with the .exe file. If you have been using the Foxuser.fbf and Foxuser.fpt files to store application-specific resource information, place the resource files in the temporary directory you create for the SetupWizard, as described later in this appendix. While the FOXUSER resource file can be included in the .exe application, the resource file is made read-only. Keep this in mind if you intend the file to be updated by the user (or the application on an automatic basis). If you do not wish to include the FOXUSER resource file in the .exe file but do need it in the application, remember to place a copy of the resource file in the temporary directory that SetupWizard will use when creating the distribution disks.

If the application you have created takes advantage of FoxPro for DOS printer drivers or specifies printer drivers with the SET PDSETUP command, the Genpd.app and Driver2.fll files must also be placed with the executable application file before SetupWizard is used to create the distribution disks.

If your application is using any .fll (FoxPro for Windows Dynamic Link Libraries) files or any files excluded when the project is built, they must also be placed with the .exe and other files for distribution. The Foxtools.fll file can be distributed with your applications.

Finally, if you are using the FoxFont typeface shipped with FoxPro for Windows, the file Foxfont.fon must also be included with the files being distributed to end users. Without this file the screen fonts calling for FoxFont will not display correctly. Like the FOXUSER file, the Foxfont.fon file is placed in the temporary directory used by SetupWizard when creating the distribution disks.

Limitations on Executable Applications

There are several limitations to the executable programs you create with the Distribution Kit. First, they cannot access all of the commands used in the development version of FoxPro. The commands not supported, listed here, are those used primarily for creating and debugging programs.

BUILD APP	MODIFY SCREEN
BUILD EXE	SET
BUILD PROJECT	SET DEBUG
COMPILE	SET DEVELOPMENT
CREATE MENU	SET DOHISTORY
CREATE QUERY	SET ECHO
CREATE SCREEN	SET STEP
FILER	SET VIEW
MODIFY MENU	SUSPEND
MODIFY QUERY	

If any of these commands are encountered in the program, either they are ignored or a message, "Feature not available," is displayed on screen. VERSION() is used to determine whether the program is running from an .exe or using the development version of FoxPro. The VERSION() function can be used in a conditional IF or CASE statement to determine whether the application is being run under the development version or as an executable application.

VERSION() will return "FoxPro 2.6 EXE Support Library for Windows" if the application has been compiled with the DK for FoxPro for Windows using the 2.5 Distribution Kit. Using VERSION(), you can create a single version of your program for both the development and runtime versions of FoxPro.

The second restriction when using the Distribution Kit to provide your clients with FoxPro applications is that certain files provided with both the development and runtime FoxPro packages cannot be distributed with your .exe files. The following files cannot be distributed with your applications:

Addicon.app	Distribution Kit
Compress.exe	Distribution Kit
Foxprow.exe	FoxPro for Windows
Foxhelp.dbf	FoxPro for Windows

Foxhelp.fpt	FoxPro for Windows
Foxhelp.hlp	FoxPro for Windows
Mssp_am.lex	FoxPro for Windows
Mssp_br.lex	FoxPro for Windows
Msspell.dll	FoxPro for Windows
Msspell.fll	FoxPro for Windows
Reserved.fll	FoxPro for Windows
Spellchk.app	FoxPro for Windows

In addition to these files, the sample files provided with your FoxPro for Windows package cannot be distributed to your clients. However, the bitmap graphics (.bmp) files can be used in your applications; they just cannot be distributed as separate files.

The last limitation when distributing applications using the DK is that some of the FoxPro system menu functions are not available to the end user. The menus and menu options that are available are listed here:

File	Close
	Save
	Save As
	Revert
Edit	All Edit options
Window	Hide
	Hide All
	Show All
	Clear
	Cycle
	The names of all open windows

Help	Contents
	How to Use Help
	Search for Help on ...
	About FoxPro
	Calculator
	Calendar/Diary
	Puzzle

To disable any of these menus or menu options, use the RELEASE BAR, RELEASE PAD, or SET SKIP OF command.

Creating Your Distribution Disks with SetupWizard

The SetupWizard is an application (.app) distributed with the DK for the purpose of taking all of the files used in your application and creating a set of files to be placed on disks for distribution to your clients. The Wizard also places a Windows-style setup program on the first disk of the set.

The Wizard allows you to select from three different sizes of disks that the files will be distributed on. It then compresses the files and even splits files into smaller files that will fit on the disks. This eliminates the problem of deciding how to fit large files (such as the 3MB Foxw25xx.esl file) on the appropriate disks and then creating a professional installation routine.

NOTE The SetupWizard can be used to create installation disks and routines for more than just FoxPro-executable files. You can use it to install plain .prg files, .app files, and so on, or even .exe files created elsewhere. The Wizard doesn't care what it is compressing and parsing out for the disks; it simply assumes that the files specified are the ones you want to install.

Before You Run the SetupWizard

The first step in creating your distribution disks is to create a temporary directory on your hard drive that will contain all of the files you want to include in the application. There can be subdirectories below this directory to separate the files into database areas, report files, or whatever you have defined in the project. Because the Wizard will compress and parse any and all files found in this directory, it should be separate from your development directory; otherwise, you may get files installed that are not part of your application.

When the user installs the disks on the destination system, the subdirectories below the initial directory will be re-created automatically, with the appropriate files placed in these directories. Because the menus, screens, and program files used in the Model Business Systems program in this book are actually compiled into the final .exe file, it is not necessary to include these directories. In this project, we have a bmps and a dbfs subdirectory under the temporary directory used for the creation of the distribution files.

Remember to place the Foxwxxxx.esl (the xxxx is the version number of the DK and must match the version number of the development version of FoxPro for Windows) file in this directory if you are creating a set of distribution disks for a FoxPro-executable application; otherwise, you will be queried by the Wizard as to the location of the support library.

Running the SetupWizard

When all of your files and subdirectories are organized the way you want them, you are ready to run the SetupWizard. (You placed the Wizard application, Setup.app, in the FoxPro for Windows default directory when you installed the Distribution Kit.) Simply enter DO SETUP in the Command window or use the Run option from the Application pulldown of the FoxPro system menu to run Setup.app.

The dialogs discussed below locate the directories where files are located or are to be placed. Once you have created one set of distribution disks, each time you run the Wizard you will be presented with the names of the directories you used the last time you created disks. This information is saved in Dksetup.ini. Use this opportunity to set up your system so that you will have to make the fewest changes each time you create a new application and distribution disks.

The first dialog displayed by the Wizard, shown in Figure B.3, asks for the name of the directory (and drive, if the directory is not on the default drive) containing the files that are to be compressed and split up. This is the temporary directory you created (along with any desired subdirectories) for all of the files to be distributed. If you do not recall the name or location of this directory, you can click the Find button or press Alt+F; a Select Directory dialog will be displayed. Once you have selected your directory, click the Next button in the bottom-right corner of the dialog box.

FIGURE B.3:

Enter the name of the directory where the files to be compressed and split are located.

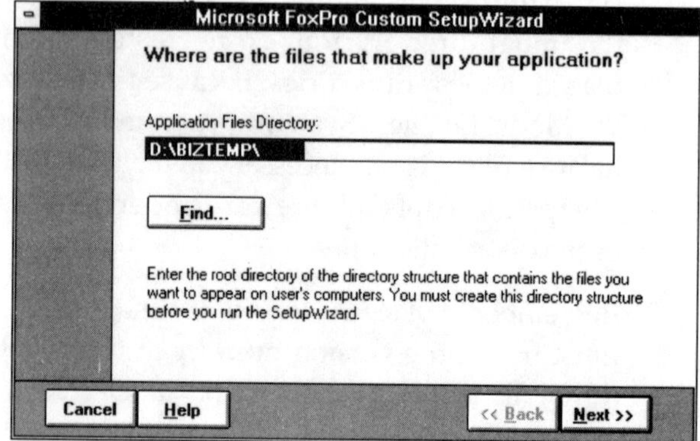

After specifying the location of the files, you are asked to specify a directory where the compressed files will be placed and the subdirectories that will contain the split files (also called Disk Images). (See Figure B.4.) This directory will be created by the Wizard if it does not already exist. When you have specified this directory, click the Next button to go on to the next dialog.

NOTE

If at any time during the setup procedure you want to go back to a previous dialog, press the Back button, which is located next to the Next button in the bottom-right corner of each dialog box. This option is available in all of the Wizard dialogs except the first.

FIGURE B.4:

Specify a destination directory for the compressed files.

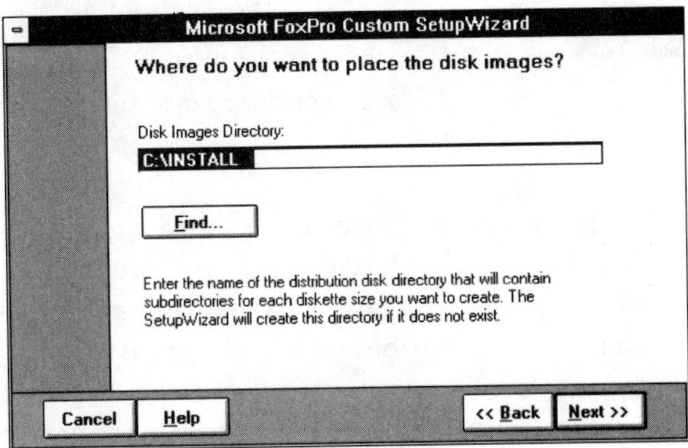

The next dialog you encounter asks you to select the sizes of the disks you intend to distribute your application on. (See Figure B.5.) You can select from 1.44MB 3.5-inch, 1.2MB 5.25-inch, and 720K 3.5-inch disks by clicking the appropriate check boxes. For each disk size you select, a subdirectory will be created under the disk images directory that you specified in the previous dialog. These subdirectories will be named disk144, disk12, and disk720 for the appropriate sizes selected.

FIGURE B.5:

Select the disk sizes for distributing the application.

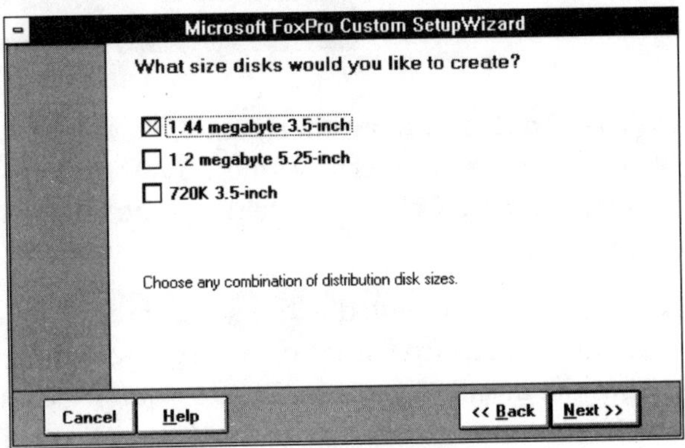

NOTE

In case you are wondering why there is no 360K 5.25-inch option, Microsoft decided that since systems using 386 or better processors are generally provided with 1.2MB or either of the 3.5-inch drives, the 360K option was not needed.

Following the disk size dialog, you are given the option to install a runtime version of Microsoft Graph with your application, as shown in Figure B.6. The Microsoft Graph program is one of the few accessories packaged with FoxPro for Windows that you can distribute with your applications.

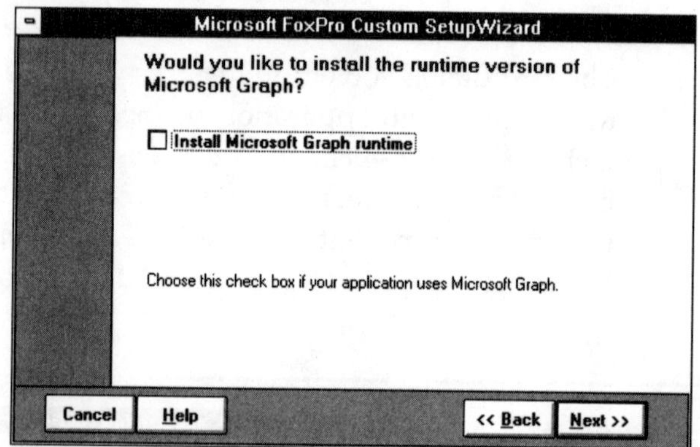

FIGURE B.6:

If your application is using Microsoft Graph to show data in a graph, select Install Microsoft Graph Runtime.

The next dialog, shown in Figure B.7, is where you specify your installation options. You indicate the directory (and drive) where you want the application and its files installed on the client's system and the Windows group in which to place the program icon.

You are also presented with a set of three installation options, where you can specify the changes the user can make to the default directory and program group during the installation. According to your selection here, the user can be allowed to change your default directory and program group, just the default directory, or neither of these. Simply check the radio button next to the installation option(s) you want the user to have and then click the Next button to continue the setup.

The next dialog (Figure B.8) is used to create the information the Windows Program Manager sees in the Program Item Properties in the Program Manager. This is where you specify the name of the application that will be run by the user, as well as other startup conditions and parameters. If you check the Suppress FoxPro Sign-on Screen box, the FoxPro logo will not be displayed when your custom application is started.

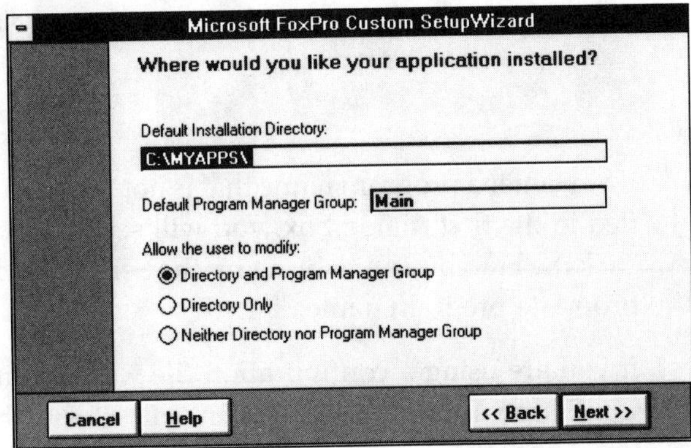

FIGURE B.7:
Enter the default installation directory and select the options users can access during the application installation.

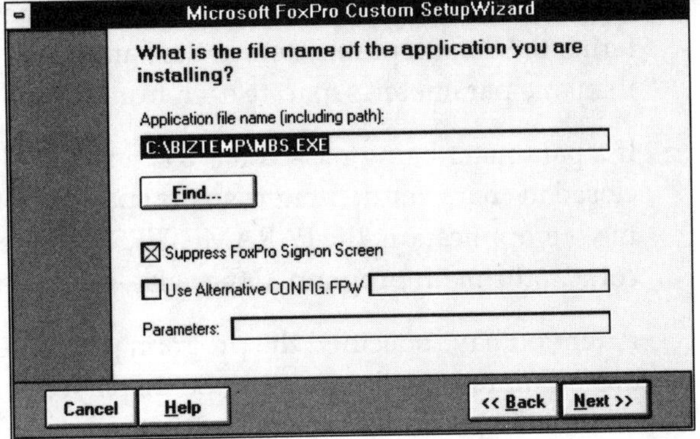

FIGURE B.8:
Specify (or Find) the application name and select other application startup options.

NOTE

While you can set the –T option in the SetupWizard or by running the Windows Program Item Properties dialog to disable the display of the FoxPro logo, the system window that is first loaded in your application shows "Microsoft FoxPro" in the title bar. To not display this title, place the TITLE = <myapp> statement in the Config.fpw file. This will display the title you indicate in <myapp> when the application is loaded.

If you enter a program name that is not found in the temporary directory you specified in the first dialog box, you will see an error message. Just click OK and then click the Find button to bring up the Select File dialog, where you can select the appropriate program name.

If you are using a configuration file with a name other than Config.fpw or if the Config.fpw file will be located in a directory other than the default program directory, check the Use Alternative CONFIG.FPW box and enter the name and/or path for the configuration file.

Another option with compiled FoxPro applications is to pass parameters at the time the program is loaded. These parameters can be set for the Program Manager by entering the default parameters in the Parameters text box. If you are specifying more than one parameter, separate each from the following with a space.

If a parameter being passed has a space included in it, the parameter must be enclosed in character delimiters so the space is not considered a parameter separator. In your application, the PARAMETERS statement must be the first line of program code in the main program. Otherwise, the parameters passed will not be loaded.

After you have specified the program properties and clicked the Next button, you are prompted for the name to be displayed with the icon in the program group when the application has been installed. (See Figure B.9.) You can use the same name you specified with TITLE in the Config.fpw or a different name. The user can change this name after the installation in the Program Item Properties function of the Program Manager.

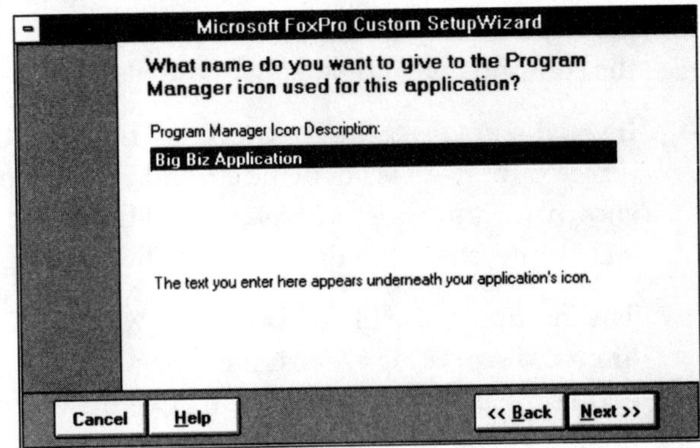

FIGURE B.9:

Enter the program title that will appear under the icon in the Program Manager.

The Wizard will let you optionally specify a program file to be run after the installation of your custom application has been completed. The program name is entered in the next dialog box, shown in Figure B.10, and can be the name of an executable program, batch file, or other valid program. As with the other dialogs, if you do not remember the name of the program to be run after the installation, click Find to open the Open dialog, where you can select the appropriate file name.

After entering an optional program you are presented with a dialog (shown in Figure B.11) where you enter a name to be displayed while the application is being installed by the end user. (If you don't enter an optional program, just press Enter.) This name can be whatever you like—perhaps Model Business Systems or Big Biz Application. You can also enter copyright information, which is placed in the About

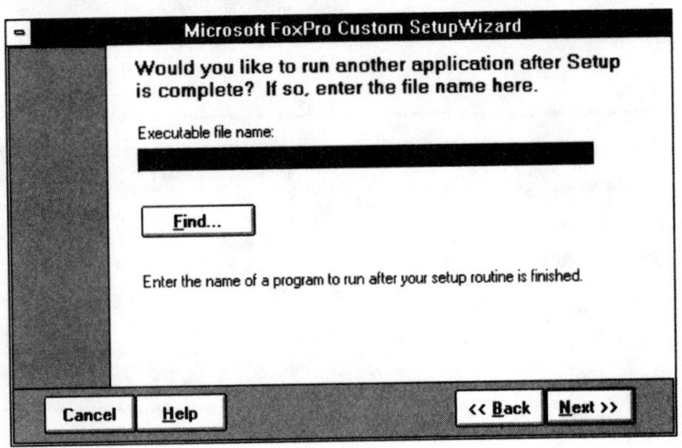

FIGURE B.10:

If you want to run a program immediately following the installation of your application, enter the name in the Executable File Name text box.

dialog in the application. At the bottom right of the dialog box shown in Figure B.11 are two buttons, labeled Back and OK. If you click OK, the SetupWizard will start the compression and parsing of the files.

If you did not place the Foxwxxxx.esl file with the application files in the temporary directory or if .esl is not in the current FoxPro default directory, the Error dialog box shown in Figure B.12 is displayed. At this point you have several options. If you select Locate, the Select dialog will be brought up so you can find the .esl file.

The location of the file will be saved with the Dksetup.ini file for future use. If you are not distributing the .esl file with your application because you know that the end user has the appropriate file or because you are using the Wizard to package a nonexecutable or non-FoxPro application, you can click Continue to proceed with the setup. If you need to get out of the SetupWizard, just select Stop.

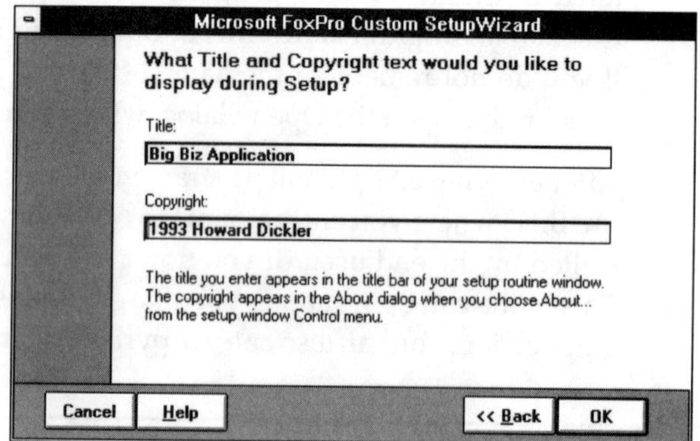

FIGURE B.11:

Enter the title and copyright text displayed in the Control window's About dialog.

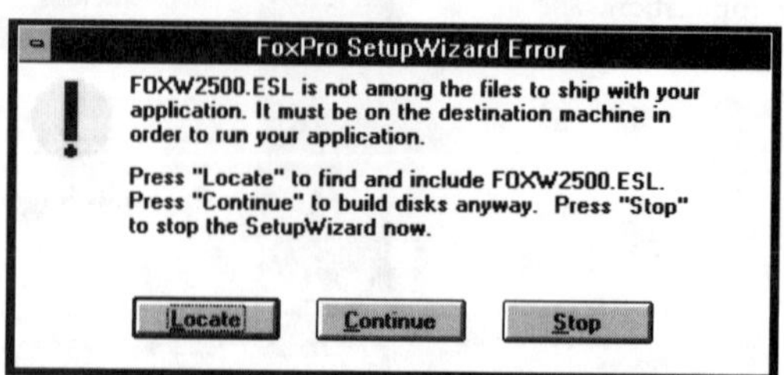

FIGURE B.12:

FoxPro SetupWizard Error box displayed when the location of Foxwxxxx.esl has not been specified

Once the Wizard has finished compressing and splitting up the files for distribution, you are shown one or more screens displaying disk and file information regarding the disk sizes you specified for distribution. You will see a separate screen for each disk size you defined, showing how many disks you will need to distribute your program and the number of files and total file size for each disk.

SetupWizard has also created a series of subdirectories under each of the diskxxx subdirectories under the compression directory you defined earlier. Under each diskxxx subdirectory is a series of subdirectories labeled disk1, disk2, disk3, and so on, matching the number of disks shown in the last screen. All you have to do is copy the contents of these final subdirectories onto separate floppy disks (disks matching the size of the diskxxx directory—disk144, disk12, or disk720).

The first disk/subdirectory already has the Windows Setup program and is used as the Setup disk for installing the program. It is not even necessary to give the disks a volume label of Disk 1, Disk 2, and so on; the Setup program reads a special file of each disk that contains the order of the disks for correct installation. The SetupWizard by itself is worth the cost of the Distribution Kit if you are distributing a large number of Windows programs or FoxPro applications.

All the settings you specified in SetupWizard are saved in the Dksetup.ini file in the FoxPro for Windows directory. The only setting that is not changed using the Wizard is that for the compression algorithm. This can be set to either 2 or 3. The default setting of 2 is the faster compression method; changing it to 3 creates smaller compressed files. The setting is expressed as

Algorithm = *n*

where *n* is either 2 or 3.

After each application has been created, two files, Dkcontrl.dbf and Dkcontrl.cdx, are created. These files keep track of information used by the Distribution Kit concerning the compressed files and how they were split. These files are overwritten each time you create a new set of disks (if you use the same compressed files directory structure).

Windows Tools Included with the Distribution Kit

There are several bonuses that come with the FoxPro Distribution Kit for Windows. Microsoft has included an application, Addicon.app, for attaching your own icons to the executable files you have created, as well as a generator for creating your own Windows-style Help files.

The Addicon application lets you specify one or more bitmap graphics, saved with an .ico file extension, that can be used by the Program Manager (or in the FoxPro application windows). The graphics can be created with the Paintbrush program (supplied with Windows), using the Save As function in Paintbrush to save the file in an icon-recognizable format.

As you may recall, FoxPro for Windows applications can use either .dbf- or Windows-style Help files. The DK comes with a Windows Help Compiler that allows you to use your word processor to create files that can then be compiled into your Help files. With this compiler and the Interface Design Guide, also provided in the DK, you can provide your applications with context-sensitive Help files using all of the standard Windows help methods.

APPENDIX

C

FoxPro 2.6 for the Migrating dBASE Programmer

C

While FoxPro for Windows 2.6 includes many enhancements that will be welcome to advanced FoxPro programmers, the lion's share of what's new in FoxPro 2.6 is dedicated to helping the hordes of programmers migrating from dBASE IV to FoxPro. For this reason, this appendix reviews what's new to FoxPro 2.6 for Windows from the standpoint of migrating dBASE IV programmers—and FoxPro programmers contracted to rework dBASE IV applications for execution under FoxPro 2.6.

TIP For a quick review of the commands and functions new to FoxPro 2.6, see the *New and Enhanced FoxPro Commands and Functions* topic in the FoxPro Help system.

Overview of FoxPro 2.6's dBASE Migration Tools

Intermediate dBASE IV users who actually employed the dBASE IV Control Center will find themselves right at home in FoxPro's new Catalog Manager, which will take over their existing dBASE catalogs and allow them to go on working with the files in their catalogs, much as they did in the dBASE IV Control Center. Those dBASE files requiring conversion—memo files, indexes, reports, screens, and label forms—are automatically converted by the FoxPro Catalog Manager's AutoMigrate program when you first open and use them. The process is seamless—just as they say in FoxPro Help—provided your forms weren't created using a variety of dBASE shortcuts for which the AutoMigrate program is unprepared. You must deal with these by modifying the converted forms in FoxPro.

TIP The FoxPro Catalog Manager will open and use existing dBASE IV Catalog (.CAT) files. There is no need to rebuild them. When you create new catalogs in FoxPro, however, you must use an .FPC extension.

The AutoMigrate program also makes the Catalog Manager important to advanced dBASE users and programmers since they must use it to convert all Screen (.SCR),

Report (.FRM), and Label (.LBL) forms included in a dBASE III or dBASE IV application for execution or modification under FoxPro. The AutoMigrate program does not overwrite the dBASE screen, report, and label design files, which must be present for FoxPro to convert the forms. AutoMigrate reads the design files and creates corresponding FoxPro design files, so you can then work with the forms using FoxPro's Screen Builder and Report Writer.

NOTE

dBASE III and dBASE IV tables require no translation unless they contain Memo fields. If they do, FoxPro makes the necessary conversion when you open them. This can be done in the Catalog Manager or from the Command window or system menu. If a table has associated index tags in a dBASE IV .MDX file, FoxPro converts them automatically when you open the table.

Intermediate dBASE IV and FoxPro users will also find the new *Wizards* quite helpful. The Wizards are a set of design tools intended to make the development of tables, queries, screen programs, and Label and Report forms semi-automatic. However, as with all such tools that make things easy, from the standpoint of programmers they are limited in what they actually do. They are no substitute for the Screen Builder and Report Writer, although they produce forms that can be modified by these more complex tools and may therefore be used as an alternative to Quick Screen and Quick Report (options built into the Screen Builder and Report Writer, respectively) for getting work under way.

Advanced dBASE programmers migrating to FoxPro will find the Wizards no less instructive than a FoxPro Quick Application. The forms they produce, the options they offer, and the simple step-by-step procedures they follow all attest to the functionality of the more complex tools you'll be using in FoxPro to create your screen programs and Report and Label forms. As with Quick Applications, which can be executed from the system menu and modified with the FoxPro Project Manager, screen programs and Report and Label forms produced by the Wizards also provide you with ideas on how things should look, now that you are programming in Windows.

TIP

Use the Screen, Report, and Label Wizards to design screen programs and Report and Label forms that approximate what you want. Where more complexity and/or different features are required, modify the resulting screen or report design files with the FoxPro Screen Builder or Report Writer. Since the Wizards themselves are FoxPro applications, they too may be regarded as examples of what you can do. You can open and examine them in the FoxPro Project Manager once you know your way around.

Just as important to the migrating dBASE IV programmer are the language enhancements—the commands and functions new to FoxPro 2.6—that will help you get your existing dBASE IV programs up and running smoothly under FoxPro. Although FoxPro's native command and function set dwarfs dBASE IV's, a few commands important to advanced dBASE IV programmers were missing in FoxPro 2.5. FoxPro 2.6 adds them. In several cases, FoxPro 2.5 commands and functions worked slightly differently than their dBASE IV counterparts. With FoxPro 2.6, the command SET COMPATIBLE DB4 has been enhanced to instruct FoxPro to mimic dBASE IV's behavior when executing these same commands and functions.

SET COMPATIBLE DB4 will help you get your dBASE IV programs running quickly under FoxPro, but leaving aside the forms that must be converted with the Catalog Manager, it won't take care of everything. There are a few other FoxPro commands you may need to employ to make your dBASE IV applications run smoothly under FoxPro 2.6. They are discussed in the section "Quick Fixes for Your dBASE Program Files" later in this appendix.

WARNING

The only major dBASE IV commands and functions not supported by FoxPro are those related to transaction processing with BEGIN/END TRANSACTION and to the dBASE IV PROTECT program. SQL also works quite differently in FoxPro than in dBASE IV. Be aware, however, of a small set of esoteric dBASE IV commands, functions, and command keywords that FoxPro 2.6 deliberately ignores—but which do not cause an error during program execution. (See the *Command and Function Differences in dBASE IV and FoxPro* and *Unsupported dBASE IV Commands or Functions* topics in FoxPro Help.)

NOTE

Coverage of FoxPro's Catalog Manager is limited in this appendix to showing how to use its AutoMigrate feature. No effort is made to explain what catalogs are or how to use the Catalog Manager as such. The new Wizards also receive no more than passing mention. As beginner tools, they are easily learned by using them and by referring to FoxPro Help as needed. In any case, if you are a migrating dBASE programmer, you already know what catalogs are, whether or not you used them in dBASE IV, and you will find the functionality of the Catalog Manager similar enough to the dBASE IV Control Center not to waste your time reading about it.

Making Your dBASE Applications Run Under FoxPro 2.6

There are three steps to making a typical menu-driven dBASE IV application run under FoxPro 2.6:

1. Converting Memo files and index tags

FoxPro handles this automatically.

2. Converting forms

This is also handled automatically, by the Catalog Manager. You may need to use the mouse, however, if you want to modify or execute multi-table forms while working in the Catalog Manager—that is, if you do not have suitable dBASE IV queries on hand for establishing the view required by the forms.

3. Opening your application's main (startup) program and making a few changes

NOTE

FoxPro reads dBASE query (.QBE) and program (.PRG) files without conversion, although it must recompile their corresponding object-code files in order to execute them. This is, of course, done automatically, just as in dBASE, when you execute the query or program.

The following pages give more ample coverage to the process of converting dBASE IV applications using the dBASE IV version of the Model Business System, featured in my *dBASE IV Developer's Handbook* (SYBEX, 1993), as an example. Bear in mind, however, that the idea here is simply to get the dBASE IV application running smoothly under FoxPro. The end result, you must be forewarned, will be bereft of the many features that give the FoxPro version of the Model Business System the look and feel of a bona fide Windows application. This much must be clear to anyone migrating to FoxPro. What's more, the converted application, developed for operation in DOS, is not likely to look nearly as good when run in Windows' graphical interface. Still, the point is to get the application running. You can then begin replacing the old dBASE IV components one by one, as discussed at the end of this appendix.

Converting Memo Files and Index Tags

dBASE and FoxPro tables are completely compatible, unless they include Memo fields, which point to incompatible memo files. So if your tables have no Memo fields, you can use the tables with either program, although the *Compatibility* topic in FoxPro Help warns against using them on a network with dBASE and FoxPro at the same time, since dBASE and FoxPro have incompatible file-locking mechanisms.

As to the memo files, the problem is that FoxPro uses them to store text as well as binary data, including graphical images, sound bites, and the like, while dBASE uses them only to store ASCII text. The storage techniques are necessarily different.

For this reason, FoxPro must convert dBASE memo files—and does so automatically when you open a dBASE table that includes Memo fields.

If you are working in the Catalog Manager, just select the Add push button when the Table list is active and use the Open dialog, shown in Figure C.1, to select and add a dBASE table to the open catalog. When you subsequently use or modify the table in the Catalog Manager, if it contains Memo fields, FoxPro wordlessly finds the dBASE memo file and carries out the conversion. On disk, the .DBT file will be gone and an .FPT (FoxPro memo file) will be found in its place.

FIGURE C.1:

Memo file conversion is automatic when you add a dBASE IV table with Memo fields to an open catalog and then use the table.

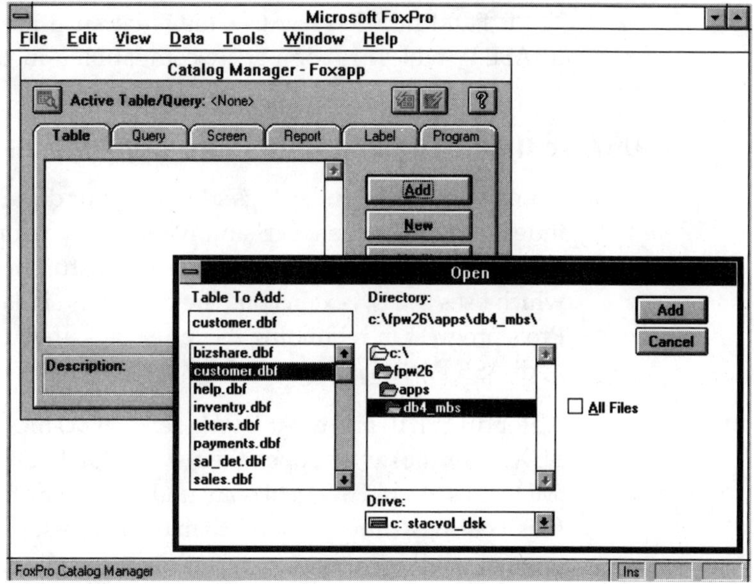

Still, you need not use the Catalog Manager to convert memo files. Anytime you open a table with FoxPro, if it has Memo fields pointing to a dBASE memo file, FoxPro will perform the conversion. However, when such a table is opened with USE <table>, issued through the Command window, in a program, or from the FoxPro system menu, FoxPro presents you with the Convert Memos dialog, shown in Figure C.2, since the action, as the message indicates, must render the table unusable in dBASE IV. (This dialog is not used in the Catalog Manager, since the Catalog Manager, in a manner of speaking, exists to convert your dBASE files.)

FIGURE C.2:

The Convert Memos dialog appears when you open dBASE IV data files containing memo files in the FoxPro Command window.

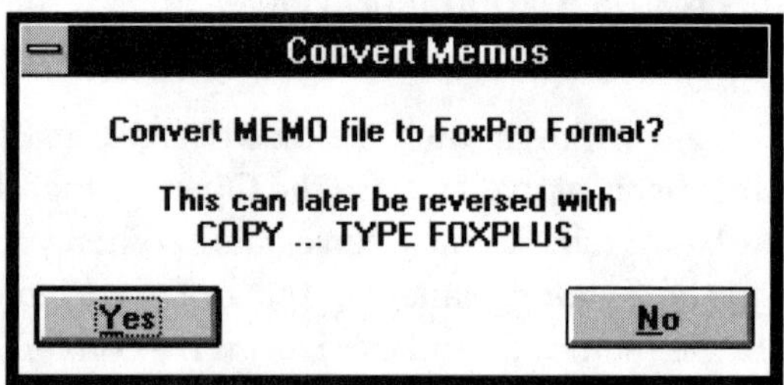

Of course, as the message in the Convert Memos dialog goes on to say, you can regain access to the table in dBASE by using FoxPro's COPY TO command with the TYPE FOXPLUS keywords. This is because FoxPlus tables and dBASE III and dBASE IV tables are completely compatible—including the memo files.

dBASE Index Tag and Index File Conversion

Don't worry about index tags stored in your dBASE IV production .MDX (multiple index tag) files. Whenever (and wherever) you open a dBASE IV table in FoxPro, FoxPro finds the .MDX file and, without disturbing it, creates its FoxPro equivalent, which uses a .CDX extension. The process is signaled by a message indicating FoxPro's progress in rebuilding the index tags. If you don't plan to use the table again in dBASE IV, you can erase the .MDX file, since FoxPro has no need of it.

As for dBASE III and dBASE IV index (.NDX) files, FoxPro converts them to its own .IDX index files as you open them with USE INDEX or SET INDEX TO. As with the .MDX files, the old .NDX files are undisturbed by the process. Non-production .MDX files, bearing a different name than their corresponding tables, must also be opened manually if FoxPro is to carry out the conversion.

Using the Catalog Manager to Convert dBASE Forms

Since most dBASE applications include any number of Report and Label forms and screen format files, the best way to begin preparing a dBASE application for execution under FoxPro is to convert the forms with the Catalog Manager. However, since screen forms require special consideration, the immediate discussion is limited to the conversion of Report and Label form files and then takes up the issues surrounding screen file conversion in the next section.

To begin converting your dBASE application's report (.FRM) and label (.LBL) files, activate the Catalog Manager, select File ➤ New Catalog, and use the Save As dialog to create a new (empty) catalog. (It is best to create a different catalog for each application and to place the catalog in the application's main directory, although a catalog can obviously include files in any directory.) To convert the dBASE IV MBS Report and Label forms, I created a catalog named DB4_MBS.FPC and placed it in the directory holding the MBS files, as shown in Figure C.3.

Strictly speaking, the Catalog Manager can convert dBASE forms without reference to the tables or multi-table views on which the forms are based. However, you will not be able to execute the forms in the Catalog Manager, and efforts to modify them (by accessing the Report Writer through the Catalog Manager) may be thwarted if you try to alter table-related elements.

This leaves you with two ways of using the Catalog Manager to perform the conversion. You can add all the tables belonging to your dBASE application to the new

FIGURE C.3:

When preparing a dBASE application to run under FoxPro, use the Catalog Manager to convert all the Report, Label, and Screen forms.

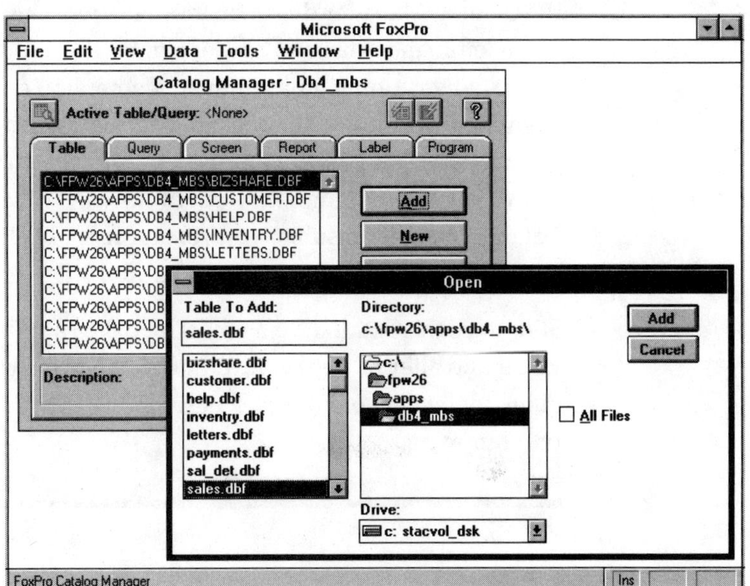

catalog, so that, prior to converting each form, you can activate the table or multi-table view on which it is based. This way you can test and/or modify the converted forms without leaving the Catalog Manager. Memo files belonging to the tables and supporting index tags will also be automatically converted in the bargain.

TIP

The additional advantage of establishing views before converting forms is that the Catalog Manager can then keep track of the data sources of the forms by storing this information in the open catalog. With this information on hand in the catalog, each time you print or modify a form in the Catalog Manager, the Catalog Manager can establish the required view. Of course, this assumes that you want to do more than simply convert the forms in the Catalog Manager.

Operation of the Catalog Manager

One thing to bear in mind about the Catalog Manager is that it is a FoxPro application. When you exit it, it saves the current environment. When you restart it, it restores the prior environment. In other words, unlike the dBASE Control Center, the Catalog Manager does not adopt the working environment set in the interactive (Command window) mode; nor, for that matter, will it maintain the environment set by running a program—whether you execute the program from the Command window or by selecting a program from the Catalog Manager's Program list. (When you run a program from within the Catalog Manager, the Catalog Manager gets completely out of the way. When the program terminates, the Catalog Manager resumes control and reestablishes its own environment, just as though you had never run the program.)

Still, since the Catalog Manager is a FoxPro application, you can attempt to revise it and alter its behavior, although this will be difficult to do without a thorough knowledge of FoxPro programming, which is very different from dBASE programming.

The alternative for those who are chomping at the bit to begin working on their converted applications in the FoxPro Project Manager is to simply use the Catalog Manager to convert the forms without troubling to add or open tables. You can then exit the Catalog Manager and test and modify the forms as needed in the Command window with MODIFY REPORT or MODIFY LABEL.

If you choose to use the Catalog Manager to establish required views prior to converting each form, begin by selecting the Add push button (when the Catalog Manager's Table list is active) to access the Open dialog and add your tables to the open catalog. Again, the Catalog Manager will convert all dBASE memo files and index tags automatically when you open their associated tables.

TIP

If the files you must add to a catalog are stored in different directories, select File ➤ Show Paths. This way the Catalog Manager will display the directory locations of all files listed in the open catalog.

Conversion of Single-Table Forms

To convert a form based on a single table, begin by opening the table with the Use (Table) push button, or double-click the table's name in the Table list to open and display the table in a BROWSE window. You can leave the BROWSE window open on the desktop as you go about your work converting the form since this is a Windows environment, not dBASE/DOS.

Next, move to the appropriate Catalog Manager tab and click the Add push button to activate the Open dialog and select the form requiring conversion. In Figure C.4, the Catalog Manager's Report tab was selected, so the Open dialog lists all available dBASE (.FRM) and FoxPro (.FRX) report design files in the selected directory.

Note that adding a form to the open catalog does not automatically convert it. You must open it for execution by clicking the Print (or Run) push button or open it for modification with Modify.

By far the easiest way to convert a Report or Label form is to select the Print push button. AutoMigrate immediately kicks in, as indicated by the appearance of a message window used to apprise you of its progress, and creates a FoxPro Report or Label form design (.FRX or .LBX) file based on the selected dBASE .FRM or .LBL

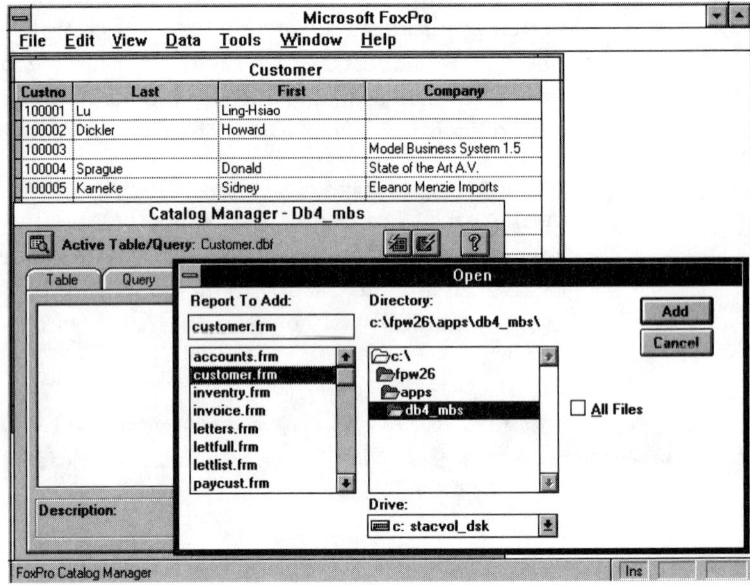

FIGURE C.4:
To convert dBASE IV reports for execution under FoxPro, add the .FRM files to the Catalog Report list.

file. (The Catalog Manager also changes the form's listing in the catalog to indicate the FoxPro .FRX or .LBX file instead of the dBASE file, although the latter is not erased from the disk.)

When the conversion is complete, the Catalog Manager Print dialog appears on the desktop. It allows you to direct the output to the printer (or to a file) via the Windows Print Manager, direct it to the Page Preview window, shown in Figure C.5, or cancel execution of the form.

TIP

If you want to convert your dBASE Report and Label forms without opening tables, use the Print push button. When the Catalog Manager Print dialog appears, just cancel the operation. (Going forward with the report will obviously result in error—although FoxPro quickly gives up and returns you to the Catalog Manager.)

As an alternative, you can select the Catalog window's Modify push button. AutoMigrate converts the Report or Label form so it can be opened for modification in the FoxPro Report (or Label) Writer, as shown in Figure C.6. Still, unless you are

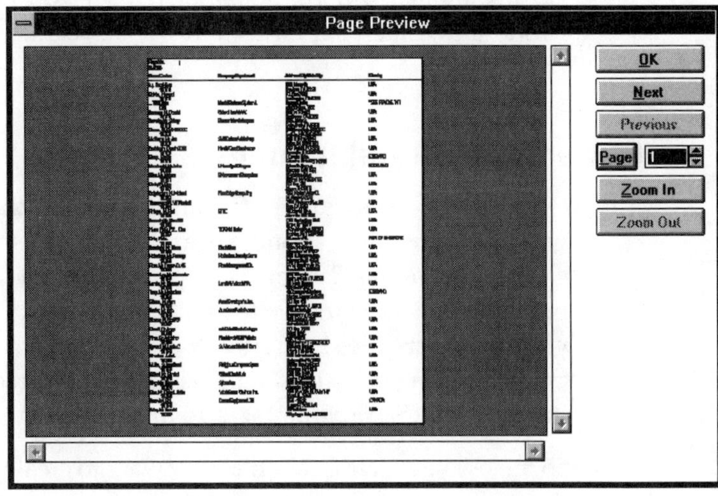

FIGURE C.5:

With FoxPro for Windows, you can display reports on the screen using the Page Preview window.

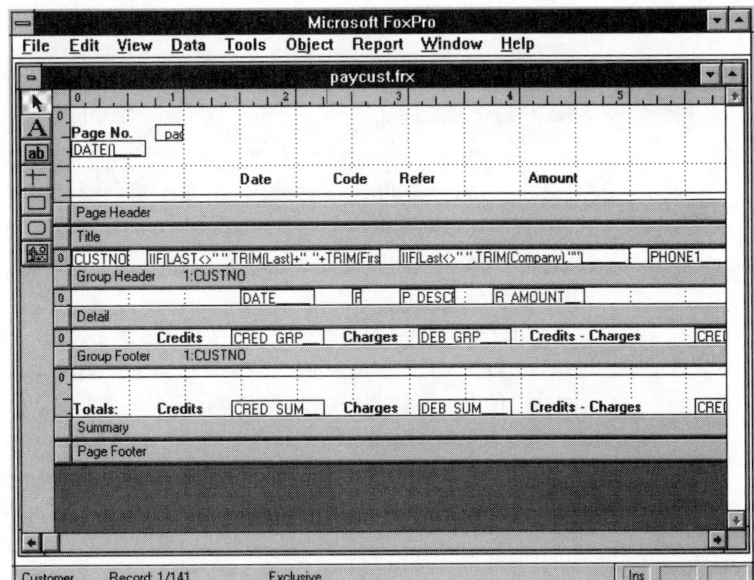

FIGURE C.6:

The Modify push button in the Catalog Manager activates the FoxPro Power Tool used to design or modify the selected file.

already familiar with the operation of the FoxPro Report Writer, it is best to put off efforts at revising your forms until you have time to explore this important FoxPro Power Tool.

Converting Multi-Table Forms

One of the downsides of the Catalog Manager is that you can't get to the Command window to set the environment, and as previously noted, you can't use programs executed from the Catalog Manager's Program tab to do it. If you want to set a multi-table view, you have to do it with a query. This will work out fine, provided you used query files in dBASE IV as an aid in writing your multi-table forms. The Catalog Manager can use them as is, although it recompiles the object code version. But most dBASE programmers, to my knowledge, never troubled with them.

So, unless you have query files—or want to create them in the Catalog Manager in the RQBE window or the Query Wizard—you might as well convert your multi-table Report and Label forms without opening any tables. Then you can exit the Catalog Manager and work with the converted forms using the Command window.

TIP

When you set a multi-file view with the View dialog in the Main FoxPro window, FoxPro outputs the commands in the Command window. The FoxPro commands establishing the view can be copied to the Clipboard and then inserted in a program. If you want a FoxPro view file instead, use CREATE VIEW <file> FROM ENVIRONMENT, just as you would in dBASE.

If you decide to build FoxPro queries in the Catalog Manager to suit your multi-table dBASE forms, you can do it quickly with the Updatable Query Wizard, which you are bound to use in any case. The other available options call on the use of RQBE/SQL-SELECT, which prepares the data by placing it all in a single table. While this is the preferred method of preparing data from multiple tables for a report in FoxPro, it is not suitable to your converted dBASE multi-table forms since they will employ alias prefixes to refer to two or more tables linked with SET RELATION. The Updatable Query Wizard, activated through the Query Wizards dialog, shown in Figure C.7, will produce the required view.

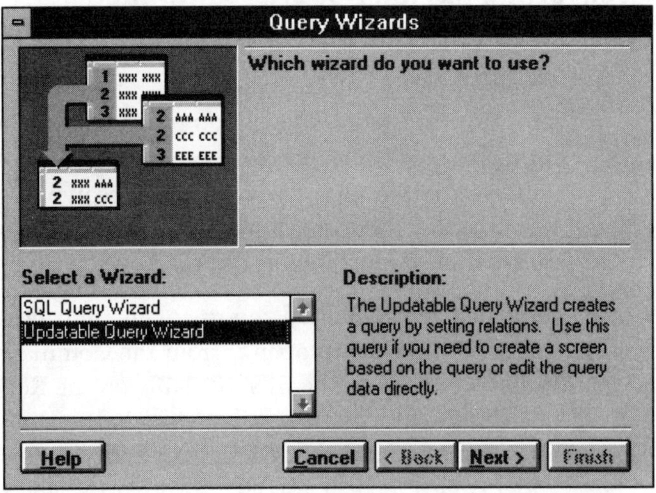

FIGURE C.7:

When creating queries in the Catalog Manager for use with your converted multi-table forms, be sure to use the Updatable Query Wizard. RQBE/SQL-SELECT will not execute the views expected by multi-table dBASE reports.

TIP

Because it works so quickly (if you know what you're doing), SQL-SELECT is the preferred tool for setting the view for reports. Since it combines all required data in a single table, it also simplifies the creation of reports, since you do not have to trouble with alias prefixes when defining report expressions and variables. Both are good reasons to consider modifying some or all of your converted multi-table forms—stripping out the alias prefixes—so they will work with SQL-SELECT. (SQL-SELECT is discussed in Chapter 12.)

Be sure to pause after converting a few forms to check them out through the Catalog Manager or by executing them from the Command window. A few difficulties may arise, owing to your use of dBASE programming techniques not anticipated by AutoMigrate. You may also be able to do more to improve the result quickly by going back to dBASE IV and revising the form before reconverting it. (Again, AutoMigrate leaves the dBASE files untouched. It creates its own report and label design files.)

When you are through converting your forms, you can move on to making whatever quick fixes are required to get your application's program files ready.

Converting dBASE Reports Containing 80+ Characters per Row

When converting dBASE reports that are defined to output more than 80 characters per row, don't panic when it appears that AutoMigrate ignored all report fields not fitting on an 8½-inch page, although this is certainly what appears to happen when you execute the report without modification. This is owing to the default Page Width setting the AutoMigrate program uses—and the Report Wizard and the Report Writer's Quick Report option, as well.

Just open the converted report for modification in the Catalog Manager or use MODIFY REPORT to open it from the Command window, and select the Report Writer's Layout dialog. It's available on the Report menu. Select the Print Setup push button to access the Print Setup dialog, shown in Figure C.8, and use the Page Size popup list to choose US Std Fanfold 14 7/8 x 11 or another option specifying a wider page. (You can also change the print orientation from Portrait to Landscape to achieve a wider page setting.) When you return to the Report Writer window, you will find the rest of your converted report fields included in the form. They were always there, but the defined page width was too small to include them.

If you intend to print the report on standard 8½- by 11-inch paper, downsize the widths of the report expressions until they fit on the 8½-inch page, and then change the Page Size setting back to 8 1/2 x 11.

Possible Areas of Difficulty with Converted Reports

When using the AutoMigrate program, I found some problems with my converted dBASE reports. Some of these areas of difficulty may be straightened out in your version of FoxPro.

- The conversion to proportional font in the converted reports may result in greater-than-desired margins between report columns since the columns must be defined to accommodate capital letters. (In proportional fonts, the letters, of course, have different sizes.) If this happens, you must modify the form and manually reduce the report expression widths as needed.

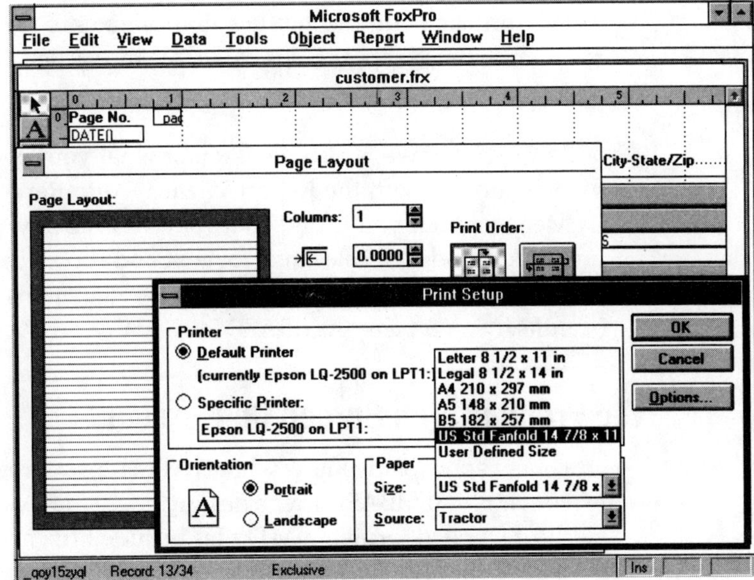

FIGURE C.8: When converting dBASE forms with 80+ character report rows, use the Report Writer's Layout dialog to change the new FoxPro form's Page Size setting. This way, all the report fields will appear in the form when it's printed or edited in the Report Writer window.

- Calculated report fields with vertical stretch don't always behave as expected in the converted report when semicolons are used to direct output to following rows in the report column. (FoxPro does support the use of embedded semicolons as in dBASE, so you may be able to straighten this out by modifying the report expression in the Report Writer.)
- Report fields with vertical stretch may not execute as expected when stacked under other report fields, owing to FoxPro's management of vertical stretch fields in a report band. You can fix the problem by modifying the report expressions after you understand the controls supplied for handling vertical stretch fields (see Chapter 13).
- Although report variables and calculations are converted without error by AutoMigrate, if the variables and calculations included in a multi-table report include unselected table fields referenced without alias, FoxPro has difficulty executing the report. (This situation occurs only if you set the environment for the report in dBASE using SET FIELDS TO, so that, when you are creating or executing the form, alias table prefixes are not required to

identify fields of unselected tables.) If you have this problem, modify the form and add the missing alias prefixes to the problem report variables and calculated report fields. Also, see the section "Using SET FIELDS Lists" later in this appendix.

In the end, there is also the issue of what your converted reports look like. If you play around with the Report Wizard, Auto-Report, or the Report Writer's Quick Menu option, you'll find that they can quickly produce reports with attractive headers and font selections for text and report data. When a dBASE report has a simple layout and includes few or no calculations, you will therefore get better results if you replace the dBASE form with a FoxPro form instead of convert it.

The Problem with Screen Conversion

Unless you already know what FoxPro screen programs are, the way AutoMigrate converts your dBASE screen design (.SCR) files won't make much sense. In dBASE, the generated format (.FMT) files include little more than @ SAY and @ GET commands specifying the data format. It is, moreover, typical in dBASE programs not to use the .FMT files with SET FORMAT TO, but to copy the @ SAYs and @ GETs directly into a program (.PRG) file. Once this is done, the .FMT and .SCR files become an afterthought. If small modifications are required in the form, they are made directly in the .PRG file. Only when a major overhaul is required does one trouble to go back to MODIFY SCREEN.

In FoxPro, on the other hand, screen design (.SCX) files and the screen program (.SPR) files they generate are everything. Instead of clipping @ SAY and @ GET commands into a .PRG file, the FoxPro programmer supplies the FoxPro Screen Builder with all the program code that would appear in the dBASE program executing the screen. The reasons for this will be clear enough after your introduction to FoxPro screen programs in Chapters 3 through 6.

Still, if your goal is to simply get your dBASE program up and running, there's really nothing to do. FoxPro supports SET FORMAT TO for downward compatibility with FoxPlus and FoxBase and will certainly have no difficulty executing @ SAYs and @ GETs in your programs. (You use your dBASE-generated .FMT files as they are.) The downside, however, is that you'll have to make do with the monospace fixed font FoxPro uses in executing your screen displays unless you revise the layout and alter the font. Such revisions are very difficult to make without the aid of a layout editor—specifically, the FoxPro Screen Builder.

Quick fixes, short of replacing the .PRG and .FMT files used in your application (for data entry and display) with more sophisticated FoxPro screen programs, are nonetheless possible. This is because the screen programs (.SPR) generated by FoxPro also include @ SAYs and @ GETs that can be clipped and moved into a bare-boned (dBASE-style) .FMT file or directly into your .PRG file. In other words, it may prove helpful to convert your .SCR files, if you have them, and then replace the code specifying your screens in your .PRG and .FMT files with the screen design code FoxPro generates in the screen (.SPR) files. The advantages of doing so are readily illustrated. Compare Figure C.9, showing the dBASE MBS Customer file entry screen, Customer.fmt, as executed by FoxPro with SET FORMAT TO and READ, with Figure C.10, showing the same screen when it is executed by the screen program AutoMigrate produces when you allow it to convert the dBASE screen. The conversion of text and data to proportional font—MS Sans Serif, 8, normal for data, and bold for titles—does a world of good, as does the placement of the form in a window.

FIGURE C.9:

FoxPro executes your dBASE screen format (.FMT) files, as well as all screen format code in dBASE programs files, without incident—but uses a monospace font.

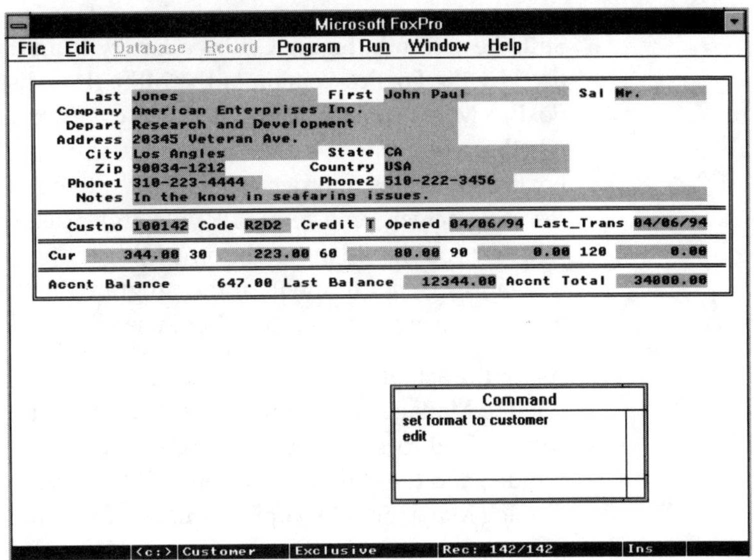

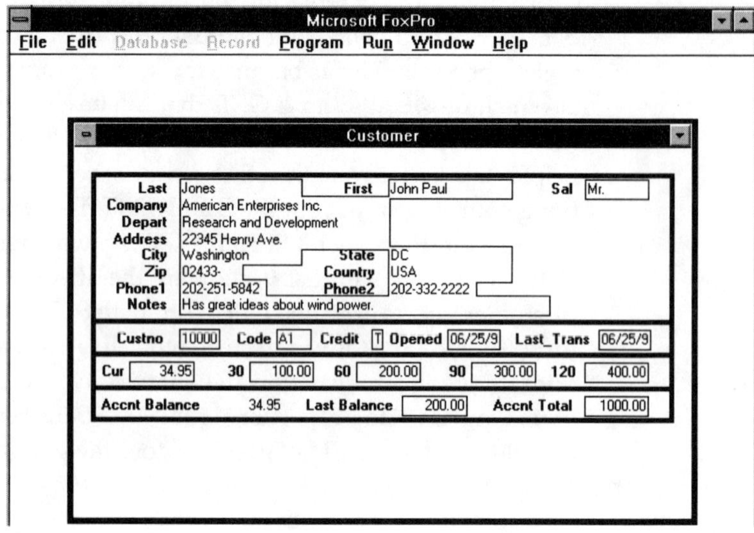

FIGURE C.10: When AutoMigrate converts your dBASE screen design (.SCR) files, it places the data format in a window and uses a proportional font for titles and data.

Still, the screen in Figure C.10 is a far cry from the Customer Data Entry window used by the FoxPro version of the MBS. (It is displayed, along with several other FoxPro MBS screens, inside the front cover of this book.) The question, then, is whether your time is better spent converting your dBASE screen design files into FoxPro .SCX files in order, subsequently, to clip the @ SAYs and @ GETs from the resulting screen program (.SPR) file and place them in an .FMT or .PRG file, or whether you should invest the time using the Screen Builder to replace your dBASE screen forms, not to mention the programs that execute them, with full-featured FoxPro screen programs, like those used by the FoxPro MBS.

As for the actual process of dBASE screen (.SCR) file conversion as executed in the Catalog Manager, it is no different than converting a Label or Report form. The resulting FoxPro screen design (.SCX) file can be modified in the FoxPro Screen Builder, and the generated screen (.SPR) program can be executed with Run in the Catalog Manager or DO <program.spr> from the Command window. (Since screen programs contain FoxPro commands, they can also be viewed and edited with MODIFY COMMAND <program.spr>, although it is not customary to edit screen program files in preference to the screen design files.) Because the resulting screen programs are intended to have functionality in the Catalog Manager, they are designed to open the table(s) on which they are based, open an application window, execute the converted screen display, and allow the operations dBASE users will associate with the EDIT command, although the effect is achieved with different commands. Owing to the conversion to proportional font, it may, of course, be necessary to resize some of the data output fields by modifying the screen layout with the Screen Builder.

TIP If you have occasion to make serious use of the Catalog Manager, you will find that the Screen Wizard produces more attractive screen programs than what you'll get by converting your dBASE screen files. In addition to a more interesting layout, it provides a set of push buttons for all available actions. Since you can modify the Wizard-produced screen design files using the FoxPro Screen Builder, you can also use them as a starting point for giving your dBASE application a real face-lift.

Quick Fixes for Your dBASE Program Files

Once you have finished converting your forms, you can begin editing your dBASE program files to execute correctly under FoxPro. This will not take much doing.

Using SET COMPATIBLE DB4

The first step in preparing any dBASE application to run under FoxPro is to add the command SET COMPATIBLE DB4 to your application's startup code. This single command instructs FoxPro to mimic dBASE's behavior in executing some 20 or so commands and functions that are implemented slightly differently in FoxPro's native state.

TIP If your application will terminate in FoxPro, add SET COMPATIBLE OFF to the application's clean-up code—unless you want FoxPro to go on behaving like dBASE when you're in the Command window.

Although you can consult the *Compatibility* topic in FoxPro Help for a complete list of the commands and functions affected by SET COMPATIBLE—or consult the entry for SET COMPATIBLE in the *Language Reference,* which actually explains how each command and function is affected—with respect to your dBASE application, it is unnecessary to do so. After all, SET COMPATIBLE makes FoxPro behave like dBASE. On the other hand, since it will be best to write new applications in FoxPro with SET COMPATIBLE OFF, you will want to know where FoxPro and dBASE differ, especially where it affects your own programming practice. By way of example, consider FoxPro's and dBASE IV's different implementations of the SELECT() function.

When you set up a multi-table view in dBASE IV, the SELECT() function opens tables in unused work areas without your having to change the current work area.

Consider the following USE commands:

```
USE customer
USE payments IN SELECT()
USE sales IN SELECT()
```

In dBASE, the first command opens Customer.dbf in the current work area, while the following two commands open Payments.dbf and Sales.dbf in unselected, unused work areas.

In FoxPro, however, the SELECT() command has two possible parameters: 1 and 0. SELECT(0) returns the number of the current work area, and SELECT(1) returns the number of an unused work area. Since SELECT(0) is the default value, the three USE commands listed above all open files in the current work area. The end result is one open table. To open all three files, as is intended in the dBASE code, you must use SELECT(1) instead—or SET COMPATIBLE DB4. The disadvantage of SET COMPATIBLE DB4, at least with respect to SELECT(), is that the dBASE usage is obviously more limited.

TIP

In FoxPro, you can also use USE <table> IN 0 to open a table in an unused work area.

Using SET FIELDS Lists

Another area of difference between FoxPro and dBASE IV of interest to most programmers is the execution of SET FIELDS TO <field list> and SET FIELDS TO ALL. Consider the following commands:

```
USE customer
IF VERS() = "FoxPro"
   USE payments ORDER custno IN SELECT(1)
ELSE
   USE payments ORDER custno IN SELECT()
ENDIF
SET RELATION TO custno INTO payments
SET SKIP ON
SET FIELDS TO ALL
SELECT payments
SET FIELDS TO ALL
SELECT customer
DISPLAY
```

When dBASE executes the DISPLAY command, it displays all fields from the Customer and Payments tables. Through the action of SET FIELDS TO ALL, issued once with each table, the fields of both tables are added to the current field list. This is consistent with both FoxPro and dBASE. But when it comes to output using the field list, FoxPro includes only those fields in the SET FIELDS TO <field list> that belong to the current table. In other words, with FoxPro, the DISPLAY command results in the output of all fields in the Customer table. To display the fields in the Payments table, you must SELECT Payments first.

Still, the advantages of dBASE IV's implementation of SET FIELDS TO were not lost on the FoxPro development team, although use of SET FIELDS is less frequent in FoxPro programming than in dBASE, owing to the availability of SQL-SELECT for preparing report data. On the other hand, when from time to time you link files together for data output, SET FIELDS TO <field list> or ALL is no help—at least before FoxPro 2.6—in establishing a multi-table field list. To achieve the same effect in FoxPro 2.5 as in dBASE with the DISPLAY command, you would be obliged to use DISPLAY FIELDS and write out the complete field list, and you would have to reenter it each time you wanted to use it with a FoxPro sequential command.

TIP

One of the additional advantages of the dBASE implementation of SET FIELDS TO, now available with FoxPro 2.6 with SET FIELDS GLOBAL, is that you don't need to use alias prefixes to identify fields of unselected tables unless they share the same name with fields of other tables included in the SET FIELDS TO <field list>. The FoxPro Report Writer and Screen Builder will also observe the current SET FIELDS list. You can generate Quick Reports, for example, that include fields from multiple tables if you use SET FIELDS TO before opening the Report Writer to include all the desired fields in the current view.

With respect to your dBASE applications, SET FIELDS will behave as it does in dBASE if you SET COMPATIBLE DB4. However, so that the dBASE implementation of SET FIELDS TO can be employed in a FoxPro program without altering the behavior of other commands affected by SET COMPATIBLE, FoxPro 2.6 now includes the command SET FIELDS GLOBAL/LOCAL. (Do not confuse this command with SET FIELDS ON/OFF, which still activates or deactivates the SET FIELDS TO <field list>.) In short, SET FIELDS GLOBAL tells FoxPro to process fields of all tables included in the SET FIELDS TO <field list> as in dBASE, while SET FIELDS LOCAL tells FoxPro to process only those fields in the SET FIELDS TO <field list> found in the current table.

NOTE

In dBASE, you can use /R to make a field included in a SET FIELDS TO <field list> read-only. FoxPro does not support this. However, if FoxPro comes across the /R parameter in a SET FIELDS TO command, instead of flagging an error, FoxPro simply ignores the parameter. (In FoxPro, you can make selected fields in a BROWSE display read-only by using the :R option in the BROWSE FIELD's list.)

UDF Execution and SET COMPATIBLE and SET UDFPARMS

With respect to the execution of user-defined functions, or UDFs, FoxPro and dBASE IV part company in two ways. In dBASE IV, if a UDF changes the current work area, dBASE IV reselects it automatically when the UDF terminates. FoxPro doesn't do this unless SET COMPATIBLE is DB4.

The other area of difference is the way parameter passing is handled—although if you want FoxPro to behave like dBASE IV, you must use SET UDFPARMS and not SET COMPATIBLE, which has no effect on parameter passing.

In dBASE IV, parameter passing is handled by reference. In FoxPro it is handled by value or reference, depending on the setting of SET UDFPARMS. Consider the following commands:

```
mem = 2
result = TEST(mem)
WAIT STR(mem+result)
RETURN

FUNCTION TEST
PARAMETER mem
mem = mem + 2
RETURN mem
```

When dBASE IV executes TEST(), WAIT always displays the value 8. This is because any changes to *mem* in TEST() are permanent. When FoxPro executes it, however, the value assigned to *mem* in TEST()—that is, 4—is returned to the calling program through RETURN *mem;* but the value of *mem* in the calling program remains what it was prior to the execution of TEST(), which cannot change it. WAIT therefore reports 6.

To make FoxPro handle UDF parameters like dBASE IV—that is, by reference—use the command SET UDFPARMS TO REFERENCE. To return FoxPro to its default practice, issue SET UDFPARMS TO VALUE.

NOTE

The handling of UDF parameters by FoxPro is not affected by SET COMPATIBLE, but by SET UDFPARMS, which was added to FoxPro with version 2.2 to give programmers greater flexibility. Bear in mind, however, that parameters passing to procedures and programs are always handled by *reference* in FoxPro, as in dBASE. You need only worry about the action of your UDFs.

FoxPro 2.6 Implementation of SET KEY TO

Besides SET FIELDS GLOBAL/LOCAL, the only dBASE-like addition to FoxPro 2.6 really affecting data processing with FoxPro is SET KEY TO [RANGE]. In dBASE IV, it instantly filtered records in a table with the aid of the master index. Its lateness in coming to FoxPro, however, is readily explained by the availability of Rushmore optimization for filtering records using available index tags. Rushmore is more far reaching than SET KEY TO, but Rushmore cannot filter records effectively in a multi-table view using the index tags of a child table. SET KEY can do this—at least by using the master index of child tables. SET KEY TO is also unencumbered with the other strictures placed on the availability of Rushmore. With SET KEY TO now available as an alternative to Rushmore, FoxPro provides the greatest possible flexibility in establishing multi-table filters. There is no need to SET COMPATIBLE to use SET KEY. It is now a standard FoxPro command, just as most migrating dBASE programmers would have it. (For more on Rushmore optimization, see Chapter 4.)

Laying Claim to the FoxPro Main Window

Unless otherwise instructed, FoxPro executes your menu-driven dBASE applications in the FoxPro main window, directly below the FoxPro system menu, as shown in Figure C.11. Just what you always wanted: two menu bars at once! Nor is the arrangement very practical, since the FoxPro system menu provides operators with powers you don't want them to have—although it would be nice to allow them use of some of the desktop tools, like the Calculator and Calendar, and even the Windows Clipboard.

The quick fix is to remove the FoxPro system menu from the desktop at the outset of your program by using the command SET SYSMENU OFF. When your program terminates, use SET SYSMENU AUTOMATIC to restore the FoxPro system menu to its normal state. (SET SYSMENU is discussed in depth in Chapter 9.)

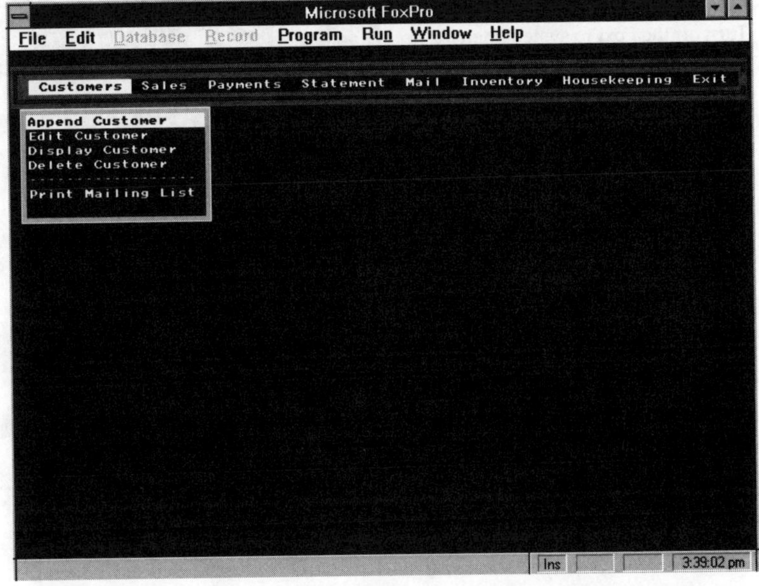

FIGURE C.11: Run without revision, FoxPro executes your dBASE applications in the FoxPro main window and places your application's menu bar directly below the FoxPro system menu.

While you're at it, however, you might as well adapt the FoxPro main window to your application by placing your application's name in the window title bar with MODIFY WINDOW SCREEN. The following command is intended to suggest other options you can use to control the behavior of the main window during program execution.

```
MODIFY WINDOW SCREEN TITLE "Model Business System" ;
    NOCLOSE FLOAT NOGROW MINIMIZE FONT "FoxFont", 10
```

The inclusion of the FONT is redundant since FoxPro uses 10-point FoxFont in executing your dBASE applications unless instructed to do otherwise. Here, you might alter the font used in the main window, although your dBASE (DOS) screens will look best with 10-point FoxFont. (MODIFY WINDOW SCREEN is discussed in Chapter 8.)

By turning off the FoxPro system menu and replacing the main window's title with your application's name, you arrive at something nearing the look your application had when executed by dBASE. Figure C.12 shows the result obtained with the dBASE MBS.

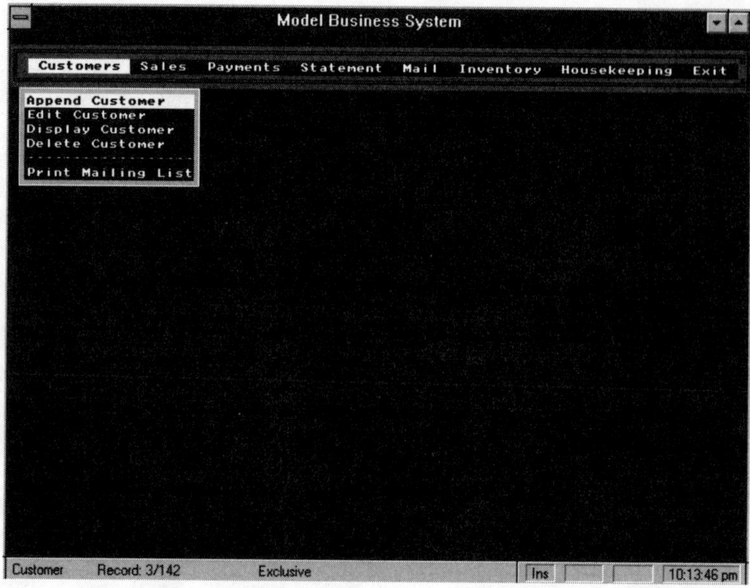

FIGURE C.12:
Turn off the FoxPro system menu and change the FoxPro main window's title to give your menu-driven application more of the look it has in dBASE.

TIP

As you will discover, running your dBASE applications in FoxPro 2.6 Windows using 10-point FoxFont will leave plenty of room at the bottom of the main window since there are more than 24 rows. For esthetic reasons, you may therefore activate a Windows-style status bar for the display of messages by using SET STATUS BAR ON. To activate the clock in the status bar, use SET CLOCK STATUS. (You may need to SET STATUS OFF to deactivate the old-style status bar, if it is activated by your application.)

dBASE Menu Bar Conundrums

If your dBASE application includes a pulldown menu system developed with the dBASE IV Application Generator, you will discover that all the pulldowns are too big. This is because they will be defined with DEFINE POPUP FROM and TO. When defining popups in FoxPro, you do not employ the TO <coordinates> clause, so FoxPro can adjust the size of the popup as needed. Use of the TO clause in the popups prevents FoxPro from doing this. The solution is to run through your main menu program and delete or comment out the DEFINE POPUP TO clauses wherever they appear.

In the following command, the DEFINE POPUP TO clause is turned into a program comment through the insertion of &&.

```
DEFINE POPUP Customer FROM 4,1 && TO 11,20
```

The result of this revision can be seen by comparing the Customers pulldown in Figure C.12, which FoxPro has sized to fit the available option, with the one in Figure C.11, where the DEFINE POPUP TO clause still holds sway.

Another problem with dBASE pulldown menus, which are primarily supported by FoxPro for downward compatibility with FoxPlus (and dBASE), is that they are not automatically cleared from the screen when a selection is made. If this should prove a problem with your application, place the commands HIDE MENU <menu bar name> and HIDE POPUP <popup name> at the outset of the programs executed through the menu bar. This will remove them from the screen until the menu bar is reactivated.

TIP

When executing your dBASE applications, you turn off the FoxPro system menu so that your dBASE menu bar will be the center of attention. But it is better by far to replace the old dBASE menu bar with a functionally equivalent FoxPro system menu. This is quickly and easily done with the FoxPro Menu Builder. You can also include any of the default FoxPro system menu options in your application's system menu. (A reading of Chapter 9 will prepare you to create a system menu for your dBASE application.)

Getting to Work

The revisions suggested above should enable you to get your dBASE application up and running quite quickly with FoxPro. Esthetic problems, however, may abound, since the color scheme used by your dBASE application may appear less satisfactory in FoxPro for Windows than in DOS. The appearance of windows with single, double, and no borders will also change, usually for the worse. A little playing around with SET COLOR TO and SET COLOR OF should help, and you can easily change the borders used by Windows.

Before you get to work, however, you are advised to look up the *Command and Function Differences in dBASE IV and FoxPro* topic in FoxPro Help so you will be aware of the minor differences between the two programs that have not been discussed in this appendix—and are not taken care of by SET COMPATIBLE. It is more than likely that none of these differences will be pertinent to your applications. This is also true of the brief list of *Unsupported dBASE IV Commands or Functions*, also found in FoxPro Help, unless your dBASE program made use of BEGIN/END TRANSACTION and related commands and functions, dBASE PROTECT, or dBASE SQL. Again, BEGIN/END TRANSACTION is not supported by FoxPro, and you must remove the commands from your application, along with ROLLBACK.

Since you will find yourself testing the converted application in a new environment with new debugging tools, you are also advised to glance at the chapter "Debugging Your Application" in the FoxPro *Developer's Guide*. Then you can get to work.

Good luck—and welcome to FoxPro!

INDEX

Note to the Reader: **Boldfaced** numbers indicate the principal discussion of a topic or the definition of a term. *Italic* numbers indicate illustrations.

Numbers and Symbols

A

B

C

D

E

F

G

H

I

J

K

L

M

N

O

Q

R

S

T

U

V

W

X

Z

Programmer's Guide to FoxPro 2.6

GET A FREE CATALOG JUST FOR EXPRESSING YOUR OPINION.

Help us improve our books and get a ***FREE*** full-color catalog in the bargain. Please complete this form, pull out this page and send it in today. The address is on the reverse side.

Name ____________________ **Company** ____________________

Address ____________________ **City** __________ **State** ____ **Zip** ______

Phone (   ) ____________________

1. **How would you rate the overall quality of this book?**
   - ❑ Excellent
   - ❑ Very Good
   - ❑ Good
   - ❑ Fair
   - ❑ Below Average
   - ❑ Poor

2. **What were the things you liked most about the book? (Check all that apply)**
   - ❑ Pace
   - ❑ Format
   - ❑ Writing Style
   - ❑ Examples
   - ❑ Table of Contents
   - ❑ Index
   - ❑ Price
   - ❑ Illustrations
   - ❑ Type Style
   - ❑ Cover
   - ❑ Depth of Coverage
   - ❑ Fast Track Notes

3. **What were the things you liked *least* about the book? (Check all that apply)**
   - ❑ Pace
   - ❑ Format
   - ❑ Writing Style
   - ❑ Examples
   - ❑ Table of Contents
   - ❑ Index
   - ❑ Price
   - ❑ Illustrations
   - ❑ Type Style
   - ❑ Cover
   - ❑ Depth of Coverage
   - ❑ Fast Track Notes

4. **Where did you buy this book?**
   - ❑ Bookstore chain
   - ❑ Small independent bookstore
   - ❑ Computer store
   - ❑ Wholesale club
   - ❑ College bookstore
   - ❑ Technical bookstore
   - ❑ Other ____________

5. **How did you decide to buy this particular book?**
   - ❑ Recommended by friend
   - ❑ Recommended by store personnel
   - ❑ Author's reputation
   - ❑ Sybex's reputation
   - ❑ Read book review in ________
   - ❑ Other ____________

6. **How did you pay for this book?**
   - ❑ Used own funds
   - ❑ Reimbursed by company
   - ❑ Received book as a gift

7. **What is your level of experience with the subject covered in this book?**
   - ❑ Beginner
   - ❑ Intermediate
   - ❑ Advanced

8. **How long have you been using a computer?**

   years ____________

   months ____________

9. **Where do you most often use your computer?**
   - ❑ Home
   - ❑ Work
   - ❑ Both
   - ❑ Other ____________

10. **What kind of computer equipment do you have? (Check all that apply)**
    - ❑ PC Compatible Desktop Computer
    - ❑ PC Compatible Laptop Computer
    - ❑ Apple/Mac Computer
    - ❑ Apple/Mac Laptop Computer
    - ❑ CD ROM
    - ❑ Fax Modem
    - ❑ Data Modem
    - ❑ Scanner
    - ❑ Sound Card
    - ❑ Other ____________

11. **What other kinds of software packages do you ordinarily use?**
    - ❑ Accounting
    - ❑ Databases
    - ❑ Networks
    - ❑ Apple/Mac
    - ❑ Desktop Publishing
    - ❑ Spreadsheets
    - ❑ CAD
    - ❑ Games
    - ❑ Word Processing
    - ❑ Communications
    - ❑ Money Management
    - ❑ Other ____________

12. **What operating systems do you ordinarily use?**
    - ❑ DOS
    - ❑ OS/2
    - ❑ Windows
    - ❑ Apple/Mac
    - ❑ Windows NT
    - ❑ Other ____________

13. **On what computer-related subject(s) would you like to see more books?**

14. **Do you have any other comments about this book? (Please feel free to use a separate piece of paper if you need more room)**

PLEASE FOLD, SEAL, AND MAIL TO SYBEX

SYBEX INC.
Department M
2021 Challenger Drive
Alameda, CA
94501

SYBEX®

Programmer's Guide to FoxPro 2.6 Companion Disk

If You Need a 3½" Disk...

To receive a 3½" disk, please return the original 5¼" disk contained in the envelope and send your written request to

Order Processing Department

SYBEX Inc.

2021 Challenger Drive

Alameda, CA 94501

Reference: 1609-4

Be sure to include your name, complete mailing address, and the reference number listed above. Otherwise, your request cannot be processed. Allow six weeks for delivery.

If Your Disk Is Defective...

To obtain a replacement disk, please refer to the instructions outlined on the warranty page at the front of the book.